■ The *Philokalia*

The *Philokalia*

A Classic Text of
Orthodox Spirituality

EDITED BY
Brock Bingaman
and Bradley Nassif

OXFORD
UNIVERSITY PRESS

OXFORD
UNIVERSITY PRESS

Oxford University Press is a department of the University of Oxford.
It furthers the University's objective of excellence in research,
scholarship, and education by publishing worldwide.

Oxford   New York
Auckland   Cape Town   Dar es Salaam   Hong Kong   Karachi
Kuala Lumpur   Madrid   Melbourne   Mexico City   Nairobi
New Delhi   Shanghai   Taipei   Toronto

With offices in
Argentina   Austria   Brazil   Chile   Czech Republic   France   Greece
Guatemala   Hungary   Italy   Japan   Poland   Portugal   Singapore
South Korea   Switzerland   Thailand   Turkey   Ukraine   Vietnam

Oxford is a registered trade mark of Oxford University Press in the UK and certain other
countries.

Published in the United States of America by Oxford University Press
198 Madison Avenue, New York, NY 10016

Library of Congress Cataloging-in-Publication Data
The Philokalia : a classic text of orthodox spirituality / edited by Brock Bingaman
and Bradley Nassif.
       p.   cm.
Includes index.
ISBN 978-0-19-539026-1—ISBN 978-0-19-539027-8
1. Philokalia. 2. Spiritual life—Eastern Orthodox Church.
I. Bingaman, Brock. II. Nassif, Bradley.
BX382.P43P55   2012
248.4'819—dc23   2011024978

For
Amanda
ἰδοὺ εἶ καλή ἡ πλησίον μου ἰδοὺ εἶ καλή
—Brock

and
Barbara
whose virtues and noble character are "more
precious than rubies" (Pr. 31:10–31)
—Brad

■ CONTENTS

'The Church,' wrote the Russian Orthodox theologian Archpriest Georges Floro-vsky, 'gives us not a system but a key; not a plan of God's City, but the means of entering it. Perhaps someone will lose his way because he has no plan. But all that he will see, he will see . . . directly, it will be real for him; while he who has studied only the plan, risks remaining outside and not really finding anything.'[1]

What Fr. Florovsky said of the Church is true equally of the *Philokalia*. It is precisely a book that gives us 'not a system but a key'; not an abstract outline of the spiritual way, but the means of ourselves undertaking the journey. It is in that sense an eminently practical book, a book that invites us to 'see directly', to explore and discover for ourselves. It provides not information but wisdom. It is not sys-tematic, and it does not attempt to offer a single, all-embracing 'theory' of the life of prayer. Yet, if read attentively and with an open mind, the texts that it contains— written by some thirty-six writers, extending chronologically over more than a millennium—have the power to alter our inner world, to effect a radical change in our will, and to reveal to us possibilities that previously we never imagined possi-ble. The authors in the *Philokalia* write, not in an academic or scholastic spirit, but on the basis of their personal experience; and they ask of us that in our turn we will read their words in a personal and experiential manner. In the phrase that Cardi-nal Newman chose as his motto, *Cor ad cor loquitur*, 'Heart speaks to heart.'

The *Philokalia* is not an easy book. We have to make the effort to climb the slopes of the mountain if we are to enjoy the view from the summit. Yet those who persist will find that the basic message of the *Philokalia* is exceedingly simple. It is summed up in the words of one of the authors close to the end of the work, Kallis-tos Kataphygiotis: 'The greatest thing that happens between God and the human soul is to love and to be loved.'[2] This basic message of mutual love is worked out in terms of the doctrines of the Trinity and the Incarnation, and in terms also of a unified, holistic view of human nature that assigns a positive role to our body. It is this mutual love that gives meaning to the recitation of the Jesus Prayer, about which the *Philokalia* has much to say; and it is this mutual love that leads ultimately, in the experience of the saints, to the vision of divine and uncreated Light. In the philokalic vision of the truth, love is both our starting-point and our end-point.

The authors in the *Philokalia* were writing in a world very different from our own, and yet what they have to say is startlingly relevant. Although this is not its immediate aim, the *Philokalia* has clear and challenging implications for the way in which we confront the major public crises in contemporary society, whether in politics, in international relations, or in the realm of ecology. For it speaks to us not only about inner prayer but also about the transfiguration of the world. It speaks about a God who is totally transcendent yet totally immanent, who is mys-tery beyond all understanding but who is also directly present in everything that he has made.

It has been said that the translation of the *Philokalia* into English 'might well be one of the greatest single contributions to perpetuating in the West what is highest in the Christian tradition.'[3] Indeed, when the first volume of extracts chosen from the *Philokalia* was published in 1951, *The Catholic Herald* commented, 'This selection is one of the most important spiritual treatises ever to be translated into English.' These are bold affirmations; but readers of the present volume, edited by Dr. Brock Bingaman and Dr. Bradley Nassif, will perhaps begin to understand why such claims have been made. The aim of the editors and contributors will be amply fulfilled if this collective work enables our readers to study the actual text of the *Philokalia* with deeper understanding and with an ever-increasing imaginative sympathy.

Kallistos Ware
Metropolitan of Diokleia

■ PREFACE

The present volume is the fruit of fine scholars from around the world, from Orthodox, Catholic, and Protestant traditions. It has been a joy working with these women and men on a project that will initiate further studies into this great collection of Orthodox spirituality known as the *Philokalia*. While we are grateful to each of our contributors for their excellent essays, we are especially grateful for the lifelong work of Metropolitan Kallistos Ware. Metropolitan Kallistos, along with G. E. H. Palmer and Philip Sherrard, has translated the first four (of five) volumes of the *Philokalia* from Greek to English over the past thirty years. His scholarship on the *Philokalia*, his lectures around the world in churches and on university campuses, and his passion for philokalic spirituality have sparked much interest in the *Philokalia*. Without his work, this volume would not have come about. Most of our contributors have utilized the English translation provided by Ware, Palmer, and Sherrard. Some have accessed the Greek version of the *Philokalia* published by the Astir Publishing Company (Athens, 1957–63), or modern critical editions.

We are also grateful to the outstanding people at Oxford University Press: Cynthia Read, Sasha Grossman, and Erica Woods Tucker. Their vision, professionalism, suggestions, and editorial input have enhanced this volume. I (Brock) would also like to express my thanks to Mark A. McIntosh, my dissertation director and mentor at Loyola University Chicago, who encouraged my research into Maximus the Confessor from the very beginning. Thanks also to Kristi Peavy, the librarian at Wesleyan College, who helped obtain Greek texts and other helpful sources for researching the *Philokalia*, and to Debra Williams, my student assistant at Wesleyan College who worked hard to put together the index. And a special thank you to my parents, John and Jan Bingaman, who have supported me for over forty years.

My (Brock's) final thanks go to my wife Amanda whose friendship, love, and strength have inspired me (and many others) over nearly two decades, and to our two children, Mia and Jakob, who bring purpose, joy, and fun to life.

I (Brad) also wish to express special gratitude to my wife Barbara whose love, prayers and cheerleading have kept me strong and steady the past twenty-three years; and to my fun-loving daughter, Melanie, whose love for life keeps me laughing—"Go Secretariat!"

Brock Bingaman and
Bradley Nassif

ABBREVIATIONS USED

CCSG	Corpus Christianorum, Series Graeca
CSEL	Corpus Scriptorum Ecclesiasticorum Latinorum
GNO	Gregorii Nysseni Opera
PG	Patrologia Graeca
SC	Sources Chrétiennes

■ CONTRIBUTORS

Frederick D. Aquino is Professor of Systematic Theology at Abilene Christian University in Abilene, Texas.

Krastu Banev is Lecturer in the Department of Theology and Religion at Durham University, UK.

Brock Bingaman is Assistant Professor of Religious Studies at Wesleyan College in Macon, Georgia.

Paul M. Blowers is the Dean E. Walker Professor of Church History at Emmanuel School of Religion in Johnson City, Tennessee.

Douglas Burton-Christie is Professor of Theology at Loyola Marymount University in Los Angeles, California.

John Chryssavgis taught theology in Sydney and Boston. A clergyman of the Greek Orthodox Archdiocese of America, he serves as theological advisor to the Ecumenical Patriarch on environmental issues.

Christopher C. H. Cook is Professorial Research Fellow in the Department of Theology and Religion at Durham University, UK.

Mary B. Cunningham is Lecturer in Historical Theology at the University of Nottingham, UK.

Verna E. F. Harrison is currently a research fellow at Holy Cross Greek Orthodox School of Theology in Boston, Massachusetts, having previously served as Assistant Professor of Church History at Saint Paul School of Theology in Kansas City, Missouri.

Hannah Hunt is Senior Lecturer in Theology and Religious Studies at Leeds Trinity University College, UK.

Julia Konstantinovsky is a British Academy Post-Doctoral Fellow at Christ Church, Oxford.

Andrew Louth is Professor of Patristic and Byzantine Studies at the University of Durham, UK; he is also a priest of the Diocese of Sourozh, Moscow Patriarchate.

John Anthony McGuckin is Ane Marie and Bent Emil Nielsen Professor in Late Antique and Byzantine Christian History Professor of Byzantine Christian Studies at Columbia University, New York; he is also a Stavrophore priest of the Orthodox Church (Patriarchate of Romania).

Bradley Nassif is Professor of Biblical and Theological Studies at North Park University in Chicago, Illinois; and a theologian of the Antiochian Orthodox Church of Syria and North America.

Mihail Neamtu is a philosopher, theologian and essayist, and is currently scientific director of the Institute for Investigation of Communist Crimes and Memory of Romanian Exile.

Kallistos Ware is a titular metropolitan of the Ecumenical Patriarchate in Great Britain.

Rowan Williams is an Anglican bishop, poet, and theologian, and is the current (104th) Archbishop of Canterbury, Metropolitan of the Province of Canterbury and Primate of All England, offices he has held since early 2003.

J. L. Zecher is a member of the Department of Theology and Religion at the University of Durham.

■ The *Philokalia*

Introduction: Love of the Beautiful

Brock Bingaman and Bradley Nassif

This book is an ecumenical collection of scholarly essays on the *Philokalia*, a title meaning "love of beauty" or "love of what is good." It suggests that God transforms human beings through love, enabling them to share in the divine beauty. The *Philokalia* is a selection of some of the noblest writings to be found in the monastic tradition of the early and Byzantine Church from the fourth to fifteenth centuries. This five-volume anthology of texts on the spiritual life was written by some thirty-six authors and was first collected and published in 1782 by two Eastern Orthodox monks of Mount Athos, St. Makarios and St. Nikodimos. Next to the Bible, the *Philokalia* is the most widely read book in the Orthodox world today.

■ A BOOK FOR ALL CHRISTIANS

The essays in this volume were written by an international team of theologians from the Orthodox, Roman Catholic, and Protestant traditions. That it is co-edited by Orthodox (Nassif) and Protestant (Bingaman) scholars lends further testimony to the fact that the *Philokalia* is a book for all Christians, not just the Orthodox. Our goal is to explore the history of the *Philokalia*, its theological foundations, and its spiritual practices—subjects that are artificially divided in the table of contents but united in reality. Our intent is to introduce readers to its background, motifs, authors, and relevance for contemporary life and thought. Our hope is that these essays will resonate with the spirit and vision of the *Philokalia*—one of deep reflection and faith.[1]

■ THE CENTRALITY OF THE GOSPEL IN THE *PHILOKALIA*

Orthodox spirituality is above all else a gospel spirituality that is centered on Jesus Christ in his trinitarian relations. The centrality of trinitarian grace in the Christian life is evident throughout all five volumes of the *Philokalia*. Nowhere is this made more explicit in the entire corpus of writings in the Eastern Orthodox tradition than in the works of St. Mark the Monk (or St. Mark the Ascetic, as he is often called). In his treatise *Concerning Those Who Imagine That They Are Justified by Works*, Mark explains the meaning of baptismal grace and how the gospel relates to the ascetical practices of keeping the commandments and overcoming the passions. Along with John Cassian, this is one of the few texts in the entire Greek patristic tradition that directly addresses the doctrines of grace, faith and works in categories that have customarily belonged to the Christian West. Mark argues that prayer, fasting, vigils and all other monastic disciplines will be dangerously misguided without a prior grounding in the "unmerited, free gift" of grace as the prime motivation for all Christian living. Salvation comes by grace through faith. It is the gift of God that does not come from doing good works. Yet the recognition of such grace instills humility that leads to works of gratitude. Grace opposes merit, but it also induces the hard work of holiness.

The goal of the Christian life as envisioned in the *Philokalia,* therefore, is not to achieve great feats of asceticism, but to love as God loves. Such love is the gift of pure prayer. Thus a major concern of the original editors of the *Philokalia,* Makarios and Nikodimos, is to stress the need for keeping the free gift of the gospel clear and central in all our thinking. The gospel of grace is the governing hermeneutic of the Christian life and, indeed, the entire collection of writings contained in the *Philokalia.*

▪ THE SCOPE AND NECESSITY OF THE BOOK

Only a selection of central issues related to the history, theology, and spiritual practices of the *Philokalia* are addressed in this book. We make no pretense of being comprehensive. On the contrary, we are keenly aware of gaps in our presentation of topics. Despite these and other shortcomings, we hope that the book will serve as a pioneering project for future generations to build on and improve.

Shocking as it is, a large lacuna exists in scholarly literature on the *Philokalia.* This we discovered in the give-and-take of research on the *Philokalia* for Dr. Bingaman's Ph.D. comprehensive exams at Loyola University Chicago, during which we worked together as student and committee member. After Dr. Bingaman made the discovery and suggested the possibility of editing a book on the *Philokalia,* we scoured the literature to confirm the range of the lacuna through extensive electronic searches. Only a few isolated scholarly articles could be found in any modern language. Thus this book was born out of scholarly necessity in our attempts to consult critical research on the *Philokalia.*

▪ RENAISSANCE IN ORTHODOX THEOLOGY

The publication of this book by the distinguished academic press of Oxford University provides further evidence that a renaissance in Orthodox theology is vigorously underway at the beginning of the twenty-first century. A rebirth of the Orthodox vision, however, inevitably brings with it the potential for serious misunderstanding. Nowhere is this more evident than in the way contemporary readers might misappropriate the spiritual teachings of the *Philokalia* and this present collection of essays. Although the two monks who compiled the *Philokalia* did so with the express intent of making Orthodox spirituality accessible to common laypeople who are not monks, they did not wish to revive or transplant the monastic culture of Mount Athos on foreign soil.

Efforts to reenact monastic life and culture in a local parish today are not only historically naïve but theologically indefensible and spiritually dangerous.

A misreading of the *Philokalia* can create a cultic, fanatical religion that once stood in lethal opposition to Jesus Christ himself. We may adopt with great profit the spiritual principles that we find in the *Philokalia*, but we need not apply its monastic practices to our lives in every historical detail.

As the twenty-first century beckons us forward, a parallel rediscovery of the spiritual treasures of the Christian East now lies before us. The *Philokalia* reemerges in a world of massive technological, social, economic, and intellectual forces that are in conflict, and interaction, with each other. There is an enormous sociological dynamic that characterizes our culture and threatens to loose us from our spiritual moorings. It is in the context of the radical changes that are taking place in our time that a joyful rediscovery of the *Philokalia* is transpiring. The fathers of the *Philokalia* present us with a paradoxical worldview. On the one hand, they remind us that Christians are to embrace all that is good and holy within our physical world and we are to contribute toward its social progress. They were not so heavenly minded that they were of no earthly good. At the same time, however, they saw the Christian life as one of countercultural engagement. They saw themselves, and all Christians, on the front lines of spiritual warfare where the heart is to be purified, the passions conquered, sin destroyed, and humanity, along with all of creation, renewed. In our quest for material well-being, the fathers of the *Philokalia* serve as a vivid reminder that our ultimate destiny is not in this world, but the next. The unseen world, in their vision, is more real, and therefore more worthy of attention, than the physical world around us (2 Cor. 4:16–17). In his article on "St. Nikodimos and the *Philokalia*," Bishop Kallistos Ware has stated their modern relevance very well. He compares the contemporary renaissance of the *Philokalia* to a spiritual "time bomb" that was set for the modern world:

> "It is surely astonishing, and also immensely encouraging, that a collection of spiritual texts, originally intended for Greeks living under Ottoman rule, should have achieved its main impact two centuries later in the secularized and post-Christian West, among the children of that very 'Enlightenment' which St. Makarios and St. Nikodimos viewed with such misgiving. There are certain books which seem to have been composed not so much for their own age as for subsequent generations. Little noticed at the time of their original publication, they attain their full influence only two or more centuries afterward, acting in this manner as a spiritual "time bomb." The *Philokalia* is precisely such a book. It is not so much the late eighteenth as the late twentieth and early twenty-first century that is the true "age of the *Philokalia*." (p. 34)

It is our hope that this collection of essays will engender further interest in the *Philokalia*, and that it will serve the original editors' purpose, inviting readers to contemplate the beauty of God and to discover the transformative power of the gospel of the kingdom. As St. Nikodimos says at the close of his preface: "Come, therefore, come. Eat of the bread of knowledge and wisdom . . . and drink a wine that spiritually gladdens the heart. . . . Come, all who are participants in the Orthodox call, both laymen and monks, all who are seeking to find the kingdom of God which is within you, and the treasure which is hidden in the field of your heart . . ."[2]

Brock Bingaman and Brad Nassif
Feast of the Transfiguration, 2011

■ PART ONE
History

1 St. Nikodimos and the *Philokalia*

Kallistos Ware

◼ AN ENIGMATIC WORK

The *Philokalia*, despite its ever-increasing popularity during the past half-century, remains in many ways an enigmatic work.[1] The title page of the original Greek edition, published in Venice in 1782—a heavy folio volume, running to 1,207 pages in double columns—refers in prominent capital letters to the patron who financed the work, John Mavrocordato.[2] But it makes no mention of the two editors, nor indeed do their names appear at any point elsewhere in the book. We happen to know with certainty who they were: Makarios of Corinth (1731–1805) and Nikodimos of the Holy Mountain (1749–1809), both of them glorified as saints by the Orthodox Church.[3] That information, however, still leaves many other questions unanswered.

The *Philokalia*, as edited by St. Makarios and St. Nikodimos, is a collection of ascetic and mystical texts taken from some thirty-six writers, extending chronologically from the fourth to the fifteenth century. What, we are immediately led to ask, do these thirty-six writers share in common? Why have the editors chosen these thirty-six, leaving out others whom we might expect to be included? What were the specific criteria determining the selection of material? In their choice of texts, were the editors guided by their personal judgment, or were they following an existing tradition? About all this we are told very little in the preface to the *Philokalia*, although it does contain a few valuable hints. The editors are for the most part deliberately self-effacing, and the publication as a whole is marked by a hidden, "apophatic" spirit.

◼ "THE HELLENO-ROMAIC DILEMMA"; THE CONTEXT OF THE *PHILOKALIA*

In order to appreciate the aim and inner unity of the *Philokalia*, let us first consider the broader cultural and religious context in which it was produced. The era in which Makarios and Nikodimos lived and worked, the latter part of the eighteenth century, constitutes a crucial turning point in the spiritual evolution of the Greek people. Notwithstanding the collapse of the Greek empire in 1453, in many respects the Byzantine period of Orthodox history—more exactly, the Romaic period—extended uninterrupted down to the late eighteenth century. The Church continued to play a central part in all aspects of national life. In the realm of theology, despite heavy Western influence, both Roman Catholic and Protestant, a patristic perspective was not altogether lost. Seventeenth-century authors such as Gabriel Severus, Meletios Syrigos, and Patriarch Dositheos of

Jerusalem used the terminology of Latin Scholasticism, but their primary point of reference was still the Ecumenical Councils and the Fathers. When looking back to the past, most Greeks took as their ideal not classical Athens but the Orthodox empire of New Rome.

As the eighteenth century drew to a close, however, there was a shift of emphasis. A different *Zeitgeist* began to prevail among educated Greeks: the spirit of modern Hellenism. The new outlook was not explicitly anti-religious, at any rate initially, but in the Neohellenic world-view the Church no longer occupied the central position that it had possessed hitherto. A more secular mind-set emerged. Church teachings and practices, hitherto accepted largely without question, began to be subjected to critical scrutiny. The protagonists of Neohellenism looked back beyond the Byzantine period to ancient Greece, drawing their inspiration from the Parthenon rather than Hagia Sophia, from Plato and Aristotle rather than St. Gregory the Theologian or St. Maximos the Confessor. They shared the Western European admiration for the Athens of Pericles, and they shared equally the Western disdain for Byzantine civilization. They looked for guidance to the Enlightenment, to Voltaire, the French Encyclopaedists, and other such representatives of the *siècle des lumières*. An appreciable number embraced Freemasonry. Many of them welcomed the French Revolution as the dawn of a fresh era of freedom and took this as their model in preparing for the liberation of the Greek nation from Ottoman autocracy.

It is not to be supposed, however, that there was an abrupt transition at the end of the eighteenth century, with the Romaic era coming to a sudden end and being everywhere replaced by the ideology of Neohellenism. The reality is far more complex. In modern Greece during the past two hundred years the two approaches have continued to coexist and overlap, and there is a subtle and pervasive interaction between them. Alexander Solzhenitsyn remarked in *The Gulag Archipelago* that the line of demarcation separating good and evil runs, not between nations or classes or political parties, but right through the middle of every human heart; and this line constantly shifts and oscillates.[4] By the same token it can be argued that the line of demarcation between the *Romios* and the Hellene runs right through the heart of every modern Greek, and this line too is constantly shifting and oscillating.

Forty-five years ago Patrick Leigh Fermor offered a witty delineation of what he styled "the Helleno-Romaic Dilemma," and most of what he says is still true today. As he rightly observed concerning the two outlooks: "All Greeks, according to my theory, are an amalgam, in varying degrees, of both; they contradict and complete each other."[5] If at the end of the eighteenth century the outstanding spokesman for modern Hellenism was Adamantios Korais (1748–1833), then during the same epoch the leading exponent of the Romaic or traditional Orthodox spirit was Nikodimos of the Holy Mountain, born just one year after Korais.

Orthodox churchmen of traditionalist outlook, during the later years of the eighteenth century, grew increasingly disturbed by the infiltration of the ideas of the Enlightenment into the Greek world. Matters came to a head with the outbreak of the Kollyvades controversy on the Holy Mountain of Athos.[6] In this both Nikodimos and Makarios were closely involved. So far as the explicit topics of this controversy were concerned, it was not a conflict between Romaic conservatism and Neohellenic innovation, but a much more restricted debate concerning liturgical practices and sacramental observance. Underlying the whole dispute, however, was the deep suspicion felt by the strongly traditionalist Kollyvades toward the Western Enlightenment and all that its influence represented in the educated Greek world.

The name "Kollyvades" is derived from *kollyva*, the boiled wheat used at memorial services for the departed (*mnimosyna*). It was over the celebration of these memorial services that the dispute initially arose. In 1754 the monks of the skete of St. Anne on the Holy Mountain began to build a new central church (*kyriakon*). To enhance their fundraising, they undertook in the customary way to commemorate the names of the departed relatives of donors. According to the Orthodox *typikon*, the appointed day for *mnimosyna* is Saturday, the day on which the dead Christ rested in the tomb. But many monks at St. Anne's needed to work on Saturdays, and in particular a number of them had to go to Karyes on that day to sell their wares at the weekly market. As the number of names to be commemorated increased, for convenience they began to transfer the *mnimosyna* to Sunday. This, the day of the Savior's resurrection from the dead, seemed to them an equally appropriate occasion on which to intercede for the departed who are awaiting their own resurrection.

This innovation displeased the more conservative monks at St. Anne's and elsewhere on the Mountain. Under the leadership initially of the deacon Neophytos the Peloponnesian (1713–84), a monk at the nearby skete of Kavsokalyvia, the traditionalist party insisted that memorial services continue to be celebrated on Saturday; hence the *sobriquet* "Kollyvades," assigned to them by their opponents. It is tempting to dismiss the whole dispute as nothing more than a fracas about a technical point of church ritual, but in the view of the Kollyvades a far more profound issue of principle was at stake: loyalty to Holy Tradition.

The Kollyvades were concerned, however, not merely with the correct day for *mnimosyna* but with other questions of more obvious importance. In particular they advocated frequent communion—"continual communion," as they termed it—by which they meant the daily reception of the sacrament, if at all possible. This was a highly unusual standpoint in the Orthodox Church at this time. Almost everywhere in Eastern Christendom communion had become infrequent: laypersons usually communicated three or four times a year, and in many cases only at Pascha, while most nonordained monks on Athos received the sacrament no more than once in every forty days.[7] The advocacy of frequent communion by the Kollyvades proved highly controversial, bringing upon them obloquy and persecution, and many of them fled or were expelled from Athos. Nikodimos, in common with Makarios, was a firm supporter of frequent communion and wrote in its defense but was not himself exiled from the Mountain.

In addition to their championship of correct liturgical and sacramental practice, the Kollyvades were also deeply devoted to the hesychast tradition of inner prayer, as taught by such fourteenth-century Athonites as Gregory of Sinai (d. 1346) and Gregory Palamas (1296–1359), and they upheld the Palamite doctrine concerning the vision of the Light of Tabor. More broadly they sought to promote a far-reaching patristic *ressourcement*, editing and publishing numerous writings of the Fathers; in this ambitious program a central and decisive place was occupied by the *Philokalia*. Here, in the patristic and Byzantine texts that they disseminated, the Kollyvades believed that they could find a "word coming forth from silence,"[8] which might serve as an antidote to the growing secularism within Greek society.

The Kollyvades looked upon this patristic heritage not as an archaeological survival from the distant past, but as a living guide for contemporary Christians. In editing the Fathers, they had a practical purpose in view. It was their hope that the *Philokalia* and other such publications would not simply gather dust on the bookshelves of scholarly specialists, but would be read by the laity as well as by monastics and clergy. As the two editors state on the title page of the *Philokalia,* the book is intended "for the general benefit of the Orthodox." In his introduction Nikodimos maintains that St. Paul's injunction, "Pray without ceasing" (1 Thess. 5:17), is addressed not merely to hermits in caves and on mountain-tops but to married Christians with responsibilities for a family, to farmers, merchants, and lawyers, even to "kings and courtiers living in palaces."[9] Unceasing prayer of the heart is a universal vocation. The best is for everyone.

Through this patristic *ressourcement,* then, the Kollyvades sought to counteract the new-fangled spirit of the *Aufklärung.* The regeneration of the Greek nation, they were fervently convinced, could come about only through a return to the authentic sources of Orthodox Christianity. Emulating Laocoön as he stood before the Trojan horse, they cried out: "Timeo Francos et dona ferentes."[10] They feared the Franks with their "enlightened" gifts. "Do not trust the West," they said to their contemporaries; "these ill-digested notions will prove in the end nothing but a disappointment and a deceit. Our only hope is to re-discover our true roots in the Divine Liturgy, in patristic theology, and in hesychastic prayer."

Such, specifically, was the standpoint of Nikodimos. Writing with reference to Roman Catholic proselytism, he stated in his great collection of the Holy Canons entitled *Pedalion* ("Rudder"), "Divine Providence has set a guardian over us."[11] The "guardian" that he had in view was none other than the Ottoman empire. His remark can be given a wider application. The Ottoman power constituted, for the Orthodox Christian faithful, a God-appointed protector not only against the emissaries of the Bishop of Rome but equally against the corruptive influences of the Enlightenment. Many traditionalist Orthodox, so far from supporting schemes to rebel against the Turks with the help of Western Europe, felt that they were better off as they were. Despite Turkish oppression, despite the dangers of apostasy and the sufferings of the New Martyrs, to whom Nikodimos had himself devoted a pioneering study,[12] the relative isolation in which the Rayahs existed under Turkish rule could be seen as a blessing. It safeguarded the Greek community from the infiltration of alien ideas, helping it to preserve intact its Orthodox identity.

As regards the immediate outcome of the controversy, the Kollyvades were only partly successful. Contrary to what the traditionalist monks of Athos had maintained concerning *mnimosyna,* in the decrees issued by the Ecumenical Patriarch Sophronios II in 1776,[13] and by the Ecumenical Patriarch Gregory V in 1819,[14] it was laid down that memorial services may be celebrated not only on Saturday but on Sunday, and indeed on any day of the week. Yet, on the far more important issue of the frequency of communion, Gregory V in his 1819 decree ruled basically in favor of the Kollyvades. Frequency of communion, he stated, is not to be restricted by any fixed interval of time, such as forty days, but in principle the faithful—provided that they are properly prepared and have made their confession to their spiritual father and been given his blessing to communicate—may receive the sacrament at each and every celebration of the Eucharist; for at each and every celebration they are invited so to do with the words, "With fear of God, with faith and love, draw near."

Unfortunately, despite the strenuous efforts of the Kollyvades, infrequent communion remained the norm almost everywhere in the Orthodox Church during the nineteenth and early twentieth centuries. There were scattered supporters of a more frequent reception of the sacrament, such as the widely revered St. John of Kronstadt (1829–1908) in pre-revolutionary Russia, and the members of the *Zoe* movement in Greece, founded by Fr. Evsevios Matthopoulos in 1907. But it was only in the second half of the twentieth century that communion on a weekly basis, or at any rate on most Sundays, became at all widespread in monasteries and parishes. It is still very far from being universal in contemporary Orthodox practice.

When I first visited the Holy Mountain in 1961, it continued to be the normal rule for nonordained monks to receive the sacrament only once every forty days. The only notable exception was the monastery of Dionysiou, where, under the influence of the great Elder Gabriel (1886–1983), abbot for nearly half a century, the monks went for communion once every two weeks, on Saturday (never on Sunday). I recall my astonishment when on that first visit I attended the all-night vigil for the feast of the Nativity of the Theotokos (8/21 September) at the Great Lavra. There was a congregation of more than a hundred, both monks and lay pilgrims. About ten priests and several deacons officiated at Vespers and Matins. But, when the time for the Divine Liturgy arrived, this was celebrated by a single priest, without a deacon; and at the moment for communion, out of the entire congregation not a single person came forward to receive the sacrament. Today, I am happy to say, the situation has changed, and at many monasteries on the Holy Mountain it is normal for the monks to receive communion several times a week.

■ "AN ENCYCLOPEDIA OF ATHONITE LEARNING": THE WORK OF ST. NIKODIMOS

The most prolific author among the Kollyvades, co-editor of the *Philokalia*, St. Nikodimos, has been justly described as "an encyclopedia of the Athonite learning of his time."[15] He was born in 1749 on the Greek island of Naxos, and at the age of sixteen he went to Smyrna, where he studied for five years (1765–70) at the Evangelical School, one of the leading Greek Orthodox educational centers in this period. He proved to be an intelligent and exceptionally industrious pupil. Moreover, he was gifted with a photographic memory, which greatly assisted him when, in later years on Athos, he had to compose many of his works without easy access to a library. It is recounted that on one occasion, when he was attending Vespers on Holy Saturday in an Athonite hermitage, it was found that they had no book with the fifteen Old Testament readings appointed for the service. Unperturbed, Nikodimos proceeded to recite them all by heart.

Returning to Naxos in 1770, Nikodimos became secretary to the local bishop. At this stage it seemed probable that he would pursue the normal career open to a young Greek with scholarly gifts and ecclesiastical interests; that is to say, he might have chosen to continue his education in the West at a Roman Catholic or Protestant university and then, returning to the Levant, he might have taken up a professorship at some "School of the Nation," eventually becoming a bishop. Instead, contacts on Naxos with three Kollyvades monks, exiles from the Holy Mountain, turned his thoughts in a different direction. Eager to learn more about the Kollyvades movement, he traveled to Hydra to see Makarios of Corinth, thus initiating the contact between the two that was to lead in due course to the publication of the *Philokalia*. Also on Hydra he came to know the Elder Silvester, another of the Kollyvades who had been forced to leave Athos. Probably it was Silvester who initiated Nikodimos into the practice of inner prayer.

These meetings awakened in the young Nikodimos a longing for monastic seclusion and hesychastic prayer. In 1775 he made his way to the Holy Mountain and here, apart from a few outside journeys, he remained for the rest of his life. He was tonsured as a monk at Dionysiou but was never ordained deacon or priest. On Athos, and throughout the Christian East in general, monasticism has always remained predominantly a lay movement. Ordination is seen not primarily as a matter of subjective "vocation," but in functional terms; in most places, only as many monks are made priest as are strictly necessary for the celebration of the services. The fact that a monk is well educated is not in itself a reason for him to receive ordination. Thus the situation of Nikodimos as a learned lay monk was and is by no means unusual in Athonite practice.

Nikodimos did not remain long at Dionysiou. In fact, almost all his time on Athos was spent not in one of the main monasteries but in various kellia or small hermitages. In this he resembled the Athonite hesychasts of the late thirteenth and fourteenth centuries, such as St. Nikiphoros, St. Gregory of Sinai, St. Gregory Palamas (save for relatively brief periods), and St. Maximos of Kavsokalyvia. While hesychast contemplation is certainly possible in large coenobia, on the whole it has flourished in the remote sketes and isolated hermit cells of the Holy Mountain.

"He repeatedly changed his place of residence," observes Fr. Gerasimos of Little St. Anne in the *vita* that he prepared for the feast of St. Nikodimos.[16] Does this betoken a certain restlessness and lack of stability in the saint's character? I think not; it is to be seen rather as an indication of his kenotic poverty and of his desire to keep himself totally free for the work of writing and editing. For seven years, it is true, he lived with one companion in an isolated hermitage that he had leased, the *kalyva* of Theonas, not far from the monastery of Pantokrator; otherwise he had no permanent home of his own, but preferred to be a guest in kellia belonging to other monks. He never sought to gather around him a group of disciples, as had been done on Athos some twenty-five years earlier by the translator of the Slavonic *Philokalia*, St. Paisy Velichkovsky (1722–94). By contrast Nikodimos had no pastoral or administrative position, no fixed base, no personal library, no circle of amanuenses and assistants. He worked alone.

In this way Nikodimos chose to reduce his existence to the barest possible essentials, depending on the hospitality of his monastic friends and on the books that he could borrow from others. He always wore sandals, never shoes, and he had no more than a single cassock. In the words of Fr. Gerasimos, "He was simple in his manners, forbearing, sweet and benign in character, devoid of possessions, meek and humble."[17] Truly he was one of the "strangers and pilgrims of this earth" (Heb. 11:13).

Nikodimos's career as an editor began two years after his arrival on the Mountain, when in 1777 Makarios of Corinth visited Athos and renewed the friendship that he and Nikodimos had begun in Hydra. According to the biographer and personal friend of Nikodimos, Hieromonk Evthymios, Makarios brought with him in manuscript form three works that he entrusted to Nikodimos for revision:

> In the year 1777 the Saint [i.e. Bishop] of Corinth Makarios arrived [on Athos], and after going on pilgrimage to the holy monasteries he came to Karyes and was given hospitality in the kellion of St. Antony by one of his fellow countrymen, Elder David. While staying there, he summoned Nikodimos and asked him to revise the *Philokalia*. In this way the blessed one embarked on the task. We may well ask: embarked on *what* task? I am at a loss and know not what to say or how to describe the spiritual struggles and excessive labors of his intellect and flesh. My mind lacks power even to guess at all that. He embarked, I say, on the *Philokalia*, and we have before us the beautiful preface that he wrote, and the brief lives, sweet as honey, of the blessed fathers. He likewise corrected the *Evergetinos* and adorned it with a fine preface. He corrected and expanded the short, all-golden work *On the Divine and Holy Continual Communion*. These the Saint of Corinth received from Nikodimos, and he went to Smyrna to raise money for the costs of printing.[18]

In due course all three works were published at Venice: the *Philokalia* in 1782; the vast ascetic anthology known as *Evergetinos*, compiled by Paul of Evergetis (d.1054), in 1783;[19] and the tract entitled *On Continual Communion*, also in 1783.[20]

Modern writers, when referring to the *Philokalia*, often speak as if Nikodimos were the chief or even the sole editor. If the account by Evthymios is accurate, however, then the part played by Makarios was at least as important as that of Nikodimos; for, according to Evthymios, the original initiative for the publication of the work came from Makarios, and it was he who selected the writings to be included in it. Nikodimos for his part revised and corrected the text, composed the eight-page general preface to the book, and wrote the brief introductory notes on each author. Evthymios does not say that Nikodimos enlarged or altered the choice of texts made by Makarios, but this is of course a possibility.

Other contemporary accounts by St. Paisy Velichkovsky[21] and St. Athanasios of Paros[22] differ from Evthymios in making no mention of Nikodimos's contribution and in treating Makarios as the sole editor of the *Philokalia*. Evthymios, however, who was in close personal contact with Nikodimos, is almost certainly more trustworthy. In particular, there are many similarities in style and content between the preface to the *Philokalia* and other compositions which are undoubtedly by Nikodimos. In other respects, however, as we shall see, Paisy provides valuable supplementary information about the preparation of the *Philokalia*.

Once embarked on literary work, Nikodimos continued to write with indefatigable energy for the remainder of his life. The quantity and range of his *oeuvre* are formidable. 'Who could recount all his labors and all his works of love?' exclaimed the Romanian monk Ioan of Neamţ, writing in 1807.[23] In the catalogue of his writings provided by Citterio, there are twenty-six major works, some extending to more than a thousand pages each; most of these are editions and translations, but they include several original writings. Citterio also lists thirty-two liturgical offices and canons and five shorter pieces, in addition to a number of unpublished compositions; there is also the saint's correspondence, little of which has so far appeared in print, but which is said to survive in manuscript.[24] Cavarnos gives a more detailed list of 109 items.[25]

Among the original writings of Nikodimos, the most important is *Symvoulevtikon Encheiridion* [*A Handbook of Spiritual Counsel*], which has been translated into English.[26] This is severe in its warnings to clergy, especially bishops; but Nikodimos had good reason to write as he did. It is severe also in its insistence upon the need to guard the senses and imagination; yet Nikodimos emphasizes at the same time that there is also a good use of the senses, when the beauty of the material creation raises our mind to God the Creator; and likewise a good use of the imagination, when it is employed in meditating on Christ's passion and resurrection. There is a valuable section on the heart and the Jesus Prayer, while the importance of studying Holy Scripture is strongly underlined.

As an editor and exegete, Nikodimos included in his scope most branches of Christian literature. In addition to his work on the New Martyrs,[27] he compiled a general collection of saints' lives for every day of the year, entitled *Synaxaristis*. He wrote commentaries on Scripture, on the Church canons,[28] and on the liturgical texts, all of them richly illustrated with patristic quotations; aided by his photographic memory, he was able to cite the Fathers with astonishing facility. The *Eortodromion* of Nikodimos, interpreting the hymnography of the great feasts, proved a valuable aid to me when working with Mother Mary of Bussy-en-Othe on *The Festal Menaion*.[29]

Equally important are the editions of the Fathers undertaken by Nikodimos. In addition to the *Philokalia* and the *Evergetinos,* on which he worked with Makarios of Corinth, he also edited the correspondence of St. Barsanouphios and St. John of Gaza, and assisted Dionysios Zagoraios with the edition of St. Symeon the New Theologian (949–1022) that was published in 1790 (this appeared under the name of Dionysios alone, but it seems to be chiefly the work of Nikodimos). By an unhappy mischance the three-volume edition of the collected works of St. Gregory Palamas, to which Nikodimos devoted much time and energy, never saw the light of day. The Greek printer in Vienna to whom the manuscript had been sent, George Makridis-Poulios, was a close associate of Rhigas Velestinlis, the protomartyr of the Greek revolution, and he was heavily involved with Rhigas in producing anti-Ottoman propaganda. When, at the prompting of the Turkish authorities, the Austrian police arrested Rhigas in 1798, they seized the stock of manuscripts awaiting publication in Poulios's office, including the edition of Palamas. Most of the text of this was lost, although the introduction by Nikodimos was recovered and eventually published.[30] The destruction of the edition of Palamas was a severe blow to

Nikodimos, and as a result the bulk of Palamas's theological work remained unpublished and neglected for the next 150 years.

A surprising genre among the writings of Nikodimos are the adaptations that he produced of Roman Catholic writings from the Counter-Reformation period.[31] The best known of these is *Unseen Warfare,* based on the *Combattimento Spirituale* of Lorenzo Scupoli (*c.* 1530–1610). Nikodimos did not claim to be himself the author of this work, but merely stated on the title page that it was "composed some time ago by a certain wise man."[32] Although of course well aware of the fact, Nikodimos refrained from pointing out that the "wise man" in question, far from being Orthodox, was actually a Roman Catholic. When Gerald Palmer (1904–84), the co-translator of the English *Philokalia,* was preparing an English version of *Unseen Warfare,* he wrote to his spiritual father the Russian Hieromonk Nikon of Karoulia (1875–1963), asking who the author of *Unseen Warfare* might be, since evidently it was not Nikodimos himself. Fr. Nikon, who had originally suggested to Gerald that he should translate the work, may well have had suspicions about its authorship; but in his reply he simply said in a charming but unhelpful manner, "This beautiful book lies open on my table each morning after breakfast."[33]

In addition to the *Combattimento Spirituale* of Scupoli, Nikodimos produced a Greek edition of the *Spiritual Exercises* of Ignatius Loyola, using the expanded version of Giampetro Pinamonti. Nikodimos's widely respected work on confession, *Exomologitarion,* is also for the most part a direct translation of two books by another Roman Catholic writer, Paulo Segneri, *Il confessore istruito* and *Il penitente istruito.*[34] The work *On Continual Communion,*[35] while drawing extensively on Roman Catholic sources, does not seem to be based on any single Western prototype.

This readiness to disseminate among the unsuspecting Orthodox public Roman Catholic works of piety, largely unchanged, is all the more surprising in that Nikodimos in his *Pedalion* upheld the view that the Roman Church lacks valid baptism, and so its members, if received into Orthodoxy, have to be rebaptized.[36] Why, then, did he choose to make use of Roman Catholic authors in this way? Certainly it cannot have been due to any ignorance on his part of the riches of Greek patristic spirituality, of which he had on the contrary an extremely detailed knowledge, as is evident from his editions of the *Philokalia* and the *Evergetinos,* of Barsanouphios, Symeon the New Theologian, and Palamas. If, then, he drew upon texts from the Counter-Reformation West, it was not because he had no other material available.

Possibly Nikodimos valued the psychological insight displayed by the Western authors as well as their warmly affective tone. He may also have considered that the techniques of discursive, imaginative meditation described by Scupoli and Loyola would help Orthodox who found the imageless, "apophatic" prayer recommended in the *Philokalia* to be largely beyond their capacity. Whatever the reason, the willingness of Nikodimos to draw upon Roman Catholic texts indicates how—despite the bitterly polemical attitude of Greek Orthodoxy toward Rome during the late eighteenth century—it was still possible for a constructive interchange to take place upon the level of spirituality.

Worn out by his unremitting literary labors, Nikodimos died in 1809, at the age of sixty, at the kellion of his friends the Skourtaioi, situated above Karyes. Here his relics are preserved, and the visitor is shown the dark and narrow inner room where he used to say the Jesus Prayer. I remember calling there in 1973, when I was received by the venerable yet lively Fr. Ananias, reputed to be the oldest monk on the Holy Mountain (he claimed to be 105, but I think that he was only 99 at that time; he eventually died in 1977). Apologizing for the somewhat simple hospitality, he explained that he had recently lost the disciple who helped him. "He had no business to die so young," said Fr. Ananias in an irritated tone. "He was only eighty-five."

Two things inspired St. Nikodimos of the Holy Mountain throughout his years on Athos. The first was a love of *hesychia*, of stillness and solitude. He found constant inspiration in Christ's statement, "The Kingdom of God is within you" (Luke 17:21), words that he quoted in the introduction to the *Philokalia*, and he devoted himself unreservedly to the quest for this inner Kingdom. Doubtless it was this longing for stillness that led him to live in the remote hermitages of the Athonite desert rather than in one of the large cenobitic houses. In the second place, however, he was not only a solitary but also, like his contemporary and fellow Athonite St. Kosmas the Aetolian (1714–79), a missionary. He sought to preach the faith not through apostolic journeys but through his writings. With good reason he is shown in engravings and icons holding a pen, with a bottle of ink at his elbow. In this way his life was marked equally by silence and by words: by words that came out of silence, and by a silence more eloquent than any words. He would have agreed, I think, with the saying, "Words are the part of silence that can be spoken."

Learned though he was, Nikodimos never wrote with an exclusively academic aim, but always with a practical and pastoral intent. Not only the *Philokalia* but almost all his works were directed to the laity as well as to monastics and clergy. The patristic *ressourcement* that he and the other Kollyvades promoted was simultaneously both scholarly and popular. Through their publications they sought to change people's lives. And it was precisely because his writings have indeed transformed the lives of countless others that in 1955, at the request of the Holy Mountain, he was officially glorified as a saint by the Ecumenical Patriarchate of Constantinople. His feast is observed on the day of his death, July 14. In the conscience of the Orthodox people he is not remembered specifically as a miracle worker; in Orthodoxy, however, the performance of miracles is in no way essential for the recognition of a saint. The grounds for the canonization of St. Nikodimos were his personal holiness and the outstanding contribution that he made to church life through his writings.

St. Nikodimos was not interested in philosophical speculation, even though he sometimes quoted texts from the Greek philosophers. He was a theologian in the patristic meaning of the term—"If you pray truly, you are a theologian," as Evagrios of Pontos (346–99) put it[37]—but he was not a "systematic theologian" in the modern Western sense. What he sought to convey was not abstract ideas but the living experience of the Church. In his writings he is above all a master of the spiritual life. He is rightly classified as a "conservative," but his conservatism was always sensitive and intelligent. Yet, despite his conservatism, by a strange parado) which often recurs in the history of the Church—the future belonged more to him than to the innovators and liberals of his day. Nikodimos's message is more relevant to the twenty-first century than that of Korais. What Fr. Georges Florovsky says of St. Paisy Velichkovsky is true equally of St. Nikodimos: "Paisy lived in the past, in traditions, and in Tradition. Yet he proved to be the prophet and harbinger of things to come. The return to sources revealed new roads and meant the acquisition of new horizons."[38]

"THESE WORKS HAVE VIRTUALLY DISAPPEARED": THE EDITORIAL POLICY OF THE COMPILERS

We now return to the questions with which we began. What criteria guided Makarios in selecting the thirty-six authors included in the *Philokalia*? What do these thirty-six have in common, which made it appropriate to include them in the volume and to exclude others? Are there master-themes throughout the *Philokalia*, which give an overall unity and coherence to the collection as a whole, and how far is it legitimate to speak of a distinctive "spirituality" of the *Philokalia*?

The general arrangement of contents in the Greek *Philokalia* gives us no help in answering these questions. Except at the very end of the work, the texts are simply placed in chronological sequence, according to the supposed dates of the various authors. There is no attempt to group the material thematically, as was done, for example, by Paul in his collection *Evergetinos*. There is also no indication which writings are best suited for "beginners" and which should be reserved for the more experienced.

The title likewise sheds little light on the scope and purpose of the work. Literally the word *Philokalia* means "love of beauty" or "love of what is good." Most commentators on the *Philokalia* therefore interpret the title as signifying love for whatever is spiritually beautiful and good, love for God as the source of all things beautiful, love for whatever leads to union with the Divine and Uncreated Beauty.[39] When applied to a book, however, the word *Philokalia* may also signify no more than "a collection of good things," an anthology. Eusebius of Caesarea, using the word in this sense, states that the third-century Bishop Beryllos of Bostra "left various *Philokalias*,"[40] and when St. Basil the Great and St. Gregory of Nazianzus assembled a collection of extracts from Origen, they gave it the title "*Philokalia*."[41] Is this, then, the meaning of the title in the case of the *Philokalia* of Makarios and Nikodimos? Is it merely an anthology, a selection of texts chosen more or less at random and then bound up for convenience within the covers of a single volume?

If the title "*Philokalia*" is ambivalent, what can be gleaned from the introduction to the work, written by Nikodimos? Here we move on to firmer ground. Without providing an explicit answer to our queries, the introduction supplies several valuable clues. First, as was already noted, Nikodimos insists that the work is addressed not only to monks and nuns but to all Christians.[42] This claim is at first sight surprising, for almost all the works in the *Philokalia* were written by monks, with a monastic audience primarily in mind. Furthermore, except in a few minor instances, the two editors have presented the texts, not in a contemporary demotic rendering—as Nikodimos does in various other publications—but in the original patristic or Byzantine Greek. This cannot have been easily intelligible to most Greek laity in the eighteenth century, or indeed to most priests or monastics. Even so, Nikodimos surely means what he says when he asserts that the *Philokalia* is intended for the Christian community as a whole.

Nikodimos offers a second clue when he states in his introduction that the *Philokalia* contains works that either are unpublished or else, if published, have grown scarce and unobtainable:

> On account of their antiquity and rarity, and because in many cases they have never been printed, these works have virtually disappeared; and, if some of them have been included in existing publications, yet the books in which they appear have become worm-eaten and totally destroyed.[43]

One criterion, then, for the selection of material in the *Philokalia* seems to have been the availability of texts in existing publications. The editors have left out the readily accessible and chosen the rare or unpublished.

This rationale helps to explain why, for instance, there is nothing in the Greek *Philokalia* from St. Isaac the Syrian (Isaac of Nineveh) (seventh century). Isaac may justly be reckoned as one of Nikodimos's three favorite authors, along with St. Maximos the Confessor (*c*.580–662) and St. Gregory Palamas. Why, then, is Isaac absent? Perhaps Nikodimos and Makarios left him out because a Greek edition of his writings, prepared by Nikiphoros Theotokis, had appeared only a few years before at Leipzig in 1770. Other authors of central importance for the Orthodox spiritual tradition, such as the Cappadocians, St. John Chrysostom, St. Dionysius the Areopagite, and St. John Klimakos—all of whom are regularly cited by Nikodimos in his *Handbook*—are likewise absent from the *Philokalia*, presumably because they too were readily available in existing publications.

Makarios and Nikodimos may also have omitted certain authors from the *Philokalia*, or assigned to them only a limited amount of space, because even as early as 1777 they had begun to plan separate editions of their writings. This is perhaps the reason why, for example, there is nothing in the *Philokalia* from St. Barsanouphios and St. John; although Nikodimos's edition did not actually appear until 1816, he may have started to prepare it at an early stage in his Athonite life. If there is relatively little from St. Symeon the New Theologian, possibly this was so because Nikodimos had begun to collaborate with Dionysios Zagoraios on the edition of Symeon published in 1790. If the choice of texts from St. Gregory Palamas appears somewhat incomplete, the explanation may be that Nikodimos had already started to project the complete edition which was later sent to Vienna and destroyed in 1798.

While pragmatic considerations of this kind may certainly have influenced the two editors of the *Philokalia*, there remains another, more interesting possibility. Perhaps in their choice of texts they were not innovating or relying solely on their personal judgment but were following an existing tradition already well established on the Holy Mountain and elsewhere.[44]

As we have noted, Evthymios, Nikodimos's biographer, asserts that, when Makarios arrived on Athos in 1777, he brought with him, already prepared, the draft version of the *Philokalia*; that is, he had selected and assembled the material before he came to the Mountain. Evthymios also gives the impression that Makarios stayed on Athos only for a relatively short time.[45] As a personal friend of Nikodimos, Evthymios is in general a trustworthy source concerning the Hagiorite's life and work, but at this point his account needs to be scrutinized in the light of evidence from Kaisarios Daponte, monk of Xeropotamou,[46] and from Paisy Velichkovsky.[47] Kaisarios was on the Mountain when Makarios came there in 1777; Paisy had left for Moldavia thirteen years earlier, but he remained in continuing contact with Athos through his disciples, whom he had left behind there. Both of them, then, may have had access to accurate information about Makarios and Nikodimos.

Kaisarios and Paisy suggest that Makarios in fact stayed on the Mountain for a considerable period. Paisy even speaks of a visit of "several years":

> The Most Reverend Kyr Makarios, former Metropolitan of Corinth [. . .] came to the Holy Mountain of Athos and found in all the libraries of the holy monasteries, through his unfathomable fervour and great striving, many such patristic books which until then he had not possessed. Above all, in the library of the most glorious and great monastery of Vatopedi he acquired a priceless treasure, a book on the union of the mind with God, gathered from all the Saints by great zealots in ancient times, and other books on prayer of which until then we had not heard. Having copied these out in several years by means of many skilled calligraphers and at no little expense, and having read them himself, comparing them with the originals, and having corrected them most surely and added the lives of all the holy writers of these books at the beginning of their books, he departed from the Holy Mountain of Athos with unutterable joy, having obtained a heavenly treasure upon earth. Then, coming to the most glorious city of Smyrna in Asia Minor, he sent to Venice at no little expense, paid for by the alms of Christ-lovers, thirty-six patristic books [. . .] and soon, as a certain person recently informed me concerning all this, with God's help the above-mentioned books will come out from the printer into the light of day.[48]

Although in this passage Paisy makes no reference to Nikodimos's share in the editing of the *Philokalia,* in other respects he seems to be well informed. If he is correct, then Makarios only made his choice of texts *after* arriving on Athos; and in assembling his material he used the different monastic libraries there. In that case, it is possible that he found on Athos, at least in an embryonic form, various "proto-philokalic" collections of ascetic texts on which he drew. Moreover, although Paisy does not mention this, Makarios may also have consulted various Athonite elders about the writings that they recommended to their disciples. In this way the selection of works in the *Philokalia* may reflect both a pre-existing written tradition and also a continuing oral tradition.

The reference to the library of Vatopedi is noteworthy, for nowhere in the *Philokalia* itself do Makarios and Nikodimos provide any information about the manuscripts which they used (in the case of some texts, they consulted more than one manuscript, for they give occasional variant readings in the margin). Professor Anthony-Emil Tachiaos has suggested that the manuscript found by Makarios in Vatopedi may have been Cod. Vatop. 605 (thirteenth century), which he may have supplemented with Cod. Vatop. 262 (fifteenth century).[49] Neither of these corresponds exactly to the contents of the printed *Philokalia* of 1782, but in any case Paisy makes it clear that Makarios worked in several libraries and drew on a number of different manuscripts. These two manuscripts, however, and others like them, definitely provide evidence of a "philokalic" tradition long before the appearance of the printed *Philokalia*. Continuing research may well bring to light other relevant manuscripts in Vatopedi or elsewhere on the Mountain.[50]

The possibility of such a pre-existing "philokalic" tradition is strongly confirmed by what is known concerning the activities of Paisy Velichkovsky during his seventeen-year residence upon the Holy Mountain (1746–63). This was of course well before the publication of the Greek *Philokalia* in 1782, and indeed before Nikodimos's arrival on Athos in 1775 and Makarios's first visit in 1777. Nikodimos and Makarios never met Paisy face to face, although they were in touch with some of the latter's followers who had remained on Athos after their master's departure, such as Schema-monk Gregory.[51] Nikodimos was so greatly impressed by what he heard about Paisy from others on the Holy Mountain that in the late 1770s he left Athos, intending to join Paisy in Moldavia, but he was forced to turn back by a storm.

Now Paisy, while on Athos, made strenuous efforts to discover copies of Greek spiritual texts which he could translate into Slavonic, or which he could use when revising existing Slavonic translations. What is truly remarkable is that almost all of the texts upon which he worked were subsequently included by Makarios and Nikodimos in the printed Greek *Philokalia*. In his letter to Archimandrite Theodosy, Paisy mentioned the following twelve authors that he translated while on Athos, all of whom appear in the Greek *Philokalia*:

> Antony the Great
> Abba Isaiah
> Hesychios
> Diadochos
> Theodore of Edessa
> Thalassios
> Philotheos
> Peter of Damascus
> Symeon the New Theologian (attributed to), *On Prayer*
> Nikitas Stithatos
> Nikiphoros the Hesychast
> Gregory of Sinai

Continuing his translation work at Dragomirna in Moldavia during 1763–75, Paisy made Slavonic versions of seven further authors, all of whom likewise figure in the Greek *Philokalia*:

> John Cassian
> Mark the Ascetic
> Neilos (i.e. Evagrios), *On Prayer*
> Makarios (in the version of Symeon Metaphrastis)
> Maximos the Confessor

Kallistos and Ignatios Xanthopoulos
Kallistos Kataphygiotis[52]

Out of the thirty-six authors in the Greek *Philokalia,* then, Paisy translated no fewer than nineteen into Slavonic, at a date before Makarios and Nikodimos had begun their collaboration. Of the remaining texts by the seventeen authors not mentioned in Paisy's letter, most are relatively brief, the only significant exception being Gregory Palamas. Thus during 1746–75 Paisy, working independently, translated into Slavonic nearly four-fifths of the material subsequently incorporated in the Greek *Philokalia* of 1782. What is more, in the account that he gave of his translation work Paisy mentioned only two authors not to be found in the Greek *Philokalia:* Isaac the Syrian and Theodore the Studite.[53]

The overlap between Paisy's translation program and the contents of the Greek *Philokalia* is so extensive that it cannot reasonably be dismissed as mere coincidence. What, then, is the explanation? Paisy's work enjoys chronological priority, and so it is impossible that he should simply be copying Makarios and Nikodimos. It is true that, after the Greek *Philokalia* had been published in 1782, Paisy seems to have made use of it in revising his translations for the Slavonic version of the *Philokalia,* titled *Dobrotolubiye,* that was published at Moscow in 1793.[54] But he had made the first draft of these Slavonic translations long before 1782. So far as the published *Dobrotolubiye* is concerned, the contents of the different texts correspond almost exactly to those in the printed Greek *Philokalia.* Whether this was also the case with Paisy's Slavonic translations before they were revised on the basis of the Greek *Philokalia,* it is not possible to say in the present state of our knowledge. Further research needs to be done on Paisy's manuscripts at Neamţ and elsewhere in Romania.

If Paisy was not simply copying Makarios and Nikodimos, what other explanation can be given for the overlap between his program and theirs? There are two obvious possibilities. First, Nikodimos and Makarios may have consulted Paisy's disciples who had remained on the Mountain, such as Schema-monk Gregory, and may have made their selection on the basis of what these disciples told them concerning Paisy's work. But Paisy himself, in the section of his letter to Archimandrite Theodosy that was quoted above, does not suggest that this is what happened. He implies, on the contrary, that Makarios undertook independent investigations in the libraries of Mount Athos, discovering "books on prayer of which until then we [that is to say, Paisy and his disciples] had not heard."[55] If Paisy was surprised by the discoveries made by Makarios, then the latter cannot merely have been copying Paisy, but—even if to some extent influenced by Paisy's example—must also have been acting on his own.

This brings us to a second possibility. If Makarios was working independently, then he may be indebted, not primarily to Paisy, but rather to the same pre-existing "philokalic" tradition on which Paisy himself had already drawn. The overlap is to be explained, at any rate in part, not by the direct influence of one upon the other, but by their joint dependence upon a common source.

Nevertheless, even though there is reason to posit the presence on Athos of such a pre-existing tradition, it cannot have been at all widely known in Paisy's and Nikodimos's day. Paisy, at his first arrival on Athos, had the greatest difficulty in finding the texts for which he was searching. His experience resembles that of Gregory of Sinai four hundred years earlier. When, at the start of the fourteenth century, Gregory arrived on Athos and sought an elder to instruct him concerning prayer of the heart, for a long time he was disappointed. His biographer, Patriarch Kallistos, records him as saying:

> I saw not a few men, endowed to the highest degree with grey hairs, with understanding and with every dignity of character; but they devoted all their zeal to the active life. If asked about stillness {*hesychia*} or the guarding of the intellect and contemplation, they said that they did not so much as know about this even by name.[56]

Paisy encountered the same problem when he came to Athos in 1746. Searching for spiritual texts that he could translate into Slavonic, he made inquiries in many monasteries and sketes, but everywhere he received what he calls "the same set answer": "Not only have we not known such books up to now, but we have not even heard of the names of such saints."[57] It was only when he visited the skete of St. Basil—at the southern tip of Athos, not far from Katounakia and Karoulia— that he found a Greek monk who was able to supply him with copies of the works for which he was looking. This same monk, whose name Paisy does not mention, also explained why these texts were so little known:

> The reason for this, in my opinion, is that these works are written in the purest Greek language, which few among the Greeks understand much of now, except for learned people, and many do not understand it at all; therefore such books have now fallen into all but complete oblivion.[58]

What Paisy was told about these spiritual texts falling into "all but complete oblivion" is fully borne out, as we have seen, by Nikodimos's statement in his introduction to the *Philokalia,* that these texts "have virtually disappeared."[59] Again and again, in the history of both the Holy Mountain and elsewhere, the tradition of inner prayer has survived only as a hidden fountain.

In all this, however, there is something further that needs explanation. It is clear from Paisy's account that, before he had met the monk at St. Basil's, he already knew what Greek texts to look for. How, then, had he originally come to learn about the existence of these texts? Evidently he had not learned about them from Greek monks on the Mountain, for according to his own testimony those whom he initially met had "never even heard of the names of such saints." If he had become acquainted with their names through reading their writings in existing Slavonic translations, the question then arises: who had introduced Paisy to these Slavonic versions?

It is not likely that he came across these texts on prayer during his four years of study (1735–39) at the Moghila Academy in Kiev, for the teaching here, as throughout the theological institutes in Ukraine and Russia at this time, was highly westernized and paid scant attention to the hesychast tradition. What, then, was Paisy's source? Almost certainly Paisy gained his initial acquaintance with hesychasm during his time in the monasteries of Moldavia (1742–46), immediately before he journeyed to Mount Athos. What is more, we can identify the spiritual father in Moldavia who turned Paisy's aspirations in a hesychast direction: it was St. Basil,

Starets of Poiana Mărului (1692–1767).[60] There was evidently a close bond between the two, for when Basil traveled to Mount Athos in 1750, he conferred the monastic tonsure on Paisy.[61]

Now Elder Basil was thoroughly familiar with the hesychast tradition. In his writings he quoted from many "philokalic" authors, such as John Cassian, Neilos, Diadochos, Maximos the Confessor, Peter of Damascus, and Symeon the New Theologian; he also composed introductions to the works of Hesychios, Philotheos, and Gregory of Sinai, all of whom appear in the *Philokalia*.[62] In all probability, then, it was through Elder Basil and his disciples in Moldavia that Paisy, prior to his sojourn on Athos, first heard about the existence of Greek writers in the "philokalic" tradition, whose works he then attempted to discover in the libraries of the Holy Mountain, initially without success. Elder Basil constitutes a vital link in the "philokalic" chain that extends back before Nikodimos, Makarios, and Paisy. In the early eighteenth century, so it seems, the teachings of hesychasm were better preserved in Moldavia than on the Mountain itself.

There is good reason, then, to believe that Makarios and Nikodimos, in their work as editors of the *Philokalia*, were not isolated pioneers but heirs to a pre-existing tradition, whose distant origins date back to the era of the fourteenth-century hesychast controversy, if not even earlier. The evidence about this "philokalic" tradition is scattered and imprecise, but further exploration may reveal other links in the chain.

■ "BE A HESYCHAST, NOT A PHANTAST": THE INNER UNITY OF THE *PHILOKALIA*

Having investigated some of the factors which may have influenced Makarios and Nikodimos in their editorial work, let us now attempt to identify the main features of the spiritual teaching contained in the *Philokalia*. Are there recurrent and characteristic themes in the book as a whole that confer upon it a genuine unity, rendering it far more than an assemblage of basically unrelated texts? To assist us in our search for this inner coherence, we will ask three questions. What kind of a readership did the editors have in view? What are the general scope and content of the work? How does it envisage the supreme goal of the spiritual quest? Hitherto we have been examining the *Philokalia* from the outside; let us now look at it from within.

1. Readership

Here the editors of the *Philokalia* insist upon two things, which seem at first sight to be, if not contradictory, then at least in mutual tension. On the one hand, they include many texts emphasizing the crucial importance of personal guidance by an experienced spiritual director. On the other hand, they state that the *Philokalia* is a book for all Orthodox Christians, whether monastic or married, whether ordained or lay. How are these two things to be reconciled? Many Orthodox Christians who are potential readers of the *Philokalia* will not have the benefit of personal guidance from a spiritual father or mother. In that case, is it safe for them to study a book such as the *Philokalia?* Is there not a danger that this "philokalic" material, if disseminated in printed form, will fall into the wrong hands?

Regarding the first point, the need for obedience to a spiritual guide, this is a leitmotif throughout the *Philokalia.* "When you have taken up your dwelling with a spiritual father and find that he helps you," states St. Theodore of Edessa (?seventh to ninth century), "let no one separate you from his love and from living with him. Do not judge him in any respect, do not revile him even though he censures or strikes you, do not listen to someone who slanders him to you, do not side with anyone who criticizes him."[63] "A person of pure faith," St. Symeon the New Theologian affirms, "will entrust everything to the decision of his spiritual father as if putting it into the hands of God. Even if you are burning with thirst, do not ask for a drink of water until on his own initiative your spiritual father urges you to drink."[64] Nikiphoros the Hesychast is no less emphatic. Speaking of the charisma of attentiveness, he says:

> Most if not all of those who attain this greatest of gifts do so chiefly through being taught. To be sure, a few without being taught receive it directly from God through the ardour of their endeavour and the fervour of their faith; but what is rare does not constitute the norm. That is why we must search for an unerring guide. [. . .] If you do not already have such a guide, you must diligently search for one.[65]

What, then, is to be done by those who meet with no success in their search for an "unerring guide?" Nikiphoros's own suggestion is that, in the absence of spiritual guidance, they should adopt when reciting the Jesus Prayer a particular physical technique, involving control of the breathing and concentration of the intellect upon the place of the heart. Most Orthodox teachers at the present time, however, consider that this technique—while in itself theologically defensible—can, if misused, have serious negative effects upon our physical and mental health. Therefore, in direct disagreement with Nikiphoros, they recommend that the technique should be employed only if a person is in fact under the immediate guidance of an experienced elder.[66]

Another possibility is to consult books such as the *Philokalia,* but the difficulty here is that general advice given in a written text will not always be applicable to the specific situation of each person. Without the counsel of a spiritual mother or father, how can I know that the instructions contained in a printed book are appropriate for me personally? For this very reason, Paisy Velichkovsky was for a long time unwilling to allow his Slavonic translations to be issued in printed form, preferring that they be circulated only in manuscript. In this way, he hoped, they would be given exclusively to those who, in the eyes of their spiritual guide, were properly prepared, whereas a printed work would be available to everyone. In this connection, he wrote to his friend Archimandrite Theodosy:

> Concerning the publication in print of the patristic books, in both the Greek and the Slavonic languages, I am seized both with joy and with fear. With joy, because they will not be given over to final oblivion, and zealots may the more easily acquire them; but with fear also, being frightened and trembling lest they be offered, as a thing that can be sold even like other books, not only to monks, but also to all Orthodox Christians, and

lest these latter, having studied the work of mental prayer in a self-willed way, without instruction from those who are experienced in it, might fall into deception. [. . .] The patristic books, and especially those concerning true obedience, sobriety of mind and silence, heedfulness and mental prayer performed with the mind in the heart, are suitable only for the monastic order and not for all Orthodox Christians in general.[67]

It was only with reluctance, under pressure from Metropolitan Gabriel of St. Petersburg, that Paisy eventually agreed to allow the printing of the *Dobrotolubiye*.

Nikodimos, however, adopted a different approach. In his introduction to the *Philokalia*, he acknowledged the problem: "Here someone might object that it is not right to publish certain of the texts contained in this volume, since they will sound strange to the ears of many people, and may even prove harmful to some of them."[68] Yet, notwithstanding the profound significance that he attached to personal guidance from a spiritual father, Nikodimos was prepared to issue the *Philokalia* in printed form. The potential benefit, in his view, far outweighed the possible risks. "Occasionally some people will go slightly astray," he admitted; but many others, provided that they embark on the task of inner prayer "with all humility and in a spirit of mourning," will derive great profit from the book.[69] If we lack a *geronta* (elder), so Nikodimos concluded, then let us entrust ourselves to the Holy Spirit; for it is he who in the fundamental sense is the one and only spiritual guide.

The basic preference of Nikodimos is not in doubt. By far the best course is to search diligently and persistently for a spiritual guide, who can give us personalized instruction. Such a guide, on the basis of his discernment of our specific spiritual state, will suggest to us which parts of the *Philokalia* we should read at each point on our journey, what we should note, and what we should for the moment pass over. But if through no fault of our own we fail in our search for an elder, this does not mean that we should lay the book aside, concluding that it is not for us. Let us invoke the Paraclete as we read, and he will guide us into all truth.

When in the early 1950s Fr. Nikon of Karoulia gave his blessing to Gerald Palmer and Evgeniya Kadloubovsky to publish the *Philokalia* in English translation, he took the same view as Nikodimos. Fr. Nikon was well aware that many readers of the English translation would be non-Orthodox or even non-Christians and that there was therefore a risk. But, in common with Makarios and Nikodimos when they dispatched the manuscript of the Greek *Philokalia* to the printers in Venice, he considered that the risk was worth taking.

2. Scope and Content

One basic and deliberate limitation in the scope of the *Philokalia* is immediately evident. The work is concerned not with outer ascetic practice but with inner prayer. Only occasionally do the authors provide directions about such matters as the rules of fasting, the hours of sleep, or the number of prostrations to be made when praying. Equally there is little about the recitation of the divine office or the ritual of the Liturgy. Where the Eucharist and the other sacraments are mentioned, their meaning is internalized. The focus of attention is not upon exterior observances but rather upon the interior guarding of the intellect (*nous*), upon the battle against passions and thoughts (*logismoi*), upon the acquisition of vigilance and stillness of heart; in short, the work is concerned, as Nikodimos emphasizes in his introduction, with the Kingdom that is within us (Luke 17:21) and with the discovery of "the inner self," fashioned in the Divine Image (Rom. 7:22; 2 Cor. 4:16; Eph. 3:16).

At the same time, however, there is no separation in the *Philokalia* between inner prayer and the sacraments. Even if the sacraments are internalized, that does not mean that they are undervalued. The significance of baptism and the Eucharist in the ascetical and mystical life is particularly clear in the *Century* of St. Kallistos and St. Ignatios Xanthopoulos, dating from the late fourteenth century. The authors commence their treatise by affirming that the foundation of all Christian life is the grace of baptism, personal and inalienable to each one of us. In our beginning is our end: the goal of the spiritual journey, they state, is "to return to that perfect spiritual recreation and renewal by grace, which was given to us freely from on high at the beginning in the sacred font."[70] Then, after discussing at length the struggle against the passions and the practice of the Jesus Prayer, the Xanthopouloi turn at the end of the *Century* to the Eucharist. Anticipating the Kollyvades, they recommend "continual communion," by which they mean if possible daily communion.[71]

Just as there is no separation in the *Philokalia* between inner prayer and the sacraments, so there is no disjunction between spirituality and doctrine. While writings of a strictly dogmatic character are not included in the *Philokalia*, the teaching on the evil thoughts and the virtues, on the invocation of the Holy Name and prayer of the heart, is regularly placed in a theological context, being linked to the doctrines of the Trinity, of creation and the fall, and to the events of Christ's saving "economy," to his incarnation, transfiguration, crucifixion, resurrection, and second coming. In this way the *Philokalia* conforms to Vladimir Lossky's criterion:

> Far from being mutually opposed, theology and mysticism support and complete each other. One is impossible without the other. [. . .] There is, therefore, no Christian mysticism without theology; but above all there is no theology without mysticism. [. . .] Mysticism is [. . .] the perfecting and crown of all theology; [it is] theology *par excellence*.[72]

In regard to the range of authors contained in the *Philokalia*, all of them belong to the Christian East. The one exception, St. John Cassian (*c.*360-*c.*430), is more apparent than real, for although he spent his later life in southern France and wrote in Latin, in his formative years he lived in Egypt, and his writings reflect the outlook of the Desert Fathers and, more particularly, the spirituality of his teacher, Evagrios. Whereas on other occasions Nikodimos made adaptations of Roman Catholic works, in the *Philokalia* he and Makarios adhere strictly to the spiritual tradition of Eastern Orthodoxy.

Yet, although there is nothing specifically Western or Roman Catholic in the *Philokalia*, there is also nothing specifically anti-Western or anti-Catholic. In the *Pedalion* Nikodimos wrote in polemical terms against the Church of Rome, but throughout the *Philokalia* he refrains from doing so. Not without reason, the Roman Catholic censors from the University of Padua, in the *licenza* or authorization that appeared at the end of the 1782 edition of the *Philokalia*, were willing

to certify that the book contains nothing *contro la Santa Fede Cattolica, "*
trary to the Holy Catholic Faith."[73] A contemporary Roman Catholic reader
surely agree with this estimate, unless he or she happens to be a determined ?
Palamite (which fortunately most Roman Catholics today are not).

Within the broad spectrum of Eastern Christian spirituality, the texts in the
Philokalia reflect predominantly one particular approach: the Evagrian-Maximian
orientation. This is immediately apparent from the omissions. There is nothing in
the *Philokalia* from Irenaeus, but that exclusion is not surprising, for in general he
was largely forgotten in the Byzantine and post-Byzantine East. More significantly,
there is nothing from Athanasius, Basil, Gregory of Nazianzus, or Gregory of
Nyssa; similarly nothing from the *Apophthegmata*, Barsanouphios, Dorotheos, and
the Greek corpus attributed to Ephrem the Syrian, and nothing from the Dionysian
writings. There are selections from the Makarian homilies, in the version of Symeon
Metaphrastis, but they are assigned only a relatively small amount of space.

There may have been, as we have suggested, practical reasons for some of these
omissions. Their cumulative effect, however, is to ensure that Evagrian-Maximian
spirituality prevails in most of the *Philokalia*. Even though only a few pages are
devoted to the works of Evagrios himself, the book as a whole makes constant use
of his threefold classification of the spiritual way into the active life (*praktiki*), the
contemplation of nature (*physiki*), and the contemplation of God (*theologia*).[74] It
also repeats in many places Evagrios's description of prayer as a "shedding of
thoughts," a laying-aside of images and discursive thinking. "When you are praying," says Evagrios, "do not shape within yourself any image of the Deity, and do
not let your intellect be stamped with the impress of any form; but approach the
Immaterial in an immaterial manner, and then you will understand."[75] This is the
interpretation of prayer that is presented, for example, by Diadochos, Hesychios,
Peter of Damascus, Gregory of Sinai, and Kallistos and Ignatios Xanthopoulos.
There are, it is true, occasional passages in the *Philokalia* that recommend imaginative meditation on the life of Christ and especially on his passion; a notable
instance occurs in the *Letter to Nicolas* by Mark the Ascetic (alias Mark the
Monk).[76] Yet in general the manner of praying advocated in the *Philokalia*, particularly in connection with the Jesus Prayer, is the "non-iconic" or "apophatic"
prayer taught by Evagrios.

Three master-themes bind together the teaching of the *Philokalia* concerning
inner prayer:

1. *Nepsis.* The centrality of this quality is at once evident from the title that
   Nikodimos and Makarios gave to their work, *Philokalia of the Holy Neptic
   [Fathers], Philokalia ton Ieron Neptikon. Nepsis*, a key concept in Eastern
   Christian spirituality, signifies inner sobriety, lucidity, alertness, watchfulness,
   and vigilance. In a remarkable passage at the start of his work *On Watchfulness
   and Holiness*, Hesychios links *nepsis* with a wide range of fundamental
   themes: with attentiveness (*prosochi*), purity of heart, guarding of the
   intellect, the Jesus Prayer, stillness, and contemplation.[77] In his introduction
   to the *Philokalia*, Nikodimos rightly characterizes *nepsis* as "all-embracing."[78]
2. *Hesychia.* Among the various qualities with which Hesychios connects *nepsis*,
   none is more important than *hesychia*, stillness or silence of the heart.[79] This

is a second unifying master-theme in the *Philokalia*. It signifies not so much outer as inner quiet, not so much the avoidance of external speech as interior freedom from images and concepts. As Gregory of Sinai expresses it, adapting the phrase from Evagrios cited above, "*Hesychia* is a shedding of thoughts."[80] *Hesychia* is thus a form of inner nakedness, of noetic poverty. The hesychast is one who strives to advance from the multiplicity of discursive thinking to the simplicity of silent contemplation. In the words of Gregory of Sinai, "Keep your intellect free from colours, forms and shapes."[81] As he writes elsewhere, "Let us seek to possess only the heart-engrafted energy in a way that is totally without form or shape."[82] Summing up his message, he says, "Be a hesychast, not a phantast."[83] In stating this, the authors in the *Philokalia* had no intention of downgrading or repudiating liturgical prayer, with its abundance of symbolic imagery. They took it for granted that the hesychast would read Scripture, recite the Psalms, and participate in the Church's sacramental life. All that they wished to do was draw attention to the possibility, alongside liturgical worship, of another way of praying that transcends the visual imagination and the reasoning brain. Evagrios's description of prayer as a "shedding of thoughts" was never intended, either by him or by others, as a comprehensive definition of all forms of prayer.

3. *The Jesus Prayer*. This state of *nepsis* and *hesychia* is acquired, according to the *Philokalia*, above all through the "remembrance [*mnimi*] and invocation [*epiclesis*]" of the Holy Name of Jesus. As is emphasized by the fourteenth-century authors in the work, the Jesus Prayer enables the intellect (*nous*) to descend into the heart (*kardia*), thus bringing about a union between the two.[84] Two points about the Jesus Prayer are consistently underlined in the pages of the *Philokalia*: the invocation of the Name should be as far as possible continuous, for its purpose is precisely to assist us to "pray without ceasing" (1 Thess. 5:17); and it should also be as far as possible unaccompanied by images and discursive thinking, for its aim is equally to initiate us into *hesychia*.

Makarios and Nikodimos include in the *Philokalia* various texts which propose the use of a physical technique to be employed with the Jesus Prayer, involving in particular the control of the breathing.[85] A disproportionate emphasis has been placed on these passages by certain Western writers, some of whom see here a form of "Byzantine Yoga." It becomes clear, however, when these passages are read in the context of the *Philokalia* as a whole, that the physical technique is no more than an optional accessory, helpful to some yet by no means indispensable. It is very far from constituting the essence of the Jesus Prayer, for this can be offered in its fullness without the use of any physical technique at all. All that is necessary in the practice of the Jesus Prayer is to invoke the Holy Name with faith and love; everything else is secondary.

Although texts in the *Philokalia* link the recitation of the Jesus Prayer with the rhythm of the breathing, nowhere is it suggested that the Prayer should be coordinated with the beating of the heart; and most Orthodox teachers regard such a practice as highly dangerous. Somewhat surprisingly, there is no reference anywhere in the *Philokalia* to the employment of a prayer rope (Greek *komvoschoinion;* Slavonic *tchotki*) in conjunction with the prayer. The use of prayer beads, in one form or another, is certainly both ancient and widespread, being found in non-Christian as well as Christian contexts; its adoption specifically in the Christian East, however, is an obscure matter that requires further investigation.[86] Certainly, as can be seen from the icons of monastic saints, the *komvoschoinion* was in common use in the Orthodox world by the seventeenth century.

While the invocation of the Holy Name is undoubtedly one of the fundamental themes in the *Philokalia,* it would be a serious mistake to regard the work primarily as a manual on the practice of the Jesus Prayer, without much else. Some of the "Little *Philokalias*" published in the West, by concentrating one-sidedly on the Jesus Prayer, risk giving a misleading impression of the total character of the work. In reality, in the first three volumes, except in Hesychios, Diadochos, and the "Discourse on Abba Philimon," there are virtually no references to the Jesus Prayer. The two authors to whom the largest amount of space is allotted in the *Philokalia,* Maximos the Confessor and Peter of Damascus (twelfth century), nowhere mention the prayer at all. It is only in the two final volumes that the invocation of the Name begins to occupy a central place, and even here most of the space is devoted to other topics.

When, therefore, the *Philokalia* is read in its entirety, it becomes evident that the editors were concerned to place the invocation of the Name in its wider ascetic and contemplative context. They did not regard the Jesus Prayer simply as a devotional "technique," to be cultivated in isolation from the Christian life as a whole. Yet even though "philokalic" spirituality cannot be reduced baldly to the recitation of the Jesus Prayer, the practice of the prayer does indeed constitute a vital unifying thread within the complex tapestry of the *Philokalia.*

3. Goal

The general aim and purpose of the spiritual life, as presented in the *Philokalia,* is plainly affirmed in the opening sentence of the introduction by Nikodimos:

> God, the blessed nature, perfection that is more than perfect, the creative principle of all that is good and beautiful, himself transcending all goodness and all beauty, in his supremely divine plan preordained from all eternity the deification of humankind.[87]

This, then, is our supreme goal as created human persons: to attain *theosis,* "deification" or "divinization." In the words of St. Basil the Great (*c.*330–79), "I am a creature that has received the command to become god."[88] We are not called merely to obey and imitate God in a moralistic fashion, but it is our vocation to participate by grace directly and organically in the divine life and glory, becoming one with the Holy Trinity in a transforming interchange of love. Such is the basic message of the *Philokalia.* The ideal of *theosis* is the most decisive of all the connecting threads that bind the *Philokalia* in unity.

This divinizing participation is understood within the *Philokalia* primarily in terms of the essence/energies distinction: union with God signifies union with the divine energies, not the divine essence.[89] As Maximos the Confessor expresses it, "We do not know God from his essence";[90] he "never issues from the hiddenness of his essence," and "according to his essence remains always a mystery."[91] Yet, while there can be no knowledge of God or union with him on the level of essence, it is possible for human beings to attain, in their relationship with God, "identity with respect to energy," to use the bold phrase of Maximos: "This identity with respect to energy constitutes the deification of the saints."[92] The implications of this distinction-in-unity between God's essence and his uncreated energies are spelt out in one of the most difficult yet fundamental texts in the entire *Philokalia,* the *Topics of Natural and Theological Science* by Gregory Palamas.[93]

It is true that only a relatively small proportion of the *Philokalia* is devoted explicitly to the essence/energies distinction. The book as a whole is very far from being simply a handbook on the Palamite controversy, just as it is much more than a manual on the Jesus Prayer. But the basic truth that the essence/energies distinction seeks to safeguard—that God is at one and the same time totally transcendent and totally immanent—underlies the *Philokalia* from beginning to end and confers upon it an integrated coherence. There is union with God but not confusion, personal encounter face to face with God but not absorption, participation in the divine but not annihilation: that is what Maximos and Palamas were concerned with affirming when they differentiated between God's essence and his energies, and that is also the living heart of "philokalic" spirituality.

I am sometimes asked: in what order should the different treatises in the *Philokalia* be read? Where should we begin? One possibility is to follow the advice of the King of Hearts to the White Rabbit in Lewis Carroll's *Alice's Adventures in Wonderland:* "Begin at the beginning, and go on till you come to the end; then stop." That plan, however, is probably not the wisest one so far as the *Philokalia* is concerned. As an alternative I suggest the following sequence, which corresponds in part, although not entirely, to the reading-list supplied in a dream to the Russian Pilgrim by his dead *starets,*[94] and to the similar list given by Fr. Nikon to the English translators of the *Philokalia;* I am indebted to Dr. Bradley Nassif for suggesting the inclusion of Mark the Ascetic [see, Introduction, "The Centrality of the Gospel" p. 3 and essay p. 87]:[95]

1. Mark the Ascetic, "On the Spiritual Law" and "On Those who Think that They are Made Righteous by Works" (*Philokalia* 1, 96–126; ET 1, 110–146).
2. Kallistos and Ignatios Xanthopoulos, "Century" (*Philokalia* 4, 197–295; ET *Writings from* the *Philokalia on Prayer of the Heart,*164–270).
3. Hesychios, "On Watchfulness and Holiness" (*Philokalia* 1, 141–73; ET 1, 162–98).
4. Evagrios, "On Prayer" (*Philokalia* 1, 176–89; ET 1, 55–71).
5. "A Discourse on Abba Philimon" (*Philokalia* 2, 241–52; ET 2, 344–57).
6. St. Symeon the New Theologian, "On Faith" (*Philokalia* 5, 73–80; ET 4, 16–24).
7. Gregory of Sinai, "On the Signs of Grace and Delusion"; "On Stillness"; "On Prayer" (*Philokalia* 4, 66–88; ET 4, 257–86).

A Spiritual Time Bomb

To what extent have the hopes of the two editors of the *Philokalia* in fact been realized? How far has the work appealed not merely to a monastic elite but to the total Christian community? Within the Greek Orthodox world, it has to be admitted, the impact of the *Philokalia* proved for a long time relatively limited. After the initial appearance of the work at Venice in 1782, more than a century passed before the Greek text was reissued in 1893, and it was not until sixty-four years later that another Greek edition commenced publication in 1957. In 175 years, then, there were only three Greek printings of the work. It is noteworthy that a standard Greek work of reference dating from the 1930s, the multivolume *Greek Hellenic Encyclopedia,* under the heading "*Philokalia*" mentions only the *Philokalia* of Origen, edited by St. Basil the Great and St. Gregory of Nazianzus, while making no reference whatever to the *Philokalia* of St. Makarios and St. Nikodimos. Only in the last fifty years has the latter become at all widely known in the Greek Orthodox world as a whole, and only in the last thirty years have translations been made into modern Greek. These have greatly increased the accessibility of the *Philokalia.* But it is significant that two centuries went by before popular versions of this kind were attempted.

Within the Slav Orthodox world, on the other hand, the *Philokalia* enjoyed a markedly different fortune. Read and cited by St. Seraphim of Sarov and the *startsy* of the Optina hermitage, it was far more influential in nineteenth-century Russia than it ever was in nineteenth-century Greece. Yet even so, following the publication of St. Paisy Velichkovsky's Slavonic *Dobrotolubiye* in 1793, twenty-nine years elapsed before a reprint appeared in 1822. A far wider diffusion, however, was enjoyed by the enlarged five-volume Russian edition of St. Theophan the Recluse, and the first volume of this, published in 1877, was reprinted no less than four times between 1883 and 1913. It was only through this Russian version at the end of the nineteenth century that the *Philokalia* began to reach a more extended audience.

Translations in other parts of the Orthodox world have been much slower in making an appearance. Not until after the Second World War did a Romanian version commence publication. Prepared by Archpriest Dumitru Staniloae (1903–93), this contains many works not included in the Greek and Russian editions. Inaugurated in 1946 and reaching its eleventh volume in 1990, it has had a decisive influence on the spiritual life of the Romanian Orthodox Church.[96] So far as the Orthodox world is concerned, then, the effect of the *Philokalia* has been profound yet slow in gathering momentum. The increase in its influence, while steady, has been very gradual.

Paradoxically the work has made its most startling impact, not in the eighteenth-century Greek world of the *Turcocratia,* not in pre-revolutionary "Holy Russia," nor yet in any of the other traditionally Orthodox countries, but above all in Western Europe and North America during the second half of the twentieth century. Here the ground was prepared by that short yet immediately appealing Russian work *The Way of a Pilgrim.* This was translated into various Western languages from 1925 onward and repeatedly reissued. Along with a few crusts of bread, the anonymous Pilgrim carried in his knapsack a large volume from which he loved to quote: the Slavonic version of the *Philokalia*, made by Paisy Velichkovsky. Intrigued by these quotations, Western readers longed to know more about the work from which they came.

Their curiosity was partially satisfied in the years shortly after the Second World War, when abbreviated versions of the *Philokalia* began to appear in English, French, German, Italian, and Spanish. An English selection, *Writings from* the *Philokalia on Prayer of the Heart*, translated by E. Kadloubovsky and G. E. H. Palmer, proved particularly successful, contrary to all the expectations of its publisher, Faber and Faber; indeed, it seems that the work would never have been accepted for publication but for the insistence of T. S. Eliot. First issued in 1951, *Writings from* the *Philokalia*, a substantial and relatively expensive book of 420 pages, was reprinted twice in the 1950s, twice in the 1960s, and no less than five times in the 1970s. It still remains in print.

In the last thirty years a further significant step has occurred. Not merely selections but complete translations of the *Philokalia*, in five volumes or more, have begun to appear in English, French, Italian, and Finnish. These too have proven to be a commercial success. Thus, through numerous translations into Western languages, the influence of the *Philokalia* has extended far beyond the Orthodox Church. Its contemporary readers belong not only to other Christian communions but also to non-Christian faiths, while an appreciable number—as the English translators have learned from the correspondence that they receive—are "seekers" not as yet connected with any religious group. It is also clear from this correspondence that the *Philokalia* appeals to many who are not in any sense specialized Byzantinists but simply persons with a sincere concern for the life of the spirit.

It is surely astonishing, and also immensely encouraging, that a collection of spiritual texts, originally intended for Greeks living under Ottoman rule, should have achieved its main impact two centuries later in the secularized and post-Christian West, among the children of that very "Enlightenment" which St. Makarios and St. Nikodimos viewed with such misgiving. There are certain books which seem to have been composed not so much for their own age as for subsequent generations. Little noticed at the time of their original publication, they attain their full influence only two or more centuries afterward, acting in this manner as a spiritual "time bomb." The *Philokalia* is precisely such a book. It is not so much the late eighteenth as the late twentieth and early twenty-first century that is the true "age of the *Philokalia*." While the life of prayer cannot be measured by statistics, it is probably true that the invocation of the Name of Jesus—so central to the spirituality of the *Philokalia*—is more widely practiced today, both in the Christian East and the Christian West, than it has ever been in the past. This development must surely be a cause of great joy to St. Makarios and St. Nikodimos.

"Not a book but a library": so Kaisarios Daponte described the *Philokalia*.[97] It is, however, a library with a specific character and an all-embracing unity. Although it has much to say about love for our fellow humans and practical compassion, its theme is not political and social action. Equally its primary subject is not outward asceticism or liturgical prayer. Its concern is rather with the "inner Kingdom" of the heart, and it shows how this "inner Kingdom" is to be explored through the acquisition of *nepsis* and *hesychia* and through the ceaseless invocation of the Holy Name of Jesus. It sets before us, as our ultimate *raison d'être*, the attainment by grace of self-transcending *theosis*, through a union of love whereby we participate in God's uncreated energies, although not in his essence. In this way it proclaims both the otherness and the nearness of the eternal; God is beyond and above the entire creation, the greatest mystery of all mysteries, yet he is at the same time everywhere present and fills all things. Although the *Philokalia* is neither exhaustive nor systematic, nonetheless these unifying master-themes justify our speaking of a distinctively "philokalic" spirituality. The work is indeed exactly what St. Nikodimos of the Holy Mountain claimed it to be: "a mystical school of noetic prayer,"[98] In the words of a contemporary Athonite monk, Fr. Nikon of New Skete, "the *Philokalia* is a work of the Holy Spirit."[99]

■ BIBLIOGRAPHY

Cavarnos, C., *St. Nicodemos the Hagiorite,* Modern Orthodox Saints 3 (Belmont, MA, 1974).

Chariton of Valamo, *The Art of Prayer: An Orthodox Anthology* (London, 1966) (Russian nineteenth-century spiritual writers).

Dupré, L., and D. E. Saliers (eds.), *Christian Spirituality: Post-Reformation and Modern,* World Spirituality: An Encyclopedic History of the Religious Quest 18 (New York, 1989), pp. 417–76 (the eighteenth-century hesychast renaissance and its influence in Russia).

Featherstone, J. M. E. (tr.), *The Life of Paisij Velyčkovs'kyj* (Cambridge, MA, 1989).

Hodges, H. A., introduction to *Unseen Warfare,* tr. E. Kadloubovsky and G. E. H. Palmer (London, 1952), pp. 13–67.

Kadloubovsky, E., and G. E. H. Palmer (trs.), *Writings from the Philokalia on Prayer of the Heart* (London, 1951).

Louth, A., "The Theology of the *Philokalia*," in J. Behr, A. Louth, and D. Conomos (eds.), *Abba: The Tradition of Orthodoxy in the West.* Festschrift for Bishop Kallistos (Ware) of Diokleia (Crestwood, NY, 2003), pp. 351–61.

Meyendorff, J., *St. Gregory Palamas and Orthodox Spirituality* (New York, 1974) (an overview of the hesychast tradition).

Nicodemus of the Holy Mountain, *A Handbook of Spiritual Counsel,* The Classics of Western Spirituality (New York, 1989).

Palmer, G. E. H., P. Sherrard, and K. Ware, the *Philokalia: The Complete Text,* 4 vols (London, 1979–95) (vol. 5 in preparation).

Pentkovsky, A. (ed.), and T. Allan Smith (tr.), *The Pilgrim's Tale,* The Classics of Western Spirituality (New York, 1999).

[Rose, S., ed.] *Blessed Paisius Velichkovsky* (Platina, CA, 1976).

Runciman, S., *The Great Church in Captivity* (Cambridge, 1968), esp. pp. 338–407 (on the general historical background).

Ware, K., *The Orthodox Way,* rev. ed. (New York, 1995), pp. 105–32 (hesychast prayer).

———, The *Inner Kingdom* (New York, 2000), pp. 75–151 (*hesychia* and spiritual fatherhood).

2 The Making of the *Philokalia:* A Tale of Monks and Manuscripts

John Anthony McGuckin

■ FOUNDATIONS

The word *Philokalia* first appeared in Christian literature in the hands of Clement of Alexandria,[1] where it means what it literally suggests at first sight: "the love for what is beautiful" (or good). It was a philosopher's term for seeking the good life and elevating canons of beauty to entice the development of the mind and soul, replacing the material goods sought after by the baser desires of human nature. But the word also had a different set of resonances which applied from patristic times and which certainly carried over into the minds of the eighteenth-century compilers of what we know today as a famous collection of ascetical texts, when they had the notion of putting it all together in imitation of longstanding and customary monastic practices. For while the *Philokalia* that we know today is perhaps the most famous compendium of Eastern monastic literature, it certainly was not the first, and indeed has not been the last. St. Gregory the Theologian uses the verb *Philokaleo* in the sense of "what one is really enthusiastic about."[2] It was he and the great St. Basil of Caesarea who compiled the first "*Philokalia*" in patristic times, a compendium of what they regarded as the best passages selected from the work of Origen of Alexandria. That collection is now known as the *Philokalia of Origen*, to reduce confusion. It is concerned mainly with principles of exegesis and was issued by the great Cappadocians as an attempt to rescue Origen's biblical reputation at a time when controversies about his name, his doctrine, and the value of his memory were already threatening to sideline his writings in the Church.

In related senses the verb also means to put things into a good order, to get them ready for use.[3] And in this sense, too, the noun *Philokalia* means in an academic context "scholarly research,"[4] careful attentiveness,[5] and particularly a "scholarly book."[6] Eusebius the historian used the word in this specific sense in the fourth century. The term *Philokalia* therefore carried associations of a scholar's love for beautiful things, but it first and foremost meant, in the patristic literature, a carefully crafted scholarly work—in other words, a compendium.

In much the same way that we need not translate "Anthology" overly literally from the Greek as a "Bouquet of Words," we can also simply accept *Philokalia* to mean more or less a "Library of the Fathers." The cognate *Philokalos* means someone who loves the beautiful, and it was used by the patristic writers to signify the double sense of one who was dedicated to literature and asceticism,[7] the two things being seen as intimately related both in ancient sophistic thought and

36

through most of the Christian tradition. The early monastic theorists in particular stood in a long line of Sophist ascetics of the ancient world. The Christian sophist, of course, relied not on the texts of the philosophers (though most of the greater fathers certainly continued reading them) but more on the sacred texts of the Bible and the growing body of patristic literature known to the monastics as the *Paterika* or the *Niptic* fathers. Engagement with the text, therefore, was always an integral part of the ascetic Christian experience—not applicable to all, at all times, but always a part of the mental and spiritual struggle (*ascesis*) of the intelligentsia among the monastic writers, those who would, over the course of the centuries, emerge as the veritable leaders and shapers of the movement. This same, age-old, juxtaposition of the love of patristic texts and the love of the ascetical life which they reveal can be seen much to the fore in all of the most notable philokalic revivals of the modern and contemporary ages: St. Paisy Velichovsky's dissemination of the Russian *Philokalia*, St. Nikodemos and St. Macarios's collation of the Greek *Philokalia*, the advocacy of the literature in the *Way of the Pilgrim*, and that modern *Philokalian*, Fr. Dumitru Staniloae, who has made of the Romanian *Philokalia* an even larger collation than any of his more famous predecessors. The combining of the love of the scholarly life with the love of the monastic traditions of prayer carried on in all of the modern translators of the *Philokalia* in English (giving the collection perhaps its widest exposure in history), and not least in the person of the most famous of the trio of Palmer, Sherrard and Ware, the learned Metropolitan Kallistos of Diokleia.

This profoundly close correlation of the ascetical monk with the lover of books is not, perhaps, something we think of immediately. We prefer the image of the simple peasant of the *Way of the Pilgrim* (in reality far from a simple peasant! for the work is not a historical diary, but a theological novel probably written by a scholarly Russian Archimandrite from St. Panteleimon monastery on Athos, to propagate *Philokalian* spirituality)—but even here the pilgrim is a literary man. The concept of the monastic "Library of the Fathers," however, has been a constant theme of Orthodox ascetical seeking. Reference to this spiritual literature, in many times where living spiritual Elders, or Startsi, were hard to come by, meant that the books could "stand in" for them temporarily.

▪ *PATERIKA* COLLECTIONS

The *Philokalia* as we know it today from its two eighteenth-century iterations, the Greek Athonite *Philokalia* and the Slavonic *Dobrotolubiye*,[8] is not a new phenomenon; It lies within a tradition that reaches back to the very foundations of the Christian monastic movement. It is the most renowned form, perhaps the only known form for nonmonastics and nonspecialist historians, of a much larger body of literature known in Orthodoxy as the *Paterika*, or collections of the writings of the fathers. This latter descriptor does not *refer* primarily to what those words would also readily mean to modern ears ("writings of the fathers" being generally understood as the dogmatic authors of the patristic era). The *Paterika* meant above all else the writings of the ascetical fathers, and chiefly on prayer, as these things had been assembled together over the course of centuries, and as monasteries wanted to make or purchase collations of the useful works for training monks, to be held in their library collections. The gathering of useful literature from the vast mountain of ascetical writings that Christianity produced meant that the numerous *Paterika* collections were always a matter of monks collating and editing: building collections of the best of the existing manuscripts that were circulating on the basis of personal recommendations. It was chiefly a matter of monks individually copying and soliciting manuscripts, for this was all in the age before print. Often the copyists were the monastic librarians. As they copied, they built up their library's holdings, and when these were sufficiently large they could solicit other manuscripts and exchange versions of other materials that they held. This process of loaning,[9] purchasing, copying, editing, and making collations continued from the time the first monasteries were built through to St. Paisy Velichovsky, and Sts. Nikodemos and Makarios: all three of them were monks who first had ink from quill pens on their fingers and later printer's ink upon their palms, for all of them lived to see the printed book replace manuscripts with monastic scribal copying.

The *Paterika* generally predate and encompass the invention of printing. This extensive corpus of monastic literature, in several different sets and collations, is also called the "Niptic Fathers." This title is from the Greek word *Nipsis*, meaning "sobriety," a concept that became prominent in Orthodox thought after the fourth-century fathers applied the word and its cognate *Sophrosyne* (wise temperance) to monastic spirituality, signifying the sober vigilance the ascetic ought to cultivate in attentiveness to God. The Niptic Fathers are thus the large assembly of Orthodox ascetical authors who wrote about the spiritual life. Over the centuries various editors collated the different ascetical writers into compendia and florilegia for monks' ready access to important formative literature. The Niptic books and *Paterika*, therefore, do not exhaust the monastic writings of the Eastern Church, which far exceed them in the amount of literature extant, but they do represent some of the most important collections of those texts which were felt to be standard and exemplary.

The earliest instances of *Paterika* were popularized in the fourth century as the monastic movement took shape. First at this formative era was the *Apophthegmata Patrum*, the sayings and deeds of the desert fathers, which were collated at Scete and other monastic centers and from there developed a wide readership in Byzantium. Latin translations were also made very early on. The fourth-century Byzantine writer Palladius, in his *Lausiac History* (stories of the monks sponsored by the Constantinopolitan aristocrat Lausos) produced an early exemplar that caused a literary sensation (not only among ascetical readers) in the imperial capital, which was added to with the *History of the Monks in Egypt*, known often as the *Egyptian Paterikon*. The genre was very popular in classical Byzantine times. Cyril of Scythopolis produced a version outlining the deeds and miracles of the Palestinian monks in the fifth century, and the *Evergetinon*, originating in the twelfth century at the large Constantinopolitan monastery of Theotokos Evergetes (Mother of God Our Benefactress), amounted to a large multivolume *Paterikon* collection that had a massive distribution and subsequently formed generations of Orthodox in the "tales and deeds of the saints." To this day many Orthodox, not otherwise connected with the monastic movement, can recount stories and legends derived from this literature, which has become part of the folk memories of different countries. Several of the *Paterika* had an influence on early Russian monasticism after the tenth century, and they continued to be produced in the later history of the Russian church. Chief among these Slavonic *Paterika* are the *Kiev Caves Paterikon* from the thirteenth century, associated with St. Mark of Pechersky Lavra; the *Skete Paterikon*, which is an old Slavonic version of the Egyptian desert literature; the *Valaam Paterikon*; and the sixteenth-century *Volokolamsk Paterikon*. There are others including Romanian and Serbian *Paterika* collections.

The *Philokalia* and *Dobrotolubiye* are, therefore, simply the two most famous examples of this ancient genre of *Paterikon*, assembled in the eighteenth century from a wide body of patristic and later medieval monastic writings. Their story begins, as does so much else about the classical age of Orthodox Monasticism, on Mount Athos. It has two versions; the first was published second (because the author largely worked in manuscript-copying modality) and the second was published first, because the authors had been deeply impressed by prior experience of modern Western print formats. The first to be discussed here is St. Paisy Velichovsky; the second is Sts. Nikodemos and Makarios.

▪ PAISY'S *DOBROTOLUBIYE*

St. Paisy Velichkovsky lived from 1722 to 1794. He was a Ukrainian by birth, but the locus of his major life's work, and his spiritual reputation, have established him as one of the greatest honorary Romanian Orthodox saints, for he is also called St. Paisy of Neamț. His life and spiritual development are full of interest, and the production of the Slavonic *Philokalia* is one of the things that gives a structure to his whole monastic existence, though his stature as one of Orthodoxy's great advocates of the hesychastic tradition extends beyond his scholarly work as collator of texts. He is a major Orthodox Higumen of the early modern age who can rank with one of the great saints of the past.[10] The saint himself wrote in his last years a sketch of an autobiography, focused especially on being a record of all the monastic communities he had founded. His disciple, the Romanian monk Vitalis, wrote the first biography in the four blank end pages of a Menaion[11] for the month of February, which was never widely disseminated. Twenty years after Paisy's death Schemamonk Metrophanes wrote of his life in Slavonic, and a large number of copies of it were made. Shortly afterwards the monk Gregory, who later became Metropolitan of Wallachia, added a short life of St. Paisy as an introduction to his book *Collection of Sayings on Obedience*. This Vita, which was printed at Neamț in 1817, placed emphasis on the remarkable leadership character of Paisy and on his superlative organizational skills.[12] It was the first work that offered an overview of his lasting importance in terms of the philokalic revival within the Orthodox Church. Later in the nineteenth century the Monk Platon compiled a full-scale biography in Slavonic which soon after was translated into Romanian and printed at Neamț in 1836. The Slavonic edition of this work was published at the Optina hermitage in Russia in 1847 and went through several other editions there,[13] establishing Paisy's reputation in Russian circles around the Optina hermitage, as well as in Romania.

Paisy was the child of a priest. He was brought up by his brother, also a priest, after his mother was widowed when he was four. He studied languages at the Kiev Mohyla Academy in his teens, and in 1741 he fulfilled a longstanding desire to become a monk, receiving the name Platon. His monastery was soon afterwards closed down because of the political stresses of the time, and he entered the Pechersky Lavra at Kiev. Here he came under the influence of the monk Ignatii, who spoke to him glowingly of the fervor of the hesychastic life he had found in Romania, and it became an ideal and a hope for him. In Lent of 1743 Paisy entered the smaller and more spiritually focused monastic environments of the Dălhăuţi, the Trăisteni, and finally the Carnul Sketes. The first two Moldovan communities were under the spiritual eldership of Starets Basil of Poiana Mărului, who became an important formative influence on Paisy's spiritual life, especially telling him about the Prayer of the Heart.[14] The third was in Wallachia. All three followed Athonite hesychast observance. In 1746, at age twenty-four, he moved to perfect his monastic experience at Mount Athos, where he made his way to the Pantocrator monastery[15] and was assigned to live in its small Kiparis Skete. Although he looked all over the mountain for a spiritual guide, he says that he could not find a single one that was advanced in the Prayer of the Heart. So he settled down once more to the solitary life and passed the next four years in quiet.

In 1750 his former Starets, Basil of Poiana Mărului, came to visit the Holy Mountain and sought out Paisy. On his advice, Paisy moved away from the strict solitary life and soon grew to be a renowned leader of a Hesychastic skete comprised of Romanian and Slavonic disciples. In 1758 Paisy was ordained to the priesthood by Bishop Gregory Rasca, and the community's rapid growth required them to move to the larger Skete of St. Elias. Paisy's community became known all over the Holy Mountain for the beauty of its services and the fervor of its monks. Paisy came to the conclusion that a critical problem affecting Orthodox monastic life in his generation was the paucity of living elders who could provide guidance in the life of prayer that was directly founded on deep personal experience. He decided then that he should turn to the fathers as if they themselves were living spiritual elders. Their writings would give him the answers to his present need to find masters and teachers. At first, not knowing patristic Greek, he set out to organize and list all the Slavonic manuscripts he could find on Mount Athos. They were largely at Panteleimon's library but he also looked elsewhere, always searching for ancient masters who could illuminate the Hesychast tradition, and especially the Prayer of the Heart and its notable exemplar, the Jesus Prayer. He found copies of the works of Hesychius of Jerusalem, Philotheus of Sinai, and Theodore of Edessa and began a handwritten collation of them. But he wrote later to Archimandrite Theodosius of the Sophroniev hermitage in Russia, that his first steps in collating the fathers were "all in vain."[16] So he set himself to learn the difficult patristic Greek and to this end studied with two of his Romanian disciples, Macarius and Hilarion, who had mastered those languages at the St. Sabas academy in Bucharest. Later, at Dragomirna, his study of ancient Greek would be further intensified.

On Athos, he presumed, it would be easy enough to get hold of numerous Greek manuscripts of the ascetic fathers, but he was soon proven wrong. He narrates that it was only in the Skete of St. Basil that he found ready access to the

Greek patristic writings on prayer. He first gathered and rendered into Slavonic the works of St. Peter Damascene, St. Anthony the Great, Sts. Gregory of Sinai, Philotheus of Sinai, Hesychius, Diadochus of Photiki, Thalassius, (Pseudo) Symeon the New Theologian, and Nicephorus the monk. This work, begun at Athos, Paisy would continue at Dragomirna, with Macarius and Hilarion leading the team of translators. It was a labor that would soon grow to become constitutive of his life's vocation. Meanwhile he also had the governance of his Skete and his disciples, and he started to introduce the recitation of the Jesus Prayer into his Typikon of observance, a move that drew criticism from other neighboring Athonite higumenoi who were deeply suspicious of the hesychastic revival he was leading. The archimandrite of the Kavsokalyvia Skete, Abbot Athanasius, attacked St. Paisy for "untraditional innovation," namely his allegedly excessive reliance on the "old Greek" manuscripts (prioritization of patristic ascetical teachings at a time when much Greek Orthodox thought had become scholasticized), and also for an excessive use of the works of St. Gregory of Sinai (thus faulting him for his emphasis on the Hesychastic school of spirituality, again at a time when this was not common monastic observance), and finally for "unauthorized liturgical innovations" (namely the use of the Jesus Prayer as part of his monastic Typikon). Each of the accusations hid behind the mask of "traditional Orthodoxy" but in fact was advocating the sleepy *status quo* from a low period in the history of Athonite life; Paisy, in contrast, was calling for a return to the true sources of Orthodox tradition: a tradition which, as he knew, was always characterized by its vitality and its freedom in the face of spiritual weariness, formalism, and hide-bound traditionalism.

In 1764 when Paisy was forty-two, Prince Gregory III of Moldavia[17] asked him to leave Athos and come to preside over the revival of monastic life in his country. So it was that he and sixty-four of his monks set sail for Moldavia and came to the Dragomirna monastery in Bucovina. Here Paisy reordered the Typikon of observances on Athonite models. His rule was a blend of the great monastic rules of Sts. Basil, Theodore the Studite, and Nil Sorsky. Great emphasis was placed in his own synthesis on attentiveness during the Psalm recitations in church, and also on simplicity, poverty, obedience to the elder, and the fervent prayer of the heart.[18] But one of the new characteristics of his Typikon here was to introduce a Catechetical Lecture, in the Byzantine fashion, where the Higumen of the monastery addressed all the monks on spiritual matters in the refectory each evening. Paisy's talks were taken from the patristic writings on prayer. He was beginning to show his particular genius for synthesizing the patristic tradition and making it live again in the contemporary spiritual lives of the monks. This was another stage of his first manuscript gathering and copying activities on Athos, and it taught him the necessity for some form of commentary on the mysteries of the hesychastic life which he had now studied from many complex masters. This development was to be taken to a new pitch in his publishing work when he later collated the Slavonic *Dobrotolubiye,* that major collection of patristic texts on prayer that would be forever afterward associated with his name and his mission, and which would continue to influence Russian and Romanian monastic life.

His work of transcribing and translating patristic sources on prayer continued uninterruptedly at Dragomirna, with monks Macarius and Hilarion leading the team of editors. While the community was resident there, the monk Raphael copied and compiled a selection of works from the ascetic fathers into Romanian. This was the first Romanian version of the *Philokalia*, the first time the spiritual fathers had been rendered into a vernacular tongue.[19] The Romanian version of this proto-*Philokalia* included writings of St. Symeon the New Theologian (including the treatise on the "Method of Prayer"[20]), Evagrius of Pontus, Dorotheus of Gaza, Gregory of Sinai, Nicephorus the Solitary, Nilus of Sinai, Starets Basil of Poiana Mărului, and the complete works of St. Nil Sorsky. The Romanian editor speaks of how his desire to elucidate and advocate the tradition of the Jesus Prayer was the whole motive behind his work of translation.[21]

The community at Dragomirna grew quickly, eventually numbering 350 monks. But Bucovina was taken forcibly into the Austrian Empire, and the monastery passed out of his hands. After the loss of Dragomirna, Paisy and his community eventually settled at Neamţ, on the vigil of the Feast of the Dormition, in 1779. The community grew to 700 monks and soon became a center for pilgrimage, but also of refugee movement, and accommodations were made for large numbers of the indigent. It was at Neamt that Paisy's literary project of the *Dobrotolubiye* really took off. Paisy established two groups of translators, editors, and copyists to work on the writings of the fathers and prepare them for editions in Romanian and Slavonic. The collections were made with a specific view to being a contemporary guide to hesychastic prayer. It was here that the concept of the Paisian *Philokalia* was born, independently of the Greek philokalic project that would precede him in print. Soon after he settled in Neamţ, St. Paisy sent his two leading disciples, the Romanian monk Gerontius and the Russian Dorotheus, to study at the Greek Academy in Bucharest so that they too could strengthen the translation team. He himself undertook translating work as a major part of his daily ascesis. He would spend the mornings giving counsel to the monks and organizing monastic affairs, and then pass much of the afternoon and evening in patristic translation. Of the thousand manuscripts possessed by Neamţ monastery, representing all its history, and in all the languages, no less than 276 were produced by the school of Paisy during this time. The majority of the translators were Romanian, only a few working in Slavonic. But Paisy himself predominantly rendered the texts into Slavonic. It was a momentous epoch in the early modern history of Orthodoxy. Unlike all the *Paterika* that had preceded him (which generally stressed the life of prayer and the need for ascetical struggles), this collection by Paisy was a focused work of editorial policy that gave precedence to the concept of the Prayer of the Heart as the chief guide and goal of the monastic life: indeed the apex of a Christian life, whether lived in the world or in the monastery.

In the early time at Dragomirna he was subjected to another attack from a neighboring monk who urged his own followers, dramatically, to seek out and throw "Paisian" philokalic literature into the local river Chasmin. Hearing this, Paisy once more composed a considered apologetic work which is now called the *Six Chapters on the Prayer of the Heart*. The opposition to Paisy's philokalic tradition and mission was soon afterward renewed by the monk Theopemptus of the Romanian Poiana Voronei hermitage. This occasioned another and final apologia from the saint's pen, addressed to the brethren of the Poiana community in 1793.[22]

In this final work he again turned to the witness of the fathers and adduced thirty-five of the ascetical writers to demonstrate that his teaching is at one with the ancient doctrine of the Orthodox spiritual fathers.

St. Paisy had been anticipated in the actual publication of a *Philokalia* by the Greek Athonite saints Macarius of Corinth and Nicodemus the Hagiorite. Paisy's reputation as a spiritual elder had already attracted the attention of St. Macarius, who had even made an attempt to join his community in Moldavia; but stormy weather forced the abandonment of that sea journey, and the intention was never realized. When Macarius and Nicodemus' great collection of the spiritual fathers was drawn to Paisius's attention, it seemed to him the perfect synopsis of his own vocational vision. Accordingly, when the Greek edition of the *Philokalia* appeared at Venice in 1782, he lost no time in making a Slavonic version of a large portion of it: twenty-four of the original thirty-six texts, but with collations of materials drawn from his own sources too. His editorial choices seemed to have been guided by a decision to omit the more "difficult" fathers such as Maximus the Confessor, and even Gregory Palamas. This issued at St. Petersburg in 1793, and also at Iasi. The original Greek *Philokalia* of Makarios and Nikodemos actually had very little impact in its first edition. It appeared "before its time" in the Greek Orthodox world, as it were. It was destined to be Paisy's Slavonic version, the *Dobrotolubiye*, that set fire to the Russian Orthodox world and brought about a veritable philokalic revolution: changing the face of modern Orthodox spirituality.

Paisy died on November 15, 1794, at age seventy-two. He was buried in the monastery church at Neamț. The Romanian Church and Mount Athos were the first to venerate him formally as a saint, and subsequently the Russian Church added his name to the Calendar of saints. A new and posthumous development of the Starets' mission came about when Neamț monastery established its own printing press and distribution center in 1807.[23] The original machinery is still visible there. Neamt press issued the Romanian version of the works of St. Ephraim in three volumes in 1818, 1819, and 1823; the Divine Ladder of St. John Klimakos in 1814; and the Ascetic Discourses of Isaac the Syrian in 1819. In 1822 a second edition of the Slavonic *Dobrotolubiye* appeared, amplifying the first with further texts taken from the Greek *Philokalia*. The majority of the original Paisian manuscript translations were never set into print, but at the beginning of the nineteenth century they were collated into a vast manuscript codex of 1,004 pages, which is now lodged as Ms. 1455 in the Library of the Romanian Academy.

▪ PAISY'S EMULATORS: ST. THEOPHAN THE RECLUSE AND THE OPTINA ELDERS

St. Paisy's life's work was taken up by a powerful school that came after him. Many of his own disciples, several of whom had become spiritual masters in their own right, took his teaching and mission back with them to Russia and the Ukraine after their Elder's death. But his readers in the next generations, and especially in the nineteenth century, assumed his vision and mission at one remove: including great saints such as St. Seraphim of Sarov, the Optina Startsi, and (later) Bishop Ignatius Brianchaninov and St. Theophan the Recluse (1815–94). St. Theophan

(Govorov), was a learned Russian monk who had spent time at the Kiev Mohyla Academy and at Jerusalem before becoming the rector of St. Petersburg Theological Academy. He was consecrated as bishop of Tambov in 1859 and then transferred to Vladimir, but in 1866 he abruptly renounced public office in the Church and was allowed by the Holy Synod to become a recluse at Vichenskii monastery. After 1872 he devoted himself more and more to strict seclusion, seeing no one but the higumen and his confessor but acting as a guide to many who sought his counsel in writing. He used his state episcopal pension to help many of the poor and also built a small hermitage chapel where he celebrated the liturgy daily. His chief form of ascesis became the translation of patristic texts. In the course of his labors, between 1876 and 1890, he made a new translation into Russian of the four-volume Slavonic *Dobrotolubiye*. He added many extra texts, making it a vastly amplified form of Paisy's work. Between 1877 and 1905 it issued in print in five volumes. Theophan showed his knowledge of, and reliance on, Nikodemos of the Holy Mountain by also translating and publishing the latter's Greek translation of the Renaissance book *Spiritual Combat* by Lorenzo Scupoli.[24]

Theophan's version, having an eye to that of Paisy and Sts. Nikodemos and Makarios, took Paisy's Slavonic prototype much further and, because of its considerable amplification, both superseded that of Paisy's 1793 edition and also showed a way forward; for many of the modern republications of the *Philokalia* (especially the twentieth-century Romanian version) have realized that what is at stake is not simply the reproduction of some past edition, but more a matter of preparing the best, most comprehensive, and practically useful collation of the major fathers who wrote on the spiritual traditions of hesychasm. Theophan restored to the vernacular Russian *Dobrotolubiye* collation St. Maximus the Confessor and St. Gregory Palamas, both of whom had been omitted by St. Paisy, and he also made extensive extracts of his own choice from other Niptic fathers. Both the Greek and Slavonic editors of the *Philokalias* had omitted the great ascetical writer St. John of Sinai (John Klimakos), probably because his work was so well known in the monasteries (he was read in the refectories throughout Great Lent). But John and the Sinaitic tradition had much to say about hesychastic prayer, and Theophan selected important passages to reflect their views. He added other texts from important missing hesychastic writers such as saints Barsanuphius and John, Dorotheos of Gaza, and St. Isaac of Niniveh. He increased the number of texts Paisy had chosen to represent from the Greek *Philokalia*, especially increasing the representation of St. Symeon the New Theologian.

The Optina fathers were also important disseminators of the *Dobrotolubiye* or philokalic tradition. Paisy's reputation among them as a master of the Prayer of the Heart and as a model Higumen needed no introduction. The image of St. Seraphim of Sarov, as practitioner of the Prayer, one who so luminously showed its effects in changing the elect disciple into a radiant icon of Christ, was also high on their spiritual horizons. The Pustyn was located at Kaluga south of Moscow, and throughout the nineteenth century it was the major locus, for Slavic Orthodoxy, of promoting the philokalic movement. Metropolitan Filaret Drozdov[25] actively encouraged Higumen Moses's ambitious publishing program there, disseminating Russian translations of Patristic works. Until the forced closure of the Pustyn in

1923 by the Soviets, it enjoyed an immense reputation as a center of living elders (especially notable among them, Sts. Leonid, Macarius, and Ambrose). Their hesychastic spirituality (the Paisian tradition revived the close connection between the Prayer of the Heart and the complete dedication of the ascetic to the direction of a spiritual Elder or Starets) attracted numerous leaders of the wider so-called Slavophile movement,[26] and writers and intellectuals such as Turgenev, Gogol, Dostoevsky, and Leontyev. Dostoevsky's *Brothers Karamazov* reflects much of what he had observed in Elder Macarius.

This great movement of hesychastic elders that came after St. Paisy passed on the tradition of the Jesus Prayer by also freeing it from the limn of the monastic life, handing it down as a precious heritage to a vast range of Orthodox lay devotees. It is a hesychastic tradition that has shown itself capable of dynamic adaptation: from the cell of the hermit to the busy life of the layperson: the invocation of the Holy Name being a healing, and a stilling, and an enlightenment in a world where the traditional supports of Orthodox life (the village church, the nearby monastery) are today few and far between. The Optina hermitage was possibly also the final home of the author who, traveling from Panteleimon monastery on Athos, and knowing the hesychastic tradition so well, composed the narrative of the "Way of the Pilgrim," putting into this popular form all the various parts of the Paisian tradition as it had been nurtured and rendered accessible to the laity in the Optina Pustyn. With this link, and indeed with the vernacularization of the texts begun with Theophan the Recluse, and a first English version of selections from Theophan's Russian *Dobrotolubiye*, and ending with the English version of the Greek *Philokalia*, the philokalic tradition truly began its voyage out of the world of the Orthodox monastic life and into much wider circles of lay involvement.

▪ THE GREEK *PHILOKALIA*: STS. NIKODEMOS AND MAKARIOS

To describe this part of the tale, we must begin again, as it were, for the three great figures of the philokalic tradition; Nikodemos, Makarios, and Paisy, were all once living close on Athos but seem never to have met. Both their sets of labors grew out of the same thirst to renew Athonite monastic spirituality by a *ressourcement*: a going back to the golden era of the great spiritual fathers. In order to do so, they needed to find manuscripts on the Holy Mountain and disseminate them. St. Nikodemos from the outset saw that this was the age of print. He was an indefatigable writer, and from the time he started to gather materials he had his eyes fixed on the Greek printing houses in Venice, who, he hoped, would bring out his labors in a good and sellable edition.

Now known as St. Nikodemos the Hagiorite, Nicholas Kallivourtsis was born in 1749 on the island of Naxos, where his boyhood home (a little cell-like dwelling in a bridge across a narrow avenue) is still shown to visitors with pride. He studied at Smyrna and then made his way in 1775 to Mount Athos, where he was tonsured as monk Nikodemos in the Dionysiou monastery. He died on Mount Athos on July 14, 1809, aged sixty, after a lifetime of scholarly activity as a canon lawyer (he assembled the influential collation of Greek canon law known as the

Pedalion or Rudder, adding much commentary of his own), as Hymnographer,[27] and as translator of numerous spiritual works and tracts, some being versions of ancient Orthodox authors[28] and others being modern Greek renditions of Italian works of devotion, such as the *Spiritual Combat* of Scupoli from 1589. He was canonized by the Greek church in 1955. His own spiritual counsels were published in English translation in 1989.[29] His relics now rest at Karyes (his own Skourtaios skete) on Mount Athos.

Nikodemos was a leading member of the Athonite Kollyvadic movement, so named from the custom of celebrating Kollyva ritual memorials for the dead,[30] but in reality a far more extensive monastic movement that sought a renewal of Orthodoxy's ancient spiritual and liturgical traditions. It was from their immersion in this movement that both he and Makarios of Corinth first understood the need to "rescue" patristic spiritual theology from the dust under which it had disappeared in Greek Church life. In line with the movement's aims, he was also an advocate for the restoration of the practice of frequent communion. His own monastic practice tended more and more in later years toward the solitary life.

Makarios of Corinth was one of the main leaders of the Kollyvadic movement on Mount Athos, to where he retreated after a short time as bishop of Corinth.[31] Makarios Notaras was born in 1731 into a rich family of the island of Hydra. He tried, against the wishes of his father, to enter the Mega Spelaion Monastery in the Peloponnesus, but was brought back home against his will, where he embarked on a deep and prolonged study of Church fathers and mystical texts. In 1764 he was elected as episcopal candidate by the Church of Corinth and was confirmed in that office by Patriarch Samuel I of Constantinople, later becoming Metropolitan there. Here he began a reformist program, attempting to raise the educational standards of the clergy and institute a school building program for the populace. The Russian-Turkish war in 1768 caused him to flee with his family for safety, and by the time he was able to resume residence in Corinth, the Phanar had confirmed the appointment of another Archbishop of the place; giving Makarios the licence to take up his residence anywhere he chose. In 1777, at age forty-six, he first came to the Holy Mountain of Athos and made contact with a twenty-eight-year-old monk, Nikodemos. Advising Nikodemos on the importance of the work for the future of the monastic revival, Makarios gave him the task of editing and preparing a good edition of the patristic texts he himself had assembled and collated from manuscripts lodged at Vatopedi monastery, as a new *Philokalia*. Makarios had earlier visited Smyrna and there persuaded the Moldo-Wallachian Voivode John Mavrogordatos to fund his philokalic enterprise. Makarios also gave to Nikodemos the task of preparing a good edition of two other book projects: a treatise he had written "On Frequent Communion,"[32] and Niptic texts from the *Evergetinos*, one of the great Paterika collections we have already noted, which finally would issue in a fourteen-volume edition[33] prepared by Nikodemos in 1783, the year after the *Philokalia* appeared—again under Makarios's instructions, and with money Makarios had secured from another supportive donor, John Kannas. It is clear, therefore, that the *Evergetinos* was the companion study to the *Philokalia* from the outset, and both were Makarios's brainchild.

While Makarios, was on Athos as a bishop *sine sede*, he was heavily involved in the Kollyvadic controversy, meeting stiff opposition from many of the more unmoveable members of the Athonite community. Nikodemos at this time was deeply impressed by Makarios's overall vision and was certainly influenced by him to assume the literary task of re-pristinating the patristic spiritual heritage as part of the movement for *ressourcement* of Orthodoxy at this period. Makarios retired to Ikaria and Patmos for a while, and after settling his father's estate back at Hydra, took up residence on the island of Chios in a hermitage after 1790. Here he wrote works of encouragement for Greeks to resist the Turkish yoke, and he composed a *New Martyrology.* He died on Chios in 1805.

Nikodemos's work, however, was not simply that of a printer's assistant. It was he who arranged all the material chronologically, writing introductions to the whole and to the various books, and adding notes in the process. The modern English *Philokalia* has purposefully omitted all this material. Nikodemos also added extra source materials, amplifying Makarios's original idea, and carrying it through to completion and publication in the bishop's absence. To this extent, both the bishop and the monk were authentically joint composers, though the initiation of the idea, the original research, and the supplying of the wherewithal fell to Makarios while the development of the idea and the sheer hard labor of editorial process fell to Nikodemos.

Their *Philokalia* gathers fathers of the hesychastic tradition from the fourth to the fifteenth centuries. The juxtaposing of the ancient writers (Evagrios Pontike and Maximus Confessor, for example) is meant to make the intellectual claim that the Byzantine Hesychastic fathers of the tradition of Gregory Palamas and Gregory of Sinai were in faithful continuity with the patristic writers, and indeed that the earlier monastic writers, at their very best, were harbingers and "prophets" of the later hesychastic teachings. The Palamite hesychastic school, of course, had several themes of its own that were reflective of late medieval conflicts over the issue of the knowledge of God. These arguments came to a head in the time of the Byzantine civil war of the fourteenth century and are synopsized in the conflict between Gregory Palamas (defending the Athonite traditions of mystical prayer) and Barlaam of Calabria, a Byzantine theologian who had accused the Athonites of heresy for claiming that they could see God's own uncreated light in the time of prayer.[34] When Nikodemos and Makarios organized all this material on prayer from the fathers and arranged it chronologically (it seems obvious to us moderns to do it that way, but in earlier times such matter had equally viably been arranged alphabetically or topically), then they were making a large claim and hypothesis: that all the valid line and spiritual pedigree of patristic teachings on prayer ran up to and through the Hesychastic fathers, to culminate in the hesychastic tradition of the Prayer of the Heart. This was the tradition to which the Athonite Kollyvadic revival belonged.

The philokalic collation of Makarios and Nikodemos gave pride of place to three leading Byzantine theologians: St. Maximos the Confessor, St. Peter of Damascus, and St. Gregory Palamas, but other important authors included Evagrios (also appearing as St. Neilos at a time when the editors did not realize the pseudepigraphy), Mark the Monk, Diadochus of Photike, John of Karpathos, Niketas Stethatos, and St. Gregory of Sinai. St. Symeon the New Theologian, receives only a few texts (largely pseudepigraphical ones and far from the best of this rhapsodic saint). This paucity was doubtless due to an inability to access good manuscripts on Athos at that time. In later years St. Makarios returned to Athos with a commission for Nikodemos to make a fuller edition of the works of St. Symeon, which he duly published in a modern Greek version. The Russian Philokalists equally lost no time in making up the deficiency in relation to St. Symeon: one of the leading voices for the spiritual tradition that most comprehensively summed up the tradition of the Prayer of the Heart: dedication to an elder, a heartfelt dedication to interior prayer, the frequent appeal to the "gift of tears," a fervent belief in the Spirit's immediacy, and an expectation of seeing God as radiant light.

The making of the *Philokalia* was, for Nikodemos and Makarios as much as it had been for Paisy, a strong defense of their own authenticity as Orthodox monastics: a brave apologetic against the current *status quo* on the Holy Mountain and elsewhere in the Orthodox corridors of power (such as Russia and Ukraine, for example) where heavily Westernized scholastic patterns of thought were in the ascendancy. To Paisy and the Kollyvadic fathers it must have seemed as if Barlaam was once more scoffing at the Athonites. The bringing together of this barrage of a response fitted their situation exactly. It was not, of course, an exact historical line of development that they thus sketched, by making the materials assume a chronological order, though it was easy to imply such a thing by the very juxtaposition of materials. The connection between Evagrios and the Hesychasts of the medieval period, for example, is more than tenuous. The presumption that Symeon the New Theologian in the eleventh century is "doing the same thing" as the Hesychasts of several centuries later is a large presumption too. But what seemed to the philokalic compilers to matter most, and what gave them their common theme of reference, is that all these authors were practical masters in the ways of prayer. For the compilers that meant above all else fervor of prayer, a dedication to the inner life: and in turn that signified to them the culmination of the whole tradition in the hesychastic movement, and particularly in its modern revival in the form of the Prayer of the Heart directed by the tradition of Eldership (*Starchestvo*).

There is much within the collection of philokalic texts, then, that is not the same as the tradition of the Prayer of the Heart. The Jesus Prayer as such is not often mentioned in the texts. But it is equally true that, issued with a view to its being a library of reference for practitioners of the Jesus Prayer, the entire corpus could be seen as offering a progressive movement from the ancient fathers, through the Byzantine masters, direct to the door of the Prayer of the Heart revival. Such was, surely, its intent. Such has been its effect ever since it was published. In the Greek world, response was muted when these large collections of the *Philokalia* and the *Evergetinos* came out. The *Dobrotolubiye*, which, as we have seen, was not just a Slavonic afterthought, or straightforward version of the Greek *Philokalia*, was really the text that launched the ship and set in motion the process of adding to the collations, rendering them from Slavonic to Russian and from manuscript to printed book. The issuing of the Greek version in its excellent later Astir Press edition, the basis then for its rendering into English, fanned the flames once more, as did the larger new collation of the Romanian

Philokalia headed by Fr. Dumitru Staniloae. Today the *Philokalia* has escaped from the monastery—for good or ill. The context the Athonite and Paisian monks always had in mind, namely that these texts would direct the spiritual life under the close advisement of a monastic elder, has now disappeared also; but the compensation is the immeasurably greater familiarity that so many people now have with the classics of Orthodox ascetical tradition. Paisy, Makarios, and Nikodemos could hardly have dreamed that their labors, so often against the grain of eighteenth-century Orthodox attitudes, would lead to such a revival, lead to such riches enjoying their greatest exposure ever in the course of the long ages of history.

3   The Influence of the *Philokalia* in the Orthodox World

Andrew Louth

The influence of the *Philokalia* can be thought of in two rather different ways. On the one hand, we can think of what one might call the reception of the *Philokalia*: how it was read, who read it, when and how and into what languages it was translated, whether the selections translated suggest different ways in which the *Philokalia* has been received and understood. On the other hand, we could think of the influence of the *Philokalia* in another way: how has the *Philokalia* affected the way its readers understand the nature of the Christian life, the nature of the Church, and even, in particular, the nature of theology? If we call the first kind of influence its *material* reception, we might (to use a word that is perhaps a sign of too great a familiarity with the English translation of the *Philokalia*!) call the second kind of influence its *noetic* reception. The material reception of the *Philokalia* is largely a matter of history—of dates and facts that can be verified, though we shall find that there are, as with any history, issues that can seem more subjective: actual translation may be fairly clear, but a more diffused influence may be more difficult to be sure about. The noetic reception of the *Philokalia* is a much more subjective matter; in exploring what is meant by noetic reception we shall encounter claims that really constitute challenges to what we consider Orthodoxy to be, what we consider theology to be. However, the material reception or influence needs to be considered first, since it provides a kind of bedrock of verifiable claims, to which the grander noetic claims will need to relate.

First of all, however, we need to establish what the *Philokalia* is, what kind of an anthology (which is what the Greek word φιλοκαλία means) it is. This question is treated in detail elsewhere in this symposium, but it is necessary to establish the main outlines here. It is, as Metropolitan Kallistos has put it, "[a] vast collection of ascetic and mystical texts by thirty-six different authors, extending from the fourth to the fifteenth century, . . . arguably the most significant Greek Orthodox book to appear during the whole of the four centuries of the Tourkokratia."[1] It was put together by St. Makarios of Corinth and St. Nikodimos of the Holy Mountain; there are varying accounts as to their respective roles in the production of the work, but it seems clear that, though the initiative and preliminary selection of texts were St. Makarios's, St. Nikodimos's role, not least in providing the introductions to the different texts and to the *Philokalia* as a whole, was significant. The selection of texts seems, however, to have represented an already existing tradition: there are what might be called "protophilokalias" that still exist in manuscripts, notably in the library of the Monastery of Vatopedi, and the translation of the *Philokalia* by St. Païssy Velichkovski must have been well under way before the publication of the work in Venice in 1782, which suggests that St. Païssy was translating a traditional body of material rather than a selection from the published *Philokalia*. We are then dealing with a traditional body of Athonite spiritual writings. Caution is required in understanding what that means, for it is also clear that this tradition was not widespread on the Holy Mountain in the eighteenth century; the tradition of hesychasm had shrunk to a trickle, apparently unknown to many of the Athonite monks, though that trickle was strong enough to nourish the renewal movement among the Kollyvades, to whom St. Makarios and St. Nikodimos belonged. So, if a tradition, then tradition as a remnant. The actual selection of texts for the *Philokalia* betrays elements of contingency. One criterion, judging from St. Nikodimos's remarks in his preface to the work, seems to have been current availability; to realize the significance of that criterion, one needs to know something of the extraordinary productivity of St. Nikodimos, who, with almost unbelievable energy, had made available an enormous array of resources from the tradition of Greek Orthodoxy: his editions of the canons, the *Pidalion*, or Rudder, of the huge ascetic anthology of the eleventh century, known as the *Evergetinos*, as well as editions of the Gaza ascetics, Sts. Barsanouphios and John, of St. Symeon the New Theologian (with Dionysios Zagoraios), and of St. Gregory Palamas (which, alas, perished in Vienna in 1798). St. Nikodimos was not alone in this work of *ressourcement*: an edition of one of the saint's favorite writers, St. Isaac the Syrian, had appeared in 1770, edited by Nikephoros Theotokis, and—then, as in the last century—Orthodox patristic *ressourcement* depended on and was inspired by Western scholarship, which had made available the works of the Cappadocians, St. John Chrysostom, St. Dionysios the Areopagite, St. John of the Ladder, and much of St. Maximos the Confessor by the end of the eighteenth century. These saints were all important to St. Nikodimos, as we know from his citations of them in his own works, such as a tract, *On Frequent Communion*, and his *Handbook on Spiritual Counsel*.[2]

Omission of authors from the *Philokalia*, therefore, does not mean that they were overlooked or excluded; it may simply mean that they were readily enough available already. Nonetheless, it was the *Philokalia* as published that exercised influence, and we need to look at what this immense body of texts represented. In some ways it might seem obvious: it is a collection of texts, presented in what St. Nikodimos thought was their chronological order, culminating in works associated with the hesychast controversy of fourteenth-century Byzantium. That controversy concerned the practice of the Jesus Prayer, and claims made by Athonite monks that through the practice of this prayer they had been granted deification and seen the uncreated light of the Godhead. Barlaam the Calabrian had ridiculed the physical techniques adopted by some of the hesychast monks, and St. Gregory Palamas had defended them, though without laying any great stress on such physical techniques. More important, Palamas had made much of the distinction in God between his essence, which is unknowable, and his activities (or energies, ἐνέργειαι) in which God makes himself known. St. Gregory Palamas is indeed one of the most important theologians drawn on in the *Philokalia*, and the work does culminate with his writings and those of his immediate antecedents (Theoliptos, Gregory of Sinai) and supporters (notably the Xanthopoulos brothers, Kallistos and Ignatios). There are two short treatises that expound the physical techniques: *The Three Methods of Prayer*, attributed to St. Symeon the New Theologian, and St. Nikiphoros the Monk's *On Watchfulness and Guarding of the Heart*, and Palamas's brief defense of physical techniques from his *Triads*. Palamas's distinction between God's essence and activities is discussed in the *150 Chapters*, but other works by Palamas defending this distinction, fundamental for Palamas's theology, are not, notably the third part of the *Triads*. While it is clearly not erroneous, then, to see the *Philokalia* as occupying a standpoint that might be regarded as hesychast, and establishing a hesychast perspective, the hesychast culmination seems a little hesitant, and to regard the *Philokalia* as a whole as representing what Germans might call the *Herkunft*[3] of Palamism or hesychasm seems unbalanced; it is not until one is two-thirds the way through the *Philokalia* that the hesychast theme of the Jesus Prayer is more than alluded to, and one needs to go still further for the Palamite distinction between essence and activities.

It seems, then, that we have to allow St. Nikodimos's scholarly propensities to weigh more heavily than his polemical aims. What we have in the *Philokalia* is an eclectic selection (eclectic partly for the contingent reasons already mentioned) illustrating the breadth and depth of the Byzantine ascetic and mystical tradition. Works that St. Nikodimos says in his introduction "have never in earlier times been published, or if they have, lie in obscurity, in darkness, in a corner, uncherished and moth-eaten, and from there dispersed and squandered."[4] Yet if there is less polemical intent in the selection, and more scholarly delight in bringing to the light of day rare works almost forgotten, the collection can hardly be called random. The inclusion of authors such as St. Diadochos of Photiki, Nikitas Stithatos, and especially St. Maximos the Confessor (to whom more pages are devoted than any other author) points to an understanding of theology in which heart and mind—devotion and rigorous thought—are united. How far it is legitimate to see such theologians—to whom one must add St. Gregory Palamas—as constituting an axis defining what one might then call a philokalic sense of the coinherence of theology and spirituality is something that may perhaps emerge as we pursue further the influence of the *Philokalia*.

The *Philokalia* was published in a period when there was a determined attempt to recover the full breadth of the tradition of Greek Orthodoxy, in which attempt St. Nikodimos played a central role. The story of the influence of the *Philokalia* does not, however, continue in Greece, which achieved independence from the Ottoman yoke in 1832, except spasmodically (there is some evidence of the continuation of philokalic spirituality inspiring some of the new martyrs in the Aegean islands—for instance, Chios, Paros, Skiathos, and Patmos),[5] but rather in the world of the Slavs. As we have already mentioned, while Sts. Makarios and Nikodimos were compiling the *Philokalia*, St. Païssy Velichkovski was already translating into Slavonic some of the works that came to be included in the *Philokalia*. When this collection was published in 1793, it was called the *Dobrotolubiye*, the word being a calque of the Greek φιλοκαλία, with no independent meaning as a Slavonic word (and thus simply suggesting to the Slav ear the meaning "love of beauty"), making clear that Païssy thought of it as a rendering of St. Makarios and Nikodimos's collection. St. Païssy had come to the Holy Mountain already aware of the tradition of hesychast spirituality. This may ultimately be traceable to the hesychast tradition of St. Nil Sorsky and the Nonpossessing monks,[6] which may have migrated to the Romanian princedoms of Wallachia and Moldavia during the time of Peter the Great and Catherine the Great. More immediately he owed his knowledge of philokalic spirituality to a Romanian elder, St. Basil of Poiana Mărului, whom he had met during his period in the monasteries of Moldavia in 1742–46, after his studies at the Moghila Academy in Kiev, and who tonsured him as a monk in 1750 on Mount Athos.[7] It used to be thought that St. Païssy had simply selected from the Greek *Philokalia* in making his translation, but it now looks rather that his selection derived from similar sources; it has remarkable parallels to the Greek anthology (and may, before publication, have been checked against the Greek text); as Metropolitan Kallistos has put it, "during 1746–75 Paissy, working independently, translated into Slavonic nearly four-fifths of the material subsequently included in the Greek *Philokalia* of 1782."[8] Nonetheless, it is striking what this one-fifth covers: the whole of St. Maximos, all the Makarian material, and the whole of St. Gregory Palamas. One can no longer think of St. Païssy as deleting this material, but it remains that his selection has a very different feel than the selection represented by the Greek *Philokalia*: the more theologically complex material is omitted, so that what is left is more straightforwardly ascetical.

The *Dobrotolubiye* in its Slavonic form was destined to have a remarkable influence. One of the intentions of St. Nikodimos, as he makes clear in his introduction, was to make the riches of the tradition represented by it available to all Orthodox Christians, married as well as monastics. Many have detected in this statement a contradiction, for many of the texts included insist on the importance of personal guidance from an experienced spiritual father (or mother), and where, outside a monastery, is such a guide likely to be found?[9] St. Nikodimos was willing to take the risk of these writings' being misinterpreted, for the sake of the benefits they would bring, which he felt would outweigh any such danger.[10] St. Païssy was more inclined to evade any such contradiction by seeking to have his *Dobrotolubiye* kept for monastic eyes; it was only at the insistence of Gabriel, Metropolitan of Novgorod and St. Petersburg, a friend of the great spiritual master St. Tikhon of Zadonsk, that the *Dobrotolubiye* was published at all.[11] It certainly seems to be the case that the advance of the *Dobrotolubiye* among the Slavs went hand-in-hand with an emphasis on the importance of spiritual fatherhood, *starchestvo*. Disciples of St. Païssy brought the *Dobrotolubiye* and its spirituality to Russia. One of the monks involved, at Metropolitan Gabriel's behest, in preparing the 1793 edition of the *Dobrotolubiye*, the monk Nazar, originally from Sarov and then refounder of the monastery of Valaam on Lake Ladoga, retired to Sarov in 1801, taking a copy of the *Dobrotolubiye* with him; through him St. Seraphim became acquainted with the *Dobrotolubiye*, though his spirituality was already indebted to the authentic tradition of St. Nil Sorsky.[12] It was the monastery of Optino, just over 100 miles to the southwest of Moscow, however, that rapidly became a center for this movement of renewal. We catch a glimpse of this influence in the early chapters of Dostoevsky's novel *The Brothers Karamazov*, in the figure of the starets Zossima, given central importance but viewed with suspicion by many of his fellow monks. Because of its accessibility from Moscow, Optina Pustyn attracted many of the intelligentsia, especially among the Slavophils; Ivan Kireevsky's sense of the paramount value of the witness of the Fathers can be seen as reflecting the influence of the *Philokalia*. For him, "The Holy Fathers speak of a country they have been to"; in their writings the Fathers bear "testimony as eyewitnesses."[13] This philokalic renewal—among both monastics and laypeople who sought spiritual succor from the monasteries—ran parallel with (whether there was any cause-and-effect, and which way round, I do not know) a program of translation from the Fathers into Russian in the course of the nineteenth century, with the result that, as Olivier Clément has put it, "at the end of the nineteenth century, Russia had at its disposal, in its own language, the best patristic library in Europe."[14]

There are two further markers of the influence of the *Philokalia* in nineteenth-century Russia that could be mentioned. First, St. Païssy's desire to preserve the *Dobrotolubiye* for monks would have been assisted by the fact that his translation was not into Russian, but into Church Slavonic. Later on in the century, between 1877 and 1889, a translation into Russian, made by St. Theophan the Recluse, was published in five volumes. It is based on the Greek *Philokalia* and restores many of the treatises omitted by St. Païssy, though not entirely. It includes from St. Maximos the *Centuries on Love*, selections from the *Theological and Economical Chapters* and the five additional "diverse" centuries, as well as the *Ascetic Book*, but not (rather surprisingly) his commentary on the *Our Father*; it includes the centuries by Thalassios and various smaller writings, two of the works of St. Gregory of Sinai, and some of the works of St. Gregory Palamas, and his *Life*, but not the *150 Chapters* or the *Agioritic Tome*. A selection of the Makarian Homilies is included from the standard set of *50 Homilies*, not, as in the Greek *Philokalia*, from the paraphrase by Symeon Metaphrastes. Furthermore, a number of authors not present in the Greek *Philokalia* are included: notably, Ephrem the Syrian, John of the Ladder, Barsanouphios, John and Dorotheos of Gaza, Isaac the Syrian and, especially Theodore the Stoudite, to whom the whole of vol. 4 is dedicated. In addition, the selections from St. Antony the Great, Isaias of Gaza, Evagrios, Cassian, Mark the Hermit, and Nilos of Ancyra are supplemented with works not included in the Greek *Philokalia* of 1782 (the additions under the name of St. Antony are no less spurious than the original item, unless one counts the selections from St. Athanasios's *Life of St. Antony*). The long work by Peter of Damascus is omitted, having been already published in Russian. The desire to add what St. Païssy had omitted (as he would have seen it) is clearly one of St. Theophan's motives. There is not much sign of serious scholarly scruples (though this might account for the substitution of Symeon Metaphrastes's paraphrase of the Makarian material). Palamas's *150 Chapters* were omitted because they contained "a good number of ideas difficult to understand or express," and the chapters of Kallistos Kataphygiotes, because they are "too subtle and largely speculative and syllogistic," as Theophan put it in his introductions to these works, and similar reasons account for the omission of chapters from Maximos, Elias Ekdikos, and Nikitas. The texts dealing with physical techniques by Nikiphoros, Pseudo-Symeon, and Gregory of Sinai have been drastically curtailed in the sections dealing with the breathing techniques, because St. Theophan had serious reservations about these techniques, as he makes clear. Theophan's own agenda is very clear, and like St. Païssy, he shows a preference for the ascetical rather than the theological or mystical. This translation by St. Theophan went into second and third editions, which have been reprinted; it is the standard Russian translation of the *Philokalia* and has been very influential not only in Russia but throughout the Slav-speaking world.

The other marker of the influence of the *Philokalia* in nineteenth-century Russia is rather different: it is a small work known in English as *The Way of a Pilgrim*, in Russian *Candid Tales of a Pilgrim to His Spiritual Father*. The story is extremely well known (that is a measure of its influence)—about a "pilgrim," perhaps better a wanderer, or *strannik*, familiar even to English readers from the pages of Tolstoy, who traveled from place to place, as many did in Imperial Russia. This *strannik*, who did try once to make a pilgrimage to Jerusalem, is presented as anxious to fulfil the Apostle's command to "pray without ceasing." After several responses that he finds unsatisfactory, he learns about, and then learns to practice, the Jesus Prayer. He also acquires a copy of the *Dobrotolubiye*—a worn and battered one, for which he pays two rubles—which he pores over every day and carries in his knapsack. The Jesus Prayer is for him a revelation and a source of joy:

> [a]nd when with all this in mind I prayed with my heart, everything around me seemed delightful and marvellous. The trees, the grass, the birds, the earth, the air, the light seemed to be telling me that they existed for man's sake, that they witnessed to the love of God for man, that everything proved the love of God for man, that all things prayed to God and sang his praise.[15]

This apparently artless work has had a tremendous influence both within and outside the Orthodox world. It famously appeared as a "pea-green book" in J. D. Salinger's *Franny and Zooey*. Recent research has revealed something of its background.[16] The familiar version is a later version—edited by St. Theophan the Recluse—who made the figure of the spiritual father, the *starets*, central. It is based on earlier material that has its context in the missionary work of an Orthodox priest, a former Old Believer, Fr. Mikhail Kozlov, among the Old Believers with whom the *stranniki* were popular. It illustrates the paradox of the issue of the accessibility of the Jesus Prayer, for St. Theophan's version, edited to bring the spiritual father into prominence, has introduced the practice of the Jesus Prayer well beyond circles in which a spiritual father could be found—even beyond the boundaries of Orthodoxy or any traditional form of Christianity.

The account of the material influence of the *Philokalia* throughout the Orthodox world must continue back in the country that can lay claim to its origins: Romania.[17] Here the story is not dissimilar to that in Russia. St. Païssy's disciples carried the tradition of philokalic spirituality from Neamţ to other monasteries in Moldavia and Wallachia; notable figures include St. Callinic of Cernica (1787–1867). The latter half of the nineteenth century saw a decline in monasticism, but the philokalic tradition continued, and in the twentieth century the tradition was found in the monastery of Sihastria, restored by the starets Ioanichie Moroï, among whose disciples were Fr. Païsie (1897–1993) and the renowned Father Cleopa (1912–98). In Transylvania another monastery, which had been destroyed in the eighteenth century by the Austrians and restored in 1935 by Metropolitan Nicolae Balan (1882–1955), Sîmbata de Sus, became a center of philokalic spirituality under its stareţ, Arsenie. In nearby Sibiu one of the professors in the Orthodox Theological Faculty was Fr. Dumitru Stăniloae, one of the first to conduct first-hand research on St. Gregory Palamas, working on the manuscripts held in Paris, where he encountered the lay Catholic intellectuals Maurice Blondel, Gabriel Marcel, and Jacques Maritain. Fr. Dumitru's lifework was to be the Romanian *Filocalia*, the first four volumes of which appeared in Sibiu between 1946 and 1948. The continuation of the venture was prevented by the communist régime, which took over in 1948, and it did not resume until 1976, appearing now in Bucharest, to which Stăniloae had moved in 1948; the final eight volumes appeared between 1976 and 1991. Fr. Stăniloae's *Filocalia* is rather different from either the Greek or Slav version. Although the authors are much the same, instead of translating the texts as they appeared in the Greek original, Fr. Dumitru went back to the original works in the many cases where only a selection or paraphrase had appeared in the Greek *Philokalia*. Instead of the "Diverse Chapters" of St. Maximos, which are for the most part a selection in the form of chapters from Maximos's *Questions to Thalassium*, Stăniloae gives the whole of the *Questions* (and, for good measure, adds the whole of what was then known of the *Quaestiones et Dubia*). Again, with St. Symeon the New Theologian, Stănilaoe gives complete translations from modern critical editions. Like Theophan in his *Dobrotolubiye*, he adds texts from Barsanouphios, John and Dorotheos of Gaza (using the critical edition in *Sources Chrétiennes* in the case of Dorotheos), includes the *Ladder of Paradise* of St. John of Sinai, and devotes a whole volume to St. Isaac the Syrian (he does not, however, include anything from Theodore of Stoudios), as well as adding a "Romanian" appendix to volume 8 (including texts from the elder Basil of Poiana Mărului and some others). In addition to his *Filocalia*, Fr. Dumitru published many other patristic texts by St. Athanasios, St. Gregory the Theologian, St. Cyril of Alexandria, Dionysios the Areopagite, St. Maximos the Confessor, St. Symeon the New Theologian, and St. Gregory Palamas. Furthermore, in all these translated works, including the volumes of the *Filocalia*, Fr. Dumitru provided succinct commentaries, and not just the introductions St. Nikodimos and St. Theophan provided in their versions. These commentaries recognize that publication in print means that there is no way of controlling who will read these texts, so that some guidance, which would ideally be provided by a spiritual father, is necessary.

The material influence of the *Philokalia* in the rest of Europe is still largely a story of the influence in the Orthodox world, though translations into English, French, German, and other languages inevitably—and designedly—reached a wider readership. In English the first volumes of translations from the *Philokalia* were made by a Russian émigrée, E. Kadloubovsky, and an English philanthropist, G. E. M. Palmer, from St. Theophan's *Dobrotolubiye*. The first volume was a selection called *Writings from the Philokalia on the Prayer of the Heart* (1951), which, as the title suggests, is mostly on the Jesus Prayer. The first part of the selection, in fact, consists of the works mentioned to the pilgrim by his spiritual father as what to read first in the *Philokalia*,[18] with a few supplements, followed in parts 2 and 3 with further selections from Hesychios of Jerusalem, Philotheos of Sinai, Sts. Barsanouphios and John of Gaza, Theoliptos of Philadelphia, and St. Philemon the Abba. It focuses on the practice of the Jesus Prayer and includes two of the treatises on the physical techniques of prayer (in St. Theophan's abbreviated form). It presents very much the devotional aspect of the *Philokalia*. A further volume, called *Early Fathers from the Philokalia* (1953), contained passages from "St. Antony the Great," St. Mark the Monk, Evagrios, St. Neilos of Sinai (in fact Evagrios's *On Prayer*), St. Dorotheos of Gaza, St. Isaac the Syrian, St. Maximos's *Four Centuries on Love* plus a selection from Theophan's selection from the seven further centuries, and a brief selection from Theodore of Edessa, with a couple of brief appendices from St. Gregory Palamas and his *Life*. Again, the emphasis is on the devotional aspect of the *Philokalia*. Along with these selections from the *Dobrotolubiye*, Kadloubovsky and Palmer also translated Theophan's revision of Nikodimos's *Unseen Warfare* (published in 1952), based on a couple of works by the Theatine Lorenzo Scupoli, which drew unusual attention to the Western affinities of the two men most associated with the *Philokalia*, itself a rigorously Orthodox selection of texts, and somewhat later Kadloubovsky (this time with E. M. Palmer) translated a work, called in Russian *Mental Art. On the Jesus Prayer*, a selection made by Igumen Chariton of Valaam mostly from the writings of St. Theophan dealing with the Jesus Prayer (1966). These further underline the practical, devotional aspect of the *Philokalia*.

Still later, G. E. H. Palmer, together with Philip Sherrard and Kallistos Ware, began to bring out an English translation of the *Philokalia* based on the original Greek version. This was a rather different venture that strove to pursue a middle course, respecting the integrity of the *Philokalia* of St. Makarios and St. Nikodimos while at the same time observing the canons of philological scholarship. Indeed, it was different, not only from Kadloubovsky and Palmer's translation of selections from Theophan's Russian, but from all the versions we have surveyed, for it made no attempt to supplement or select from the text of the original *Philokalia* of 1782; there were only two kinds of changes: first, critical editions, where available, were used, rather than the text produced in 1782, and second, Nikodimos's prefaces (even his preface to the whole work) were replaced with their own, reflecting the views of current scholarship with regard to date, authenticity, and so forth. This work entailed two significant changes from the original version: the selection from St. Antony was relegated to an appendix, since none of it is authentic, or even Christian, and *On Prayer*, ascribed to St. Neilos, is restored to Evagrios. In many cases, too, pseudonymity is acknowledged. This edition, projected in five volumes, is still incomplete.[19]

The story in France is very similar, save for one matter: while the story of the English *Philokalia* tells of the endeavors of Orthodox scholars and translators (just one assistant translator was Catholic), the French story begins with a selection presented by a Catholic, reminding us how much the movement of recourse to the Fathers—*ressourcement*—in France was primarily a Catholic movement, from which Orthodox benefited (and to some extent inspired).[20] This short book, *Petite Philocalie de la Prière de Cœur*, translated and introduced by Jean Gouillard,[21] consists of brief selections from a wide range of writers from the *Philokalia*—twenty-one in all. Right from the beginning we sense a certain freedom, inspired by scholarly considerations: the chapters ascribed to St. Antony are replaced by a selection from the *Apophthegmata Patrum*; Evagrios is represented by a selection from his *On Prayer*, ascribed in the Greek *Philokalia* to St. Neilos; the selection from the Makarian Homilies abandons the Metaphrastic version reproduced by Nikodimos and gives a selection from various more authentic collections, including the Coptic cycle, which aligns the saying of the Jesus Prayer to breathing; Barsanouphios and John, Isaac the Syrian, and John of the Ladder are also included; and the treatises on the physical techniques are not missing. The title suggests a devotional anthology focusing on the prayer of the heart, and this is made unavoidable by the very brevity of the selections. The complete text of the *Philokalia* was published by the Dean of the Institut St.-Serge between 1979 and 1991 and was re-edited in two volumes and presented by Olivier Clément in two volumes in 1995.[22]

The story of translations and editions could go on, but let us leave that for now. What we have seen is a more complex story than we might have expected. It is not the story of the translation and edition of some *editio princeps*, rather it is the story of the spread and influence of a way of prayer and a way of life, represented by a group of texts that take different forms and themselves emerge from various collections about which we are as yet not well informed. There are certain features that characterize the "*Philokalia*" in all its forms: the practice of the Jesus Prayer as a way of attaining the prayer of the heart is a constant, sometimes exclusively so, at other times as the heart of an approach to God that embraces a much wider range of texts than would be included under the term "devotional"; the sense that the hesychast controversy and the Palamite defense of the hesychasts was a determining event for Orthodox prayer, spirituality, and theology; a sense of a continuing tradition that can be traced back to the fourth century, at least, a tradition that one must call "patristic"; a sense of this tradition as a living tradition, passed on from generation to generation, and not simply a tradition of texts. What does all this add up to? How is one to characterize what we have called the "noetic" influence of the *Philokalia*?

The difficulty of identifying the "philokalic" collection is not just a perhaps rather complex problem; it is rather intrinsic. The very freedom with which the various anthologies calling themselves the "*Philokalia*" have been fashioned—with a still somewhat fluctuating core, with various works added or overlooked for a variety of apparently contingent reasons, with a critical sense that varies from the minimal (though never altogether absent: even the Slavonic *Dobrotolubiye*, though primarily devotional, still has a sense of critical allegiance to the Greek manuscripts on which it is based) to a desire to present texts in the most up-to-date critical form (as in the diaspora, and also with Fr. Dumitru's Romanian version)— points to the fact that the texts are not self-sufficient but witness to a living (though sometimes only just living) tradition of prayer, understood as an ascetic and mystical exercise ("the practice and contemplation of ethical philosophy") by which, in synergy with the grace of the Holy Spirit, "the mind [intellect, or $\nu o\hat{\upsilon}\varsigma$] is purified, illuminated and brought to perfection," as it is stated on the title page of the 1782 Greek edition. This tradition of personal prayer and asceticism that both presupposes the sacramental life of the Church (as St. Nikodimos's introduction makes clear) and makes possible a genuine engagement in that sacramental life of grace is what is fundamental. This means that we have to be aware, not just of the material succession of the various editions of the *Philokalia*, but of the living flow of the tradition of prayer (which the monastic life is intended to foster but which is not restricted to the monastic order) throughout the ages, if we are to appreciate the noetic influence of the *Philokalia*. We need, therefore, to pay attention, not just to movements of life and thought clearly associated with the textual tradition of the *Philokalia*, but also to movements anterior to, or even apparently independent of, that textual tradition. We need to pay attention to the movement centered on Optina Pustyn in nineteenth-century Russia, the revival of philokalic piety in mid-twentieth-century Greece, with elders such as Joseph, Païssios, Porphyry, Aimilianos, the philokalic revival in Romania, associated with Fr. Stăniloae's translation, the revival of monasteries in the early part of the twentieth century that endured persecution under the communists, and other similarly obvious examples of the influence of the *Philokalia*. But we need to pay attention, too, to Sarov and St. Seraphim, even though the saint's spiritual roots go back before anything identifiably philokalic, to other movements of monastic renewal in eighteenth- and early nineteenth-century Russia, which prepared the soil, as it were, for the seeds of the *Philokalia*, to the movement of intellectual renewal associated with Solov'ev, Florensky, and Bulgakov—and even with Dostoevsky—partly because of the importance for them of Optino, and partly for the role the tradition of prayer manifest in hermits and elders played in their understanding of the Christian life (Fr. Florensky's devotion to his *starets*, Isidore, or the role of hermits in Fr. Bulgakov's return to the faith). We might also think of St. Nektarios of Aegina, even more evidently Fr. Justin Popovich of Serbia, whose theology breathes an authentically philokalic spirit; and certainly of St. Silouan of Mount Athos, his disciple Fr. Sophrony, and *his* disciples.[23]

I will conclude by suggesting, very tentatively, what might be meant by a philokalic style, or tenor, of theology. It seems likely that it was in response to his encounter with the *Dobrotolubiye* that the Slavophile Ivan Kireevsky came to speak of the Fathers as bearing "testimony as eyewitnesses" and speaking of "a country they have been to."[24] A sense of the patristic tradition as our inheritance as Christians seems to me central to the *Philokalia*, and in several ways: objectively, there is a sense of who the Fathers are, and the inclusion of St. Maximos and St. Gregory Palamas, in particular, makes it clear that the great patristic witnesses revered by us Orthodox—the great hierarchs and universal teachers, St. Basil the Great, St. Gregory the Theologian, and St. John Chrysostom, Sts. Athanasios and Cyril of Alexandria, St. Gregory of Nyssa, celebrated by the Church, together with St. Maximos, in the latter part of January (with St. Photios not far away)—are prominent in this their native land, but remembered alongside ascetics and mystics who live out the theology they proclaimed; but subjectively there is the sense of the Fathers as precisely our fathers (and in principle) mothers, those to whom we owe our faith, those who have nurtured us in the Faith. Furthermore, we participate in this tradition not just by learning (though learning is important, as St. Nikodimos's example makes clear), but by praying, by living out the theology we discern and proclaim. The *Philokalia*—as both text and life—initiates us into a participation in the divine life, the divine energies, by—as we have just heard—a process of purification, illumination, and perfection. That terminology, that process, is also applied by the Fathers to the activation and practice of the *spiritual senses*, the ways in which we perceive by feeling, sensing, the movement of the Holy Spirit, in ourselves, in others, in the world. What we are seeing here is something that goes beyond reading and understanding and is more like participation and assimilation. In Father Sophrony's book on St. Silouan, there is a passage that tells of conversations a Roman Catholic priest visiting the Holy Mountain had with a learned monk of St. Panteleimon. To his question about what the monks at the monastery read, the reply is a list of "philokalic" fathers and some modern Russian saints. The priest is astonished: "With us it's only professors who do." When the conversation is repeated to St. Silouan, the saint replies that he could have told the priest "that our monks not only read these books but could themselves write their like. . . . But if these books were somehow or other to disappear, then the monks would write new ones." St. Silouan's point is that the monks assimilate the books in their lives. Elsewhere he speaks of the "taste" by which the movements of the Spirit can be discerned, and how necessary it is to have a spiritual father who has acquired this taste: "He who has savored the Holy Spirit recognizes the taste of grace."[25]

These thoughts recall the closing paragraph of the introductory letter of Fr. Pavel Florensky's *The Pillar and Ground of the Truth*:

> The indefinability of Orthodox ecclesiality, I repeat, is the best proof of its vitality. . . . There is no concept of ecclesiality, but ecclesiality itself is, and for every living member of the Church, the life of the Church is the most definite and tangible thing that he knows. But the life of the Church is assimilated and known only through life—not in the abstract, nor in a rational way. If one must nevertheless apply concepts to the life of the Church, the most appropriate concepts would be not juridical and archaeological ones but biological and aesthetic ones. What is ecclesiality? It is a new life, life in the Spirit. What is the criterion of the rightness of this life? Beauty. Yes, there is a special beauty of the spirit, and, ungraspable by logical formulas, it is at the same time the only true path to the definition of what is orthodox and what is not orthodox.
>
> The connoisseurs of this beauty are the spiritual elders, the *startsy*, the masters of the "art of arts," as the holy fathers call asceticism. The *startsy* were adept at assessing the quality of the spiritual life. The Orthodox taste, the Orthodox temper, is felt but it is not subject of arithmetical calculation. Orthodoxy is shown, not proved. That is why there is only one way to understanding Orthodoxy: through direct orthodox experience. . . . [T]o become Orthodox, it is necessary to immerse oneself all at once in the very element of Orthodoxy, to begin living in an Orthodox way. There is no other way.[26]

There we find a succinct statement of the true philokalic tenor of theology; it is in tracing that that we trace the noetic influence of the *Philokalia*.

4

Conversing with the World by Commenting on the Fathers: Fr. Dumitru Stăniloae and the Romanian Edition of the *Philokalia*

Mihail Neamtu

■ THE HISTORICAL CONTEXT

Born in Transylvania at the beginning of the twentieth century, Dumitru Stăniloae grew up as the son of a pious family of Orthodox Christians.[1] Without any pretense or critical interrogations, their peasant life followed the laws and customs of traditional Christianity. Prayer, fasting, and quite an intense perception of the sacred permeated an agrarian form of existence. In rural Transylvania, crucifixes marked the crossroads of Orthodox and Catholic villages, while religious festivals punctuated the annual calendar.[2] This landscape provided an important contrast to the urban life, which the young Dumitru Stăniloae discovered during his theological studies at the University of Cernăuţi (present-day *Chernowitz,* Ukraine).

In 1922, early in his university career, he made his first acquaintance with the scholastic perspective on church dogmatics, inherited as such from the nineteenth-century theological handbooks. The latter's dry, rigid, and nonsacramental approach to the divine mystery quickly disappointed Dumitru. Following his post-graduate research in Athens (1927) and Munich (1928), Stăniloae discovered the spiritual riches of the Byzantine tradition, best exemplified by the works of St. Gregory Palamas (1296–1359).[3] In the late 1930s, encouraged perhaps by the first signals of the neopatristic movement, Dumitru Stăniloae began to translate some of Palamas's works (the second and the third treatise of Palamas's first *Triads*; the extended *Apology*; the fifth *Antirhetikos*). Though married, Fr. Stăniloae was eager to deepen his knowledge of monastic spirituality. The patristic wisdom taught him that the perfect knowledge of God stemmed from an intimate communion with the Holy Spirit, and not from hypothetical musings regarding the created order (as with physics, mathematics, and other natural sciences).

Western theology, on the other hand, flirted with the notion of *scientia* or *Wissenschaft,* following the paradigm imposed by, respectively, René Descartes (1596–1650) and Immanuel Kant (1724–1804).[4] This meant that a systematic discourse in the realm of theology had to resemble the scientific approach to the created order of things. Such an attitude not only preserved the old scholastic taxonomies, but it also gave more space to doubt and criticism with respect to the first sources of theology: the Bible and its interpretative tradition.[5] Of course, many Christian circles responded immediately to this threat of reifying the subject of theology. Rationalism came under the attack of fideism. These wars canonized the division between "heart" and "mind" which division, in turn, promoted the clash between pietism and intellectualism. In order to survive within a secular milieu, academic theologians came to reject the early Christian "subjectivism" while favoring a historicist approach to Church history, Christian ethics, and Christian dogma.[6]

■ THE LURE OF MONASTICISM

By favoring historicism over Christian subjectivism, most of Stăniloae's professors accepted the inevitable separation between their scholastic knowledge of Christian doctrine and the traditional forms of Eastern Orthodox practice. From a sociological perspective, the world of ordinary churchgoers seemed strange to many Church bureaucrats and pedantic scholars. In the eyes of many clergymen or secular intellectuals, the consubstantial relationship between asceticism, liturgy, and dogma was far from being obvious. Outside the rural area, orthodoxy and orthopraxy seemed even more disconnected. Few Christians understood the metaphysical depth of Eastern Orthodoxy, just as many intellectuals had little more than scorn for the century-old habits of church rites.[7] It was in this context that Fr. Stăniloae felt the need to embark on his mission: to show how Christian piety needed to be grounded in contemplation, and how true theology was intrinsically linked to a specific set of sacramental, ascetic, and narrative practices. Ultimately, this undertaking was an attempt to bring together the life of rural Christianity and the wide cultural horizon of urban communities, which were already marked by the alert pace of modernization.

Fr. Dumitru Stăniloae was not alone in thinking along these lines. By the early 1940s an old monastic site in Bucharest (Antim Monastery) staged an important experiment under the heading, "The Burning Bush Conferences." On a regular basis, religious people, whether laymen or members of the clergy, gathered together in order to discuss the link between the world of humanities and the sphere of theological reflection.[8] Under the guidance of a Russian refugee and hieromonk known as Ivan Kuligin, many doctors, poets, university professors, painters, musicians, architects, philosophers, and monks prayed, conversed, and studied together. Persecuted by the Soviet agents of terror, Fr. Kuligin imparted to his Romanian friends the spiritual tradition in which he was brought up at Optina Pustyn in Russia. At the Antim Monastery from Bucharest, they all shared the same desire to unearth the treasures of early Christianity. They learned how the experience of God required inner compunction and the practice of incessant prayer. Since Fr. Stăniloae was a resident of Sibiu (Transylvania), he had only a distant knowledge of the Burning Bush Movement, but its message inspired him. He himself was very close to a circle of monks from Sâmbăta Monastery (Fr. Arsenie Boca, Fr. Serafim Popescu, and others) located in the lower Carpathians, in Transylvania.[9]

The literary encounter with the neopatristic movement and his discovery of the Palamite corpus in the early 1930s brought Father Stăniloae very close to the pristine wells of Church monasticism. The evils of World War II, the danger of fascism and eventual tyranny of communism, and the tragic history of the Eastern European countries encouraged Fr. Stăniloae to pursue more vigorously his decision to translate the *Philokalia* corpus. In the mid-1940s he initiated a lifelong project that, by the early 1990s, numbered more than five thousand pages. The road to completion was long and strenuous. Fr. Stăniloae's mature years had been punctuated by political harassment, professional isolation, imprisonment, and a great degree of solitude. However, his intellectual achievements were nothing short of impressive.

■ THE ROMANIAN EDITION OF THE *PHILOKALIA*

The Western reader should bear in mind that Stăniloae's edition of the *Philokalia* differs from the first Greek edition published by St. Nicodemos of Athos and St. Macarios of Corinth in Venice in 1782. The Romanian translator and editor decided to enrich the original material with some significant *supplementa*. The first volume (published in 1946) includes Evagrius of Pontus's treatise *On Prayer* and Mark the Ascetic's essay *On Baptism*. The second volume (1947) incorporates St. Maximus the Confessor's dissertation *On the Ascetic Life*, his *Chapters on Love*, as well as the *Quaestiones et Dubia*. The third volume (1948) includes the *Quaestiones ad Thalassium* (replacing *Various Chapters*, present in the Greek edition). Volumes four (1948) and five (1976) preserve the format of Nikodimos's edition. The sixth volume (1977), however, displays St. Symeon the New Theologian's 225 theological and practical chapters, moral chapters, together with a selection from among the *Ethical Discourses* (1 and 5). The sixth volume ends with St. Nikitas Stithatos's 300 chapters on ascetic praxis, natural contemplation, and theological knowledge, on top of his commentary, *On Paradise*. The seventh volume is dedicated to St. Gregory Palamas (*The Triads* II. 2–3; *On the Godly and Deifying Participation*). The eighth volume (1979) opens with a number of translations from Ignatius and Kallistos of Xanthopol, Kallistos Angelicudes, and Kallistos Kataphygiotes. This book closes with Fr. Stăniloae's survey of the history of hesychasm in Romania, based on texts and hagiographical documents related to St. Vasile from Poiana Mărului, St. Calinic from Cernica Monastery, and Iosif from Văratec. The ninth volume (1980) includes *The Ladder* of St. John Climacus, together with Abba Dorotheos of Gaza's *Instructions* (i–xiv) and *Letters* (1–2). The tenth volume (1981) incorporates Stăniloae's rendering of the Greek version of St. Isaac the Syrian's *Ascetic Writings*. The eleventh volume (1990) contains the writings of Abba Barsanuphius and John. The twelfth volume (1991) incorporates Abba Isaiah the Solitary's writings, dating from around the fourth century.[10]

What can we make of Fr. Stăniloae's decision to present the works of St. Maximus the Confessor as part and parcel of the Romanian edition of the *Philokalia*? What was the point of extending so much the initial scope of this monastic library? In part, we may assume that he wanted to draw the attention of the Romanian intelligentsia to the caricature of Orthodox Christian liturgical practices and traditions inherent in their thinking, that is, their equating of the sacramental life of the church with meaningless superstitions and purely ritualistic endeavors.[11]

Fr. Stăniloae wanted to circulate the *Philokalia* not only among the hardcore ascetics, but also among the members of the Church hierarchy and of the intellectual elite, who insisted only on the social contribution of religion to the common
good.[12] Fr. Stăniloae's selection struck the perfect balance between the very
practical texts, which taught Christians the lesson of obedience to God, and the
highbrow contemplative passages, which gave important insights into Christian
metaphysics and cosmology. The story of friendship and reconciliation under
the Savior Jesus Christ met with a sophisticated account of human nature, cosmic
beauty, and transcendent order.

Unlike other patristic editions published by Western scholars, Fr. Stăniloae's
version of the *Philokalia* does not elaborate much on philological, textual, and
historical matters.[13] A standard volume in the Romanian series of the *Philokalia*
opens with a short historical presentation of the authors and their respective
works. Fr. Stăniloae discusses the circulation of the oldest manuscripts, the
style of the author, as well as their belonging to a specific monastic school.
From our contemporary perspective, Stăniloae's scholarly proficiency could not
compete with the high standards set by the "Sources Chrétiennes" team in Paris
and Lyon, for example. Fr. Stăniloae's translations from Greek are accurate and
his introductions, while based on Western scholarship, remain quite reliable
(with a few exceptions). However, his main goal was not to debate the complex
genealogy of some opaque texts, but rather to inform his modern audience
about their enduring message. The Romanian theologian shared the concerns
of his own generation and therefore, did not hesitate to speak the language of
French existentialism or German phenomenology. Despite his anti-Catholic bias,
Fr. Stăniloae's initial commentaries make references to Western authors such as
Martin Heidegger (1889–1976), Maurice Blondel (1861–1946), Louis Lavalle
(1883–1951), and Ludwig Binswanger (1881–1966). These Western writers helped
him translate into a modern literary jargon some of the most profound monastic
insights into the human psyche.[14] Among other authors of Orthodox literature,
Fr. Stăniloae's open position remains almost an exception.

In the wake of the Soviet takeover of Romania, Fr. Stăniloae refrained from
quoting openly such writers. After being forcefully removed from the position he
held in the Department of Theology of the University of Sibiu (1947), the Communist authorities sent him to Bucharest under strict surveillance. Irregularly, Fr.
Stăniloae continued to meet with certain members of the Burning Bush Movement. They shared innocent impressions regarding various readings in the realm
of monastic theology and Christian spirituality. On June 14, 1958, the Romanian
branch of the Communist secret police (*Siguranța*, and later *Securitatea*, equivalent to the Soviet NKVD and later KGB), in a second wave of arrests, captured
more Burning Bush sympathizers. Four months later, on November 8, 1958, Fr.
Stăniloae was detained and later sentenced to five years in prison because of his
alleged "obscurantist propaganda."

On January 15, 1963, the Communist authorities released Fr. Stăniloae from the
dreadful prison of Aiud. It was in these very difficult personal circumstances that
he resumed his work on the *Philokalia*, drafting his comments carefully. Reading
between the lines, however, one can detect very subtle allusions to the liberating

power of faith, as opposed to the dictatorship of materialism (be it tied to the Marxist dialectics of history or to the mere consumerism of the Western world).

Nobody questions the huge impact of Fr. Stăniloae's work on the Eastern Orthodox culture. Some of his commentaries have been translated into modern Greek and French. Most of them remain available in Romanian, proving that

> [o]ne can be a theologian without exclusivisms and without concessions. [. . .] For his entire life, and especially in the last decades, he has been an extraordinary bridge between worlds. He was surrounded by numerous laymen, painters, writers, people who felt the need to visit him and to look for his advice; I have also frequented him for a while, through some artist friends. Through his discreetly radiant presence, as well as his translations in the *Philokalia*, he helped us all to survive the times we experienced. Reading the *Philokalia* helped me to get through the difficult years of dictatorship. I survived spiritually and intellectually by talking to others who were also reading the *Philokalia*.[15]

It would be impossible to summarize here the multifaceted nature of Fr. Stăniloae's observations, clarifications, and interpretations of the *Philokalia*. They comprise references to Christian doctrine, theological anthropology, soteriology, biblical exegesis, ecclesiology, and ethics. Fr. Stăniloae's richest notes and observations occur during the second part of his completion of the *Philokalia* project. The same goes for other annotations found in his Romanian translations of St. Cyril of Alexandria (376–444), of St. Maximus the Confessor (580–662), and of St. Symeon the New Theologian (949–1022).

Given the space limit, we shall focus here on the moral teaching extracted from Fr. Stăniloae's slow and penetrating reading of the monastic sources.

■ ETHICAL LESSONS FROM THE *PHILOKALIA*

Christian life begins precisely where our slavish dependency on material needs ends. This is perhaps the core lesson of the *Philokalia*. The archetypal monk is presented as an unusual creature in this world, whose life does not depend on political promises, tribal allegiances, collective theft or exploitation, immanent fears, and common anxieties. His entire existence is a protest against the worldly addictions to sex,[16] power,[17] wealth, buzz,[18] and prestige.[19] The monk imposes no financial burdens upon future generations, inasmuch as he tries to reconcile communities found in disagreement with respect to their common past.[20] He consumes little and gives away much to the poor. He receives no subsidies for his manual labor and accepts no pension, health care, or other social benefits from any secular body. The monk is, in the best sense of the word, an autarkic creature.

The *Philokalia* presents the image of the perfect monk neither as a self-absorbed hippy figure nor as a fake Messiah spreading radical slogans about saving the planet. Freedom, for a Christian monk or nun, means, first, to have confidence in God, to fight the passions of the soul, and to be reluctant toward any human promises. Fear of God is the beginning of wisdom, but Fr. Stăniloae does not understand this fear simply in negative terms: its purpose is not tyrannical, but rather didactic, making one aware of God's incessant presence in the life of the world.[21]

The monastic ethics is grounded in personal responsibility: toward God, toward oneself, and toward one's neighbor and community. This fundamental principle is opposed to the collectivist rhetoric of entitlement, according to which the self must be seen as the exclusive product of various anonymous social relationships. It is no surprise that the *Philokalia* does not know and does not employ the language of human rights. The rhetoric of human rights detached from the cultivation of divine responsibilities is what brings about the death of the spiritual life and the collapse of Christian culture.[22]

Even less does the *Philokalia* confuse the fundamental freedoms with which human being is endowed by God, with the social rights acquired by a particular minority of people at a given time in history. The *Philokalia* develops a theological understanding of equality: God does not judge on the basis of external appearance of man, and therefore, He hearkens to the prayer of the rich and of the poor, of the wealthy and of the dispossessed, of the intelligent and of the dim-witted. This equality, however, does not endorse an egalitarian, nonhierarchical perception of the world. Individual liberty is respected for its potential development into the service of the supreme Good.

The practice of virtues aims at the purification of our bodily senses, of our imagination, and of our heart. This requires conversion and self-scrutiny. The sacrament of confession performs precisely this work while showing the great power of God in our very weakness.[23] To confess one's sins and failures means to admit our intrinsic finitude and brokenness, while being open to the eternal mercy of God in Jesus Christ. The Holy Spirit supports this "progressive work,"[24] which brings human being from a broken life to the stature of those made perfect in the image of Christ. The search for immortal beauty is not separated from the pursuit of goodness, which is why theological aesthetics depends upon an ethics of moderation.

Unlike many modern philosophical tracts, the *Philokalia* treats human beings as complex entities, endowed with potential for both greatness and baseness, for holiness and damnation. One finds here neither Thomas Hobbes's gloomy and one-sided perspective on human being (*homo homini lupus*), nor the rosy commentaries of Jean-Jacques Rousseau, regarding *le bon sauvage* of the premodern civilizations. The *Philokalia* recognizes the ubiquity of evil and celebrates the possibility of overcoming sin through Christ. The Fathers warn us, however, against any blind attachment toward one particular virtue, which may be acquired at the expense of others. The wholeness of Christ is discovered only when the virtues complement each other. "The progress towards virtue is an incessant struggle against the adverse waves of selfishness," writes Fr. Stăniloae.[25] Every decision to practice a particular virtue is met with resistance within ourselves. The desire to forgive encounters in its path the formidable force of resentment, while the will to preserve one's chastity "wakes up" the opposite attraction toward fornication.[26] An Orthodox perspective suggests, however, that the gradual increase in virtue cements the very dynamics of deification.

The acquisition of virtues is not an end in itself, but rather a means to deepen our conversation with God. And where God abides, there is also sublime beauty and infinite goodness.

■ INNER BEAUTY AND INCORRUPTIBLE GOODNESS

Initially one might perform good deeds out of a natural inclination or perhaps because of a blind and unproblematic faith. Perseverance in the cultivation of virtue, however, leads toward a superior knowledge of the invisible world. A strong personal faith grounds one's constancy of behavior in a quiet heart. This is not, however, an apology for the utilitarian appropriation of Christian faith. One should not confuse fideism with orthodoxy, or reduce the experience of faith in God to the realm of emotions. Faith is, according to Fr. Stăniloae, an even subtler form of cognition than the empirical knowledge of material things. Why? Because "only in faith the personhood of the Other is revealed."[27] This revelation of our neighbor's personhood avoids reducing human otherness to an ontic and anonymous reality.[28]

Fr. Stăniloae compares faith to the ocular experience: if sin blurs the contours of one's vision, the practice of virtue widens the horizons of intelligibility. The "sinful man cannot see God because his soul is too thick,"[29] and therefore lacks the diaphanous mind (and, often, body) of the blessed saints. On the contrary, faith and virtue are "like an eye in which God's light, power, and goodness are present both directly and in a reflected manner."[30] The same gradualism explains here the transition from mere faith to perceptive knowledge, sustained and intensified by prayer. Neither Christian ethics nor theological epistemology can be conceived in the absence of this fundamental act of piety. Prayer, in Fr. Stăniloae's generic terms, ranges from psalmody and liturgical chanting to quiet recollection in one's cell.[31] However, the peak of contemplation[32] is reached by those abiding in *hesychia* ("stillness") through the practice of the Jesus Prayer. "When our intellect pulls itself together and abandons the multitude of worldly things, it is united in Christ and it prays within Him."[33] The incessant prayer used by the monks frees the mind from all fears, anxieties, addictions, and other materialist forms of bondage. "We cannot conquer death unless we strengthen our inner spirit by the invocation of the name of Jesus."[34] Doing this enables us to live within the "horizons of infinity, pure love, and authentic progress."[35] Finally, the dispassionate soul lands onto the shores of stillness and joy. The fulfillment of the divine commandments brings about an immediate joy,[36] just as the false promises of sin trigger a sense of melancholy, irritation, or sadness. In this way, the soul that manages such a feat resembles a temple in which the divine glory dwells undisturbed by evil thoughts and foul desires.

For those Christians living in the world, matters such as health, public dignity, and respect for property may represent legitimate issues of concern. However, these needs cannot justify individual or societal indebtedness to corruptible factors, such as fashion, idols, consumerism, ideological passions, atheistic forms of welfare, or any other redemptive promises made by the secular order. The monk inhabits a culture of humility, which remains at odds with the slavery imposed by purely materialistic goals. If the *Philokalia* has an important value for the moral and spiritual edification of the modern age, it does so because its various authors provide us with a radical perspective: the authentic encounter of God dissolves all utopian desires to build a paradise on earth. The sphere of immanence cannot replace the heavenly kingdom, which must be taken by force (Matthew 11:12). To die together with Christ on the Cross means to pay by way of repentance an unexpected visit to our inner hell—that is, to descend into our darkest self, and from there to recognize the imperative need for healing, transformation, and redemption.[37]

Fr. Stăniloae's commentaries on the *Philokalia*, moreover, tell us that, in its post-lapsarian condition, humankind displays an extraordinary capacity for self-delusion.[38] This vice begins by one's taking at face value the "good promises" made by any external agent other than God himself, who made himself known to us in his incarnate Word, through the Holy Spirit. One's own lustful or greedy fantasy, a flattering neighbor or friend, or even the abuse of some social programs—they prosper in a culture of duplicity, where most of the promises made cannot be delivered. The *Philokalia* reminds every revolutionary that no human being can bring about more than a very limited amount of good into the world. Most of the time, we betray ourselves and fail to meet the best expectations entertained by our friends, colleagues, relatives, and neighbors. The remedy for the earliest symptoms of self-delusion is contained in humility and continual penance. More than an exercise in sincerity and an experience of public shame (occasioned by the presence of the Other), the act of confession builds up courage and boldness.[39]

■ SELF-KNOWLEDGE AND IMMEDIATE TRANSPARENCY

The power to confess one's sins also demonstrates the saintly transparency of the true Christian soul.[40] Those who have overcome the temptation of vanity have nothing to hide.[41] Rivalry and hypocrisy, however, are the most widespread currency in worldly affairs, from which divine love and genuine desire to communicate with the neighbor are absent. Egalitarian envy (which is often justified by ideological means) incites us to measure incessantly our own progress on the ladder of virtues. This perverse self-evaluation inevitably leads us to fall. In contrast, a heart touched by the spirit of compunction will shy away from any obsession with worldly standards of felicity (measured by celebrity, money, worldly acquisitions, power, sexuality, or material comfort).

When assisted by divine grace, self-knowledge improves one's dialogue with God and with humankind. The *Philokalia* calls for self-scrutiny as part of a more general strategy involved in the unseen warfare. Within a monastic setting, particularly, the Church gatherings are not meant primarily for socialization, which often disappears into gossip and irrelevant (if not irreverent) talk. Those engaging in tittle-tattle show little concern for their own personal improvement, while being eager to mock others' shortcomings and blunders. In contrast, the Church is the place where genuine dialogue and self-expression, together with love, joy, and fellowship, are celebrated for their own sake. Without such preparation, any intellectual enterprise, social work,[42] or missionary activity becomes fruitless.

By not judging our neighbor, we do not question the existence of real hierarchies of value, just as we do not endorse moral and epistemic relativism. Being silent about our brother's sins has a pedagogical meaning. Virtue cannot blossom in the absence of freedom— and this is why God's power was revealed in Christ's utmost humility. Nobody can be forced to appropriate the paradox of Christ's phenomenality: His light can blind the disciples, whereas His discretion perplexes the strangers. Not to judge the other means, first, to be alert with respect to one's own personal faults.[43] It also means to be aware that every human person remains, in its very uniqueness, a perfect mystery. Sociology, economics, or behavioral psychology can provide us with useful distinctions and typologies. However, a spiritual father will always recognize the invisible heart of each human person, going thus beyond the warnings of worldly prejudice and stereotypes.

▪ PRELIMINARY CONCLUSIONS

Fr. Dumitru Stăniloae's commentaries on the *Philokalia* have been written from an apologetic perspective. They show the relevance of Orthodox Christianity in a modern world, which was torn apart during the twentieth century between the excessive idealization of individual freedom, on the one hand, and the horrific manipulation of collective identity (through fascism, tribal nationalism, and communism), on the other. The *Philokalia* emerges as an important document that presents human nature from a nonideological perspective. Man's original call to freedom, self-knowledge, love, and perfection is incompatible with any partial description of our humanity, which sees the latter always trapped into the laws of biology, social engineering, or economics. The *Philokalia* rejects any such form of determinism, while praising God's power to break through the cycles of nature (understood here as a fallen creation).

Stăniloae's exegesis speaks to the world while remaining profoundly Christocentric and deeply imbued with the Spirit of the Fathers themselves. Fr. Stăniloae reveals how the monastic teachings of purification, illumination, and deification could bring about hope and salvation into a heart wrecked by despair, pride, and despondency.

One could argue that, at times, Fr. Stăniloae's apologetics was shaped by confessional bias and rhetorical clichés (such as the reduction of Roman Catholic spirituality to mere legalism). His polemical remarks are, nonetheless, valuable, as they constantly emphasize the specificity and the uniqueness of Orthodoxy among all the other offers made available on the global free market of spirituality. The reason why mystical writers of the Christian Orient should never be confused with the mystical authors of the Far East,[44] says Stăniloae, lies in the sound theological grammar, which the former embrace and which the latter do not have.

The commentaries in the Romanian edition of the *Philokalia* underscore the connection between the dogmas established by the Church councils and the ascetic practices validated throughout the ages by the patristic tradition. Systematic theology and Christian ethics, one could say, are brought together in order to inspire the lay reader as well as the clergy or those individuals belonging to a monastic order. It was this great achievement that earned Fr. Stăniloae the title "Doctor Philocalicus."

PART TWO
Theological Foundations

5   The Luminous Word: Scripture in the *Philokalia*[1]

Douglas Burton-Christie

> 'His majesty is upon Israel' (Ps. 68:34. LXX)—that is, upon the intellect that beholds, so far as this is possible, the beauty of the glory of God Himself. 'And this strength is in the clouds' (Ibid.), that is, in radiant souls that gaze towards the dawn. In such souls it reveals the Beloved, He who sits at the right hand of God and floods them with light as the sun's rays flood the white clouds.'[2]

There is a deep stillness at the heart of everything. Out of that stillness arises a Word, fierce, tender, luminous. The Word partakes of this stillness and cannot be apprehended apart from it. Only by entering the soul, taking root there and becoming part of the fabric of one's life can the Word live and shine in us.[3] Only in this way can the mystery of the Incarnation, the Word made flesh, come alive in us, in the world.

Such is the vision of life and Spirit that the *Philokalia* presents—a vision of the soul illuminated from within by the creative, redemptive power of the Word and radiating forth with its own spiritual power. This is a vision that the *Philokalia* shares with the Christian spiritual tradition as a whole, a vision grounded in the fundamental mystery of the Incarnation. However, in its ceaseless attention to the need for disciplined spiritual practice, and its insistence on the importance of such practice to the full realization of the Word in the life of the soul, the *Philokalia* makes a distinctive contribution to this tradition. Opening oneself to the Word, coming to live in the Word entails, for the *Philokalia*, confronting oneself honestly and deeply, embarking upon an utterly involving, lifelong process of transformation. Every page of this great work insists on this fact. To interpret the Word, then, is a profound existential struggle, one that promises to bring about in the life of the interpreter the promise, long cherished by the Eastern Christian spiritual tradition, of *theosis* or divinization. In both its practical advice and theoretical reflections, the *Philokalia* invites the one who would realize this promise to risk everything for the sake of this luminous, transformed life.[4]

Hesychios the Priest, cited above, gives beautiful expression to this vision in his treatise *On Watchfulness and Holiness*. For Hesychios, as for the *Philokalia* as a whole, this new, luminous existence is mediated by Christ the Word and enables the soul to experience a continuous awareness of union with the divine. This is the life to which the contemplative is called, and which the one who learns to "guard the intellect" may come to know:

> The guarding of the intellect may appropriately be called "light-producing," "lightning-producing," "light-giving," and "fire-bearing," for truly it surpasses endless virtues. . . . Those who are seized by love for this virtue . . . are enabled to become just, responsive, pure,

holy and wise through Jesus Christ. Not only this, but they are able to contemplate mystically and to theologize; and when they have become contemplatives, they bathe in a sea of pure and infinite light, touching it ineffably and dwelling in it.... Such [persons] alone truly call upon God and give thanks to Him, and in their love for Him continually speak with Him.[5]

But how does this happen? How is one brought to this place of awareness of oneself as bathing in a "sea of pure and infinite light"? Almost every page of the *Philokalia* is devoted to addressing this question, to helping the one who seeks to know God to find a way to uncover the mystery of the divine light hidden within. And while there is considerable variability among the many writers whose works comprise the *Philokalia* concerning the most fruitful approach to this question and the practices most likely to yield genuine transformation, the tradition is united in its conviction that knowledge of the Word is essential. There is a similar broad consensus regarding the conviction that true knowledge of the Word cannot arise without the practice of vigilance, or what Hesychios calls "the guarding of the intellect." This is, for the *Philokalia*, the appropriate and necessary response to what has been given in the Incarnation: a sustained practice of attention to everything within and without that draws us near the Word or obscures its luminous power. Ascetic practice cannot, in this sense, be separated from the work of interpretation. Nor can either of these practices be understood without reference to the fundamental truth revealed in the Incarnation of the Word or apart from the ultimate end of our efforts to know the Word: "touching and ineffably dwelling in" the divine light.

The *Philokalia*'s vision of the Word is finally mystical in character. And utterly encompassing of reality as a whole. "We practice the virtues," says Evagrios, "in order to achieve contemplation of the inner essences [logoi] of created things, and from this we pass to contemplation of the Logos who gives them their being; and He manifests Himself when we are in the state of prayer."[6] Here Evagrios points to a theological conviction whose origins can be traced back to the earliest moments of the Christian tradition, namely that the whole of existence is brought into being and sustained by the Word (Jn. 1:1). To attend to the Word, to understand how it beckons to us in our experience of the created world, the work of discernment, in our meditation on scripture, and in prayer, is at the heart of the spiritual vision the *Philokalia* expresses and seeks to cultivate. It is in this sense that one can affirm the centrality of scripture to the *Philokalia*'s spiritual vision while also acknowledging the significance of the Word's more capacious and varied manifestations. In what follows, this larger, more encompassing vision of the Word will ground my reflection on the *Philokalia*'s understanding of the authority and power of scripture. This great spiritual classic never ceases in its insistence on the importance of cultivating an awareness of the presence of the Word as a continuous part of one's life, of learning to apprehend the divine at the heart of everything.

■ APPREHENDING THE WORD: CONTEXT

There is hardly a page of the *Philokalia* in which one does not encounter an allusion to scripture or a teaching about its efficacy or meaning or a reflection (direct or indirect) on the significance of the Incarnation of the Word. In this sense, the

Philokalia can be said to be Logo-centric. Still, the broad assumptions underlying the *Philokalia's* approach to scripture are not always, at least to the contemporary reader, either self-evident or entirely consistent. For this reason, some reflections on the context in which scripture is understood and interpreted in the *Philokalia* are in order. Three elements of this context are particularly important for understanding the teaching of the *Philokalia* on scripture: the theological, the practical, and the hermeneutical.

I have already alluded to the significance of the Incarnation for understanding how the *Philokalia* conceives of the significance of scripture in the life of the one who seeks to know and live in God. As with many critical theological ideas from the ancient Eastern Christian tradition, the doctrine of the Incarnation exists not in isolation but as part of a fabric of thought and practice that can be apprehended only as a whole. In the case of the Incarnation, this means acknowledging its significance not only as an expression of what God has done in salvation history, but also as a crucial part of the ongoing spiritual life of the Christian community. To speak of the Incarnation is to reckon with the mystery of *theosis*, with the notion that the destiny of every baptized Christian is to be divinized, taken up into the life of God. St. Symeon the New Theologian (949–1022), echoing the famous formulation of Athanasius of Alexandria, gives eloquent expression to this truth in his "One Hundred and Fifty-Three Practical and Theological Texts."

> What is the purpose of the Incarnation of the Divine Logos which is proclaimed throughout the Scriptures, about which we read and which yet we do not recognize? Surely, it is that He has shared in what is ours so as to make us participants of what is His. For the Son of God became the Son of man in order to make us human beings sons of God, raising us up by grace to what He is by nature, giving us a new birth in the Holy Spirit and leading us directly into the kingdom of heaven. Or, rather, He gives us the grace to possess the kingdom within ourselves (cf. Luke 17:21), so that not merely do we hope to enter it, but being in full possession of it, we can affirm: "Our life is hid with Christ in God" (Col. 3:3).[7]

Here we have a highly compressed vision of Christian life at the center of which is the Incarnation of the Word into human flesh. This particular understanding of the Incarnation, in its full theological significance, can be traced back at least to the Council of Nicea in 325. What is striking about Symeon's expression of this idea in the *Philokalia* is how profoundly the truth of the Word incarnate is integrated into a distinctive understanding of the spiritual life. The Word entered into our condition so that we might be raised up to His exalted status, so that we might be divinized. Nearly every reference to the Logos or scripture in the *Philokalia* depends upon this insight for understanding how our relationship with the Word can transform us, can restore us to our original image and likeness. To meditate or ruminate upon the Word, to recite it, to seek out its hidden meanings, to practice it is to open oneself to God's radical redemptive power. It is to be drawn, gradually but imperceptibly, into the life of the Word.

This theological intuition, rooted in a sense of Christian life as grounded in the Word and always tending toward renewal in God mediated by the Word, helps to account for the *Philokalia's* insistence on the *practical* importance of engaging and orienting oneself toward the Word. One of the most fundamental forms of such practice is attending to the power of scripture, something that the *Philokalia* never tires of advocating. Most often the immediate context for this practice was monastic life. For the sake of this life, notes John Cassian, "the reading and study of scripture are readily undertaken."[8] But the monk did not encounter scripture only through reading and study, for the Word was often *heard* rather than read. So too was scripture spoken or recited, as for example in the common practice of psalmody, the simple recitation of the psalms, a practice that profoundly shaped the monk's apprehension of scripture.

"The rule of [one] holy Elder" we are told, "was as follows. During the night he quietly chanted the entire Psalter and the Biblical canticles. . . ."[9] While such a practice may not have been the norm for all monks, it suggests the kind of intimate familiarity with scripture that came from this practice. It is also worth noting that the Jesus Prayer, one of the most ancient and important prayer traditions in the *Philokalia*, was itself a form of prayer rooted in the mindful repetition of a Gospel text. And throughout the *Philokalia*, one hears endless exhortations simply to *practice* the teachings of scripture. "Understand the words of Holy Scripture by putting them into practice," counseled St. Mark the Ascetic.[10]

Such practice was hardly simple, for engaging scripture was understood as one element of a complex and demanding ascetic life. One encounters many places in the *Philokalia* where the attention to scripture is seen as occupying a crucial position within a more wide-ranging set of ascetic practices. St. John of Karpathos declares confidently, "Nothing so readily renews the decrepit soul, and enables it to approach the Lord, as fear of God, attentiveness, constant meditation on the words of Scripture, the arming of oneself with prayer, and spiritual progress through the keeping of vigils."[11] Here the practice of meditation on scripture is understood as central to the work of renewing the soul, but also complementary to other related practices. Indeed the capacity to meditate fruitfully on the words of scripture, John seems to suggest, is dependent on certain crucial practices such as prayer and the keeping of vigils, as well as dispositions of the soul, such as fear of God and attentiveness. To the extent that one opens oneself to God deeply and honestly, one will be able to hear and respond to the scriptures. The tradition embodied in the *Philokalia* was also careful to note the limits of certain ascetic practices, and the danger of imagining that such practices were sufficient by themselves to transform one's awareness and kindle a sense of intimacy with God. "Bodily fasting alone is not enough to bring about perfect self-restraint and true purity," said John Cassian. "It must be accompanied by contrition of heart, intense prayer to God, frequent meditation on the Scriptures, toil and manual labor."[12] Here, meditation on scripture is understood to be a grounding, integrating practice oriented toward bringing about greater awareness of the meaning and purpose of one's whole spiritual life, a practice that could help one avoid a superficial attachment to certain outer forms of ascetic discipline.

Ultimately, such mindful practice was believed to lead one toward a rare and precious depth of awareness. "Spiritual knowledge," says St. Diadochos of Photiki, "comes through prayer, deep stillness and complete detachment, while wisdom comes through humble meditation on Holy Scripture and, above all, through grace given by God."[13] The precise meaning of Diadochos's distinction between "spiritual knowledge" and "wisdom" is not clear, for they seem here to be kindred forms of knowledge that come to one who is advanced in such spiritual practice. Still, it is noteworthy that wisdom, which comes "from grace given by God," arises in the life of the one who engages in "humble meditation on Holy Scripture." Here one sees clear evidence of the particular power and authority the teachers in the *Philokalia* often ascribed to scripture and to the practices that helped the monk gain true knowledge and understanding of it. Meditation on scripture could yield *wisdom*.

But how could one gain such wisdom? How could one learn to *interpret* the scriptures so that they yielded their wisdom? And what precisely did such wisdom consist of? These are hermeneutical questions, and the teachers in the *Philokalia* were acutely sensitive to them, for challenge of interpreting scripture was bound inextricably to the process of coming to know and experience God. And while there are many warnings to be found in the *Philokalia* against the dangers of un-necessary speculation in relation to scripture and the need for simply putting the scriptures into practice, there was nevertheless a deep interest in understanding how to read and respond to the scriptures in a way that would allow them to yield fruit in the life of the monk. The way the *Philokalia* frames this interest can be traced back to Origen of Alexandria's profound investigations into the nature and purpose of scripture in the late second and early third centuries. Especially impor-tant in this regard was Origen's influential distinction between the literal and spir-itual meanings of the text. As for Origen, what mattered most to the teachers in the *Philokalia* was the spiritual or allegorical meaning of scripture—how its teachings could be applied to the inner life of one seeking God. Maximos the Confessor gives clear, succinct expression to this fundamental hermeneutical orientation: "All sacred Scripture can be divided into flesh and spirit as if it were a spiritual man. For the literal sense of Scripture is flesh and its inner meaning is soul or spirit. Clearly someone wise abandons what is corruptible and unites his whole being to what is incorruptible."[14]

As this observation makes clear, the primary significance of this understanding of scripture as operating on two levels of meaning has to do with what it will mean for one seeking to know God through the scriptures. Just as no one truly seeking God will remain satisfied with what is corruptible, but will instead seek the incor-ruptible, so too the perceptive reader of scripture will always seek its inner meaning, its "soul or spirit." It is for the sake of living against this infinite horizon that the monk should seek to become an adept reader of scripture, suggests Maxi-mos. This is what we were created for and what we truly long for. To the one who has learned to read scripture attentively and has become sensitive to the different levels of meaning revealed there, this becomes clear: "though Holy Scripture, being restricted chronologically to the times of the events which it records, is limited where the letter is concerned, yet in spirit it always remains unlimited as regards the contemplation of intelligible realities."[15]

Still, this beautiful vision of scripture as mediator of profound spiritual knowl-edge was not clear to all, and the *Philokalia* devotes considerable attention to the problems arising from the apparently widespread and habitual orientation toward a purely literal reading of scripture. St. Symeon the New Theologian sounds a strikingly skeptical note about how many of those who set out upon the spiritual path are able to interpret scripture adequately. "Many read the Holy Scriptures and hear them read," he says. "But few can grasp their meaning and import."[16] It is difficult to judge from such comments whether the inability to read and interpret scripture on the spiritual level was really so pervasive. But clearly, for St. Symeon and other teachers of the *Philokalia*, the challenge of helping those seeking God to go deeper in their reading of scripture was always present. St. Peter Damaskos acknowledges this problem in his own way in his depiction of what it means to embody wisdom: "The true sage is he who regards the text as authoritative and discovers, through the wisdom of the Spirit, the hidden mysteries to which the divine Scriptures bear witness."[17] The range of terms used to describe what the true interpreter of scripture is seeking—soul or spirit, intelligible realities, meaning, hidden mysteries—is suggestive of the richness of the hermeneutical process itself. It is not a particular truth that the interpreter is seeking to uncover (like solving a puzzle), but a depth of life and awareness that allows one to stand before God honestly and freely.

It is no wonder that the process of interpretation of scripture is so challenging, for in our encounter with the text, suggests the *Philokalia*, we bring the whole of who we are—our limitations and blindness as well as our still-emerging capacity to see and know. And scripture itself is structured in a way that only gradually can we learn to see the deeper mysteries it contains. This, suggests St. Peter of Damaskos, is one of its primary benefits to us.

> For the Logos wishes to transmit things to us in a way that is neither too clear nor too obscure, but is in our best interests. St. John Chrysostom says that it is a great blessing from God that some parts of the Scriptures are clear while others are not. By means of the first we acquire faith and ardour and do not fall into disbelief and laziness because of our utter inability to grasp what is said. By means of the second we are roused to enquiry and effort, thus both strengthening our understanding and learning humility from the fact that everything is not intelligible to us.[18]

Without struggle, and a sense that some things in scripture are simply beyond our immediate understanding, we might never be impelled to search deeper, to uncover those hidden parts of ourselves and of scripture that can lead us to God. But without a place to stand, without some basic understanding, even if this understanding is superficial, we might lose our way altogether. So yes, the distinction between the letter and the spirit is real and suggests the ever-present challenge of reading scripture on different levels and advancing beyond whatever level we find ourselves in at present. But for Peter of Damaskos, as for many other teachers in the *Philokalia*, the simpler, more literal way of reading scripture is not always to be disparaged. The Logos can communicate to us through this means as well and can lead us on from there to a more profound and encompassing awareness of the truth revealed in scripture. Even so, some of the mysteries in scripture, the writers of the *Philokalia* suggest, will always remain beyond our grasp. But this is also useful, for it deepens our humility.

This frank acknowledgement of how challenging it can be to read and interpret scripture in a way that honors its profundity and reach suggests something crucial about the *Philokalia*'s entire approach to scripture—namely that reading and interpreting scripture always take place as part of a far-reaching and demanding spiritual struggle. The teachers in the *Philokalia* speak of this struggle in different ways, but there is a widely shared recognition that one cannot achieve a mature knowledge of oneself or God without reckoning with those parts of oneself that are as yet unhealed; or, to use the most common terminology in this tradition, one must be prepared to struggle with those aspects of one's being that are still under the sway of the passions or demons. Reading scripture deeply and honestly was believed to be one of the most important means of achieving freedom from the power of these anomalous forces and acquiring the true self-knowledge that is among the most important expressions of this freedom. Yet the teachers of the *Philokalia* recognized that, in the early stages of the spiritual life at least, one's capacity to read and understand scripture with true discernment was often obscured by one's relative lack of freedom and self-knowledge. Thus the capacity to read and interpret scripture and to open one's mind to the luminous, saving presence of the Word could only deepen as one's self-knowledge and freedom deepened. Reading in this sense meant engaging in an ever more searching struggle to know oneself and to open the mind to the luminous presence of the Word.

Nikitas Stithatos articulates this hermeneutical principle succinctly in his treatise *On the Inner Nature of Things and on the Purification of the Intellect*: "The reading of the Scriptures means one thing for those who have but recently embraced the life of holiness, and another for those who have attained the middle state, and another for those who are moving rapidly towards perfection."[19] His careful elaboration of these three "stages" of interpretive insight makes it clear how closely one's capacity to read and understand scripture is bound to the depth of one's self-knowledge or wisdom. The true or full meaning of scripture is simply not accessible to one who has not yet purified his mind through the long, hard struggle of ascetic practice and prayer. Such knowledge is open only to one who has cultivated a capacity to read scripture with discernment. As Maximos the Confessor notes, regarding what it means to read deeply: "Discrimination is the distinctive characteristic of one who probes [the scriptures]." For Maximos, as for many other teachers in the *Philokalia*, such "probing" of the scriptures was part of a much more encompassing commitment to probe *everything* and to seek at the heart of everything the mystery of God. Maximos describes the search this way:

> [The one] who examines the symbols of the Law in a spiritual manner, and who contemplates the visible nature of created beings with intelligence, will discriminate in Scripture between letter and spirit, in creation between inner essence and outward appearance, and in himself between intellect and the senses; and in Scripture he will choose the spirit, in creation the inner essence or *logos,* and in himself the intellect. If he then unites these three indissolubly to one another, he will have found God: he will have come to recognize, as he should and as is possible, the God who is Intellect, Logos and Spirit.[20]

This extraordinary vision of spiritual knowledge encompasses every aspect of reality; nothing is excluded. It suggests that for the one who possesses the capacity to see with discernment, everything can be perceived and experienced as part of one indissoluble whole. To see this deeply is perhaps possible only for those who, as Nikitas says "are moving rapidly towards perfection to find God." Still, this vision of spiritual knowledge boldly lays forth what is possible for all those who cultivate their capacity to read and take in the whole of reality with discernment.

The *Philokalia* recognizes that many of those just embarking on the spiritual path will not yet have cultivated this capacity and will find themselves struggling with more basic questions. Among the most important of these questions was learning to discern, among the various thoughts, musings and fantasies that flowed through the mind, those that were most harmful to the soul, and what if anything one could do to keep them from completely overwhelming the monk. Nighttime, when the vigilance that is possible during the waking hours becomes difficult to sustain, could be especially challenging. The *Philokalia* contains many accounts of monks expressing their sense of fear and vulnerability in the face of the demons, especially as the hour of sleep approached. A text from *A Discourse on Abba Philimon* takes up this question with remarkable sensitivity and practical insight. In response to a brother who complains of seeing "many vain fantasies" in his sleep, Abba Philimon counsels: "Before going to sleep, say many prayers in your heart, fight against evil thoughts and don't be deluged by the devil's demands; then God will receive you into His presence." This basic preparation, a kind of preventative vigilance, is to be accompanied if possible by further exercises. "If you possibly can," says Philimon, "sleep only after reciting the psalms and after inward meditation. Don't be caught off your guard, letting your mind admit strange thoughts; but lie down meditating on the thought of your prayer, so that when you sleep it may be conjoined with you and when you awake it may commune with you (cf. Prov. 6:22)."[21]

This text reflects a widely shared belief among the teachers of the *Philokalia* concerning the practical efficacy of psalmody, whose benefits were believed to include protection from the attacks of the demons and a growing sense of integration and peace. This particular teaching reveals how and why such protection was believed to be so crucial. The thoughts or passions with which the monks struggled were experienced as being both devious and tenacious, insinuating themselves into those parts of the soul where one was most vulnerable and susceptible and requiring of the monk the most serious and sustained self-reflection and resistance. The power of psalmody to help one resist such assaults was rooted first of all in the authority of scripture itself. To stand in the Word, to repeat it over and over, to gradually absorb its power and wisdom into one's being was to be drawn, little by little, into the presence of God. But the monks recognized that while the simple repetition of the words of scripture had a certain efficacy, the real power of the practice depended on the extent to which one was prepared to bring one's entire being to the work—thus the significance of the recommendation to recite the psalms together with "inward meditation," that is, with awareness and attention. If the assaults of the demons in the form of unruly thoughts and fantasies could unbalance and overwhelm the mind, how much more necessary was it to practice psalmody with such care and attention that the power of the text could penetrate and inhabit the depths of one's mind, even what we would refer to as the subconscious mind? Only one who practiced psalmody with such assiduous attention could hope to experience peace and security even in the depths of night when the conscious mind was no longer able to maintain vigil.

Why was it so difficult to pay attention? And why did it matter so much if the mind should wander during psalmody or prayer? Also, what if anything could be done to redirect or focus the mind? The *Philokalia*'s insistent attention to these questions reflects the importance this tradition attributed to the need to purify the mind. Watchfulness and stillness are the terms most often used in the *Philokalia* to describe this work. The cultivation of these habits or dispositions was seen as having crucial importance for learning to apprehend the truth of scripture and the presence of God. Nikitas Stithatos describes the kind of confusion that can take hold in the soul of one who has not learned to practice attention when reciting the psalms. "As you pray and sing psalms to the Lord," he says, "watch out for the guile of the demons. Either they deceive us into saying one thing instead of another, snatching the soul's attention and turning the verses of the psalms into blasphemies, so that we say things that we should not say; or, when we have started with a psalm, they cause us to skip to the end of it, distracting the intellect from what lies between; or else they make us return time and again to the same verse, through absent-mindedness preventing us from going on to what comes next."[22] Here we have an almost comical catalogue of the problems that arise from inattention: inadvertent blasphemy, absent-minded forgetfulness, and pointless repetition. Anyone who has ever become lost in the midst of a simple recitation of a prayer or psalm will recognize this account. And the message is clear: mere repetition or rote memorization of scripture is not enough. The one who recites scripture in this way is wasting his time. In fact he may do more harm than if he had never undertaken such a practice at all.

Nikitas considers this question important enough that he devotes considerable attention to it in his writings. One question that seems to have come up for at least some of his readers concerns the difference between quality and quantity in reciting scripture. On the face of it, this seems a simple question: the quality of one's recitation will always take precedence over sheer quantity. Nikitas does in fact affirm this. But he is sensitive enough to the importance of the monastic regime of chanting and reciting psalms that he does not dismiss the concern with quantity out of hand. "Quantity is very important in the prayerful recitation of psalms," he acknowledges. But he is quick to add this caveat: "provided that it is accompanied by perseverance and attentiveness." Ultimately, he says, it is "the quality of our recitation [that] gives life to the soul and makes it fruitful." Here one sees an acknowledgement of the significance of what was simply a fact of life for Christian monks: a great deal of their time was taken up with the repetitive task of chanting or reciting psalms, a practice that likely felt tedious or even pointless at times for some of those to whom Nikitas addresses himself. There may well have been some who thought that it would be better not to recite so many psalms, while others advocated completing the full regime of psalms. Clearly there was some tension around this issue and questions raised about how best to cultivate an authentic spirit of prayer while practicing psalmody. And while Nikitas does not dismiss the potential value in reciting a large number of psalms, he is quick to note the importance of the monks' intention, here described as "perseverance and attentiveness." It is the presence of these habits during psalmody that accounts for its "quality" and the value of this practice to the soul. "Quality in psalmody and prayer," he says, "consists in praying with the Spirit and with the intellect (cf. I Cor. 14:15). We pray with the intellect when, as we say prayers and recite psalms, we perceive the meaning hidden in the Holy Scriptures and thence garner in the heart a harvest of ever more exalted divine thoughts. . . . This is the fruit of prayer, begotten through the quality of their psalmody in the soul of those who pray."[23]

Psalmody, a fundamental element in the rhythm of the monastic life, must be informed by and in turn inform true prayer if it is to bear fruit in the life of the monk. This is the recurring teaching of the *Philokalia*. For this to happen, Nikitas suggests, the monk must be vigilant in his attention to the words he is reciting, alert and open to the revelatory power contained in those words. This is what it means to pray the psalms "with the Spirit and with the intellect." Nikitas does not attempt to describe the particular technique that enables this to occur. Rather, he simply insists that the mind is capable of such deep concentrated attention and that the one who practices psalmody must seek to open himself or herself to it as far as possible. This is the only way that the "meaning hidden in the Holy Scriptures" or "exalted divine thoughts" can be perceived and known. What exactly is meant by these expressions? To what kind of experience do they point? Nikitas does not say. But they are suggestive of the deep and abiding sense of God's presence that readers of the *Philokalia* sought and sometimes found. Ultimately, it is the presence or absence of Spirit that allows one to judge whether psalmody has the potential to bear fruit. This fundamental criterion also helps one to arrive at a judicious conclusion concerning the matter of quantity and quality in psalmody. "Where the fruit of the Spirit is present in a person," says Nikitas, "prayer is of like quality; and where there is such quality, quantity in the recitation of psalms is excellent. Where there is no spiritual fruit, the quality is sapless. If the quality is arid, quantity is useless: even if it disciplines the body, for most people there is no gain to be got from it."[24]

The *Philokalia* everywhere points to the inextricable bond that exists between the ongoing spiritual development of the monk and the knowledge and experience of God that could arise through the reading and recitation of scripture. The importance of this bond transcended psalmody to include every encounter with scripture, which the teachers of the *Philokalia* were eager to point out always carried with it the potential to transform one. Stillness was believed to be especially fruitful in this regard. St. Peter Damaskos calls stillness "the highest gift of all" and insists that "we all need this devotion and stillness, total or partial, if we are to attain the humility and spiritual knowledge necessary for the understanding of the mysteries hidden in the divine scripture and in all creation."[25] Elsewhere he elaborates on this idea, noting that "unless a person attends to what is said in divine Scripture, he will gather but little fruit, even though he sings or reads them frequently. 'Devote yourself to stillness and know,' it is written (Ps. 46:10), because such devotion concentrates the intellect: even if it is attentive for only a short time, none the less it knows 'in part,' as St. Paul puts it (I Cor. 13:12)."[26] Here, stillness and attention are almost synonymous with one another. To be still in one's mind is to have the capacity to pay attention, to take in experience deeply and fully, including the experience of reading and reciting scripture. But such stillness was immensely difficult to achieve and sustain. Only the one who entered into the hard, demanding work of ascetic practice and continuous self-reflection could hope to arrive at such a place. But even a partial realization of such stillness could be beneficial, helping to create a space in the mind where the knowledge of God could begin to take hold in one's life.

▪ PRACTICE: REALIZING THE WORD OF GOD

The longing to deepen one's knowledge of God through an assiduous and attentive reading of scripture is one of the fundamental and recurring concerns of the *Philokalia*. The extent to which the teachers in the *Philokalia* examined the *means* by which this could be realized in the life of the monk, especially the inner discipline and transparency required to reach a place of inner stillness, suggests the depth of their commitment to discover how the Word could truly come to illumine the soul and transform one's life. It is in this sense that their more speculative hermeneutical interests can be seen as complementing a fundamentally practical concern, namely the possibility that one's entire life—one's consciousness as well as one's activities, indeed one's very self—could be reoriented to conform with the vision of spiritual unity found in scripture. In fact, there was a strong conviction among many of the teachers in the *Philokalia* that apart from such transformation, all attempts to interpret scripture or discern its hidden meanings were bound to be fruitless. One's reading of scripture had to be reflected in a transformed existence.

Maximos the Confessor offers a bracing reminder of the importance of such practical application of scripture, not only for the individual but also for the larger community. "If the words of God are uttered merely as verbal expressions, and their message is not rooted in the virtuous way of life of those who utter them," he says, "they will not be heard. But if they are uttered though the practice of the commandments, their sound has such power that they dissolve the demons and dispose men eagerly to build their hearts into temples of God through making progress in the works of righteousness."[27] Maximos is reminding his readers that those who seek God not only read scripture and hear it proclaimed, but will in the course of their lives sometimes be called upon to teach it, speak of it, or proclaim it to others. But what makes such speech authentic, meaningful? For Maximos, this requires that one allow the words upon which one meditates to penetrate one's mind and character. They must be integrated into one's life. Otherwise, the words that one speaks (or the gestures of one's life, for that matter) "will not be heard." They will be meaningless, perhaps harmful. However, if they are uttered "through the practice of the commandments," that is, through the effort to live in accord with them, to embody their truth in one's life, such words have tremendous power and efficacy. They possess the authority to help one resist, even banish demons; they also have the power to inspire others to transform their lives. Such is the compelling force of authentic witness.

This concern to enter fully into the life of the Word and to have one's entire life permeated by its presence is also expressed in the recurring attention the *Philokalia* gives to the importance of *performing* the text. One catches a glimpse, in this teaching, of the reality of community life out of which the *Philokalia* arose and to which its teaching is continuously directed. The question of what it meant to *live* the Gospel usually meant trying to understand how to embody in one's life the fundamental biblical injunction to love. The teachers of the *Philokalia* reflected deeply on this question, not only by engaging in an effort to understand what kind of ascetic disciplines and meditative practices could help to free the soul to love, but also by asking what simple, concrete gestures could deepen the hold of love on one's life, help one to live *in* love. What does it mean, for example, to regard one's neighbor as oneself? Symeon the New Theologian takes this as one of the crucial questions for reflecting on whether we have come to understand the scriptures. "We who have been commanded to regard our neighbor as our self (Lev. 19:18; Luke 10:27) should do so not for one day only," he says, "but for our whole life. Similarly, we who have been told to give to all who ask (Matt. 5:42) are told to do this for our whole life." This deceptively simple statement captures what was for the *Philokalia* one of the most significant and challenging dimensions of spiritual practice: the importance of learning to live with a total, encompassing commitment to the other. One sees here a reflection of the *Philokalia*'s characteristic orientation toward life, toward God, and toward one's neighbor—one that rejects half-measures as inadequate, that seeks instead to cultivate a way of living that is whole-hearted and complete.

Symeon offers an uncompromising vision of what this concept will mean in practice, inviting his readers to consider the extent to which they are prepared to open themselves to this challenge. "Whoever regards his neighbor as himself," he says "cannot bear to possess more than his neighbor. On the other hand, if he has more and does not give unstintingly until he himself becomes as poor as his neighbor, he fails to fulfill the Lord's commandment. And if someone wishes to give to all who ask, but rejects one of them while he still has a penny or a scrap of bread, or if he does not act towards his neighbor as he would like other people to act towards him, he too is failing to fulfill the Lord's commandment."[28] This is a severe and demanding teaching, and one can imagine readers flinching at what it would mean for them to take it seriously. But Symeon appeals not simply to an ethical imperative, one that may well seem unrealizable, but to something we already know and feel: the one who regards his neighbor as himself "cannot *bear* to possess more than his neighbor," he says. We already carry within us, he seems to suggest, the knowledge and desire that will be required of us if we are to fulfill this Gospel injunction. We do not wish to possess a penny or scrap of bread more than our neighbor possesses. It pains us to do so. Our conscience is already alive to the importance of learning to live with and for our neighbor. All that remains is to respond to this prompting, from scripture and from deep within our own souls. Not once or occasionally, but for "our whole life."

Symeon and many other teachers in the *Philokalia* recognize how difficult it is to learn to live this way. "Who can do all this?" one imagined interlocutor exclaims. Striving to live in this way seems likely to open one to a never-ending stream of requests and demands from others. Who could bear this? Who could live up to such a standard? Symeon addresses this very real concern by reframing the question. It is not a matter of having to perform an endless series of tasks, he says, but rather of learning to inhabit the truth of scripture so deeply that one's entire being will be oriented toward the other utterly and completely. The right response will make itself clear. In order for this to be possible, Symeon says, it is crucial that one learn to live in the truth of what he calls the "comprehensive commandments" and "comprehensive virtues" which contain within them all the more particular commandments and particular virtues. Thus, he says, "he who sells what he has and distributes it to the poor (cf. Mt. 19:21), and who once and for all becomes poor himself, has fulfilled at once all the more particular commandments." In practical terms, such a person will find himself not only unable to give alms to those who ask for them, but not obliged to do so. The point of this teaching is not to "erect a fence around the law" and carefully delimit what a person is obliged to do in a given situation. Rather it is to encourage careful reflection on the question of what it means to live deeply and fully within the truth of the "comprehensive commandments." There is profound freedom in such a life, freedom that brings with it the capacity for an open, spontaneous response to any situation that arises.

This principle also applies to the life of prayer. Symeon notes that "someone who prays continuously (cf. I Thess. 5:17) has in this act included everything and is no longer obliged to praise the Lord seven times a day." There are potential dangers to such teaching, for it can be taken as a license to simply avoid disciplined practice altogether. But this is clearly not Symeon's intention. He wishes rather to open up a horizon of thought and practice in which the monk can begin to imagine the possibility of life in God as a continuous, unbroken reality. To this end, he expresses in this same text what is among the most vivid and stirring visions of a transformed life in the *Philokalia*, rooted in the idea that one can so deeply *inhabit* the truth of scripture in one's life that one becomes a kind of sacred text. "He who has acquired consciously within himself the Teacher of spiritual knowledge (cf. Ps. 94:10) has gone through all Scripture, has gained all that is to be gained from reading, and will no longer have need to resort to books. How is this? The person who is in communion with Him who inspired those who wrote the Divine Scriptures, and is initiated by Him into the undivulged secrets of the hidden mysteries, will himself be an inspired book to others."[29] Here we see the ultimate end or fruit of the simple practices of psalmody and attentive reading of scripture described throughout the *Philokalia*. Such reading, grounded in stillness and brought to a point of clarity through a deepening purity of intellect, creates a space in which the Word can enter and dwell in and gradually transform the soul.

▪ CONCLUSION

This vision of spiritual transformation is at the heart of the *Philokalia*'s understanding of what it is to know and encounter the Word of God. Grounded in a profound apprehension of the truth of the Incarnation of the Word, and brought to life through the simple practice of reciting psalms and the ongoing struggle to integrate the Word into one's life, the *Philokalia* invites readers into a way of reading scripture that leaves out nothing, that encompasses everything. Gradually, the teaching suggests, one can learn to be more and more sensitive to the Word's presence and significance, in scripture, in the created world, in community, and in one's own soul and to live in the awareness of this great mystery. To read scripture in this way is to be brought to the threshold of a great and transforming knowledge. Symeon the New Theologian says that "if a monk has truly withdrawn from the world and its affairs and has come to Christ, if he is fully conscious of his calling and has been raised to the heights of spiritual contemplation through the practice of the commandments, then he will look unwaveringly on God and be well aware of the change that has taken place in him."[30] Nikitas Stithatos says, "The practice of God's commandments will lead the spiritual contestant to such heights that on the day when he becomes perfect in virtue he will be filled with quiet delight and will reign with a pure mind in Zion."[31] This is the true meaning of the Incarnation of the Word, alive and luminous in a transformed soul, filling the whole world with that light.

6 Concerning Those Who Imagine That They Are Justified by Works: The Gospel According to St. Mark—the Monk

Bradley Nassif

"Sell all that you have, and buy Mark the Monk." This widely reported saying within monastic circles was recorded in a Byzantine manuscript in the fourteenth century.[1] It indicates the immense popularity of Mark's works in the Christian East. Mark the Monk, also known since the sixteenth century as Mark the Ascetic or Mark the Hermit, flourished around CE 430 (parameters ranging 430–535).[2] Today, however, he is a little known Father of the church. Scholars and general readers alike remain unaware of his existence, let alone his significance in the history of Christianity, both East and West. If he is known at all, it is usually because three of his extant works appear in volume one of the *Philokalia*: *On the Spiritual Law, Concerning Those Who Imagine That They Are Justified by Works*, and the *Letter to Nicolas the Solitary*. This essay will offer an interpretation of Mark's treatise titled *Concerning Those Who Imagine That They Are Justified by Works* (hereafter abbreviated as *Justified by Works*).

THE CENTRALITY OF THE GOSPEL

Why should this treatise matter to readers of the *Philokalia* today? Two reasons can be given: First, Mark's ascetical theology is directly relevant to Christian living. It lays before us the church's understanding of the gospel as it relates to grace, faith, and good works in the Christian life. Mark, and the compilers of the *Philokalia* (Sts. Makarios and Nicodemus), want us to understand the vital importance of keeping the gospel *clear and central* to all our acts of Christian obedience.[3] Based on the content of this treatise, a central purpose of the placement is to stress once and for all that *the gospel is the governing hermeneutic of all Christian spirituality.*[4] Mark's message is that all ascetic efforts of prayer, fasting, almsgiving, and church life will be dangerously misguided without a prior understanding of the free gift of grace as the foundation for all Christian living.

Although Mark is the leading author in the *Philokalia* who makes this point, he is certainly not the only one. Other writers of the *Philokalia* repeat Mark's urgent call to keep the gospel clear and central to the Christian life, and they cite him as an authority to emphasize this point. For example, in the treatise purported to be from John of Damaskos, the author speaks of Mark as the "wisest of the ascetics." Philotheos of Sinai ranks him among the "great fathers and teachers" of the church.

Those who explicitly cite Mark's treatise *Justified by Works* include Sts. Hesychios the Priest, Theodore the Great Ascetic, (Pseudo) John of Damaskos, Philotheos of Sinai, Peter of Damaskos, Symeon the New Theologian, Nikephoros the Monk, Gregory of Sinai, and Gregory Palamas.[5] These writers unanimously agree that unless one has a clear understanding of salvation as the unmerited gift of God's grace, good works can be a damnable manifestation of subtle pride and self-reliance. Hesychios the Priest stresses this point by incorporating paragraphs 2–8 of *Justified by Works* into paragraphs 79–82 of his own treatise titled *On Watchfulness and Holiness*. In those passages, Hesychios repeats Mark's central teaching that "the kingdom of heaven is not a reward for works, but a gift of grace prepared by the Master for His faithful servants."[6] Likewise Diadochos of Photiki emphasizes the centrality of the gospel in his treatise *On Spiritual Knowledge*. His work closely parallels Mark's essays *On Baptism* and *Justified by Works*.[7] Peter of Damaskos also cites Mark's *Justified by Works* to make the point that the only works that are truly "good" are those that come from God's unmerited grace.

> And, lastly, the more one tries for one day to do something good, the more one is a debtor all the days of one's life, as St. Mark has said; for even if the ability and desire to do good are one's own, the grace to do it comes from God. It is only because of this grace that we are able to do anything good; when we do it, then, what have we to boast about? If we boast, it shows that we imagine we have done something good simply through our own strength and that we unjustly condemn those incapable of doing the same.[8]

Thus Mark's teaching on the relation between grace, faith, and works[9] in *Justified by Works* may be regarded as a crucial and widely accepted doctrine among the great Fathers of the church across the centuries and throughout the pages of the *Philolakia*.

The second reason that *Justified by Works* is so relevant to all readers of *The Philokalia* today is that it promotes Christian unity. It has particular relevance to contemporary ecumenical dialogue between Eastern Orthodoxy and the Christian West. Along with the works of John Cassian, *Justified by Works* is the only other text I know of in the entire Greek patristic tradition that gives focused attention to the theological relationships between grace, faith, and works in the Eastern Church's understanding of salvation. These are distinctive categories that have characterized the theological controversies of the Christian West off and on for centuries. This is not to say, however, that Mark is a proto-Protestant or that he is writing against the Pelagians. His opponents clearly are not identical to those of Augustine or his Medieval and Reformation children. Rather, *Justified by Works* is directed toward a heretical group of monks known as the Messalians (discussed below).

The title of Mark's treatise *Justified by Works* leads one to think that its subject is the Pauline doctrine of "justification." But as we shall see, that is not the subject Mark deals with. He particularly does not explore the forensic aspects of the doctrine of "justification by faith" as interpreted by Martin Luther and others in the Christian West. Yet Mark's treatise clearly supports—by implication—the most important ecumenical agreement between Catholics and Lutherans since the sixteenth century: the 1999 document titled *The Joint Declaration on the Doctrine of*

Justification by the Lutheran World Federation and the Catholic Church. Mark serves as a constructive bridge between Eastern and Western Christianity by grounding unity in the truth of the gospel. In this way, the *Philokalia* offers a way out of the dead end of modern ecumenism, which has stressed common social action as the grounds for Christian unity.

▓ RECEPTION HISTORY OF MARK THE MONK

Before we analyze *Justified by Works*, it will be helpful to see how Mark the Monk has been received in the history of Christianity so we can avoid the interpretive mistakes that have been made on his works in the past. Augustine Casiday has surveyed the history of the reception of the Markan corpus in his Introduction to the newly published English translation of his writings.[10] Casiday tells us that ancient historians and hagiographers in the first millennium of Christian history regarded Mark as one of the greatest figures of Christian monasticism.[11] In the sixteenth-century Reformation of the Christian West, Casiday observes, "It appears to have been taken for granted by both sides of the debate that Mark was indeed proto-Protestant in his understanding of grace."[12] Casiday cites Samuel Schelwig (1643–1715), a Lutheran professor of dogmatic theology who was broadly familiar with Mark's writings. Schelwig was part of a line of Protestants who found Mark's emphasis on the utterly free gift of God's grace to be congenial with the Protestant view. Schelwig argued that Mark's faith was consistent with the Lutheran profession as well as John Chrysostom, Jerome, and Augustine. In 1688 he wrote a pamphlet titled *Theological Theses on Justification and Good Works*, excerpted from the work *On Those Who Think They Are Justified by Their Own Works* of Mark the Hermit, *a saint and ancient writer, illustrated with brief notes.*

Robert Bellarmine (1542–1621) and other theologians of the Catholic Counter-Reformation represent the Roman trend to discourage people from even reading Mark, and urged extreme caution if they did. In combating Protestantism, Bellarmine tried to identify Mark with an ascetic of the same name dating back to 906 rather than the early fifth century. But the modern Catholic specialist on Mark, Georges de Durand, O.P., rejects Bellarmine's dating as "a dishonest and ineffective ruse."[13] He contends that Bellarmine would have known about Photios's citation of Mark in the ninth century. By making Mark later than was generally accepted, Bellarmine was attempting to discredit his writings because he believed they reflected a proto-Protestant perspective.

▓ MARK AND MESSALIANISM

In the Introduction to Mark the Monk in the *Philokalia*, Kallistos Ware tells us that Mark's spiritual teaching "is directed particularly against the heretical Syrian movement of Messalianism."[14] At the risk of historical oversimplification, the paragraphs below provide a description of Messalianism[15] that form the background of our analysis of Mark's treatise *Justified by Works*. Three areas of Messalianism are especially relevant: The general characteristics of Messalianism, Messalianism and baptism, and the relation of Messalianism to Pelagianism.

The Messalian Movement

Messalianism comes from a Syriac word *messalleyane*, meaning "those who pray" (*Euchites* from the Greek). The name is based on a trait, not on a person. References to Messalian persons or practices appear in the 370s first in Mesopotamia, then in Asia Minor with the controversy peaking in the 420s and 430s. Yet the movement periodically appears in various regions between the fourth century and the end of the Middle Ages. In their extreme wings, Messalians are also known in the later ancestry of the Slavic Bogomils in the East, and Cathars or Albigensians in the West. The Messalians were condemned by a variety of church councils and Fathers from the fourth to fourteenth centuries. The most important condemnation came from the ecumenical Council of Ephesus in 431 where the bishops anathematized certain Messalian propositions found in their ascetical book called the *Ascetikon*.

The Messalian movement is so regionally and historically diverse that it is impossible to give a single "one-size-fits-all" definition that covers every variation of its theology. They did not seem to be a defiant sect within the church. In fact, even to call it a sect or a movement is to ascribe more internal coherence than the extant evidence can sustain.[16] To use a scientific metaphor, it is better to think of Messalianism more as a liquid than as a solid. Messalianism is a term that represents broad monastic inclinations, tendencies, imbalances, and particular heresies than a full-blown heretical system in such groups as the Arians or Monophysites with all their variations and complexities.[17] Although we cannot do justice to every historical variation within the movement, we can describe some of the most common characteristics of Messalianism in the fourth and fifth centuries, as well as a number of particular beliefs that seemed to have formed the object of Mark's polemical arguments against them. In nearly all his writings, Mark has their teachings in mind even though he does not mention the Messalians by name.

The major thrust of the Messalians was their challenge to the church as a sacramental body. They minimized the efficacy of baptism and the Eucharist while downplaying the church hierarchy. One group, known as the "righteous," emphasized asceticism and manual labor while the other, known as the "perfect," was based almost exclusively on a life of prayer and the absence of manual labor. John Meyendorff explains:

> According to *Liber Graduum* [= *The Book of Steps*, an anonymous 4th century Syriac collection of 30 discourses on the Christian life], the Christian community is divided into two distinct groups: the "righteous" and the "perfect." The "righteous" alone are obligated to practice good works, help the poor and, in general, fulfill the commandments of standard Christian morality. The "perfect ones" receive special gifts of the Spirit and, as a consequence, stand above manual labor and good works, and even above fasting and asceticism. They possess what the Messalians called "true love" and the vision of God, which made it superfluous for them to fulfill the external demands of ethical commandments. The sacraments themselves are of no use to the "perfect."[18]

These are just a few of the salient points about Messalianism that are relevant to Mark's treatise *Justified by Works*. As we will see, both groups appear to be in view in *Justified by Works*, although the "righteous" seem to be in the foreground.

More specific information on the Messalianism that Mark refutes can be obtained by turning to Mark's treatise *On Baptism* and by comparing the doctrinal relations between Messalianism and Pelagianism.

Baptism in Mark and the Messalians

With regard to baptism, Kallistos Ware tells us that "Mark, although he never mentions the Messalians by name, is the anti-Messalian writer *par excellence*, and this is true above all in his work *De baptismo* [*On Baptism*]."[19] The main concern of Mark's anti-Messalian preoccupation in this treatise is to stress the *perfection* or *completeness* (τέλειος) of holy baptism. Mark's point is that ascetical efforts can add nothing whatsoever to the completeness of baptismal grace. Mark describes this "completeness" in three ways: First, baptism entirely removes our sinful condition by cleansing us (καθαρίσμος) from original sin and all personal sins. In Messalianism, ascetic struggles, particularly continual prayer, can alone uproot sin and expel the active demon that remains within us as part of our Adamic inheritance.[20] Second, baptism confers spiritual freedom (ἐλευθερία). Mark rejects the Messalian belief in a post-baptismal demonic presence within the heart of the believer.[21] Third, baptism confers the indwelling (ἐνοικήσις) Christ and the Holy Spirit within the heart of the believer; we can never "add" anything to that baptismal grace. By contrast, in Messalian teaching, baptism brings about, at most, the coexistence of good and evil within us, while the devil still remains deep within our hearts.[22]

Messalianism: The Pelagianism of the East

John Meyendorff observes, "It is, indeed, true that the Messalians were, in a sense, the Pelagians of the East."[23] The connection between Pelagianism and Messalianism, therefore, is especially relevant for the interpretation of Mark's treatise *Justified by Works*. Here is where the polemics of the Reformation misappropriated Mark's work by interpreting him in isolation from the Messalian context of his day. It is also where Mark's theology of grace sets him apart from the Latin tradition represented by Augustine and his Lutheran and Calvinist children.

In an article "Messalianism and Pelagianism," Andrew Louth compares the two as quasi-monastic movements that felt that the "Great Church" failed, or was in danger of failing, to deal with how humans can work out their relationship with God. Louth puts the matter succinctly:

> They were both controversies that forced men to clarify their understanding of *grace*. The doctrine of grace in the West is conditioned (at least in part) by Pelagianism. . . . Something similar is true of Messalianism in the East—not I think in quite such a thorough-going way—but nonetheless "Messalianism" is the kind of taunt that you throw at your opponent's head, if it is his doctrine of grace you are concerned with. Put somewhat more crudely than I want to put it: The doctrine of grace in the West is anti–Pelagian, in the East it is anti-Messalian.[24]

These two controversies about grace in the fifth century ran parallel with each other even though they were independent from each other, one in the East and one in the West. Yet they had far more differences than similarities. In Pelagianism, good works originate from a human will that is believed to be free from inherited guilt and a corrupted human nature. Good works come from a good human nature that imitates Christ and obeys the precepts of the Bible. Grace is essentially God's forgiveness of personal sin and the strengthening of our wills to imitate perfection. In Messalianism, ascetic struggles, particularly continual prayer, can alone uproot sin and expel the active demon that remains within us as part of our Adamic inheritance. Grace does not eradicate or disempower original sin or the powers of darkness within us. These, so it seems, are the essential differences between the Pelagian and Messalian doctrines of grace and good works.

■ CONCERNING THOSE WHO IMAGINE THAT THEY ARE JUSTIFIED BY WORKS

Now that we have surveyed Mark's place in the history of interpretation and situated his work in the context of his day via the Messalian and Pelagian movements, we are ready to interpret *Justified by Works*. Without attempting a full analysis, we will focus on its master theme: the gospel of grace. The following analysis will attempt to explain the text's literary characteristics, the title of the treatise, and Mark's theology of righteousness as both the gift and task of God's grace.

Literary Characteristics

The literary genre that Mark uses to set forth his teaching in *Justified by Works* is variously referred to as "apophthegms," "centuries," "chapters" or "sayings." These are different words that simply refer to a collection of short sentences or paragraphs about a given topic. The genre originated in pagan literature but was later adopted by monastic writers as a preferred method of discourse. Mark is one of several authors who use this diadactic method in the *Philokalia*. Others include Evagrios, Diadochus of Photike, Maximos the Confessor, Symeon the New Theologian, Gregory Palamas, and others. This communication style has several advantages and disadvantages for the beginning reader of the *Philokalia*. The main disadvantage is that it can be frustrating for a reader who expects a clearly organized, systematic presentation on a given topic. The "sayings" genre can frustrate readers because it abruptly changes topics without warning and at times comes across as uneven, illogical, repetitious, or puzzling. The advantages of this genre, however, are that it presents the teaching in a concise, memorable form. It forces the reader to think about the connections between the various ideas presented and to put into practice those parts they do understand even if they are unable to make sense of the whole. So beginning readers of the *Philokalia* should not get discouraged by this teaching method but should approach the literature in the same ascetical spirit as the book itself: with patience, thoughtfulness, and prayer. It is largely a matter of breaking the ice.

Justified by Works is best understood in relation to two other treatises by Mark, titled *On the Spiritual Law* and *On Baptism*. *Justified by Works* likely forms the second of a two-part work, the first part titled *On the Spiritual Law*.[25] *On the*

Spiritual Law is an interpretation of St. Paul's phrase "law of the Spirit" given in Romans 7:14. There Mark defines Christian freedom not as "lawlessness" but as "obedience to the law of freedom." He describes the life of Christian perfection in 201 monastic "sayings." The "sayings" affirm that the laws of freedom, and the grace that enables one to put them into practice, come from Christ. In its sequel, *Justified by Works*, Mark takes these laws and applies them more fully against the Messalians. Together these two treatises form the foundation for a fuller development of Mark's sacramental theology that is given in his later treatise titled *On Baptism*, which was described above in the section *Baptism in Mark and the Messalians*. Thus there is a progressive connection among these three treatises by Mark. Of the three, *Justified by Works* stands in the middle. On the one hand, it rejects the Messalian notion of "merit" through the principles of "the law of the Spirit" that Mark gave in his first treatise, *On the Spiritual Law*. On the other hand, *Justified by Works* leaves unfinished the fuller development of sacramental theology that Mark will eventually take up in *On Baptism*.

Topical Outline

The following is a basic summary of the topics covered in *Justified by Works* which was given, with some modifications, by Claire-Agnes Zirnheld.[26] The numbers that appear next to each topic, and in the remainder of this essay, refer to the "sayings" in the new English translation of *Justified by Works* by Tim Vivian and Augustine Casiday in *Counsels on the Spiritual Life*, pages 113–39 (see endnote 1).

The Practical Outworking of Baptismal Grace:
Purpose of the Treatise, Saying #1 (hereafter only numbers given)
Commandments and Obedience, 2–6
Spiritual Labor, 7–9
Discernment, 10–11
Knowledge and Practice, 12–16
Repayment or Divine Sonship, 17–24
Practice of the Virtues, 25–27
Silence (*hesychia*), 28–30
Prayer, 31–39
Repentance, 40–41
Obligations, 42–44
Forgiveness, 45–47
Intentions, 48–50
Trials and Discernment, 51–54
Feelings of Grace, 55–57
Discernment, 58–80
Movements of the Intellect, 81–86
Advice for Spiritual Leaders, 87–92
Grace, 93–100
Passions, 101–10
Compensation, 111–18

A Telling Title

The title of this work indicates its purpose and content. We offer an expanded paraphrase to capture its intended meaning: *Regarding Those Messalians Who Wrongly Imagine That Their Lives Are Made Righteous as a Due Reward for Their Works.*

Are Messalians the enemies of the gospel that Mark opposes in this treatise? A close exegesis of the title in the original Greek is critical to the interpretation of the entire document, because the crux of the Messalian error that Mark refutes is revealed by it. Vivian and Casiday translate it as *Concerning Those Who Imagine That They Are Justified by Works*, but Palmer, Sherrard, and Ware translates it *On Those Who Think That They Are Made Righteous by Works*. Both translations are possible renderings of the Greek $Περὶ\ τῶν\ οἰομένων\ ἐξ\ ἔργων\ δικαιοῦσθαι$. The words "made righteous" ($δικαιοῦσθαι$) reveal the error of Mark's opponents. But what is meant by this term? The term $δικαιοῦσθαι$ has been translated as "to be justified" (Vivian and Casiday's translation[27]) and "to be made righteous" (Palmer, Sherrard, and Ware's translation). For Catholic and classical Protestant readers of this treatise, both of these translations will quickly evoke the Reformation debates over the forensic nature of "justification by faith." In Reformation polemics, the debate centered on whether or not the Scriptures use the verb "justify" ($δικαιόω$) to denote "divine acquittal of a believer through a legal declaration of being made right with God" (Luther and Calvin), or a believer who is "made holy through moral acts of righteous behavior" (Council of Trent). These issues are crucial and should not be disregarded simply because they have never been debated in the Greek patristic tradition. Additional concerns over whether or not

Mark is a proto-Protestant further introduce an unwarranted anachronistic association. Mark simply uses the term δικαιόω synonymously as "righteous" or "justify" with no significant theological difference implied. Justice and righteousness
are virtually equivalent in this treatise as well as in most of Greek patristic thought.
In fact, Mark rarely uses the word or its cognates and never gives us a precise definition of the verb anywhere in the treatise. The only clues we have that can elucidate Mark's understanding of the term δικαιόω are the ascetical teachings he gives
in *Justified by Works* and its companion volume *On the Spiritual Law*. The sayings
in these two treatises will shed light on what Mark meant by the term δικαιόω in
the title of *Justified by Works*. The main sayings that are relevant to the determination of the meaning of this word are the following:

The preface to saying #1 of *On the Spiritual Law*:

> Since you have often desired to know what the Apostle (that is, St. Paul) means when he
> says that "the law is spiritual" [Rom. 7.14], and what knowledge and practice is fitting for
> those who wish to keep the spiritual law, we have spoken about it to the best of our ability.

This text states that the purpose of the treatise *On the Spiritual Law* is to explain
Paul's meaning of Romans 7:14 as it relates to Christian living. The role of "the
spiritual law" is to create not lawlessness, but Christian freedom. To drive the
point home, Mark adds the sequel volume *Justified by Works* to make it clear that
obedience to Christ can in no way *earn* the reward of salvation. Thus the term
"justify" or "made righteous" (δικαίοω) in the title of *Justified by Works* does not
refer to a divine acquittal of guilt. Rather it refers to the error of those Messalians
who imagined that a *righteous life* is given as a *reward* to those who practice good
deeds and ascetical disciplines. Mark rejects this notion and insists that a life of
righteousness comes about only as a gift of God's grace that is freely given in baptism through faith in the cross of Christ.

As Meyendorff noted earlier (see *Messalianism* above), according to the *Liber
Graduum*, the Christian community is divided into two distinct groups: the "righteous" and the "perfect." One must be careful, however, not to overgeneralize about
this feature of the "perfectionist" strand of Messalianism. In the *Liber Graduum*
many of the "perfect" share in the "good works" of the "righteous." Those who are
devoted exclusively to prayer appear to be an elite group within the elite "perfect."
The "righteous" alone are obligated to practice good works, help the poor, and, in
general fulfill the commandments of standard Christian morality. The greatest
number of sayings found in Mark's rebuttal appear to be directed mainly, though
not exclusively, toward them rather than the "perfect" ones. The "righteous" whom
Mark refutes are those who view baptism, fasting, asceticism, the practice of the
virtues, and other spiritual works as meritorious. To that extent, their definition of
grace is akin to the Pelagian error of the West. *Justified by Works* is therefore the
most anti-Pelagian-like treatise of all Mark's writings.

Although the type of Messalianism that Mark counters is primarily the "righteous" form, Mark does seem to include in his rebuttal the "perfectionist" strand
in which the only good work that matters in the Christian life is the life of
prayer. Saying #17 seems to be an allusion to this group: *Some, without keeping
the commandments, think they are keeping the faith, while others, keeping the*

commandments, expect to receive the kingdom as a reward owed to them. Both are deprived of the kingdom. Thus the errors of the "righteous" are primarily in view while not excluding those of the "perfectionists."

Finally, saying #1 of *Justified by Works* openly states the purpose and direction for the entire treatise.

> In the texts that follow, the erroneous beliefs of those outside the faith will be refuted by those who are well grounded in the faith and who fully recognize the truth.

Again, this text does not identify the Messalians by name, but we can be certain that they are the ones Mark is addressing. He tells us that his refutation is directed toward "the erroneous beliefs of those outside the faith." That these must be the Messalians is supported by internal and external evidence. The internal evidence given in saying #1 states that these people are "those outside the faith" (Ἡ τῶν ἔξωθεν κακοπιστία). These are not Christians whom Mark considers insiders. Their faith is "outside" (ἔξωθεν) the commonly known beliefs of Mark's ecclesial community "who are well grounded in the faith and who fully recognize the truth [ἐπεγνωσκότων τὴν ἀλήθειαν]." The external evidence in support of a Messalian audience can be deduced from Mark's other treatise *On Baptism*. The characteristics of Messalianism that occur there appear also in *Justified by Works* but with added features. Kallistos Ware has established the Messalian background of the treatise *On Baptism* in his article referred to above, so we need not restate the evidence here. The relevant conclusion to draw from this is that Mark knew Messalian doctrine well enough to refute it in *On Baptism*, and that refutation provides collaborating evidence for Mark's other polemic against them here, which is born out from the title of *Justified by Works*, saying #1 and the sayings that follow it.

The Markan Center of *Justified by Works*

The beginning and end of the treatise function as bookends that describe the entire work as an ascetic essay on "the free gift of grace." At end of his last saying, #211, Mark tells us that in the foregoing work he has attempted to explain only a "few" of the "many ordinances of the spiritual law." In other words, the 210 precepts he previously gave are rooted in the liberating work of the spiritual law in the life of the believer. These 210 precepts are "spiritual" because the Spirit brings freedom to all who have repented, believed the gospel, and been baptized. Such freedom comes as a gift of grace, not as a reward for works. At the beginning of *Justified by Works*, Mark offers what amounts to a summary statement of the entire treatise. In saying #2 he makes two key points that summarize the center of his thought. That center can serve as the organizing structure for our interpretation of the central point of Mark's thesis, namely, that righteousness is both a "gift" and "task" of God's grace.

> Saying #2: The Lord, wishing to show that every commandment is obligatory but that sonship is a gift bestowed on human beings by means of his own blood, says, "When you have done everything that you were ordered to do, say, 'We are worthless slaves, we have done only what we ought to have done'" [Lk. 17:10]. Thus the kingdom of heaven is not a reward for works but is rather a master's gift prepared for his faithful servants.

Righteousness as a Gift of Grace

Saying #2 above summarizes the main point of Mark's treatise. He tells his readers that "sonship" and the "kingdom of heaven" is "not a reward for works" but a "gift of grace" bestowed on the believer "by means of His [Christ's] own blood." The term "sonship" (υἱοθεσίαν) is a Pauline concept (Romans 8:15, 23; 9:4; Galatians 4:5; Ephesians 1:5). It denotes divine adoption into the family of God on the basis of faith in Christ and His work on the cross. Prior to conversion, humans are seen as spiritual orphans who are in need of adoption into God's family. Through repentance, faith, and baptism (Romans 6:1–12), humans become sons and daughters of God by grace. Salvation is a free gift of adoption; it is not a "reward" for righteous deeds. Sayings #3–4, 19–20, and 23 reinforce this point:

#3. A slave does not demand freedom as a reward, but rather satisfies his master as someone who is indebted to him and who waits for his freedom as a gift.

#4. "Christ died for our sins in accordance with the Scriptures" [1 Cor. 15:3], and to those who serve him well he gives freedom as a gift, for he says, "Well done, good and faithful servant; since you have been trustworthy in a few things, I will put you in charge of many things. Come share in your master's joy" [Mt. 25:21].

#19. If "Christ died for us in accordance with the Scriptures" [1 Cor. 15:3] and "we do not live for ourselves but for him who died and was raised for us" [2 Cor. 5:15], it is clear that we are obligated to serve him until our deaths. How then can we consider sonship something owed to us?

#20. Christ is Master by essence and is Master by divine dispensation, because he has brought into being those who did not exist, and with his own blood has redeemed those who were dead in sin [Jn. 1.3] and has given the gift of grace to those who thus believe [Rom. 5:9; Rev. 5:9].

#23. Every good work that we do through our own nature causes us to abstain from its opposing evil, but without grace it cannot increase our holiness.

These texts refute the Messalian notion that a righteous life comes about as a due reward given by God for faithful Christian living. On the contrary, Mark maintains that spiritual labors can benefit one's life only by God's grace. Human effort in and of itself is worthless, because "without grace it cannot increase our holiness." The point of these passages is clear: Sonship, the kingdom of heaven, spiritual freedom, and good works that lead to holiness can never be earned, but rather they are gifts of God's grace freely given to those who believe and are baptized.

In sayings #17 and 21–22 Mark adds further arguments against Messalian doctrine by affirming that God is not a dealer bound by contract. He does not reward one for a life of fasting, prayer, and all other good works.

#17. Some, without keeping the commandments, think they are keeping the faith, while others, keeping the commandments, expect to receive the kingdom as a reward owed to them. Both are deprived of the kingdom.

#21. When, therefore, you hear Scripture say, "He will reward each person according to his works" [Ps. 62:12; Mt. 16:27], it does not say that works deserve hell or the kingdom, but rather that works are done out of faith or lack of faith in him. Christ repays each person not as a businessman fulfilling his contracts but as God, our Creator and Redeemer.

#22. We who have been considered worthy to receive the washing of regeneration offer good works not as repayment, but as a means of preserving the purity that has been given to us.

Mark repeatedly uses the synonyms "reward" (μισθός, in sayings #2, 3, and 17), "repay" (ἀποδίδωσιν in 21), and "recompense" (ἀνταπόδοσιν in #22). In all cases the terms convey the idea of remuneration. They refer to someone who "pays back a debt" that is owed. In these instances, the Messalians wrongly imagined that God owed them the blessings of salvation as a reward for their works of righteousness. Mark replies that those who have been baptized "offer good works not as repayment, but as a means of preserving [φυλακὴν] the purity that has been given to us." The term φυλακή means "guard, watch over." Good works are a necessary means of guarding or protecting the purity of our salvation that has been granted in baptism, but they should never lead us to think that God will repay us for them.

If the gifts of salvation do not come as a reward for good works, how then is salvation received? Mark is very clear: Sayings #2, 19, and 24 indicate that salvation comes only through faith in the work of Christ on the cross.

#2 ". . . sonship is a gift bestowed on human beings by means of his own blood."

#19 If "Christ died for us in accordance with the Scriptures" [1 Cor. 15:3] and "we do not live for ourselves but for him who died and was raised for us" [2 Cor. 5:15], it is clear that we are obligated to serve him until our deaths. How then can we consider sonship something owed to us?

#24 "Christ, through the cross, gives sonship as a gift."

In short, Mark is neither a Messalian nor a Pelagian. Salvation is a free gift of God's grace given in baptism to all those who believe in the gospel on the basis of the shed blood of Christ offered on the cross. He believes that no amount of good works can ever earn us the kingdom of heaven or the right to become adopted sons and daughters of God. The so-called "righteous" Messalians had distorted the gospel by imagining that God owed them the righteous life they sought through their ascetical efforts.

Righteousness as a Task of Grace

Mark maintains that every true Christian conversion has consequences. There are at least three overarching consequences connected with baptism that Mark identifies in *Justified by Works*: First, good works are a response of gratitude rooted in "the spiritual law" or "the law of freedom"; second, grace is secretly hidden in the heart of the baptized but requires keeping the commandments in order for that grace to be consciously revealed in the heart of the believer; third, ascetical labors are the duties of sonship and faithful service to Christ. We will look at each of these in turn.

Mark first tells us that the "law of freedom" enables the mind of the ascetic to do good works out of a heart of gratitude for the salvation he received through Christ.

#16 The mind carries out many good and bad things without the body, whereas the body can accomplish none of these things without the mind, since the law of freedom goes into effect before a person does something.

#211b We have come to a place where we now understand, out of many, these few ordinances of the spiritual law. The Great Psalm [Ps. 119] constantly instructs us to learn them and to sing psalms without ceasing to the Lord. To him be the glory, forever and ever. Amen.

As was noted earlier, saying #211b comes at the end of the treatise and looks back on the previous 210 sayings, which Mark deems as a mere "few ordinances of the spiritual law." All the good works and monastic disciplines that he described in the 210 sayings are expressions of the "law of freedom." True ascetical life flows from the law of freedom.

Second, in sayings #56, 85, and 210 Mark affirms that grace is secretly hidden in the heart of the baptized and requires one to keep the commandments in order for grace to be consciously experienced.

#56 Grace has been mystically [μυστικως] bestowed on those who have been baptized in Christ and becomes active in them to the extent that they keep the commandments. Grace never ceases to secretly help us but it is up to us, as far as it lies within our own power, to do good or not to do good. Grace first rouses the conscience in a manner that conforms to God's wishes; that is how even evildoers have repented and come to please God. Again, grace may be hidden in a neighbor's advice. There are times when it also accompanies one's thoughts when one is reading and, as a natural consequence, teaches the mind the truth about itself. If, therefore, we do not hide the talent that has in consequence been given to us [25:20–25], we shall without a doubt enter into the Lord's joy.

#85 Each person baptized in an orthodox manner has mystically [μυστικως] received the fullness of grace, but each person is fully assured [πληροφρειται] of grace afterwards to the extent that he keeps the commandments.

#210 Every word of Christ demonstrates God's mercy and justice and wisdom, and their power penetrates those who willingly listen to his words. That is why the unmerciful and the unjust, who listened unwillingly to the wisdom of God [1 Cor. 2:7–8], were not able to understand it but even crucified Christ for speaking it. Therefore let us also see whether we listen to him willingly, for he said, "The person who loves me will keep my commandments and will be loved by my Father, and I too will love him and will reveal myself to him'" [Jn. 14:21]. Do you see how he has hidden his self-revelation in the commandments?

The Greek terms that have been bracketed above frequently reappear in Mark's treatise *On Baptism*.[28] *Justified by Works* and *On Baptism* express the same teaching regarding the "mystical or hidden" (μυστικως) nature of grace in the baptized and the need for one to have a "conscious awareness" (πληροφρειται) of it that comes by keeping the commandments. Mark believes that baptismal regeneration is the decisive foundation for spiritual life and that new birth may be hidden in the life of the believer. But Mark does not develop the doctrine of original sin and its consequences in *Justified by Works* as he does in *On Baptism*.

A third and major theme of Mark is that keeping the commandments is a "duty" of sonship and a "debt" of faithful service to the Master. Sayings #2 and 4 quoted above under *Righteousness as a Gift of Grace* capture the inseparable relationship between the "gift" and "task" of God's grace. Mark develops this theme further in the following sayings which are strongly anti-Messalian:

> #17 Some, [an elite group among the 'perfect'?] without keeping the commandments, think they are keeping the faith, while others, [the 'righteous'?] keeping the commandments, expect to receive the kingdom as a reward owed to them. Both are deprived of the kingdom.

> #18 A master has no obligation to reward his slaves, nor, on the other hand, will those who are not faithful servants receive their freedom.

> #22 We who have been considered worthy to receive the washing of regeneration offer good works not as repayment, but as a means of preserving the purity that has been given to us.

> #24b–25 Avoiding sin is something that comes naturally; it is not something done in exchange for the kingdom. A person can barely maintain what comes to him naturally, while Christ, through the cross, gives sonship as a gift.

Throughout the discourse, Mark freely roams through various topics, explaining in one place how righteousness is a gift of God's grace while, in another place, exhorting readers to a variety of spiritual deeds. The *Topical Outline* of *Justified by Works* given above lists a wide range of virtues and vices that Mark develops. To elaborate on Mark's teaching about prayer, repentance, trials, the passions, and other topics would require a separate essay. All these subjects, however, must be interpreted within the context of Mark's anti-Messalian intent. That intent seeks to purposely undermine his readers' self-confidence in their own good works so that the ascetical life can be rooted in grace from start to finish.

The Goal of Grace: To Love as God Loves

The penultimate goal of *Justified by Works* is to instill humility by recognizing God's grace. Without a firm grounding in the gift of grace, Mark knows that Christians will be tempted to spiritual pride. Whenever the faithful practice fasting, vigils, prayer, the patient acceptance of wrongs, or any other task of grace discussed in this treatise, they cannot claim that they have done more than what God requires. The best we can say is that we have only done what was our duty. That is why Mark invokes the need for humility. True humility does not lead to self-praise or to self-condemnation, but to gratitude:

> #103 Humility consists, not in condemning our conscience, but in recognizing God's grace and compassion.[29]

The emphasis on ascetical rigor as the task of grace leads Mark to underscore the final goal of the Christian life. The aim of the ascetic life is not to merit the Kingdom of God or to engage in great ascetical feats as if they were ends in themselves, but *to love as God loves*. That is why grace opposes merit while inducing the hard work of holiness. The final goal is to cultivate love for God and others through the practice of inner silence (ἡσυχία). The simple "stilling of one's thoughts" is a fourth-century description of the more developed practice of *The Jesus Prayer* in later centuries. The last saying puts it all together:

> Saying #211: The most comprehensive of all the commandments is the love of God and of one's neighbor [Mark 12:30–31], which is maintained by abstaining from material things and through stilling one's thoughts. . . . We have come to a place where we now understand, out of many, these few ordinances of the spiritual law.

If one approaches *Justified by Works* in the same spirit of humility that we find here, we too will share the enthusiasm of those earlier monks in the fifth century who urged one another to "Sell all that you have, and buy Mark the Monk."

7 The Theological World of the *Philokalia*[1]

Rowan Williams

"The ascetical writings collected in the *Philokalia* have a tremendous success in some esoteric groups that are supremely indifferent to the life, death and resurrection of Jesus Christ." So wrote Fr. Alexander Schmemann in that profound and luminous little book, *The World as Sacrament*.[2] The sentiments are very characteristic; they can be found reiterated in a number of places in the Journals[3] as part of a general and deeply felt suspicion of Athonite elitism and a precious and self-conscious spirituality which deserved all of the Nietzschean polemic against a religion which created unreal feelings for unreal objects and so took away the essential distinctive sign of Christianity—the eschatological joy of the sacraments, announcing the transfiguration of this world. Thus you will find him deploring "the reduction of everything in Orthodoxy to the 'Fathers' and 'Spirituality'! . . . The triumph nowadays of a sectarian 'only'! Only the Fathers, only 'Dobrotolubie,' only typikon. Boredom, mediocrity and lack of seriousness and talent in it all."[4]

It is apparently a severe indictment of the world of spiritual vision and counsel we are examining—and perhaps it is one that would be shared by other theologians impatient with spiritual preciousness and wary of what might seem to relativize or sidestep the sacramental reality of life in the Church. But it may be possible to show that what is being criticized by Schmemann is a way of approaching these texts which systematically avoids their broad theological vision, reducing them to just that limited and self-enclosed "spirituality" which he always claimed not to understand. Schmemann's own theology of the sacramentality of the world in Christ is, I should want to argue, exactly where we should begin in rereading the *Philokalia,* and exactly where a thoroughgoing theological reading will lead us back again.

But there is of course a double risk in addressing this subject. Apart from the danger of presumption in dealing with it outside the specific context of spiritual practice and the acquisition of discernment, there is the obvious risk involved in someone formed largely by Western spiritual and intellectual currents attempting to trace the chief features of these Eastern sources. In all that follows, the reader must bear these dangers in mind. But in a context where spirituality and doctrine are still regarded as separate matters by so many, it may not be a waste of time to try to show how the contemplative practice to which the *Philokalia* is a guide both presupposes and reinforces a set of beliefs about God and creation. For the authors of the *Philokalia,* revelation was essentially the gift of a wisdom which opened up fresh possibilities for human action—or, more accurately, which restored possibilities lost by human sin and ignorance. The person examining himself or herself in the light of these texts is a person learning how to live truthfully in the world as it really is; and such truthful living is not possible without both the self-manifestation of God and the self-giving of God into human activity. There is no "spirituality" free of doctrine, and the fashionable modern opposition between spirituality and religion is meaningless in the context of the *Philokalia*.[5] The health and maturity of the human spirit are dependent on purified awareness, "watchfulness," *nepsis*, the key concept of the *Philokalia*, and such awareness is necessarily a matter of being alert to false and imprisoning accounts of who and what the human subject is—and of who and what God is.

One other introductory observation. In what follows, I have concentrated a good deal (though not exclusively, especially in the later parts of this essay) on the earlier texts in the *Philokalia*, simply because they are the ones in which the vocabulary and thought-world of the later selections are most vividly mapped out. Many of the most copious texts in the later sections add little to the substance of the theological analysis of the human subject and of the development of contemplation outlined earlier; some are, in effect, recastings of earlier ones (or of comparable texts such as John Klimakos).[6] Where they add significantly to the theology of the whole corpus is in two areas: the practical outworkings of the underlying concepts of hesychastic prayer, and (especially in the texts from Gregory Palamas) some fresh and bold proposals for better understanding the character of divine action and relation.

I

Given what has just been said about the need for awareness of false accounts of the human and the divine, a good place to start is with the idea of nature in the *Philokalia*. For anything to be natural is for it to be as God intends, to be in the state in and for which God created it. Hesychios (I, p. 194) summarizes the classical view of this idea toward the end of his treatise *On Watchfulness and Holiness* (#179): the natural state of human beings is the "beauty, loveliness and integrity" of the first creation. Quoting Athanasius's *Life of Antony*, Hesychios accepts the identification of holiness with the "natural" state, which is clear perception. But the condition we experience as habitual is the opposite of clear perception: it is a state of bondage to images that are seen or sensed as objects for the mind's satisfaction. The intelligence[7] can receive impressions in two basic ways, defined by Mark the Ascetic (*On the Spiritual Law*, #87, I, p. 116) as "passionate" or "objective" (*monotropos*, literally "in a single or simple mode"; the significance of this notion of "simple" perception will be apparent in our later discussion) We may perceive objects either as related to the unreconstructed needs of the human self or as related to the single intelligible purpose of the creator. It is a distinction rooted in the analyses offered by Evagrios, whose treatise on "discrimination" (otherwise familiar outside the philokalic tradition as *On Thoughts*)[8] had distinguished between thinking of the things of the world with and without desire and had (#7, I, pp. 42–43; cf. #4, p. 40) elaborated this concept further in terms of the differences between angelic, diabolical, and human awareness. The angel knows the "essence" of things—though "meaning" might be a better rendering: how they work in the providence of God in the natural order and how they serve the purpose of God in the historical order as well. The demon is aware of a thing only as something to be acquired and used for profit. Human awareness is initially and primitively just the registering of the image of an object without either meaning or craving attached. So what watchfulness entails is awareness of the moment at which this bare "human" consciousness becomes diabolical, becomes bound to the acquisitive mode of perceiving; and the implication is that what will stabilize the mind is the infusion of angelic awareness, seeing the things of the world in their true—that is, symbolic—significance and using them accordingly (cf., for example, Maximos, *First Century on Love* #92, II, p. 63). This is a "natural" state in that it relates human consciousness to the real significance of things. And this allows us to say that the world as it is has nothing in it that is intrinsically evil, whether in soul or body: everything has the capacity to convey the divine intelligence and so to be related to human intelligence in its proper state (Maximos, *Second Century on Love* #76 ff., II, pp 78–79). For the human intelligence—and thus the life that intelligence organizes—to be natural is to perceive the world as comprehensively significant; and because the world is significant in relation to God, it cannot take its significance from its potential for self-directed or self-serving human use.

This concept may illuminate the Maximian doctrine (e.g., *First Century on Love* #71, II, p. 60) that our love is properly directed toward the nature of other human beings, since this is one and the same for all. Love cannot be dependent on circumstance or attitude; we do not love perfectly if our love depends on someone's positive relation to us, but only when we accept the variety and instability of how others treat us or regard us. In this attitude we follow the example of Christ, who suffered for all; like Him we can offer hope to all, even if we cannot dictate their response to this offer. Behind this in turn lies the conviction that God's love in general must be a love for human nature in its pristine glory: with the righteous, such love affirms and rewards a nature exercising its own proper gifts, with the unrighteous it shows compassion for the loss of "natural" dignity (Ibid. #25, p. 55). In other words, as with the world of things, so with the world of other human subjects: the significance of other human beings depends not on what they do, least of all on what they do to make me secure or comfortable, but on what they intrinsically are. It may seem at first as though Maximos is commending an essentially impersonal kind of love, love for humanity in general; but in fact the exact opposite is the case. Love depersonalizes when it treats the neighbor as significant primarily in relation to myself; it is rightly directed toward the unique reality of the person when it sees the other in relation to God—as, in the proper sense, symbolic, a living sign of the creator, irreducible either to generalities or to the other's specific significance and usefulness for me.

Thus a coherent and subtle picture is built up of the natural activity of human intelligence. As Maximos says at the end of the *First Century on Love* (#97, p. 64), the restored human consciousness is either looking at human affairs without craving and the desire to dominate, or looking at the principles and processes of the world in their God-given order, or opening itself to the light of the Trinity. It is, in other words, receptive to what is actually there, to the human and the nonhuman world in their primordial relation to God, and to God as the source of the web of significance, of meaningful interaction and interdependence, which makes the universe a system of mutual gift and enlightenment. And in Maximos's scheme, this process is evidently connected with the conviction that we cannot know God "in essence" but only by participating in His act or energy (e.g., *First Century*, #96, 100, p. 64, *Third Century*, #22–27, pp. 86–87). To know the "essences" of things is simply to know their meaning in relation to God's action in the universe; but God's "significance" is what it is, dependent on no contingent and particular thing. To know God can only be to know Him in His character as the giver of significance through His action of self-bestowing—in what is revealed of His life in Trinity and in His acts of creation and providential sustaining. The not-knowing which is central to the true contemplative enterprise is here both a "referral" of the meaning of all things to God and an acknowledgement that God's "meaning" is within Himself alone. When we turn to the texts from Gregory Palamas in the later parts of the *Philokalia,* it is important to remember that the famous "essence-energies" distinction is not primarily a solution to a metaphysical problem (there are many complications in treating it as such)[9] but a way of codifying this vision of a world in which all meanings rest on a divine act whose own meaning can never be specified with reference to anything else, whose being is never therefore to be thought of as functional to any specific created agenda or narrative.

To return for a moment to the matter of humanity's natural state, it is clear that the early philokalic authors understand this as a capacity for nonpassionate (nonacquisitive, non-self-directed) awareness of the world comparable in some sense to God's perception of the world (which is by definition disinterested, since God needs nothing from the world and is not given either being or intelligibility in terms of or in relation to the world). This capacity is obscured; indeed it could be said that the essential character of sin or fallenness in the *Philokalia* is our inability to see the world, including our fellow-humans, without "passion," without the compulsion, that is, to see them in terms of our own supposed needs and fantasies. It is Diadochos of Photike who, in his treatise *On Spiritual Knowledge*, gives one of the most suggestive accounts of what the Fall effects. We discover, says Diadochos, in the course of our growth in illumination by the Spirit, that human sensation is primitively one and undivided (#25, 29, I, pp. 259, 260–61). In unfallen humanity, the variations of bodily sensation among the five senses are due only to the varying needs of the body—that is, they are diverse aspects of a single disposition of receptivity (the *monotropos* condition already noted in the vocabulary of Mark the Ascetic). The body's receptivity is not separate from that of the intelligence. But in the fallen state, perception has become divided. This division is not, it seems, simply a division of body from soul or sensible from intellective, but a division between self-oriented and other-oriented perceiving. Both bodily sense and intelligence are split between their natural openness to things as they are (to the "symbolic" world, to use the Evagrian phrasing mentioned earlier) and the compulsion to obscure this true perception through selfish will, through the "passionate" consciousness which replaces the reality with a simulacrum, a passion-laden perception that is designed to serve the self's agenda.

Thus, for Diadochos, the gift of the Holy Spirit in baptism and the life of grace thereafter is the restoration of simplicity. "The form imprinted on the soul is single and simple" (Ibid. #78, I, p. 280). The morally complex and spiritually strenuous condition of the baptized person is not a sign that there are two "powers" at work still within us (Diadochos is determined to avoid any suggestion of the alleged Messalian model of two spirits within the believer), but the somewhat paradoxical mark of the gradual process by which simplicity establishes itself as normal. Continuing battle is a different matter, he says, from captivity (#82, p. 283). At first in the new world of the Spirit, we cannot think good thoughts without being aware of their opposite: this is the continuing legacy of Adam's split consciousness.[10] We know the good in contrast to the destructive possibilities which we cannot forget (because they have been so habitual to us). In one of Diadochos's characteristically vivid images, we are like a man facing east at dawn in winter: the sun rises and warms him in front while he is still aware of the chill at his back. But the illustration shows that this is not a picture of two powers fighting within the soul, but a phase in the steady expansion of grace to fill soul and body. The renewed perception given to the believer allows us to be confident that a process is in hand which is out of our control but directed firmly toward a new wholeness. In another memorable image, Diadochos speaks (#89, p. 288) of baptismal grace as the divine artist's monochrome sketch; it is for us in conscious collaboration with the Spirit to fill in the colors. And, "when the full range of colours is added to the outline, the painter captures the likeness of the subject, even down to the smile."

The artist is painting the likeness of the divine original: if we pursue the metaphor in detail, its implication is that God is painting a self-portrait in the elements of human nature, beginning with the act of decisive liberation which makes the whole enterprise possible, continuing with the distinctive and complex way in which human freedom energized by the Spirit in turn becomes an image of divine freedom, and so of divine love also. What the fuller implications of this picture might be for a theology of the Trinitarian life is something to which we shall be returning, but for now the point is that we are habitually held back in what might rather awkwardly be called the natural process of becoming natural. The capacity we possess in virtue of our humanity, according to Evagrios, the capacity for passion-free or passion-neutral perception, is naturally oriented toward the "symbolic" consciousness of specific things and persons in their relation to God. And as a result of Adam's divided perception, the introduction into human awareness of the perception of the world as symbolic only of the self's imagined needs, we need restoration. Habituated to this false awareness of the world, we have become forgetful of our nature and have to be awakened and to keep awake; as Mark the Ascetic observes (*On the Spiritual Law* #61–62, I, p. 114), forgetfulness is a form of ontological deficiency, a step toward self-destruction, a state of mind that is not only absorbed in unreal objects but is itself a shadow existence. Forgetting your nature is death; awareness is the condition for life. When Christ's gracious action has opened the way to "natural understanding" (Mark, *Letter to Nicolas the Solitary*, I, p. 149), the dual habits of contrition and gratitude keep before us the nature we had almost lost and preserve us from defeat by the passion of lust and anger which—to use an awkward but helpful phrasing—de-realize other things and persons, making them either objects for possession and manipulation or objects of hatred and fear. Keeping the commandments so as to preserve baptismal purity, not out of hope for reward (e.g., Mark, *On Those Who Think That*

They Are Made Righteous by Works, #23, #57) is the precondition for that openness to the full life of the Spirit in contemplative vision which is the fully natural state of human life. "He who seeks the energies of the Spirit, before he has actively observed the commandments, is like someone who sells himself into slavery and who, as soon as he is bought, asks to be given his freedom while still keeping his purchase money" (Ibid. #64, p. 130). As Maximos argues (*Second Century on Love* #4ff., II, p. 65), practical virtue, obedience to the commandments, detaches our intelligence from "passionate" thinking; we are trained to respond to the world around us without allowing our self-serving instinct to distort. But this is only a step towards the radical receptivity to God's life which is experienced in "undistracted prayer," pure eros toward God (Ibid. #6, II, pp. 65–66). In other words, obeying the practical precepts of God's commandments, the acquiring of virtuous habit, keeps us alert to our true nature in such a way that we both guard against the entry into the intelligence of passionate perceiving and keep the door open to the Spirit's work which activates the deepest potential of the intelligence, the Christ-reflecting potential (about which, again, more later).

There is, incidentally, what may seem to be a surface contradiction between this picture and that suggested by the *Gnomic Anthology* of Ilias the Presbyter, a work probably from around 1100, where there is a sequence of texts on the relation between ascetic practice and contemplation (*Anthology* IV, esp. 33–60, III, pp. 52–55) apparently implying that some arrive at contemplation by way of asceticism and some come first to contemplation and move on to asceticism (see in particular #57: "Where people of greater intelligence are concerned, contemplation precedes [*proageitai*] ascetic practice, whereas in the case of the more obtuse, ascetic practice precedes contemplation"). However, the translation is misleading here. It is quite clear from the whole section that contemplation is the superior state and that—as Maximos and others had insisted—*praktike* alone cannot take us beyond the ethical realm and deliver renewed spiritual vision. It is also clear that the contemplative habit cannot be arrived at without the steady presence of *praktike* (cf., for example, #77, III, p. 57). Thus the verb *(proago)* translated "precede" in the controverted passage (#57, III, p. 55) has surely to be read as "takes precedence" or "is more highly valued or preferred"—i.e., not in a temporal sense. The properly enlightened value contemplation more highly, the "more obtuse" prefer the more manageable or measurable activity of asceticism—and are accordingly more at risk of never realizing what they are called to and equipped for. In an intriguing anticipation of Teresa of Avila at the end of the *Interior Castle*, Ilias (#56) contrasts the ascetic who wants to "depart and be with Christ" so that their struggles may be at an end, with the mature contemplative who is content to live in the present moment, both because of the joy it contains and because of the good that may be done to others.[11] The contemplative is the person who has arrived at the place where they stand in the world, the person present to the God who is present in all times and places; the "pure" ascetic is the person who refuses the present for the future. This refusal has its place, dialectically, in the process of growth—so much is clear from any texts in this tradition—but the point of it is the return to present actuality as seen and sensed "in God."

The natural state of the human intelligence is thus a level of "mindfulness" which is essentially opposed to the irrationality of passion. "Irrationality" here means simply out of alignment with what is truly the case—arbitrary, "mindless" love or hate, or a desire for what is not needed (Maximos, *Second Century* #16, II, p. 67). What is natural is, once again, receptivity to what is, grounded in the conscious acknowledgement of what one is oneself. And if I recognize myself as God's image, my intelligence as participating in the contemplative perceiving exercised by God toward the world, I recognize both the possibility of "innocent," passion-free, perception and the calling to enlarge this toward Evagrios's "angelic" awareness, the unified and symbolic consciousness that connects us with the inner life of the contingent world. The merely human in Evagrios's schema is naturally open to the angelic or supernatural.

But the vocabulary is fluid in this area. Mark (*On Those Who Think* . . . #90, I, p. 132) characterizes the restored natural state as one in which we acknowledge not only that we are in the image of God but also that we are ourselves the source of our own difficulties: natural awareness is mindfulness of our fragility, our capacity not only for dispassionate knowledge but also for passion. Natural awareness includes the knowledge that we may become unnatural in our intelligence, forgetting that our troubles arise from within (even if they are activated by the demonic forces) and projecting them on to others so that conflict and resentment arise. Self-awareness means that we become ready to receive what is "above nature," the fruits of the Spirit. It is clear that any search here for a tightly consistent lexicon of nature and supernature is misplaced. Natural intelligence is simply truthful intelligence. In the unfallen state of "nature" this would mean an openness to passion-free relation to the world which would lead into the perception of the causes of things, the structure of divine wisdom embodied in creation. But the division of consciousness has made this state problematic: we have been lured into passionate perception. Natural awareness now is the awareness of inner dividedness, the coexistence of the possibility of passion-free, unselfish, knowing and acting with the possessive fantasizing that enslaves intelligence and traps us in forgetfulness and unreality, and thus ultimately in death. The practice of the commandments teaches us to identify and fight against selfish and forgetful habits by recognizing the behaviors that exemplify passion; and the self-awareness arising from ascetic practice properly understood reminds us of the deeper truth of our own nature and its possibilities and prepares us for the liberation given by the Spirit—a stage of experience that cannot be guaranteed by any amount of asceticism but that cannot take root without the habits of self-examination and self-control.

This state helps us make sense also of the superficially puzzling language of Isaiah the Solitary about passion that is "according to nature" (*On Guarding the Intellect* #1, and cf. 18, 19, 25; I, pp. 22, 25–27). Anger at the intrusion into the intelligence of alien habit is a precondition for the "re-naturalizing" of the intelligence—by way of releasing the proper use of *epithumia*, desire, towards God (Ibid. 25)—and so is itself in a sense natural. The general point is found in Evagrios (*On Discrimination*

#15, 16, I, pp. 47–48) and Cassian (*On the Eight Vices*, I, p. 83), who uses the same language as Isaiah about anger "according to nature": "natural" anger is the repudiating of what is unnatural in the intelligence, i.e., self-serving habits of mind. It is a theme that has quite a long ancestry in Platonic and Stoic discussion and in, for example, the spiritual theology of the Cappadocians,[12] but it is here given a more specific analysis. Diadochos (*On Spiritual Knowledge* #6, I, p. 254) attempts a useful terminological refinement by speaking of an "incensive" response (*thumos*) that is free from anger (*aorgetos*). When this response is engaged in the battle against irrational passions, the believer must be silent; only when calm is restored can words of praise again be uttered (#10, p. 255). The example of Jesus is cited (#62, p. 272), as He is three times said in John's Gospel to have been moved and troubled (Jn. 11:33, 12:27, and 13:21): he chooses to let his spirit be disturbed by anger against evil and death, even though he does not need his will reinforced by this reaction. The implication is that he makes his spirit vulnerable in this way to remind us that there is a proper use of anger directed against the unnatural effects of evil. A pity, Diadochos adds, that Eve did not use anger against the serpent's temptation. The essential point is simply that anger used against any other person is unnatural—not least because it implies that the source of our problems or failures is in someone else's acts and dispositions (cf. the brief and crystal clear enunciation of this idea by Peter of Damascus, *Spiritual Reading*, III, p.156). But it is not even that we are encouraged to be angry with ourselves in the ordinary sense. Just as we are told to love our nature and the nature of all people, our anger rightly used is an anger about the devastation of nature overall: it is something like a cry of protest against the freedom we have all lost. This also illuminates why compassion is said to be the best specific against anger (e.g., Evagrios, *On Discrimination* #3, I. p. 40; cf. Maximos, *Third Century on Love*, #90, II, p. 97): the "incensive power" rightly used is in effect compassion, an intense protest against another's suffering or slavery. To be "natural" in this connection is to recognize that our restoration to liberty is not purely a matter of reasoning: the positive effect of the divided self is that the debased and forgetful caricature of humanity to which we have become so accustomed can be an object of both reflection and emotion to the convalescent soul. The process of becoming natural is energised by thought and feeling alike, and the passionate or instinctual dimensions of the inner life can be deployed in an unselfish way to push us further toward proper dispassion, which is the gateway to love, in the well-known phrase of Evagrios.[13]

One final point is worth underlining about the restoration of nature, a point already touched on in various ways. Restored nature draws together the scattered powers of perception and reestablishes simplicity; and this means that the body as well as the intelligence is involved. Isaiah speaks of a new and inseparable union between body, soul, and spirit brought about by the Holy Spirit (#18, I, p. 26); and Diadochos sees the "single and simple perceptive faculty" bestowed by the Spirit as allowing the intelligence to share its joy with the body (*On Spiritual Knowledge* #25, I, p. 259). In other words, although we generally think of what might be called a renewed or restored "attitude" toward what is seen and sensed, the philokalic vision is of bodily senses themselves working in a somewhat different way. What this might mean is not clear—though there are other traditions of meditation, notably certain Buddhist disciplines, which would echo the idea and might offer some lines for investigation. The point is clearly connected with the teachings of Symeon the New Theologian and the fourteenth-century hesychasts about the physical sensing of uncreated light, but this is not, I think, the only thing in mind here.

But the mention of this quietly recurrent theme in the *Philokalia,* the renewal of the body in the restored simplicity of the life of the Holy Spirit—the theosis of the body in Maximos's terms (*Second Century on Theology* #88, II, p. 160)—provides a helpful focus for grasping one of the controlling ideas in the anthropology of the *Philokalia.* We are not yet natural. Instead of envisaging "nature" as a basic condition that can straightforwardly be recovered or released, the texts present a more nuanced and psychologically complex picture. Created with certain capacities, we have in one sense irretrievably lost our starting point. We have known division and cannot behave as if the divided intelligence could be ignored or overcome by wishing it so. We are as a consequence living in some degree of unreality; we are not really here. The body's habitual response to stimuli has become either defense or absorption (anger or lust), so that we are chronically unable to exist as part of an interdependent created order. To learn to do so requires us to be educated in how we identify destructive behavior (keeping the commandments) and so to check these habitual responses. In the process, something begins to happen to the instinctive life of aggression and desire which reconstitutes it as a positive discontent with the present state of slavery. We recognize that we actively and profoundly want something other than the life of passion and fantasy. And that uncovered or reconstituted wanting is our opening up to the life for which we were made and which is made accessible to us once again in baptism, in the identification of ourselves with the self-giving Word of God incarnate. Beyond this, it is the Spirit who acts for the transformation of our awareness, physical and mental, so that the simplicity for which we were designed may pervade our intelligence. Throughout that lifetime's labor, the awareness of the gulf between what we may be and what we have made of ourselves continues to act as a goad to preserve the habit of self-questioning and penitence. We do not simply stop being divided; we learn to use our very dividedness to cast into a stronger light the possibility of a proper presence in and to the world and its maker.

The intelligence that has not yet remembered itself is not yet truly embodied. Our problem, if this reading of the *Philokalia* is correct, is not that we are embodied spirits, but that we are *incompletely* embodied spirits—that is, that we are as yet unable to live in this material and mutable world without clinging to our impressions, distorting our impressions, or compulsively marking out our territory. The things of the world—and our human neighbors in the world—appear either as food or as threat to the ego. Unless we become able to receive the truth of what is before us as it stands in relation to God, not to us, we are failing to be embodied in the sense of being properly part of creation: we are caught in an implicit idolatry, the effort to separate ourselves from the order of which we are a part.

Numerous scholars of early and mediaeval Christianity, such as Peter Brown, Margaret Miles, and Caroline Walker Bynum,[14] have in recent years challenged the cliché that patristic theology and ascetic practice simply internalized a radical opposition between body and soul borrowed from Platonism. We have been reminded that the body is understood as that which connects us to the world, as that which speaks and symbolizes the truth that is being realized in the spirit, and so on. Schmemann, in a memorable passage in his Journals,[15] insists that proper instruction in Christianity "should start with the body. In the body, everything is given for communication, knowledge, communion." The intriguing recent work of David Jasper[16] argues that the body in early monastic spirituality is above all the sign of a "kenotic" abandonment of pretensions to spiritual power, so that bodily ascesis becomes a way of "reducing" the self to the limitations of the body, not an effort to transcend them. But what lies behind all of this is the belief, articulated in some of the earliest of the philokalic writings, that what needs to be overcome in human consciousness is the alliance of "perception," whether bodily or mental, with self-interest. The body's needs, sensations, and impressions are capable of being freed from the compulsion either to devour on the one hand or to expel or repulse on the other. Ascetic practice and contemplation alike are the means by which this freedom is sustained, though, as we have seen, we cannot achieve our own liberation by our own efforts; we are always responding to the gift of renewal offered us in Christ and the Spirit.

And it is significant that when Hesychios spells out what watchfulness or mindfulness practically entails, he turns to the Jesus Prayer as the activity that above all brings together action and contemplation. It is an action, an ascetical practice, in one sense; but it is also the means of sustaining contemplative self-awareness. "Letters cannot be written on air; they have to be inscribed in some material if they are to have any permanence" (*On Watchfulness and Holiness*, #183, I, p. 195): the Jesus Prayer is an "inscription" of watchfulness in the rhythm of the human body. It invokes the presence which makes it ultimately impossible to live in a divided state, the presence which cannot coexist with demonic fantasies: "He does not allow them to project in the mind's mirror even the first hint of their infiltration" (Ibid. #174, p. 193). As Diadochos further explains (*On Spiritual Knowledge*, #59, I, pp. 270–71), the invocation of the Name is the activity through which the intelligence is held and stabilized when all images and concepts of God have been laid aside. Evagrios's teaching that the contemplative comes to see the light of his or her own intelligence (as in *On Discrimination* #18 and #52, for example, I, p. 49) is here linked to the practice of the Jesus Prayer: what we come to see in our hearts as a result of consistent practice is the fire of Christ's presence burning away "the filth which covers the surface of the soul." And when passion has distracted us afresh, we can recover the freedom of our intelligence by simply beginning the action again, saying over the words until the intelligence "catches up" with their meaning (Diadochos, Ibid. #61, p. 271; something of the same underlies the advice in the *Discourse on Abba Philimon*, II, pp. 344–57, esp. pp. 347–49, and it becomes the foundation of later teaching on the practice of the Prayer—as, famously, in the narrative of the nineteenth-century Russian "Pilgrim").[17] Like children repeating words they do not understand, we say the words, waiting for the Spirit to help us in our weakness (Diadochos refers to Rom. 8:26).

Thus if we ask what the natural life is for human beings, one very straightforward answer is that, in practice, it is a life in which the intelligence is anchored in the constant invocation of the Name of Jesus. This practice, to pick up Hesychios's image, keeps the mind's mirror clear. And to understand this is to open up a further dimension of the theology of the *Philokalia*, which is simply the centrality of the belief that the essential activity of the intelligence is always and already grounded in the indwelling Word of God, so that what baptism does is to set free the indwelling Word to shape as it ought the life of the human agent. It is this process which also allows, in some of the medieval material (notably in Nikitas Stithatos and Gregory of Sinai; see, e.g., IV, pp. 144, 213, 220, 237) the analogy between contemplative practice and the Eucharist: the mature intelligence both offers and receives the Lamb of God and "becomes an image of the Lamb as he is in the age to come" (Gregory of Sinai, *On Commandments and Doctrines*, #112, IV, p. 237). Granted that an explicit Eucharistic theology is not an obvious major theme in the *Philokalia*, there are connections here which need drawing out as regards the "Eucharistic" character of the invocation of the Name of Jesus and of the assumption that the prayer of the specific contemplative is the prayer of Christ in His Body.

The second part of this essay deals with how all this opens up the underlying Trinitarian theology of the *Philokalia*. So far we have seen how the teaching of the *Philokalia* presupposes a many-layered analysis of human consciousness at the center of which lies a very particular reading of the meaning of the image of God in us. It is an anthropology which goes far deeper than the conventional assumptions so often made by Christians and non-Christians alike about the division of body and soul or intellect and emotion; and in positing a fundamental unity of perception of what is lost in the Fall, it challenges all fragmented accounts of human knowing and sensing and insists that a restored humanity must be one in which bodily experience is given meaning. Doing this involves both the capacity to see the material world as "symbolic," as communicating the intelligence and generosity of the creator, and the transformation of the body itself in its capacity to receive and manifest divine life. Restored humanity is humanity properly embodied, and this embodiment includes the freedom to relate to the things and the persons of the world as they are in relation to God. It is in this connection that the spirituality of the philokalic tradition may rightly be seen as the foundation for a social and environmental ethic capable of addressing the major public crises of our own time.[18]

The anthropology of the *Philokalia* has some obvious resonances with certain currents in both modern and postmodern philosophy. Its avoidance of a fixed account of human nature in terms of a static content sounds initially very congenial to an intellectual culture suspicious of metaphysical models of "humanity-as-such"; and the idea of embodiment as a project rather than a given is also potentially intriguing for the contemporary theorist eager to deconstruct simplistic and uncritical views of the body. But a degree of caution is in order. The relative indeterminacy of the human intelligence and its embodied expression implies no scepticism about truth. What is often difficult for the contemporary intellect is to see that the contemplative tradition, in relativizing conceptual mastery and finality, is laying claim to another level of truthfulness. The world really is as it is; there is an "objective" state of affairs in the universe, and it is truly related in every aspect to its maker. But our own truthfulness is more a matter of learning how to exist as a conscious but dependent part of that real or true order than it is of achieving a comprehensive and accurate picture of it, let alone of its maker. Truthfulness is a habit of receptivity, and it entails what I have been calling, in the wake of Evagrios, the ability to read the world symbolically—which does not mean reading it, in full-blown medi-eval style, as a collection of allegories, but understanding how to receive its diversity as the gift of a freely self-bestowing divine agency. This is where it is crucial for understanding the *Philokalia* to see how the ideal works of a renewed simplicity or singleness of apprehension, free from the anxious question of how I am to exercise power and impose meaning in my environment, human or otherwise.

The echoes of this approach in the Augustinian distinction between scientia and sapientia merit more exploration, insofar as Augustine is trying to identify a knowing that is not function-bound, not dictated by the question of how an object can usefully relate to me. But the philokalic texts establish this in closer connection with the practices of self-awareness, *nepsis,* which teach us to ask of every impression or sensation how far I am turning it into something other than itself by tying its significance to my needs and projections. Very much at the center of the philokalic vision is the conviction that the ideal and purposed state of being for the human intelligence, its "natural" life, is a welcoming receptivity to the other, without the violence that seeks either to possess or exclude. To quote Schmemann once more, for the baptized person is in Christ, "The world is again his life, not his death, for he knows what to do with it";[19] everything is now "given to us as full of meaning and beauty" (Ibid., p. 142). It is as we think through the implications of this as the natural, God-reflecting state of human intelligence that we may begin to see how this entire picture requires in turn a particular understanding of the divine nature and persons. To this we shall now turn in more detail.

■ III

For the created intelligence to become natural is for it to be anchored in the life of the Holy Spirit, which is also the life of the Word, the eternal divine intelligence which is the ground of all created intelligence. Thus Mark (*On Those Who Think . . .,* #225, I, p. 145) describes the ascetic as called to keep on knocking at the door of *Christ's* internal dwelling—the natural intelligence within us that is being restored by the Spirit's grace. To be adopted children in and through the eternal Son is the essence of what baptism confers, a theme prominent in Mark and Diad-ochos and richly developed in Maximos: what we aim at is not the perfect keeping of the commandments as some sort of human achievement, but the freedom to receive the gift of Christ being formed in us and to guard it by means of our watch-fulness (see, for example, Mark, *On Those Who Think . . .* #2, 64 ff., Diadochos, *On Spiritual Knowledge,* ##26, 61, 97–98, pp. 260, 271–72, 293–94). The implication is that our adoptive relation to the Father is a matter essentially of doing what Christ eternally does. Evagrios had said that in sharing the death of Christ through our death to self-oriented passion, we come to share Christ's contemplation of the Father (*On Discrimination,* #17, I, p. 49, echoed by Neilos, *Ascetic Discourse,* p. 201), and Diadochos, *On Spiritual Knowledge* #61, I, pp. 271–72, as we have noted, specifically connects the Spirit-aided repetition of the Name of Jesus (understood in terms of the promise in Romans 8:26 that the Spirit will express to God what we cannot express in words through our own prayers) with the cry of "Abba," which characterizes the Spirit's indwelling (Rom. 8:15, Gal. 4:6).

In other words, what the early philokalic authors are assuming is that the natural state of the intelligence is one in which the divine Word is free to live and act within the created subject: noetic prayer is the prayer that Christ offers in us. Thus also the sense in which the intelligence in us is the image of God cannot properly be abstracted from the recognition that the noetic image is a created mode of sharing in eternal contemplation; the image is not a static correspondence but an active participation in eternal love.

Maximos picks up this idea and develops it at various points in his *Centuries on Theology*, linking it to the paschal theme that has been adumbrated in Evagrios and elsewhere. Christ is "buried" in us as we bury all that has crucified him—our passions and even our intellectual conceptions—so that it is Christ alone who rises in us, marking the dawning of the "eighth day" of creation, the mystical fulfilment of the process of God's work in us (*First Century on Theology* ##63–67, II, pp. 126–27). He is constantly dying and rising in us, crucified in our weakness, raised in our purification (*Second Century on Theology* #27, II, p. 144). The eternal Word is the "mustard seed" of the gospel text (Mt. 13:31–32), containing all things in potentiality; it is sown in the human heart and when that heart is purified by the Spirit, the "energies" of all things are awakened (Ibid., ##10–11, II, pp. 140–41). Because all fullness is eternally in Christ, that fullness becomes ours when we open ourselves completely to his gift (Ibid. #21, II p. 142). Thus our failure to grow spiritually is a sort of imprisonment of Christ in ourselves, a crippling of his freedom (Ibid., #30, II, p. 145). He seeks to be incarnate in our virtues, and, in our contemplation, to return to his original and eternal state (Ibid., #37, II, pp. 146–47); we ascend with him to the Father, while also constantly being ready not to despise following him in "incarnating" what we are through communicating the mystery to others (Ibid., ##46–49, 55, II, pp. 148–49, 150). At the end of the second of the *Centuries on Theology*, Maximos explains Paul's language about having the *nous* of Christ (I Cor. 2:16) in terms of perfect alignment with and sharing in the eternal act of noetic contemplation which is Christ's. It is not that we acquire something "extra" to our humanity or that something in our humanity is supplanted by grace, let alone that we somehow reproduce the unique union in Christ of divinity and humanity; simply that we are taken into the fullness of Christ's eternal life, just as we are taken into Christ's Body in our life within the baptized community (##83–84, II, pp. 158–59). In this way, we inherit the Kingdom of God or of Heaven, since this is nothing other than the life of Christ within us (Ibid., #91ff., II, pp.161–62), and body and soul are brought into final harmony through this indwelling (Ibid., #100, II, p. 163).

So, to return briefly to the themes already outlined in the first two sections of this essay, our proper and natural openness to all things, the free, renewed, non-possessive vision of the world which is given in the life of grace, is ultimately the contemplative energy of the second person of the Trinity within us, directed toward the Father and the world inseparably. The divine image may be spoken of in terms that seem remote from Christology, static or dualistic,[20] but the governing theological theme is clear. The journey toward the natural condition of the intelligence is a journey toward the uncovering of the act of Christ at the center or ground of created intelligence. Hesychios's language about keeping the interior mirror clear is taken up and refined further by Philotheos of Sinai (*Forty Texts on Watchfulness* #23, III, p. 25: the mirror of the intelligence is meant to reflect "Jesus Christ, the wisdom and power of God the Father"; when it is clear, we can see all things in the intelligence, since we can see that the Kingdom is within us—clear echoes of Maximos here. In the same vein, Philotheos can say that, for the mature contemplative, there is "another activity" going on within, the energeia of Christ (Ibid., #37, III, p. 30). And Peter of Damascus stresses the fact that when we do the will of the Father we are assimilated to the Son (*A Treasury of Divine Knowledge*, III, p. 84), though he is less strong in his language than some others as to the actual embrace of created activity within the action of the Son.

In defining the action of the Son in this way, as the eternal contemplation of the Father, shared in the Spirit with the created intelligences that mirror this eternal life, the philokalic writers are setting out a very clear and distinctive approach to how the unity and plurality of divine life may be thought (however imperfectly). The relation of the eternal Logos to the Father begins to be understood—insofar as it ever can be—as we grasp the character of the selfless receptivity which is given us in the life of grace, the universal and dispassionate love (love that is neither defensive nor possessive) which allows us to be indwelt by the sheer reality of what is before us. Freed from the distortions of anger and possessive desire, we embrace in love and thanksgiving a world and a divine reality which are literally nothing but gratuitous gift or bestowal. And in entering such a state, or at least, as we might say, becoming able to imagine it as possible for us, we come to see something of what the exchange of life and goodness might be in that divine life which necessarily and eternally knows nothing of self-possession or self-withholding, nothing of the fear of loss or of absorption, but is the loving and joyful apprehension of sheer otherness.

▪ **IV**

Maximos speaks of the contemplative's prayer as characterized by *eros* (*Second Century on Charity*, #6, II, p. 65); and the implication—given what has just been said about the alignment of human contemplation with the eternal contemplation of the Father by the Son—seems to be that we could in some way speak about perfect mutual *eros* as the mark of the Trinitarian life. There is another passage, not in the *Philokalia*, where Maximos affirms that God in some sense participates in the *eros* toward Himself that He has planted in human hearts (Amb. 48, PG 91, 1361B). But it is not until relatively late in the Byzantine period that there are signs of this implication being drawn out. It is Gregory Palamas who takes up these leads and pursues them in the direction of a systematic theology of intradivine *eros*. And, although there are later writers who echo the hints of Maximos on the divine origin of human *eros* toward God (as, for example, in the chapters *On Prayer* of Patriarch Kallistos, ##21–22, pp. 327–29 of the Greek edition, as yet untranslated), Palamas's schema does not seem to have been developed—perhaps not surprisingly, given that it is both complex and tantalizingly briefly spelled out.

Much has been written about various aspects of the theology of Palamas's *Capita* (*Topics of Natural and Theological Science and on the Moral and Ascetical Life*, as the title is rendered in the English translation of the *Philokalia*); and recent scholarship, especially the distinguished work of Reinhard Flogaus,[21] has opened up the complex question of the degree of dependence on Augustine's *De trinitate* in sections of this work. But this particular focus alone does not exhaust the unique interest of Palamas's treatment of the Trinity here. In sections 34 to 40 (IV, pp. 359–64), we have a model for the threefold divine life and for the image of that life in the created human subject that does not simply correspond either to an Augustinian pattern or to earlier Eastern ideas, but is, arguably, a creative fusion of these very diverse elements. And what is significant for our present purposes is that it is a model recognizably developing some of the leading themes of earlier philokalic material in respect of clarifying the theological basis of contemplative or hesychastic practice.

The basic structure is this. God is supremely and eternally *nous*, intelligence, and essentially or by definition "goodness": this intelligence is, or has within it, wisdom and life, which are inseparable from goodness. They are conceptually but not in reality distinguishable, united in divine simplicity. If we speak of divine intelligence generating divine wisdom, a *logos* or object of intelligence coextensive with intelligence itself, we speak of that which is indistinguishable in its goodness from its source but distinguished simply by its relation as derived from the act of intelligence. *Logos*, it appears, is the "content" of eternal intelligence expressed as what intelligence itself understands—intelligence producing that which mirrors itself. Eternal *logos* is eternal self-knowledge. Palamas appeals (#35, IV, pp. 360–61) to the analogy of our own internal *logos* in a way that strongly evokes Augustine's interior *verbum*. But he goes on to say that we cannot conceive of an intelligent self-awareness such as we have just sketched as deprived of "life" or "spirit"; and these terms seem to mean what we might call conscious mutual involvement, an eternal flow of life between the two terms that is not exhausted by talking about the basic relation of derivation. "The Spirit of the supreme Logos is a kind of ineffable yet intense longing or *eros* experienced by the Begetter for the Logos born ineffably from Him, a longing experienced also by the beloved Logos and Son of the Father for His Begetter; but the Logos possesses this love by virtue of the fact that it comes from the Father in the very act through which He comes from the Father, and it resides co-naturally in Him" (#36, IV, p. 361). St. Gregory is clear about the single procession of the Spirit (Ibid. IV p. 362), but equally clear that the Spirit is the mutual joy or bliss of Father and Son, turned in love to each other.

Thus he can go on (#37, IV p. 362) to explain how this concept shapes our understanding of the divine image in ourselves. Our created intelligence yearns for the content of what it spiritually understands; just as *logos* is born from the intelligence, so is *eros*, and the latter is present even when the former is inchoate or obscured. What is more, this erotic impulse is what sets us apart from the angelic orders and constitutes us more in the image of God than they are (#38–39, pp. 362–63): our *eros* generates and sustains life in the body and, despite its "intellectual" character, cleaves in love to the body, which it does not want to abandon. And it is this body-related *eros* which becomes so dangerous for fallen humanity, when the intellective and the erotic energy are not properly directed toward the eternal prototype. The human subject is always at some level aware of its *eros* toward God, but unless the erotic identification with the body is rooted in the desire for God, it degenerates into a self-love that fragments the "inner world" of the subject as trinitarian image (#40, IV, p. 364) and dooms the body to death—so that the fact that the body does not at once decay when the spirit has rebelled is the result of the providence of a just God who chooses, so to speak, to honor His own intention of giving life and to postpone the punishment that ought to follow in the course of nature (#46–48, pp. 367–69, #51, pp. 370–71).

Unmistakeably there are Augustinian resonances throughout these chapters, but what is most significant is the way in which the vocabulary of *eros* is deployed. Palamas implies that there is in the divine life an analogical foundation for the awareness of the incompleteness of the self in finite experience. Our intelligence is not simply *satisfied* with its self-awareness; it acknowledges the unfinished character of this awareness and longs for completion through relationship with its infinite source and archetype. And, in an idiom that is undoubtedly very bold in theological terms, Palamas posits, not an "incompleteness" within God, which would be wholly untenable for him as for the entire orthodox tradition of belief, but what we might call an eternal desire to exist *in* the other that is at the same time never consummated by any collapse into an undifferentiated identity. The "desire" of the Father to be in the Son, to bestow all that is His as Father upon the Son, is never completed in the sense of pouring Himself out without remainder or relation into the life of this divine Other. He is eternally confronted with the sheer otherness of the Son whom He generates. Likewise the response of the Son to the Father is not a simple abjection and self-cancelling: it is again a desire to give life "into" the other that is never exhausted. The otherness of the persons of the Trinity to each other is irreducible, and for that very reason their relation may be imagined as *eros*, as "yearning" rather than consummation, since no amount of self-abnegating love can abolish the eternal difference—which would in fact be to abolish love itself.

But in what sense can we then, with Palamas, see this *eros* as "hypostatic," as actually a divine person? The role of the Spirit as conceived in this model could be said to be the excess of excessive love itself. The Father begets the Son as that which is wholly other to Him as Father and thus cannot ever "absorb" the Son or be absorbed *by* the Son in His love, since that love is itself the ground of this absolute otherness, an otherness constituted not by any essential difference, any distinctness in predicates or qualities, but by the sheer self-giving of "goodness." But this means that when goodness has, so to speak, taken cognizance of its self-giving character in the generation of the otherness of the Logos, this does not exhaust the self-giving act of goodness: generative love does not merely see itself in the mirror of the Logos, a love going out and returning to its source in a way that closes a circle; it returns to itself from the other in a way that displays the inexhaustibility of its own generative or "productive" agency. It is reflected back to itself as, precisely, the love that cannot ever be absorbed in the other, thus the love that can never be expressed simply as gift and return. For the Father to generate the Son, Palamas says, is for the Father to give to the Son the life that is already in Him as Source, the life that is not capable of being absorbed in the other. The excess of love that generates the Son begets in the Son the same excessive love, a love that is not contained in the binary relation of giving and responding but "overflows" eternally.

This is the "life" that is designated by the name of "Spirit." Eternal intelligence sees itself in the Logos and because it sees *itself,* it sees its own uncontainable excess, already overflowing as the reality of *eros* and *zoe* that cannot be reduced to either the begetting or the begotten agency but is an equally eternal dimension of God's reality (it does not seem right to speak of a "residue" here, which sounds much too passive, yet one might defend the word as indicating what is *not* spoken of just by speaking of the Father's begetting of the Son).

These are matters—we hardly need reminding—that strain the limits of what we can say. But it is essential to try to follow them through in this connection insofar as they frame what Palamas wants to say about our own spiritual *eros.* We carry the image of the Trinitarian life: that is, we are not only intelligent and self-aware, we are carried out from ourselves in excess. The Logos exists in us only as that which moves us to excess, "self-transcendence," if you want a rather stale technicality—that is, the Logos exists in us only as animated by *eros,* by the spirit which urges us to give to and live in the other. This is supremely about giving to and living in the divine Other, living in communion with the Father through Christ in the Spirit; but the tantalizing reference to the relation of all this to the body suggests that the Logos within us exists in a state of self-giving love toward that which is radically "other" to the life of intelligence or spirit—toward the bodily world which it is called to make significant, to transform into a living sign of the Trinitarian mystery of love. Our own *eros* toward what our divinely gifted intelligence can receive, our *eros* toward the harmony and meaningfulness of the universal Logos, is never restricted to simply being drawn into the Son's response to the Father, since that response in eternity is always overflowing into another "otherness."

In relation to Maximos's language about divine and human *eros,* what Palamas in effect adds is that for the human subject to "mirror" the divine is not simply for human *logos* to participate in the eternal Logos, but for that human *logos* to be activated by *eros,* the dynamic of the Holy Spirit, in its unending urge to immerse itself in the foundational mystery of *nous* itself, which images and participates in the eternal self-giving intelligence that is the divine Source, the Father. Or in other words, for humanity to bear the image of the Son, to have the Son's life at the heart of finite human awareness, is what it means for it to bear the image of the Trinity; we cannot make sense of a humanity that is in the image of one divine person in isolation. We know that by the eleventh century the convention had developed of describing the divine image in humanity as threefold—*psuche noera, nous,* and *logos* (Nikitas Stithatos, *On Spiritual Knowledge* #8, IV, p. 141), or *nous, logos,* and *pneuma* (Gregory of Sinai, *On Commandments and Doctrines,* #31–32, IV, p. 218), which is closer to Palamas. But Palamas's originality is in doing very much what Augustine does in the *de trinitate*: moving from a discourse about the divine image which is essentially about correspondence (Gregory of Sinai's assimilation of the three persons to the three aspects of human subjectivity might risk that if left without supplement) to a discourse which places at the center the *relation* of image to prototype as the crucial and irreducible element in a fully theological account of the divine image in us.[22]

A fully theological account: to put it like this is to be reminded of that sense of *theologia* that is familiar to us from Evagrios's much-cited dictum (*On Prayer* #45,

I, p. 62) that "If you are a theologian, you will pray truly. And if you pray truly, you are a theologian." A "theological" account of the divine image has, in such a light, to be one that begins and ends in the attempt to put into words the relationship that exists between God and the created *eros* of the human self, the relationship that is renewed by the gift of baptism and the practice of watchfulness and *hesy-chia*. And what the *Philokalia* overall presumes is that this relationship is grounded in an eternal contemplative reality—the contemplation of the Father by the Son, the contemplation of the Son's radical "otherness" by the Father, which together define the shape of creation's relation to the creator and more specifically the rela-tion of the finite *nous* to the infinite intelligence of God. Human nature—in the sense traced in the earlier sections of this study—is as it is because it has at its center an impulsion toward union-in-otherness; it has the Logos at its heart. The liberation and purification of this impulsion, this "erotic" drawing toward the source without which it is incomplete and imprisoned in unreality, allow the Logos to exist freely and transformingly within the created subject, and thus to shape the relation of that created subject not only to God but also to the rest of the universe, human and nonhuman. But we do not adequately grasp what it means to speak of the divine image in us unless, with Palamas, we see that the presence of the image of the Logos in us implies the image of the Trinity as a whole. Our inner life is both an energy directed by the Spirit through the Logos toward the Father *and* a mirroring in its own workings of the interplay of *eros* between intelligence in its deepest and most comprehensive sense and *logos*, the awareness of intelli-gence's content. The mind loves God and also loves itself loving God; in so doing, it loves the love of God for the world and thus (an advance here on the Augustin-ian model) loves its own embodied life which it seeks in turn to shape into the likeness of divine love. So the focal encounter with God in hesychastic prayer gradually "unfolds" into a remarkably wide-ranging agenda for anthropology and ethics. The doctrine of the image is very far from being a bald statement of some supposed correspondence between human and divine and is seen to be insepa-rable from the practical—you could even say "evangelical"—question of how we are freed from the passions, freed for that openness to the other that is stifled by craving and aggression.

And it is this rootedness in the "erotic" mutuality of the Trinity that helps us make sense of the fact that hesychastic prayer is not a static gazing into a static void but a steady expansion of desire beyond any thought of satisfaction or ultimate identification or absorption. If the life of the Trinity is an unending openness to the inexhaustible other, then this, "stretched out" in the conditions of our temporal existence, is the constant growing toward the imageless depths of God's otherness, with all that this implies about the abandonment of any imagined world in which the individual's desires are the arbiter of meaning, and the satisfying of those (uncriticized) desires is the arbiter of what is to be said about "natural" fulfilment. If—to borrow a phrase I have used elsewhere in discussing some parallel themes in the work of St. John of the Cross[23]—the *eros* of the contemplative is a "desire for the desire of the Word," it is a desire for what can, axiomatically, never be gained or contained, a desire for its own frustration, you would say if you were beginning from the distorted picture of desire we habitually resort to.

In a recent essay by Christoph Schneider on "The Transformation of Eros: Re-flections on Desire in Jacques Lacan," which seeks to bring some contemporary psychoanalytic theory into conversation with Maximos the Confessor,[24] the point is made that the liturgical and ascetical idiom of the Christian East has the re-sources to break through the highly problematic accounts of the relation of self to other that are offered by Lacanian analysis. If the only alternatives for human mat-uration and liberation are being subordinated to the "Law" of the Other (with the consequent erotization of transgressing the Law) or redrawing the map of desire so that the subject can find satisfaction in a detached and limited version of what the Other desires, there is never in fact a properly developed relation with the genuinely Other as it is. Schneider suggests that the classical Orthodox account of relation with God posits a divine desire that, because it is identical with the inmost structure and directedness of the subject, may be "appropriated" by the subject for mimesis without subjugation (and its attendant resentment and drift to the desire of transgression); yet at the same time, the infinite otherness of the divine act and divine "desire" means that this appropriation is never a collapse into uninterrupted or unchallenged identity, a static interior life. "The loving Other unceasingly plays [*sic*; perhaps an error for "places"] highly specific and highly personalized possibil-ities in the subject's way, which, if they are actively received and actualized, con-tribute to its flourishing and spiritual well-being".[25] Other Orthodox writers have made a similar point, among them Nikolaos Loudovikos, who has stressed the significance in Eastern theology of separating *eros* from the idea of "self-fulfilment" and the will to power and insisting on its association with *ekstasis* and thus *keno-sis*[26]—an association much discussed in modern Orthodox theology, from Lossky to Zizioulas. But the roots of this idea are firmly in the philokalic vision, which sees the fundamental pattern behind the entire universe as that of loving presence-in-the-other, a contemplative immersion in the other that never turns into identity yet is wholly devoid of defense and aggression. All that can be said about the Trin-ity pivots around this pattern; and the philokalic connection between the eternal contemplation that is the act of the Logos and the essential or natural orientation of the created self means that we can without absurdity speak of the created self living out the adoptive grace of baptism as the place where the Trinitarian life locates itself within the world—and also speak of the awareness of the baptized person as located within the divine vision of things.

So Nikitas Stithatos can say at the end of his century *On Spiritual Knowledge* (#100, IV, p. 174) that the hesychast "standing outside all things . . . will dwell within all things," having been united with the Father through the Logos and led into this union by the work of the Spirit. Watchfulness or mindfulness of who and what we are, and of what is the nature of the various delusions that make us misuse the world we inhabit, preserves us from slipping back into "impassioned" perspec-tives on our environment and our neighbors, and also warns against associating our relation to God with specific images or sensations. If what we are is beings created for the limitless enlargement of desire without possession, we are most "natural" when most free from manageable images of the divine. Yet—in the cen-tral paradox of Christian teaching—this affirmation of the imageless character of God is bound up inseparably with a doctrine that seems to many to make extravagant claims for the positive knowledge of the divine: the doctrine of the Trinity. It is only when that doctrine is firmly located within the attempt to articulate what happens in contemplation that the apparent contradiction disappears: it is this doctrine of God which alone sets out why the self-emptying involved in something analogous to *eros* is the grain or contour of reality itself, why the abandoning of possession or control as an ideal is the fundamentally *truthful* response to the world we inhabit. *Hesychia* and mindfulness dissolve the fiction that the world is constituted by a solidly boundaried self confronting solidly boundaried objects which must be catalogued and filed. They insist that we see the self as never outside relation, never the source of life and meaning as an individual, separable entity. They prescribe a new way of seeing which is the proper outworking of the baptized identity, when the *eros* of the Spirit is bestowed to shape our lives in union with the Logos. Living this identity more and more radically shows us what we cannot help saying about the God who makes this possible: that His life is the defining source and archetype for all the loving contemplation of otherness that is realized in the world by finite intelligences.

The theological world of the *Philokalia*, the indwelling of the created mind in the God whose own identity is mutual indwelling and so makes possible the indwelling of the mind in the world and the world in the mind, is encapsulated—unsurprisingly—by Maximos, one of the most exceptionally creative minds represented in the collection, and it is appropriate to conclude with his words.

"God, who created all nature with wisdom and secretly planted in each intelligent being knowledge of Himself as its first power, like a munificent Lord gave also to us men a natural desire (*pothos*) and longing (*eros*) for Him, combining it in a natural way with the power of our intelligence (*logos*). Using our intelligence, we struggle so as to learn with tranquillity and without going astray how to realize this natural desire. Impelled by it we are led to search out the truth, wisdom and order manifest harmoniously in all creation, aspiring through them to attain Him by whose grace we received the desire" (Maximos, *Fifth Century of Various Texts*, #100, II, p. 284).

8 Tradition and Creativity in the Construction and Reading of the *Philokalia*

J. L. Zecher

I first thought of writing this essay when I began studying the *Philokalia* a year ago. I read through it carefully, took copious notes, and then sat down to write a chapter for my doctoral thesis about the role of death in the *Philokalia*. It was at this point that I realized I had no idea how to approach an anthology of this sort. How would I arrange my chapter? By author? By era? Should I retain Nicodemus's order, or "correct" it historically? Should I compare and contrast various authors, or attempt to synthesize their statements? Was I, in fact, looking at a haphazard group of texts or a coherent whole? These are the sorts of questions which have puzzled other commentators before me and which will, I suspect, haunt every careful reader of the *Philokalia*. They are, in many ways, the same questions that occur to a reader of Scripture. Reading the *Philokalia* feels very much like exploring a topic in the Bible—one has to balance numerous voices, a vast underlying history, and always the drive toward an ultimate unity. As with scriptural interpretation, my confusion ultimately resolved into a fundamental question about *tradition*—here not simply the history behind the text, but the process by which the whole is formed and received, bequeathed and inherited—those diachronic processes give rise to a synchronic text. Tradition becomes a source of authority, opening as it does claims to legitimacy for authors, texts, and practices which can be shown to square with what has gone before. It is, however, far from static. Tradition expresses itself constantly through living practices, through new works and ideas which arise within it. Tradition is, in a sense, the *context* within which one becomes free to *create*— but not to innovate. Innovation I will here define as a creative act which breaks out of its context in the drive toward newness. Innovation has as its exemplars Nietzsche's "tempters" while creation for its has the *Philokalia*'s various editors over the last three centuries.

When discussing Scripture, a focus on "tradition" leads inevitably to consideration of the text as *canon*, in the sense of a rule or norm. That is, the tradition of Scripture lies entirely behind the "final form" which can then be privileged as the location of meaning and value for readers. The group of texts joined together in the "canon of Scripture" ("canon" now as "list") becomes the "canon" for interpretation, the source and proper subject of the *regulae fidei* which govern its readership.[1] The *Philokalia* has no one final form, though, and its list of authors can hardly be called "closed." "Tradition" is therefore far more nebulous with regard to the *Philokalia*, since we can hardly apply to it the strictures of a *canon*, or allow ourselves the luxury of a "final form," but the extent to which we may call the *Philokalia* a coherent whole is the extent to which it represents or even constitutes a tradition—a tradition both of writing and of practice. Simultaneously, as we remain open to polyphony, to the different pitches and timbres of the various authors, the levels of interpretation and selection which have gone into fashioning this coherent whole, we can begin to understand how *tradition* gives way to *creativity*, both as something recognized in its contributors and cherished among its readers.

I must be clear at the outset about two things. First, I do not wish to place *tradition* in opposition to *creativity*. Rather, I will show how, for the editors and readers of the *Philokalia*, tradition *demands* creativity. Unity and polyphony coexist in the *Philokalia*'s coherence and, indeed, collude together to create its dynamic and profound picture of ascetic spirituality. This essay explores the *interaction* of tradition and creativity both in the editorial creation of the *Philokalia* and in the complex task of reading it. Second, this essay will not present new historical research or hitherto unknown information. Rather, it will reflect on what we already know of the *Philokalia* and draw a few conclusions about which we can approach it as creative readers.

■ CONTINUITY AND COMPLEXITY

Kallistos Ware concluded an article on the spirituality of the *Philokalia* thus:

> Without being exhaustive or systematic, the *Philokalia* possesses none the less a genuine unity and coherence of its own. Far more than a group of disparate texts bound together at random in a single volume, it is indeed what its editors St. Makarios of Corinth and St. Nikodimos of the Holy Mountain claim it to be: "a mystical school of noetic prayer."[2]

Ware is certainly correct in his assessment—the *Philokalia* is neither haphazard nor fortuitous. It presents the roots, buds, and fruit of an established tradition, harvested by some of the most learned theologians in the history of the Orthodox Church. Neither, as Ware implicitly suggests, is it *canonical* in the sense that Scripture may be called canonical. The *Philokalia* is neither complete nor closed. Its editors presume a much larger tradition of texts, practices, and community, within which this anthology may be usefully studied and its ideas applied. Nevertheless its perceived authority and stunning popularity throughout the Orthodox world (albeit greater in Romania, the Slavic lands, and Europe than in Greece) collude to give an aura of something more than coherence— of continuity and canonicity—to the *Philokalia*. That is, the *Philokalia* represents the nexus of spiritual revival which took place in the eighteenth century and which dominated the spirituality of, for example, Russia in the nineteenth and a much wider sphere in the twentieth.[3] Thus the *Philokalia* may be perceived as describing a tradition which, if not incorporating the totality of Orthodox spirituality, certainly represents its highest ambitions and most pregnant possibilities.

It may be argued, as Andrew Louth does in his contribution to this volume, that the *Philokalia* offers not a rule of texts, but one of practices. It speaks to a tradition of spiritual practice and operates, therefore, as a sort of reference work or source-book, ready for consultation. Nevertheless, the *Philokalia* presents textually the picture of a continuous trajectory of spiritual practices. Its breadth and historical organization give the impression at once of historical development leading toward a climax but also of a deeper stability, that over the millennium leading to Palamas, ascetics all struggled with similar temptations and shared similar spiritual hopes. It drives toward Gregory Palamas and his disciples as the zenith of Hesychastic prayer. [4] From Antony the Great through to Gregory Palamas, the unity which Ware rightly finds in the *Philokalia* resides in the impression given of a trajectory of practices and writings, as well as, ultimately, the authority of a tradition which develops within, and as the fruition of, Orthodox Christian asceticism. In a sense the coherence of the *Philokalia* results from the fact of its existence *as an anthology*—that is, as a synchronization of diachronic activities, an enforced, detemporalized, juxtaposition of elements drawn in from across wildly disparate times and places. The reader is implicitly invited to *find* the unifying principle in any anthology. Reading through this series of works by often famous ascetics and theologians on similar topics, using generally consistent vocabulary and progressing in (roughly) chronological order, one finds oneself at last with the great Byzantine Hesychasts—Gregory of Sinai, Gregory Palamas, the Xanthipouloi. Looking back, one begins to feel that Hesychast spirituality sprang up not in the twelfth century, or even the tenth, but in the fourth—in the *Philokalia*'s arrangement Palamite Hesychasm culminates a tradition which begins, tellingly, with Anthony the Great: the "mystical school of prayer" belongs not to Nikodemos and Makarios, nor even to the Byzantine Hesychasts, but to the whole Christian ascetic tradition. It is, I think, equally telling that the text attributed to Anthony in the *Philokalia* is spurious: the appearance of continuity is, at least to some extent, illusory. The *Philokalia* gives, therefore, the impression of *continuity* and, therefore, of a shared and coherent *tradition,* and yet one can discern a polyphony underlying or, at least informing, its coherence.

This essay will reflect on ways in which the *Philokalia* may be called "traditional." It will explore first the unspoken contextuality of the *Philokalia* to show how this may be appreciated as constructing a trajectory of thought within tradition and will argue that this selective construction is a *creative* act. It will then elaborate four modes of interaction with tradition: how the editors of the *Philokalia* reflect, crystallize, discover, and create tradition. It does so in order to open up the ways in which the *Philokalia* is *creative*. And, because its construction is the result of a creative process, so also, I contend, is its readership—a fact of which the *Philokalia*'s various editors and translators have made use in order to express their own ideas through redaction of a "traditional" text. I will begin with the Greek *Philokalia* of Makarios of Corinth and Nikodemos the Athonite and will only explicitly widen the field to include other editions rather late in the essay. In this way, I shall attempt to show that it is precisely in the careful exercise of creativity that the *Philokalia* offers tradition to its editors and readers.

▪ CONTEXT: WHAT THE *PHILOKALIA* IS NOT

To begin apophatically—as is only appropriate in such a situation—it is worth thinking about the silences in the *Philokalia*. These, as Kallistos Ware and, in this present volume, Andrew Louth (among others) have pointed out, the *Philokalia* has a number of puzzling, if not troubling, holes in its authorial roster. Aside from its obvious lack of dogmatic authors, such as the Cappadocians or John Chrysostom, whose absence is explained by the purpose,[5] we would seek in vain for those like Isaac the Syrian, John Climacus, and the Gaza fathers (Barsanuphius, John, and Dorotheus). Ware and others agree that such authors are missing from the *Philokalia* because they were readily available at the time of its publication—Nikiphoros Theotokis's edition of Isaac and Rader's edition of Climacus, among others, had appeared during the preceding century or so.[6] From a historical standpoint, this explanation is, I think, sufficient. I want to reflect on what it tells us about the nature of the *Philokalia*.

If the editors leave texts and authors out of their collection precisely because those texts and authors are available, then we can say very simply that the *Philokalia* is not intended to be exhaustive. The *Philokalia* does not attempt to found a new community or create a new monastic rule or *typikon*, nor does it propose a new liturgy or even liturgical reform, nor does it, except in very limited ways, give recommendations for quotidian ascetical practices.[7] Neither Makarios nor Paissy nor Nikodemos were radicals in that sense—one could hardly accuse the Kolly-vades of being innovators.[8] The *Philokalia* instead appears *within* a larger tradition. Its selectivity extends even to works known and loved by Hesychasts. To take one example, Gregory of Sinai recommends reading of a certain sort, citing Climacus as his authority:

> Read works of the fathers related to stillness and prayer, like those of St. John Klimakos, St. Isaac, St. Maximos, St. Neilos, St. Hesychios, Philotheos of Sinai, St. Symeon the New Theologian and his disciple Stithatos, and whatever else exists of writers of this kind. Leave other books for the time being, not because they are to be rejected, but because they do not contribute to your present purpose, diverting the intellect from prayer by their narrative character.[9]

Gregory has in mind reading which directly concerns the practices associated with Hesychasm. The works he recommends leaving aside appear to be saints' lives and perhaps dogmatic works. Importantly, he does not reject them as value-less but simply as tangential to the project of ceaseless prayer. Perhaps more interesting is the list of recommended authors. While Maximus, Nilus, Hesychius, Philotheus, Symeon, and Niketas all appear (at least in selections) in the *Philokalia*, neither Climacus nor Isaac (the Syrian) is present. Thus, the selectivity of the *Philokalia*'s editors should not be seen as a rejection but as an assumption of wider reading and education on the part of their intended readers. As Louth points out, "the *Philokalia* has a particular purpose, but it presupposes the whole context of Orthodox monasticism, or better, of faithful Orthodox living, especially the Divine Liturgy."[10] They would (in all likelihood) have access to Clima-cus, to Isaac, to the Gaza fathers, to Basil of Caesarea, and all the other works which are commendable and, indeed, utilized by philokalic authors. The *Philokalia assumes* a wider tradition as context and therefore does not speak about it directly.

As its editors select from a broader tradition, the *Philokalia* offers hermeneutical parameters for would-be readers. Not only do silences suggest contours outside of which interrogation will fail but, by asking what is not included, readers may come to understand better what the editors considered to be *uniquely* important and, in a sense, unavailable elsewhere for Hesychastic practices. We are, I think, silently encouraged to be careful what questions we put to this particular anthology. It does not, nor would it claim to, hold answers to every question. Matters of dress, of diet, of liturgical practice—these cannot be fruitfully asked of the *Philokalia*. Although such matters are undoubtedly relevant to those who would cultivate *hesychia*, the *Philokalia* remains resolutely silent on them because its content begins where these leave off. Those asking such questions may be able to construct them fancifully from the material of the *Philokalia*, but what emerges will not be "philokalic." The *Philokalia* is necessarily *incomplete*, a fact which would remain true no matter how many authors or works an editor includes, because, insofar as tradition ever finds its expression in lived existence, it is ongoing and developing and therefore always "incomplete."

So far, I admit, I have made no new claims. I will go one step further: the act of contouring a "tradition within a tradition," even as it relies on previous efforts to do so, is a *creative* act. The act of selection is creative, silence equally so, because both help develop and contour particular themes, motifs, and resonances between texts included in the anthology. Selection is, to put it simply, the means by which one *creates* an anthology and *derives* meaning from what emerges. This creative act belongs properly to the reader but is prepared by the editor—they collude together to create the world of the anthological text.

To take one example: despite his rather frequent quotations and allusions, Niketas Stethatos's heavy reliance on Climacus cannot be explored within the *Philokalia* itself, as the *Ladder* was not selected for inclusion. Instead, we find Stethatos appearing not long after Symeon Metaphrastes's paraphrases of Ps-Macarius, works which Niketas may or may not have read. He was, likewise, undoubtedly familiar with Maximus the Confessor but certainly not with the *Capita Varia* as they appear in the *Philokalia*.[11] From a historical perspective, we do best to look at his explicit use of sources to clarify Stethatos's thinking, but as readers of this anthology, we are free to interpret Niketas in terms of the Metaphrast and the *Capita Varia*—we can understand him "philokalically" as part of a picture of spirituality emerging from the interaction of texts chosen out of the larger tradition. We are, however, also free to understand him more "historically" in terms of his reliance on Climacus, since the *Philokalia* invites or at least allows us to read within the larger Orthodox tradition. We have the space needed to construct meaning and to interpret philokalic texts with reference either to the world of the anthology or the larger world within which it took shape. Ultimately, we may do both and the reader's creative act resides precisely in developing and holding together these two levels of interpretation.

The *Philokalia*, then, is precisely what it claims to be: an anthology, etymologically a selection of things which the editors found beautiful and therefore loved above others—and, like the canon of Scripture, when read as a whole the *Philokalia* becomes a world unto itself. Tradition within tradition means here world within world, a created world of meaning within a received world of practice and doctrine.

We turn now to four ways in which the created world of the *Philokalia* interacts with the received world of Orthodox tradition—four ways in which the *Philokalia* may be called "traditional." When one is discussing "tradition" and the *Philokalia*, there are two aspects which must constantly be held together. The first regards practice, and here we have to do with the content of the *Philokalia*: to what extent do its texts refer to ideas and practices whose validity has been witnessed (or can be sanctioned) by the Eastern ascetic tradition at large. The traditionality of philokalic spirituality is a topic well and often explored. The second aspect, rather less considered except in its barest historical form, concerns the traditionality of anthologizing activity itself. I will explore the primarily latter in perhaps unusual ways: I will generally not ask who else anthologized, or when or for what purposes, but rather how tradition informs the creation of an anthology and what sort of tradition emerges in one.

Representing Tradition

Formally, the principle of anthologizing which one finds in the *Philokalia* represents a tradition that extends a millennium back from Makarios and Nikodemos, and that is reflected in important ways in several of the *Philokalia*'s contributing authors. Very generally, Makarios and Nikodemos had a tradition of anthologizing behind them which extended at least to the sixth century in the form of *florilegia*, often used as supporting arguments in doctrinal disputes—among the most famous being those deployed on both sides of the Iconoclast Controversy.[12] Paul Evergetinos's vast *Synagoge*, compiled in the twelfth century, is a famous example of later compilations of edifying ascetic writing, though any *Geronticon* or *Patericon* would fit the mold. However, neither *Synagoge* nor *Paterica* were limited thematically, while *florilegia* were traditionally doctrinal. The *Philokalia*'s editors drew on these traditions but with a uniquely spiritual-thematic principle of selection and, of course, Nikodemos's historical-critical sensibilities, as its organizing principles. Although even in this regard, works like those of Peter of Damascus and, according to Placide Deseille, Hesychast compilations in the fourteenth century preceded the *Philokalia* in anthologizing works around ascetical or spiritual themes rather than doctrinal ones.[13] More proximally, Makarios and Nikodemos most likely worked under the influence and perhaps even inspiration of Paissy Velichkovsky's prior philokalic translation work, which likely took place during his stay on Athos between 1746 and 1763, though his *Dobrotolubiye* would be published ten years after Makarios's and would take account of their work.[14] Thus, the activity of "anthologizing" was not original to Makarios and Nikodemos, and so, from a textual perspective, the *Philokalia* can be considered as a representative—albeit a particularly successful and influential one—of a much longer tradition extending in some form to at least the sixth century.

Moreover, this general tradition found specific expression in certain of the authors included in the *Philokalia*. Nikiphoros the Monk's work *On Stillness and the Guarding of the Heart* consists primarily of well-known stories of various Desert Fathers and quotations of later ascetic writers—Antony the Great, Abba Arsenius, Saba, Mark the Monk, John Climacus, Isaiah of Scetis, Isaac the Syrian, among others. For each story or quotation, though, Nikiphoros gives his own, notably Hesychast, interpretation which relates the story to interior guard and silence. For example, Nikiphoros refers to Saba's habit of giving cells to the infirm but making the healthy build their own, and he interprets this to mean that Saba "required his disciples to keep watch over the intellect." He appends similar commentaries to each story or quotation he records—for some his interpretation is quite likely, for others (like Saba) more fanciful, a point to which I will return below.[15] At the end of this litany of authors, Nikiphoros offers a few of his own thoughts—he put himself at the end, a contemporary example of a tradition extending to the first generation of monastics. The sense one has here is that tradition is a source of authority and a criterion by which to judge contemporary practices. Each author, then, who dares to offer his own experience or advice or interpretation, attempts to find his own place in that tradition. In doing so, however, he acts similarly to his forebears, who also sought to find themselves within tradition but, in doing so, continued and elaborated it as well.

Much like Nikiphoros, neither Makarios nor Nikodemos contributes anything to the *Philokalia*, apart from the Introduction and brief notices on each author.[16] They efface themselves and, if one examines the original publication, one cannot find their names on it. The editors sought to disappear so as to focus the reader all the more on the spiritual tradition on display in the *Philokalia*. Indeed, the contents of the *Philokalia* are traditional, its authors acknowledged by generations of Orthodox Christians, sealed by councils, and approved by later authors. Yet it was Makarios's and Nikodemos's editorial work which enabled a new or, at least, revived, engagement with that tradition and which would, if only in a limited way through organization, shape readers' interaction with it. In this sense, too, the editors of the *Philokalia* represent tradition—they follow their forebears in what had become a traditional means of expressing and legitimating theological, spiritual, and ascetical claims. The editors of the anthology were people who strove, in their daily life and in their thought, to be faithful to the ideas and practices which were handed down to them.[17] Their creation of the *Philokalia* was in no way an attempt at something "new." It was an attempt (and, especially for Nikodemos, part of a much wider effort) to be faithful and to help others be faithful to the Orthodox theological and spiritual tradition encapsulated in the writings of the Fathers. The appeal to tradition as source of authority was made not in the hope of legitimating innovation, but to point to the soil of current practices and to find a meaning in them richer for having deep roots. Thus the creation of the *Philokalia* can be described not simply as "representing" tradition, but as an act of carrying on tradition and an offering given to tradition.

Crystallizing Tradition

The *Philokalia*, by utilizing sources already approved and used by Hesychasts, and especially by Palamite Hesychasts, sets its approval on a particular ascetical-spiritual tradition which had already developed within the larger Orthodox tradition. Though not exhaustive even from the perspective of Hesychast tradition, the *Philokalia* both responds to and offers afresh a "canon" (in the sense of rule) of which *sort* of texts are valuable for Hesychast practices. It effectively distills Hesychast tradition—which can itself be seen as a sort of distillation of Orthodox asceticism—and the result is, as Louth puts it, a "certain complexion," an entrance into "the world of the fathers from a particular direction, so to speak."[18] The direction is one determined by the great theological figures of the thirteenth and fourteenth centuries—an orientation of ascetic practice and spirituality directly toward Hesychasm. Thus, first, the *Philokalia* does not represent Orthodox tradition as such, no matter how much the anthology witnesses to it. Rather, it represents a particular interpretation, an understanding of tradition operative among Hesychasts. Specifically, it represents the ascetic tradition as *developing* toward a Hesychast end—the editors are unapologetic about the fact that "Jesus Prayer" does not appear in many of the *Philokalia*'s early authors. Nevertheless, this development is an elaboration, not an innovation: the themes remain constant even as they are unfolded more and more toward Palamas. We return to the creativity behind the *Philokalia*, here the implicit work of interpretation which Hesychasts gave to Orthodox ascetic spirituality presented silently in the *Philokalia*.

Given the likely existence of prior Hesychast anthologies and the work done by Paissy prior to the publication of the *Philokalia*, it can hardly be called novel in the nature of the activity or the scope of the texts chosen. It was not Makarios or Paissy or Nikodemos who cut the *Logoi* of Isaiah of Scetis together into the twenty-seven texts on *Guarding the Intellect* which appears near the beginning of the *Philokalia*.[19] They included, it seems, a text which had been put together and used by previous Hesychast authors. It does not exactly represent Isaiah's own thought—who devoted none of his *Logoi* specifically to the topic of νῆψις—but the interpretation which was given him by Hesychast authors and was, therefore, something which Paissy and Makarios could approve and include in their Hesychast collections. If we may call the piece attributed to Isaiah a Hesychast interpretation of his spiritual contribution, then its inclusion in the *Philokalia* represents an acceptance of that interpretation. Thus the *Philokalia* in its selectivity *crystallizes* a prior interpretation of tradition. The editors' selectivity was a way of being faithful not only to Orthodox tradition generally but, in terms of content, to the Hesychast tradition which inspired them.

However, as I will argue below concerning subsequent editors of the *Philokalia*, crystallization does not imply stasis. As crystals expand by repeated iterations of the same pattern, the *Philokalia* remains open to incorporation of further texts in the same spirit. Likewise, as crystals have a rich variety of patterns, the *Philokalia* remains open to the theological concerns and even agendas of its readers. The *Philokalia* draws its legitimacy from that of the tradition on which it draws but becomes, in its turn, a source and criterion of legitimacy for later writings—it gains, for better or worse, the value of a *canon*. It portrays a trajectory of tradition, and readers are invited to interpret whatever else they read in light of the "complexion" shaded by the *Philokalia*.

Recovering Tradition

Of course, it is well and good to say that the Hesychast tradition pre-existed Paissy's, Makarios's, and Nikodemos's work and that they simply distilled it. The situation that these men encountered, however, seems to have been rather more dismal. Under *Tourkokratia*, monastic life was a shadow of its former Byzantine self. Education especially had suffered, and there were few monks, it seems, who could even read the Atticized Greek of the authors included in the *Philokalia*. In his Introduction, Nikodemos laments that the manuscripts that were used to create the anthology were neglected, dusty, and "moth-eaten."[20] While it is hard to know whether the practices had withered, the spiritual sources certainly seem to have dried up. The creation of the *Philokalia*, then, required a rediscovery of tradition, and the result can be called a *recovery* of tradition. That is, it is not itself the recovery of Hesychast practice, but it certainly provides an invaluable support to would-be Hesychasts. Indeed, it provides a support which, at the time of its publication, was otherwise unobtainable. As was noted above, this rationale helps explain why Makarios and Paissy chose the particular texts they did for inclusion: if they were otherwise available, they did not need to be included in the *Philokalia*. The other rationale given above, that selections were at least in part based on previous collections, fits as well. The *Philokalia* could function as a desk-reference of the hard-to-find ascetic works which were and are so valuable to those who would practice Hesychastic prayer.

In this sense its incompleteness, to which I have alluded above, is a virtue of sorts. The *Philokalia* points beyond itself. It exists to aid its readers and to inspire them to further reading and reflection. As other works become available, philokalic readers would have the opportunity to get hold of them—the *Logoi* of Isaiah of Scetis, the *Ambigua* of Maximus Confessor, the original *Homilies* of Ps.-Macarius, other works of Mark the Monk, Symeon the New Theologian, Gregory Palamas, as well as those of the spiritual luminaries of their own day: people who, influenced by the spirituality found in the *Philokalia*, made it their own and thus "rediscovered" tradition for themselves. Theophan the Recluse, Silouan the Athonite, his disciple Fr. Sophrony of Essex, as well as Fr. Cleopa of Sihastria or Justin Popovic in Serbia—These men and many others find tradition through the *Philokalia* and so the "discovery" begun by Paissy, Makarios, and Nikodemos continues afresh in each reader, finding new and unique expressions in the experiences of every budding Hesychast.

Yet there is a tension at work in the philokalic recovery of tradition. It is striking that Nikodemos and Makarios envisioned the *Philokalia* as a work for all Christians yet presented it in a form of Greek quite difficult to read. Only a couple of very late pieces, which were likely already translated into *demotike*, are incorporated. Everything else remains in its Byzantine form—often dense, highly complex

Greek, such as one finds in the works of Maximus the Confessor and Gregory Palamas, two of the largest and, arguably, most important contributors. Yet it was monks' (and, presumably, seculars') ignorance of Byzantine Greek which Paissy credited for the neglect of these sources in the first place.[21] Now it is possible for those with knowledge only of *demotike* to read Byzantine Greek—particularly those, like monks and pious seculars, familiar and comfortable with the Greek liturgy and hymnody of the Orthodox Church. Yet Byzantine Greek would still present many difficulties for readers, and only in the later twentieth century was the *Philokalia* finally made available in modern Greek. We may ask, then, how accessible—how *available*—Makarios and Nikodemos made their "rediscovery" of tradition.

Ware is quite right that the current situation in which, at long last, after the really incredible efforts of numerous translators, the *Philokalia* is available to all those people Nikodemos hoped would read it—that at last Nikodemos must be quite content that his vision has been realized.[22] But why didn't he realize it himself? I would suggest that we look to Paissy Velichkovsky's own reticence about publication for the answer.

Paissy had been translating philokalic texts into Slavonic long before Makarios and Nikodemos published the *Philokalia* in 1782.[23] However, his *Dobrotolubiye* did not appear until 1793, and only then under pressure from Metropolitan Gabriel of St. Petersburg. Paissy, we read, was afraid lest these texts fall into the wrong hands—if the casual reader attempted what they enjoined, he was sure only of ending up in delusion and demonic despair. His was a fear which Nikodemos understood, though he did not share it so much. So Paissy began allowing a sort of underground manuscript circulation—only those deemed worthy by monks already in possession of the *Dobrotolubiye* would see it. In this way, he could certainly ensure that readership was ready for what the *Philokalia* had to say. But such methods could hardly allow for the wider dissemination for which Makarios and Nikodemos, among others, yearned—though Nikodemos was at least cognizant of the sort of fears expressed by Paissy. When Paissy did publish the *Dobrotolubiye* in 1793, it was in Slavonic (and thus linguistically more inaccessible to Russians than Byzantine Greek to Greeks!) and would only be translated into Russian by Theophan the Recluse between 1887 and 1889.[24] There was a tension from the outset, then, between a desire to present the traditional sources of ascetic spirituality, on the one hand, and a desire to maintain a select and worthy readership, on the other. I would suggest that Makarios and Nikodemos steered a middle course: publish the *Philokalia*, present the works and establish them more permanently in the wider literary consciousness, but leave them in a form so difficult that reading would require great labor. Thus, anyone could have access to spiritual writings, but only those willing to put in the necessary effort would actually utilize it.

This is to say that the editors "recovered" tradition in such a way as to safeguard it. The practices and their underlying spiritual principles would be available, but would, in keeping with the claims of philokalic sources themselves, require effort to obtain. The key lay in either limiting readership (as Paissy attempted) or culling readers through language itself, as Nikodemos did.[25] The reader is given constraints of one kind or another, so that the opening up of tradition operates within

proper bounds. Each reader, that is, becomes free to "discover" Hesychast tradition, but only to do so within the constraints laid down by the demands of
Hesychasm itself.

Creating Tradition

Even as it represents, crystallizes, and recovers tradition, the *Philokalia* also *creates*
tradition. I will here describe the core claims of this essay: that the *Philokalia*
cannot be anything but a creator of tradition and, therefore, foster creative readership. I noted above that an anthology, particularly when read as a whole, creates
resonances between included pieces. By resonances I mean not only overt inter-
textual relations such as quotations and allusions, but the echoes of ideas and
vocabulary, of themes and motifs, which a reader cannot help but notice when
reading one text after another, particularly within a coherent and deliberate collection. Some resonances emerge simply by means of juxtaposition. For example,
when one has Diadochos of Photiki's definitions in hand, it is difficult not to want
to apply them to other texts in the same collection. It is questionable, however,
whether Maximus the Confessor, in his *Capita de Caritate* means by love "growing
affection for those who abuse us."[26] Yet, in context of the *Philokalia*, where these
two texts appear in reasonably close proximity, we are invited to read one in light
of the other. Thus, the simple fact of an anthology suggests at least some new and,
so far as the contributing authors are concerned, unintended, resonances.

There are other points which emerge, though, in the layered nature of the texts
peculiar to the *Philokalia*. That is, the anthology not only includes well-known
works by major figures (such as the pieces by Mark the Monk and Symeon the New
Theologian), but also texts which represent prior interpretations of ascetic authors.
Isaiah of Scetis, as is noted above, devoted no *logoi* to "the guarding of the intellect." The piece in the *Philokalia* stands, in isolation, at one remove from Isaiah's
own thought: it is cut together and therefore represents someone else's interpretation of Isaiah. One may say the same of the five hundred *Capita Varia* attributed to
Maximus the Confessor. These are cut together from a variety of his works—edited
down, reordered, and put back together in "centuries." A third obvious example is
Symeon Metaphrastes's cutting and *paraphrasing* of Ps-Macarius's homilies.
Symeon seems to have worked from two different collections of the Macarian
Homilies and not only cut them together into six thematically defined "discourses,"
but paraphrased parts so as to make these six new "discourses" flow coherently.
Interpretation has given way to creation in the texts chosen for the *Philokalia*. As
these sorts of texts are incorporated into the anthology, they too offer voices to the
chorus. But the voices heard by the reader are not exactly those with which Isaiah,
Maximus, and Macarius once sang. Thus the resonances which emerge from their
juxtaposition with other texts are even further removed from any kind of authorial
intent or originating historical milieu.

As complex texts enter the chorus, the resonances and echoes which the reader
hears become something else new as well—now Symeon Metaphrastes's paraphrase of Ps-Macarius may be read in light of Maximus the Confessor, whose
works certainly post-date Macarius but who did influence the Metaphrast. To

carry our example further, we may note that Gregory of Sinai adduces Isaiah of Scetis and John Climacus to affirm the methods of prayer enjoined by an unknown author—though the piece *On the Three Methods of Prayer* is attributed (falsely) in the *Philokalia* to Symeon the New Theologian.[27] Isaiah, it may be said, seems never to have suggested methods of prayer similar to those found in Ps-Symeon and, later, in Gregory. Gregory's reliance on Isaiah suggests now that Isaiah may be read in light of Gregory or, at least Symeon the New Theologian. This suggestion is made all the more likely when one encounters not the *logoi* of Isaiah, but the cutting utilized by Nikiphoros the Monk and included in the *Philokalia*. The themes which this cutting brought out in Isaiah carry through and find further elaboration in later authors such as Nikiphoros and Gregory, but that elaboration can, in a synchronic compendium, now color also earlier texts to which the reader may turn immediately.

The complex historical relations between these men are now flattened into the ordering of chapters in a single work wherein each may be read in light of the other. The *Philokalia*'s intended use as a reference work only serves to highlight the reader's a-directional approach. Now one reads one chapter or author, now another—in order, out of order, whatever that may even mean. The historical trajectory of development—already a particular interpretation of the ascetic tradition—expands into a harmonizing synchronicity wherein each text can influence and be influenced by every other. Editor and reader know the ending which the authors did not, so she reads the themes developed later back into those who wrote earlier. Isaiah of Scetis is now not only an influence on Gregory of Sinai, but Gregory of Sinai suggests how to interpret Isaiah of Scetis; the same may be said of Macarius, Maximus, and the Metaphrast. Indeed, we could find these complex echoes and influences between all the texts of the *Philokalia*. None exists on its own. Every author is now part of a larger whole in which he must take his place. This is the finding of oneself within a tradition which was discussed above, only now it is not the author who places himself in the tradition, it is the editor and, even more, it is the reader. The reader interprets these texts together and so creates the relationships between them which must be called a *tradition*.

In these ways, among others, the editors of the *Philokalia* effectively create a tradition which did not previously exist. The diachronic development, the various voices singing along, which lies behind the *Philokalia* is ultimately incommensurable with the symphony which the anthology creates, as the inclusion (without comment) of Evagrius suggests. The heretic is, at least as far as these works are concerned, a theologian. Of course, it is not the editors who imbue their anthology with meaning. Neither Makarios nor Nikodemos creates the resonating relationships among their chosen texts. To some extent the authors themselves do that through quotations and allusions. But, most important, their juxtaposition within a single work necessitates the relationships. However, these must remain illusory or at least latent, until the reader begins to do the work of interpretation. It is, I think, not just the editors, but the readers who can, at least within the specific bounds of an anthology like the *Philokalia*, affirm with Gregory of Sinai that "Assuredly, the words of the saints never disagree if they are carefully examined."[28] From a historical perspective Gregory's words are almost laughably absurd. The saints most certainly disagree on many matters. Many of those disagreements are even enshrined in the *Philokalia*. But by their incorporation the reader is invited toward a new synthesis, a synchronization of elements which allows for new, coherent meanings. The effect of all this is to make the *Philokalia* something new yet very old, a tradition created from traditions, a coherence which imposes itself on polyphony by the very fact of its existence.

■ READING CREATIVELY: WHICH *PHILOKALIA*?

The *Philokalia* was not intended for scholarly research. Certainly, it can be useful for those ends, but its intended use was as a guide, a reference work, an aid to spiritual development. It was meant to be read as part of one's life in the Church, expressed most perfectly in one's relationship of obedience to a spiritual father. Whatever ideas and practices it may offer, the *Philokalia* points continually beyond itself. It serves first as a reminder of the pilgrim's own eagerness with which he first opens its pages and, very probably, his spiritual father's advice to do so. It inspires him to further reading, to intensified activity, to seek out holiness in others, in books, in himself. I mean that the *Philokalia* not only represents the creative drive of its editors and, further back, its contributing authors, but it also serves to inspire a creativity in its readers. To be traditional, if one takes Makarios, Nikodemos, and Paissy, as examples, is to be creative.

Readers of the *Philokalia* have certainly found this for themselves. A brief catalogue of other editions and translations of the *Philokalia* will make my point, as subsequent editors represent, I think, philokalic readers *par excellence*. Paissy's Slavonic *Dobrotolubiye*, whose organization and contents differ somewhat from Makarios's and Nikodemos's, was translated into Russian by Theophan the Recluse. It is actually quite likely that Theophan translated the Greek *Philokalia*, since his *Dobrotolubiye* incorporates much material, including large portions of Maximus the Confessor, which was included by Makarios but not by Paissy. Theophan thus began with *ressourcement* but continued by making a few important changes himself to the contents—editing out some pieces and adding others. Why did he make the changes? Theophan was not comfortable with some of the techniques enjoined in the Greek *Philokalia*—he found some portions (such as Palamas's *150 Chapters*) too difficult and some (such as the breathing techniques of Ps-Symeon) too scandalous. So in some cases he edited them out entirely (as with the *150 Chapters*) and in others he expurgated them (as with Ps-Symeon, Nikiphoros the Monk, and Gregory of Sinai). He added a good deal of material from the Desert Fathers as well as selections of Climacus, Isaac the Syrian, and the Gaza Fathers. The effect is one of "sharply accentuating the ascetic aspect of the *Philokalia* while reducing the speculative and mystical aspect."[29] In both cases, he measured what he received against his own judgment and experience and edited it accordingly. He had room, and felt he had room, to create.

In the twentieth century, two different versions further illustrate in very different ways the same principle of editorial creativity. The Romanian version, pioneered by Fr. Dumitru Staniloae, is almost triple the length of the Greek, and, instead of selections, includes complete works—one does not read the

Capita Varia, but the complete *Quaestiones ad Thalassium* of Maximus the Confessor, for example. Moreover, Staniloae incorporated material from modern and contemporary Orthodox luminaries—Silouan the Athonite, Justin Popovic, and others. He *continued* the *Philokalia*, in the same spiritual mode and, in contrast with Theophan, a personal focus on its "speculative and mystical aspect," and so from later tradition he added whatever he thought useful while from the tradition already represented in the *Philokalia* he expanded its selections so that Romanians could enjoy wider access to philokalic sources.[30] At the risk of generalizing, Staniloae represents, perhaps, a Makarian spirit.

The English version, undertaken by Kallistos Ware, Phillip Sherard, and G. E. H. Palmer, represents a rather different continuation, perhaps more in the spirit of Nikodemos. These men brought their scholarly, critical sensibilities to bear on the anthology and so they substituted critical editions where available, they provided their own introductions (which often give very different historical information from what Nikodemos had), and, in perhaps the boldest move, relegated the piece attributed to Anthony the Great to an appendix—that most vestigial organ of modern scholarship.[31] They aimed to bring Makarios's and Nikodemos's work to a new audience, but to offer at the same time the best of their own talents, and so they "corrected" Nikodemos's work in light of modern scholarship. I suspect that Nikodemos, with his own curious critical streak, would approve of their creative reworking.

Theophan, Staniloae, and the English translators all strive to continue the work begun by Paissy, Makarios, and Nikodemos. They each do so in different ways, in accordance with their own spiritual, scholarly, and personal experience and talents. All of these have sought to *be* traditional and to locate themselves within the tradition which they then offer to others. In doing so, each editor has created something new, yet entirely in the spirit of the tradition which he has sought to continue. The space for creativity is, it seems, coterminous with tradition itself.

▪ A BRIEF CONCLUSION: CREATIVITY AND ITS LIMITS

The editors of the *Philokalia* make it their own because, as readers, they are free to do so. They create even in the act of recovering and offering again something they perceive as traditional. They are right to do so, and they are guaranteed their creative license by the nature of the *Philokalia*. Yet their creativity is also contoured by the limits imposed by the *Philokalia* itself—it demands always a consciousness of one's responsibility toward the larger Orthodox tradition. The repeated warnings about the need for a spiritual father describe most perfectly the limits of creativity: creativity among readers must be exercised *and* corrected from within the Church—from a sacramental, prayerful, and always *guided* perspective. The *Philokalia* was always a creative work precisely in its traditionality—in the unflagging loyalty to the Orthodox Church, and especially to the ideals of Hesychasm which inspired its editors. Its very traditionality ultimately offers safe space for readers to exercise creativity within the same ecclesial context and, in so doing, to continue traditions and make them thrive.

The *Philokalia* as a book is dead—it is a text like any other, closed and doomed to become as moth-eaten as those manuscripts which Nikodemos describes. Such is the fate of every book. But its practices—the traditions general and specific—of ascetic spirituality and thought to which it witnesses—these are very much alive. Tradition continues to live and thrive precisely as each reader of the *Philokalia* makes it her own, whether she does so in her own use of the Jesus Prayer, or in editorial or translatory work, or in simply finding inspiration from it for wider reading, deeper contemplation, and a richer life in the Church—all purposes for which, after all, the *Philokalia* was first created.

9 Becoming a Spiritual World of God: The Theological Anthropology of Maximus the Confessor

Brock Bingaman

> The [person] who has struggled bravely with the passions of the body, has fought ably against unclean spirits, and has expelled from [their] soul the conceptual images they provoke, should pray for a pure heart to be given [them] and for a spirit of integrity to be renewed within [them] (Ps. 51:10). In other words, [they] should pray that by grace [they] may be completely emptied of all evil thoughts and filled with divine thoughts, so that [they] *may become a spiritual world of God, splendid and vast,* wrought from moral, natural and theological forms of contemplation.[1]

▨ INTRODUCTION

The work of Maximus the Confessor, the seventh-century Orthodox theologian known for his profound synthesis of theology and spirituality and his opposition to Monothelitism, is like a river that runs into and feeds many of the diverse streams within the *Philokalia*. One indicator of his importance and influence in the *Philokalia* (assembled by St. Nikodimos and St. Makarios) is seen in his being assigned more space than anyone else in the collection, with his work making up most of the second volume of five in the English translation by Palmer, Sherrard, and Ware.[2] The work of Maximus included in the *Philokalia* presents a theological vision of the human calling in the world. Within this theological vision are many interconnected aspects, much like the various tiles that together make up a large mosaic. Therefore, Maximus's reflections on human being in Christ or theological anthropology are connected deeply to his meditations on the Trinity, Christ, and the creation and re-creation of the cosmos.[3]

The purpose of this essay is to consider some of the salient features of Maximus's theological anthropology, to provide a map of sorts that leads the reader of the *Philokalia* through some of the key themes in Maximus's anthropology. In other words, this chapter is meant to be read alongside the writings of Maximus that are included in the *Philokalia*. Informed by some of the leading modern scholarship on Maximus, this essay explores aspects of Maximus's s anthropology, including the cosmological, christological, soteriological, and eschatological dimensions.[4] In the spirit of the *Philokalia*, a book intended for the spiritual development of monks and laypeople alike, this essay ponders the question, *What does Maximus teach us about becoming a spiritual world of God, splendid and vast?* That is, what can we learn from Maximus's teaching in the *Philokalia* about what it means to be human, to be created, recreated, and indwelt by God?

■ CREATION: THE COSMOS

Maximus speaks about creation in a number of his various works in the *Philokalia*. Yet one text in particular, his *Fourth Century on Love*, provides a helpful summary of his cosmology.[5] Looking briefly at Maximus's view of creation in general will provide a cosmological context for his anthropology. In the first section of this century, there are eight discernible elements of cosmology. The first is *creatio ex nihilo*.[6] In line with orthodox Christian tradition, Maximus asserts that God created the world out of nothing. This sovereign act of God, according to Maximus, amazes the human mind and demonstrates the limitless magnificence of God. This view expresses the superiority of God over all creation, as well as the idea that God does not need any pre-existent material in order to create. It safeguards the distance and distinction between God and creation.[7]

A second cosmological element concerns creation because of God's will.[8] This view, which is closely related to creation out of nothing, emphasizes that the world was created according to God's sovereign will, not because of obligation or any other external factor. Linked with the idea of creation by God's sovereign will is Maximus's theology of the *logoi*.[9] Based on the Stoic idea of *logos spermatikos*, merged with early Christian Logos theology, Maximus builds on the teaching of Origen and Pseudo-Dionysius as he constructs his own vision of the *logoi*. For Maximus, the *logoi* are the divine ideas for all things that have received their being from God. Not only are these principles of differentiated creation preexistent in God, as God's thoughts, but they are divine wills or intentions. In short, Maximus's teaching on the *logoi* underscores the goodness of a diversified creation, brought about by God's free will, and unified in the incarnate Logos, as we will discuss below when we look more closely at the incarnation.

The third element in Maximus's cosmology is creation because of God's benevolence.[10] In addition to creation out of nothing and creation because of God's will, Maximus explains that God's creative activity is rooted in divine goodness. These interconnected facets of Maximus's cosmology maintain the sovereignty of God over all created being, the goodness of diversified created existence, and the notion that this differentiated existence is part of God's *good* plan. Unlike some Origenists who tended to view diversified existence as a result of the fall (a notion considered in the next section), Maximus asserts that the reunification of all things through communion with the Logos is an original divine intention, something interrupted by humanity's fall into sin.

A fourth element in Maximus's cosmology is creation by the Word. A few things should be mentioned here. First, Maximus explains that God creates through God's coessential Logos and Spirit. The creation of all things is a trinitarian work, as Maximus reiterates in other texts included in the *Philokalia*.[11] Second, as is noted above, creation through the Word or Logos involves Maximus's multifaceted teaching on the *logoi*. Among other things, Maximus's teaching on the *logoi* in relation to the Logos demonstrates God's purpose to create a world of differentiated creatures, independent creatures that find their unity in relationship to the Logos. The *logoi*, those divine ideas or intentions in the mind of God, are dynamic realities that radiate from God, the Creator and Cause of all. According to another text of Maximus in the *Philokalia*, *Second Century on Theology*, God and the *logoi* may be compared to the center of a circle as the indivisible source of all the radii extending from it. This comparison suggests that the principles of created beings (the *logoi*) are centered in God, and that God is the unifying center of the whole creation.[12] Third, through contemplation in the Spirit, believers are enabled to see the Logos in the *logoi* of creation. In biblical, parabolic language, Maximus says that the *logoi* are perched like birds on the outstretched branches of the massive Logos tree.[13] Therefore, those who are in communion with Christ are enabled to see the *logoi*, the world of differentiated creatures, in light of their integral connection to the Logos.[14] As Lars Thunberg explains, Maximus interweaves the above strands, showing how creation by the Word underscores the differentiation and unification of the *logoi* in the Logos, as well as the deep relationship between cosmology and the economy of salvation. "Creation by the Word thus implies to Maximus not only a positive evaluation of creation," says Thunberg, "but the inclusion of the latter in a purpose of universal unification, on the basis of the Incarnation by grace of the Logos, in which all the [*logoi*] of things abide."[15] Through this perception of the world based on the Logos and *logoi*, Maximus highlights that God intended to create a world of differentiated creatures, that they are unified through their relationship to the Logos, and that created nature is dynamic or energetic on the basis of its relationship to the Creator.[16]

In addition to creation through the Word, a fifth aspect of Maximus's cosmology can be seen: creation on the basis of God's prudence.[17] Building on the distinction between prudence and wisdom found in Aristotle and Evagrius, Maximus asserts the apophatic approach to God and God's creation. While Maximus speaks about the Creator giving "being to and manifesting that knowledge of created things which already existed in him from all eternity," God's prudence or practical wisdom transcends the human intellect ($\dot{\upsilon}\pi\grave{\epsilon}\rho$ $\nu o\hat{\upsilon}\nu$) and is beyond human comprehension.[18] As we proceed, we will see how Maximus also utilizes this apophatic approach in his anthropological, christological, and soteriological reflection.

A sixth element of Maximus's cosmology concerns creation as an act of God's condescension.[19] In Maximus's view, the act of creation conveys a number of important things that will help us better understand his anthropology as it unfolds. First, creation is good because God is its Cause. As an "astonishing sea of goodness," God is the unsearchable, fathomless source of all being.[20] Further, while God is the transcendent and ultimately unknowable cause of all that exists, God enters into a deep relationship with creation by simply giving it existence. The work of creation is an act of condescension on God's part, an act of divine goodness and love. Not only does God grant creatures existence, but God the Logos actually indwells all of creation, as is illustrated in Maximus's Logos-*logoi* theology. Moreover, utilizing the Aristotelian idea of motion, Maximus suggests that the movement of rational beings toward God, who is their unifying end, signifies their development. This movement as an opportunity for growth conveys the idea that all of creation is oriented toward God, who is its benevolent cause. What's more, the condescension of God through the act of creation, in which the immovable God realizes God's creative power in motion, reinforces Maximus's positive opinion about motion.[21]

The next element in Maximus's cosmology—the notion that every creature is a composite of substance and accident—will also shed light on Maximus's anthropology as our study continues. Here a succinct summary is given that will come into play particularly when we look at Maximus's teaching on deification.[22] For Maximus, God is pure being or substance, while creatures are given qualified being with the possibility for participation in something more than general being. Thus the concept of being or substance has an inherent dynamic element. Moreover, as a category of creation, substance is characterized by limitations, conditions of limited ability which belong to all creatures. In Maximus's view, being (*ousia*) as existence is something that must be realized in an act of self-fulfillment. This point gives rise to Maximus's teaching on being, well-being, and ever-being, which basically spells out how one's substantial potentiality is realized through their intentional energies and the active grace of God. Creaturely existence is, therefore, the gift of participation in God's own being, goodness, wisdom, and life. This conception of creaturely existence enables Maximus to speak of the self-realization and transcendence of substance in ways that underscore the goodness and grace of the Creator, the dynamic potentiality of nature, the divine purpose of a differentiated creation, and the notion of God as the *telos* toward which all creatures are moving. Based on this dynamic understanding of creaturely being, Maximus argues that by human freedom (the gnomic will) human beings are able to transcend nature without violating it, and to realize their created purpose, which is union with God or deification. As we will see, this union is made possible for humanity through the coming of Christ, through the hypostatic union of his human and divine natures.

The eighth and final point of Maximus's cosmology that is important for an understanding of his anthropology is that creation is in need of divine Providence.[23] In short, and in line with what we saw previously, Maximus accentuates the dynamic dimension of creaturely life, distinguishing between the principle of nature (λόγοσ φύσεωσ) and the mode of existence (τρόποσ ὑπάρξεωσ). For Maximus, the principle of nature is immutable, while the mode of existence is variable and open to the possibility of realization. These distinctions play an important role in Maximus's christology, his understanding of Christ's two natures, and how the incarnation opens up new possibilities for human beings in relationship to him. The notion of "mode of existence," like the transcendence of substance considered above, paves the way for Maximus to speak of an ongoing incarnation of Christ in the virtues of those who are in communion with him. As Thunberg suggests, this "does not interfere with nature, but calls forth natural powers of human nature, so that the boundaries of the latter are reached and the human person may experience, by grace, the transcendence which is properly called deification." This perspective "leads, finally, to consequences in the understanding of the freedom of the individual. . . . Consequently, persons are developing and variable in their modes, though their natural operation is immutable in accordance with the immutability of the principle of their nature."[24] Therefore, sketching some of these elements of Maximus's teaching on creation provides a context in which to analyze his anthropology.

Creation: The Human Person

In view of Maximus's basic understanding of the creation of the cosmos, we turn now to his teaching on the creation of the human being in particular. As Hans Urs von Balthasar and others have pointed out, Maximus is perhaps the most world-affirming of the Greek Fathers.[25] His view of the created world, as we have just seen, underscores that creation is the good work of a benevolent God, that creatures are graced with being, and that humans are called to transcend nature and realize their full potential through communion with God in Christ. Thus, we already see the intrinsic connections between Maximus's positive evaluation of the material world in general and that of human existence in particular. In this section, we will see this in greater detail as we look at Maximus's understanding of the relationship between body and soul in human being, as well as his teaching on the image of God in humanity.

Body and Soul

Modern scholarship has shed light on Maximus's multifaceted teaching on the human person. While we are focusing on Maximus's teaching in the *Philokalia*, here we look briefly at his broader work, including a few texts in and outside of the *Philokalia*. In these texts, a number of key aspects of his anthropology can be seen. One is the indissoluble unity of body and soul. Unlike the general trends within Origenism that proposed the doctrine of the preexistence of the soul, a double creation, and a punitive view of embodiedness, Maximus argues for the coexistence of body and soul from the beginning. Building on the biblically grounded ideas of Gregory of Nyssa, Maximus contends that human bodies are good, that their creation is rooted in the foreknowledge of God, and that their coexistence safeguards both divine sovereignty and a positive view of the world in its differentiation.[26] For Maximus, "it is impossible for either the soul or the body to exist before the other or indeed to exist after the other in time."[27] The body and soul, therefore, are intrinsically related to one another.[28]

Additionally, Maximus is careful to distinguish between body and soul. Working with concepts from Aristotle, Nemesius of Emesa, and Leontius of Byzantium, Maximus stresses that the relationship between body and soul is one of both deep unity and distinction. To illustrate this point, Maximus suggests that the relationship between body and soul is somewhat analogous to the unity of the human and divine natures in Christ. Utilizing insights from Chalcedonian christology, a practice that pervades his work, Maximus understands the relationship between body and soul in terms of *perichoresis*. Body and soul interpenetrate one another, yet in their union they remain unconfused.[29]

Dichotomous and Trichotomous Terms

In his anthropological reflection, Maximus speaks of the composite nature of human beings in both dichotomous and trichotomous terms. While he seems to prefer speaking of human ontology in terms of body and soul, Maximus does at times speak of mind, soul, and body.[30] Taking up the concepts of his predecessors who employ both dichotomous and trichotomous thinking, including the Apostle Paul, Origen, Gregory of Nyssa, and Evagrius, Maximus describes the dynamism of human existence as mind, soul, and body. This is not intended to be a literal metaphysical distinction, but a description of the various elements involved in human existence. What is particularly important to recognize is the way Maximus stresses the unity of human being, the positive evaluation of the body and its permanent relationship to the soul (in line with 1 Cor. 15:35–57), and the careful, creative ways that Maximus appropriates the ideas of his predecessors to emphasize a holistic understanding of the human person.[31]

Furthermore, there is the important concept of the human being as microcosm and mediator. In short, Maximus employs the image of microcosm to describe the human being, made up of body and soul, as a picture of the created universe, a "little world" that reflects the material and spiritual aspects of creation. Maximus also speaks of the human being as a universal mediator whose vocation is, following the example of Christ, to unify all of creation with the Creator.[32]

Nous: The Contemplative Part of Humanity

Along with Maximus's ideas on the relationship between body and soul is his understanding of *nous* (νοῦσ). According to Maximus, *nous* (mind or intellect) is the contemplative part or organ in humans that is primarily responsible for relating to God. *Nous* is to be harmonized with the passible elements in humans, leading to a contemplative understanding of creation, and to realizing one's union with the Trinity. For Maximus, *nous* represents the human being as a whole (in relation to body and soul), and it establishes the true Godward orientation of the entire human person. Identified with the soul, and representative of the whole person, *nous* can be understood as our "thinking subject" (as von Balthasar suggests) or as our "spiritual subject" (according to Thunberg).[33] As will be seen below, Maximus speaks of *nous* being purified by grace and advancing toward God through the threefold way of practical asceticism, contemplation of nature, and mystical union with God (*praktike, phusike,* and *theologike*).[34]*Nous* is, therefore, one way that Maximus speaks of the personal aspect of human existence, bringing together the ideas of something that is beyond nature, that represents inner unity and the capacity or means by which we relate to God.[35]

Further Ideas on Body and Soul

When we focus specifically on Maximus's work in the *Philokalia*, we find a number of other significant elements in his teaching on the human body and soul. His *Texts on Love* are particularly helpful in this respect. For Maximus, body and soul are both created by God and for God,[36] and are good.[37] Further, it is the soul that gives motion to the body.[38] Maximus consistently contrasts body and soul, even asserting that the soul is nobler than the body. Consequently, the one who values the body more than the soul (and the world created by God more than the Creator) is an idolater.[39] The three aspects of the soul—the incensive, the desiring, and the intelligent—are powers that can be used negatively (in sin) or positively (in holy living, in accord with true nature).[40] According to Maximus, these powers of the soul are healed or restored to their created purpose through spiritual practices: almsgiving heals the soul's incensive power; fasting withers sensual desire; and prayer purifies the intellect and prepares it for contemplation.[41] While some modern readers may be troubled by the apparent severe treatment of the body or the superior view of the soul, one should keep in mind that Maximus acknowledges the limited value of bodily asceticism[42] and asserts the goodness of all created things, including both body and soul.[43] Moreover, as we will see in Maximus's teaching on deification, the body and soul live together in harmony, as God intended, when focused on and energized by love for God and neighbor. While, according to Maximus and others included in the *Philokalia*, the soul may exert its influence on the body, the two are created to work together harmoniously. They exist in vital relationship to one another, forming an integrated, composite whole, and are an essential and irreducible unity.[44]

The Image of God in Human Beings

What Maximus has to say about the image of God in human beings is another crucial element in his theological anthropology. Looking at his teaching on the εἰκόνα θεοῦ or *imago Dei* that is included in the *Philokalia*, we can make several observations. The first concerns the reality that the image of God is *within us*. Accordingly, in his *Second Century on Theology*, Maximus describes the image of God within humanity in incarnational, eschatological, and even artistic terms. He explains that before his visible appearance in the flesh, the divine Logos was present among the Old Testament patriarchs and prophets in a spiritual manner, prefiguring his coming incarnation. After his incarnation, the Logos is present in a similar fashion to spiritual beginners, in leading them to perfection, and to the spiritually mature, "secretly pre-delineating in them the features of His future advent as if in an *icon*."[45] Thus the image of God in the spiritually mature functions as an icon, a work of divine art that offers glimpses into the glory of Christ and his church at the Second Coming. The general idea behind this image is reminiscent of 1 Jn. 3:2: "Beloved, we are God's children now; what we will be has not yet been revealed. What we do know is this: When he is revealed, we will be like him, for we will see him as he is."[46]

In another philokalic text, Maximus says that if we are made in the image of God, then we are to become the image of ourselves and of God, losing our attachment to material things, so that we may commune with God and become gods.[47] Maximus links this realization of the divine and human elements in us to growth in love, as we will see below in his teaching on the role of love in deification. Therefore, according to Maximus, as we become more like God, we become our true human selves, and this process is evidenced in love for God and others. Additionally, Maximus speaks about the saints living in accordance with nature, and how their doing so coincides with putting on the whole image of the heavenly (cf. 1 Cor. 15:49).[48] For Maximus, human nature bears the image of God, and when it is liberated from its tendencies to attach itself to created things and is united to God through the Spirit, then it finds rest in *the* Image, the divine Archetype in whom creatures find the Sabbath rest for which they long. Thus an interesting tension is at work within Maximus's conception of the divine image. As Maximus explains, the divine image is drawn to the one living a holy life while at the same time being drawn by it. The importance of this reciprocal dynamic will become clearer as we consider the centrality of the incarnation in Maximus's theological anthropology.

A second observation that can be made about Maximus's teaching on the image of God in human beings is the distinction he makes between the divine image and likeness, a tradition stemming from early Christian theologians, including Irenaeus and Origen.[49]

In his *Third Century on Love*, Maximus reflects on God's creation of rational creatures, and how God communicated to them the divine attributes of being, eternal being, goodness, and wisdom. Maximus explains that the first two characteristics—being and eternal being—are granted to human essence. The second two—goodness and wisdom—are placed within human volitive faculty or power of the will. Therefore, what God is in God's essence, the creature may become by participation. Maximus proceeds to elucidate how these divine attributes correspond to the creation of human beings in the image and likeness of God (cf. Gen. 1:26). Human beings are made in the image of God, since our being is in the image of God's eternal being. That is, while our being is not without origin, our being is without end. Furthermore, we are made in the likeness of God, since we are good in the likeness of God's goodness and wise in the likeness of God's wisdom, since God is good and wise by nature, and human beings are so by grace. Therefore, Maximus concludes his meditation by saying, "Every intelligent nature is in the image [εἰκόνα] of God, but only the good and wise attain [God's] likeness [ὁμοίωσιν]."[50]

In another philokalic text, *First Century on Theology*, Maximus offers further reflection on the distinction between the divine image and likeness, underscoring once again how humanity's created nature is perfected through right use of the will. Maximus says

> If a person's intellect is illumined with intellections of the divine, if [their] speech is unceasingly devoted to singing the praises of the Creator, and if [their] senses are hallowed by unsullied images—[they have] enhanced that sanctity which is [theirs] by nature, as created in the image of God, by adding to it the sanctity of the divine likeness that is attained through the exercise of [their] own free will [γνωμικὸν].[51]

According to this passage, Maximus suggests that every person is created in the image of God, but only those whose intellects, speech, and senses are centered on and infused with God build up that essential holiness which is theirs by nature of existence. Maximus ponders the links between the creation of human beings in the divine image and their growth in the divine likeness according to free will in his exposition, *On The Lord's Prayer*. He explains, "Naturally endowed with the holiness of the divine image, the intelligence urges the soul to conform itself by its own free choice to the divine likeness."[52] Therefore, Maximus continues the tradition of distinguishing between the divine image and likeness in human beings, underscoring the important role that the will plays in being shaped and transformed into the divine likeness.

Along with the distinction between the divine image and likeness in human beings is a third feature of Maximus's teaching on the *imago Dei*: it is linked with the soul. As was noted in our consideration of Maximus's treatment of the body and soul, the soul or intellect is the highest human faculty, the organ of contemplation that enables a person to experience and know God as well as the inner principles of created things.[53] In some of the texts we have examined, this relationship between the divine image and likeness in humanity and the soul is evident. In the text quoted above from *First Century on Theology*, Maximus maintains that there is a correlation between the intellect and the image of God. When the intellect is illumined with divine insight, Maximus argues, it grows in holiness and manifests the divine likeness.[54] Furthermore, in a meditation on Luke 2:34 regarding the destiny of Jesus and the falling and rising of many in Israel, Maximus offers a spiritual interpretation that speaks to the relationship between the divine image and the soul. He explains that the "fall" refers to those who seek to understand creation and scripture according to the senses and in a literal manner, without the spirit of grace. The "resurrection" describes those who contemplate God's creatures and God's words in a spiritual manner. This, Maximus says, is accomplished by "cultivating in appropriate ways only the divine image that is within the soul."[55] This linking of the divine image with the soul is also found in another philokalic author who appropriates the Evagrian tradition, St. Diadochos of Photiki, when he says that the intellect dwells in the very depths of the soul and constitutes the innermost aspect of the heart.[56] For Maximus, along with many other teachers in the *Philokalia*, the intellect is the highest faculty in human beings, the organ of contemplation or eye of the heart (as the *Makarian Homilies* say[57]) through which one experiences and understands divine truth.

A fourth characteristic of Maximus's teaching on the divine image and likeness in humanity deals with the fall and renewal of human beings. Since the fall and renewal are examined more thoroughly in the following sections, here we consider only a few texts that shed light on Maximus's teaching on the divine image. In the *First Century of Various Texts*, where Maximus discusses passages and themes from Gregory of Nazianzus and Gregory of Nyssa,[58] Maximus ruminates on how the divine image was replaced by a likeness to animals. He explains that pleasure and distress, desire and fear, and what they produce, were not originally created as parts of human nature and experience. Following Gregory of Nyssa, Maximus suggests that these things were introduced after humanity's fall from perfection, since they infiltrated into that part of our human nature which is least endowed with intelligence. Through pleasure, distress, desire, and fear, the divine image in humanity was at the time of Adam's transgression replaced immediately by an evident likeness to animals. As a result of the obscuring of the original dignity of the intelligence, human nature was subjected to the ongoing chastisement of these fatuous elements to which it had opened the door.[59] In another text from the *First Century*, Maximus discusses how one's mode of life produces a garment that reveals whether a person is righteous or wicked. The righteous person, through the power of the Spirit, fashions a garment of incorruption interwoven in accordance with virtue and intelligence. This garment clothes the soul, making it beautiful and resplendent. Conversely, the wicked person who is controlled by the desires of the flesh interweaves a filthy, soiled garment (cf. Jude 23). The inner disposition of this person is marked by a conscience deformed by the constant recollection of evil impulses and actions arising from the flesh. Unlike the clean garment that protects and beautifies the virtuous soul, this filthy garment that stinks of the passions wraps around the soul, imposing on it a form and image that is contrary to the divine.[60] From these two texts, therefore, we learn that at the fall the divine image in humanity was replaced by a likeness to animals, and that one's mode of living can form either a beautiful life of virtue in accord with the divine image or a life that reeks of sin and soils the divine image. On this note, we turn to a more detailed consideration of the Fall in Maximus's thinking.

■ THE FALL

Our discussion of Maximus's teaching on the image (and likeness) of God in human beings—including the relation between image and likeness, between the divine image and the soul and between the divine image and human volition—leads to his understanding of the Fall. Maximus's teaching on the Fall that is included in the *Philokalia* is multifaceted and insightful. One thing that can be seen in Maximus's understanding of the Fall is that human beings were created to enjoy communion with God. *The Fourth Century of Various Texts* explains that when

> God the Logos created human nature He did not make the senses susceptible either to pleasure or to pain; instead, He implanted in it a certain noetic capacity [$\delta \acute{u} \nu \alpha \mu \iota \nu$] through which [people] could enjoy Him in an inexpressible way. By this capacity I mean the intellect's natural longing for God.[61]

In Maximus's view, God planted in human nature an intellectual ability to find delight and pleasure in God, to experience joy and fulfillment through communion with the Trinity. The intellect, that contemplative organ that resides in the depths of the human soul, is created with an innate desire for God, an idea that echoes the psalmists who speak of the soul thirsting for God in a dry, weary, and waterless place, or of the soul longing for God as a deer longs for flowing streams (Ps. 63:1; 42:1). This notion of the soul's natural longing for God is something Maximus draws from scripture and from his theological predecessors, including Gregory of Nyssa and Pseudo-Dionysius.[62] However, as we know from the narrative of Genesis, the texts in which Maximus roots his thinking, human beings did not properly follow this natural longing for God but turned in another direction to seek fulfillment.[63] Human nature, created with free will and a capacity to obey God, deviated from God's plan and consequently found itself under the influence of disordered desire.

This brings us to a second feature of Maximus's perspective on the Fall, that human beings were seduced by the Devil and self-love.[64] Described by Maximus as a spawn of sin and the father of iniquity who through pride expelled himself from divine glory, the Devil is responsible for getting Adam and Eve expelled from Paradise. The serpentine figure described in the third chapter of Genesis is portrayed by Maximus as jealous of both human beings and God, as well as intent on luring man and woman away from God's purposes. The Devil, Maximus explains, is jealous of God's power being seen in the deification of man and woman, and jealous of human beings' attaining virtue and becoming participants in the divine glory.[65] Beguiled from their original state, in which their whole selves, soul and body, would find true delight and genuine satisfaction through communion with God, Adam and Eve chose death rather than true life.[66] The craftiness of the Devil, which deceived Adam and Eve in a malicious and cunning way, provoked them through self-love (φιλαυτία; *philautia*) to sensual pleasure, leading to the disordering of their original state.[67] This disruption of humanity's original condition, in which love for God and love for neighbor preserved harmony in creation, was the result of a trio of evil instigators: ignorance, self-love, and tyranny. Maximus says that from ignorance comes self-love, and from self-love comes tyranny over one's own kind. These are established by the Devil in human beings when the soul's three powers (the intelligence, the incensive, and desire) are misused.[68]

Utilizing the image of the two trees in the garden found in Genesis 2–3, Maximus reinforces the role that the Devil played upon the free will of Adam and Eve, tricking them into the pursuit of sensual pleasure through self-love. In the *Second Century of Various Texts*, we read a number of interesting things about these two trees, things that further inform us about Maximus's conception of the Fall and its relation to his overall anthropology. In these texts, the tree of life is said to produce life, while the "other tree" produces death. Moreover, the tree of life symbolizes wisdom, which is characterized by intellect and intelligence. The tree of the knowledge of good and evil is opposite to wisdom, lacking intelligence, and based on sensation.[69]

Stemming from Maximus's understanding of humans created as noetic soul and sentient body, he offers an anthropological interpretation of the two trees. The tree of life symbolizes the soul's intellect, which is the seat of wisdom. The other tree represents the body's power of sensation, understood to be the seat of mindless impulses. Accordingly, human beings were commanded by God not to directly involve themselves with these impulses, yet they did not obey. For Maximus, the intellect is capable of discriminating between the spiritual and the sensible, between the eternal and the transitory. The intellect, functioning as the soul's discriminatory power, urges the soul to focus on spiritual realities and to transcend sensible things. The two trees also represent different expressions of discriminatory power. Those who simply distinguish between pain and pleasure in the body, and thereby embrace pleasure but avoid pain, eat of the tree of the knowledge of good and evil. Those who distinguish noetically between the eternal and the transitory obey the divine command and eat from the tree of life. This drawing from wisdom associated with the intellect and soul urges one to seek the glory of the eternal and avoid the impurity of transitory things.[70] Bringing these various elements together, the main idea in Maximus's teaching on the two trees is that God's design for humanity—unceasing communion and unity between God and all

creatures—was interrupted by the misuse of free will. The reparation of this misuse, as Maximus's teaching on asceticism and deification makes clear, involves
spiritual discernment, detachment from material things, the healthy pain of mortification through ascetic exercises, and the right use of human freedom in pursuit
of God and the common good.

Consequences of the Fall

In addition to considering how Maximus interprets the Fall and how this interpretation informs his anthropology, we turn to consider briefly some of the consequences of the Fall. As we have seen, Maximus asserts that human volition is
rooted in divine freedom. One expression of the image of God in human beings
is the freedom to choose between obedience and disobedience to God, between
love for God and love of self, between worship of the Creator and worship of
creation.[71] Exploiting the will, Maximus argues, the Devil provoked human beings through self-love to the pursuit of sensual pleasure. As a result, human beings
are separated in their wills from God and from one another. Humanity has been
divided into many opinions and deluded by many fantasies.[72] If human beings
had obeyed God's command from the beginning, then virtue would have naturally flowered in the human heart, and union with God through love would have
been realized. Instead, disobedience brought about a cosmic breach, a series of
divisions between creatures, and between creatures and Creator.[73] Along with
these rifts resulting from human disobedience, the Fall misaligned the human
faculties that were designed to contemplate spiritual realities and lead to union
with God. Because of the Fall, Maximus asserts, the Devil riveted the attention
of these faculties to visible things, so that human beings were preoccupied with
sensible things and acquired no understanding of what lies beyond the senses.
This misuse of free will, leading to deceit and self-absorption, is healed by the
grace of the Holy Spirit.[74] The Spirit breaks the unhealthy attachment of the
faculties to material things and restores them to their original state. Only then
are men and women enabled to move beyond being captivated by visible things,
to search out divine realities, and to fulfill their vocation as human beings.[75]
Moreover, because of humanity's microcosmic and mediatory role in the universe, as composite beings consisting of body and soul (or matter and spirit), the
consequences of the Fall spread through the created order. The disobedience of
man and woman brought about the sentence of death on all nature. Human beings were intended to bring all created things into harmony and union with
God, but now human beings, apart from divine grace, lead created things toward
death. By succumbing to and cooperating with the deceit and trickery of the
Devil, human beings take part in destroying the works of God and dissolving
what has been brought into existence.[76] Finally, through the Fall of man and
woman, the physical mode of human life is changed and marked by pleasure and
pain.[77] Human beings were intended to live eternally, but as we saw above in a
number of texts, they chose temporal, sensible pleasure and introduced pain
into human life, accompanied by a law of death. Death is therefore something
that puts an end to a trajectory outside of the divine purpose for man and

woman. It is the culmination of pain. However, human beings are still created to live, and after the Fall, sexual intercourse is the means to life, something that exemplifies sensual pleasure and that results in birth through pain. Humanity, therefore, finds itself imprisoned by the law of death and the law of pleasure, which govern the end and beginning of physical life. In Maximus's view, through Christ the tyrannical rule of these laws is broken, and human beings are freed to experience new life and to fulfill their created purpose. To this theme of salvation in Christ we now turn.

■ SALVATION

The Incarnation

Thus far our discussion of the interconnected dimensions of Maximus's anthropology has considered: his understanding of a created universe that is good, indwelt by the divine Logos, and destined for union with God; his teaching on the creation of the human person as a unity of body and soul, made in the image and likeness of God; and his interpretation of humanity's Fall from communion with God, resulting in personal and cosmic fragmentation. This brings us to what is most central in Maximus's theological anthropology: the mystery of Christ. In Maximus's theological vision of the universe and human life, Christ is the *axis mundi*, the center around which all things revolve. As John McGuckin asserts, for Maximus the incarnation of Christ is the "high point of all human history . . . the dynamic method and means of the deification of the human race; a spiritual re-creation of human nature that allows individuals the freedom needed to practice virtue, since all humans were formerly enslaved by passions."[78] In this section we will examine Maximus's teaching on the incarnation as the foundation of his soteriology and his anthropology. By looking at a number of important elements in Maximus's reflection on the incarnation, we will see how Christ renews human nature, undoes the effects of the Fall, and enables human beings to experience the grace of deification.

Key to Understanding All Things

The first element of Maximus's teaching on the incarnation that informs his understanding of salvation and human being is found in one of his better-known and evocative philokalic texts. Maximus explains:

> The mystery of the incarnation of the Logos is the key [Τὸ τῆς ἐνσωματώσεως της τοῦ Λόγου μυστήριον] to all the arcane symbolism and typology in the Scriptures, and in addition give us knowledge of created things, both visible and intelligible. [The one] who apprehends the mystery of the cross and the burial apprehends the inward essences of created things; while [the one] who is initiated into the inexpressible power of the resurrection apprehends the purpose for which God first established everything.[79]

The image that Maximus suggests is the incarnation as *the* key that unlocks the secrets of scripture and creation.[80] More specifically, these three christological motifs—the incarnation, crucifixion, and resurrection—provide the hermeneutical key that opens up the deepest meanings of scripture, and the *logoi* and *telos* of creation. As Paul Blowers puts it, according to Maximus's vision of the world and its salvation,

> the incarnation of the Second Person of the Holy Trinity in Jesus of Nazareth holds the secret to the foundations—the architectural *logoi*—of the created cosmos, its destiny after the fall of created beings (the mystery of *redemption*), and the transcendent end [τέλος] of creation (the mystery of deification) wherein the prospect of ever more intimate communion with the Trinity is opened up.[81]

In other philokalic texts, Maximus reiterates this idea of the incarnation as the means to understanding God's salvific purpose and plan for humanity and all of creation. For example, Maximus says that the great counsel of God the Father, the unspoken and unknown mystery of the divine plan, was revealed through the incarnation of the Son. By taking on human flesh, the Son becomes the messenger of the great pre-eternal counsel of the Father, disclosing the divine plan and even enabling others to join him in spreading the knowledge of this message.[82] In another text, Maximus says that the wisdom of God is revealed in Christ's becoming by nature a true man, the justice of God is shown by his assumption of a passible nature identical to ours, and the might of God is demonstrated through the suffering and death of the eternal Logos.[83] Therefore, the knowledge of Christ opens the human mind to perceive God's wisdom, justice, and power, as symbolized in scripture and creation. Experiential knowledge of Christ, the incarnate Logos, is the hermeneutical key that unlatches the hidden storehouses of divine spiritual wisdom and power.

Act of Love

In addition to the incarnation as the ultimate means to understanding God's purpose for human beings and all of creation, is the notion that the enfleshment of the Logos is an act of love. To illustrate, Maximus says that in God's love for humanity, God became man so that through the incarnation human nature would be united to God and prevented from promoting more evil, from being at strife, from further dividing itself, and from having no rest because of the instability of its will and purpose.[84] In a further text, in which Maximus elucidates the law of grace, he says that despite the fact that we were God's enemies because of sin, God loved us so much more than God's very own self that God became man. Although God is beyond every being, explains Maximus, God entered into our being, without changing, and supra-essentially took on human nature, in order to reveal God among human beings as well as pay the penalty of sin which was ours. Consequently, this law of grace, rooted in God's love for wayward humanity and expressed in the incarnation, teaches us how to love others and to be more concerned for them than we are for ourselves.[85] Furthermore, Maximus says that a person's ability to deify her- or himself is correlative with God's becoming man through compassion for humanity's sake.[86] God's saving activity through the mystery of the incarnation is therefore motivated by love and compassion for

God's creatures. This love, as Maximus emphasizes throughout his writings, undergirds God's re-creation of the human race and serves as the clearest example of selfless love that human beings are to follow.

Work of the Trinity

A further aspect of Maximus's teaching on the role of the incarnation in God's plan of salvation concerns the Trinity. In particular, Maximus, along with the other theologians in the *Philokalia*, insists that the incarnation is the cooperative work of the Trinity. Jaroslav Pelikan has underscored the way that Maximus roots his theology in christological and trinitarian thinking, calling it a "Trinitarian-Christocentrism."[87] This overriding theme that pervades his work is seen clearly in his reflection on the trinitarian cooperation that occurs in the incarnation. In the introduction to his exposition of the Lord's Prayer, Maximus says that the prayer includes requests for all that the divine Logos brought about through his self-emptying (*kenosis*) in the incarnation, and the prayer instructs us on how to acquire the blessings that God the Father provides through the mediation of the Son in the Holy Spirit. Weaving these various strands together, Maximus suggests that the Father, Son, and Spirit work together through the incarnate mediation of the Son, bringing about divine revelation, reconciliation, and communion between humanity and God.[88] Later in his exposition, Maximus reiterates that the incarnation is a work of the Trinity. He says that theology (*theologia*), the active participation in the realities of the divine world and the realization of spiritual knowledge,[89] is taught to us by the incarnate Logos of God, since he reveals in himself the Father and the Holy Spirit. "For the whole of the Father and the whole of the Spirit," Maximus states, "were present essentially and perfectly in the whole of the incarnate Son. They themselves did not become incarnate, but the Father approved and the Spirit co-operated when the Son [himself] effected [his] incarnation."[90] This trinitarian portrayal of the incarnation, with all its technical details and emphases,[91] is crucial for Maximus's teaching on the deification of human beings, as we will see below.

Kenosis

In addition to the trinitarian perspective on the incarnation, Maximus speaks regularly of the self-emptying of Christ and its relation to the salvation of humanity. In the text we considered previously, Maximus speaks of the spiritual riches that flow out of Christ's self-emptying in the incarnation. Pondering the counsel of God mentioned in Psalm 33:11, Maximus proposes that perhaps this text speaks prophetically of "the unfathomable self-emptying of the only begotten Son which [God] brought about for the deification of our nature."[92] For Maximus, the kenotic incarnation of the Son has been part of God's eternal plan to renew humanity and all of creation.[93] Toward the end of his meditation on the Lord's Prayer, Maximus urges readers to focus prayerfully on the mystery of deification, "which shows us what we were once like and what the *self-emptying of the only-begotten Son through*

the flesh [οἴους ἡμᾶς ἡ διὰ σαρκὸς κένωσις τοῦ μονογενοῦς ἀπειργάσατο]
has now made us." Maximus argues that this prayerful consideration of the Son's
kenosis and its deifying effects will reveal to us "the depths to which we were
dragged down by the weight of sin, and the heights to which we have been raised
by [his] compassionate hand."[94] Maximus concludes that prayerful contemplation
on the self-emptying of Christ, and the bipolar outlook this cultivates (on humanity's nadir and zenith), engenders greater love for God who prepared and accomplished this salvation for us with such wisdom.

Ongoing Incarnation

Along with Maximus's teaching on the incarnation as the key to understanding all
things, as an act of divine love, as a trinitarian work, and as the self-emptying of
Christ, is the idea that the incarnation continues to occur within believers. In the
First Century of *Various Texts on Theology, the Divine Economy,* and *Virtue and
Vice,* Maximus asserts that the "divine Logos, who once for all was born in the
flesh, always in his compassion desires to be born in spirit [ἀεὶ γεννᾶται θέλων
κατὰ πνεῦμα] in those who desire him."[95] Maximus goes on to explain that the
Logos becomes an infant and forms himself in the believer through the virtues.[96]
The Logos reveals only as much of himself as he knows the believer can accept.
The limited manifestation of his own greatness in each believer is not due to his
lack of generosity, but is based on the receptive capacity of those who long to see
him. "In this way," Maximus continues, "the divine Logos is eternally made manifest in different modes of participation [τοῖς τρόπος τῶν μετοχῶν], and yet
remains eternally invisible to all in virtue of the surpassing nature of his hidden
activity."[97]

In another philokalic text, where Maximus speaks of a balance of dispositions and an inner unity that reflect the holiness of the divine image and likeness, he explains that this is how one participates in the kingdom of God and
becomes a translucent abode of the Holy Spirit. Through grace and free choice,
the believer's soul becomes the dwelling place of Christ: "In souls such as this,
Christ always desires to be born in a mystical way, becoming incarnate in those
who attain salvation."[98] Thunberg argues that Maximus's teaching on Christ's
presence, birth, and embodiment in the virtues demonstrates that human perfection has two sides. First, it includes restoration, integration, unification, and
deification; and second, it includes divine inhabitation in human multiplicity.
This double emphasis is found whenever Maximus reflects on the theme of
Christ's ongoing incarnation in believers and is based on Maximus's late Chalcedonian theology with its emphasis on *communicatio idiomatum* and *perichoresis*
(or the sharing of attributes and the interpenetration of the divine and human
natures in Christ). Thus Maximus understands that the incarnation of the Logos
and the deification of humanity are two sides of the same mystery.[99] In light of
these elements of Maximus's teaching on the centrality of Christ and the mystery of his incarnation in the re-creation of human beings, we turn to his
teaching on deification.

■ **DEIFICATION**

Through Participation in God

Based on his vision of the incarnation of the Word as the key to understanding all things, an act of divine love, a trinitarian work, the Son's *kenosis*, and the ongoing incarnation in believers, Maximus develops his nuanced teaching on deification. Before we examine his interpretation of deification, a few comments are in order. First, as Kallistos Ware demonstrates, the doctrine of deification is the unifying thread that runs through the entire *Philokalia*.[100] Accordingly, this strand is found interwoven through much of Maximus's work. Further, Thunberg argues that Maximus's teaching on deification summarizes his whole theological anthropology.[101] In view of these things, this section explores a number of key features in Maximus's teaching on deification. The first is that deification occurs through participation in God. In a text we examined above, the *Third Century on Love*, Maximus explains that when God created rational beings, they were endowed with four divine attributes: being, eternal being, goodness, and wisdom. The first two were granted to their essence (*ousia*), the second two to their volitive faculty, "so that," Maximus explains, "what [God] is in [God's] essence the creature may become by participation."[102] As Norman Russell states, "By attaining likeness to God 'so far as is possible to humankind,' by participating in the divine attributes through the virtuous exercise of the will, human beings become what God is while still remaining creatures." This exceeds "moral achievement brought about by ascetic endeavor because the mystery of love in which the believer participates is that which has succeeded the law and the prophets—that is, Christ himself."[103] It is important to remember, however, that this divinizing participation signifies union with the divine energies, not the divine essence.[104]

In a further text, a meditation on the spiritual meaning of the seven spirits that rest on the Lord (Is. 11:2), Maximus says that wisdom (the seventh spirit) represents an indivisible union with God. Through this union, the saints attain the actual enjoyment of the things for which they long, and they become god by participation and immersion in the secret flow of God's mysteries.[105] Elsewhere, Maximus speaks to the relationship between deification and creaturely participation in God. He interweaves thematic threads on the soul's salvation as the consummation of faith, the revelation of what one believes, and the interpenetration (περιχώρησις) of the believer with God, who is the object of belief. Through this interpenetration between believer and God, one returns to their origin, which is the fulfillment of human desire and an ever-active repose in God, the object of desire. This repose, which is uninterrupted enjoyment of God, includes participation (μετεχόμεν) in supranatural divine realities, so that the participant becomes like (ὁμοίωσις) that in which she participates. Maximus explains that this likeness involves an identity *with respect to energy* (κατ᾽ ἐνέργειαν) between the participant and that in which she participates on account of the likeness. Maximus asserts, therefore, that this "identity with respect to energy constitutes the deification of the saints."[106]

Maximus also speaks of deification in terms of the believer's assumption into the divine. This occurs through the practice of the virtues, true faith, genuine fear of God, and natural contemplation, which, working together, lead to spiritual ascent into God.[107] This spiritual ascent into God, Maximus explains in his exposition on the Lord's Prayer, occurs as we trust in God, forgive the sins of others, and follow Christ, who leads us upward in love and holy desire. Those who follow Christ, in obedience to the Father's will, are made co-worshipers with the angels, reflecting their God-centered behavior in heaven. Then Christ "leads us up still further on the supreme ascent of divine truth to the Father of lights, and makes us share in the divine nature (cf. 2 Pet. 1:4) through participation by grace in the Holy Spirit" [ἀπ᾽ ἐργαζομένου φύσεως κοινωνοὺς, καὶ θείας ἀ περγαζομένου φύσεως κοινωνους, τῇ κατά χάριν μεθέξει τοῦ Πνεύματοσ].[108] Through this deifying participation in the divine nature, we become children of God, are cleansed from sin, and encircle the Father and Son, who grant us being, movement, and life (cf. Acts 17:28). Thus, as we saw in Maximus's teaching on the incarnation as a cooperative work of the Trinity, here we find the same trinitarian emphasis and structure. Deification, which extends the grace of the incarnation to all believers, is accomplished through participation in the transforming energies of the Spirit, as they are led in the ascent to God and into conformity to the likeness of the Son.

Through the Incarnation of the Word

In addition to deification in terms of participation in God, is Maximus's insistence that deification is made possible through Christ's incarnation. The Logos, Maximus says, descended to the earth and ascended to heaven for our sakes. Through his incarnation, the Logos has attained all that a human being can. The Logos became son of man and human so that he might make humans gods and the children of God. Because of the incarnation of the Logos, Christians are empowered to believe that they will reach the place where Christ is, where he has gone to the Father as a human forerunner, paving the way for others to follow. In the end, as Maximus understands Ps. 82:1 (LXX)—God will stand "in the midst of the congregation of gods"—that is, among those who have been saved and deified through the incarnation of Christ.

Reciprocity

A further aspect of Maximus's teaching on deification that is rooted in Christ's incarnation, concerns the notion of reciprocity. A few particular texts illustrate this. A passage from the *First Century of Various Texts*, mentioned previously, reads:

> A sure warrant for looking forward with hope to the deification of human nature is provided by the incarnation of God, which makes [man and woman] god to the same degree as God himself became man. For it is clear that he who became man without sin (cf. Heb. 4:15) will divinize human nature without changing it into the divine nature [χωρὶς τῆς εἰς θεότητα μεταβολῆς τὴν φύσιν θεοποιήσει],

and will raise it up for his own sake to the same degree as he lowered himself for [humanity's] sake. This is what St. Paul teaches mystically when he says, ". . . that in the ages to come [God] might display the overflowing riches of [divine] grace" (Eph. 2:7).[109]

And in the *Fifth Century of Various Texts*, Maximus states:

> We are told that God and [humans] are exemplars [παραδείγματα] of each other. [Humanity's] ability to deify [themselves] through love for God's sake is correlative with God's becoming man through compassion for [humanity's] sake. And [humanity's] manifestation through the virtues of the God who is by nature invisible is correlative with the degree to which [one's] intellect is seized by God and imbued with spiritual knowledge.[110]

These passages evince the interrelatedness between the incarnation of God and the deification of human beings, between the Logos becoming human so that humans might become divine. This idea of reciprocity between incarnation and deification is rooted in the Greek Fathers, including Athanasius and the Cappadocians, who develop it further.[111] Within these texts, one can hear echoes of Athanasius's axiom—"The Logos became man in order that we should become gods."[112] Moreover, we also find the notion of reciprocity between the divine attributes and the human virtues, in the same way that Christ's incarnation and humanity's deification correspond to each other.[113] This, as we have seen, is reinforced in other passages where Maximus speaks of the continual incarnation of Christ that occurs in the virtues of individual believers:

> The divine Logos, who once for all was born in the flesh, always in his compassion desires to be born in spirit in those who desire him. He becomes an infant and molds himself in them through the virtues.[114]

> The qualities of the virtues and the inner principles of created beings are both images of divine blessings, and in them God continually becomes [human]. As his body he has the qualities of the virtues, and as his soul the inner principles of spiritual knowledge. In this way he deifies those found worthy.[115]

> In souls such as this [those that resemble God by grace and become abodes of the Holy Spirit] Christ always desires to be born in a mystical way, becoming incarnate in those who attain salvation, and making the soul that gives birth to him a virgin mother.[116]

Therefore, in these various texts that convey the aspect of reciprocity between Christ's incarnation and humanity's deification, as well as the divine characteristics and the human virtues, we can make several observations. First, it is the incarnation of God that makes deification possible. Through the union of divine and human nature in Christ, human beings are enabled to participate in the divine nature. Second, Maximus's understanding of Chalcedonian christology informs his teaching on deification. Thus the divine Logos who became human will divinize human nature *without changing* it into the divine nature. Maximus's use of Chalcedonian terms—*asynchtôs, atreptôs, adiaretôs, achoristôs* (no confusion, no change, no division, no separation)—helps him safeguard the integrity of the natural. Louth sees this practice as a thoroughly consistent "Chalcedonian logic" that

Maximus employs as he spells out the way that the hypostatic unity between the divine and human nature in Christ becomes the basis for the deification of woman and man.[117] Likewise, John Meyendorff argues that the "doctrine of deification in Maximus is based upon the fundamental patristic presupposition that communion with God does not diminish or destroy humanity, but makes it fully human."[118] Third, as Christ was born in the flesh, he is also born in spirit, in an ongoing fashion within the life of the believer. As was noted previously, this notion of Christ being formed in the lives of Christians is found in Gal. 4:19. It seems that Maximus is building on this image and working out further details in terms of the doctrine of deification.[119]

Pneumatological and Eschatological Dimensions

In addition to deification through participation in God's energies, which is made possible through Christ's incarnation, is the pneumatological aspect of *theosis*. As the primordial creation and the incarnation of the Logos are trinitarian works, so is deification. The human person is recreated, made a new creation, through the Holy Spirit. In his exposition of the Lord's Prayer, Maximus explains: "The Logos bestows adoption on us when he grants us that birth and deification which, transcending nature, comes by grace from above *through the Spirit*."[120] Within the broader context of this meditation on the Lord's Prayer, Maximus speaks of seven mysteries, with each one corresponding to a different facet of deification.[121] The adoption bestowed by the Logos, which is the second mystery, is brought about by baptism. One is therefore adopted as a child of God by grace through the Spirit. As the text goes on to make clear, this adoption is maintained by the help of God's Spirit as one pursues the moral life through the practice of the commandments. In this gracious work of God through the Spirit, one is enabled to transcend nature, through the self-emptying (*kenosis*) of the passions, and to experience the mystery of deification.

Another text from this meditation on the Lord's Prayer sheds further light on the role of the Spirit in deification. In this text, Maximus says that the Logos leads us up on the ascent to the Father, enabling us to share in the divine nature (2 Pet. 1:4) through participation by grace *in the Holy Spirit*. Because of this participation, Maximus explains, we are called children of God, are cleansed from sin, and worshipfully encircle the God who extends such grace to human beings.[122]

Along with this pneumatological aspect is the *eschatological dimension* of deification which Maximus develops. Russell suggests that Maximus, in a way that resembles Origen and Gregory of Nyssa, portrays the journey toward God as a dynamic *diabasis* without end. Through the moral life one is oriented toward God. And on account of participating in the Holy Spirit through baptism, Christ graces the believer to live in close companionship (συμβίωσις) with him, ultimately taking him or her to the point of sharing in the attributes of the Father. Therefore, in Maximus's perspective, deification is understood as an ascent toward higher levels of unity and ever increasing intimacy with God. In view of our consideration of Maximus's teaching on the Fall, deification may also be understood as a return to our origins. As Maximus explains, the divine likeness that was lost on account of Adam's sin was restored to humanity through the incarnation and holy life of Christ. This divine likeness is recovered by believers through their compan-ionship with Christ and by seeking their destiny in him.[123] However, this is not simply a return to our origins.[124] For Maximus, salvation through Christ's incarna-tion, holy life, and resurrection brings about a new creation, one that encompasses and outstrips the original creation.[125]

A further text speaks to this eschatological dimension of deification. In the *First Century on Theology*, Maximus reflects on the symbolic meaning of the eighth day following the seven days of creation. In one sense, the eighth day signifies the res-urrection of Christ, and in another sense, it represents the blessed, abundant inner life of the mature Christian. The six days in the creation narrative symbolize dif-ferent stages in the ascetic life, culminating on the sixth day with the contempla-tion that discerns the inner principles of all things subject to nature and time. The seventh day signifies the conclusion of the contemplative life, when the believer enters into the rest of God.[126] Maximus proceeds:

> But if [one] is also found worthy of the eighth day [they have] risen from the dead—that is from all that is sequent to God, whether sensible or intelligible, expressible or conceiv-able. [They experience] the blessed life of God, who is the only true life, and [they become] god by deification.[127]

Linked to the eschatological dimension of Maximus's teaching on deification, where the image of returning to God and entering into God's eternal sabbath are found, is his understanding of the Transfiguration of Christ, which leads us to the next point.

A Holistic Process: Body and Soul

As we are seeing, Maximus's teaching on deification has pneumatological and eschatological dimensions. That is, deification or participation in the divine nature is accomplished through the work of the Spirit and is a fulfillment of the spiritual life in Christ, offering a foretaste of the age to come. Consequently, Maximus sug-gests that the Transfiguration of Christ illustrates the way that deification, while not fully realized in this life, offers a preview of the full transformation of believers that will occur in the age to come. Maximus explains that Christ is experienced in two forms. The first, which is more common and popular, is a perception of Christ that is limited to the normal state of his earthly life, in which his "beauty" is not discerned (Isa. 53:2). This is consonant to beginners or *praktikoi*. The second form, which is more hidden and rare, is the perception of Christ in his transfigured glory. Those who become like the apostles Peter and John are the ones who experience the spiritual beauty of Christ as one "fairer than the children of men" (Ps. 45:2). These are the spiritually advanced, the *gnostikoi*.[128] Maximus continues:

> The first is an image of the Lord's initial advent, to which the literal meaning of the Gos-pel refers, and which by means of suffering purifies those practicing the virtues. The second prefigures the second and glorious advent, in which the spirit of the Gospel is apprehended, and by which means wisdom transfigures and deifies those imbued with spiritual knowledge: because of the transfiguration of the Logos within them "they reflect with unveiled face the glory of the Lord" (2 Cor. 3:18).[129]

Those who cultivate the life of virtue with great resolve are inspired by the first advent of the Logos, which cleanses them from impurity. Those who through contemplation have their intellect raised to the angelic state acquire the power of the second advent, which produces dispassion and incorruptibility.[130]

In the latter part of this second century, Maximus reflects on the question of what the state of perfection of the saints in the kingdom of God might be like. Does it involve progress and change or is it a fixed condition? And what will become of the relationship between body and soul? Speaking conjecturally, Maximus suggests a parallel between the development of the body and that of the soul. In the physical development of the human person one takes food first for growth and then for sustenance. Maximus continues:

> In the same way the reason for nourishing the soul is also twofold. While it is advancing along the spiritual path, it is nourished by virtue and contemplation, until it transcends all created things and attains "the measure of the stature of the fullness of Christ" (Eph. 4:13). Once it has entered this state it ceases from all increase and growth nourished by indirect means and is nourished directly, in a manner which passes understanding. Having now completed the stage of growth, the soul receives the kind of incorruptible nourishment which sustains the godlike perfection granted to it, and receives a state of eternal well-being. Then the infinite splendors inherent in this nourishment are revealed to the soul, and it becomes god by participation in divine grace, ceasing from all activity of intellect and sense, and at the same time suspending all the natural operations of the body. For the body is deified along with the soul through its own corresponding participation in the process of deification [καί ἑαυτῇ τὰς τοῦ σώματος συναποπαύσασα φυσικὰς ἐνεργείας, συνθεωθέντος αὐτῇ κατὰ τὴν ἀναλογοῦσαν αὐτῷ μέθεξιν τῆς θεώσεως]. Thus God alone is made manifest through the soul and the body, since their natural properties have been overcome by the superabundance of [God's] glory.[131]

Among other things, this passage further illuminates the eschatological aspect of deification, the perfection of the saints, and the *holistic understanding of deification*. The body and the soul are transformed *together* in the process of deification as illustrated in the Transfiguration of Christ. As Meyendorff has pointed out, deification for Maximus means a participation of the "whole person" in the "whole God."[132] Therefore, the unity of body and soul becomes the vehicle through which the glorious revelation of God shines forth in the world. Moreover, in our consideration of the Fall, we noted that because of humanity's mediatory role in creation, being composed of a soul and a material body, human sin resulted in cosmic divisions. All of creation was affected negatively by human disobedience to God. Conversely, with the coming of enfleshed Logos and his life of obedience that restored what was broken through Adam, the deification of human being means the transfiguration of the wider cosmos. The divinization of woman and man as body and soul corresponds to the deification of the whole creation. The new creation in Christ, brought about by the Father and through the Spirit, encompasses all things.[133]

Grace, Faith, Love

Along with the holistic emphasis in Maximus's teaching on deification is another crucial element: his conviction that deification is the gift of a gracious God, appropriated by faith and most clearly understood in terms of love. This idea is evident in a number of the texts already considered, but here we highlight a few other passages that reinforce these ideas. Maximus asserts that God made human beings so that we might partake of the divine nature (2 Pet. 1:4), share in God's eternity, and become like God (1 Jn. 3:2) through deification by grace. And it is through deification by grace that we are reconstituted.[134] As we have seen at various points, human beings are not by nature able to accomplish their own deification, since they are unable to grasp God. The act of conferring deification on believers is within the power of divine grace alone.[135] In a passage where Maximus discusses the three sets of laws in the world—the law of nature, the written law, and the law of grace—he explains that those who do not spiritually contemplate scripture fail to understand all three laws. Conversely, those who spiritually contemplate scripture, nourish the soul with the virtues, discern the inner principles of created things, and feast the mind on the wisdom of God will understand, rejoice, and hope in the deification given by grace according to the new mystery of grace in Christ.[136] Thus, not only is the process of deification a gift of grace that remains out of reach without divine assistance, but deification cannot even be understood without God's illuminating wisdom into the mystery of grace in Christ. For Maximus, the notion of deification is so permeated with grace that he consistently refers to it as "the grace of deification" ($\tau\grave{\eta}\nu\ \tau\hat{\eta}s\ \theta\epsilon\acute{\omega}\sigma\epsilon\omega s\ \chi\acute{a}\rho\iota\nu$).[137] And through the deification of human nature, God puts on universal display the riches of divine grace for all to behold (Eph. 2:7).[138]

Coupled with this insistent emphasis on deification by grace is the accompanying truth, that one is transformed by the deifying energies of God through faith. In a meditation on the two laws—the law of the flesh and the law of the Spirit (Rom. 7:23)—that are related to the body and soul, Maximus speaks of deification by faith. He explains that the law of the flesh functions according to the senses, while the law of the Spirit functions according to the intellect. By virtue of the senses, the first law automatically attaches one to matter, whereas the second law, by virtue of the intellect, brings about union with God. Therefore, the person who does not doubt in her heart (Mk. 11:23), that is, does not vacillate in her intellect and interrupt the union with God that has been brought about by faith, has already experienced deification through union with God by faith. Empowered through this union with God by faith, she is enabled to displace mountains (Mt. 17:20), which symbolize the will and the law of the flesh. According to our own natural powers, this feat is impossible, but with divine assistance through faith, the law and the flesh are moved and union with God is realized.[139] Moreover, as we saw in Maximus's teaching on the Fall, the first human neglected the divine, divinizing, and immaterial birth by choosing what was immediately attractive to the senses, in preference to the spiritual blessings that were not yet revealed. Because of this preference, humans were condemned to a bodily generation that is without choice, material, and subject to death. Therefore, created man and woman cannot become children of God and god by grace through deification, unless they are first, through their own free choice, begotten in the Spirit by means of the self-loving and independent power that dwells naturally within them.[140] As Thunberg maintains, for Maximus deification is not the fruit of human activity but of God's activity. Human beings can only receive it, voluntarily. The role of the will in this process is understood as a "voluntary outpassing," something that affirms clearly that Maximus underscores the importance of free will. Thus there "is a divine *perichoresis* into those who are holy, but it has its counterpart in a *human consent to the process.* [One] as it were suffers it to happen."[141]

Intrinsically linked to Maximus's understanding of deification as a gift of God's grace that is received by faith is the central role that love plays in the process. In a series of reflections on the excellencies of love and its function in the deification of human beings, Maximus says that love is the consummation ($\tau \acute{\epsilon} \lambda o \varsigma$) of all blessings, since all who walk in love are led toward and united with God, who is the ultimate cause of every blessing. Appropriating the Pauline triad from 1 Cor. 13:8, Maximus explains that faith is the foundation ($\beta \acute{\alpha} \sigma \iota \sigma$) of hope and love, that hope is the strength of the two preeminent gifts of love and faith, and that love is the completion of the other two. He goes on to say that the most perfect work of love and the fulfillment of its activity is to bring about an exchange between those it joins together. Through love, their distinctive characteristics are united and their respective conditions are adapted to each other. "Love makes [humans] god, and reveals and manifests God as [human], through the single and identical purpose and activity of the will of both."[142]Further, stemming from his reflection on the Shema (Deut. 6:5; Lev. 19:18; Mt. 22:37–39), Maximus elucidates why love is supreme among all blessings. It joins God and human beings together, and it makes the Creator of human beings manifest as a human being through their deified likeness to God. This is, in Maximus's estimation, the actualization of the twofold commandment to love the Lord your God with all your heart, soul, and might, and to love your neighbor as yourself.[143] Utilizing the Pauline triad in another text, Maximus stresses again the connection between deification and love, this time in terms of the spiritual ascent. He says that the perfect practice of virtue is produced by faith and reverence for God. And focused natural contemplation as one embarks on the spiritual ascent to God is produced by hope and understanding. Finally, deification through assumption into the divine is produced by perfect love and an intellect that is voluntary blinded, through its transcendent state, to created things.[144]

The Goal of Life

Along with his teaching on the grace of deification through faith and love, Maximus envisions deification as the ultimate goal of human life. In his *Commentary on the Lord's Prayer*, Maximus speaks of deification as the true end for which humanity was created. This, according to Maximus, is not his own personal opinion, but what scripture reveals about the counsel of the Lord (Ps. 33:11). Commenting on the counsel or salvific plan of the Lord, Maximus says:

Perhaps the counsel of God the Father to which David here refers is the unfathomable self-emptying of the only-begotten Son which [God] brought about for the deification [τὴν ἐπι θεώσει] of our nature, and by which [God] has set a limit to the ages.[145]

According to Russell, this passage speaks of deification as the goal for which humanity was created. Moreover, it highlights the notion of the reciprocal relationship between the incarnation of the Word and the deification of humanity. "The kenosis of the divine Son took place in order to bring about the theosis of the human person,"[146] Russell explains. Deification is the *skopos* or salvific goal of the divine counsel, and this is the primary reason for learning the Lord's Prayer and putting it into practice in everyday life. Within the Lord's Prayer, as we saw above, are the seven great new mysteries of the New Dispensation: theology, adoption as children by God's grace, equality with the angels, participation in eternal life, the restoration and unification of human nature, the abolition of the law of sin, and the destruction of the evil one's tyranny. Through appropriating each of these mysteries, believers experience a different aspect of the process of deification. This is what Christians keep before them as they pray the Lord's Prayer: the goal of deification, sharing in the divine nature through participation by grace in the Holy Spirit.[147]

Because deification is the sole true end of human life, the destiny of the ascending journey toward God, to stop short of this end is tragic. In his discussion of this in terms of the intellect that moves incessantly toward God and experiences the pleasure of the soul's marriage with the Logos, Maximus says that to be deprived of this marriage is endless torment.

> Thus when [one] has left the body and all that pertains to it, [one] is impelled towards union with the divine; for even if [one] were to be master of the whole world, [they] would still recognize only one real disaster: failure to attain by grace the deification for which [one] is hoping.[148]

If the failure to reach ever-deeper union with God, which is at the heart of deification, is catastrophic, then attaining deification is the supreme delight, the fulfillment of all desires, and the essence of the kingdom of God.[149] While the sacramental and ecclesial symbolism is not explicit in these (and related) passages from *On the Lord's Prayer*, Russell argues that it is there, albeit in a more implicit fashion.[150] We know, from Maximus's other writings, that baptism and the Eucharist are the primary means of participating in the divine life. Therefore, deification, the ultimate goal of human life, is of course not simply a private affair worked out between individual believers and God. This kind of individualistic thinking and practice (over against a communal perspective) is foreign to Maximus. One place where this process is most clearly seen is in *The Church's Mystagogy*. In this meditation on the mystical meanings of the liturgical and sacramental life of the church, Maximus transplants Evagrian spirituality into an ecclesial context.[151] This is another example of how Maximus seeks to synthesize and refine the ideas of his predecessors (in this case Evagrius and Pseudo-Dionysius),[152] as he reflects on deification as the goal of human life.

■ CONCLUDING REMARKS

The aim of this essay has been to guide readers of the *Philokalia* through some of the major themes in Maximus's theological anthropology. Working our way through a number of Maximus's key texts in the *Philokalia*, we analyzed interconnected aspects of his anthropology, including the cosmological, christological, soteriological, and eschatological dimensions. Informed by leading scholarship on Maximus, we began by considering his teaching on the creation of the cosmos out of nothing, noting Maximus's emphasis on the goodness of the material world created by a sovereign, benevolent God. This provided a cosmological context in which to examine his teaching on the creation of the human person. Accordingly, we looked at Maximus's vision of human being as a unity of body and soul, and as a creature made in the image and likeness of God. Next, we investigated Maximus's interpretation of the Fall of man and woman, from unbroken communion with God to seduction by evil into self-love, resulting in personal and cosmic fragmentation. We then explored Maximus's vision of the salvation of humanity. We saw first that Christ's incarnation—as the key to understanding all things, as an act of divine love, as a trinitarian work, as the Son's *kenosis*, and as an ongoing reality—is the foundation and paradigm for humanity's re-creation. Second, we reflected on elements of Maximus's teaching on *theosis*, including deification through participation in God, through the incarnation of the word, and as a reciprocal dynamic. We also considered its pneumatological and eschatological dimensions, as well as deification as a holistic process, as something based on grace, faith, and love, and as the ultimate goal of life. In line with Maximus's theological vision of human being, we considered these various themes while pondering the question, How are we to become a spiritual world of God, splendid and vast? Along with the other authors in the *Philokalia*, Maximus's teaching on the human person demonstrates that theological reflection and spiritual practice belong together. As we search out the essence of what it means to be human according to Maximus's theological vision, we are challenged to cooperate with divine grace as we are transformed into a glorious world in which the triune God is pleased to dwell.

10 The Ecclesiology of the *Philokalia*

Krastu Banev

> The *Philokalia* is an itinerary through the labyrinth of time, a silent
> way of love and gnosis through the deserts and emptinesses of life,
> especially of modern life, a vivifying and fadeless presence. . . . It must
> be stressed, however, that this spiritual path . . . cannot be followed in
> a vacuum. Although most of the texts in the *Philokalia* are not
> specifically doctrinal, they all presuppose doctrine even when they do
> not state it. Moreover, this doctrine entails ecclesiology. It presupposes
> a particular understanding of the church and a view of salvation
> inextricably bound up with its sacramental and liturgical life.
>   —(*Philokalia*, "Introduction" to the English translation)[1]

A "silent way" but one which cannot be followed "in a vacuum." Philip Sherrard
and Kallistos Ware, now Metropolitan of Diokleia, are emphatic that the ascetic
way presented in the *Philokalia* is at the same time both doctrinal and ecclesial.
The clarification introduced here is also a warning. Even when the texts "do not
state it," they "presuppose" a very particular set of doctrinal beliefs and their ecclesial manifestation. What this refers to is, of course, the dogmatic and liturgical
framework of the Orthodox Church, and in particular the longstanding tradition
of the Holy Mountain, Mount Athos, itself a continuation of the earlier monastic
traditions in Egypt and Palestine. To establish the essential connection between
asceticism, doctrine, and ecclesiology is important because the loss of one of these
three will ultimately lead to a distorted view of salvation. The "silent way," if followed
"in a vacuum," will lead to a dead end. And if the first readers of the *Philokalia*
were not in need of such a warning, readers today, especially those living in "the
deserts and emptinesses" created by individualism and consumerism, certainly do.
For the temptation to take the philokalic message as yet another anti-depressant
tablet is nowhere stronger than in our modern Western society. It is, therefore, in
this modern context that we first observe the need to reflect on the "ecclesiology"
of the *Philokalia*.[2]

The issue that troubles modern ecclesially minded readers of the *Philokalia*
seems to be that of the collection's emphasis on individual spirituality which, so it
appears, undermines the salvific role of the community of believers, the church.
The central tension here is between prayer understood as the liturgical act of the
whole church and the nonliturgical private discipline of prayer. Thus Fr. Alexander Schmemann famously rejected what he called the "refined narcissism" of
those Orthodox people who use quotations from the *Philokalia* in their church
bulletins. He saw the main problem as the "singling out of spirituality as a thing in
itself," and denounced the "spiritual madness" of those Orthodox people who "study

163

spirituality."[3] A little more nuanced is the view of the renowned Greek theologian Christos Yannaras. In a recent Christmas interview for the Russian Christian magazine "КИФА" ("Cephas"), Prof. Yannaras criticized individualist approaches to the *Philokalia*:

> We have in Greece parishes with 90,000 parishioners. These are not a parish. People are more united at a football match than in parishes of this size. In my opinion, this is where the main problem lies. We cannot resolve major theological problems remaining suspended in the air. . . . Do you permit me to be a little provocative? I will ask you a question: Have you ever thought why the *Philokalia* is so popular today in the West? If you read the *Philokalia*, you will see that the church is not mentioned, it is absent. If according to the *Philokalia* the mind is united with the heart, then all is well. You do not need anything else—not the church, not the Eucharist. I do not speak of the patristic texts in the anthology which are deep and important. The problem is with the choices made over the selection of texts. These choices were not made in an ecclesial spirit.[4]

Just as with the rest of Prof. Yannaras's theology, this passage is not to be read as a simple criticism of the "bad" West. It should be read as belonging to the genre of self-criticism: the cited reflection is made in an interview for a Russian Orthodox magazine and deals with current parish life in Greece. This fact demonstrates that Yannaras's criticism of Christians who remain "suspended in the air" is aimed at the Orthodox themselves: first in Greece, then in Russia, and then in the West. In his analysis, what informs both the composition and the reading of the *Philokalia* on its native Orthodox soil is the exclusive, and thus negative, concern for individualistic piety. In another place, the now Metropolitan Kallistos Ware has also criticized some of the abbreviated modern Western editions of the *Philokalia* which concentrate only on the prayer of the heart, as if it were possible to practice it as a spiritual technique in an ecclesiological and doctrinal vacuum.[5] The "Introduction" to the English translation of the *Philokalia* also emphasizes the need to see the collection in the context of the church "bound up with its sacramental and liturgical life." This warning can be viewed as a direct response to the kind of criticisms voiced so characteristically by both Schmemann and Yannaras. For Yannaras, the choices over the selection of texts "were not made in an ecclesial spirit" and St. Nikodimos was the person responsible for this apparent lack of an ecclesiological dimension.[6] Sherrard and Ware's response was that all the texts "presuppose doctrine" which in turn "entails ecclesiology."

To think about the "ecclesiology" of the *Philokalia* is to presume that there are ways of defining the *Philokalia* as a church book. And yet, as Yannaras and Schmemann point out, the *Philokalia* does not have much to offer in terms of ecclesiology: since broadly speaking the focus of the collections is on the prayer of the heart, as practiced by individual Christians, the church per se is seldom mentioned. One can therefore entertain the view that the *Philokalia* offers alternatives to mainstream church-based Christian practice: a sort of gnostic private route for the spiritual specialist, with corresponding special techniques. Nevertheless, in the remainder of this essay I shall oppose the claim that philokalic prayer ignores normal church life or renders church participation unnecessary. My contention will be that the *Philokalia* is a fundamentally ecclesial book. The exposition will follow a division between what can be called the "implicit" and the "explicit" ecclesiology of the *Philokalia*.

∎ IMPLICIT ECCLESIOLOGY

We begin analyzing the implicit ecclesiology of the *Philokalia* with a discussion on the origins of the term, the composition of the collection and the role played by its editors and translators. This demonstration of the ecclesial background of all the stages in the life of the collection will help us to uncover the implicit ecclesiology of the *Philokalia*.

As a patristic term, "*Philokalia*" has a clearly identifiable ecclesial provenance. The literal meaning of the Greek word φιλοκαλία (as well as of the Slavonic "доброτολюбіе") is "love of beauty" or "love of what is good," and thus by extension "love of God," the ultimate source of goodness and beauty. Used of books, φιλοκαλία designates an "anthology of good and beautiful things," and this is precisely the meaning given to it in the fourth century by St. Basil of Caesarea and St. Gregory of Nazianzus for their collection of extracts from Origen's writings.[7] In the eighteenth century, the same title with the same meaning was chosen for the anthology of Greek patristic writings on prayer prepared by St. Makarios of Corinth (1731–1805) and St. Nikodimos of Mt. Athos (1749–1809). Published in Venice in 1782, this new *Philokalia* quickly became the main literary witness to the tradition of personal non-liturgical prayer, known as "prayer of the heart," as it was lived in the Christian East. With the almost simultaneous translation into Slavonic and then modern Russian, the new *Philokalia* spread across the vast expanse of Russian Orthodoxy. It was with a copy of this *Philokalia* in his bag that the pilgrim of *The Way of a Pilgrim* crossed imperial Russia (including, at that time, Poland and the Ukraine) living as a stranger and devoting his whole time to prayer.[8] The story of the pilgrim, however, is also the story of the continuous growth of the philokalic tradition. Its popularity in nineteenth-century Russia was immense. In the twentieth century it was translated into all the major European languages becoming, in the estimation of one of its English translators, "the most significant Greek Orthodox book to appear during the whole of the four centuries of the Tourkokratia."[9] Both St. Makarios and St. Nikodimos were practicing members of the Orthodox Church, strong advocates of frequent communion in line with the program of the Kollyvades movement.[10] Their lives were spent under the spiritual care of the Ecumenical patriarchate, which eventually numbered them among the saints. The "ecclesiology of the editors," if we are permitted to use the phrase, cannot be questioned. Their intention, as the title page of the first edition states, was to offer their work for the benefit of the entire community of Orthodox faithful (εἰς κοινὴν τῶν ὀρθοδόξων ὀφέλειαν), an expression which signifies the fullness of the church including both ordained and lay people as well as the monastics. The emphasis of the collection as a whole is on prayer as a universal Christian vocation. Among the selected authors, not all but still a significant number were ordained clergy, including both monk-priests and bishops. All these elements implicitly suggest that the *Philokalia* was a clearly ecclesial undertaking.

But more than just a church-run project to gather church-related materials, the *Philokalia* was also conceived as having a very particular ecclesial purpose. It was intended, as St. Nikodimos tells us in his "Introduction," to help *practicing* Orthodox Christians to arrive at a fuller understanding of the meaning of their church observances. The majority of his fellow Christians, St. Nikodimos lamented, "are troubled about many things: about bodily and active virtues, or, to speak more truly, exclusively about the tools for securing the virtues; and they neglect the one thing needed, keeping guard over the intellect and pure prayer."[11] In his "Introduction," St. Nikodimos reminds his readers that the purpose of all Christian life is "deification," which is infinitely greater and more exciting than just the keeping of church observances. Humanity is called to contemplation and union with God by grace, something which escapes verbal expression and is solely a matter of living experience. Those who understand will understand, repeatedly add the saintly authors in the *Philokalia*, clarifying that, if you are still lacking understanding, pure prayer and your cell will teach you! Thus the entire collection was seen by Nikodimos as an aid to rediscovering the true meaning of the church rites (fasting, liturgical prayer, charity) by rekindling the grace received in baptism. The work is to be undertaken by each Christian individually and is defined as the "inner action" or "inner work" (the usual Greek and Slavonic terms are ἐσωτερική ἐργασία, внутреннее делание). This inner work takes place within what the Apostle Paul had defined as "the inner man" or "the inner self" (Rom. 7:22; 2 Cor. 4:16; Eph. 3:16). St. Luke's Gospel announced that "The kingdom of God is within you" (Lk.17:21), and in keeping with this proclamation St. Nikodimos sees the purpose of the *Philokalia* in offering guidance to practicing Christians on how to come yet closer to Christ the King, who through baptism abides in the "kingdom" of their hearts. The individual sanctification advocated by the *Philokalia* does not exclude the church, for it presupposes, first, baptism, and then all other church sacraments and observances.

These observances, however, when understood philokalically, are not simply matters of individual Christian duty, but steps on the ladder that reaches up to the gates of the Kingdom, a ladder of heavenly joy. Thus the fifth-century bishop and theologian Diadochos of Photiki speaks of the two types of Christian joy:

> Initiatory joy is one thing and the joy of perfection is another. The first is not exempt from fantasy while the second has the strength of humility. Between the two joys comes a "godly sorrow" (2 Cor. 7:10) and active tears.[12]

The second stage of active tears "between the two joys" comes when the first inspiration and the initial power of baptismal grace diminish and the strength of true humility is not yet in sight. It is precisely at this stage that the *Philokalia* is particularly effective. This more profound ecclesiological role of the *Philokalia* presupposes a complex anthropological and theological awareness. It presupposes not only the reception of baptism in the church, but also the acceptance of the ecclesial vision of deified humanity, particular to the Eastern Christian tradition. There is thus a deep doctrinal level which implicitly supports the whole philokalic endeavor. This doctrinal level is connected with the tradition, which maintains that the Christian God is both beyond and yet near, both the inaccessible Creator *and* the Sustainer of life whose embrace everyone can feel. This distinction between the divine nature (inaccessible) and the divine energies (accessible) was made explicit in the Hesychast controversy. What this amounted to was nothing short of a revolution of religious thought, for it postulated that humanity's relationship with God is a matter not of "obligation and moral duty" but of "participation in divine life": Christianity is not a "religion" but a "mystagogy." When St. Nikodimos objected to his contemporaries' limited understanding of what their life in church was about, he was keen to stress that ecclesial observances are not simply a matter of Christian obligation or duty. Rather, they are the means to achieving the desired union with God, or deification. But to speak of deification and to remain a Christian monotheist is possible only if one's beliefs are in harmony with the doctrinal tradition of the Fathers of the Eastern church, from the great Cappadocians to St. Gregory Palamas.[13] Like modern chemical pencils that work on only the correct type of paper, the ascetical way of the *Philokalia* is visible only against the solid doctrinal ground of the Eastern Orthodox church.

At this juncture we arrive at the requirement for quite specific spiritual training. Does the above mean that the *Philokalia* should not be offered to the general reader since the required anthropological and theological awareness is not present in all people at all times? When faced with this problem, the original compilers and translators of the anthology held two different opinions: St. Makarios and St. Nikodimos decided in favor of the average Greek-speaking Christian; the translator into Slavonic, St. Paisy Velichkovsky, decided against this saying that the book is suitable only for a monastic readership.[14] St. Paisy's restraint was governed by his belief that the advice found in the *Philokalia* should always be measured against the advice of a spiritual father (and seekers of such advice are found mainly among the monastics). St. Paisy's opinion was based on his long experience as a spiritual child and then a spiritual father both in Moldavia and on Mt. Athos. There he had learned that spiritual advice, just like medicine, cannot be given in abstraction: every case is individual and has to be decided in consultation with one's spiritual father (doctor). It is said that it was only under strong pressure, from the then metropolitan of St. Petersburg, that St. Paisy agreed to bring his translations into the light of day, in print.

On the Greek side things were different. St. Nikodimos tells us in his prologue that he is aware of the danger but is convinced that it presents no major obstacle:

> Even if occasionally some people go slightly astray, what is surprising in that? For the most part this happens to them because of their conceit. . . . But, trusting rather in Him who said, "I am the way and the truth" (Jn. 14:6), let us embark on the task [of inner prayer] with all humility and in a spirit of mourning. For, if a person is free from conceit and the desire to please others, even though the whole evil host of demons attacks him, yet they cannot approach him. . . . Draw near, all of you who share the Orthodox calling, laity and monks alike, who are eager to discover the kingdom of God that is within you, the treasure hidden in the field of the heart [cf. Mt. 13:44], which is the sweet Lord Jesus.[15]

Thus St. Nikodimos insists that the *Philokalia* is to be offered to the general public. But this proposal in itself does not resolve the issue raised by St. Paisy. If the

Philokalia is to be read "in the world" and not just in monasteries, who is going to fill the place of the spiritual father for the people in the world? St. Nikodimos does not give a direct answer to this question. The answer that suggests itself as a result of the discussion so far is that the spiritual director of the general reader is the church herself. By participating in the life of the church, in its sacraments, services, and works of charity, every Christian is given all the instruction needed, if only they are prepared to receive it. The strength and importance of this personal link with the church is visible above all in the life of St. Nikodimos, whose devotion to the church is exemplary. Among his many writings—he has been called "An encyclopaedia of Athonite learning"—a very large and yet for the most part still unpublished section is comprised of liturgical songs, offices for saints and for the Mother of God. This in fact is the only original contribution he has made, given the fact that the rest of his work (including the *Philokalia*) consists mainly of translations and commentaries. Thus, as is demonstrated in the case of its editor, the *Philokalia* does not exclude the church from its vision but, on the contrary, fully supports it.[16]

With this conclusion the implicit ecclesiology of the *Philokalia* acquires a very important role. The collection is not just a church enterprise for practcsing church members. Its medicinal quality is fully effective only in the church, as the church safeguards the integrity and vitality of the medicine. Finally, it is the church that assumes the role of spiritual guide for the nonmonastic readers of the *Philokalia*.

▪ EXPLICIT ECCLESIOLOGY

We have so far been engaged with assembling the evidence for what was called the "implicit" ecclesiology of the *Philokalia*. It is now time to show that the *Philokalia* does talk overtly about the church, and that in fact it has quite a lot to say on the subject. When we find explicit references to the church, these are concerned mainly with: (a) doctrinal formulations, services, and singing, (b) fasting, charity, and hospitality, and (c) the sacraments (baptism, Eucharist, confession, and ordination). Often these three pools of references are neglected when generalizations on the (lacking or only presupposed) ecclesiology of the *Philokalia* are made. Thus one way of reading our title—"The Ecclesiology of the *Philokalia*"—is to think that once the direct references to the church celebrations and observances are brought to light, the fundamental ecclesial character of the *Philokalia* will become plain and obvious to all. With this aim in view, we will analyze the explicit references to the church in the *Philokalia*.

1. Church Doctrine and Church Services

An important ascetical principle guides the resoluteness of the philokalic authors as to why Christians are to accept wholeheartedly the doctrinal formulations of the church. The *Discourse on Abba Philimon* (one of the Egyptian desert fathers, fourth to fifth century) contains the following lapidary advice: "Recite the holy Creed of the Orthodox faith before you fall asleep. For true belief in God is the source and guard of all blessings."[17] St. Peter of Damaskos (eleventh to twelfth century) was also emphatic that one should readily accept the teachings of the church. He thus argued that true spiritual safety comes from following the mind of the whole community of faith, the church:

> It is on this account that with firm faith and by questioning those with experience we should accept the doctrines of the Church and the decisions of its teachers, both concerning the Holy Scriptures and concerning the sensible and spiritual worlds. Otherwise we may quickly fall because we walk according to our own understanding.[18]

The ascetical principle behind the strong views expressed by Abba Philimon and Peter of Damaskos is that to follow one's own mind is intrinsically wrong for the monk. This principle is made explicit in the monastic spirituality of the Christian East, going back to the home of Abba Philimon, the Egyptian desert. Outside of the *Philokalia*, one does not need to look further than the "Introduction" to the alphabetical collection of the *Apophthegmata* to discover that in the understanding of its monastic editors the calling of the monk was above all one of rejection of personal opinion in the spirit of obedience to the teaching of the fathers.[19] In the passage quoted above, this obedience is also ecclesiological: it entails acceptance of the "doctrines of the Church."

After church doctrine, the *Philokalia* addresses also practical questions related to the performance of the church services and to singing in church. For the sake of bringing to light the explicit ecclesiology of the *Philokalia,* we will need a few extensive quotations. Again, the *Discourse on Abba Philimon* offers some very good examples:

> Say the daily prayers laid down by the holy fathers. By this I mean, try to recite the Third, Sixth, and Ninth Hours, Vespers and the night services. Strive to keep your mind undistracted, always being attentive to your inner thoughts. When you are in church, and are going to partake of the divine mysteries of Christ, do not go out until you have attained complete peace. Stand in one place, and do not leave it until the dismissal. Think that you are standing in heaven, and that in the company of the holy angels you are meeting God and receiving Him in your heart.[20]

> When the good brother heard this, his soul was wounded by divine longing; and he and Abba Philimon went to live in Sketis where the greatest of the holy fathers had pursued the path of sanctity. They settled in the Lavra of St. John the Small. . . . And by the grace of God they lived in complete stillness, unfailingly attending church on Saturdays and Sundays but on the other days of the week staying in their cells, praying and fulfilling their rule.
>
> The rule of the holy Elder (Philimon) was as follows. During the night he quietly chanted the entire Psalter and the Biblical canticles, and recited part of the Gospels. Then he sat down and intently repeated "Lord have mercy" for as long as he could. After that he slept, rising towards dawn to chant the First Hour. Then he again sat down, facing eastward, and alternately chanted psalms and recited by heart sections of the Epistles and Gospels. He spent the whole day in this manner, chanting and praying unceasingly. . . . His intellect was often lifted up to contemplation, and he did not know if he was still on earth.[21]

These quotations speak for themselves, and their ecclesiology is obvious: one is not to understand the spiritual message of the *Philokalia* without the church, without

its patterns of regular daily worship, the reading of Scripture, the chants and the oft-
repeated prayer "Lord have mercy," In the context of the monastic tradition of the
desert, we can safely infer that the Eucharist is also included as part of Elder Philimon's
rule of "unfailingly attending church on Saturdays and Sundays."

On the subject of singing church hymns, Peter of Damaskos is perhaps the best
person to turn to. Let us be reminded that he is one of the principal authors in the
collection, whose texts fill up the largest section, and yet he does not talk about the
Jesus Prayer. So the emphasis on church hymns is even more important here. He is
the only writer who quotes complete sections of the Greek Orthodox hymn books.
He weaves seamlessly into his discourses "On contemplation" whole passages from
the services for Holy Week, Matins for the major feasts, Vespers and Matins for the
eight tones of the week, and Compline. Here are a few illustrations:

> O virgin-born, do not cast me away, harlot though I am; do not spurn my tears, O joy of
> the angels; but receive me in my repentance O Lord, and in Thy great mercy do not reject
> me a sinner.[22]

> Have mercy on my brethren and fathers, on all monks and priests everywhere, on my
> parents, my brothers and sisters, my relatives, on those who have served us and those
> who serve us now [the officiating priests], on those who pray for us and who have asked
> us to pray for them, on those who hate us and those who love us, on those whom I have
> injured or offended, on those who have injured or offended me or who will do so in the
> future, and on all who trust in Thee. Forgive us every sin whether deliberate or uninten-
> tional. Protect our lives and our departure out of this world from impure spirits, from
> every temptation, from all sin and malice, from presumption and despair, from lack of
> faith . . ., Give rest to our fathers and brethren who have departed this life before us, and
> through the prayers of them all have mercy on my unhappy self in my depravity. See
> how feeble I am in all things: rectify my conduct, direct my life and death into the paths
> of peace, fashion me into what Thou wilt . . .,

> Give peace to Thy world, and in ways best known to Thee have mercy on all. Count me
> worthy to partake of Thy pure body and Thy precious blood, for the remission of sins,
> for communion in the holy spirit, as a foretaste of eternal life in Thee with Thine elect,
> through the intercessions of Thy most pure Mother, of the angels and the celestial
> powers, and of all Thy saints; for Thou art blessed through all the ages. Amen

> Most holy Lady, Mother of God, all celestial powers, holy angels and archangels, and all
> saints, intercede for me a sinner. God our Master, Father almighty, Lord Jesus Christ, the
> Only-begotten Son and Holy Sprit, one Godhead, one Power, have mercy on me a
> sinner.[23]

> After praying in this way you should immediately address your own thoughts and
> say three times: "O come, let us worship and fall down before God our King." Then you
> should begin the psalms reciting the *Trisagion* after each subsection of the Psalter,[24] and
> enclosing your intellect within the words you are saying.

Peter of Damaskos is here praying with the prayers of the church—*mot à mot*—
they have become *his* prayers. His is a prayer for the whole world, and then for "my

unhappy self," preparation for the reception of Holy Communion is after the petition "Give peace to Thy world, and in ways best known to Thee have mercy on all." The way Peter of Damaskos's quotations are interwoven with the rest of his inspired exhortations suggests that he is quoting from memory, very much as happens with Scriptural quotations throughout the *Philokalia*. It is the subject of another dissertation to examine how the Word of God had become the native language of the fathers in the *Philokalia*. But with Peter of Damaskos we have a striking, and to my knowledge unique, example of the words of the church becoming the language of personal prayer.

2. Church Fasts and Social Outreach

On the question of church fasts and social outreach, our next witness is St. Symeon the New Theologian (949–1022).[25] "The New Theologian" was originally an ironic nickname given to him by the opponents of his devotion to his spiritual father, St. Symeon the Pious. The philokalic tradition has, however, accepted the name and confirmed the spiritual greatness of the New Theologian. He is remembered especially for his unforgiving attitude to spiritual indolence. This is displayed in the following characteristic injunctions: "Never go to communion without tears."[26] "Take care never to receive communion while you have anything against anyone, even if this is only a hostile thought."[27] "You should arrive first at the church services, especially matins and the Liturgy, and leave last, unless forced to do otherwise."[28] The original Greek *Philokalia* contains only a small section from his writings, the *Practical and Theological Texts*. For our purpose, of interest are those passages in which St. Symeon gives us information on the ecclesial observances of his day. We begin with a citation on the fasting periods:

> You should observe the great Lenten fast by eating every third day (not counting Saturdays and Sundays), unless there is a major feast. During the other two main fasts— before Christmas and before the Feast of the Dormition—you should eat every other day. On the remaining days of the year you should eat only once, except on Saturdays and Sundays and on feast days, but do not eat to repletion.[29]

Symeon was clearly a zealous advocate of strict monasticism. Nevertheless, his strictness did not prevent him from knowing how to be a good guest—"you should eat what is put in front of you, no matter what it is, and take wine with uncomplaining self-restraint"[30]—and how to relate positively to the rest of God's created world:

> Visit the sick, console the distressed, and do not make your longing for prayer a pretext for turning away from anyone who asks for your help; for love is greater than prayer. Show sympathy towards all, do not be arrogant or over-familiar, do not find fault with others, or ask for anything from the abbot. . . . be respectful towards all priests, attentive in prayer, frank and loving towards everyone. . . .[31]

We note here the emphasis on including the church: "all priests" and so by implication their flocks. Symeon moreover affirms that the desire for prayer should never be used as an excuse to sever contact with those who are in need for, in his memorable phrase, "love is greater than prayer." In another place Symeon develops his idea even further, declaring that "We, the faithful, should look upon all the faithful as one single being, and should consider that Christ dwells in each of them. We should have such love for each of them that we are willing to lay down our lives for him."[32] The reason given for this command of universal love is that Christ dwells in each believer. From here, in Symeon's view, comes the assurance of the church's entry into God's Kingdom. The gift of the Holy Spirit, on the other hand, is received by the church on earth as a pledge of the eternal heavenly blessings to come:

> The Church—the bride-to-be composed of all the faithful—and the soul of each of us receive from Christ, the bridegroom-to-be, only the pledge of the Sprit. The eternal blessings and the kingdom of heaven are given subsequent to this earthly life, though both the Church and the individual soul have the assurance of them through the pledge they have received.[33]

Here the ecclesiology is very clear; it even includes one of the rare definitions of the church in the *Philokalia*. In St. Symeon's characteristic words, the church is the bride-to-be of Christ composed of "all the faithful" and, simultaneously, of "the soul of each" individual. The soul is thus presented as a microcosm of the church.[34] As a corollary to this parallel definition we can affirm that the perfection of the soul, aimed at by St. Symeon and the other philokalic authors, is at the same time a perfection of the church. Thus there can be no real opposition between the *Philokalia* and the church. Ultimately, they both strive for the same eternal blessings: union with Christ, the Bridegroom, in the gift of the Spirit.

3. Sacraments and Celebration of the Eucharist

In the philokalic vision, the union with Christ in the *eschaton* includes a foretaste of the blessings in the present: this foretaste is to be found in the sacrifice of the Eucharist and in the other celebrations of the church. St. Symeon the New Theologian gives us the following in relation to the Eucharist and ordination:

> A certain priest-monk, who had full confidence in me as his friend, once told me this: "I have never celebrated the Liturgy without seeing the Holy Spirit, just as I saw Him come upon me when I was ordained and the metropolitan said the prayer while the service-book rested on my head." When I asked him how he saw it at that time, and in what form, he said: "Undifferentiated and without form, except as light. At first I was astonished, beholding what I had never beheld before; and as I was asking myself what it might be, the light said to me, its voice heard only by the intellect: 'Thus have I appeared to all the prophets and apostles, and to those who are now the saints and the elect of God; for I am the Holy Spirit of God.' To him be glory and power to the ages. Amen."[35]

When discussing the celebration of the Eucharist, for example, the *Philokalia* lays emphasis simultaneously on the personal sanctity/repentance of the celebrant and on the greatness of the mystery which is celebrated. In other words, church life requires inner holiness, the fruit of philokalic striving and wisdom: it is not that either precludes the need for the other, but rather that the two things go together, each depending on the other. Let us consider two examples from St. Theognostos. In an important passage devoted to the daily celebration of the Eucharist he says:

> Remember that you look daily on the salvation of God which, when he saw it but once, so terrified and amazed Symeon the Elder that he prayed for his deliverance (cf. Luke 2:29). If you have not been assured by the Holy Spirit that you are equal to the angels and so an acceptable intermediary between God and humanity, do not presumptuously dare to celebrate the awesome and most holy mysteries, which even the angels venerate and from whose purity many of the saints themselves have in reverent fear drawn back. Otherwise you will be destroyed because of your pretense to holiness.[36]

St Theognostos's advice on the importance of personal sanctity for those actively involved in the ecclesial celebrations is later repeated in the form of a story:

> There was once a monk-priest who had a reputation for piety and was held in honour by many on account of his outward behaviour, though within he was licentious and defiled. One day he was celebrating the divine Liturgy and, on reaching the cherubic hymn, he had bent his head as usual before the holy table and was reading the prayer, "No one is worthy . . .," when he suddenly died, his soul having left him in that position.[37]

Thus, contrary to certain standard generalizations, the *Philokalia* does talk overtly about the church and, in fact, has quite a lot to say on the subject. The unambiguous and direct references to the church demonstrate that the *Philokalia* has a well-defined ecclesial character. Its ecclesiology is not just presupposed, or implicit, but on the contrary, also quite explicit. This explicit ecclesiology, however, has its own distinct characteristics. The quotations from St. Theognostos give us the general flavor quite well. The sound is one of warning. Thus we hear St. Symeon the New Theologian give the following lapidary advice: "Do not pull down your own house because you want to build a house for your neighbor."[38] Taken in the context of the monastic life of prayer, this simple remark reveals a great deal about how the philokalic authors approached both life in general, and life in the church in particular. When the *Philokalia* does talk about the church, the message is always one of caution: unless the spiritual powers of Christians are well ordered, their external church observances are of no effect.

▪ CONCLUSION

We have now demonstrated the implicit and explicit ecclesiology of the *Philokalia*. We have shown, first, that the *Philokalia* presupposes the church, because the authors it includes are church people and saints, because the compilers and first translators are church people and saints, and because it is addressed to practicing church people who, it is hoped, are also on the way to sainthood. And, second, that the *Philokalia* does talk frankly and overtly about the church, directly mentioning church creedal formulations, the daily liturgical office, the sacraments, the singing of church hymns, charity, hospitality, and love. Thus we can conclude that the dichotomy between the *Philokalia* and the church is a false one: there is no contrast. Inner prayer and church participation are both necessary expressions of the same attention to God.

But if the ecclesiology of the *Philokalia* is so obvious, why the question at all? The apparent contrast has emerged from a misuse of the collection especially in the twentieth and the twenty-first century with the rise of economic consumerism and its parallel methods for individual spiritual satisfaction. The overwhelming corrective for this impression is the implicit one discussed in the first part of the exposition. The whole background, genesis, conception, execution, and intention, as well as the translations of the *Philokalia* are patently ecclesial. Even though the collection may appear to be offering or advocating something newer or better, a superior spirituality, it is only in the sense of self–criticism which is always part of the church's fundamental mission. The *Philokalia* is part of the internal movement for renewal which the church must always have if it is to be the church. The *Philokalia* is thus a clue to the inner meaning of church observances, as St. Nikodimos wrote; but it is not a replacement for them. It advocates neither a breakaway movement, nor a quietist elite. The explicit endorsements of ecclesial life and participation, on which we focused in the second part of the exposition, are the result of the implicit allegiance: a book so rooted in the ecclesial life and project of the church cannot but, sooner or later, evince signs of its fundamental source and orientation. The explicit section is therefore, in a sense, only an assemblage of internal evidence for and illustrations of the implicit arguments. The *Philokalia* is thus a fundamentally ecclesial book. It is a manual to sanctity and a door to salvation; one of the many that lead to the treasures of God's house, the church.

The short Life of Maximos of Kafsokalyvia, hermit on the Holy Mountain, provides a fitting conclusion to our exploration illustrating the point that pure prayer, the central concern of the whole *Philokalia*, is one of the gifts treasured and transmitted in the church. In a conversation with St. Gregory of Sinai (1255–1346), St. Maximos described how he had received the gift of pure unceasing prayer while venerating—in church—an icon of the Mother of God:

> From my youth, I had great faith in my Lady the Mother of God and I often prayed to her with tears asking her to give me the grace of pure prayer. One day, when I had gone, as my custom was, into the church, I repeated my prayer to her with all the warmth of my heart. Then, when I lovingly kissed her holy icon, I felt in my chest and in my heart a strange warmth, like a flame which came from the icon, and which did not burn, but which covered me like a dew. . . . From that moment on, dear Father, my heart began to say the prayer within itself, and my mind delights in the sweetness of remembering Jesus continually. . . . Since then, the prayer has continued without interruption in my heart.[39]

11 Evagrius in the *Philokalia* of Sts. Macarius and Nicodemus

Julia Konstantinovsky

Recent new studies and translations of Evagrius Ponticus (ca. 345–99) have been prolific, and the research into the somewhat puzzling "Evagrian phenomenon" is clearly ascending.[1] One aspect of Evagrius's legacy in need of elucidation is the significance of his presence in the intricate "spiritual classic,"[2] the 1782 *Philokalia of the Holy Neptic Fathers* (Ἡ Φιλοκαλία τῶν ἱεροων νηπτικῶν) of Sts. Macarius and Nicodemus. Why is an inquiry into the philokalic *Evagriana* desirable? In addition to further clarifying nuances of Evagrius's "Greek" legacy, an evaluation of his presence within the "philokalic" context will clearly yield a new insight into the mindset of the editors regarding the "flow," continuity, and diachronic interaction between ideas within the ascetic Christianity in the East: from its late-ancient Egyptian roots, through to the early-Medieval ascetic constructions within Constantinople, Syria, and Palestine, to the late-fourteenth-century Byzantine asceticism of St. Gregory Palamas, to final culmination in the eighteenth-century Greek spiritual revival under "Turcocratia," for the sake of which the *Philokalia* project arose. Consequently, an analysis of Evagrius's contribution to the collection goes a considerable way toward establishing a more general conceptual framework for an evaluation of the entire 1782 *Philokalia* project itself, so that the following key issues may be clarified:

- If Evagrius is *essential* to the philokalic project, what is the *essence* of the *Philokalia* itself, the elusive "philokalic *spirit*"?
- A connected issue concerns the editors' rationale behind "assembling" the collection: why include these specific Greek ascetic works while excluding others, no less seminal and classic? Why represent Evagrius by specifically the four (or even three) works that made it into the collection and not others?
- A further related question regards the nature of the conceptual links between Evagrius and other authors within the anthology: did the assumed connection act as a possible selection criterion for the entire anthology?
- Finally, are we to view the *Philokalia* as "closed" or open-ended, that is, to what extent is the *Philokalia* "a thing in itself"? In this respect, how are we to use it today?

■ EVAGRIUS'S PLACE IN THE *PHILOKALIA*: ESTABLISHING THE PARAMETERS

The original 1782 edition of the *Philokalia* of Sts. Macarius and Nicodemus contains four works by Evagrius in the original Greek: three under Evagrius's own name and one, *The Chapters on Prayer: 153 Texts*, under that of the fifth-century spiritual director St. Neilus of Ancyra—a common attribution throughout the Middle Ages.[3] The following Evagrian works are listed as those by Evagrius himself: *Outline Teaching on Asceticism and Stillness in the Solitary Life*; *Texts on Discrimination in respect of Passions and Thoughts*; *Extracts from the Texts on Watchfulness*.

Chronologically ordered, the philokalic collection dates from the great fourth-century Egyptian masters all the way to the expounders of the fifteenth-century hesychasm.

Within this sequence, Evagrius occupies a place of prominence. He is third in the list of the thirty-six "contributors" making up the collection: following (Pseudo-)Anthony's treatise *On the Character of Men and on the Virtuous Life* and St. Isaiah the Solitary's *On Guarding the Intellect*. The collection could actually legitimately *open* with Evagrius, since we now know what the editors did not: that the attribution of the first treatise to St. Anthony is spurious, while the second work, by Abba Isaiah, should probably be moved further up the time-line, somewhere to the early fifth century.[4] However, even placed third, Evagrius in the *Philokalia* immediately strikes us as someone enjoying an especially honorific status.

First, within the collection he is both one of the "earliest" and part of an ascetic tradition that is the "earliest" and archetypal: the tradition of the Desert Fathers. In terms of its ideals of the solitary life of *apatheia* and *virtue* and encompassing legendary figures of the likes of St. Anthony the Great and St. Macarius of Alexandria, fourth-century Egypt remained foundational and formative to subsequent Christian ages—an opinion that the editors of the philokalic collection evidently strongly upheld. While preserving a variety of the ascetic practices—the ascetic life in the village, the eremitic, semi-eremitic, and cenobytic ways of life, some of which were strikingly harsh—Egyptian monasticism in itself was never regarded as being on the margins of orthodoxy. On the contrary, ancient sources about Egypt consistently represent it as being generally normative, in terms of both ascetic practice and doctrinal "orthodoxy."[5] These sources, to which Egyptian asceticism gave rise, themselves enjoyed a quasi-"best-seller" status of normative orthodoxy. Notable among them are the *Apophthegmata Patrum*, the *Historia Lausiaca*, and numerous other *historiae monachorum* and travel accounts.[6]

Second, Evagrius's place of honor within the collection is based upon his biographical connection with the great undisputed lights of orthodoxy: the three "Cappadocian" theologians, especially Basil the Great and Gregory the Theologian. According to the original introduction to the philokalic works of Evagrius, which was composed by St. Nicodemus of the Holy Mountain, Evagrius was something of a "younger Cappadocian": he enjoyed a quasi-familial connection with Basil and Gregory, having been ordained reader by the former and deacon by the latter. The connection places Evagrius within the illustrious holy company of saints and teachers of the church, guaranteeing his own impeccability. Yet, historically Evagrius's ties with the Cappadocian theologians are easily deconstructible: the commonness of life, purpose, and theological vision between Evagrius and his teachers becomes disrupted around the year 382. Evagrius's post-Constantinople I writings, notably *The Gnostic Chapters* and *the Great Letter* (=the *Letter to Melania*) are strikingly novel and un-"Cappadocian" in terms of their Christology, cosmology, and anthropology.

The key question arising at this point is this: what was the editors' reason for the inclusion of precisely these Evagrius texts, leaving out the rest of his voluminous *oeuvre*? This *aporeia* is subsumed within a more general one: what was the editors' overall rationale for the inclusion and exclusion of texts within the *Philokalia*?

■ EVAGRIUS'S "PHILOKALIC" WORKS AND THEIR MANUSCRIPT SOURCES

Looking at the manuscript sources for Evagrius's and other texts within the collection is germane to this key question. Once this task is completed, it will then be imperative to assess the internal content of the philokalic *Evagriana*.

The discrepancy in the textual attribution, signaled above, with only three of Evagrius's philokalic text—*Outline Teaching on Asceticism and Stillness in the Solitary Life*, *Texts on Discrimination in Respect of Passions and Thoughts*, and *Extracts from the Texts on Watchfulness*—attributed to him, and the *Chapters on Prayer* erroneously placed within the *oeuvre* of St. Neilus, is telling. It is informative with regard to the level of the editors' awareness of the histories behind the texts and personalities they engaged with, as well as the amount of time and scholarship they were able to put into the editing of their collection. In fact neither appears to have been extensive. The individual texts that were gathered eventually to form the 1782 *Philokalia* were not entirely the choice of the editors themselves. Neither were Sts. Macarius and Nicodemus, in their task of bringing the collection together, concerned with in-depth philological or even theological assessment of the texts that came to be included in the collection. In picking their authors and texts, the editors were to a considerable extent conditioned by the source manuscripts at hand. Thus the nature of their attribution of Evagrius's texts reflects the fact that the first three texts came from a manuscript source different from that of the *Chapters on Prayer*. As first discovered by Antoine and Claire Guillaumont, the three Evagrian works grouped together by the editors all come from the same manuscript. This is an unknown (probably Athonite) manuscript, closely related to the Lavra M 54 (Athos 1745).[7]

The codex M 54 of the Great Lavra is an enormously lengthy manuscript, of a small format (210x150 mm), containing 476 leaves, 26 lines in one page. Being a recent manuscript, it is on paper. According to notes in the margins, its history is as follows. It appears to be from Smyrna, not Mt. Athos. At the close of the eighteenth century the manuscript belonged to a certain Anthymos, an official in Smyrna. It was only in 1844 that it was donated to the Athonite monastery Esphigmenou. While it is unknown how and when the manuscript came into the possession of the Great Lavra, it is clear that it was not on Athos at the time when Sts.

Macarius and Nicodemus were gathering the texts for their philokalic collection. Yet, the manuscript has striking affinities with the *Philokalia of the Neptic Fathers*. Almost all of the texts contained within this huge manuscript are on the subjects of prayer, *nepsis*, and the guarding of the heart. It thus in itself constitutes one of the numerous "*Philokaliae*" before the *Philokalia*,[8] containing a long-established canon of patristic hesychast texts. The establishment of this canon is inseparable from the work of St. Gregory Palamas, the "Palamite" councils in Constantinople, and the overall triumph of St. Gregory's views in the Eastern Christendom in the second half of the fourteenth century.

One practical corollary of this victory was the sharp rise of the prestige and popularity of the Greek monastic texts on *hesychia* and the spiritual prayer. This resulted in a heightening of the manuscript production of these texts in the Greek Christian East. The work of copying and collating manuscripts containing writings of St. Gregory and his predecessors continued for as long as the remembrance of St. Gregory's teaching on the inner life, based on centuries-long mystical tradition, was in zenith. It may be unclear at which point the influence of the "Palamite" ideas started to wane, yet it seems undisputed that it did. This evidences from the fact that the majority of the Greek manuscripts on *nepsis* found at present on Mount Athos go back to the parent manuscripts that were produced between the late fourteenth–early sixteenth century, and not later than this.[9] Since the Lavra M 54 originates from Smyrna and was not located on Mt. Athos in the late 1770s–early 1780s, the editors would probably not have been able to use this particular manuscript as their source. Instead, they must have utilized a source closely related to it and one to which they had access at the time of their preparation of the edition. As is reflected in the Lavra M 54, a substantial part of all the works and authors included within the 1782 philokalic collection were copied from this one unknown manuscript.[10] With regard to Evagrius's works in the *Philokalia*, the three texts that the *Philokalia* lists as authored by him are found in the Lavra M 54 in the same order and textual form (save for very slight alterations administered by the editors) as in the manuscript.

As was previously noted, notably absent from the Lavra M 54, and in all probability from the source manuscript, is Evagrius's *Chapters on Prayer*. The problem surrounding the manuscript history for this work will be dealt with within the eagerly awaited Introduction to a critical edition and a French translation of the *Chapters*, currently under preparation by P. Géhin for the *Source Chrétiennes* series. Likewise absent from the Lavra M 54 are the following authors within the *Philokalia* who also were pivotal to the dissemination in the Greek-speaking Byzantine world of Evagrius's ideas on the spiritual life: Cassian (*Philokalia*, vol. 1), Diadochus of Photike (vol. 1), and Maximus the Confessor (vol. 2).

It is clear that the discovery of the Lavra M 54 as a manuscript extremely closely related to a large portion of the *Philokalia* presents the work of Sts. Macarius and Nicodemus in a new light. They did not conduct their work in a vacuum, nor did it arise out of nothing. Furthermore, it is no longer correct to credit Sts. Macarius and Nicodemus with being the inventors of the *Philokalia* project itself. In their work, they would have drawn on the immense wealth of ascetic patristic material contained in innumerable manuscript collections of apophthegmata and parenetic kephalaia, soul-edifying stories and lives of holy ascetics, treatises of spiritual council, and ascetic rules. Consequently, the rationale behind the *Philokalia* was not entirely their own. To a considerable degree, they accepted what was already there in their manuscript sources, notably the parent manuscript of the Lavra M 54. The latter source was convenient, since it contained a considerable list of edifying texts by famous saintly authors, with a great number of works dealing precisely with the editors' preferred subjects. All the editors had to do was pick out of the entire manuscript the specific portion of it dealing especially with the guarding of the intellect. Consequently, the scope of their creativity in shaping up their collection was much more restricted than has long been assumed.

▪ EVAGRIUS'S TEXTS IN VOLUME 1 OF THE *PHILOKALIA*

As is noted above, save for the *Chapters on Prayer*, the first volume of the *Philokalia* contains the same texts, in identical versions and order, as the Lavra M 54. Thus Lavra M 54 contains:

1. *The Foundations of the Monastic Life*, whose full title in the Greek of the *Philokalia* and the Lavra M 54 manuscript is Εὐαγρίου ὑποτύπωσις μοναχικὴ διδασκαλία πῶς δεῖ ἀσκεῖν καὶ ἡσυχάζειν. Beside the *Philokalia* the work is also in PG 40. 1252d–1264c, entitled in Latin *Rerum monachalium rationes*, and in Greek ΕΥΑΓΡΙΟΥ ΜΟΝΑΧΟΥ, ΤΩΝ ΚΑΤΑ ΜΟΝΑΧΩΝ ΠΡΑΓΜΑΤΩΝ ΤΑ ΑΙΤΙΑ ῾ΥΠΟΤΥΠΟΣΙΣ, ΚΑΙ ΚΑΘ°ΗΣΥΧΙΑΝ ΤΟΥΤΩΝ ΠΑΡΑΘΕΣΙΣ.

[Evagrius in the *Philokalia* and in the later Greek tradition: based on the manuscript tradition, Evagrius's credentials with the Byzantines were centred upon the opinion current in the Eastern Church that Evagrius was one of the "Cappadocian Fathers" and also one of the "Desert Fathers," who undertook the task of recording their sayings. Thus, some rather early (12th c.) florilegia containing his works, in particular the *Practicus*, which also found its way into Nicodemus's collection, are listed under the name of Εὐαγρίου Καππαδόκου ἀποφθέγματα περὶ τῶν μεγάλων γερόντων.[11]]

Beginning with: Ἐν τῷ Ἱερεμίᾳ . . . the text ends with: ἀκατάπαυστον ἀναπέμπει τὸν ὕμνον, σὺν τῷ ἀνάρχῳ αὐτοῦ πατρὸς καὶ τῷ παναγίῳ. . .°. The version contained in the *Philokalia* and the Lavra M 54 is the integral text of this Evagrius's work, with the concluding "with His Father Who is without beginning, and the All-holy Spirit" phrase being a later addition. The concluding phrase, which is absent from other renditions of the work, such as the *Patrologia Graeca* version,[12] as well as from the original text,[13] seems to shimmer with tantalizing possibilities of meaning. One possible explanation is that the phrase represents an intention on the part of subsequent generations of scribes and interpreters of Evagrius to render the treatise more acceptable with regard to the Trinitarian and Christological opinions it seems to express. It is hardly surprising that Athonite and other Eastern Orthodox monasteries should be storing in their libraries precisely this version of the text whose orthodoxy is thus enhanced.[14]

2. *On the Thoughts* (Περὶ διαφόρων πονηρῶν λογισμῶν and *De diversis malignis cogitationibus* in PG 79.1200d–1228c.) By contrast with the PG and other, more

common, manuscript versions, the Lavra M 54 and the *Philokalia* do not bear the familiar "*Περὶ λογισμῶν*" title. Instead the work is presented with the following lengthy heading: *Εὐαγρίου μοναχοῦ μαθητοῦ τοῦ μεγάλου Βασιλείου παρ᾽ τοῦ καὶ τὴν τοῦ ἀναγνώστου σφραγῖδα εὤληφε, παρὰ δὲ Γριγορίου τὴν τοῦ διακόνου χειροτονίαν, κεφάλαια περὶ διακρίσεως παθῶν καὶ λογισμῶν.*

This introduction to Evagrius's second treatise within the *Philokalia*, the Lavra M 54 manuscript and thus, in all probability, the source manuscript appears to also be used by St. Nicodemos for the general biographical note introducing Evagrius's works within the collection. Both the title of Evagrius's second philokalic work and his biographical note emphasize Evagrius's quasi-familial connection with the two of the three great Cappadocian lights: Basil the Great and Gregory Nazianzen, from the late fourth century onward, universally regarded as pillars of doctrinal and ascetical orthodoxy and unquestionably saints. Clearly, Evagrius's association with these powerful ecclesiastical figures provides a formidable advocacy of Evagrius's own elite status in Greek Christian ascetic tradition and therefore of his inclusion within the collection. Once again, no mention is given to the cloud of suspicion associated with his name from the aftermath of the First Origenist controversy, through the 553 condemnations, and into the Byzantine late middle ages.

Commencing with *Τῶν ἀντικειμένων δαιμόνων . . .,* the text concludes with: *ὄψει εὖ προσευχῇ.* It is noteworthy that the philokalic version of the work is incomplete and generally is not a good text of this Evagrian work. Despite its attribution to St. Neilus, the PG version of the text is preferable to the philokalic one in terms of the text's completeness.[15] In a large number of other manuscripts, not used in the PG version, *On the Thoughts* is passed under Evagrius's own name.

To take a closer look at the matter, the version of the treatise that found its way into the *Philokalia*, as well as the Lavra M 54, belongs within the so-called "Tradition of St. Neilus" for this work. If the completeness of the text is an evaluative factor, this is not the best manuscript tradition for this specific Evagrian work, since *all* texts of the treatise within this tradition are incomplete.[16] Thus, while the version used in the Lavra M 54 and the philokalic collection consists of 23 chapters, the full text counts 43 chapters in all.[17] Another feature of this manuscript branch for the *On the Thoughts* is that in it some manuscripts attribute it to St. Neilus while others to Evagrius. It therefore seems to be on account of the Evagrian attribution of this work within the source manuscript (this is proven by the same attribution within the Lavra M 54) that the *Philokalia* lists the work under Evagrius's rather than St. Neilus's name. Once again, this finding suggests that the compilers of the *Philokalia* followed their source manuscripts, copying texts and attributions without questioning the trustworthiness of their available sources. A further characteristic of the St. Neilus tradition for the *On the Thoughts* is that the manuscripts within the tradition that attribute the work to St. Neilus often *also* contain Evagrius's *Chapters on Prayer*, which they likewise attribute to St. Neilus.[18] Had the editors of the *Philokalia* broadened their search for the Evagrius-St. Neilus manuscript tradition, they may well have come across evidence enabling them to conclude: (1) that both *On the Thoughts* and the *Chapters on Prayer* had been authored by a single author, and (2) that this author was in fact Evagrius and not St. Neilus. It therefore appears that the editors had neither the opportunity nor the desire to cast their net wider, in order to accomplish a better job in philological and historical scholarship. That they failed to see a connection between the *Chapters on Prayer* and the treatise *On the Thoughts* is proof that they knew little of the true identity of Evagrius or the extent of his *oeuvre*.

The extensive manuscript tradition of the *Evagriana* appears to have been unknown to them, despite the probable presence on Mt. Athos, at the time of their work on the collection, of numerous manuscripts containing other, possibly fuller, texts of Evagrius's works, which may also have been correctly attributed to him. Instead the editors settled for including only a small number of Evagrius's works, and these often in imperfect textual versions. Clearly they did so on account of the restricted manuscript resources that were available to them at the time of their quest. These resources and the manuscript tradition from which they stem constitute a very limited Evagrian environment.

3. *On the Thoughts* is followed by a very short text consisting of only five chapters. These are in fact a small selection from a much longer Evagrius treatise: the *Practicus*. The *Practicus*'s chapters in the *Philokalia*, the Lavra M 54, and, in all probability, the prototype manuscript are the chapters: 29, 32, 91, 9, 4 and 15 of the full version, in this order. This philokalic selection from the *Practicus*, which begins with Τοῦ αὐτοῦ ἐκ τῶν νηπτικῶν κεφαλαίων . . . and ending with . . . Οὕτω δεῖ ἀεί; . . . καὶ οὐκ ὠφέλιμα᾽, can be seen as in many ways an imperfect rendition of the flow of Evagrius's ideas as they unfold in this work, since the full text of the treatise numbers 100 chapters. The text is contained in the *Patrologia Graeca* 40.1220c-1236c, 1244b-1252c; 1272a-1276b. Here the work is entitled: in Latin, *Institutio sive paraenesis ad monachos*, and in Greek, attributed to St. Neilus: ΤΟΥ ΑΥΤΟΥ ΕΝ ΑΓΟΙΣ ΠΑΤΡΟΣ ΗΜΩΝ ΝΕΙΛΟΥ ΠΑΡΕΙΝΕΣΙΣ ΠΡΟΣ ΜΟΝΑΧΟΥΣ.

Once again, the editors' reason for including precisely this portion of the work at the end of their "Evagrian" section was simply that this same selection from the *Practicus* was found in their source manuscript at the end of the manuscript's Evagrian section, all of which is reflected in the Lavra M 54. Beside the actual edifying content of the text, the original scribe's rationale for concluding the "Evagrian" section of his manuscript with this particular text appears to have a lot to do with the practicalities of manuscript copying. In the Lavra M 54, as probably within its prototype manuscript, the *Practicus* excerpt fills out the final part of the Evagrian section. Now the prototype of the Lavra M 54 (as well of the substantial part of the *Philokalia*) itself must have been composed of numerous smaller manuscript compilations of the florilegia type. The hypothetical smaller manuscript that may have contained just a selection of Evagrius's works probably used a small portion of the *Practicus* at the very end of the manuscript to fill out the remaining space. That *Practicus* is written in the genre of the *kephalaia* made it a good candidate for this specific role: an assembly of short pithy maxims can be interrupted and divided far easier than a continuous text. A frequent feature of a Byzantine manuscript is filling out the space at the end with a shorter concluding text. This would be either a complete small work or an excerpt from a longer one. The scribe would add this text at the end of his manuscript not solely on account of the text's edifying contents but also in order to fill out the few remaining blank pages or even lines.

Alternatively, entire manuscripts could be constituted by a number of excerpts from longer works by well-known authors. Such a handwritten book would thus constitute something akin to a portable library of excerpts from highly sought-after treatises and authors, usually collected around a certain edifying subject or personality. In situations of need when monks were compelled to travel or perhaps move away to escape persecution, they would carry such portable libraries with them. Transported in the luggage of traveling scholars, the manuscripts moved and were disseminated around focal areas of the Eastern empire's Christian ascetic orbit. This was one of the ways in which diverse bodies of ascetic literature, under the names of "Macarius," "Ephrem," "Isaiah," "Evagrius," or "Evagrius-Neilus," were formed and circulated between monastic libraries in the Christian East.[19]

Returning to the compilation of the *Philokalia*, it is clear that, far from being original or starting from scratch in their work of compiling the *Philokalia*, Sts. Nicodemus and Macarius were guided by centuries-old manuscript traditions, in particular some of the pre-existing traditions around Evagrius's *oeuvre*.

4. The fourth Evagrian text within the collection is the *Chapters on Prayer*, an ascetical manual dedicated to the subject of the hesychastic prayer. Beside the *Philokalia*, the work is also found in the PG 79.1165–1200, where it is likewise attributed to St. Neilus of Ancyra. Belonging within the Neilus-Evagrius tradition, in subsequent ascetical monastic traditions, later Byzantine as well as medieval Russian, the treatise was widely celebrated as foundational with regard to the potency and the beneficial nature of its instruction upon striving for Christian perfection through the work of prayer. Its high ranking within the Greek ascetical tradition is manifested by the frequency with which the treatise recurs in Byzantine ascetical florilegia. In particular, the work is contained in manuscripts housed within high-profile Athonite libraries of Greek and Slavic monasteries, such as the libraries of the Vatopedi, St. Panteleimon, and Chilandar monasteries.[20] In the Russian ascetic tradition, the high popularity of the work evidences from its presence in the library of the influential Volokolamsk monastery.[21]

The manuscript tradition for this work of Evagrius in the *Philokalia* is complex. The work is not present in the Lavra M 54 and, in all probability, not in its source manuscript. For this work, the editors of the collection must have used another, unknown, manuscript source(s). Beside the *Philokalia*, the work is printed in PG, where it is attributed to St. Neilus: PG 79.1165a-1200c. The oriental Evagrian tradition (Syriac and Armenian) proves Evagrius's authorship of the work. On the internal consistency of the work with the ideas of Evagrius, see I. Hausherr, *Le Traité de l'Oraison d'Évagre le Pontique (Pseudo-Nil)* (in RAM 15, 1934). A critical edition of the *Chapters on Prayer* is currently in preparation by P. Géhin for the *Sources Chrétiennes*. When it finally appears, one hopes that the introduction to the edition will shed light upon the murky question of the manuscript tradition for this work.

▓ STS. MACARIUS AND NICODEMUS'S
METHOD OF WORK

It thus makes sense to conclude that the saintly compilers of the *Philokalia* were not interested in minute philological-historical archaeology. Their knowledge of their authors was limited to the information contained within the few source manuscripts they chose or were able to employ. It appears that in their quest the compilers were not driven by the spirit of inquiry in the modern academic sense. Instead of attempting an in-depth research into manuscript sources, the saintly editors carried out a different sort of task, whereupon they appear to have relied, in a seemingly uncritical fashion, upon a relatively small number of centuries-old florilegia of ascetic texts available to them. As a result, the apparent limitations in terms of historicity that the *Philokalia* manifests go back all the way to its source manuscripts which the eighteenth-century editors simply copied. These manuscript source volumes were themselves complete *Philokalia*–type florilegia collections, among which were the specific genres of types of compilations focusing specifically upon the subject of personal Christian perfection through spiritual prayer.

▓ THE MANUSCRIPT SOURCES OF THE *PHILOKALIA*

The question of the manuscript sources for the philokalic *Evagriana* is part of the bigger and inveterate question about the sources for the entire *Philokalia*. Beside the prototype for the Lavra M 54 volume, can anything more be suggested toward identifying at least some of the *Philokalia*'s prototype manuscript sources? Like the majority of the sixteenth- to eighteenth-century editors, Sts. Nicodemus and Macarius do not state their manuscript sources. In his important entry "Philocalie" in the *Dictionnaire de spiritualité*, Metr. Kallistos Ware signals the problem, pointing out that, in their Introduction to the collection, the editors of the *Philokalia* say nothing with regard to their method of collecting their materials.[22] What seems likely, however, is that it was "newer," post-tenth-century, manuscripts that on the whole would have been more readily available on Mount Athos in 1780s, at the time of the editors' work on the collection.[23] This must have equally been the case with regard to the specific manuscript compilations Sts. Nicodemus and Macarius used for their *Philokalia*. Regarding the original manuscript collections that eventually gave rise to the copies and new collections that Sts. Macarius and Nicodemus were able to use, in all probability these would have been first produced in the thirteenth to fourteenth-centuries. There are a number of reasons for this. The first one is the intellectual and spiritual renaissance, and consequently an increase in manuscript copying, that marked the post-restoration period in Byzantium.[24] The durability of paper that was beginning to be used at this time may be another: paper manuscripts lasted longer and therefore were copied more. There may be a further reason, however, for a profusion of manuscripts produced, specifically on the subject of *hesychia*, around later fourteenth to fifteenth centuries. This was the time of the aftermath of the "Palamite" councils[25] and the victory of the views of the Athonite hesychast monks, who maintained that personal deification was the essence of Christian life. It may thus be tempting to see the triumph of hesychasm as expounded by St. Gregory to be the catalyst that inspired a spiritual ascetic revival in the years to come, and not merely in Greek but among Slavic audiences as well. All of this would have given rise to prolific manuscript production specifically of florilegia on hesychia, inwardness and mental prayer. Thus, the catalogue of the Slavonic manuscripts of Chilandar[26] alone cites numerous manuscript collections of different authors (*Зборники*) and volumes of collected works by individual authors (*Слова*) on the subjects germane to hesychia, all from the late fourteenth century. Despite its being speculative, this increase in publishing may be evidence that, in addition to active copying and compiling of books on hesychast subjects, the keen interest for hesychasm caused an increase in translations of Greek hesychastic texts into Slavonic around this time.[27] This development would make St. Gregory Palamas, whose corpus in the *Philokalia* is one of the bulkiest, a special inspirational figure behind the entire *Philokalia* project and the Byzantine reception of the Greek *Evagriana*.

▪ THE SPIRITUAL CONTENT OF THE PHILOKALIC *EVAGRIAN*

If texts on personal spiritual rebirth were the *Philokalia* editors' guiding interest, what about the content of his works that secured Evagrius's inclusion within the *Philokalia*? Of course, centuries prior to the rise of the *Philokalia*, the four works of Evagrius that were in the collection had already been considered classic spiritual texts and were being included in numerous collections. Yet this initial inclusion, despite the 553 condemnations, of Evagrius within the Byzantine soul-edifying canon itself would have been at least in part based on the character of the writings.

Leaving the *Chapters on Prayer* aside for the moment, one notable feature of the philokalic *Evagriana* as it appears in Athos M 54 is that the three works in question seem to be in an order corresponding to a conceptual progression consistent with Evagrius's tripartite ascending *praktikê-theôria-theologia* pedagogy. Commencing with subjects integral to more practical and bodily asceticism, *praktikê*, which is intended for relative beginners (*Outline Teaching on Asceticism*), the instruction within *On the Thoughts* then proceeds to much more advanced ascetical subjects, such as the mechanism of fallen sense-perception, the spiritual warfare, and the contemplation (*theôria*) of the spiritual principles of creation. There are even passages treating of the ultimate mystical visionary states corresponding to *theologia*.[28] The spiritual progression is recapitulated in the short five excerpts from the *Practicus*, which in all probability are also served as a physical conclusion to the Evagrian section within the source manuscript. At this point it is expedient to revisit the content of these Evagrian works in some detail.

▪ 1 OUTLINE TEACHING ON ASCETICISM AND STILLNESS IN *THE SOLITARY LIFE*

Unusually to Evagrius, the work is composed as a discursive text rather than a series of *kephalaia* (Evagrius's trademark). Nevertheless it is also typically Evagrian, in that his classic tripartite gradation of the spiritual life is discernible here. The work's predominant preoccupation with practical asceticism, rather than the more exalted spiritual pursuits of contemplation, suggests it was meant for beginners on the ascetical journey, those at the stage of the *praktike*.[29] Nevertheless, without spelling out what is the essence of it, the treatise is unambiguous that practical asceticism is but a means to an end, which is the life of stillness, *hesychia*.

Voluntary exile (pp. 33–34 in the English translation) is treated as fundamental to the life of stillness. To withdraw (*anakhôrein*) from the society is the first prerequisite for the solitary life. The opening paragraphs link together allegorical readings of Jer. 16:1–4 and 1 Cor. 7:33–4. In the latter passage the Apostle warns about the troubles of the married lifestyle. Consequently the life of celibacy is a *sine qua non* for the life of stillness and a necessary part of the "exile." Abstention from marriage, preferably in the life of virginity, is necessary for the person to escape the turmoil and material concerns of the "worldly" lifestyle. However, Evagrius points out, the celibacy of the monk consists not primarily in the absence of a wife and physical procreation, but in abstention from "fleshly thoughts and lusts" (σαρκικῶν λογισμῶν καὶ ἐπιθυμιῶν, π, p. 38 line 13 of the Greek text) of The monk's "exile" and "stillness" therefore is not purely physical withdrawal from places and societies. It rather signifies abandoning worldly ways of life, full of material cares, for the sake of fostering an "immaterial" and "carefree" (ἄϋλον καὶ ἀμέριμνον) state of the mind. The true "exile," then, is spiritual. It consists in a certain attitude of the mind and is a subjective state. Although addressing the earliest stages of the monk's education, the treatise thus paves the way for Evagrius's essential axiom: the *entire* life of stillness, from its inception to culmination, concerns the cultivation of the spiritual self.

Food, Human Relationships, Labor, and Fasting

The treatise then goes on to address in detail the practicalities of the monastic life. These are regulations on food intake, material possessions, relationships with others, manual labor, and fasting. Thus, in his eating habits the monk is exhorted to maintain a "sparse and plain diet," not seeking out "a variety of tempting dishes." Possessions are to be reduced to the necessary minimum, as acquisitiveness and prehensility destroy the tranquillity of the mind. While hospitality is an essential requirement of Christian love, relationships with relatives and former friends may be practiced only with discretion (pp. 38–40 of the Greek text). Yet the company of the "men of peace, spiritual friends and holy fathers" is to be cultivated (p. 41 of the Greek). While manual labor is essential, the monk is to guard himself against becoming excessively engrossed in selling and buying (Ibid. p. 41). While the proliferation of this detail may appear somewhat tedious, it was all extremely important to the monastics and communities benefiting from this council. All of this detail has a point, for Evagrius's overruling concern is to instil within the inexperienced minds the need to be truly both truly free and responsible. Discernment ought to be practiced above all else. Evagrius's guiding principle even at these inceptive stages of training is encourage the pupil to watch the effect a specific decision has upon the state of one's mind. The mind's peaceful disposition, rather than rules themselves, is the goal. Even at the beginner's level, Evagrius prioritizes the life of the spirit/mind over that of the dead letter.

Demons

Demons are another prominent subject in the *Outline*. The warfare against the spiritual adversary is the stern reality of the life of the monk, who is to be "a soldier of Christ" (Χριστοῦ στρατιώτην). The treatise especially warns against the "demon of listlessness" (cf. p. 41 of the Greek text), presumably as a particular temptation assailing predominantly junior monastics.

Staying in One's Cell

The monk's cell is his fortress protecting him against temptations. One is to remain within the cell as much as possible. Yet again, Evagrius's concern here is not about outward decorum but the inner spiritual tranquility of the mind: it is only valuable to remain in one's cell inasmuch as it safeguards the concentration of the mind (cf. καθεζόμενος ἐν τῷ κελλίῳ σου συνάγαγέ σου τὸν νοῦν, p. 42 of the Greek text).

The Ultimate Goal of the Monastic Life

Characteristic of his gradual pedagogy, Evagrius refrains in this work for the beginners from fully disclosing the ultimate goal of the monastic life. This goal is presented in general terms as an experience of "the immortal fruits of the heavenly life" (ἀθανάτους τῆς αἰωνίου ζωῆς . . . καρπούς, p. 39 in the Greek text). The indistinctness of this language contrasts with potent and clear definitions of the peak of the monastic life observable in other Evagrius works, aimed at those more proficient in spiritual gnosis. By contrast the two philokalic treatises immediately following the *Outline* narrowly identify the goal and peak of the monastic life as the spiritual knowledge of God and luminous theophanic experiences.

Properly Evagrian Concepts: Matter and the Mind

It is thus clear that, despite being a manual for the more simple-minded, the *Outline* is concerned with advanced spiritual subjects such as the contrast between "matter" and "mind." Evagrius refers to "matter" (*hulê*) as the fundamental obstacle to the life of the spirit, which in his vocabulary is the "spiritual intellect"/"mind" (*nous*). As regards the former, the monk is defined as one "who has renounced all materiality/matter of this world" (πᾶσαν ὕλην τοῦ κόσμου, p. 39 of the Greek text). This "materiality" is not at all the physical creation itself but a certain grossness of the spiritual *nous*, whereby its spiritual tranquility, unity, and intentness upon the divine realities is disorientated and disrupted by demonic assaults. Evagrius's theological anthropology of the immaterial mind/intellect as the most preeminent part of the human composition, in which imageless prayer takes place,[30] is fundamental to the entire subsequent hesychastic tradition. The doctrine of the immaterial intellect/mind as the quintessence of man is integral to the entire *Philokalia*, even though Evagrius is not its only author.[31] It is no exaggeration to suggest that all of the collection's five volumes pay special attention to the cultivation of the spiritual intellect as the very spiritual essence of humanity. Evagrius's opening philokalic treatise announces right at the inception of the collection what constitutes a matter of special importance to the hesychast and by extension the editors of the *Philokalia*.

Theology and Christology Proper

Regarding Evagrius's specific theology and Christology, of which the compilers of the collection seemed unaware, the work at least hints at his trademark distinction between God (as the Father and the Logos), on the one hand, and on the other hand, the created Jesus Christ.[32] This appears to be manifested by the work's finale. The manuscript tradition for the *Outline* points to a short and plain conclusive doxology as the treatise's original ending: "For to God be the glory forever. Amen" (Ὅτι τῷ Θεῷ ἡ δόξα εἰς τοὺς αἰῶνας. Ἀμήν), which makes no mention of Christ as one of the three divine persons of the Trinity. By contrast, the Byzantine tradition on which the *Philokalia* draws replaces this finale with a traditionally Triadological formula which refers to Christ as one divine person of the Trinity on a par with the Father and the Spirit:

> For it is He whom the whole spiritual host and the choir of angels serve with fear and glorify with trembling; and they sing in unceasing praise to Him [Christ], together with the Father who has no origin, and with the all-holy and co-eternal Spirit, now and ever through all the ages. Amen.[33]

Even though throughout the treatise he seems careful not to bring his anomalous Christology to the notice of junior monastics, one might argue that the fully blown Triadological formula of the kind found in the philokalic version of the work would be more than what Evagrius would have been willing to accept: after all, Jesus Christ was "not consubstantial with the Trinity."[34] The laconic doxology to God alone, without a Triadological formula that included Christ within the company of the divine persons, may have been a special point Evagrius wished to make even in a work intended for beginners, in preparation for their more advanced training in spiritual mysteries as outlined in his *Gnostic Chapters*. The Evagrian philokalic tradition, which arose subsequently to the 553 condemnations, glosses over and roots out any hint of such Christology. While this may be a distortion of Evagrius's authentic message, this strategy of the unknown Byzantine copyists and editors also redeems him for the later Byzantine Christianity.

▪ 2. ON THE THOUGHTS

The next Evagrius philokalic work is *On the Thoughts*. In comparison with the *Outline*, this is a more advanced manual for desert-dwellers, with a specific emphasis upon the spiritual work of the monk: the spiritual warfare against the demonic assaults, and the guarding of the intellect. The philokalic version of the work is significantly (by 18 chapters) shorter than the full original, with chapters 24–37 and 40–43 18–37 of the original left out in the philokalic version. Notwithstanding, the shorter version retains (and probably accentuates) the core foci of the original: a fascination with the human mind/soul and its operation; the search for the divine self-manifestations in creatures as the mind's proper function; the role of sense perception in the formation of thoughts and concepts in the mind; finally, dispassion as precondition to the contemplation of the *logoi* of beings. All of these key ideas became fundamental points of the "grammar of hesychasm" to the subsequent Greek hesychast tradition. In this sense, the work in its entirety is quintessentially "hesychastic."

The Purified Mind as the New Adam

The mind's exalted role within the human composition dominates the treatise. Using allegorical interpretation of sacred texts by pressing them into interpretations illustrative of his own doctrines of the monastic combat and prayer, Evagrius presents the human mind (*nous*) as our "helmsman" (τὸν κυβερνήτην) in the dangerous voyage of the human life. The mind-helmsman is in turn guided through the raging sea of life by the Lord himself.[35] Conflating Gal. 3:28 and Col. 3:10–11, Evagrius presents the voyage's final destination and goal as the formation in us of the "new man" (ὁ νέος ἄνθρωπος). It is Evagrius' idea that this comes about and the "new man" arises in our soul when the resemblance to Christ which is ontologically in-built within the human makeup, becomes refreshed and polished back to its divinely ordained brightness. The image of Christ in our soul thus renewed, this transformation in turn culminates in our becoming healed and whole again. This means that all the fallen divisions within the human kind and each individual person, as listed in Col. 3:11, are annulled, being united back together in Christ, who becomes "all and in all."[36] So far these may seem traditionally Pauline and early Christian views of redemption as conformity to the image of Christ in us. Evagrius, however, then superimposes a strictly ascetical perspective by making it clear that the "new man" in us is is our purified mind, brought back to the state of harmony and noetic capacity through prayer.[37] This is yet another elaboration of Evagrius's key tenet that the quintessence of humanity is humanity's spiritual mind/intellect. Every other component of the human being, notably the body and its senses, is secondary in importance to the mind. One stands or falls by the state of one's soul/mind.

The Spiritual Warfare: Thoughts and Concepts in the Mind

A further major theme of the philokalic *On Thoughts* is the spiritual warfare against the invisible demonic adversary. The battle against demonic temptation is conducted within the mind of the ascetic; the mind, then, is the battleground. But the mind is also the battle trophy: all of the monk's effort is directed at guarding the mind's tranquility and purity—the prerequisite of dispassion and gateway to contemplation. When the invisible demons wage war against the ascetic, it is a battle of the minds: demonic against human. In it demons endeavor to pollute normal human thoughts and concepts. To win the battle, it is imperative that the ascetic know the normal workings of his mind from their distortions. The doctrine of the normal thought formation and of the mechanism of its demonic subversion is perhaps the most essential of all Evagrius's ascetic doctrines and one that proved enormously influential in subsequent Byzantine centuries. Thus it is safe to suggest that, in one manner or another, all of the *Philokalia*'s authors manifest familiarity and build upon Evagrius's catenae of vices and virtues and the eight principal evil thoughts. Eastern Christian ascetics attached categorical importance to the monk's ability to stay in command over the whirlpool of thoughts and concepts in the mind.[38] Evagrius's writings are extremely important in this regard, as he is the first truly rigorous ideologist of a doctrine that was handed down to later generations of ascetics, largely unchanged.

Thoughts Natural and Unnatural

While the minutiae of Evagrius's catalogue of thoughts and images disturbing the mind have been extensively studied,[39] one aspect of this psychology, especially prominent in the treatise *On the Thoughts*, needs to be revisited. According to Evagrius, to think is a natural property of the rational soul. Through normal sense perception, thoughts, images and concepts are formed in the mind. This activity of the mind is neutral with respect to virtue or vice. Sense perception and thought process, then, are not reprehensible in themselves.

Evagrius further maintains that there are "evil" thoughts as well as "good" ones, which are benign, innocent, and pure (cf. *Thoughts* 16). The essence of the monastic striving lies in the ascetic's guarding and protecting the good thoughts in his mind from the evil and demonic ones, like the good shepherd cherishes the sheep, guarding them from the wolves:

> The Lord has entrusted the concepts [*noemata*] of this age to man as a kind of sheep to a good shepherd. For it is said: "He gave the world to his heart";[40] to help him, He joined to him the irascible part and the desirous part, so that with the former he would put to flight the representations that are from the wolves, and with the latter he would cherish the sheep.[41]

The "Cutting Off" of Evil Thoughts?

This invisible warfare to protect the mind is conducted by "cutting off" the evil thought"s energy inspired by the demons.[42] However, which thoughts are evil and how are they to be cut off? *Thoughts* 20 (19 in the full version) is crucial in expounding this tenet so fundamental to the later Byzantine ascetical hesychasm. Evagrius is categorical that, as God's creation, material things and bodies are good and beyond reproach. Also normal is the mind's activity of processing and storing the images of external objects, later to recall and meditate on them through memory. Normal sense perception, however, is subverted when, on demonic instigation, passion (cf. avarice, in *Thoughts* 20) is introduced into the mind's normal activity of image creating. This passion then unbalances and wrecks the tranquility of the mind. Thus:

> Suppose, for instance, that a thought full of avarice [ὁ τῆς φιλαργυρίας λογισμός] is suggested to you. Distinguish between the component elements: the intellect which has accepted the thought, the intellection of gold [τὸ νόημα τοῦ χρυσοῦ], gold itself, and the passion of avarice [εἰς τὸ φιλάργυρον πάθος]. Then ask: in which of these does the sin consist? Is it the intellect? But how then can the intellect be the image of God? Is it the intellection of gold? But what

sensible person would ever say that? Then is gold itself the sin? In that case, why was it created? It follows, then, that the cause of the sin is the fourth element, which is neither an objective reality nor the intellection of something real, but is a certain noxious pleasure [ἡδονή τις μισάνθρωπος] which, once it is freely chosen, compels the intellect to misuse what God has created. It is this pleasure that the law of God commands to cut off.[43]

This is a brief nutshell account of the birth of sin in the soul. Sin comes about when we let an image of an object become entangled with a passion associated with it (lust, hatred, or avarice). The exact same theory, with some elaborations, came later to be employed by Byzantine ascetical writers, notably Maximus the Confessor.[44] According to Evagrius, then, a properly monastic "work" is the guarding of one's mind, which consists of guarding the "good thoughts" and "cutting off" the "bad" ones. The "good" thoughts are the impressions and concepts of external things not mixed with passion, while "bad" ones are those that have an element of passion attached to them. "Guarding the intellect" involves making evil thoughts good, by separating the "passionate" component from the equation.[45]

Pure Prayer

What, however, is the purpose of this minute scrutiny of one's own thoughts? The stakes, to Evagrius, are high. An intellect/mind infested with impassioned thoughts lacks the detachment prerequisite for the mind's ascending to the level of spiritual contemplation and—the highest state of all—pure prayer (ἡ καθαρὰ προσευχή).[46] According to Evagrius, then, the following logical concatenation applies: a passionate thought kills the dispassion of the mind; this in turn prevents grace from coming; without grace the contemplative goal of asceticism is unattainable. In what sense is pure prayer the hesychast's goal? Even though the treatise provides no "cataphatic" explanation of how "pure prayer" is conducive to luminous immaterial visions, nevertheless it is clear that, to Evagrius, the visions of light manifested during prayer are equivalent with participation in the divine life. Consequently, pure luminous prayer is the prize—and fruit of—the life of stillness, *hesychia*.

▪ 3. EXTRACTS FROM TEXTS ON WATCHFULNESS

The remaining third text listed as Evagrian in the *Philokalia*, although a short five-chapter selection from the *Practicus*, nevertheless treats of the most fundamental subjects of hesychia: chapters 2 and 3 summarize Evagrius's entire pedagogical vision: the spiritual knowledge and contemplation for the mature; practical virtue for the beginners (chapter 2); the presence of love begets dispassion (chapter 3). The remainder of the excerpt concerns rather the beginner stage.

▪ 4. CHAPTERS ON PRAYER

As was mentioned above, this work of Evagrius comes from an unknown manuscript source different from that of the preceding three works. In its source manuscript, the work must have been mistakenly attributed to St. Neilus—the attribution that, together with the text itself, was then copied by the editors of the collection. Evidently the editors did not consider Evagrius's own mention, at the conclusion of the philokalic *On Thoughts* 22, of a treatise on prayer authored by him, as a reference specifically to the *Chapters on Prayer* within the St. Neilus collection. Rather than negligent oversight, this perhaps was simply the editors' executive decision to trust the sources available to them and when possible opt for minimal alterations.[47] As was pointed out above, in the late eighteenth century an entire list of Evagrius's works would not have been well known, because of the sixteenth-century ecclesiastical condemnations and subsequent reattributions of his texts.

In terms of its thematic content, the work seems to be addressed to a spiritually proficient readership of the kind intended for the treatise *On the Thoughts*. In fact there are clear conceptual overlaps and parallels between the two, accentuated by Evagrius's own cross-reference to *Prayer* in *Thoughts* 22. This is especially the case with regard to the key ascetic principle, so prominent in the entire *Philokalia* collection, of the need to regulate the thought-activity in the mind. Just like the *Thoughts*, the *Chapters on Prayer* is adamant that key ascetic striving must be to clear one's mind of all persistent, delusional, and obsessive preoccupations, by dissociating the mind's intellections from the passionate content attached to them. The *Chapters on Prayer*, however, develops the subject further, by actually spelling out that the ascetic's battle for the purification of the mind is conducted *entirely* for the sake of finding true prayer and for no other reason. Thus:

> He who wishes to pray truly [ἀληθῶς] must not only control his incensive power and his desire, but must also free himself from every impassioned thought [νοήματος ἐμπαθοῦς] (*Chapters on Prayer*, 54).[48]

It then goes on to make an even more radical claim that, for prayer to be "true," one is to leave behind not merely the evil and impassioned thoughts, but the dispassionate thoughts as well, and in fact *all* preoccupation with the created order altogether:

> One who has attained dispassion [ὁ ἀπαθείας τετυχηκώς] has not necessarily achieved true prayer. For he may still be occupied with simple [=dispassionate] thoughts [ψυλοῖς νοήμασι] and be distracted by the information they provide and so be far from God (*Chapters on Prayer*, 56).[49]

This is Evagrius's celebrated foundational teaching on "imageless prayer." The reason for this radical divestiture of the mind of all conceptual content is that only the naked mind is able to approach God in prayer. God alone is the proper "destination" of prayer, which is "the ascent of the intellect to God" (*Chapters on Prayer*, 36).

One more key characteristic of the work makes it stand out as being foundational to the entire philokalic tradition. This is its conception of the essence of Christianity and of Christian theology as being fundamentally experiential—a key principle within the *Philokalia*. To impress this upon his audiences, Evagrius coins his famous pithy maxims: "If you are a theologian, you pray truly [ἀληθῶς]; if you pray truly you are a theologian."[50] And: "prayer is the mind's conversation [ὁμιλία] with God."[51] Clearly, Evagrius himself was a "true theologian" and man of prayer in this sense: his teaching on the "true prayer" was based on experience and practice.[52] It appears, however, that, while attractive, this experientialism also carries with it the danger of doing away with attention to doctrinally correct propositions, so long as the experience of the divine is present. The philokalic tradition on the whole was willing to accept Evagrius's experiential emphasis as correct and proper and to integrate it within the overall Byzantine and Orthodox ascetical theology. Moreover, in subsequent Byzantine hesychastic synthesis, Evagrius's experientialist streak is realigned with mainstream orthodoxy when it is reinterpreted in strictly Christocentric terms akin to the tradition of Pseudo-Macarius: later hesychastic theologians conceive of imageless prayer essentially as the Jesus Prayer.

PART THREE

Spiritual Practices

12 The Place of the Jesus Prayer in the *Philokalia*

Mary B. Cunningham

In their introduction to the first volume of the English version of the *Philokalia*, the translators suggest that, more than anything else, it is the Jesus Prayer that confers unity on the work as a whole.[1] This article will attempt to determine whether this statement is true, exploring the extent to which the various writers whose works were included in the eighteenth-century anthology are guided by the inner principle of the "prayer of the heart," with its focus on the name of Jesus, and whether they are consistent in their understanding of its meaning and function.

When studying the *Philokalia*, it is important not only to look at the individual texts from which it is composed, but also to consider the work as a whole. Thus, whereas different writers within the *Philokalia* may express diverse ideas about the Jesus Prayer, the compilers of the anthology, Sts. Nikodemos and Makarios, may have viewed their contributions as presenting a unified vision of the spiritual life. Similarly, it should be borne in mind that the texts contained in the spiritual anthology have commanded a variety of audiences over the centuries. In the first instance, texts such as Diadochos of Photike's treatise *On Spiritual Knowledge* were usually addressed to a small group of disciples, or sometimes an individual monk, attached to the spiritual teacher.[2] When selected for inclusion in the *Philokalia*, however, these works reached a much wider audience, both monastic and lay, which has continued to read and practice their teachings up to the modern period. It is important to keep these separate contexts and audiences in mind while exploring the place of the Jesus Prayer in the *Philokalia*. Both diversity and unity play parts in its overall nature; it seems likely that its compilers were fully aware of this fact, perhaps perceiving the anthology as a rich tapestry woven from variegated threads.

We begin this investigation by defining the Jesus Prayer, before proceeding to analyze its treatment in the texts that make up the *Philokalia*. The prayer takes various forms, ranging from the simple invocation of the name of Jesus to the longer version that has come to be regarded as the classic one: "Lord Jesus Christ, Son of [the Living] God, have mercy on me [a sinner]."[3] It appears, on the basis of the texts that survive, that the earlier writers who refer explicitly to the prayer, such as Diadochos of Photike and Hesychios the Priest, knew only the shorter version.[4] *A Discourse on Abba Philemon*, which may have been written between the sixth and seventh centuries, appears to be the first text to refer to the fully developed form of the Jesus Prayer, that is based on the words of the publican in the parable (Luke 18:13): "God, be merciful to me a sinner."[5] As Lev Gillet, Kallistos Ware, and others have pointed out, the longer version of the Jesus Prayer includes various elements, which together form a rich synthesis of Orthodox Christian doctrine and devotion.[6] The three names, "Lord," "Jesus," and "Christ," remind us of the mystery of God's incarnation and Trinitarian existence; more than that, however, they represent an invocation, or reminder, of his continuing presence in the human heart. As Gillet puts it, "the name of Jesus is not just the employment of a magical formula, for no one can use this name effectively if he does not have an inner relationship with Jesus himself."[7] The second (and later) half of the prayer brings the penitent Christian into the Lord's presence. Here we open up our hearts to his mercy, hiding nothing and seeking forgiveness. Whereas the publican's petition may provide the most obvious scriptural foundation for this part of the prayer, there are innumerable other sources for it in the Old and New Testaments, including especially many of the psalms.

Various scholars, including Irenée Hausherr and Gillet, have already traced the history of the Jesus Prayer;[8] the *Philokalia* illustrates this background since it includes a number of texts in which it plays an important role. As we have already seen, Diadochos of Photike, who flourished in the fifth century, was the first ascetic writer to refer explicitly to the prayer. He calls it "a weapon against Satan's deception,"[9] "the remembrance of God,"[10] and "the pearl of great price" (cf. Mt. 13:46).[11] Diadochos makes it clear throughout his treatise *On Spiritual Knowledge* that he is referring to the shorter form of the prayer, as we see in his touching comparison between a mother who teaches her child to say "father" and the soul that, with the help of divine grace, teaches the intellect to repeat the words, "Lord Jesus."[12] For Diadochos, the Jesus Prayer, or simple invocation of the name, acts both as a method and as a goal in the ascetic life. Later spiritual writers, whose works appear in the final volumes of the *Philokalia*, express a more developed understanding of the prayer's role in hesychastic practice. For them, the Jesus Prayer in its longer form (usually "Lord Jesus Christ, Son of God, have mercy on me") both induces and then itself becomes a state of continuous "mindfulness" of God. Some writers, such as Gregory of Sinai, who was a contemporary of Gregory Palamas in the fourteenth century,[13] describe the physical techniques such as deep breathing and gazing toward the heart or navel that may help to induce this state.[14] The justification for this practice lies in scripture, especially in the concept of constant prayer (I Thess. 5:17). As Gregory of Sinai and others teach throughout the *Philokalia*, the process will eventually, with the grace of God, lead to the desired goal. When the devout Christian has learned to keep the name of Jesus Christ continually in mind, she or he will eventually lose all sense of self and be absorbed into a state of joyful union with God. Theoliptos of Philadelphia, who lived and taught in the late thirteenth and early fourteenth centuries, writes of this state as follows:

> Such are the characteristics of true mindfulness of God. Prayer is the mind's dialogue with God, in which words of petition are uttered with the intellect riveted wholly on God. For when the mind unceasingly repeats the name of the Lord and the intellect gives its full attention to the invocation of the divine name, the light of the knowledge of God overshadows the entire soul like a luminous cloud.[15]

Let us now attempt to trace some of the ways in which various contributors to the first four volumes of the *Philokalia*,[16] beginning with Diadochos of Photike in the fifth century and ending with writers such as Gregory of Sinai in the fourteenth, understand the Jesus Prayer. The development from a simple invocation of the name of Jesus to a full penitential prayer between these periods has already been noted; in addition, we shall explore various authors' understanding of the uses and outcome, or goal, of the Jesus Prayer. Whereas individual writers express different ideas about these two aspects of the prayer, it would be incorrect to suggest that one developed out of the other in the course of time. Diadochos and Hesychios of Jerusalem, in the first volume, are just as insistent on the mystical goal of meditative prayer as later monastic teachers are. In this sense, the Jesus Prayer contributes fully to the unity of the *Philokalia*. Nevertheless, it is also important to explore how individual writers fit this form of contemplation, or "prayer of the heart," into their wider understanding of hesychastic practice. In the discussion that follows, we shall examine first the role of the Jesus Prayer as an aid, or method, of meditative prayer and second, its place as the final goal itself, according to the various contributors to the *Philokalia*. As a result of this short study, it may then be possible to draw some conclusions about the role of the Jesus Prayer in the *Philokalia* as a whole.

To begin with the function of the Jesus Prayer in ascetic practice, it is noticeable that many writers in the *Philokalia*, both early and late, see it first as a tool, or "weapon," for combating the passions and thoughts that assail those who are attempting to pray. Diadochos of Photike, as we have already seen, describes vividly the way in which Satan attacks the intellect both at day and night. He counsels his readers to "[cleave] fervently to the remembrance of the holy and glorious name of the Lord Jesus and [use] it as a weapon against Satan's deception."[17] Mental images represent one form of such demonic assault, according to this writer. Diadochos counsels his readers to concentrate on the "glorious and holy name," "Lord Jesus," with such intensity that they are not distracted by images or thoughts.[18] Hesychios the Priest, who may have been active in the eighth or ninth century, also addresses the problem of mental distraction and advises ascetics who are troubled by this simply to invoke Christ.[19] It is not always clear in these earlier texts whether their authors mean the Jesus Prayer (that is, the name of Jesus) when they use the phrase, "the Prayer of Jesus Christ."[20] It is possible that in some contexts they are referring to the Lord's Prayer, or prayer to God the Father, that was given by Christ to his disciples (Mt. 6:7; Lk. 11:2–4).[21] For most writers, however, it is the invocation simply of the name "Jesus Christ," that acts as the most effective barrier against distracting thoughts and images. Ilias the Presbyter writes, for example, that "the single-phrased Jesus Prayer bridles unruly thought."[22]

The concept of the Jesus Prayer as a weapon against distracting thoughts is not confined to the earlier Fathers whose works appear in the *Philokalia*. Nikiphoros the Monk, who carried out a hesychastic life on Mt. Athos in the second half of the thirteenth century, writes in his treatise *On Watchfulness*:

> You know that everyone's discursive faculty is centred in his breast; for when our lips are silent we speak and deliberate and formulate prayers, psalms and other things in our breast. Banish, then, all thoughts from this faculty—and you can do this if you want to—and in their place put the prayer, "Lord Jesus Christ, Son of God, have mercy on me," and compel it to repeat this prayer ceaselessly.[23]

Gregory of Sinai, writing slightly later, explicitly compares the prayer to military weaponry, counselling:

So when thoughts invade you, in place of weapons call on the Lord Jesus frequently and persistently and then they will retreat: for they cannot bear the warmth produced in the heart by prayer and they flee as if scorched by fire.[24]

Gregory of Sinai is in fact one of the most technical spiritual writers of the later Byzantine period. The treatises in the fourth volume of the *Philokalia* deal not only with methods such as the Jesus Prayer for banishing unruly thoughts, but also with the physical process, known as the "psychosomatic method," of hesychastic prayer. Gregory sees the spiritual development of individual Christians as beginning with the sacrament of baptism, which confers the energy of the Holy Spirit, and reaching fruition through the practice of the commandments and prayer, along with continuous invocation of the Lord Jesus. All of these actions, but especially those involving prayer, bring "warmth and joy to the intellect and [set] the heart alight with an ineffable love for God and man."[25]

In fact this passage, which moves from the practical uses of the Jesus Prayer to its happy outcome, serves to introduce the second topic, namely, the purpose or goal that is achieved by constant remembrance of Christ. It is clear that all of the writers included in the *Philokalia* who refer to the Jesus Prayer see it not merely as a tool for inducing pure contemplation, but also as the outcome itself. A few examples will suffice to show that the means in fact *becomes* the end in this process. Diadochos of Photike stresses throughout his treatise the love and longing for God that characterizes the whole spiritual experience, the connection between the intellect's focus on the Jesus Prayer as a way of eliminating mental images, and the discovery that this invocation is in fact the final goal of contemplation.[26] Hesychios the Priest conveys in the following passage the sense that the prayer represents the beginning, middle, and end of contemplation:

Attentiveness is the heart's stillness, unbroken by any thought. In this stillness the heart breathes and invokes, endlessly and without ceasing, only Jesus Christ who is the Son of God and himself God.[27]

Hesychios is describing here the state of mindfulness for which every ascetic strives. Distracting thoughts and images have dissipated, driven out by the intellect's attention to the prayer. In the resulting stillness, the heart is able to focus constantly on that name, breathing, invoking, and in fact becoming one with Jesus Christ, who is God.

One important aspect of the Jesus Prayer, when it has become this deep, meditative state, is that it should become continuous, as the apostle Paul recommended (I Thess. 5:17). Most of the writers in the *Philokalia* recognize that whereas this goal is desirable, it is not always easy to maintain. The *Discourse on Abba Philemon*, which provides one of the few narrative treatments of this subject, suggests remedies for the problem. First the author recommends that monks at all times, whether asleep, awake, eating, drinking, or working, be meditating either on the psalms or on the full version of the Jesus Prayer, "Lord Jesus Christ, Son of God, have mercy on me."[28] This text suggests, in a quite believable manner, that even when ascetics have experienced the state of contemplation when the intellect has transcended "knowledge of created things and is united with God,"[29] it may wander away again into distractions such as thoughts and passions. St. Philemon recommends a variety of methods for returning to stillness, including not only the Jesus Prayer, but also psalmody, chanting of the liturgical offices, and the recitation of scripture. Occasionally, and only after much ascetic struggle, the vision of divine reality may be granted: this is "wholly inexpressible; words cannot describe it, nor the ear grasp it. To compare the true light to the rays of the morning star or the brightness of the moon or the light of the sun is to fail totally to do justice to its glory and is inadequate as comparing a pitch-black moonless night to the clearest of noons."[30]

Later contributors to the *Philokalia* also imply that whereas it may start as an invocation, the Jesus Prayer becomes one with its subject, Christ himself. A passage from Theoliptos of Philadelphia's treatise *On the Inner Work in Christ* was quoted earlier, in which the author describes the knowledge of God "overshadow[ing] the entire soul like a luminous cloud."[31] Theoliptos goes on to say that such a state of contemplation is followed by a sense of love and joy: intellect, mind, and soul, in their attentiveness to God, are drawn to serve and love him. Later in the same treatise he writes that once it has reached this blessed state, "[the intellect's] sole activity is to invoke the Lord's name in the depth of itself with continuous recollectedness, as a child repeats the name of his father."[32] Gregory of Sinai, who acknowledges throughout his treatise *On Prayer* the difficulties of maintaining an undistracted, meditative state, describes the goal in one memorable passage, as follows:

> Authentic prayer—the warmth that accompanies the Jesus Prayer, for it is Jesus who enkindles fire on the earth of our hearts (cf. Lk. 12:49)—consumes the passions like thorns and fills the soul with delight and joyfulness. Such prayer comes neither from right nor left, nor from above, but wells up in the heart like a spring of water from the life-quickening Spirit.[33]

As all of these passages demonstrate, the goal of contemplation, which may be assisted not only by the Jesus Prayer but also by other physical and mental practices, is characterized by joy, love, and a sense of union with Christ. The metaphors that many writers use, including images such as fire, warmth, flowing water, and so on, convey the fact that this visionary experience involves the whole human person. The more technical hesychastic writers, such as Nikiphoros the Monk and Gregory of Sinai, suggest that a process takes place in which the intellect, which has been dislocated, returns and becomes one with the heart. For these writers, the various aspects of the human person, including the physical, intellectual, and spiritual, are all involved in the process of deification. They therefore evoke aspects of creation, which are themselves a part of God's revelation to humanity, in their descriptions of the mystical goal that is reached through contemplation.

To return to the questions that were posed at the beginning of this article, which concerned the unifying role of the Jesus Prayer in the *Philokalia* and the extent to which individual writers are consistent in their ideas about the prayer, it is possible now to draw a few conclusions. First, as we have seen, the form of the prayer appears to have changed over the centuries, with a simple invocation of the name of Jesus being replaced—or at least supplemented—by a longer, supplicatory prayer. Apart from this difference, however, the various contributors to the *Philokalia* are consistent in their presentation of the uses and goal of the prayer. Spiritual teachers from the fifth through the fourteenth century recommend the Jesus Prayer as a method for combating the thoughts and mental images that assail the human mind at all times. As Diadochos of Photike and most of his successors argue, the repetition of the Jesus Prayer (in any of its various forms) serves to recall the intellect from its wandering thoughts and to focus it on Christ. With practice, this form of prayer eventually becomes continuous, to the extent that the ascetic becomes mindful of God when awake, asleep, or performing daily tasks. This is a manifestation of St. Paul's concept of "constant prayer," which the writers of the *Philokalia* see as a true dialogue with Christ. Finally, as we have seen, these teachers are consistent in their understanding that the goal of contemplative prayer is reached when the Jesus Prayer stops being experienced as a dialogue and becomes a state of deep communion with God. The seamlessness of this transition is conveyed in a number of writings, as they describe the constant repetition of the name of Christ turning gradually into a sense of unity with him. Joy, love, and warmth are experienced in this spiritual state; the words that were used to address Christ have finally given way to silence; and there is a sense that he is fully present in the one that prays. It is at this stage that the Jesus Prayer truly becomes "the prayer of the heart": the intellect and soul have returned to the place where they belong, which is in the heart.

The *Philokalia* thus does display considerable unity in its teachings on the Jesus Prayer. The English translators' claim that it is the prayer itself that gives the *Philokalia* inner unity goes further than this simple statement, however. On the basis of this brief study, it seems possible to agree with their conclusion, for the following reasons: first, as we have seen, the Jesus Prayer lies at the heart of the method, focus, and ultimate goal of ascetic practice, according to many of the writers whose works appear in the *Philokalia*. This idea represents much more than the simple repetition of the name, Jesus Christ, or of the short prayer that is addressed to him. As all of these writers make clear, Christ, as the incarnate Lord and Son of God, lies at the heart of Christian revelation. The Christian life, which can be perfected through ascetic labor and the grace of the Holy Spirit, finds its meaning in him; deification can be attained only by focusing one's intellect and heart continuously on Christ. The Jesus Prayer is not simply a formulation of words. It is aimed at returning the human person to the experience for which she or he was originally created, namely, union with the One who was begotten as the Second Adam, in the image and likeness of God. It is in this sense that the Jesus Prayer becomes a unifying thread that runs right through the five volumes of the *Philokalia*. It represents the means and the end of all ascetic endeavor, whose arduous practices may ultimately be rewarded by the mystical goal of union with Christ.

As a final conclusion, it is perhaps worth making a few further observations. They are offered in the hope that this article, although representing work in progress, will stimulate further research in the field. First, it is worth noting that in spite of the overall unity that is displayed in the various writers' views of the Jesus

Prayer throughout the *Philokalia*, the differences in their ways of expressing these ideas require investigation. We have noted only in passing, for example, the brevity with which earlier writers treat the technical aspects of contemplative prayer, as opposed to thirteenth- and fourteenth-century ideas on the subject. A second topic that would merit study is the extent to which individual writers explore the theological implications of the mystical experience. The ninth- or tenth-century Sinaite monk Philotheos states in his *Forty Texts on Watchfulness* that the enlightened heart is "enabled to contain within it the uncontainable God."[34] In the fourteenth century the hesychastic controversy provoked debate about the extent to which ascetics may participate in the uncreated energies of God; the role of the Jesus Prayer in this context is worthy of more detailed investigation than has been possible in the space of this article.[35] Third, it is worth asking why some of the most important contributors to the *Philokalia*, such as Maximos the Confessor, Symeon the New Theologian, and Gregory Palamas, do *not* devote much attention to the Jesus Prayer. There can be no doubt that they, like other spiritual writers in the Byzantine tradition, were concerned with hesychastic practice, contemplation and mystical union with God. However, the Jesus Prayer does not receive explicit treatment in their writings. This omission remains puzzling.[36]

Finally, at the beginning of this article we raised questions about the various audiences of the *Philokalia*. So far, we have studied the various texts in the anthology more from the point of view of their contemporary audiences than of the readers who continue to make use of them today. It is clear that most of these texts were originally aimed at monks and nuns, both coenobitic and solitary, who had the benefit of spiritual teachers who would help them to practice ascetic exercises including the Jesus Prayer. The same can probably be said of the *Philokalia* as a whole when it was compiled in the eighteenth century. Quite quickly, however, and especially after translations of the anthology began to be circulated in Russia, Romania, and elsewhere, the *Philokalia* began to be read and followed by lay Orthodox Christians. The nineteenth-century narrative known as *The Way of the Pilgrim* provides vivid testimony of the book's reception by a simple Russian peasant, who absorbed above all its teachings about continuous prayer and the Jesus Prayer.[37] Metropolitan Kallistos of Diokleia has wisely counseled modern readers of the *Philokalia* to seek spiritual guidance before attempting to carry out hesychastic methods including deep breathing and lengthy meditation on the Jesus Prayer.[38] The power of such practices, as we have seen, might be overwhelming for someone who is inexperienced in contemplation of this kind. It is worth recalling Zooey's wise counsel to his sister Franny in the novel by J.D. Salinger:

> If you are going to say the Jesus Prayer, at least say it to *Jesus*, and not to St. Francis and Seymour and Heidi's grandfather all wrapped up in one. Keep him in mind if you say it, and him only, and him as he was and not as you would like him to have been . . . who besides Jesus really knew which end was up? Nobody. Not Moses. Don't tell me Moses. He was a nice man and he kept in beautiful touch with his God, and all that—but that's exactly the point. He had to keep in touch. Jesus realized that there *is* no separation from God.[39]

202 ■ SPIRITUAL PRACTICES

Expressed in colloquial American English and set in the context of a disjointed secular world in which Franny is experiencing some form of emotional crisis, Salinger succeeds in conveying here the reason why the Jesus Prayer confers inner unity on the *Philokalia*. Invocation of Jesus, in whatever verbal form it takes, bridges the gulf between God and human beings. Jesus Christ is present in the heart of every human being even though most may not recognize this fact. The invocation of Christ, when understood properly, thus lies at the heart of all Christian prayer and ascetic endeavor.

■ FURTHER READING

Gillet, Lev. (A Monk of the Eastern Church). *On the Invocation of the Name of Jesus* (Springfield, IL: Templegate Publishers, 1985).

Hausherr, Irénée. *The Name of Jesus. The Names of Jesus Used by Early Christians. The Development of the Jesus Prayer*, trans. Charles Cummings (Kalamazoo, MI: Cistercian Publications, 1978).

Kallistos of Diokleia, Bishop. *The Power of the Name. The Jesus Prayer in Orthodox Spirituality* (Oxford: SLG Press, 1974; new ed. 1986).

Louth, Andrew. "The Theology of the *Philokalia*," in J. Behr, A. Louth, and D. Conomos, eds., *Abba: The Tradition of Orthodoxy in the West. Festschrift for Bishop Kallistos (Ware) of Diokleia* (Crestwood, NY: St. Vladimir's Seminary Press, 2003), 351–61.

Maloney, George, S.J. *Prayer of the Heart. The Contemplative Tradition of the Christian East* (Notre Dame, IN: Ave Maria Press, 1981; rev. ed. 2008).

A Monk of the Eastern Church. *The Jesus Prayer* (Crestwood, NY: St Vladimir's Seminary Press; rev. ed. 1987).

Sjögren, Per-Olov. *The Jesus Prayer*, trans. Sydney Linton (London: SPCK, 1975).

13 Uses and Abuses of Spiritual Authority in the Writings of St. Symeon the New Theologian

Hannah Hunt

The three texts in volume four of the *Philokalia* which are attributed to Symeon the New Theologian give copious advice on the Orthodox practice of spiritual direction (specifically denoted as spiritual fatherhood) and insist that such direction derives from a conscious awareness of the indwelling divine spark. Of the three texts, the first is the only one whose authorship is acknowledged as being solely by Symeon. "On Faith" equates to *Catechesis 22* to be found in a modern edition in *Sources Chrétiennes*.[1] This discourse provides some of the key autobiographical statements by Symeon; its inclusion within the *Philokalia* affirms the significance within the canon of spiritual writings of Symeon's insistence on a spirituality which derives totally from experience of God, as well as the seminal role of the spiritual father in the pneumatic growth of the Christian. It depicts the advent of "George" to the monastery, possibly around 970.[2] Specific references to Mark the Hermit (d. 430 near Ancyra) link Symeon's text to its desert root while highlighting the wisdom of his spiritual father in introducing him to such texts. The quotations given here by Symeon derive from the text "Of those who think that they are made righteous by works," and "On the Spiritual Law" is also referred to obliquely. Both these texts are translated in volume one of the *Philokalia*, denoting a common heritage from eremitical sources, a commonality of written style as well as content.

"The One Hundred and Fifty-Three Practical and Theological Texts" is an amalgam of texts by Symeon the Younger. Numbers 1–118 derive from the *First Theological Chapter*;[3] numbers 119–52 have been persuasively demonstrated to be by Symeon's spiritual father Symeon the Studite, known as Eulabes,[4] and the closing chapter is a record by Nicetas Stethatos of Symeon the younger's teaching. This style of writing in "sentences" is widespread, from the desert tradition onwards; Evagrios may be one model for such transmission of pithy aphorisms.

"The Three Methods of Prayer" is almost certainly not by Symeon, but its inclusion as a treatise on hesychastic methods of prayer again places Symeon within a continuum of spiritual advice within the Orthodox church.[5] A convincing argument against authorship by Symeon is the relative absence in it of much favorable mention of *penthos*, which he normally mentions with frequency as a marker of spiritual enlightenment. The question of what physical posture should be adopted for prayer, and the integration of the physical body with the spiritual life in prayer, are much written about in philokalic literature. Within writings more convincingly authored by Symeon, there are occasional references to bodily posture and the integration of the physical person into devotional activity. In "On Faith," the third piece of advice he claims to have received from the writings of Mark the Monk is about the inadequacy of praying with the body alone.[6] In "The Three Methods of Prayer," in addition to discussion of the merits of various types of prayer, there is a focus on obedience. The depiction of the final stage of contemplation as "that of the old man with grey hairs"[7] obliquely refers the reader to an elder, who is to be the "unerring guide."[8] Symeon's contribution to the later hesychast movement is often perceived retrospectively; John McGuckin describes him as a kind of fore-runner of the fourteenth century hesychast movement" despite not having authored the texts on methods of prayer.[9] Monastics had written about contemplative prayer practices since the time of the desert fathers onwards; Gregory of Sinai's "Two Methods of Prayer," (echoes of which may be found in the later pages of the *Philokalia* volume 4), represents, with Gregory Palamas, its flowering. The introductory notes to Palamas's text in the *Philokalia* volume 4 stress that such prayer should be undertaken only under appropriate spiritual guidance.[10] Comparisons are sometimes drawn between hesychastic prayer and the contemplative practices of non-Christian eastern religions of yoga,[11] and modern scholarship from social sciences also makes connections between the Christian practice and other forms of meditation.[12]

Among orthodox writers, Symeon is perhaps unusual in that his "external" life was shaped by three significant prompts all pertaining to his relationship with his spiritual father, who is known in the tradition as both the Studite and Eulabes.[13] Symeon himself was both spiritual child and spiritual father, and he writes from both perspectives.[14] The autobiographical content of the *Treatise on Faith* is one of many instances of Symeon's writing overtly or covertly about his encounters with spiritual direction in the monastery.[15] This autobiographical element functions not so much as a boast about his noetic battles as affirmation that teaching is valid only when based on personal experience. This conviction dominated his writings and brought him into conflict with the ecclesiastical authorities; it is this experience, together with the mystical nature of his experiences, which formed a link to the later Hesychast Movement. Like Symeon, Gregory Palamas interpreted the injunction in Ex. 20:12 to "honor your father and mother" as being even more appropriately applied to your spiritual father; he continued the practice by exegeting biblical teachings about family to suggest the priority of desert constructs of spiritual rebirth into a family of pious righteousness rather than worldly bonds.[16] Symeon's status "on the prophetic margins" of the Church to which he was devoted was due in no small part to his teachings on spiritual fatherhood.[17]

Recent additions to scholarship about Symeon's life include those of Alfeyev and Golitzin.[18] The seminal treatise on confession (a crucial document in terms of transmitting both the tradition he inherited and his own exegesis of it for his spiritual children) is now available in modern English translations of Holl's original edition[19] and other sources by both Golitzin[20] and Turner.[21] The *Ascetic Discourse* of Symeon Eulabes has now been edited and translated into French.[22]

Symeon's lifespan virtually overlaps the reign of the great Macedonian Emperor Basil II as well as the humanist Michael Psellos;[23] he formed a bridge between established traditions of monasticism rooted in desert practice[24] and the Byzantine court at the height of its power, a place of uneasy tensions between conflicting sources of authority and power. The synergy of charism (represented by the mystical experiences of monks who may not be ordained) and synodical oversight is longstanding.[25] Both parties claim authority, and the contest can be resolved to some extent by recognition of the different roles of each claimant. John Chryssavgis explains this relationship cogently: "Synods and Bishops are sources of authority which operate primarily in cases of conflict and necessity, that is in abnormal situations such as the condemnation of heresy . . . Ecclesial authority is the experience of the mystery of God in Christ through the Spirit who guides the Church."[26] This distinction resonates strongly with Symeon's oft-cited insistence on empirical experience of God, which he finds articulated in the witness and ministry of his spiritual father, Eulabes, who was not ordained. As a spiritual father himself, Symeon models an unquestioning reliance on a guide who has had direct experience of God and who therefore commands the obedience shown by Jesus to his heavenly father. In different texts we find Symeon asking for the right guide, thanking God that he has provided such a reliable helper,[27] and advising his own monks to find a similar guide.[28] We frequently find comments such as: "Send me a man who knows You so that, by serving and obeying him with all my strength as I would You, and by doing his will as I would Yours, I may be well-pleasing to You, the only God."[29]

Symeon's actions and teachings contributed to the rich sociopolitical mix of the late Byzantine church by integrating some aspects of secular literary conventions, such as autobiography, into his catechetical writing and hymnody. Apparently, from the time of Alexios the Studite autobiographies served almost to replace saints' lives; this change can be readily related to the extensive autobiographical material in Symeon's writing. Michael Angold suggests that the reason Symeon cloaked his identity in the pseudonym "George" was the already contentious nature of his assertions about the validity of the mystical encounter.[30] By the time Symeon as abbot was recording his early life experiences, he had encountered sufficient friction with ecclesiastical authorities to have evolved a sophisticated ability to integrate political expediency and spiritual insight. His place within Byzantine society is marked by uniquely strident assertions about an alternative hierarchy to that of emperor and patriarch—namely, the charismatic "golden chain" of the illuminated spiritual athlete who passes his mystical insight from one generation of spiritual child to the next, a chain of guidance which based its authenticity solely on mystical, light-filled visions of God. The image of the golden chain appears throughout the patristic tradition from Gregory Nyssa onward. Symeon sees *penthos* (contrition and tears of spiritual grief) as axiomatic of genuine spiritual illumination and he makes frequent reference to it in his writings, especially those which relate to Eulabes. Such weeping is modeled in some of the psalms, and in the New Testament by Peter's bitter weeping (Mt. 27:24) and the tenderly expressed penitence of the Sinful Woman in Lk. 7:35–47.[31]

Within Byzantine monasticism, the practice of spiritual fatherhood was widespread and based on longstanding tradition: in writing about it, Symeon acknowledges previous sources both directly and indirectly.[32] The earliest recorded monastic *vita* contains affirmation of the role of spiritual fatherhood, suggesting that it should be seen as normative to spiritual development even in eremitic contexts.[33] Spiritual fatherhood became for Symeon one of two "supreme princi-ples of his thought."[34] The mere presence in his life of Symeon Eulabes, however, constituted as much of a "source" as any textual tradition, in line with the indis-solubility of *praxis* and *theoria* in orthodox religious thought.[35] Symeon's own witness to Eulabes as spiritual father emphasises his charismatic rather than ecclesiological authority, noting that "I was myself a disciple to such a father, one who did not have the ordination from men, but who brought me by the hand—or better, by the spirit—into discipleship."[36] After a noviciate at the Stoudios, he became established as abbot of St. Mamas, where he put into practice the experi-ences and teachings of his elder, but no actual *typikon* exists for the monastery.[37] Rather what we have are records, in his catecheses and hymns, of examples of charismatic experience rooted always in biblical teaching and an insistence on penitence. This, as much as the insistence on experience, shaped his own spiritual parenting.[38]

While from a spiritual or theological perspective, the purpose of a spiritual father was to prompt salvation, historical perspectives on the situation in tenth-century Byzantium reveal other considerations. For example, Rosemary Morris argues that "contrary to theological teaching, the possession of a spiritual father in Byzantium was often not so much a mark of spirituality as of social distinction."[39] There are many nuances here; just as spiritual pride may prompt a person to seek a "superior" spiritual guide, so social class may suggest that mere acquisition of a spiritual father may impress other people within the secular world.[40] Having the "right" guide might display social advantage; just as in the imperial court which fostered the adolescent Symeon's political career, so in Byzantine monasticism there was also a role for patronage.[41] And while monasteries focused on the spiri-tual health and growth of monks, they also offered other forms of education, espe-cially at the Stoudios where Symeon was guided by Eulabes as a young man, on several occasions.[42]

Byzantine monasteries were complex societies; various versions of family life and friendship shaped their structure and social dynamics. In some places, a system of *metochia* existed whereby a couple of monks managed "individual households";[43] some monasteries amounted to a family business, with various members of extended families occupying or even founding the same monastery.[44] Symeon's contemporary, Michael Psellos, advocated a basis of *philia* in place of familial relationships. While this was found in some Byzantine monasteries, it may in fact be no more than a form of nepotism or favoritism; Browning dismisses this concept of *philia* as "the Byzantine equivalent of the old school tie."[45] Systematic and personal friendships were certainly involved in monastic formation but these would normally be fairly open. What was distinctive about that between Eulabes and Symeon was the mutual expectation of exclusivity, an intense loyalty that left no space for other social engagements. It was exactly the scenario likely to foster suspicion of a "cult."[46]

Axiomatic to the practice of spiritual fatherhood was the replacement of any vestige of loyalty to birth family in favor of a new commitment to the spiritual father, as an extension of renunciation of the world.[47] Symeon's renunciation of his birth family as part of what was to be left behind is a *topos* much developed in his biography. The biblical basis for this includes Lk. 14:26, which encourages the replacement of flesh family with a "new" bond, and 1 Cor. 4:15,[48] which invokes the image of fatherhood: "Though you have countless guides in Christ, you do not have many fathers." Adherence to this rule effectively transferred authority to the spiritual father, from not only the birth family but the wider church.[49] Monastic life therefore has at its heart a practice which the modern world readily reads as a cult; namely, the removal of the aspiring spiritual athlete from the outer world and especially his or her birth family.[50] Contact with such "worldly" social groups (or, more important, attachment to them) was actively discouraged as antithetical to spiritual growth. The response to this situation by the families left behind is also noted, and demonstrates not only the strength of emotional bonds but the conflicting ties and expectations of secular and religious life. Symeon's overt preference for the heavenly father over his father on earth is repeated throughout his texts and is clearly inherited from the teaching of Eulabes.[51] As is noted above, Symeon's place in the continuum of such teaching is demonstrated by echoes to be found in the writings of Gregory Palamas and Gregory of Sinai. Symeon's biography suggests that the disappointment expressed by his birth father over the son's decision to enter the monastery may owe as much to the frustration of paternal hopes for a political career as to providing filial support for his declining years.[52]

The metaphor of spiritual parenting and engendering of ascetic life is overt in Symeon's writings on spiritual fatherhood and is a key requirement of a spiritual father. Other roles or titles set out the requirements for authentic spiritual guidance and the purpose of it; the elder should act as *anadochos* (akin to sponsor or godparent) with an emphasis on bearing the burdens of the child in a manner which goes beyond the requirement on all Christians to do so (Gal. 6:2, Rom. 15:1).[53] As a spiritual father, Symeon declares dramatically his sacrificial love for his "child"; "I will die if God overlooks you [my child]. I will hand over myself to the eternal fire in your place if He deserts you."[54] Symeon's own *Letter on Confession* gives an extensive list of appropriate qualities, in conscious imitation of John of Sinai's *The Pastor*, which acts as a companion piece to the eponymous *Ladder of Divine Ascent*.[55] The elder should act as navigator[56] and physician.[57] The *Letter on Confession* repeatedly portrays the process of spiritual direction as one of healing; a victim of spiritual assault needs "a sympathetic and compassionate physician . . . and intercessor and friend of God."[58] The resonance here to the Good Samaritan suggests perhaps the outsider status of the spiritual father. Other roles include that of intercessor, mediator, and confessor.[59]

The spiritual father should be seen as Christ-like, and adherence to him is in *mimesis* of Christ's obedience to his Father;[60] the elder's advice should be seen as coming directly from God.[61] The image derives from a sense of Christ as the prototype of the "physician of souls and bodies,"[62] in his care for his flock, but also as the model of the son of God who was obedient to his Heavenly Father. A commonly found image, which like the *mimesis* of Christ roots the whole practice of spiritual direction in its biblical sources, is that of the elder as a new Moses, leading spiritual children from the bondage of sin.[63] The invocation of Moses gives prophetic status to the charismatically illuminated elder, which accords well with the uneasy coexistence of charismatic and ecclesiastical leadership in late Byzantine society. The spiritual father is elevated to a status of angelic[64] or Godlike significance; Symeon recounts that "the young man" accepted the recommendation to read Mark the Monk "as though it had been sent by God Himself,"[65] and that "He did all these things as if God Himself had told him so."[66] This idea is overtly stated in Climacus, in common with many of the definitions of spiritual fatherhood.[67] *Mimesis* is traditionally the means by which learning took place, from the time of the disciples onward.[68] We see here the potential seeds of excessive veneration: Symeon, giving thanks for his spiritual father, writes: "As for my fellow-worker and my helper—thy holy disciple and apostle—I reverenced him as Thee who hast created me. I honoured and loved him with my soul."[69]

The extravagant nature of Symeon's diction here is not unusual; in a *Catechesis* entirely devoted to Eulabes, he asserts that his elder "shone like the sun,"[70] a scriptural reference which in itself suggests the quasi-divine nature of his elder. The apostolic claim was not singled out for criticism by ecclesiastical authorities, but shows clearly the extent to which Symeon believed in the authenticity of his elder's spiritual authority and its place within a continuum from Christ's obedient submission to his father's will.

Christ is invoked, too, in the absence of a spiritual father; you should not assume that a spiritual father will be granted whenever you want one, so if you cannot find one you should simply raise your eyes constantly to Christ, Symeon recommends.[71] Christ, in his obedience to God, is set out as the prototype of the spiritual relationship.[72]

Just as in the modern world the spiritual traveler is urged not to actively seek particular spiritual fathers but to accept the one they have been given by God,[73] similarly, elders are discouraged from actively seeking out pupils. The assumption is that the golden chain of spiritual fatherhood will naturally draw the right child to the right elder at the right time, so the process is not one of pursuit but of discernment and intuition. The spiritual child in turn becomes a spiritual father. As Stithatos puts it: "Such a rebirth comes through obedience to a spiritual father, for if we do not first become pregnant with the seed of the Logos through the teaching of such a father and through him become children of God, we cannot be spiritually reborn." He continues that this system was modeled by Christ's twelve disciples as the start of the golden chain of spiritual saints.[74] The engendering of spiritual children is advocated as an appropriate alternative to physical parenting.

At the heart of the relationship between spiritual father and child is obedience. This reorienting of authority and loyalty clearly risks undermining the status and role of the abbot, metropolitan, or even emperor when taken to extremes. As so often occurs, worldly and spiritual demands conflict with each other; Symeon advocates obedience not to secular or even ecclesial authority but to charism. The Lord's obedience unto death (Phil. 2:8) is invoked as providing the model for monastic obedience, which is "the best ornament of the monk."[75] The biblical model sows the seed for the vast body of desert and patristic teaching on refocusing of a penitent's will, which would have been available to Symeon and his precursors. It also forms the bedrock of modern spiritual direction.[76] In John Climacos's *The Ladder of Divine Ascent* the longest chapter and a rung early on the ladder is entitled *On Obedience*. Climacos presents obedience as spiritual freedom rather than a guilty response.[77] Climacos in turn may have found such teaching in the writings of Pachomius, Diadochus, Barsanuphius, and John of Gaza. The desert fathers make it clear that obedience is not to a rule (even where one exists, given that most of these writings derive from eremitic rather than coenobitic contexts); it exists as part of a continuum of Christ-like obedience not to an abstract concept of "authority" but to a specific person. Among the *Apophthegmata*, it is common to find statements such as that of Mius: "Obedience responds to obedience. When someone obeys God, God obeys his request."[78] The *Apophthegmata* abound with examples of obedience as an essential relinquishing of the will, not necessarily as denoting excessive ascetic practices but as an unquestioning acceptance that one's father's insights were blessed and to be obeyed. The spiritual child demonstrated this obedience partly by acting as a servant to the elder.[79] In the case of Eulabes and Symeon, far from the elder requiring great feats of fasting and vigil, he was noted for being a moderate disciplinarian; the obedience came through the younger Symeon's humble acceptance that excessive practice might not be what was required.[80] The injunctions of your spiritual father might even be deliberately absurd or incomprehensible, such as John the Dwarf being told to water a piece of wood.[81] The spiritual child who plants his feet on the "rock of obedience to his spiritual father" builds on solid foundations.[82] The child must act in complete confidence in the guidance of his spiritual father, as denoted by the title of Symeon's *Hymn 4*.[83] Obedience to the spiritual father is "axiomatic of the relationship," as far as Symeon the younger was concerned.[84] Later fathers, especially those within the hesychastic tradition, continued to draw on this synthesis of desert and patristic teaching. Gregory of Sinai places obedience as the third of five rungs of the spiritual ladder.[85]

As we have seen, at the heart of spiritual fatherhood is the unquestioning devotion to the elder. Where this attachment becomes a focus on that person himself as a focus for veneration rather than as a conduit of grace, then delusion and corruption may occur. (This is what is contested in the case of Elder Ephraim in St. Anthony's monastery, Arizona, discussed below.) Symeon potentially encouraged excessive devotion to his father by his assertion that ordained members of the church have become corrupt and that personal charism (denoted through penitent tears and accompanied by taboric illumination) has replaced the automatic capacity of all clergy to hear confessions and remit sin. This issue has been much debated; in essence, it was the norm for monks to make their confession to the abbot but laity could confess to nonordained monks. Symeon subverts this custom by insisting on the need to restrict the hearing of confession to those who are charismatically gifted with the ability to loose sins. For Symeon, the appropriateness of hearing confession (and thus the authority to confer absolution of sins) rests solely with those who "possess direct experience of the Holy Spirit."[86] The practice of lay confession to monks was normalized, according to the *Letter on Confession* 11, because of the corruption of clergy.[87] The *hypotyposis* of the Studite monastery prescribed for monks a daily examination of thought before the hegumen, with confession to a chosen elder being a practice reserved for the laity.[88] One of the traditional roles of the spiritual father was to act as confessor to his "child": a good confessor is identified by his prayerful intercession (with tears) on behalf of his child.[89]

Symeon's apparent circumvention of the established church as the agent of re-mission of sins and therefore gateway to salvation was highly controversial. His biography presents various reasons for his veneration of Eulabes being seen as a "cult," though ironically Nicetas Stethatos's affirmation of the concept of a charis-matic hierarchy de facto militates for a rather hagiographic account of Symeon's life, as well as a degree of arrogance in positioning himself as a link also in the golden chain.[90] Trained by Symeon, he argues that "the real bishop is the one who has knowledge."[91] In his writings for his monks, Symeon frequently portrays Eula-bes as a living saint. *Catechesis 6(7)* refers to Eulabes as "a saint . . . who received within himself the wholeness of the Paraclete."[92] He is "equal to the great and exalted saints,"[93] and we also find honorary references such as "When the saint saw me."[94] After Eulabes's death, Symeon commissioned an icon and instituted lit-urgies in his honor.[95] Partly as a result of this action, he was sent into exile and largely ignored by the church until after his death. The mere presence of such an icon was an indication that Eulabes was being depicted as an intercessor or medi-ator, which was a common practice in the Byzantine period[96] and was at the heart of Symeon's teaching on penitence as the means to salvation.[97] In an attempt to mollify those who accused him of instituting a cult of Eulabes, Symeon had the words "the saint" removed from the icon he had commissioned.[98] Suggestions that the spiritual father be viewed as Christ-like are given further weight by modern parallels of opposition to the "cult" with the battles of iconodules for acceptance of the veneration of icons in the Byzantine period.[99]

Although much is written about what constitutes good spiritual direction, the literature also gives warnings and illustrations of its reverse.[100] The classic desert quality of discernment is invoked as the means by which an individual should decide whether or not to accept guidance from a particular spiritual father.

The main stumbling block to fruitful spiritual direction was lack of discern-ment; in his fourth letter, Symeon highlights a concern about self-delusion on the part of those who offer guidance, addressing it to "one of the self-appointed teachers who attribute apostolic dignity to themselves while lacking the grace with it from above."[101] True teaching, he asserts, comes from neither men nor angels but from spiritual grace.[102] Fruitful spiritual direction requires an appropriate response on the part of the spiritual child; humility and obedience are at the forefront of their engagement with the process, but discernment is needed also to ensure that the spiritual father is authentically gifted with spiritual insight.

The dangers of bad spiritual direction are spelled out in the *Letter on Confes-sion*; an "inexperienced physician" may be overly severe. Equally dangerous is the practice condemned in one of his *Ethical Discourses* to offer "inappropriate sym-pathy" so that the spiritual invalid might "think [you] are getting better when in fact you are still ailing."[103] Those who pretend spiritual superiority "differ in no way with respect to the invisible motions of their soul from those who are the most extravagant in malice."[104] But the key crime is to attempt to teach or direct from a position of ignorance of the indwelling spirit.[105]

Such apparent spiritual arrogance may underlie a contentious example of spir-itual fatherhood in the twenty-first century in North America, where an allegation of abuse of the practice was publicly aired. Spiritual direction features strongly in the Orthodox church of today and is explicitly linked to biblical examples such as Acts 8:31, where an Ethiopian reader of the OT asks Philip to explain the text.[106] Much of it is offered not within the parish context but in local monasteries; indeed, Chryssavgis suggests that the "chief social role" of monasteries today is to provide opportunities for spiritual direction, which is normally sought here rather than from scholars.[107] Just as in the Byzantine empire, spiritual fathers had an uneasy relationship with secular counterparts, straining the boundaries between church, empire, and monastery, so in modern America in particular there have been some anxieties about the choices made by young men and women choosing to adopt a spiritual kinship which takes them away from birth families and communities. Ironically, this situation exactly replicates Symeon's own life choice; his parents were reluctant to let him become a monk.[108] Further conflict arises from the rivalries between different ethnic autocephalous branches of the modern orthodox church. Both the Greek and Russian Orthodox churches question the point at which adherence to an elder becomes a cult; the danger of spiritual pride leading a secular person to assume that only a particularly renowned elder is worthy of his confession and obedience. The *plani* (or *prelist*, to adopt the Russian term) of self-delusion is articulated by excessive piety and the inability of those involved to distinguish between what happens in monasteries and how this true tradition is outworked in parish life, where different constraints and imperatives apply.[109]

Father Theologos Pantanizopoulos (born Niko) entered the Greek Orthodox monastery of St. Anthony, in the Sonoran Desert of Arizona,[110] where his spiritual father is Elder Ephraim, a disciple of Elder Joseph the Hesychast. Despite Ephraim's Athonite roots, his role as spiritual director has been challenged by the secularized parents of the young man in question, whose autobiographical notes chart a growing awareness of monastic calling in terms and on a timescale which mimic that of Symeon himself. Like his tenth-century counterpart, he enjoyed the worldly temptations of his own society while beginning to explore a religious alternative; like Symeon, he explored several options and returned from time to time to his birth family before finally committing himself to a monastic life. Like Augustine before him, he enjoyed the support of two friends who were also seeking an alternative to sex and drugs; they were known as "the three musketeers" because of their close friendship. Like Symeon, Father Theologos cites patristic sources (in this case, John Climacus) as a source for his inspiration. He was allegedly treated for depression and physical ailments within the monastery, using herbal rather than allopathic medicines.

Concern for obedience, humility, and a rightly oriented and proportionate piety are classic desert concerns, as was noted above. However, these qualities sit uneasily with modern secular agendas, and when they are observed within contemporary society, the Orthodox practice of traditional pastoral relationships may make the church vulnerable to accusations of deviancy or cult. Using conventional eastern Christian methodology, Chryssavgis attempts a rationale for modern problems by drawing on patristic models; St. Chrysostom, he notes, condemns the delusion of superiority in his *Homily on the Hebrews* 34, 1.[111] He also discusses the Justinian model of "cooperation" between the earthly kingdom and heavenly hierarchy.[112] He is also open to the insights of modern psychotherapy; the powerful emotions which may flow between a spiritual father and his parishioner may demonstrate "transference and countertransference" rather than genuine love, he notes.[113] The classic anxiety about discernment of true enlightenment is raised, with the possibility of both pseudo-direction and misdirection being concerns for modern folk.[114]

Concern is also expressed about the fact that modern modes of communication lend themselves particularly easily to the dissemination of inappropriate gossip about church affairs and individuals.[115] It is pertinent that the troubling case of Father Theologos was aired by his parents through internet postings,[116] and a television broadcast in February 2006 on KVOA Channel 4.[117] In turn the young man's account of events was posted in a 25-page posting on the Athos in America website.[118] The spiritual father in question, Elder Ephraim of Philotheou, has a facebook page dedicated to him, and videos of his spiritual advice appear on You Tube.[119] The issue continues to be debated on electronic fora such as monachos. net, which featured a report of a speaker on "Cult Mentality—a Threat to Individual Responsibility in the Church."[120] Although the furore about this particular incident has quieted, the challenge presented to the modern world by the moral and religious traditions of orthodoxy remains, not least because within orthodoxy there can be no division between a theoretical approach and the outliving of doctrinal understanding.

Whether in modern America, Mount Sinai, the monasteries of Constantinople, or the steppes of Russia, orthodox Christians have sought and continue to seek the right guide for the pathway toward salvation. The choice of fatherhood as a model for spiritual engendering and mentoring carries heavy connotations; intrinsically biblical in origin, it demands a radical shifting of human allegiance from the birth family to a new social and political community, where discernment and unquestioning obedience replace any more domestic criteria for acceptance within a family unit. Symeon's reworking of the desert tradition places his use of spiritual fatherhood into the vortex of state/church relationships in his day, and his insistence on the authority of charisma forges links in the chain between the Hebrew prophets, John the Forerunner, Christ himself, the hesychasts, and mystics of subsequent centuries, the hidden *staretz* of soviet Russia. The concept is gendered, in a world which ostensibly seeks to emancipate women; it is subjective and mystical, in a world which better understands the concrete and material. As a human construct, it is vulnerable to abuse, misunderstanding, neglect, and decay. As a means of sharing the divinity of Christ, it remains the bedrock of orthodox spirituality.

■ BIBLIOGRAPHY

Alfeyev, Hilarion. St. *Symeon the New Theologian and Orthodox Tradition*. Oxford: Oxford University Press, 2000.
———. "St. Symeon the New Theologian, St. Symeon the Pious and the Studite Tradition." *Studia Monastica* 36 (1994): 183–222.
———. ed. *Syméon le Studite: Discours Ascétique*, trans. Louis Neyrand, Sources Chrétiennes, no. 460. Paris: Editions du cerf, 2001.

Angold, Michael. "The Autobiographical Impulse in Byzantium." *Dumbarton Oaks Papers* 52 (1998): 225–57.

Browning, Robert. "Enlightenment and Repression in Byzantium in the Eleventh and Twelfth Centuries." *Past & Present* 69 (Nov. 1975): 3–23.

De Catanzaro, C. J. (tr.) *Symeon the New Theologian: The Discourses.* New York: Paulist Press, 1980.

Chariton, Igumen. *The Art of Prayer: An Orthodox Anthology.* tr. Elizabeth M. Palmer. London: Faber, 1966.

Chryssavgis, John. *Soul Mending: The Art of Spiritual Direction.* Brookline, MA: Holy Cross Orthodox Press, 2000.

Deferrari, Roy J. *Early Christian Biographies.* Fathers of the Church, Catholic University of America, 1952.

Golitzin, Hieromonk Alexander. "Hierarchy versus Anarchy? Dionysius Areopagita, Symeon the New Theologian, Nicetas Stethatos and Their Common Roots in Ascetical Tradition." *St. Vladimir's Theological Quarterly* 38.2 (1994): 131–79.

Golitzin, Alexander. *St. Symeon the New Theologian: On The Mystical Life: The Ethical Discourses.* 3 vols. Crestwood, NY: St. Vladimir's Seminary Press, 1995–1997.

Gouillard, Jean. "Syméon le Jeune, le Théologien." In *Dictionnaire de théologie catholique* 14.2, 2941–59. Paris: Librairie Letouzey et Ané, 1941.

Graef, Hilda. "The Spiritual Director in the Thought of Symeon the New Theologian." In *Kyriakon: Festscrift for J. Quasten* (vol. 2), ed. Patrick Granfield and Josef A. Junmann, 608–14. Münster Westfalen: Ascehendorff, 1970.

Hausherr, Iréné. *Direction Spirituelle en Orient Autrefois.* Rome: Institutium Orientalium Studiorum, 1955. Translated as *Spiritual Direction in the Early Christian East,* tr. Anthony P. Gythiel. Kalamazoo, MI:, 1990.

Hausherr, Iréné, and Horn, Gabriel. "Un Grand Mystique Byzantin: Vie de Syméon le Nouveau Théologien par Nicétas Stéthatos." Rome: *Orientalia Christiana* XII (45) (1928): lvi-lxvii.

Hausherr, Iréné. (ed). "La Méthode d'Oraison Hésychaste." Rome: *Orientalia Christiana* IX -2 (36):1927.

Holl, Kurt *Enthusiasmus und Bussgewalt beim griechischen Mönchtum: Eine Studie zu Symeon dem neuen Theologen.* Leipzig: Hinrichs, 1898.

Hunt, Hannah. "Byzantine Christianity." In *The Blackwell Companion to Eastern Christianity,* ed. Ken Parry, 73–93. Oxford: Blackwell Publishing, 2007.

———. *Joy-bearing Grief: Tears of Contrition in the Writings of the Early Syrian and Byzantine Fathers.* Leiden: Brill, 2004.

———. "The Reforming Abbot and his Tears: *Penthos* in Late Byzantium." In *Spirituality in Late Byzantium,* ed. Eugenia Russell, 13–20. Cambridge: Cambridge Scholars, 2009.

Kazhdan, Alexander. "State, Feudal, and Private Economy in Byzantium." *Dumbarton Oaks Papers* 47 (1993): 83–100.

Krausmüller, Dirk. "The Monastic Communities of Stoudios and St. Mamas in the Second Half of the Tenth Century." In *The Theotokos Evergetis and Eleventh-Century Monasticism,* ed. Margaret Mullet and Anthony Kirby, 67–85. Belfast: Belfast Byzantine Texts and Translations 6.1, 1994.

Krivochéine, Basil. *In the Light of Christ: Saint Symeon the New Theologian, Life—Spirituality—Doctrine.* New York: St. Vladimir's Seminary Press, 1986.

Louchakova, Olga, and Warner, A., "Via Kundalini: Pyschosomatic excursions in transpersonal psychology." *The Humanist Pyschologist* 31 (2–3) (2003):115–58.

Luibheid, Colm, and Russell, Norman. *John Klimakos: The Ladder of Divine Ascent.* New York: Paulist Press, 1982.

Maloney, George. (tr.) *Hymns of Divine Love by Symeon the New Theologian.* Denville, NJ: Dimension Books, 1975.

Matus, Thomas. "Symeon the New Theologian and the Hesychast 'Method.'" *Diakonia* 10 (1975): 260–70.

McGuckin, John Anthony. "The Notion of the Luminous Vision in 11th Century Byzantium: Interpreting the Biblical and Theological Paradigms of St. Symeon the New Theologian." In *Acts of the Belfast Byzantine Colloquium*, 1–34. Belfast, 1996.

———. "Symeon the New Theologian." In *Encyclopedia of Greece and the Hellenic Tradition*, ed. G. Speake. London, 2000.

———. "Symeon the New Theologian and Byzantine Monasticism." In *Mount Athos and Byzantine Monasticism*, ed. Anthony Bryer and Mary Cunningham, 17–35. Aldershot: Ashgate, 1996.

———. "St. Symeon the New Theologian (969–1022): Byzantine Spiritual Renewal in Search of a Precedent." *The Church Retrospective*, Studies in Church History no. 33, 75–90. Oxford: Boydell Press, 1997.

———. "Symeon the New Theologian: His Vision of Theology." *Patristic and Byzantine Review*, 3.3 (1984): 208–14.

———. "Symeon the New Theologian's Hymns of Divine Eros: A Neglected Masterpiece of the Christian Mystical Tradition." *Spiritus: A Journal of Christian Spirituality* 5.2 (2005) 182–202.

McGuckin, Paul. (tr.) *Symeon the New Theologian: The Practical and Theological Chapters and the Three Theological Discourses.* Kalamazoo, MI: Cistercian Publications, 1982.

Morris, Rosemary. *Monks and Laymen in Byzantium, 843–1118.* Cambridge: Cambridge University Press, 1995.

———. "The Political Saint of the Eleventh Century." *Studies Supplementary to Sobornost 5* (1981): 43–50.

———. 'Spiritual Fathers and Temporal Patrons: Logic and Contradiction in Byzantine Monasticism in the Tenth Century.' *Revue Benedictine* 103 (1993): 273–88.

Neyrand, Louis, and Paramelle, Joseph (trs.) *Hymnes, Syméon le nouveau théologien* Sources Chrétiennes, 3 vols. 156, 174, 196. Paris: Editions du cerf, 1969–73.

Oikonomides, Nicolas. "The Holy Icon as an Asset." *Dumbarton Oaks Papers* 45 (1991): 35–44.

Palmer, George. E. H, Sherrard, Philip, and Ware, Kallistos. (trs.) the *Philokalia*. 4 vols. London: Faber & Faber, 1979–95.

Paramelle, Joseph. (tr.) *Symeon the New Theologian Catéchèses.* Sources Chrétiénnes, 3 vols. 96, 104, 113. Paris: Editions du cerf, 1963–65.

Sommerfeldt, John. R. (ed.) *Abba: Guides to Wholeness and Holiness East and West* Kalamazoo, MI: Cistercian Publications, 1982.

Špidlík, Tomáš. "Syméon le Nouveau Théologien." In *Dictionnaire Spiritualité* 14, 1387–1401. Paris: Beauchesne, 1990.

Sturrock, John. *The Language of Autobiography: Studies in the First Person Singular.* Cambridge: Cambridge University Press, 1993.

Talbot, Alice-Mary. "The Byzantine Family and the Monastery." *Dumbarton Oaks Papers* 44 (1990): 119–29.

Turner, H. John M. *The Epistles of St. Symeon the New Theologian* Oxford: Oxford University Press, 2009.

———. *St. Symeon the New Theologian and Spiritual Fatherhood* Leiden: Brill, 1990.

———. "St. Symeon the New Theologian: His Place in the History of Spiritual Fatherhood." *Studia Patristica* XXIII (1989): 91–5.

Ward, Benedicta. *The Sayings of the Desert Fathers: The Alphabetical Collection* Kalamazoo, MI: Cistercian Publications, 1975.

Ware, Kallistos. "The Mystery of God and Man in St. Symeon the New Theologian." *Sobornost* 6/4 (1971): 227–36.

———. "Tradition and Personal Experience in Later Byzantine Theology." *Eastern Churches Review* 3.2 (1970): 131–41.

■ WEBSITES

St. Anthony's Greek Orthodox Monastery website. Online. Available: http://www.stanthonysmonastery.org/index.php. April 19, 2010.

"Orthodox Monasticism is not a cult." Athos in America website. Online. Available: http://www.athosinamerica.org/. April 19, 2010.

Paffhausen, Hieromonk Jonah. *5 Good Reasons Not to Visit a Monastery.* Again Magazine (issue not stated). Online. Available: http://kiev-orthodox.org/site/english/722/. April 19, 2010.

Young, Priest Alexey. *"Understandest thou what thou readest" The Place and Importance of Spiritual Direction.* Online. Available: http://www.roca.org.OA/142/142p.htm. April 19, 2010.

14 Hope for the Passible Self: The Use and Transformation of the Human Passions in the Fathers of the *Philokalia*

Paul M. Blowers

To embark on exploring the healing and the *transformation* of the human passions (πάθη) in the writings of the *Philokalia* could appear to some readers a dubious project. Many will remember principally the keywords signifying suppression—such as "self-control" (ἐγκράτεια), "mortification" (νέκρωσις), and especially "dispassion" (ἀπάθεια)—in the *Philokalia*'s treatment of the passions in the spiritual life. In addition, there is the close association of the passions with demonic infestation and the battle with illicit thoughts. Passions are catalogued as "vices," targeted for spiritual warfare. The eleventh-century Studite monk Nicetas Stethatos calls them the "Red Sea" that has to be crossed in order to attain to divine knowledge and holy bliss.[1] Meanwhile the *Philokalia*'s texts are mostly instructions concerning the immediate existential challenges of achieving spiritual maturity and tranquility (ἡσυχία), not scholastic works of theological anthropology treating in detail the origins, anatomy, and potential tractability of the passions.

The Fathers of the *Philokalia* nevertheless remained beholden to a broad stream of early Byzantine ascetical doctrine—I would identify it as a theologically and christologically "chastened" humanism—which considered the passible faculties to be rooted in the human constitution and potentially salutary, and which championed the wise use (χρῆσις) of the passions, even the transformation of the passible faculties themselves, in the mystery of deification. To understand this theologically refined humanism and its impact on the *Philokalia*, we will first consider at some length two crucial currents within that stream. One, certainly, was the Alexandrian heritage of Christian paideia, the education of the soul, articulated in Clement and Origen, later Didymus the Blind, all of whom addressed the healing and retraining of the passible self in the direction of assimilation to God (ὁμοίωσις θεῷ). A second crucial current was the cumulative tradition of Greek patristic theological anthropology, with its concentrated analysis of the origins and "economy" of human passibility (πάθος; τὸ παθητόν). In this connection, Gregory of Nyssa and Maximus the Confessor loom very large.

▪ ALEXANDRIAN AND CAPPADOCIAN PAIDEIA: EMOTIONAL THERAPY AND THE CONVERSION OF HUMAN DESIRE

Clement and Origen were not alone in constructively engaging Greco-Roman traditions of philosophical psychology and asceticism, but indisputably they were pioneers, and the better studies have shown how they imposed significant critical filters on pagan paideia and "psychagogy" in their efforts to contextualize Christian asceticism philosophically.[2] Even if they left a mixed taste in the mouths of their Byzantine successors (e.g., Maximus the Confessor, living on the other side of the Origenist Controversy, mentions Clement by name, but never Origen), their work was formative.

1. Consideration of the Moral Psychology of the Passions and Passible Faculties

Largely through the Alexandrians, Christianity gained its earliest bridge to the longstanding Greco-Roman discussions of the ontology, physiology, and, most important, the morality of the human passions. In ancient moral psychology, Stoics had debated whether the passions were errant mental judgments ($\kappa\rho\acute{\iota}\sigma\epsilon\iota\varsigma$) of the appearances of things, or diseased states ($\pi\acute{a}\theta\eta$) of the soul, or both.[3] To include them *within* the domain of the mind, or $\acute{\eta}\gamma\epsilon\mu o\nu\iota\kappa\acute{o}\nu$, rather than treat them as purely extrinsic agitations, seemed inevitable if their subjects were to be held morally accountable for them.[4] Cicero and Seneca even considered them voluntary if in fact they could be controlled or eradicated.[5] Though much Stoic attention famously focused on the emotions as destabilizing annoyances—especially the cardinal passions of desire ($\epsilon\pi\iota\theta\upsilon\mu\acute{\iota}a$), pleasure ($\acute{\eta}\delta o\nu\acute{\eta}$), fear ($\phi\acute{o}\beta o\varsigma$), and grief ($\lambda\acute{\upsilon}\pi\eta$)[6]—there was room still for the "short list" of $\epsilon\acute{\upsilon}\pi\acute{a}\theta\epsilon\iota a\iota$, designating not so much "good passions" as reasonable affective states conducive to the moral health of the soul.[7] There was room as well for a select few emotions worthy of the "novice" but not the advanced Stoic sage.[8]

Platonists meanwhile carried forward their master's reflection on the passions as rooted in the body (*Phaedo* 66C) but also implicating the lower soul's desiring ($\epsilon\pi\iota\theta\upsilon\mu\eta\tau\iota\kappa\acute{o}\nu$) and irascible ($\theta\upsilon\mu\iota\kappa\acute{o}\nu$) faculties, which, rightly conditioned and trained, could contribute to the cultivation of virtue.[9] They inherited as well Plato's acknowledgment of the soul's engrained passion or yearning ($\acute{\epsilon}\rho\omega\varsigma$) for beauty as a *sine qua non* of its mobility and moral orientation.[10] All told, there was considerable variability among Stoic and Platonic positions on the passions, thus leaving latitude for a Middle Stoic writer like Posidonius of Apamea (second century B.C.E.), for example, to err with Platonists in seeing the passions as rooted in faculties of the lower soul rather than as faulty judgments within the mind.[11]

Clement and Origen were thoroughly conversant with these Stoic and Platonic speculations on the ontology and morality of the passions. Clement, who echoes the Stoic definition of a passion as "an impulse [$\acute{o}\rho\mu\acute{\eta}$] that exceeds or overextends reasonable limits, an impulse impervious to reason," and the passions generally as "an unnatural movement of the soul in defiance of reason,"[12] also positions them outside the ἡγεμονικόν within the so-called "carnal spirit" (πνεῦμα σαρκικόν).[13] But he sides with Posidonius, Galen, and certain Middle Platonic writers in denying that passions are errant mental judgments, connecting them instead with the soul's desiring (τὸ ἐπιθυμητικόν) and irascible (τὸ θυμικόν) faculties.[14] This was an important nuance for later *Philokalia* authors since, over and beyond the pejorative associations with illicit carnal passions, these passible faculties could still be considered intrinsically neutral or indifferent (ἀδιάφορα) and thus capable of being "used" to morally virtuous or vicious ends.

For his part Origen, followed by Didymus the Blind and Jerome, explored the morality of what some Stoics called προπάθειαι ("pre-passions"), the first stirrings or involuntary movements of affect that could, if not checked, become full-fledged passions. Origen and Didymus treat these as morally innocent unless reason gives them consent, allowing them to progress into culpable emotions.[15] They are naturally human, and well attested in the Bible. Even Jesus experienced them in the trepidation of Gethsemane, proving all the more his profound identification with humanity.[16] Origen and Didymus take a bold step beyond the Stoics, however, in identifying the προπάθειαι with nascent "thoughts" (*cogitationes* = λογισμοί), which, in the negative sense, can denote the morally tainted *suggestiones* that remain innocent agitations (*commotiones*) so long as we inhibit them from becoming more. These can arise from within our own hearts or else be inspired by demons, and if the "first movements" (*primi motus*) of something like intemperance stir within us, and we indulge them further, the demons can capitalize and lead us to sin.[17] Didymus speculates that the προπάθειαι are induced by "ideas" (ἐνθυμήματα), potentially disrupting impressions or judgments that likewise can be implanted by the Devil.[18] In the worst case scenario, bad thoughts or ideas can overwhelm ascetics, driving them into an array of vicious passions—a doctrine famously passed from Origen and Didymus to Evagrius Ponticus and other authors of the *Philokalia*. Conversely, however, the soul might still be disciplined to give full assent to healthy λογισμοί conducive to virtue.

2. Emotional Therapy and the Radical Reorientation of the Soul's Desire

Emotional therapy through *philosophia* had deep roots in Hellenistic moral thought. If the passions arose from faculties (δυνάμεις) proper to the soul, there were appropriate reconditioning exercises that could be enlisted for the sake of emotional (and moral) health. The Greco-Roman schools had several *cognitive* therapies for managing the passions, some of which had definite parallels in Christian writers.[19] Clement of Alexandria showcases Christian therapies in his *Paedagogus*, in which he depicts Christ the Logos as the ultimate instructor and physician for the "philokalic" soul:

> While there is one course of training [ἀγωγή] for philosophers, another for orators, still another for wrestlers, so too there is an excellent disposition [διάθεσις] derived from Christ's pedagogy that obtains in the free will that cherishes moral beauty [φιλοκάλῳ προαιρέσει] ... The training of the Logos is not overstrained but is of just the right intensity [εὔτονος]. The Logos is called Savior precisely because he has

found rational medicines [λογικὰ φάρμακα] for our human sensibility and health, and because he looks for just the right moment to reprove evil, to expose the roots of the passions, to excise irrational desires, to point out what we should avoid, and to provide the antidotes of salvation for all who are diseased.[20]

In the *Paedagogus* the "healing of the passions" (ἴασις τῶν παθῶν) comes through measured responses to concrete situations liable to inflame corrupt passions.[21] The goal is moderation or modulation—μετριοπάθεια—en route to the godlike dispassion [ἀπάθεια] enjoyed by the perfected Christian gnostic.[22] Standing securely in a broad-based philosophical tradition of "care of the self," Clement nonetheless recurs to the Mosaic Law along with the New Testament for the definitive constraints, directives, and encouragements in ascetical discipline.[23] Vying with heterodox Gnostics, the dialectical relation he establishes between radical self-mortification and salvific transformation of embodied human nature is extraordinarily intense, nowhere more so than with respect to the struggle with desires (ἐπιθυμίαι), sexual and otherwise. Clement readily honors, for example, a Stoic distinction between "appetite" (ὄρεξις), as a natural and useful faculty of the soul, and as an irrational and illicit "lust" (ἐπιθυμία).[24]

But could the passible faculties be integrated into the cultivation of virtue? The Stoic notion of good "use" (χρῆσις) of the emotions, and Aristotle's teleological approach to virtue, in which emotions and appetites can be recruited to aid the will in practicing virtues,[25] register in Clement but not prominently. For example, fear (φόβος), a cardinal passion for Stoics, can for Clement find healthy use as reverent fear of God, convertible to love.[26] Hope (ἐλπίς), a throwaway emotion for Stoics (save for philosophical novices),[27] and considered respectable by Philo but only as a *propatheia* of joy,[28] becomes for Clement the very "soul" and "blood" of faith.[29] And yet Clement, having commended the Apostles for learning so much from their impassible (ἀπαθής) Lord, suggests that they reached a gnostic perfection wherein they were no longer affected "even by such movements of the passions as seem good, like courage [θάρσον], zeal [ζῆλον], joy [χαράν], and desire [ἐπιθυμίαν]."[30]

It is much more the Cappadocian Fathers, especially Basil and Gregory of Nyssa, who rework the Stoic principle of good and bad *use* of the passions in the context of the spiritual life.[31] Basil states that with desire, anger, and the like, "each becomes a good or an evil for its possessor consistent with its mode of use [χρήσεως];" and he especially underscores irascibility's utility for indignation against evil as well as for vigor in practicing virtue.[32] Both of these uses are well attested in the *Philokalia*. Gregory of Nyssa too imagines not only anger but the passions of the desiring faculty—even greed—as useful and virtuous if properly directed.[33] Indeed, irrational passions can be transmuted into forms of virtue: "anger into courage, cowardice into caution, fear into obedience, hatred into aversion from evil, the faculty of love [ἡ ἀγαπητικὴ δύναμις] into the desire [ἐπιθυμία] for what is truly beautiful."[34] Among the Fathers of the *Philokalia*, Maximus the Confessor is prominent, as we will see further on, in developing the notion of the good use of the passible faculties or of the "ideas" (νοήματα) that underlie the passions—particularly in the shadow of Christ's vanquishing of the culpable passions and his right use of fear and other potentially salutary emotions.

Especially sensational for the later history of monastic devotion, however, was the Alexandrian and Cappadocian recovery of Platonic *eros* as a transformative Christian virtue. For Origen (who readily acknowledged Scripture's frequent avoidance of "erotic" language) and later Gregory of Nyssa, this was hardly philosophically outlandish since, as both demonstrate in their *Commentaries* and *Homilies on the Song of Songs*, a higher vision of *eros* was sanctioned by the Song's own allegory.[35] The Song projected not an acquisitive or possessive *eros* but a powerful passion integrating the soul's "natural" desiring element (τὸ ἐπιθυμητικόν), indeed its whole appetency, into the urge for transcending and "ecstatic" intimacy with God through the Logos-Bridegroom. This ideal of a deifying *eros*, further enhanced by Pseudo-Dionysius the Areopagite, again finds expression, as we will demonstrate, in Maximus and other Fathers of the *Philokalia*.

■ THE DIALECTICS OF HUMAN PASSIBILITY IN GREEK PATRISTIC THEOLOGICAL ANTHROPOLOGY

The *Philokalia* presupposes a rich tradition of Greek patristic theological anthropology canvassing major themes relating to the origins, anatomy, and economy of the passible faculties. Considerable speculation focused on prelapsarian human nature created in God's image, and whether the passible faculties were created in a virtuous state or only in consequence of the Adamic fall. If the latter, was this result purely punitive on God's part, or were these faculties intended to serve a rehabilitative and salutary function? Would they, moreover, be eschatologically transfigured and deified?

These are enormous issues, and this discussion will be restricted to two key figures, Gregory of Nyssa and Maximus the Confessor, whose perspectives were especially decisive for the *Philokalia*.[36] Gregory's importance lies in having established a careful dialectical relationship between the prelapsarian, postlapsarian, and eschatological conditions of the passible nature. Realizing the dilemma that even if passions were a consequence of the Fall, somehow passibility must have also factored into the original lapse, Nyssen famously posits that the Creator instilled passible faculties in human nature *in prevision of the Fall*,[37] which were punitively "stunted" after the Fall with the imposing of the "garments of skins" (Gen. 3:21), symbolizing mortality, irrationality, and liability to deviant passions.[38] Gregory also scrupulously distinguishes between the natural affective faculties of ἐπιθυμία and θυμός, as appetites (ὀρέξεις) or drives (ὁρμαί) under reason's hegemony, and the base passions (lust, rage, pleasure, envy, etc.) that betray the fallenness and abuse of those faculties.[39]

And yet fallenness is hardly the last word, for Gregory envisions human "nature," endowed with the image and likeness of God, as intrinsically dynamic and open to perpetual transformation.[40] The frontier of that nature, moreover, is not simply a process of recovering the lost, prelapsarian state but an adventure of "rebirthing" the self through the virtuous exercise of free will.[41] In the ascetical process of assimilation to God, human nature—including the passible faculties—must constantly be stretched beyond its own limits, finding its ultimate definition through perpetual ecstatic change and divinization.[42] Human desire, in all its dimensions, takes center stage as the vehicle for this transformation. Indeed, as

Rowan Williams has observed, the whole passible nature participates because Gregory's ideal of human fulfillment is "not the extirpation of inferior faculties, but a controlled and integrated use of all that is human." Deification, in this sense, is not purely a contemplative journey but begins out of the precarious and restive state of human nature, with the dramatic "stirring of desire" and longing for divine beauty.[43] It is in exactly this context that Gregory can affirm, as was noted above, the prudent use of the passions in the spiritual life. Sorrow, fear, ire, hope, mercy, passion (*eros*), and a wide range of affections give texture and depth to the soul's pursuit of God in a scenario of human transformation that is not only moral and ascetical but also aesthetic, dramatizing the unfolding beauty of human nature in its eschatological fullness and newness. Indeed, Gregory projects that in the transcendent deified state, the passions are eternally transmuted into holy desires for God and receptors of supernal grace.[44]

Maximus the Confessor in turn provides a crucial bridge between Nyssen and the *Philokalia*. He establishes the same dialectical relation between basic human passibility ($\pi \acute{a} \theta o \varsigma$)—at the core of which is the creature's "natural" desire for God[45]—and the stray passions, beginning with pleasure and pain, which stemmed from the Fall.[46] Maximus also defers to Gregory when he writes:

> The passions . . . become good in those who are spiritually earnest once they have wisely separated them from corporeal objects and used them to gain possession of heavenly things. For instance, they can turn desire into the appetitive movement of the mind's longing for divine things, or pleasure into the unadulterated joy of the mind when enticed toward divine gifts, or fear into cautious concern for imminent punishment for sins committed, or grief into corrective repentance of a present evil. In short, we can compare this with the wise physicians who remove the existing or festering infection of the body using the poisonous beast, the viper. The spiritually earnest use the passions to destroy a present or anticipated evil, and to embrace and hold to virtue and knowledge. Thus . . . the passions become good when they are used by those who *take every thought captive in order to obey Christ* (2 Cor. 10:5).[47]

Like Gregory, Maximus adopts an essentially *teleological* approach to the passions. He spends less time than Gregory reflecting on the lost prelapsarian paradise, since, in his view, Adam squandered his faculty of spiritual pleasure at the instant he was created ($\mathring{a}\mu a \ \tau \mathring{\omega} \ \gamma \acute{\iota}\nu\epsilon\sigma\theta a\iota$),[48] thus consigning his human posterity to an ongoing history of ascetical recovery and renewal. Yet this history proves to be precisely the theater of God's transformative and deifying grace. As Maximus suggests, echoing Gregory, the infinite God stretches to infinity the desire of those who enjoy God through participation ($\delta\iota\mathring{a} \ \mu\epsilon\tauo\chi\mathring{\eta}\varsigma$).[49] By extension that includes the entire passible self: "Let our whole intellect be directed toward God, tensed by our incensive power [$\tau \mathring{\omega} \ \theta \upsilon\mu\iota\kappa \mathring{\omega}$] as if by some nerve, and fired with longing [$\mathring{\epsilon}\pi\iota\theta\upsilon\mu\acute{\iota}a\varsigma$] by our desire at its most ardent [$\tau \mathring{\eta} \ \kappa a\tau' \ \mathring{a}\kappa\rhoo\nu \ \mathring{\epsilon}\phi\acute{\epsilon}\sigma\epsilon\iota$]."[50] The glory of deification, itself a "supernatural passion" ($\mathring{\upsilon}\pi\mathring{\epsilon}\rho \ \phi\acute{\upsilon}\sigma\iota\nu \ \tau\mathring{o} \ \pi\acute{a}\theta o\varsigma$),[51] is the transfiguration of *all* the capacities of human nature: intelligent, volitional, and affective.[52]

In both Gregory and Maximus, moreover, the transformation of the passions cannot be understood apart from its christological dimension, since it is essentially the manifestation of *incarnational* grace. The New Adam brings to human flesh the pure integrity of unfallen (and eschatological) human nature, being born of a virgin, born free of deviant passions but appropriating the innocent ones associated with survival,[53] and submitting ἐπιθυμία and θυμός to his refiner's fire.[54] And yet in the flesh he also accomplishes something unprecedented, utterly new—a new mode (τρόπος) of humanity.[55] His suffering, and his death as the ultimate "passion," prove to be agents of re-creative grace because of the pure freedom of Christ to "use" the fear of death redemptively[56] and to use death itself "to turn the end of our natural passibility—which is death—into the beginning of our natural transformation to incorruption."[57]

■ THE USE AND TRANSFORMATION OF THE PASSIONS IN THE *PHILOKALIA*

This somewhat detailed (but hardly complete) foray into Alexandrian and Cappadocian paideia, and into the dialectics of human passibility in Greek patristic theological anthropology, has aimed at identifying two crucial traditions of reflection on the predicament and promise of the human passions in the background of the *Philokalia*. Within the *Philokalia*, Evagrius and John Cassian, Mark the Monk, Maximus, later Hesychius the Priest, Peter Damascene, Nicetas Stethatos, Gregory of Sinai, and Gregory Palamas, bear especially strong witness to these traditions but nearly all the *Philokalia* authors reveal their impact.

1. Getting at the Root of Things: Trumping Thoughts with Thoughts

Self-knowledge, including insight into how passions arise and operate, was a staple of early Christian and Byzantine asceticism. As was noted earlier, Origen and Didymus, drawing upon Stoic moral psychology, gave considerable attention to the various components of the passions, beginning with the involuntary "first movements," the preliminary προπάθειαι or "thoughts" (λογισμοί) that remain morally innocent unless allowed to fructify into culpable passions. Evagrius makes a veritable ascetical science of the λογισμοί, and other authors in the *Philokalia* follow suit, cataloguing the thoughts by various configurations.[58] In his *Texts on Discrimination* (selected from his *On Thoughts*, Περὶ λογισμῶν) he targets the primal thoughts of gluttony, avarice, and vainglory, whence arise other, secondary thoughts and passions, which can be connected respectively to the desiring and irascible faculties. Demonic intrigue lying behind the thoughts and the power of salacious mental images to linger in the memory further complicate the monk's ability to preempt thoughts; and it is a matter of intense mental discipline and graced discrimination (διάκρισις) to stem their tidal wave.[59]

Mark the Monk and other *Philokalia* authors speak frequently of the components enabling thoughts to become illicit passions.[60] Involuntary "provocations" (προβολαί) or thoughts and "momentary disturbances" (παραρριπισμοί) approximate the *propatheiai* and yet remain inculpable unless the intellect entertains them and gives them assent; and involuntary "prepossession" (πρόληψις) occurs when a former passion lodges in the memory, poised to tempt again.[61] One text erroneously attributed to John Damascene details the stages from involuntary temptation to voluntary passion:

Provocation (προβολή) is simply a suggestion coming from the enemy, like "do this" or "do that," such as our Lord Himself experienced when He heard the words "Command that these stones become bread" (Matt. 4:3) . . . [and] it is not within our power to prevent provocations. *Coupling* [συνδοιασμός; = συνδυασμός] is the acceptance of the thought [λογισμοῦ] suggested by the enemy. It means dwelling on the thought and choosing deliberately to dally with it in a pleasurable manner. *Passion* [πάθος] is the state resulting from coupling with the thought provoked by the enemy; it means letting the imagination brood on the thought continually. *Wrestling* [πάλη] is the resistance offered to the impassioned thought. It may result either in destroying the passion in the thought—that is to say, the impassioned thought—or in our assenting to it. As St. Paul says, "The flesh desires in a way that opposes the Spirit, the Spirit in a way that opposes the flesh: the one contrary to the other" (Gal. 5:17). *Captivity* [αἰχμαλωσία] is the forcible and compulsive abduction of the heart already dominated by prepossession [προλήψεως] and long habit. *Assent* [συγκατάθεσις] is giving approval to the passion inherent in the thought. *Actualization* [ἐνέργεια] is putting the impassioned thought into effect once it has received our assent. If we can confront the first of these things, the provocation, in a dispassionate way [ἀπαθῶς], or firmly rebut it at the outset, we thereby cut off at once everything that comes after.[62]

The Fathers prescribe an array of practices (fasting, vigils, psalmody, prayer, etc.) to defend against such provocations, but often the best defense is a good offense, counteracting the demons by commanding the *use* of the imagination, recollection, thoughts, and at bottom the free will. "Involuntary thoughts arise from previous sin; voluntary ones from our free will," says Mark the Monk.[63] For Evagrius and later Peter Damascene, who distinguish between "demonic" (evil), "human" (neutral), and "angelic" (spiritual) thoughts,[64] bombarding oneself with salutary mental images and λογισμοί is crucial. Angelic thoughts gleaned from contemplation of the true purposes or principles (λόγοι) of created things (including human nature itself), thoughts derived immediately from our free will, and "natural" thoughts (e.g., love of children) can all displace demonic ones.[65] It is perilous business, as Evagrius exemplifies with the freely willed thought of godly hospitality, which the Tempter can surreptitiously mutate into the thought of hospitality merely for display, effectively subverting a noble thought with the passion of vainglory.[66] As Peter Damascene advises, even the spiritual knowledge gained from angelic-inspired contemplation must be honed by patience, humility, and hope born of faith amid the continued seduction of the intellect.[67]

The ascetic can also use memory to recall demonic machinations and so avoid them by anticipation, and can make positive use of the desiring and irascible faculties (discussed below). For Maximus as well as Evagrius, it is especially a battle of mental representations (νοήματα), the mind's conceptual pictures of sensible objects, which are more intellectually developed than the λογισμοί though closely related.[68] It is incumbent on the mind to "use" these mental representations rightly in order to be spiritually well-adjusted to sensible things and thus use them rightly as well.[69] Conversely, both Maximus and Gregory of Sinai observe that "misuse" (παράχρησις)—first of internal faculties, second of external objects—is at the root of deviant passions.[70]

2. The Virtuous Use of Ire and Desire

Many of the Fathers of the *Philokalia* recall the primary dialectical relation, noted earlier with Gregory of Nyssa and Maximus, between the prelapsarian passible faculties of human nature in their integrity and the stunted and disordered condition of those faculties after the Fall. As Gregory of Sinai states:

> When God through His life-giving breath created the soul deiform and intellective, He did not implant in it anger and desire that are animal-like. But He did endow it with a power of longing and aspiration, as well as with a courage responsive to divine love. Similarly when God formed the body He did not originally implant in it instinctual anger and desire. It was only afterwards, through the fall, that it was infested with these characteristics that have rendered it mortal, corruptible, and animal-like.[71]

The *Philokalia* throughout emphasizes restoring the prelapsarian state of the soul's faculties, a process which is effected only through *incarnational* grace. Not only is there healing for the passions in the invocation of the name of Jesus,[72] and in the constant meditation on the depth of Christ's *kenosis*,[73] but Christ himself must enter the soul with his "threefold gift of peace" (John 14:27), which mends the soul's three powers [ἐπιθυμία, θυμός, λόγος] and "brings it into triadic perfection and unites it with Himself."[74] According to Gregory Palamas, the indwelling Christ heals from the ground up, starting with desire, since unsatisfied desire fuels the incensive faculty, and since these both must be healed for the intellect to be healthy.[75] This striking inversion of the more typical model of reason's ruling the two passible powers indicates the critical importance of the *natural* use of these faculties. The goal is perfect integrity: "For just as the intellect does not reject the passions that surround it, but uses them in accordance with their true nature, so the soul does not reject the body, but uses it for every good work."[76]

With irascibility (θυμός), Evagrius and John Cassian, citing abundant Scriptures, note at once its precariousness and its profound utility in waging fervent warfare against demons and vicious passions.[77] The very first lines in the *Philokalia*, from Isaiah the Solitary, are a summons to such righteous indignation, and the redirection of anger into exercising courage or mounting a defense against wicked thoughts is among the most consistent themes in the entire anthology.[78] The aim is not simply regulation of ire and desire, but their liberation and utter transformation as well. In Maximus's words:

> The incensive power and desire . . . are to be treated like the servant and the handmaid of another tribe (cf. Lev. 25:41–42). The contemplative intellect, through fortitude and self-restraint, subjugates them for ever to the lordship of the intelligence, so that they serve the virtues. *It does not give them their complete freedom until the law of nature is totally swallowed up by the law of the spirit*, in the same way as the death of an unhappy flesh is swallowed up by infinite life (cf. 2 Cor. 5:4), and until the image of the unoriginate kingdom is clearly revealed, mimetically manifesting itself in the entire form of the archetype. When the contemplative intellect enters this state it gives the incensive power

and desire their freedom, transmuting desire into the unsullied pleasure and pure enravishment of an intense love for God and the incensive power into spiritual fervour, an ever-active fiery *élan*, a self-possessed frenzy.[79]

The use and transformation of desire is crucial because it cuts to the very heart of the soul's nature and teleological orientation. This too depends on the incarnational grace of Christ, who "in His deep-seated love dilated the appetitive aspect of the soul so that it can partake of the blessings of eternal life."[80] Maximus especially emphasizes that the irascible faculty should serve desire and that if ἐπιθυμία can be transmuted into passion (ἔρως) for God, ire too can be converted into divine love (ἀγάπη).[81] Perpetuating the evocative love language of Origen and Gregory of Nyssa in their works on the Song of Songs, many Fathers of the *Philokalia* find indispensable the use of deep-seated desire (ἐπιθυμία; ἔρως) to ignite the soul's longing for God in the mystery of deification. The soul must be "wounded" (cf. Song 2:5; 5:8) by longing and love as it recollects God's graciousness.[82] As in Origen and Nyssen, the line between godly passion (ἔρως) and charity (ἀγάπη) breaks down. Diadochus and Maximus, among others, strongly insist on the social dimension whereby this profound love of God vanquishes self-love (φιλαυτία) and overflows into warm affection and love for neighbor.[83]

Some writers speak openly of desire's "ecstatic" aspiration. Desire for God is thoroughly *natural* for the soul, but it must by grace be stretched beyond its own limitations. It must be ravished.[84] Diadochus calls for fierce realism here. The ascetic who is being transformed through the love of God "is both present in this life and not present in it," remaining in the body but propelled by intense longing, and by the energy of the Holy Spirit, toward ecstasy; and yet in this sublime state the soul is vulnerable to diabolically induced pride at its exalted experience, and only the activity of the Spirit internal to the soul's love can authenticate its rapture.[85] Meanwhile, says Pseudo-Macarius, ecstatic monks should be all the more aware of their profound debt to Christ;[86] and other authors too hinge this ecstasy of desire on continued remembrance of God and on contemplation and imitation of the incarnate Christ.[87] Ultimately ecstasy is but the upshot of the holistic transformation of the passible self:

> Rapture means the total elevation of the soul's powers towards the majesty of divine glory, disclosed as an undivided unity. Or again, rapture is pure and all-embracing ascent towards the limitless power that dwells in light. Ecstasy is not only the heavenward ravishing of the soul's powers; it is also complete transcendence of the sense-world itself. Intense longing for God—there are two forms of it—is a spiritual intoxication that arouses our desire. As just remarked, there are two main forms of ecstatic longing for God: one within the heart and the other in the enravishment taking one beyond oneself. The first pertains to those who are still in the process of achieving illumination, the second to those perfected in love. Both, acting on the intellect, transport it beyond the sense-world. Such longing for the divine is truly a spiritual intoxication, impelling natural thoughts towards higher states and detaching the senses from involvement with visible things.[88]

3. Godly Fear, Sorrow, Joy, and Hope

For all of its teaching on self-control, the *Philokalia* has much to say about godly affections, some of which are converted vices. Here two of Stoicism's four cardinal passions, fear (φόβος) and grief (λύπη), rise to stardom as indispensable elements of Christian devotion. And here too is one of the clearest evidences of the Bible's profound imprint on the *Philokalia*, whose authors scoured its narratives of virtuous emotions, emotions they prescribed for "re-performance" in their own communities and contexts. Examining their prescriptions, however, we discover that the Bible's godly emotions often assumed unique nuances and complexions in Byzantine asceticism.

The fear of God, for example, appearing abundantly in Scripture as reverence and awe as well as anticipation of divine judgment, becomes in monastic usage the emotional skeleton of the penitential life. In the Bible, "the fear of the Lord is the *beginning* of wisdom" (Ps. 110:10, LXX; Prov. 1:7; 9:10; Job 28:28) while in its purity it also "endures *forever*" (Ps. 18:10, LXX). And while "there is no deficiency in those who fear God" (Ps. 33:10, LXX), there is also the testimony that "perfect love casts out fear" (1 John 4:18). Certain *Philokalia* authors astutely reconciled these texts by distinguishing variant forms of "fear" and projecting a pattern of maturing fear of God. John Cassian sets the precedent by differentiating the mere dread of divine punishment that motivates beginners in the spiritual life and the advanced fear that gives way to hope and ultimately to consummate love of God.[89] Diadochus, guarding against ascetical overconfidence in the wake of the Messalian Controversy, sees reverent fear as only gradually giving way to perfect love and as its essential underpinning.[90] Theodore the Great Ascetic conversely sees loving desire as fueling and perfecting godly fear,[91] while Maximus, Peter Damascene, and Theodore all imagine an ultimate fusion of godly fear and perfected love after growth beyond mere dread of judgment.[92] Nicetas, however, sees fear actually transmuting into desire and thereby becoming the supreme catalyst of perfect love, as "it makes the soul not only fearless and full of love for God, but also the very mother of the divine Logos [in the soul]."[93]

As is so often the case in the *Philokalia*, the transformation of the passions, a gift of the Spirit, is actualized through the co-inherence and mutual conditioning among the sanctified emotions themselves—a principle reminiscent of Clement's (and the Stoics') doctrine of the "mutual implication" (ἀντακολουθία) of the virtues.[94] For the *Philokalia*'s reader, the "chicken-or-egg" quandary is common since one emotion can appear as both the cause and the product of another; and each one really represents a complex emotional state aspiring to become dispositional rather than experientially momentary in the dynamic progress of the soul.

If fear and love condition each other in Byzantine asceticism, so do godly grief and joy.[95] The *Philokalia*'s rich vocabulary of penitential sorrow—compunction (κατάνυξις), mourning (πένθος), tears (δάκρυα), grief (λύπη), repentance (μετάνοια)—bespeaks the multifaceted experience of contrition for sin, complemented by the deep joy of renewing grace. Several authors draw upon the seventh-century Sinaite John Climacus, who in his *Ladder of Divine Ascent* coined a new Greek word, χαρμολύπη, "joyous sorrow," to describe contrition's bittersweet character.[96] It is in many respects the emotional threshold of the ascetical life and a barometer of its authenticity and depth. Opposed to the vicious passion of self-pity or dejection (λύπη; *tristitia*), or bereavement at the loss of worldly goods, godly sorrow is the patently virtuous expression of grief.[97] Compunction is the pang of sorrow for one's sinfulness, and the flow of tears, a gift from God, comes with the painful recognition of alienation from God and of one's spiritual poverty,[98] but also with jubilance at the divine mercy shown the penitent.[99] These are primal, Adamic tears that relive the tragedy of the Fall and the expulsion from paradise.[100] They cleanse the passible faculties and the intellect, purify the conscience, mortify the body, and restore spiritual virginity.[101] They flow not only for oneself but for all of fallen humanity ("the grief of all Adam").[102] Indeed, these tears water a new creation. "As from Eden," writes Nicetas, "from you flows another stream of compunction, divided into the four streams of humility, chastity, dispassion, and undistracted prayer; and it waters the face of God's entire spiritual creation (cf. Gen. 2:10)."[103]

The godly joy (χαρά) that arises from deep repentance can certainly manifest itself as sublime jubilation, much like a spiritual ecstasy.[104] Yet because of the deep link with contrition, it still retains sobriety and never becomes complacent or overconfident. Not unlike what we saw in the process of maturing fear of God, Diadochus declares that "initiatory joy is one thing, the joy of perfection is another. The first is not exempt from fantasy, while the second has the strength of humility. Between the two comes a 'godly sorrow' (2 Cor. 7:10) and active tears; 'For in much wisdom is much knowledge; and he that increases knowledge increases sorrow' (Eccles. 1:18)." Thus the soul goes through the necessary refiner's fire of its joy.[105]

As was noted earlier, ancient Stoics considered hope (ἐλπίς) an expendable emotion, worthy only of beginners in the philosophical life. The *Philokalia*, however, presupposes hope as one of the established "theological virtues" and concurs with Clement that it is a life-blood of faith that the Christian never outgrows. In a sage piece of hyperbole, John of Karpathos claims that "it is more serious to lose hope than to sin," as is evidenced in the defeatist Judas, a nonstarter in spiritual warfare who fell into despair and hanged himself.[106] There is a message as well for the experienced ascetic who has battled thoughts and passions. In a subtle but incisive dictum Mark the Monk says, "He whose mind teems with thoughts lacks self-control; and even when they are beneficial, hope is more so."[107] Hope is the makings of endurance, not only instilling confidence in God amid the toils and trials of ascetical life, but also embodying its eschatological orientation and aspiration.[108] As Diadochus posits, hope lies "midway between sadness and joy," gladdening the soul amid its sense of abandonment during temptations, but also helping to guard its joy from becoming presumptuous.[109]

■ CONCLUSION: THE PASSIONATE FACE OF *APATHEIA* IN THE *PHILOKALIA*

I indicated at the beginning of this essay that many readers are prone to equate the teaching of the *Philokalia* on the human passions with prescriptions of self-control and suppression. Clearly, however, this is not the last word, for as we have seen, its

writers still have much to say about the "economy" of human passibility, the transformation of the passible faculties, and the role of godly emotions in a Christian's
spiritual formation.

In fact the cumulative approach of these authors to the use and transformation
of the passions wholly redefined the Stoic ideal of *apatheia*. Though even some
Stoics recognized that stabilization rather than total annihilation was the realistic
goal in dealing therapeutically with the passions, the weight of their moral psychology, εὐπάθειαι aside, went against making the use of robust emotions a major
component of the philosophical life. The Byzantine Fathers celebrated the fact that
in the composite hypostasis of Jesus Christ, God was remaking human nature with
a grace that penetrated its disintegrated elements. God in his *kenosis* was doing a
new thing precisely by assuming human passibility. "In exchange for our destructive passions," writes Maximus, "he grants us his life-giving Passion as a cure to
save the whole world."[110]

The *apatheia* of the *Philokalia*, in turn, not only differs from Stoicism but is
the very antithesis of the modern colloquial notion of "apathy." It is the salvific
engagement of the passible faculties, drawing them into the magnetic field of
transforming incarnational grace. The negative dimension of *apatheia*, the vanquishing of destructive thoughts and passions, remains a pervasive theme still in
the *Philokalia*, especially through the widespread influence of Evagrius and Maximus. Hopefully, however, we have shown that for the *Philokalia* overall, *liberation from* deviant passions is one thing, and the *liberation of* passibility itself
another.

John Cassian and other writers famously avoided the term *apatheia*, preferring the less controversial and more obviously biblical ideal of "purity of heart."
It is mistaken, however, to deem this term purely a correction of Evagrius and
others who freely employed *apatheia*. For one thing, as Jeremy Driscoll has
demonstrated from Evagrian works outside the *Philokalia*, Evagrius himself had
a multifaceted conception of *apatheia*: e.g., as *virtue* habituated in the passible
faculties, or as "purity of heart" in the prudent pursuit of spiritual knowledge.[111]
In his treatise *On Prayer* in the *Philokalia*, he ties *apatheia* closely to passionate
love (ἔρως) of God.[112] Furthermore, Cassian's own "purity of heart" is itself
multidimensional, entailing ascetical purification, an equation with love, the experience (emotion) of tranquility in the liberation from sinful passions, and
contemplative vision of God.[113] Little surprise, then, that a later writer such as
Hesychius would be able to use both *apatheia* and "purity of heart," and further
associate purity of heart with inner vigilance (νῆψις) and a host of other godly
emotions and virtues: "joy, hopefulness, compunction, sorrow, tears, an understanding of ourselves and of our sins, mindfulness of death, true humility, unlimited love of God and man, and an intense and heartfelt longing for the
divine."[114] *Apatheia* is in sum the union and intersection of *all* the virtues,
according to Peter Damascene.[115]

The Fathers of the *Philokalia* recognized that *apatheia*, a gift of grace, was a
beginning and a middle (or instrumentality) as well as a final goal, indicating its
dynamism within the spiritual life.[116] Were it only an end, it would be marked by
immunity to disturbing passions, but the fact is that the dispassionate Christian

ascetic is still vulnerable to passions and to trials[117] and is tempered precisely by suffering.[118] "Do not say that a dispassionate man cannot suffer affliction," says Mark the Monk, "for even if he does not suffer on his own account, he is under a liability to do so for his neighbor."[119] Such captures well the deep association of *apatheia* and love, both of God and of all humanity. Some writers call *apatheia* the beginning of love,[120] others call love the beginning of *apatheia*.[121] Egg or chicken, the point is the same; the two are inseparable. In the culmination together of love and dispassion, says Maximus:

> there is no difference between his own or another's, or between Christians and unbe-
> lievers, or between slave and free, or even between male and female. But because he has
> risen above the tyranny of the passions and has fixed his attention on the single nature
> of man, he looks on all in the same way and shows the same disposition to all. For in him
> there is neither Greek nor Jew, male nor female, bond nor free, but Christ who is "all and
> in all" (Col. 3:11; cf. Gal. 3:28).[122]

Long after Maximus, Nicetas too portrays *apatheia* as an outflowing of love, aspiration, and spiritual freedom, a transcendence still fully grounded in bodily existence:

> When you approach the frontiers of dispassion—attaining a right view of God and the
> nature of things, and according to your growth in purity ascending to the Creator
> through the beauty of his creatures—you will be illumined by the Holy Spirit. Enter-
> taining kindly feelings about all men and always thinking good of all, you will look on
> all as pure and holy and will rightly esteem things both human and divine. You will
> desire none of the material things that men seek but, divesting yourself of worldly sense-
> perception by means of the intellect, you will ascend towards heaven and towards God,
> free from all impurity and from every form of servitude, aware in spirit only of God's
> blessings and His beauty. Thus, full of reverence and joy, and in indescribable silence,
> you will dwell in the divine realm of God's blessed glory, all your senses transformed,
> and at the same time you will live spiritually among men like an angel in a material
> body.[123]

Nicolas Berdyaev (1874–1948), the provocative Russian "personalist" philos-opher, expressed deep frustration with the traditional asceticism and monasti-cism of Eastern Christianity, decrying its eschatological orientation and otherworldliness. He censured Maximus and other Byzantine ascetics for abstracting passionate spiritual love "from the emotions and from all concrete-ness and individuality," and for hardening it into a method of transcendence bereft of emotional warmth.[124] Whatever the justice of his criticism of monasti-cism in his own time, surely Berdyaev failed to see the depth and breadth of what Maximus, representing well the heritage of the *Philokalia*, calls "the blessed pas-sion of holy love" (τὸ μακάριος πάθος τῆς ἁγίας ἀγάπης),[125] and with it the *apatheia* embodying the glorious healing and transformation of the human pas-sions. Indeed, I would contend that the *Philokalia*'s bold vision of the passionate face of love and *apatheia*—its hope for the passible self—remains one of its great-est legacies in all ages, and one of the Orthodox tradition's greatest gifts to ecu-menical Christianity.

15 Healing, Psychotherapy, and the *Philokalia*

Christopher C. H. Cook

The *Philokalia* identifies the passions as a fundamental concern of the spiritual life, a concern which must be properly understood if the barrier that they present to progress toward the goal of human existence is to be effectively addressed. The exact nature and properties of the passions and the proper means of addressing and overcoming them are presented, as one would expect from forty or so authors writing over a span of more than a thousand years, in diverse ways. On a canvas of more or less consistent philosophical and theological assumptions about Christian anthropology, a rich variety of images, symbols, metaphors and allegories is used to paint a passionate picture of the human predicament and its solution. Amid this plethora of images is that of the compassionate physician treating the ailing human creature whose very life is drained by the multiplicity of wounds and diseases that comprise the passions. Although it might be stretching things too far to claim that this image is universal and consistent throughout the texts of the *Philokalia*, it would certainly seem to be an important image, among other images, and it is found in both the earliest and latest texts and in texts by all of the major contributors.

What, then, is the nature of the pathology that the *Philokalia* diagnoses? Fundamentally, the passions are themselves, collectively and individually, understood as being a kind of disease, or sickness, of the soul.

Thus:

- In *On the Eight Vices*, John Cassian refers to unchastity, avarice, anger, dejection, and listlessness as sicknesses.[1]
- Neilos, in his *Ascetic Discourse*, refers to sin as being like a protracted illness, and to the passions as causing a disease of the soul.[2]
- John of Karpathos, in *For the Encouragement of the Monks in India who had Written to Him: One Hundred Texts*, refers to the sicknesses of unbelief and despair, and of rebellion against God.[3]
- In *On the Character of Men and on the Virtuous Life*, attributed in the *Philokalia* to Antony the Great, the greatest sickness of the soul is said to be not knowing God, and Godlessness and love of praise are said to be "the worst and most incurable disease of the soul."[4]
- Thalassios the Libyan, in *On Love, Self-Control, and Life in Accordance with the Intellect*, asserts that "The soul's disease is an evil disposition."[5]
- Abba Philimon is quoted as saying that "Thoughts about vain things are sicknesses of an idle and sluggish soul."[6]

- In *On the Practice of the Virtues, Contemplation and the Priesthood*, a text attributed in the *Philokalia* to Theognostos, reference is made to "the sickness of the passions."[7]
- Ilias the Presbyter, in Part I of *A Gnomic Anthology*, contrasts the "hidden sickness," "in the depths of consciousness" with the possibly healthy outward appearance of a soul.[8]
- Symeon Metaphrastis, in the *Paraphrase of the Homilies of St. Makarios of Egypt*, refers to "the sickness of evil and ignorance."[9]
- Nikitas Stithatos, in *On the Inner Nature of Things and on the Purification of the Intellect*, refers to sickness of the soul (or "psychic illness") in a general sense and to lack of faith specifically as a disease of the soul.[10]
- Gregory Palamas, in *To the Most Reverend Nun Xenia*, distinguishes between passions which belong to human beings "by nature," and therefore are good, and the misuse of these passions which provides evidence of sickness of the soul.[11]

These philokalic references to sickness and disease show great diversity. However, they also show a more or less consistent understanding of the human condition as giving evidence of a kind of pathology of the soul. This evidence is closely associated with, if not actually identified with, the activity of the passions. In fact, even if these explicit metaphors were not used, the account of the passions provided by the *Philokalia* would arguably invite the use of medical metaphors such as disease, sickness, and illness. The passions are portrayed as causing pain and dysfunction in the spiritual life,[12] as being contrary to nature,[13] and as leading to death[14] if left untreated.

The *Philokalia* also employs medical metaphors in respect of the treatment of the passions. Thus, medicines effective in treatment of the diseased soul include:

- Anger (when properly used against evil thoughts)[15]
- Fear of God[16]
- Salvation[17]
- Guarding the intellect (by remembrance of sins, mindfulness of death, meditation on the passion of Christ, and remembrance of blessings)[18]
- Ascetic discipline[19]
- Tears[20]

More generally, healing of the soul is described as being brought about through meditation and prayer,[21] the compassion of God,[22] pain and suffering,[23] the passion of Christ,[24] wisdom,[25] and reproof.[26] Specific remedies for specific passions include almsgiving for the healing of the soul's incensive power,[27] spiritual knowledge for the healing of mental dejection,[28] humility for envy and self-conceit,[29] solitude for conceit and vanity.[30] But again the whole tenor of the *Philokalia* is one of the healing of the human condition, and even where this is implicit rather than explicit, or where other kinds of metaphors are used, it would still seem appropriate to understand the *Philokalia* as offering a kind of therapeutic repertoire, or pharmacopeia, for the treatment of the soul afflicted by the passions. Thus, ascetic discipline, prayer (including the Jesus prayer), psalmody, and guarding of the heart might all be understood as therapies for the soul.

The aim of therapy, the healing of the soul, might at one level be understood as achieving dispassion. In this sense, the aim of philokalic therapy can in many places appear very similar to that of Stoic philosophy, the elimination of the passions. But the *Philokalia* does not stop here, for its authors understand dispassion only as a means to a theological end, the goal of pure prayer, or union with God. While the doctrine of deification was not definitively formulated by Gregory Palamas until the fourteenth century, and is treated explicitly by relatively few authors of the *Philokalia*,[31] nonetheless throughout the *Philokalia* well-being is understood theologically, whether in terms of hesychia, illumination of the intellect, blessedness, pure prayer, or openness to God, rather than purely psychologically or philosophically in terms of thoughts or ideas.

In the second century of *Two Hundred Texts on Theology and the Incarnate Dispensation of the Son of God*, Maximos the Confessor provides a more detailed account of the healing process:

> If you are healed of the breach caused by the fall, you are severed first from the passions and then from impassioned thoughts. Next you are severed from nature and the inner principles of nature, then from conceptual images and the knowledge relating to them. Lastly, when you have passed through the manifold principles relating to divine providence, you attain through unknowing the very principle of divine unity. Then the intellect contemplates only its own immutability, and rejoices with an unspeakable joy because it has received the peace of God which transcends all intellect and which ceaselessly keeps him who has been granted it from falling (cf. Phil. 4:7).[32]

This account of healing appears to reverse or undo the pathology of the passions that Maximos describes elsewhere.[33] Maximos seems to understand a process by which thoughts or images become impassioned by a kind of cathexis or attachment of a passion to a thought/image. In the healing process, this attachment is broken. But the healing process is more radical than this, for having uncoupled thought processes from the passions it goes on to engage them in a contemplation of the "manifold principles relating to divine providence" and then, through a process of "unknowing," to the divine unity itself. Here there is a transcending of the intellect, a transcending of the multiplicity of thoughts, in the unity of God.

If the *Philokalia* presents a school of therapy for the soul, designed to bring about its healing, it might well be argued that the *Philokalia* is a kind of manual for psychotherapy. However, once the word "psychotherapy" is used, with all its more modern connotations of Freudian and post-Freudian therapies designed to explore the unconscious, and of the cognitive-behavioral therapies based on cognitive and behavioral scientific psychology, we realize at once how the *Philokalia* is both similar to and radically different from what we now call, in the Western world, psychotherapy.

On the one hand, the *Philokalia* shares with contemporary psychotherapies a concern with "inwardness" and with self-reflective awareness, a suspicion about the motives that lay behind apparently innocent or well-intentioned actions, and a keen attention to the content and processes of cognition. Even some of the methods look very similar—especially those that betray a Stoic model of the passions (or in the case of contemporary psychology the emotions) as being fundamentally based upon thoughts (or cognition). For example, the identification of thoughts/judgments that lead to fear might be a concern of both the cognitive therapist and the disciple of the *Philokalia*,[34] remembrance of death is also effectively a cognitive strategy for changing patterns of thought, and ascetic discipline might be considered a kind of behavioral therapy orientated toward changing patterns of thought as well as lifestyle. Even the philokalic injunctions to obedience and submission to an elder or spiritual guide find their parallels in the therapeutic relationship with a therapist, who is seen as having greater wisdom, knowledge, and experience in matters of the inner life.

On the other hand, contemporary psychotherapies are based on very different theoretical frameworks and aim at very different ends. While differences in theory might be surprisingly more superficial than they first appear, there are undoubtedly important differences. The Freudian tripartite model of the psyche as comprising id, ego, and superego, for example, is not so very different from the Platonic model of appetitive, incensive, and rational parts of the soul, a model which influenced both Freud and the authors of the *Philokalia*. Or again, both the cognitive therapist and the authors of the *Philokalia* emphasize the importance of a self-reflective awareness of thought processes which will lead to greater understanding of how to identify aberrant patterns of thought and develop healthy ones. The scientific rationalism of the cognitive therapist is not necessarily so far removed from the philosophical and contemplative reasoning of the philokalic practitioner when consideration is limited only to matters of cognitive analysis. But when consideration is broadened to include ultimate concerns, the atheistic assumptions of Freud and the cognitive-behaviorists contrast strongly with the philokalic world of personal spiritual forces which draw the human creature inevitably toward, or away from, a telos which is firmly located in the Divine. Moreover, the end of human beings in relationship with God involves the authors of the *Philokalia* in a contemplative "unknowing" which ultimately transcends human rational thought. This transcendence is completely lacking, at least from Freud and the more scientific cognitive-behavioral schools of therapy, if not from all of the schools of therapy which have emerged since the work of pioneers such as Freud, Skinner, and Ellis.

Differences are perhaps nowhere more apparent, however, than in the accounts that are given in the secular psychotherapies and in the *Philokalia* of the relationship of suffering to therapy and the healing process. In order to give this comparison more careful consideration, it is necessary first to say a little more about what the goals of the secular psychotherapies are.

Jerome Frank has suggested:

> The goal of all forms of psychotherapy is to enable a person to satisfy his legitimate needs for affection, recognition, and sense of mastery through helping him to correct the maladaptive attitudes, emotions, and behaviour that impede the attainment of such satisfactions. In so doing, psychotherapy seeks to improve his social interactions and reduce his distress, while at the same time helping him to accept the suffering that is an inevitable aspect of life and, when possible, to utilize it in the service of personal growth.[35]

While psychotherapy seeks to reduce distress, it also recognizes that suffering is an inevitable aspect of life and that acceptance of suffering that cannot be relieved will be an important goal of therapy, alongside reducing it where it can. Where possible, however, a higher goal is hinted at, the goal of "personal growth," a goal toward which the acceptance of inevitable suffering may take the patient closer. The exact form that this personal growth might take is not specified, although it would appear to have something to do with the enabling of satisfaction of personal needs and the achieving of a "sense of mastery." Exactly how these goals might be achieved will vary from one form of therapy to another.[36]

Although there is not space here to survey exactly how personal growth is understood in all the different kinds of psychotherapy, Carl Rogers has provided an account which might be considered typical of many:

> . . . the individual becomes more integrated, more effective. He shows fewer of the characteristics which are usually termed neurotic or psychotic, and more of the characteristics of the healthy, well-functioning person. He changes his perception of himself, becoming more realistic in his views of self. He becomes more like the person he wishes to be. He values himself more highly. He is more self-confident and self-directing. He has a better understanding of himself, becomes more open to his experience, denies or represses less of his experience. He becomes more accepting in his attitudes toward others, seeing others as more similar to himself.
>
> In his behaviour he shows similar changes. He is less frustrated by stress, and recovers from stress more quickly. He becomes more mature in his everyday behaviour as this is observed by friends. He is less defensive, more adaptive, more able to meet situations creatively.[37]

For Rogers, this growth takes place when a troubled, conflicted person is provided with a certain type of relationship, one which is characterized by genuineness, acceptance, and empathy.[38] However, in other forms of psychotherapy it might be facilitated by resolution of inner conflicts, symptom reduction, or modification of patterns of thought. What would seem to be the common thread is that psychotherapy aims to reduce distress and suffering where possible, to enable acceptance of and adaptation to stresses that cannot be changed, and to achieve a greater sense of self-confidence and self-mastery which is concerned with the satisfaction of personal needs, including the need for harmonious and mutually fulfilling interactions with others.

We may again note that there is much common ground here with the model of therapy that is presented in the *Philokalia*. The *Philokalia* is also concerned with the correction of maladaptive attitudes, emotions (or passions), and behaviors. The *Philokalia* is concerned with acceptance of suffering, improved social interactions, and personal growth. It is concerned with self-awareness and realism about self and experience of the world. At least insofar as ascetic discipline is a form of self-control, it is also concerned with self-mastery. However, alongside these parallel concerns, we must also note that the *Philokalia* is an anthology of texts concerned with the life of prayer and that its ultimate goal is one of deification, or union with God. This central theological preoccupation, and its recognition of the need for the grace of God in order to achieve it, renders its school of therapy radically different from secular psychotherapy. If the psychotherapies are, by and large, "talking cures," the *Philokalia* offers a "praying cure." If the former aim to increase self-confidence, the latter aim to increase confidence in God:

> Humility consists in constant prayer combined with tears and suffering. For this ceaseless calling upon God for help prevents us from foolishly growing confident in our own strength and wisdom, and from putting ourselves above others. These are dangerous diseases of the passion of pride.[39]

This difference is brought out when we consider how suffering is dealt with differently in psychotherapy and in the *Philokalia*. While suffering might constitute the reason for seeking psychotherapy, and its reduction and management might constitute the therapeutic objectives of psychotherapy, in the *Philokalia* we find that it is fundamentally a part of therapy. This point becomes especially clear in the works of Maximos the Confessor, the second largest single contributor to the *Philokalia*, although it is by no means confined to these texts.

For Maximos, the healing process is facilitated primarily by the suffering of Christ in his passion, but necessarily also by the willing participation of human beings in this suffering. Thus, for example, in the fourth century of *Four Hundred Texts on Love*, he writes:

> The aim of divine providence is to unite by means of true faith and spiritual love those separated in various ways by vice. Indeed, the Saviour endured His sufferings so that "He should gather together into one the scattered children of God" (Jn. 11: 52). Thus, he who does not resolutely bear trouble, endure affliction, and patiently sustain hardship, has strayed from the path of divine love and from the purpose of providence.[40]

Elsewhere, in the first century of *Two hundred texts on theology and the incarnate dispensation of the Son of God, Written for Thalassios*, Maximos associates a process of suffering which "purifies those practicing the virtues" and which then leads to contemplation, dispassion, and deification, with a Christological model of the appearance of Christ in human and then transfigured forms.[41] Human suffering thus presents both a healing opportunity to share in the human suffering of Christ and also a healing path by which to progress to contemplative prayer, dispassion, and ultimately deification.[42]

Maximos clearly does not see suffering as the only prescription administered by the Divine Physician of Souls.[43] The efficacy of the treatment is also dependent upon human compliance.[44] Neither is specific suffering deliberately brought about by God with the purpose of imposing treatment. Maximos refers to suffering as caused by human sin,[45] misfortune,[46] the devil,[47] and the passions.[48] It is the fool who regards either God or other human beings as responsible, says Maximos.[49] However, in the fourth century of *Various Texts on Theology, the Divine Economy, and Virtue and Vice*,[50] Maximos differentiates between two kinds of suffering. The one kind is a part of a "pleasure-pain syndrome," where pain in the soul results from pleasure in the senses. This pain, associated with indulgence of the passions, was introduced by Adam, through the Fall. The other kind of suffering, which brings about healing of this syndrome, is a pain in the senses which is associated with pleasure in the soul. This is the suffering which is associated with pursuit of virtue and which was introduced into the world through the incarnation of Christ. Thus, Maximos writes:

> For through His passion He conferred dispassion, through suffering repose, and through death eternal life. By His privations in the flesh He reestablished and renewed the human state, and by His own incarnation He bestowed on human nature the supranatural grace of deification.[51]

According to Maximos, then, the suffering associated with the human condition is intimately tied up with the pleasure associated with the passions. If the passions are pleasurable, they are also noxious, or hostile.[52] The healing of this suffering is brought about through a Christological therapy, which is both concerned with the sharing of Christ in human suffering, freely chosen, and also with human sharing in the suffering of Christ, also freely chosen for love of him.

As is noted above, the repertoire of therapies offered in the *Philokalia* is much broader than this Maximian perspective on participation in Christ's suffering alone might imply. It includes, for example, obedience and spiritual discipline, remembrance of death, psalmody, watchfulness, and prayer. However, in every therapeutic modality the *Philokalia* has its points of radical difference from contemporary secular psychotherapy. These differences are most obviously and pervasively theological, finding their justification in scripture, doctrine, and Christian tradition rather than in any anthropocentric outcomes, understanding a dependence upon the grace of God rather than the activities of human beings as essential for the process of healing, and finding a Divine telos as the only ultimately important goal of healing.

In the example just examined, of the Maximian understanding of the therapeutic role of suffering, the difference from secular psychotherapies is not only theological but also strikingly Christological. A Christological element to the therapy of the *Philokalia* may be identified more widely, as for example in the use of the Jesus Prayer or the significance of the transfiguration of Christ for understanding the illumination of the intellect.[53] Even where it is not explicit, there is arguably always an implicit Christology lurking in the background, as in the case of the temptation of Christ in the wilderness as a model for ascetic discipline.[54]

The *Philokalia* is also personal in a way that the contemporary psychotherapies are not. It is true that the philokalic importance of the personal relationship of the Christian disciple with a spiritual father finds its parallel in the significance accorded to the therapeutic relationship between patient and therapist in virtually all psychotherapies. Similarly, relationships with other human beings are important for the growth of Christian virtue in the *Philokalia*, and for understanding and healing dysfunctional relationships in psychotherapy. However, the world of the *Philokalia* is rich with other personal and spiritual beings with whom the disciple is also in relationship, including both angels and demons as well as, most importantly, God himself. An instructive example here might be found in the growing popularity of the practice of mindfulness in secular psychotherapy.

Mindfulness, in this context, has its origins in the traditions of Buddhism.[55] It is not easily defined and is susceptible of varying definitions, but it is "to pay attention in a particular way."[56] The attention is generally understood to be focused on present experience and often also implies a degree of acceptance of this experience, however difficult that may be. It is sometimes also associated with a degree of ineffability. It is now seen as having an evidence-based role in a variety of forms of psychotherapy from dynamic to cognitive-behavioral, and finds a place in stress management as well as in the treatment of anxiety and mood disorders, addiction, and even psychosis. The common features of mindfulness and hesychia, or stillness, as understood in the *Philokalia* are immediately apparent. For example, both are associated with bodily discipline and avoidance of distractions,[57] and both are associated with a degree of ineffability. However, as the authors of the English translation of the *Philokalia* make clear in their glossary, hesychia is fundamentally a state of relationship with God—of listening or being open to God.[58] Where the English word "mindfulness" appears in the translation of the *Philokalia*, it usually refers explicitly to mindfulness of God.[59]

While mindfulness as employed in secular psychotherapy has some important commonalities with hesychia and mindfulness in the *Philokalia*, they may be distinguished both by the theological context and, importantly, also the greater personal and interpersonal nature of Christian hesychia as contrasted with the more impersonal and intrapersonal nature of Buddhist/secular mindfulness. In hesychia, the Christian is drawn toward a relationship with God in Christ. In mindfulness, the Buddhist is in a more or less impersonal state of attentive awareness. These differences reflect the theological contrast between the Christian understanding of the contingency of creation upon a personal creator, and the Buddhist understandings of impermanence of all things and in particular of "non-self," or absence of any enduring entity such as self or soul.

The differences between the *Philokalia* and secular psychotherapies, about which much more could doubtless be said than space allows for here, might be summarized as being the difference between what is essentially a "talking cure" and what is essentially a "praying cure." The former is anthropocentric. The latter is pervasively theocentric and specifically Christocentric.

What, then, are the implications of the *Philokalia* for the Christian understanding of healing and for the practice of psychotherapy?

1. Christian healing is a fundamentally theocentric and Christological process which does not necessarily imply freedom from suffering, or even reduction of suffering, in human terms. However, it does understand a therapeutic process whereby suffering itself becomes a part of the healing process. As Maximos would have it, the passion of Christ becomes a means of the healing of human passions.

2. The passions are "hostile pleasures." They reflect a distraction from Divine purpose, a drawing into relationships with things and people which are superficially rewarding but ultimately a cause of human suffering. To try to find a balm for human suffering among the pleasures of wealth, sexual indulgence, or self-satisfaction is therefore somewhat like trying to put out a fire with gasoline!

3. Psychotherapy is concerned with psychological processes, with thoughts, emotions and passions, whether viewed from a secular perspective or seen through the lens of the *Philokalia*. However, secular psychotherapies are concerned primarily with the improvement of psychological well-being, whereas the *Philokalia* is concerned primarily with spiritual well-being understood in a personal and Christocentric way. The *Philokalia* keeps a positive perspective about the ultimate goals around which most secular psychotherapies either prefer to remain silent or else are nihilistic.

4. Although the therapy offered by the *Philokalia* is not primarily concerned with reducing psychological suffering, this does not imply that the reduction of psychological suffering might not be achieved by application of the therapy that the *Philokalia* prescribes. Similarly, at least in certain circumstances or on some occasions, secular therapies might usefully and legitimately be appropriated by Christians to this end. Indeed one might imagine that Christian love will always be concerned with bringing such relief where possible. The warning that the *Philokalia* offers is that this relief should not be the final end of therapy, or one that is pursued to the ultimate harm of the person concerned.

5. If secular psychotherapy is a "talking cure," then the *Philokalia* offers a "praying cure." Prayer, understood as relationship with the Divine, leading eventually to union with God, is both the means and end of the therapy that the *Philokalia* prescribes.

It is interesting that counseling and psychotherapy are increasingly open to consideration of a spiritual dimension of human well-being, and yet that the possibility of prayer within the context of a therapeutic relationship seems to be increasingly controversial.[60] While the concept of spirituality is elastic enough to accommodate widely varying ideas of what the spiritual goals of therapy should be, prayer is an inescapably theistic and personal encounter. The *Philokalia* was published at a time when the European enlightenment was challenging not only ideas of whether and how God might be known, but even the extent to which anything at all can confidently be known by the human subject. While it arises from an Eastern context within which such concerns were hardly voiced at all, or even completely unknown, yet its self-reflective approach to the need to question and interpret human thoughts, and ultimately to find transcendence beyond them, works remarkably well as a means of seeking healing in our present age.

The present secular age within which we live[61] is inward looking and radically reflexive if also at times surprisingly naïve about the goodness that it expects to find within the human self. To this context, the *Philokalia* brings a means of being self-reflective which is both critical and realistic, aware of immanence and transcendence, psychologically sophisticated, and yet spiritually directed.

■ BIBLIOGRAPHY

Frank, Jerome D. "What Is Psychotherapy?" In *An Introduction to the Psychotherapies*, ed. S. Bloch, 59–76. Oxford: Oxford University Press, 2006.
Mace, Chris. *Mindfulness and Mental Health*. London: Routledge, 2008.

Moore, J., and C. Purton. *Spirituality and Counselling: Experiential and Theoretical Perspectives*. Ross-on-Wye: PCCS Books, 2006.

Palmer, G. E. H., P. Sherrard, and K. Ware. The *Philokalia: The Complete Text Compiled by St. Nikodimos of the Holy Mountain and St. Makarios of Corinth*. Vol. 2. London: Faber & Faber, 1984.

Poole, R. and C.C.H. Cook (2011). "In Debate: Praying with a Patient constitutes a Breach of Professional Boundaries in Psychiatric Practice." *British Journal of Psychiatry* 199 (2): 94–98.

Powell, Andrew, and Christopher MacKenna. "Psychotherapy." In *Spirituality and Psychiatry*, ed. Chris Cook, Andrew Powell, and Andrew Sims, 101–21. London: Royal College of Psychiatrists Press, 2009.

Rogers, Carl R. *On Becoming a Person: A Therapist's View of Psychotherapy*. London: Constable, 1975.

Sinkewicz, R. E. *Evagrius of Pontus: The Greek Ascetic Corpus*. Oxford: Oxford University Press, 2003.

Taylor, Charles. *A Secular Age*. Cambridge: Belknap, 2007.

16 The *Philokalia* and Regulative Virtue Epistemology: A Look at Maximus the Confessor

Frederick D. Aquino

> A pure intellect sees things correctly. A trained intelligence puts
> them in order. A keen hearing takes in what is said.[1] When like the
> patriarchs we learn to dig wells of virtue and spiritual knowledge
> within ourselves by means of ascetic practice and contemplation, we
> will find within us Christ the spring of life. . . . The Logos of God is
> the way (cf. John 14:6) for those who run the course of virtue in
> their ascetic life nobly and vigorously, swerving neither to the right
> through self-esteem, nor to the left through proclivity to the
> passions, but directing their steps in accordance with God's will.[2]

Some philosophers have recently called for a character–based virtue epistemology that gives attention to the nature and internal structure of individual intellectual virtues, clarifies their particular role in the cognitive life, and explains how they contribute to intellectual flourishing.[3] This essay follows a similar logic and explores how select ascetic virtues (e.g., love), as demarcated in the works of Maximus the Confessor (one of the authors in the *Philokalia*), factor into the process of cultivating the deiform self, how they regulate the path to deification, and how they contribute to the goal of attaining divine likeness. These ascetic virtues are traits that form excellent persons and enable them to move from potency (image of God) to actuality (likeness of God). As I hope to show, Maximus's account of the threefold path to deification is a fitting example for pursuing a constructive task of this sort.

However, putting Maximus—a seventh-century mystical theologian—in conversation with recent work in virtue epistemology might seem a bit odd, out of place, or, at best, a kind of hermeneutical cherry-picking. What does his ascetic and mystical theology have to do with contemporary epistemology, given the general characterization of the latter as a discipline that is primarily concerned with fleshing out a theory of knowledge? At first, one might question such a constructive adventure, but my contention is that the current landscape of epistemology is more expansive than one might think and even more suitable to theological appropriation than in times past. In this regard, I hope to develop a constructive link between Maximus's account of the threefold path to deification and a regulative approach to virtue epistemology.

To this end, the essay is structured in the following way. The first section offers a brief overview of the sprawling territory of contemporary epistemology and clarifies how Maximus's account of the threefold path to deification coheres, to some extent, with the recent emphasis on developing a regulative approach to virtue epistemology. The second section shows how Maximus's conception of divine philosophy (an ascetically grounded pursuit and love of divine wisdom) shapes his account of the threefold path to deification. Progress toward divine likeness includes practice of the virtues, contemplation of God in and through nature, and direct perceptual knowledge of God, The third section explains the connection between the practice of the virtues and the natural movement of the intellect. The fourth section, unpacks Maximus's understanding of the relationship between the virtue of love and knowledge of God. A connection of this sort produces a praiseworthy desire for God (e.g., an appetite for knowledge of God), draws the intellect to its proper source of illumination, and makes possible a unified movement toward participation in the divine life. The fifth section closes with a suggestion about how a constructive link between Maximus's conception of the threefold path to deification and a regulative approach to virtue epistemology opens up a viable trajectory for future research in philokalic studies.

▪ DEIFICATION AND THE SPRAWLING TERRAIN OF CONTEMPORARY EPISTEMOLOGY

Epistemology, broadly conceived, entails philosophical reflection on particular cognitive aspects and endeavors of human life. The landscape includes, but is not limited to, developing adequate accounts of our cognitive faculties (e.g., memory, reason, sense-perception), belief-formation, knowledge, truth, rationality, justification, warrant, understanding, wisdom, the evaluative qualities of cognitive agents (e.g., the intellectual virtues), and the social dimension of cognitive activities (e.g., testimony, epistemic evaluation, inquiry).[4] Moreover, the vast range of epistemic ends warrants clarifying what each aspect of cognition constitutes in its own right and perhaps understanding their interrelations (e.g., the relationship between truth and understanding). As a result, a more expansive conception of epistemology recognizes both "a plurality of epistemic values and goals"[5] and diverse strategies for achieving these goals.[6] The point here is not to determine whether epistemic value monism (e.g., whether the acquisition of true beliefs is the primary, if not only, goal, aim, or value of epistemology; whether sense making is the primary, if not only, goal, aim, or value of epistemology) or epistemic value pluralism (e.g., whether truth is one among many other epistemic goals) is the more appropriate strategy for ordering these goals.[7] Rather, the diverse and expansive landscape of contemporary epistemology allows for greater focus on individual goals in their own right and on their interrelations.

Within this sprawling territory, a regulative approach to epistemology focuses principally on the questions of how intellectual and social practices shape the formation of cognitive agents and of how intellectual virtues contribute to cognitive flourishing. In this regard, Robert Roberts and Jay Wood have recently proposed a regulative approach to epistemology that gives particular attention to individual intellectual virtues. Drawing from Nicholas Wolterstorff's work on Locke, they note the distinction between "rule-oriented" (e.g., Descartes) and "habit-oriented" (e.g., Locke) versions of regulative epistemology. The former concentrates on the "procedural directions for acquiring knowledge, avoiding error, and conducting

oneself rationally," while the latter focuses on the "habits of mind of the epistemi-
cally rational person" or on the process of "*training* that nurtures *people* in the
right intellectual *dispositions*."[8] Notwithstanding the different emphases here,
the common ground lies in the attempt to provide an apt "response to perceived
deficiencies in people's intellectual conduct" and therefore "generate guidance for
epistemic practice."[9]

The aim of a regulative approach to epistemology, constructively envisioned by
Roberts and Wood, is not to employ the virtues to resolve traditional problems in
epistemology (e.g., the debate between externalism and internalism; the problem
of skepticism; the dispute between foundationalism and coherentism), nor is it to
identify the necessary and sufficient conditions of these character traits. Rather,
the goal is to provide an extended analysis of particular virtues (e.g., love of knowledge, intellectual firmness, courage and caution, humility, autonomy, generosity,
and practical wisdom), and in so doing, enlarge "our practical understanding of
the inner workings of the intellectual life."[10] Seen in this way, a regulative approach
to epistemology is "particularly attentive to the character traits of the excellent
epistemic agent."[11]

How, then, does the *Philokalia* (a collection of texts ranging from the fourth to
the fifteenth centuries), or more specifically Maximus, fit into a contemporary discussion of this sort? In general, the editorial selection of texts in the *Philokalia*
reflects a deep interest in clarifying the intellectual, theological, and environmental conditions under which people *ought* to pursue the goal of divine-likeness.[12]
The ideal of deification, as a unifying thread that the *Philokalia* charts, calls for the
purification, illumination, and perfection of the intellect.[13] In this regard, Maximus is no exception (in fact no other writer takes up as much space as Maximus
in the *Philokalia*). Undergirding his conception of deification is a vision of how
one *ought* to be formed—morally, liturgically, philosophically, and theologically—
and of the route that enables one to make progress toward fulfilling the ultimate
end of human existence—divine likeness. Deification is not simply another way of
talking about or one among many expressions for salvation. Rather, it is the final
end of salvation.[14] The regulative path to deification, for example, includes the
purification of the intellect through virtuous and contemplative practices, the
transfiguration of the whole creation, the assimilation of particulars to universals,
direct perceptual experience of and participation in the life of God, and a divinely
infused "passion" that sustains communion with God.[15]

In particular, a constructive link between Maximus and a regulative approach
to virtue epistemology, as I hope to show, lies in adding cognitive agents to the list
of epistemic evaluation and highlighting the requisite virtuous and contemplative
practices that guide both human inquiry about God and the path toward actual-
izing divine-likeness. The focus here is on how these practices foster an appetite
for knowledge of God—the beautiful, the exalted, and the excellent (the meaning
of the term *Philokalia*)—and ultimately enable the deiform self to participate in
the life of God. An approach of this sort recognizes (perhaps comparable to what
some epistemologists have recently intimated) that "the life of the intellect is just
as much a matter of loves, concerns, desires, emotions, and the like as the other
parts of our lives."[16] In this regard, Maximus acknowledges the difference between

intellect, emotion, and volition, though, as we will see, he rejects the notion that each can be ultimately severed from one another, especially in terms of the goal of being conformed to and participating in the life of God. Reintegration of the self, in other words, entails the transformation of the whole person. As one genuinely hastens toward and stretches toward God "step by step,"[17] one discerns how bringing together the rational, emotional, and volitional reaffirms the true nature, dignity, and nobility of human existence and thus how the highest possibility—assimilation to God—becomes an actuality.

▦ THE THREEFOLD PATH TO DEIFICATION: A MATTER OF DIVINE PHILOSOPHY

Maximus's account of deification envisions a threefold path that begins with the practice of the virtues (πρακτική), moves to the process of deciphering the logos in and through the created world (θεωρία), and is consummated in theology (θεολογία). The threefold path is also described as ascetic or practical philosophy (πρακτικὴ φιλοσοφία), natural philosophy (φυσικὴ φιλοσοφία), and theological philosophy (θεολογικὴ φιλοσοφία).[18] The first stage of the path involves the cultivation of the virtues, thereby fostering stability, purifying the self from false notions (e.g., the redirection of the passions), and forming a praiseworthy desire (or a holy passion) for God that leads to contemplation.[19] The second stage is contemplation of God in and through nature (e.g., understanding the inner structure or inner principles of the natural order, or discerning "harmonious wisdom" in creation[20]). As a result, the intellect, will, and the senses are connected more holistically. However, virtuous practices are indispensable for engaging in the second stage of the process; they enable the person to undertake focused contemplation of God, self, and world. The third stage entails direct perceptual knowledge of (participation in the energies of) the triune God. Experiential knowledge of this sort, for Maximus, pertains primarily to the future state of deification. The deiform self "is granted the grace of theology when, carried on wings of love beyond these two former stages, it is taken up into God and with the help of the Holy Spirit discerns—as far as this is possible for the human intellect—the qualities of God."[21]

Theologia (stage 3), then, presupposes the backdrop of virtuous (stage 1) and contemplative (stage 2) practices. In *Quaestiones ad Thalassium* 22, for example, Maximus clarifies the difference between the cognitive and volitional activities of the self in this world (e.g., the ages of the incarnation in which humans now live) and the future state of deification (e.g., the ages of deification in which God alone will transform humanity). A distinction of this sort, however, suggests that virtuous and contemplative practices are "taken up" (not necessarily overcome) in the future state of deification.[22]

> Existing here and now, we arrive at the *end of the ages* as active agents and reach the end of the exertion of our power and activity. But in the ages to come we shall undergo by grace the transformation unto deification and no longer be active but passive; and for this reason we shall not cease from being deified. At that point our passion will be supernatural, and there will be no principle restrictive of the divine activity in infinitely deifying those who

are passive to it. For we are active agents insofar as we have operative, by nature, a rational faculty for performing the virtues, and also a spiritual faculty, unlimited in its potential, capable of receiving all knowledge, capable of transcending the nature of all created beings and known things and even of leaving the "ages" of time behind it. But when in the future we are rendered passive (in deification), and have fully transcended the principles of beings created out of nothing, we will unwittingly enter into the true cause of existent beings and terminate our proper faculties along with everything in our nature that has reached completion. We shall become that which in no way results from our natural ability, since our human nature has no faculty for grasping what transcends nature.[23]

Deification, as the final end of human existence, is a graced mode of experiential knowledge. However, the passivity or supernatural passion in the future state of deification "is really for Maximus an eternal perfection of the active faculties of human nature that are primed for communion with God."[24] The "true dialectic" here is that of continuity with creation (e.g., practicing the virtues is in accordance with the natural movement of the intellect) and the transcendence of the created order (e.g., God is the only one who is capable of deifying humans).[25] Accordingly, the future state of deification is the fulfillment and perfection of antecedent modes of knowledge (e.g., theological truths deduced from causes in *theoria* or natural philosophy).[26]

Understood in this way, the virtues play an integral role in the process of pursuing knowledge of God. Regulating the inner and outer workings of the self in order to fashion or transform "the knower by that which is known"[27] is precisely the rationale for linking the virtues and knowledge of God. Accordingly, those who desire to acquire knowledge of God (participate in the divine energies and exhibit divine likeness) *ought* to "possess as well a rich store of virtue gained through [their] conduct."[28] The logos of God leads "to spiritual knowledge those who, in their unsullied pursuit of the ascetic life, have nobly traversed the whole way of the virtues."[29] Virtues such as faith, self-mastery, long-suffering, patience, fear of God, humility, dispassion, and love foster a stable disposition that leads to contemplation, which "finds its fulfillment in illumination and ultimately in perfection or union with God or *theosis*, deification."[30] Furthermore, linking virtue and knowledge in this way enables the deiform self to enter into "God's light" (ἐν φωτὶ τῶ θεῶ).[31] That is to say, virtue is "the form in which knowledge appears to us, but knowledge is the center that holds virtue together. Through them both, virtue and knowledge, one single wisdom [σοφία] comes into being."[32] So, the process of cultivating and embodying virtuous dispositions purifies one from misguided or false notions, enables one to advance in knowledge of God, and opens up the possibility of receiving divine wisdom.

By linking virtue and knowledge of God in this way, Maximus rejects the claim that "divine philosophy" belongs to those who attempt to reach God through contemplation (or intellect) alone without engaging in the process of ascetic formation.[33] Alternatively, ascetic formation (e.g., the struggle involved in cultivating and embodying virtuous dispositions) is a precondition for rendering apt theological judgments, for perceiving correctly the divine in and through nature, and for participating in the life of God. A "true philosopher" in this regard is one who learns how "to rectify" misguided desires and how to move from self-love to a stable and intense longing for God.[34] Self-love (the mother of vices or of the passions) creates instability that ultimately results in the disintegration of the self.[35] Conversely, those who engage in divine philosophy with a pure heart "derive the greatest gain from the knowledge it contains. For their will and purpose no longer change with circumstances, but readily and with firm assurance they undertake all that conforms to the standard of holiness."[36]

Maximus's conception of divine philosophy, especially as it pertains to the generation of regulative practices, the ascetic formation of praiseworthy dispositions, and the goal of participating in the divine life, emphasizes the mutuality and interrelatedness of *praktike* and *theoria*.

> Ascetic practice and contemplation mutually cohere in one another, and the one is never separated from the other. On the contrary, ascetic practice shows forth through conduct the knowledge derived from contemplation, while contemplation no less displays rational virtue fortified by practice.[37]

Understood in this way, *praktike* plays an integral role in the formation of cognitive agents of deification. The self is purified from false notions and misguided passions, and, "all the virtues co-operate with the intellect to produce [an] intense longing for God."[38] Though it is certainly a prerequisite for engaging in contemplation, *praktike* is more "than merely a stage which has to be passed, before the mind may perform its higher contemplative functions."[39]

In the *Mystagogia*, for example, Maximus emphasizes the inextricable relationship between *praktike* and *theoria*. He divides the rational part of the soul into mind (νοῦς) and reason (λόγος). The former is the intellectual faculty that contemplates and communes with God. Its aim is to acquire divine knowledge, truth, and wisdom. The latter is the faculty that cultivates virtue, actively pursues goodness, and renders apt judgments (*phronesis*) about concrete matters. As we have seen, ascetic virtues play a fundamental role in enabling the self to make progress toward divine likeness. The contemplative side of things "can happen only when the human 'architecture' is restored to its right hierarchical structure. Reason, again, is a practical faculty which governs [regulates] the activity of the soul."[40]

The pairing of *praktike* and *theoria* (one of the five pairs listed in *Mystagogia* 5) reflects Maximus's view that humans, as a creative unity, are called to live in accordance with the logos embedded in nature and to embody the qualities of God.[41] Those who engage in virtuous and contemplative practices "are unified in their one object, though they may tend toward it under different aspects. This will be the ultimate basis why, apart from the example of the Incarnation, one must always insist on having both theory and practice."[42] Though truth and goodness are distinct goals (*desiderata*), both are connected with and reveal the same reality.

Maximus's conception of divine philosophy, then, requires the formation of the whole person (e.g., the deification of the body as well as of the soul). It upholds the mutual coherence of *praktike* and *theoria*, especially since humans were created to be holistic and their proper end is to participate in the qualities of God (e.g., truth and goodness).[43] When moved by truth and goodness, the self "becomes united to the God of all in imitating what is immutable and beneficent in his essence and activity by means of its steadfastness in the good and its unalterable habit of choice."[44] As a result, divine philosophy does not depict *praktike* merely as preparation for *theoria*. Rather, virtuous and contemplative practices enable the self to move toward participative knowledge of God (*theologia*).

■ THE NATURAL MOVEMENT OF THE INTELLECT: FROM POTENCY (IMAGE) TO ACTUALITY (LIKENESS)

Clarifying the connection between the natural movement of the intellect and the final end of humanity is also crucial to Maximus's account of the threefold path to deification. Movement in this regard is understood positively as an "inherent power," "natural activity," "passion," or "irrepressible activity" that directs, impels, and tends toward the "perfect fulfillment" of humanity's final end.[45] In this sense, passion (e.g., as redirected desire) plays a positive role in forming the right state of mind and moving the intellect toward its proper end. Negatively speaking, passion is an impulse that diverges from the natural movement of the intellect, such as in the misuse of human cognitive faculties or in the failure to cultivate "natural powers."[46] This is precisely why a properly regulated use (or perfection) of our cognitive faculties is crucial for fostering a praiseworthy desire for God and ultimately for moving the self toward participation in the divine life.

Maximus's conception of the natural movement of the intellect envisions a complementary relationship between human cognitive activity and the work of divine grace. Redirecting the intellect to its proper end, in other words, does not necessitate shutting down the physical (e.g., natural faculties) in order to open the spiritual, nor does it require the activity of a secret sense (or appending a supplementary intellect to our own mind). As the following passage aptly summarizes, the process of receiving divine wisdom calls for genuine human cognitive activity:

> We are not permitted to say that grace alone brings about, in the saints, insight into the divine mysteries without any contribution from their natural capacity to receive knowledge. . . . The point is that the grace of the Holy Spirit does not bring about wisdom in the saints without the receptivity of their intelligence, does not give knowledge without their ability to grasp the Word, does not give faith without the stability of mind and the confident readiness to face the still-unrevealed future in hope. . . . For the grace of Holy Spirit never destroys the capabilities of nature. Just the opposite: it makes nature, which has been weakened by unnatural habit, mature and strong enough once again to function in a natural way and leads it upward toward insight into the divine. For what the Holy Spirit is trying to accomplish in us is a true knowledge of things. . . . For as the Logos accomplished divine works in the flesh, but not without the cooperation of a body animated by a rational soul, so the Holy Spirit accomplishes in the Saints the ability to understand mysteries, but not without the exercise of their natural abilities or without their seeking and careful searching for knowledge.[47]

The natural movement of the intellect accordingly includes the employment of faculties such as reason and sense perception.[48] Yet these cognitive faculties need to be matured, trained, and realized, the result of which is discernment, dispassion, wisdom, and knowledge. To put it in contemporary terms, the "mature functioning of the epistemic agent depends on and makes use of the faculties, but the dispositions that are needed for high-level functioning are not the faculties alone, but the epistemic skills and virtues that are built on them."[49]

Maximus's cosmic theology undergirds his account of the conditions under which the self moves toward its reintegration and its conformity to God. The state of becoming (γένεσις) in which body and soul come together simultaneously "to form a particular person"[50] issues in movement (κίνησις) that has contemplative rest in God as its ultimate end. Everything that comes into existence is not "self-moved" but is "subject to movement."[51] Since becoming precedes movement, it seems "impossible to have movement before something has come into being."[52] God is the only unmoved reality that "fills all things, and everything that was brought from non-being to being is moved (because it tends toward some end)." Understood in this way, movement implies that humans have "not yet come to rest in that which is ultimately desirable."[53] Consequently, no created thing can be at rest until it has achieved its proper end.

As a result, the natural movement of the intellect, positively envisioned, is fundamental to the process of pursuing and being conformed to the ultimate good. Contemplative rest (epistemic stability, the fulfillment of human longing) in God (the ultimate good) is the end toward which humans are called to move. Attaining this end requires rational, emotional, and volitional maturation, especially since the actualization of goodness is "a goodness that is yet to come not one that existed once and was corrupted."[54] Accordingly, the deiform person draws on "wisdom and reason," and "by appropriate movement" seeks to understand his or her "proper beginning and cause."[55] The key is fostering a "firm and steadfast disposition, a willing surrender, so that from the one from whom we have received being we long to receive being moved as well. It is like the relation between an image and its archetype."[56] Undergirding such a process is the distinction that God is the only "existent Being" while humans "exist in potentiality before they exist in actuality."[57]

Maximus envisions the transition from potency to actuality (the formation and development of human agents of deification) in terms of a threefold pattern of human development (parallel, for example, to his conception of the cosmic schema of becoming, movement, and rest): (1) the logos of being (τὸ εἶναι), (2) the logos of well-being (τὸ εὖ εἶναι), and (3) the logos of eternal well-being (τὸ ἀεὶ εὖ εἶναι). The first mode, as we have seen, refers to the state of created existence in which body and soul come together simultaneously, and this kind of activity itself constitutes change, a natural movement (by the proper use of human cognitive faculties) toward the achievement of a particular end.[58] The second mode denotes the aptitude for well-being in which humans strive to acquire divine likeness through virtuous and contemplative practices.[59] The third mode is identified with eschatological existence in which the agent of deification will be "translated by grace unto eternal well-being."[60] The middle term (well-being) is couched between being and eternal well-being. However, a natural movement of this sort is not in and of itself capable of deifying the person; it needs grace, not as an add-on but as a fundamental ingredient to enable the agent to conceptualize and experience the reality of its existence. Being and eternal well-being, in other words, are the sole gifts of God.

What Maximus seems to have in mind is the regulation, education, and healing of the passions, not the eradication of them. The passions, under the influence of God's grace, can be "transformed into divine love."[61] This is precisely where the virtues play a crucial role in reconstituting and moving the self from potency to actuality. When the intellect strays from its "natural motion," the requisite steps toward its reorientation, purification, illumination, and perfection come, as we have seen, by cultivating the virtues and by engaging deeply in contemplative practices.[62] The one "who participates in virtue as a matter of habit unquestionably participates in God, the substance of virtues," and "to the inherent goodness of the image is added the likeness."[63] Formed in this way, the self employs "the passions to destroy a present or anticipated evil, and to embrace and hold to virtue and knowledge."[64] Thus, the process of educating the passions demands a well-formed character that renders the self "fit to participate in God."[65]

The natural movement of the intellect, then, entails internalizing the virtues, employing cognitive faculties properly, deciphering the principles of being in and through nature, and growing in the desire to experience directly and participate in the qualities of God.[66] Accordingly, the process of learning how to discern things correctly is fundamental to the goal of making progress toward deification.[67] Sharpening faculties and redirecting desire enable the human agent of deification to perceive, discriminate, and discern. When "sown by God with seeds of virtue," the cultivated self is "able to bring forth the power to see with knowledge what is in front of it, through a religious attention to contemplation."[68]

■ LOVE AS REGULATIVE LINK AND SYNTHETIC POWER

Reintegrating the self along these lines requires in particular a synthetic power that solidifies other virtues, draws the intellect to its proper source of illumination, and aids in navigating a unified movement toward divine likeness. For Maximus, no other virtue in this regard has a higher priority than love, especially since it undergirds the reintegration of the self and, as a manifestation of divine grace, elevates "human beings to deification." In fact, the deifying power of love has the regulative function of bringing together "all good things that are recounted by the *logos* of truth in the form of virtue."[69] It heals the self of its divisive tendencies by gathering "together what has been separated, once again fashioning the human being in accordance with a single meaning and mode."[70] Moreover, love, with this transformative process in mind, is "the goal of every good, being the highest of goods with God, and source of every good."[71] Consequently, people shaped in this way become an embodiment of divine goodness; they make progress in accordance with the *logos* of truth and "unite in themselves the torn fragments of nature. This is the true and blameless divine wisdom of the faithful, the goal of which is the good and the truth."[72]

The kind of formation envisioned here constitutes a process of "training in love."[73] Nevertheless, love is not concerned merely with the moral formation of the self, nor is it simply the finished product of the first stage (*praktike*) of the path to deification. It is also linked with the quest for knowledge of God and accordingly carries intellectual activity toward communion with God.[74] As a "holy state" (or a "blessed passion"), love "binds the intellect to spiritual contemplation," disposes it to prefer knowledge of God (e.g., mystical experiential knowledge of God) to all other things, and enables it to pursue "such knowledge ardently and ceaselessly."[75] With this in mind, deifying illumination is "engendered by love for God."[76] "Just as the thought of fire does not warm the body, so faith without love does not actualize the light of spiritual knowledge in the soul." Or "just as the light of the sun attracts a healthy eye, so through love, knowledge of God naturally draws to itself the pure intellect."[77] Understood in this way, love for and knowledge of God are integrally related to the intellectual formation of the agent of deification.

Along these lines, a virtuously formed mind, sustained by self-control and moved by love, withholds itself from and rectifies "impassioned fantasies and impulses."[78] In fostering epistemic stability of this sort, the power of love liberates the intellect from vices (e.g., arrogance), "equips it to advance in knowledge," and thus enables the deiform self to grow in its capacity to perceive divine mysteries.[79] Progress here requires aligning the quest for knowledge of God with evaluative qualities precisely because the goal of being immersed in the divine life presupposes maturation of the person. In this sense, the aim is not simply to accumulate knowledge about God or about the threefold path to deification, though these are important to the process of attaining divine likeness. More exactly, the ultimate end is "the transposition and transmutation of those found worthy into a state of deification" in which they will become directly acquainted with and participate in "God's deifying energy."[80] As the knower, in other words, becomes more acquainted with the known, the former is changed by participatory knowledge in the latter.

With this in mind, the deiform self must be volitionally open and formed through virtuous and contemplative practices in order to share in the divine life. These "conceptually loaded"[81] practices, as we have seen, regulate how a person *ought* to pursue the path to deification, though, as the following passage shows, perceptual acquaintance with God entails a different mode of knowledge.

> The scriptural Word knows of two kinds of knowledge of divine things. On the one hand, there is a relative knowledge, rooted only in reason and ideas, and lacking in the kind of experiential perception of what one knows through active engagement; such relative knowledge is what we use to order our affairs in our present life. On the other hand, there is truly authentic knowledge, gained only by actual experience, apart from reason and ideas, which provides a total perception of the known object through a participation [$\mu\acute{\epsilon}\theta\epsilon\xi\iota\varsigma$] by grace. . . . By "rational knowledge of God" I mean the use of the analogy of created beings in the intellectual contemplation of God; by "perception" I mean the experience, through participation, of the supernatural goods.[82]

The gift of participation is the consummation of volitional and cognitive activities. One can certainly obtain truths about God from the natural world. Acquiring beliefs in this way, however, falls short of the kind of direct apprehension or perception that Maximus describes in *theologia*. In other words, a *person* may infer that God exists (e.g., a person may be psychologically disposed to believe the proposition that God exists) without deriving this knowledge from an actual encounter with God. Even so, rational knowledge of this sort "can motivate our desire for the participative knowledge acquired by active engagement."[83] Its overall purpose is "to awake in us a desire for mystical participation; but it is also designed to purify the soul in a positive way and prepare it for the transcendental experience."[84]

A fundamental distinction, then, holds between participating in what is real and trying to understand, explain, and infer things about this reality. The former (perceptual knowledge of God) comes by experiential acquaintance with God and not simply (or only) by argument (e.g., the process of providing reasons to justify the belief that God exists).[85] Knowledge of God in this sense is not secured by sitting back and waiting for the evidence for God's existence to be produced, or as the result of viewing the evidence for God in a noncommittal way.[86] Instead, the deiform person needs to be volitionally open and engaged in virtuous and contemplative practices to receive perceptual knowledge of God.

■ CONCLUDING REMARKS

Maximus envisions the threefold path to deification more in diachronic than in synchronic terms. The deiform person takes up virtuous and contemplative practices over time, and in so doing, acquires an appetite for, learns to discern, and participates in what is beautiful, true, and good. Presupposed here is an ascetic-oriented struggle in which the self strives through these practices to achieve the goal of divine likeness. The point is not to suggest that all domains of inquiry need to follow the same process. Rather, a regulative approach to deification stipulates the conditions under which humans can flourish. The virtues in particular constitute forms of excellence that contribute both to the ongoing reintegration of the self and to the process of making progress toward divine likeness.

My proposal offers a suggestion about how one might form a constructive link between Maximus's conception of the threefold path to deification and a regulative approach to virtue epistemology, and how one might open up a viable trajectory for future research in philokalic studies. In particular, I think that we need to reorient religious epistemology to the question of what it means for humans to inquire about God and to what extent transformative practices are key for acquiring knowledge of God. As we have seen, ascetic formation and acquiring knowledge of God are inextricably linked to one another. Searching for God in this manner does not happen from a neutral perspective; rather, human agents must open themselves up to being cognitively and volitionally transformed. Accordingly, a time-slice depiction of Christian belief (e.g., the evaluation of beliefs in isolation from the actual practices and processes of Christian formation) will not suffice as an explanation of the cognitive aspects of deification. Instead, we need to pay closer attention to the role that struggle plays in our efforts to think theologically and to be conformed to the object of our inquiry.

What we see in Maximus is a profound connection between rigorous ascetic practices and an intellectual quest for God. He envisions intellectual formation in more holistic terms and therefore does not separate philosophical reflection and theological inquiry from spirituality or moral formation. A connection of this sort seems to pervade the collected texts in the *Philokalia*. As we have seen, love for and knowledge of the beautiful, the exalted, and the excellent are deeply intertwined.

In this regard, I have highlighted the role that the ascetic virtue of love plays in guiding the cognitive agent on the path to deification. More specifically, this essay has explained how Maximus's integration of love and knowledge fits within his account of deification. Rightly formed ascetic dispositions help the deiform person see clearly and make progress toward divine-likeness. Accordingly, the process of cultivating the virtues and of seeking to know God (both conceptually and experientially) requires a robust set of regulative practices.

17 Women in the *Philokalia*?

Verna E. F. Harrison

At the front of Graham Speake's book about Mount Athos is a photograph of an icon. The Mother of God is depicted standing upon the holy mountain with its many monasteries. One of her hands is raised in prayer, and the other holds a staff that identifies her as an ephor, one of the overseers of Athos.[1] In other Athonite icons she is presented as abbess of the confederation of monasteries. What then is her role in the spiritual lives of monks who turn their eyes prayerfully toward these icons? Surely they ask her to pray for them and protect them, then thank her for answering their prayers. But how do they relate to her as their abbess? She lived a virtuous virginal life, so surely the monks reflect on her example and seek to follow it. Perhaps they find her offering them guidance or direction in other, more specific ways as well.

Mount Athos, where spiritual writings were preserved for a thousand years and collected in the *Philokalia*, is a confederation of monasteries, sketes, and her-mitages for monks. Women, even Byzantine empresses and even devout nuns, have not been allowed to set foot there. In the *Philokalia*, St. Mark the Ascetic (fifth century) explains the rationale behind this ban. Concerned about the dangers of unchastity, he advises that "it is very helpful for young monks not to meet women at all, even though these women are considered saintly."[2] Moreover, even the remembrance of women can be dangerous for a monk, as St. John Cassian (ca. 360–ca. 435) explains: "The way to keep guard over our heart is immediately to expel from the mind every demon-inspired recollection of women—even of mother or sister or any other devout woman—lest by dwelling on it for too long the mind is thrown headlong by the deceiver into debased and pernicious thoughts."[3]

So women have been excluded from visiting the holy mountain, yet on the Greek mainland, not far from Athos, there are communities of nuns living the same way of life and often guided by the same spiritual fathers as their brothers on the mountain. Like the monks, they benefit from reading the *Philokalia*. So do monastic and lay women and men throughout the world. Needless to say, many of these readers who are women themselves or meet them frequently cannot take literally the advice of Mark the Ascetic and John Cassian, cited above.

What can readers find specifically about women in the *Philokalia*? They will find advice to monks about chastity, a few exhortations to pray to the Mother of God, and a letter of St. Gregory Palamas (1296–1359) to the nun Xenia about the monastic way of life. Yet little is said explicitly about a specific feminine identity or vocation. Although women readers today may be looking for such material, the *Philokalia* does not provide it, at least not directly. This exclusion in itself is a significant point.

In fact, the reasons for this silence go deeper than the absence of women among the Athonite monks who were the anthology's editors and their original intended audience. The writings included in the *Philokalia* actually directed readers' attention elsewhere. The four volumes we have in English provide advice in endless variations on guarding the thoughts, practicing virtues, avoiding vices, and persevering in prayer. These activities are presented as the most important tasks not only for monks but for all human beings. These activities and the progress toward God to which they lead manifest the authentic human identity that all people alike share. All are called to attain the same goal, the likeness of Christ, regardless of gender, race, ethnicity, and other human differences. In this affirmation, the *Philokalia* offers a prophetic message to today's world, characterized as it is by postmodern fragmentation.

This chapter will show how the *Philokalia* invites people to undertake a spiritual journey in which their gendered experience undergoes a profound transformation. First, they are called to lay aside the divisiveness associated with the split between male and female and to perceive and embrace the unity of humankind. Second, they are asked to overcome the passions of temper and desire, with the inner conflicts and distortions they cause, and to focus their attention toward God and God's kingdom. Finally, they are to embody a universal human vocation of virgin motherhood and give birth to Christ spiritually. Thus, the beginning task of monks and nuns is to renounce a sense that who they are is grounded in their maleness or femaleness, as distinct from their humanity made in God's image, which can reject vices, practice virtues, and contemplate God. Their task is also to renounce participation in bodily procreation. And yet, at the end of their journey their generative faculty reemerges transformed into a capacity to bring forth the virtues, and indeed to bring forth Christ.

■ **HUMAN UNITY**

The *Philokalia* is concerned with attaining unity within oneself as well as unity with others. However, its authors sometimes perceive the gender distinction as a cause of both internal and interpersonal division. Ilias the Presbyter (twelfth century?) says, "One living in a state of self-division cannot avoid the distinction between male and female; but this distinction may be accomplished by one's living in a state of self-unity, when the distinction between male and female is suppressed through attaining the divine likeness in Christ Jesus (cf. Gal. 3:28)."[4] Ilias is a succinct and enigmatic writer. He may mean that the division between male and female occurs within a single human person. Or it may point allegorically to the polarity between anger and desire, which can pull a person in different directions. This standard allegory is described in texts by Evagrius the Solitary (ca. 345–399) and St. Maximus the Confessor (580–662), discussed below. Citing Gal. 3:28, Ilias contrasts the gender distinction with the goal of monastic striving, the state of unity and completeness that is likeness to Christ.

Maximus, a profound theologian and a teacher of monastic life, provides most of the texts in volume two of the *Philokalia*, and he speaks of gender in several different ways. In the *Second Century on Love*, he explains how one who has attained likeness to Christ can perceive how all people are alike.

For him who is perfect in love and has reached the summit of dispassion there is no difference between his own and another's, or between Christians and unbelievers, or between slave and free, or even between male and female. But because he has risen above the tyranny of the passions and has fixed his attention on the single human nature, he looks on all in the same way and shows the same disposition to all. For in him there is neither Greek nor Jew, male nor female, bond nor free, but Christ who "is all, and in all" (Col. 3:11; cf. Gal. 3:28).[5]

Maximus lists several seemingly insurmountable divisions in human society, those based on property, faith, the institution of slavery, and above all gender. Like Ilias, he sees the passions as causing and exacerbating these divisions. He draws the reader's attention to the humanity common to everybody. Maximus hints that the perception of social divisions may actually cause or exacerbate these divisions themselves, and moreover the passions cause divisions within the self that result in this perception and then become projected onto others. And interestingly, for Maximus the unity within the self that has attained Christ's likeness grounds the perception of others as one and alike. That is, one who has Christ within also sees Christ in everyone he or she meets. As people grow spiritually, the presence of Christ within the self and others becomes more prominent than the presence of human characteristics that fall short of the Lord's wholeness.

▪ ALLEGORIES OF TEMPER AND DESIRE

The church fathers use allegory in many ways, often in the interpretation of scripture. Allegory frequently serves to build a bridge between the words of a biblical text and the needs or concerns of readers at a particular time and place. Allegories are made to fit specific contexts, so the same words can serve as allegorical signifiers for different things in different settings. In one place Maximus uses "women" as an allegory for virtue, love, and union with God,[6] all supremely positive realities in the Philokalia.

In other cases, allegories become standardized in the course of history. These linkages between a signifier and the thing it represents are then repeated and can be easily recognized within the tradition. For instance, the pair "male and female" frequently represents the two nonrational powers of the soul: temper[7] and desire. In accordance with age-old cultural stereotypes of the aggressive man and the sensuous woman, the male then stands for temper and the female for desire. These two powers of the soul are often discussed in the Philokalia, and in the English translation they are clearly defined and described in the glossary at the end of each volume. The authors of the Philokalia recommend that our intellect be allied with God and guide our temper and desire so that they become virtues. Then our inner being will become a unity as all its drives work together to serve God instead of pulling us in different directions. Thus temper and desire can become either good or evil, depending on how we use them. In this context, intellect, the most valuable faculty, is allegorically neither male nor female. Temper and desire work in different ways but appear to be of equal, ambivalent value. This scenario is vastly different from a use of allegory that can be described as sexist, in which "male" represents virtue and "female" represents sin or evil.

■ FROM MALE AND FEMALE TO CHRIST'S LIKENESS

In a consideration of intellect, temper, and desire, Evagrius makes use of the allegory discussed in the last paragraph to introduce Gal. 3:28. Significantly, he says that intellect itself needs to be purified, because like the emotional faculties it can be misused.

> Observe how the Physician of souls . . . corrects our temper through acts of compassion, purifies the intellect through prayer, and through fasting withers desire. By means of these virtues the new Adam is formed, made again according to the image of his Creator—an Adam in whom, thanks to dispassion, there is "neither male nor female" and, thanks to singleness of faith, there is "neither Greek nor Jew, circumcision nor uncircumcision, barbarian, Scythian, bond nor free; but Christ is all, and in all" (Gal. 3:28, Col. 3:10–11).[8]

Here, temper and desire are retrained by a difficult practice; one chooses to make them do the opposite of what they would prefer. Anger must turn to compassion and desire to fasting. The result is a new Adam who is neither male nor female but bears the likeness of Christ. Such an Adam can be a model and a head for men and women equally, as can the Christ of Gal. 3:28.

In *On the Lord's Prayer*, Maximus reflects at greater length on the same points. In this important passage, he interweaves the exegesis of Gal. 3:28 with the story of the wonder-working prophet Elijah. As he often does, he begins by looking toward the goal, God's kingdom.

> If the indestructible power of the pure kingdom is given to the humble and the gentle, who will be so lacking in love and so completely without appetite for divine blessings that he will not desire the greatest degree of humility and gentleness in order to take on the imprint of the divine kingdom, so far as this is possible for humans, and to bear in himself by grace an exact spiritual likeness of Christ, who is by nature the truly great King? In this likeness, says St. Paul, "there is neither male nor female" (Gal. 3:28), that is, there is neither temper nor desire.[9]

Here Maximus, like Evagrius, uses Gal. 3:28 to contrast the two impassioned drives of the soul, allegorized as "male and female," with the unity in Christ's likeness that is the life of God's kingdom. This fascinating interpretation of the verse would appear to be a distinctive characteristic of the *Philokalia*.

Maximus continues with a description of the imbalance and distortion of a soul in which anger or desire has run amok. Instead, he says, the aim is for the intellect, without these emotional drives, to be in control. Then he offers as an example Elijah, who "advanced freely towards God, unencumbered by attachment to any created thing."[10] Maximus adds that the prophet's soul was undivided by passions, and his will was a unity. As he continues, he uses a patristic approach to exegesis, not a modern historical method:

> Elijah knew that in the disciple of Christ there must be no imbalance of dispositions, for such diversity is proof of a lack of inward unity. . . . He who already lives and moves and has his being in Christ (cf. Acts 17:28) has annulled in himself the production of what is

imbalanced and disunited: as I have said, he does not bear within him, like male and female, the opposing dispositions of such passions. In this way, the intelligence is not enslaved by the passions and made subject to their fickleness. Naturally endowed with the holiness of the divine image, the intelligence urges the soul to conform itself by its own free choice to the divine likeness. In this way the soul is able to participate in the great kingdom that exists in a substantive manner in God the Father of all, and to become a translucent abode of the Holy Spirit.[11]

Maximus adds that the soul that has attained such a state "resembles God" and preserves the blessings it has received, thus remaining stable.

The Confessor drew from Evagrius's thought, and like him links male and female with passions, disunity, and distortion, while he links unity, stability, and likeness to Christ with a condition no longer characterized by the gender distinction. In our text, Maximus draws this conclusion, speaking of the soul that has attained Christ's likeness.

> For the soul that through the grace of its calling resembles God keeps inviolate within itself the substance of the blessings bestowed upon it. In souls such as this Christ always desires to be born in a mystical way, becoming incarnate in those who attain salvation, and making the soul that gives birth to Him a Virgin Mother; for such a soul, to put it briefly, is not conditioned by categories like those of male and female that typify a nature subject to generation and corruption.[12]

Maximus suggests here that as the human person advances toward Christ's likeness, the characteristics of male or female are not simply blotted out; rather, they are transformed into a sublime kind of femininity, virgin motherhood. This means that the human capacity to generate new life, which ordinarily requires the cooperation of a man and a woman, becomes transformed into the work of one human who has attained wholeness. Following the example of the Virgin Mary, she or he brings forth Christ, though spiritually, not physically. St. Gregory of Nazianzus (ca. 329–ca. 390), whose works were well known to Maximus,[13] made the same point succinctly in his Christmas homily. "Christ comes from a Virgin; women, practice virginity," he urged his listeners, "that you may become mothers of Christ."[14] Gregory's advice is directed to women, but Maximus addresses the same advice to monks, and the inclusion of his text in the *Philokalia* addressed it to the monks of Mount Athos. They saw themselves as invited to follow Mary's example in a very specific way. This is a significant reason why they would regard the Mother of God as abbess of the holy mountain.

■ WHY VIRGIN MOTHERHOOD?

Yet why does Maximus say that the categories "male and female" characterize "a nature subject to generation and corruption"? Recognizing that the reader would be surprised by this claim, he says in the very next sentence, "Let no one be shocked to hear me speak of the corruption that is inherent in generation."[15] He explains that in those entities that "come into being and pass away," such as fallen, mortal humans, "one will clearly see that generation begins with corruption and ends with corruption."[16] Then he again speaks of the passions, adding that they accompany the generation of a child and observing that they also result in disintegration and death. Such is the condition of "male and female." Again citing Gal. 3:28, he contrasts this condition with unity of will and purpose, virtue, and Christ's likeness.[17]

Maximus's attitude toward marriage and family life expresses an exclusively monastic perspective. His approach appears unfortunate today, given that faithful marriage often lacks support from the culture that surrounds it and needs the support of the church. Married people, like monks, are engaged in spiritual struggle, and the family lives in community every day. The two paths both lead toward God's kingdom. St. Symeon the New Theologian (949–1022), another contributor to the *Philokalia*, wisely observed that the real issue is not whether marriage or monasticism is better but what God has called each of us to do.[18]

However, Maximus explains his point about corruption further in discussing a theme characteristic of his ascetic theology, the pleasure-pain syndrome.[19] In our fallen condition, he says, when we engage in pleasures, the result is pain. Then, to relieve our pain, we engage in more pleasures, and so we are caught in a vicious circle that leads to death. Maximus's primary example of this phenomenon is once again human generation, which ends in death, since those who are born will die. He adds that Christ came and provided us with a new birth that leads instead to eternal life. Thus, for Maximus, Christ's birth from a virgin is itself a salvific act. It inaugurates a new kind of generation that others can imitate. This idea may allude to baptism, as freeing people from the death sentence inherent in the pleasure-pain cycle.

Yet to say that Christ's birth is salvific implies the idea of monastics giving birth to Christ spiritually. For the church fathers, virgin motherhood is more than an escape from the vicious circle of coming to be and passing away. Rather, it is supremely positive.[20] Gregory of Nyssa speaks of what such spiritual birthgiving involves.

> Birth comes not from blood, nor from the will of man or the will of the flesh, but from God only (cf. John 1:13). And this occurs when one conceives through the aliveness of the heart the incorruptibility of the Spirit and gives birth to wisdom and justice and holiness and redemption. For it is possible for everyone to become truly a mother of these [virtues], as indeed the Lord says somewhere: "The one doing my will is my brother and sister and mother" (cf. Matt. 12:50, Mk. 3:35).

What place, then, does death still have in such offspring? In them, mortality is truly defeated by life; and the virginal life seems to be an image of the blessedness of the age to come, bringing in itself many identifying marks of the good things stored away through hope.[21]

Gregory adds that a life of virginity brings closeness to God, participation in the life to come, likeness to the angels, and communion with the saints. A comparison between this passage in its context and Maximus's thought as discussed above suggests that he was familiar with it. He develops some of Gregory's themes further.

As Gregory explains in *On the Beatitudes* 4, virtues such as those listed here, "wisdom and justice and holiness and redemption," are in the first place divine attributes.[22] Christ possesses all the virtues, and our human task is to participate in them, which amounts to participation in him. In other words, to bring forth acts of virtue is to give birth to Christ spiritually. Gregory sees such birthgiving as the fruit of virginity.

Elsewhere he makes the further point that virginity is characteristic of the whole Trinity, beginning with the "incorruptible Father":

> Indeed it is a paradox to find virginity in a Father who also has a Son begotten without passion. And virginity is grasped together with the only-begotten God, the supplier of incorruptibility, since it shone forth with purity and dispassion in his begetting. And again, the Son, conceived through virginity, is understood as an equal paradox. And in the same way one perceives virginity in the natural and incorruptible purity of the Holy Spirit. For when one names the pure and incorruptible, one signifies virginity by another name.[23]

So, Gregory argues, since all three divine persons are incorruptible, they are by definition virginal. The Father loses nothing in begetting but remains whole and undiminished, and his Son, too, comes forth whole, from a single parent.

As Gregory sees a parallel between the Father and the Son, so also there is a parallel between the Father's begetting of the divine Son in eternity and the Virgin Mary's bearing of the same Son as human within history. Her childbirth can be compared to the divine begetting because it also shares wholeness and unity. In Greek this connection is clearer than in English, since a single verb, $\gamma\epsilon\nu\nu\alpha\eta\omega$, is used for "to beget" and "to bear," depending in whether a father or a mother is the subject. For example, in the Chalcedonian Definition, our Lord Jesus Christ is said to be "generated [$\gamma\epsilon\nu\nu\eta\theta\epsilon\eta\nu\tau\alpha$ = born or begotten?] before the ages from the Father in his divinity and in the last days . . . of Mary the Virgin Theotokos in his humanity."[24] The same verb names both the divine and human generations, and it is not even repeated in the second phrase. The Chalcedonian Definition is a creedal statement well known in the Orthodox Church from the fifth century onward, and an inspiration for Maximus's theology. So the parallel between Christ's two generations had long been familiar to him.

So for Maximus, virginal begetting and bearing are the same kind of procreation; they directly parallel each other. In the Trinity, the Son comes directly from the essence of the Father. Appropriately, the closest human image of this divine generation is Mary's virginal birthgiving. Thus for Maximus, virgin motherhood emerges as a new paradigm for human procreation because the ultimate model to be followed occurs in the Trinity itself. Christ's mother followed God the Father's example as far as is humanly possible in giving birth to the same Son, and so she became a model for others. Her motherhood is paradigmatic for all humans, especially nuns and monks.

In fact, in virginal generation, the contrast between male and female and their coming together play no part in producing the offspring. Instead, virginal generation transcends the polarity between male and female. The ways of engendering of God the Father and Mary parallel each other, just as monks and nuns live the same way and follow the same path, though in separate communities, and they bring forth the same virtues, or indeed bring forth Christ. Therefore Maximus believes that virginal generation is the goal of human generativity for both men and women. Virginal generation is specific to Mary's motherhood, and yet it is not only feminine; it also belongs to God the Father, who is symbolically masculine, though in reality he is beyond gender.

In the *Philokalia*, Gregory Palamas (1296–1359) clarifies and extends the connection between the Trinity and the virginal life. Here he may have drawn from Gregory of Nyssa, *On Virginity* 2, cited above, which was written a thousand years earlier.

> If you are capable of it, embrace the path of virginity, so that you may become wholly God's and may cleave to Him with perfect love, all your life devoting yourself undistractedly to the Lord and to what belongs to Him (cf. 1 Cor. 7:32), and in this way anticipating the life to come and living as an angel of God on earth. For the angels are characterized by virginity, and if you cleave to virginity you emulate them with your body, in so far as this is possible. Or, rather, prior to them you emulate the Father who in virginity begot the Son before all ages, and also the virginal Son who in the beginning came forth from the virginal Father by way of generation, and in these latter times was born in the flesh of a virginal Mother; you likewise emulate the Holy Spirit who ineffably proceeds from the Father alone, not by way of generation, but by procession.[25] Hence, if you practice true chastity in soul and body you emulate God and are joined to Him in imperishable wedlock, embellishing every sensation, word and thought with virginal beauty.[26]

This passage summarizes clearly much of what earlier Greek patristic writers have said about virginity. Gregory Palamas adds the obvious conclusion, that the aim of human existence is to become a bride of Christ. Again, a feminine symbol, made flesh above all in the Mother of God, is the paradigm, not for nuns only but also for the monks of Mount Athos.

■ **CONCLUSIONS**

We have examined some of the more interesting references to women and gender in the *Philokalia*, though this paper cannot claim to have covered the topic exhaustively. From the few texts we have studied, what conclusions can we draw? Let us note first that the anthology focuses attention on other aspects of the human condition, not on gender. Moreover, it expresses an exclusively monastic perspective. The following conclusions must be understood in this context.

1. Ilias the Presbyter, Evagrius the Solitary, and Maximus the Confessor all interpret Gal. 3:28 dynamically. In other words, at the beginning of the spiritual journey, people are male or female. They are in a state of disunity and disorder, and their minds are pulled in different directions by the passions. Their aim is to progress to a point where "there is neither male nor female" but each person is "all one in Christ Jesus" (RSV), that is, unified, with the intellect guiding the emotional faculties and being supported by them. Then the whole person is united to Christ and brings him to birth through virtuous actions. So here the movement from fragmentation to union is understood primarily as occurring *within* the human self. Fragmentation means inner conflict, but the aim is to move toward having all

one's human capacities work together to serve God. This goal can be interpreted to mean that to live in Christ is to leave behind the culturally constructed limitations of our gender identity. That is, it means beginning with the virtues that may seem connatural to us as women or as men but then growing to acquire the virtues associated with the other gender as well. Christ's humanity is whole and complete, so he embodies all the virtues, and Christians are called to become like him through union with him.

2. As Ilias and Maximus explain, the fragmentation occurs both within each human person and among human persons. Perception is what connects the inner realm to the outer world. So one who is inwardly obsessed with gender or sexuality will have a distorted view of others that overemphasizes or misperceives their gender and perhaps their sexuality. Such misperceptions, or the need to guard novices against them, may be a reason why the monks spoke so negatively about being in the presence of women. Such distorted perceptions result in disordered interactions with one's neighbors in deeds as well as in thoughts. The *Philokalia* teaches us to focus on other aspects of ourselves, on diagnosing and redirecting our unruly thoughts and passions, and on developing our abilities to practice virtues and to pray. When we struggle consistently in these areas, we will learn to see ourselves as humans made in God's image, and thus we will come to view our neighbors in the same way. The *Philokalia* dares to pose a question to today's men and women: To what extent is our intense focus on gender issues a symptom of internalizing our culture's passion-driven malaise?

3. In the tradition of patristic allegory, Evagrius and Maximus link the emotional faculties, temper and desire, with male and female. But is there a deeper reason for it? Perhaps men appeared to the church fathers as more aggressive and women as more sensuous. These appearances may result from genes, from cultural formation, or both; for whatever reason the same stereotypes exist today. Men and women have been trained from childhood in bad habits, yet the *Philokalia* can teach them to redirect their attention and turn toward God. Despite the stereotypes, there are plenty of angry women and sensuous men, too. Another question the anthology poses is: To what extent is our sense of who we are as men or women bound up with a tangle of passion-driven presuppositions, thoughts, and emotions?

4. In Gal. 3:28, "male and female" is the starting point and "Christ Jesus" is the goal, according to the *Philokalia*. So Christ is contrasted with male and female. Does this mean that he is without gender? As with any Christological question, a convincing answer will be complicated. To be sure, his divinity is beyond gender, but what about his humanity? To become incarnate and live a specific human life must have meant to assume one gender or the other. In Christ, this is maleness. Yet this raises a deeper question: what is the relationship between maleness and humanity as such? Between the specific and the universal? We cannot answer such questions here,[27] but let me suggest a way of approaching them. The *Philokalia* interprets "Christ Jesus" in Gal. 3:28 as the goal of monastic striving, that is the fullness of human perfection, encompassing all the virtues. In this context, "male and female" are incomplete parts of that complete humanity. We each begin with some parts, and perhaps each person starts with a different set, but over time we

are called to acquire more. Christians believe that Christ was born with the whole of human perfection. Significantly, the philokalic interpretation of Gal. 3:28 avoids any identification of human perfection with maleness. Let us consider whether the Christ of the Gospels embodied some perfections and practiced some virtues that appear to us as feminine.

5. If the goal is to become like Christ, it is also to become like Mary his mother, as Maximus and Gregory Palamas say. This means acquiring both masculine and feminine perfections. Indeed, the Mother of God, like her Son, must possess the perfections of both genders. Virginal generation bypasses the need for both male and female parents; it is wholeness giving birth to wholeness. Though birthgiving is the work of a female, virginal generation somehow surpasses gender. The ultimate example is God the Father, who transcends everything human. In the Byzantine Christmas services, which have been sung on Mount Athos for many centuries, the following Psalm verse is chanted repeatedly and sets the theme: "From the womb before the morning star have I begotten thee."[28] The liturgical context shows that this verse refers both to Christ's generation from the Father in eternity and to his generation from Mary at a moment in time. Yet how can the Father, who was never incarnate, be said to have a womb?[29] Virginal generation is like fatherhood in that it initiates the child's life without any prior biological source, and it is like motherhood in that the child comes forth from the parent's own being, as from a womb. In a word, it is beyond gender limitations. Here there are more questions: Does the Mother of God, like her Son, encompass the perfections of the other gender as well as her own? Does virginity make this possible? Monastic life may facilitate this wholeness for men and for women in the course of a lifetime, since both have the same vocation.

6. The spiritual journey described in the *Philokalia* passes through different stages. At the beginning one is either male or female, beset by passions, and in need of transformation. Then, through many struggles over time, one's attention is refocused on prayer and on God. At the end, one is united with Christ, or becomes like the Mother of God, or both. The gender distinction is an active concern at the beginning, though one's understanding is distorted by the passions. One identifies oneself as either male or female. In the middle the focus on these matters is laid aside, and one does the prayer and work characteristic of monastic life. And then, at the end, gender comes back, but everyone possesses the perfections of both male and female, not just half.

And yet, this perfection can also be described as symbolically feminine, though it still involves a transcendence of gender. According to Maximus, one arrives at virgin motherhood, and, like a mother, brings Christ forth. According to Gregory Palamas, one becomes united with Christ the Bridegroom. Thus one becomes a bride of Christ, unequivocally symbolically feminine. Thus Gregory of Nyssa calls Paul the bride in the Song of Songs.[30]

Could this be the goal of the monks on Mount Athos? Yes, but not exclusively. The *Philokalia* tells us that the monk is also called to be a soldier, a profoundly masculine identity in ancient and Byzantine times. St. Philotheos of Sinai, for example, makes extensive use of the metaphor of spiritual warfare.[31] It follows that once distorted perceptions of gender are laid aside, each person is called to become perfected in both masculine and feminine ways.

18 Solitude, Silence, and Stillness: Light from the Palestinian Desert

John Chryssavgis

▨ I. INTRODUCTION: READING BETWEEN THE LINES

It has always amazed me that a selection of the *Letters* of Barsanuphius the Great and John the Prophet was never included in the spiritual anthology of Saints Nikodemus of the Holy Mountain and Makarios of Corinth. In some ways, this absence of the great Gaza elders from a treatise of such profound authority is not by accident; for, surely it was not out of ignorance. Perhaps this omission reflected the humble deference of the elders themselves, who spent their entire lifetime avoiding visibility and recognition.

Nikodemus himself became well aware of the importance and influence of the two Old Men, having produced an edition of their entire correspondence—850 letters in total, together with a detailed biographical and theological introduction—at Venice in 1816, albeit several decades after the appearance of the *Philokalia*. The title of that publication, edited by Nikodemus and based on several Athonite manuscripts, was "Very Beneficial Book Containing Responses to Various Questions by the Holy Fathers Barsanuphius and John, carefully edited and enriched with the lives of the saints." It would be helpful, then, to consider some of the insights of these renowned elders, whose counsel is distinguished by a rare sense of balance, which is not always immediately evident in much of the often overwhelming and more rigorous teaching of the *Philokalia*.

Indeed, a consideration of the fundamental convictions of the two Gaza elders on the notion of spiritual life—especially relating to the fundamental concept of *hesychia* extolled and championed by the *Philokalia*—highlights the way in which the *Philokalia* assumes an understanding and appreciation of the broader range of the ascetic tradition. Therefore, this classic, albeit beloved anthology should not be idealized—or idolized—as the complete or ultimate word on the discipline of silent prayer. It is surely in the same vein that one should understand the absence of—even the 27th Step *On Stillness* from—the *Ladder of Divine Ascent* by St. John Climacus, which otherwise exercises such profound influence on many of the writers in the *Philokalia*. In this regard, I have focused on the gift of silence in Barsanuphius and John as indicative of the way in which self-understanding and self-knowledge lead to and can never be dissociated from the spiritual worldview and deeper knowledge of God. Silence is also a way of connecting the notion of self-love with love for others as well as with divine love, without which self-righteousness may readily be identified with self-hatred in the ascetic life.

There are, in all, six references to Barsanuphius of Gaza in the *Philokalia*: five of these are in volume 4, while the last is in volume 5. In volume 4 Gregory of Sinai mentions Barsanuphius by name in his own "Very Beneficial Chapters," where there are two references concerning psalmody. Moreover, in the same volume, a text attributed to Symeon the New Theologian, "On the Three Methods of Prayer," contains a reference to Barsanuphius on the same topic. Finally, in the fifth volume, Kallistos and Ignatios Xanthopouloi mention Barsanuphius three times in their work titled "On Those Who Choose to Live in Stillness," citing general advice from the "great old man" on the spiritual struggle, his classical teaching on "not reckoning oneself as anything" (*to apsepheston* [τό αψήφιστον];[1] in this case, the verbal variant: *to apsephesthenai* [τό αψηφισθῆναι]), and finally quoting a passage from *Letter* 119 in their section on "the fruit of internal prayer."

The full text of the *Letter* cited by the Xanthopouloi brothers, where the specific words quoted are highlighted, reads as follows:

> Letter 119. Response by the same Great Old Man to the same brother, when a thought was sown within him that not abstaining from food was preventing him from reaching what had been promised.
>
> It is not because I wish to abolish abstinence and the monastic discipline that I am always telling your love to perform the needs of your body as necessary—far be it for me! Rather, I am saying that, **if the inner work does not come to our assistance after God, then one is laboring in vain on the outward self.**[2] For that is why the Lord said: "It is not what goes into the mouth that defiles a person, but it is what comes out of the mouth that defiles." (Matt. 15:11) **Indeed, inner work with labor of heart brings purity, and purity brings true stillness of heart, and such stillness brings humility, and humility renders a person the dwelling-place of God, and from this dwelling-place the evil demons are banished,**[3] together with the [passions] devil who is their captain, as well as their shameful passions. **Then, that person is found to be a temple of God, sanctified, illumined, purified, graceful,** filled with every fragrance and goodness and gladness; and that person is found to be a God-bearer, or rather is even found to be a god, according to the one who said: "I have said, you are gods, all children of the Most High." (Ps. 81:6, John 10:34) Therefore, do not let the thought, or rather the evil one, trouble you, that bodily foods prevent you from attaining to those promises. No; for they are holy, and evil cannot issue from good, but only from those things that come from the mouth. The things, then, that come from inside the heart (cf. Matt. 15:18–19) are the ones that prevent and hinder a person from arriving swiftly at the promises that lie before us. Therefore, when you carry out your bodily needs, do not have any doubts, but do whatever your inner nature can do to labor and humble its thoughts. Then, God will open the eyes of your heart in order to see "the true light" (John 1:9) and to understand the words: "I am saved by grace" (Eph. 2:5) in Christ Jesus our Lord. Amen.

The above-mentioned "inner work" or "labor of the heart"—as a journey toward purification, illumination, and sanctification—lies at the very core of the spiritual life in the *Philokalia*. Purity of the heart (*kardia*) or concentration of the mind (*nous*), the control of the passions or conquest of the vices, as well as the intellectual or physical methods adopted in watchfulness and prayer: all are achieved by means of solitude, silence, and stillness. For "prayer of the heart" and "prayer of the intellect" do not exist in themselves; they denote a process of intimate relationship—with one's surroundings, with one's community, and ultimately with God. They presuppose an intense sense of vigilance with regard to the physical surrounding of one's external solitude, the activity of inward silence, and the way of utter stillness.

This chapter on the one hand explores some of the fundamental insights and basic lessons about silence, as formulated by Barsanuphius and John, thereby illuminating a fundamental principle in the tradition of the *Philokalia* through the eyes of these elders from sixth-century Gaza.[4] After all, it is important to recall that fourteenth-century hesychasm is not simply the result of a few exceptional individuals, such as Gregory of Sinai (1260s–1346) or Gregory Palamas (1296–1359), who crown the fourth volume of the *Philokalia*;[5] nor does the hesychast movement merely imply a somewhat broader selection of mystical writings, such as those included in the extraordinary anthology of the *Philokalia*. It is also an organic extension and natural continuation of countless unknown hermits and numerous other writers, whose lives and lines are not officially recorded in the *Philokalia*. The editors of the English translation of the *Philokalia* recognize this fact in their introduction to volume 1: "Hesychasm . . . is far more than a local historical movement dating to the later Byzantine centuries. On the contrary, it denotes the whole spiritual tradition going back to the earliest times and delineated in the *Philokalia*."[6]

Had Nikodemus of the Holy Mountain discovered the manuscripts of Barsanuphius and John prior to the publication of the *Philokalia* in 1782, there is a distinct possibility that he would have included selections from their spiritual correspondence in the opening volume of his anthology, just as he chose to incorporate excerpts from the little known writings of their revered Palestinian predecessor, Abba Isaiah of Scetis, who died in Gaza toward the end of the fifth century (491). However, before examining the wisdom of these elders on vigilance and silence, it is helpful briefly to explore their characteristic lifestyle in early sixth-century Gaza, which surely shaped their thinking and clearly influenced subsequent monastic teaching about solitude and stillness.

■ II. THE MONASTIC LIFESTYLE IN PALESTINE AND GAZA

We do not know exactly when—or, indeed, why—the Great Old Man, Barsanuphius, entered the hilly region of Thavatha (*Letter* 61), presumably from Egypt, choosing to lead there the enclosed life of a recluse in a small cell. We do, however, know that from this position he counseled numerous ascetics, who were gradually attracted by the Great Old Man's extraordinary reputation for discernment and compassion. Some time between 525 and 527, the Other Old Man, Abba John the Prophet, came to live beside Barsanuphius, sharing the same lifestyle and supporting the same ministry.

Barsanuphius and John were the continuation and, in many ways, an incarnation of the principles treasured in the early Egyptian desert. In particular, Barsanuphius was clearly shaped by the Evagrian notion—contained in the anthology of the *Philokalia* and comprising the entire worldview of the *Philokalia*—that the monk was "apart-from all and yet a part-of all."[7] By not opening his door to the elderly Egyptian monk who requested to see him (in *Letter* 55), Barsanuphius was in fact leaving the door open to everyone! Certain aspects of this lifestyle are of course reminiscent of earlier patterns in Judaean monasticism, geographically and spiritually familiar to Barsanuphius and John.[8]

Their custom of communicating in silence—surely a significant dimension of communication in writing—through someone else, as a measure of protecting their solitude, also finds a precedent in Abba Isaiah, who would regularly communicate during the fifty years of his own seclusion in the same region through Peter the Egyptian. However, Isaiah would never quite reach the same exclusive measures as Barsanuphius and John; nor would this system of contact and conversation with his disciples constitute a central element in his spiritual ministry. Still, this form of counseling was neither altogether original nor entirely exceptional in the region.

Curiously, the "invisibility" and "inaccessibility" of Barsanuphius and John became the very reasons for their visible eminence and attraction.[9] The lifestyle that they both experienced and encouraged included a balance of solitude and silence:

> You too should live in stillness for five days of the week and be in the company of your brothers for the other two days. And if your sitting in solitude is indeed according to God, that is to say if you come to know what you want from sitting in your cell, then you will not fall into the hands of the demon of vainglory. For a person who knows what one has come to do in a particular city desires that alone and does not divert one's heart toward anything else, otherwise one will fail in that which one seeks. (*Letter* 211)

Both of these unique elders exercised extraordinary influence on generations of monastics throughout the world, including Mt. Athos. Evidence of this impact lies in the numerous manuscripts that survive in monasteries, revealing the wide appreciation and dissemination of the correspondence. Although the Muslim invasions of Palestine left little or nothing in that region to remind one of the monastic or Byzantine presence and influence,[10] nevertheless the correspondence was known in early ninth-century Constantinople, the oldest manuscripts originating on Mt. Sinai and dating from the tenth century. Several manuscripts were preserved on Mt. Athos from the eleventh through the fourteenth centuries; Nikodemus of the Holy Mountain had direct access to these documents.[11]

The fundamental concepts, and even key terms, so highly valued in the *Philokalia* are developed in a unique way by the Gaza elders, who contribute invaluable insights and avoid pitfalls normally associated with such notions as silence and prayer.[12] Without the balanced context provided by these elders, basic virtues such as prayer and discipline may be misinterpreted as individual struggles and selfish feats, far removed from any need for and gift of grace.[13] After all, it is helpful to recall that the image of spiritual struggle is ultimately one of embrace and love (as in the icon of Israel and the angel of God). In a sense, anything that we do in the spiritual struggle—just as everything we do in life—is a reflection of this love, whether as the experience of its fullness or else of its failing. In the journey of spiritual struggle, the ascetic learns how to balance the demands of nature with the endowment of grace. The ascetic struggle is to learn how to love, how to share, and especially how to let go; the goal is to understand when our passions interfere with our relationships, when we are selfish and hurt others or when we have to step back and refashion ourselves, when we give ourselves to another (and how much of ourselves we are daring to give) or when we play games and manipulate.

What is it, then, that the soul desires to learn through solitude, silence, and stillness? What are the spiritual variations of monastic seclusion and communal relations in the search of the roots of *Philokalia* as "the love of divine beauty"?

■ III. THE WAY OF THE SOUL

The *Philokalia* acknowledges that there is a blurred line of demarcation between the virtues of solitude, silence, and stillness:

> Some of the fathers have called this practice stillness of the heart, others attentiveness, others the guarding of the heart, others watchfulness and rebuttal, others again the investigation of thoughts and the guarding of the intellect. But all of them alike worked the earth of their own heart, and in this way they were fed on the divine manna.[14]

Yet Barsanuphius and John do draw distinctions between solitude,[15] silence,[16] and stillness.[17] Indeed, underlying these three disciplines is the importance of taking time to examine the various aspects of the soul and the particular principles that govern them. Self-knowledge is the heart of solitude, the basis of silence, and the center of stillness.[18]

In our age of instant communication and immediate gratification, we seem to know less about ourselves, and about the motives behind our actions, than any other subject. Somewhere on that long trail between childhood and adulthood, many of us have lost touch with the vital skills that permit us to know ourselves. Perhaps part of the problem is that we have set impossible goals, which can be met only by angels. The spirituality of the desert taught the Gaza elders that perfection is for God alone; we are called neither to forego nor to forget our imperfection. The fragility and vulnerability of life itself reveals the priority of confronting and embracing our inner desires and personal weaknesses.

Barsanuphius and John certainly comprehend the ways of the soul that struggles to know or understand itself as well as the wiles of temptation that often detract or distract. Indeed, they appreciate the fact that, unless we take the radical step of surrendering familiar connections and concepts through an act of *xeniteia*, whereby we enter the foreign territory and learn to speak the foreign language of solitude, then we cannot begin to articulate the language of the soul. The Gaza elders are therefore aware that, while there are as many ways of knowing our selves as there are human beings, the differences between us are in fact very slight.

Furthermore, Barsanuphius and John recognize that specific rules and spiritual regulations determine the depth of solitude, silence, and stillness. Often our lives are complicated by rules and regulations; we are burned out and afraid to be alone, unable to listen, unwilling to love. The *Philokalia* underlines the fact that, through and in silence, God is the one who first listens and loves.[19] Barsanuphius and John propose simple and practical ways of learning this truth by "sitting in the cell" (*Letter* 172), practicing silence during conversation (*Letters* 470, 481), and "beginning to practice stillness" (*Letter* 211). The spiritual life is a way of breaking bad habits and establishing new ones in their place:

> To cut off one's own will while sitting in the cell is to despise fleshly comfort in all things. (*Letter* 173)

Barsanuphius adopts the image of constructing a house in order to describe the arduous struggle (*Letters* 52, 71, 207, 535)[20] and continual effort (*Letter* 41)[21] involved in the practice of silence and stillness:

> If you wish to construct your home, first prepare the material and all other necessary things. Then, it is up to the professional builder to come and build the house.[22] The necessary building materials for such a construction include firm faith[23] for the building of walls, luminous wooden windows that allow in the light of the sun to brighten the house, so that there may be no darkness inside. These wooden windows are the five senses.[24] . . . Furthermore, you need the house to be covered by a roof, . . . symbolical of love for God, "which never ends" (1 Cor. 13:8). . . . Finally, the house requires a door, which allows the person dwelling there to enter inside and to be protected. When I speak of a door, brother, you should understand the spiritual door, namely the Son of God,[25] who says: "I am the door" (Jn. 10:9). (*Letter* 208)

In the house of the soul, then, the essential quality of solitude is awareness or vigilance; the essential quality of silence is listening or obedience; and the essential quality of stillness is intimacy or love.[26] There is no obedience without vigilance; and there can be no intimacy without solitude. When these three qualities coexist, then the ascetic struggle enables us to discover the deep soul and to take our soul with us wherever we go:

> When you arrive at the point of stillness, then you shall find rest with grace, *wherever you may happen to withdraw*. (*Letter* 789)

▪ IV. SOLITUDE: THE DOOR TO THE SOUL

Solitude—or, as Niketas Stethatos calls it, "taking up one's abode in the desert"[27]— is what allows us the time and the space to become alert to others and ourselves. For Peter of Damascus, solitude is the principal form of discipline, "consisting . . . in living a life without distraction, far from all worldly care, removing ourselves from human society . . . instead having one concern."[28] For Gregory Palamas, lack of solitude "shatters that one-pointed concentration of the intellect, which constitutes the inward and true monk."[29] Therefore, as Nilus the Ascetic counsels, solitude should be "embraced [as] the mother of wisdom."[30] For Barsanuphius and John, it is a prerequisite in the way of spiritual progress (see *Letter* 616). In response to someone requesting prayers, Barsanuphius writes:

> Brother, do not compel me to speak when I desire to venerate stillness and silence. (*Letter* 69)

And to a monk inquiring whether he should accept money in order to feed the poor, Abba John is equally radical, apparently uncharitable: you are to avoid this . . . "even if you see someone dying in front of your very cell!" (*Letter* 619) Both elders appreciate how easily love and service are used as excuses to avoid the inner work of transformation. They recognize how even prayer can become a pretext to circumvent the difficult work of solitude and silence (see *Letter* 739). This is why Abba John will also state:

> As far as almsgiving goes, not everyone can bear the application of this virtue, but only those who have reached stillness through mourning for their own sins. (*Letter* 618)

Unfortunately, however, we tend to confuse self-knowledge with self-absorption. In reality, self-knowledge leads away from self-absorption toward a sense of "forgetting oneself."

> Brother, show complete hatred in order to acquire complete love; show complete estrangement in order to acquire complete intimacy; abhor adoption in order to receive adoption; surrender your will in order to perform your will; cut yourself away and bind yourself; put yourself to death in order to give life to yourself; forget yourself and know yourself. Then, behold, you will have the works of a solitary. (*Letter* 112)

Curiously, while we encourage the need for knowing and loving others, we less frequently reward knowing ourselves in solitude. Barsanuphius reiterates the stark conviction of Abba Alonius: "I and God are alone in this world" (*Letter* 346).[31] Barsanuphius states: "Being alone and laboring a little is of more benefit to you than being with others" (*Letter* 359). Indeed, we are never less alone than when we are alone:

> Brother, you are not alone in your struggle. . . . For there are many others, who are struggling with you in their prayers (cf. Col. 4:12). (*Letter* 832)[32]

Knowing why we do what we do facilitates the awareness also of why other people do what they do, and in the end the acceptance of other people as they are (see *Letter* 316). Narcissism is not too much self but rather insufficient knowledge of our true self. People who are self-absorbed normally suffer from too little rather than too much self. The antidote to self-centeredness is self-awareness. This is why Gregory of Sinai knows that "nothing so fills the heart with contrition and humbles the soul as solitude embraced with self-awareness."[33]

We often seek intimacy by facing in the wrong direction. Instead of looking inwardly, we turn outwardly toward others. So the isolation of solitude should serve as the first step to intimacy or communion with other people. "Brother, when you are alone in your cell, examine your heart, and you will discover whence this hardness [toward your brother] came to you" (*Letter* 614). The notion of silence and prayer as a mirror of one's soul is certainly a fundamental concept of the *Philokalia*.[34] Intimacy begins from within, and it reflects the inner world of the soul. It is the solid ground from which we are able to reach others, even God Himself. According to an apocryphal saying attributed to Jesus in the *Gospel of Thomas*:

When you make the two one,
And make the inside like the outside,
And the outside like the inside,
And the upper side like the underneath . . .
Then the kingdom is at hand.

Solitude, then, is the great stabilizer. It is like a secret compass in our relationships with God, with others, and with ourselves. It enables us to distinguish between personal sharing and "people-pleasing" (*anthropareskeia*, ανθρωπαρεσκεια); the latter is to be strictly avoided (see, for example, *Letters* 260–61 and 824–25). Solitude leads to silence, which is nothing but "the restraining of one's heart from giving and taking (Phil. 4:14), from people-pleasing and other such things" (*Letter* 314). Solitude is about being, and not simply doing. It renders the soul attentive and receptive. It smashes the idol of prayer as "not working" when we do not receive what we want. Prayer does not want; it simply wonders and humbly waits.

> Do not despair at the labor [of being alone], and you shall find humility. . . . If you are humbled, you will receive grace; and if you receive grace, this grace will assist you. (*Letter* 359)

Barsanuphius and John are clear about the fact that when prayer is answered, it is never in ways that we might expect. "God will arrange the matter in a way that you do not know" (*Letter* 359). In fact, prayer is answered in ways that transcend—perhaps even devastate—a self-reliance that seeks immediate attainment of premeditated goals. Thus solitude is hardly identified with selfishness; solitude dissolves self-centeredness; it is not reckoning oneself as anything at all (what Barsanuphius and John call τό αψήφιστον):

> Be carefree from all things; then, you will have time for God. Die to all people; this is true exile. Moreover, retain the virtue of not reckoning yourself as anything; then you will find your thought to be undisturbed. (*Letter* 259)

Barsanuphius and John continually walk a delicate tightrope between the devil of instant vainglory (see *Letter* 204) and the blue sea of despair:

> When a person descends to humility, that person discovers progress. Remaining in your cell only renders you useless if you remain without affliction. When we are carefree prematurely, our enemy prepares turmoil instead of tranquility, in order to bring us to the point of saying: "I wish I had never been born!" (*Letter* 692)

They often explicitly recommend balance, "not moving to one or another extreme, but journeying rather in the middle way" (*Letter* 314).

> Neither being bold in one's silence nor despising one's silence in times of distraction; this is truly the middle way. (*Letter* 315)

However, progress in the way of the soul takes toil and time. We do not change suddenly, magically becoming new people, with our old faults forgotten. We can never run away from who we are; we can never escape temptations and passions:

our temper, vanity, fear, envy, delusion, or arrogance. Barsanuphius advises us "never to enter the cell on the pretext of cowardice, but only at the proper time" (*Letter* 434). John adds:

> When you come to silence by means of ascetic struggle, then it is good. However, when this is not the way that you come to it, but rather keep silent out of fear for any turmoil, then it is harmful. (*Letter* 481)

Ultimately, the degree to which we are able to acknowledge and accept others will be limited to the degree that we can understand and tolerate ourselves. We are more united to each other through our weaknesses and shortcomings than through our strengths and successes.

In the solitude of the cell, through temptations and tensions, the ascetic becomes painfully aware of what is lacking. There, the ascetic is haunted by the absence of love and yearns for the depth of communion. The cell symbolizes the safe haven of the soul, which one never leaves and where one can always willingly return in order to discover more and more of the authentic self, irrespective of how painful an ordeal or how agonizing a struggle this may be. Such a discovery through solitude eventually becomes a fountain of healing. Embracing solitude in the loneliness of the cell (and, by extension, the soul) means knowing what you think, understanding how you behave, and finally accepting others without the need to defend oneself. It is assuming responsibility without the least sense of self-justification. It is the source of authentic vulnerability and openness.

In this respect, namely in the above-mentioned sense of vulnerability or openness, solitude also connects with the Cross of Christ (see *Letter* 185). Indeed, John writes, "that is when one reaches silence, [precisely] when one bears the Cross" (*Letters* 314, 320).[35] People who have been pushed, to the "breaking point," whether by personal suffering or by difficult circumstance, frequently have a richness of vision that is less apparent in those without any conflict. Indeed, the reality of conflict as a constant and crucial part of life is difficult to accept. Yet, how we experience tension and ambivalence deeply affects how we accept ourselves and others. The truth is that God may be discerned in the very midst of these tensions and trials.

Solitude reminds us that the soul is not a conflict-free zone where we can evade or ignore the perils of the world and the temptation of the soul.

> In the cell, we feel pain and compunction. What prevents compunction from coming to you is your own will. If a person does not cut off one's own will, then the heart does not feel pain. (*Letter* 237)

No wonder the Gaza elders underline the need to "rejoice in the Lord, rejoice in the Lord, rejoice in the Lord" (*Letter* 10). While "we cannot be without affliction ... we have been commanded instead to 'give thanks in all circumstances' (1 Thess. 5:18)" (*Letter* 96). It is here that solitude meets service, and the cell opens up to the whole world.

There is no limit to the hours of silence. However, one should bear everything that comes one's way with thanksgiving. . . . This is what constitutes compassion. (*Letter* 315)[36]

■ V. SILENCE: THE WAY TO THE SOUL

If solitude endows us with a quality of awareness and vigilance, silence educates us in the art of listening and attentiveness. The *Philokalia* underlines the importance of using few words. St. Theodore the Ascetic is explicit about this:

Expel from yourself the spirit of talkativeness. For in it lurk the most dreadful passions: lying, loose speech, absurd chatter, buffoonery, obscenity. To put the matter succinctly, "through talkativeness, you will not escape sin" (Prov. 10:19), whereas a silent man "is a throne of perceptiveness" (Prov. 12:33). Moreover, the Lord has said that we shall have to give an account of every idle word (cf. Matt. 12:36). Thus silence is most necessary and profitable.[37]

Physical contact and verbal communication are as much associated with intimacy and love as silence is. In solitude, the space between ourselves is important; so too is the space between our words in silence. This space is always necessary; therefore, "silence is always more admirable" (*Letter* 36), "always better" (*Letter* 697), "glorious above all else" (*Letter* 469), "good in every case" (*Letter* 283), "more necessary and more beneficial than everything" (*Letter* 314). The same truth is evident in the *Philokalia*: "Silence is more valuable than speech";[38] it is "indescribable."[39] This is why Barsanuphius claims that silence is actually demanded of us by God (*Letter* 603); he would never say this of stillness, which is a gift (*Letter* 94). Solitude provides the space and the capacity to listen to and soak up what another person is saying and conveying. This is so because we bring to relationships the same self that we are (or are not) in touch with when we are alone. Indeed, the elders harshly rebuke those who complain about losing any spiritual gifts attained in solitude—including silence—when they happen to be with other brothers! (*Letter* 268)

Silence is a skill whereby we acknowledge that what is going on in someone else's world matters. Otherwise, the river of connection between "me" and "you" may render the force of my own desires and prejudices more "conscious" in my mind and in my heart. As a result, I create my own version of you, with little if any chance of contact or connection.

Another Christ-loving layperson asked the same Old Man (John): Sometimes, I happen to be in conversation with someone, and suddenly my thought is distracted, so that I feel that I am alone and ultimately I forget what that person has just said. Not because my intellect is transferred somewhere else, but because it is simply beside [full of?] itself. . . .

This is a diabolical temptation. . . . However, if one freely reveals this to the other person in conversation, saying: "Forgive me; for I was distracted by the devil," then the devil is put to shame and the temptation ceases. After that, you may continue the conversation with vigilance. (*Letter* 692)

These elders recognize that where there is an impoverished self, there is also an endangered relationship. Silence is the criterion of truthfulness, integrity, and balance. For Elias the Presbyter:

> A sense of the right moment and a sense of proportion go hand in hand with an intelligent silence. Truth is the banquet of all the three together.[40]

Now, Barsanuphius and John are well aware that in order to achieve self-knowledge, we need to trust at least one other person:

> From this you may learn whether you are living like the others in the monastic community; by not doing anything of your own will, eating neither alone nor with the brothers, but doing whatever you have been ordered without any discussion. (*Letter* 250)
>
> Doing something through the abbot is always a lesser wrong . . . . However, doing something alone always brings a double warfare, not only from the heart but also from other people. (*Letter* 324; cf. also 173)

Obedience is essentially an act of listening attentively; it is the art of listening closely (*hypakoe*).[41] Mark the Ascetic already alluded to the dangers of extreme isolation, when one "relies on one's own judgment with no one else as witness."[42] Barsanuphius is certain that "when you hasten to do something on your own, then the resulting silence is from the devil" (*Letter* 93). In brief, the basic advice is almost reminiscent of a good "prep school" education: "It is never good to speak before being asked" (*Letter* 698). However, the goal is not to restrain or repress the will; it is to strengthen and stabilize the will:

> Feel neither arrogant if your words are accepted, nor grieved if your words are rejected. (*Letters* 698 and 738)

Obedience is the measure and criterion of authentic solitude and silence:

> If you wish to learn whether you are being hurt or receiving benefit by staying on your own, then adopt this as a sign. If you are staying there as a result of obedience, you may be certain that you are benefiting. (*Letter* 248)

Of course, the fine balance between isolation and intimacy is ultimately impossible to attain without divine grace. Authentic silence and stillness are a reflection of the fellowship that exists in the Holy Trinity:

> Now, if you prepare your house [of silence] in this way . . . [the Son of God] will come with the blessed Father and the Holy Spirit, and will make a home with you (cf. John 14:23), teaching you what stillness is and enlightening your heart with ineffable joy. (*Letter* 208)

Moreover, the fine balance between isolation and intimacy is extremely difficult to sustain without a spiritual director. Through someone else's belief in our self, we begin confidently—that is, by the act of confiding and confessing—to rediscover the solid ground within. Sharing our thoughts and temptations openly with at least one other person enables us to become familiar with the desires and conflicts that drive our behavior. Furthermore, being prepared to listen to and accept the reality of our nature and our self renders us more aware of (and more caring toward) other people. The opportunity to go within in order to learn and grow at one's pace is ultimately the chance also to become aware of the presence of others and attentive to them.

One reason for sharing with others is that most of us are harsher critics of ourselves, striking the most painful blows against ourselves at just the time when we most require tolerance and compassion, virtues that characterize the Gaza elders. And, while obedience goes against the grain to much of our contemporary notions of liberation and independence, when someone is unable to build up from even the smallest patch of solid ground, then terms like "freedom" and "will" have little resonance.

Frequently citing Galatians 6:2, Barsanuphius and John emphasize that responsibility for "the burdens of others" is critical to growing spiritually. Assuming and acknowledging responsibility for the consequences of one's thoughts and actions implies not blaming others, who as a result become less threatening to us.

> To come to perfect silence, one must first endure insults from other people, as well as despise, dishonor and hurt . . . in order that the labor may not be in vain (cf. 1 Thess. 3:5). (*Letter* 185)

Silence, then, is the alphabet in the language of tolerance and love. Under the steamroller of our words, intimacy may sometimes be crushed!

Barsanuphius prefers silence; John, however, confesses that he loves conversation:

> My babbling does not allow me to keep silent without replying; for I have an uncontrolled tongue. (*Letter* 211)

Indeed, John claims: "Since we have not yet reached the point of walking the way of the perfect, on account of our weakness, we should in fact speak" (*Letter* 469). After all, as he observes elsewhere:

> As for the silence, of which the Fathers speak, you do not even know what this is. Not many people know at all. For this silence is not a matter of shutting one's mouth. There may be someone who speaks tens of thousands of words that are useful; and this is reckoned as silence. There may be another who speaks only one idle word, and this is reckoned as trampling the Savior's teachings. (*Letter* 554)[43]

This balance between solitude and society distinguished the nearby monastery, where Barsanuphius's scribe, Seridos, served as abbot. Cells opened up to windows that allowed for conversation with visitors; and monks were encouraged to support the needs of those outside the community, including lay persons and family relatives—"not in order to please people or to seek praise, but out of purity of heart" (*Letter* 595).

Finally, Abba John is the first to refer to the concept of "nonsilence" *(to asiopeton,* or *to me siopan),* when one is silent but does not honestly manifest one's thoughts and, therefore, remains unhealed (*Letter* 320). Both silence and speaking can be false. When our theology is disconnected from others, when it does not relate to this world, it is a false language, a miscommunication. Barsanuphius and John have little tolerance for spiritual chatter (cf. *Letter* 36) that renders God small and manageable. They do not offer a recipe book for healing and salvation. Seductive as the "quick-fix" may be, Barsanuphius and John know that human beings are unpredictable, far too complex for this approach to bear long-term benefits. The more possible it is to predict someone, the less of a real person one has become. Beware the person who always has the answer!

▪ VI. STILLNESS: THE RESURRECTION OF THE SOUL

Solitude and silence finally issue in the mystery of stillness; indeed, they are "the foundation of stillness."[44] For Gregory of Sinai, stillness is so "eloquent"[45] that anyone desiring to know the mysteries should "cleave to stillness."[46] For Abba Philemon in the *Philokalia*, "the only path leading to heaven is that of complete stillness."[47] And for Niketas Stethatos, it is "the upper room,"[48] "the knowledge of the mysteries of God . . . the abyss of divine intellections, the rapture of the intellect, intercourse with God, an unsleeping watchfulness, spiritual prayer . . . solidarity and union with God."[49] For this is the moment when we realize that God is the ground of our being (cf. Jer. 10:10), "the solid rock of our foundation" (*Letter* 345), before whom we are no longer afraid of "being frail" or of "being nothing" (cf. *to apsepheston* in *Letters* 227, 259, 271, 604). Abba John says: "Wherever there is stillness . . . there also God dwells" (*Letter* 454). And Barsanuphius claims that stillness is a spiritual gift, given by God "in its proper time" (*Letter* 208).[50]

Stillness closely relates to death. It also reflects our expectation of the age to come. Be vigilant, Barsanuphius advises: "Pay attention to yourself and expect your impending death" (*Letter* 256).

> The cell is a cemetery. . . . It is the place of rest . . . a sanctuary inasmuch as it contains the dwelling-place of God! (*Letter* 142)

Stillness can almost feel like death, also resembling the slow, silent growth of roots spreading deep in the ground—furtive, yet formative. Barsanuphius likens "perfect stillness" (*Letter* 6) to "the arrival of a ship in a harbor, where it no longer fears dangers, distress or the onset of winds" (*Letters* 8–9).

There is nothing simplistic or sluggish about the cultivation of stillness."[51] Living life to the full comes only when the ultimate concerns have been faced, namely meaninglessness and death.[52] How we face or avoid these concerns has profound consequences on our experience of solitude, silence, and stillness. Remembrance of death is a crucial virtue in the ascetic life, a daily and tangible reminder of our weakness and imperfection. If we want to come out of life nice and polished, we need simply to think of death. There is hardly an outwardly sense of perfection in nursing homes and hospices. Remembrance of death allows brokenness to be revealed truthfully so that the lie may split wide open and the healing may begin.

Nevertheless, stillness is not merely something frightening; it is, above all, something sacred. Stillness is closely associated with the desire for "life in abundance" (Jn. 10:10), beyond "mere survival." Most of us tend to deny the relation between death and stillness by entering a whirl of activity that makes death either improbable or else impossible. Stillness is like waiting respectfully and reverently.

It is a renewing sense of anticipation, an overture to heavenly resurrection. In stillness, we are aware of being alive, and not dead—of having needs and temptations and of being able to face and embrace these without turning elsewhere. In stillness we are not empty; we are not alone; we are not afraid. "In stillness, [we] know that God is" (Ps. 46:11)[53]—an experience that may occur in a split instant or develop over an entire lifetime.

Finally, stillness introduces an apophatic element to the way of intimacy and love. This is why Gregory of Sinai claims: "Stillness requires above all . . . love with all one's heart and strength and might."[54] Citing Isaac the Syrian, Peter of Damascus links "the state of stillness" with "freedom from discursive thought."[55] In this regard, silence and stillness become greater than love itself.[56] In the *Philokalia*, Thalassius the Libyan closely links "stillness and intense longing for God."[57] Indeed, through stillness comes the refreshing suggestion of approaching God and others by "not knowing" them. If we are fixed to our preconceptions about God or our fears of people, then we may never enjoy perfect stillness (see *Letters* 6, 496). When we "know" someone, we have already shut our eyes to that person's constant process of change and growth. We limit ourselves by rooting others only in the past and not rejoicing in their potential. In the isolation of solitude, we can risk being who we are; in the echo of silence, we can risk facing the other person as he is; and in the intimacy of stillness, we can embrace the other person in his entirety, in his eternal dimension—beyond what we can ever comprehend, tolerate, or merely find useful. For, then, we are—to adopt the phrase of Nicephoros the Monk—"wounded by love."[58]

▪ VII. CONCLUSION

According to a legend preserved in the *Historia Ecclesiastica* of Evagrius Scholasticus, at the time of Evagrius's writing (c. 593), some fifty years after the presumed death of Barsanuphius, the Great Old Man was believed to be still alive. When the Patriarch of Jerusalem ordered the cell door opened, a consuming fire flashed out of the cell.[59] The silence of Barsanuphius proved stronger than death itself; it would prove profoundly influential for generations of monastics and laity interested in pursuing the way of beauty, prayer, and silence promoted in later centuries by the anthology of the *Philokalia*.

Solitude, silence, and stillness are monastic virtues that present us with subtle yet significant variances of the wonder of the soul and the wound of the heart. In many ways they constitute an equivalent, in application and practice, to the Evagrian threefold distinction between *praktike, theoria*, and *theologia*.[60] Nevertheless, Barsanuphius and John offer a fresh and alternative perspective of this world, not an occasion to escape the reality of this world. In defining the three stages of the solitary life, they underline the fact that we can be authentically attached only when we have become completely detached. This is essentially the experience of letting go and of trusting. It is the ability to forget oneself in an effort to reach out to another person. Indeed, solitude, silence, and stillness relate to every detail, to "every matter and conduct and concern" in our life (*Letter* 52). Every relationship demands the same closeness and separateness, the same acceptance and space.

In this respect, the three stages of the solitary life defy the paradoxical or ideological clash sometimes highlighted between the ideal of silence and the reality of verbosity in the desert tradition. Such was the way of silence found among the desert Fathers transmitted through Evagrius of Pontus and Nikodemus of Mount Athos.; the same silence was also the ultimate prize treasured in the *Philokalia*;[61] and this silence was the teaching echoed and expressed by Barsanuphius and John, who likewise claimed that "one should be with others as if not being with them" (*Letter* 173).

■ NOTES

■ Foreword

1. "The Catholicity of the Church," in Georges Florovsky, *Bible, Church, Tradition: an Eastern Orthodox View,* Collected Works, vol. 1 (Belmont, MA: Nordland, 1972), pp. 50–51, citing B. M. Melioransky.

2. *Chapters* 25: in the Greek "Astir" edition of the *Philokalia* (Athens: Papadimitriou, 1957–63), vol. 5, p. 16; this work will be included in vol. 5 of the English *Philokalia,* which is still in preparation.

3. Introduction to E. Kadloubovsky and G. E. H. Palmer, *Early Fathers from the Philokalia* (London: Faber and Faber, 1954), p. 15.

■ Introduction

1. Two helpful books for beginning students of the *Philokalia* are Anthony M. Coniaris, *A Beginner's Introduction to* the *Philokalia* (Minneapolis, MN: Light and Life, 2004); *Philokalia: The Bible of Orthodox Spirituality by Anthony M. Coniaris* (Minneapolis, MN: Light and Life, 1998); Anthony M. Coniaris, *Confronting and Controlling Thoughts According to the Fathers of* the *Philokalia* (Minneapolis, MN: Light and Life, 2004); Allyne Smith, *Philokalia: The Eastern Christian Spiritual Texts. Selections Annotated and Explained* (Weedstock, Vermont: Skylight Paths, 2006). For topical studies on various subjects, see Basileios S. Stapakis, the *Philokalia: Master Reference Guide* (Minneapolis, MN: Light and Life, 2004).

2. See the English translation of St. Nikodimos' proem by Constantine Cavarnos, the *Philokalia: Writings of the Holy Mystic Fathers in Which Is Explained How the Mind Is Purified, Illumined, and Perfected through Practical and Contemplative Ethical Philosophy* (Belmont, MA: The Institute for Byzantine and Modern Greek Studies, 2008), 39.

■ Chapter 1

1. The present work is a revised version of my article "St Nikodimos and the *Philokalia,*" originally published in Dimitri Conomos and Graham Speake (eds.), *Mount Athos the Sacred Bridge* (Oxford, 2005), pp. 69–121. I have included some material from another of my articles, "The spirituality of the *Philokalia,*" in *Sobornost incorporating Eastern Churches Review* 13: 1 (1991), pp. 6–24.

2. On the Greek editions and the various translations of the *Philokalia,* see Kallistos Ware, "philokalie," *Dictionnaire de Spiritualité* 12 (1984), cols. 1336–52. For supplementary information on the Slav and Romanian versions, see Dan Zamfirescu, *A Fundamental Book of European Culture* (Bucharest, 1991), pp. 8–22; V. Pelin, "L'opera di Nicodemo l'Aghiorita in Romania," in A. Rigo (ed.), *Nicodimo l'Aghiorita e la Filocalia,* Atti dell' VIII Convegno ecumenico internazionale di spiritualità ortodossa, sessione bizantina, Bose, 16–19 settembre 2000 (Magnano, 2001), pp. 243–51; E. Citterio, "Nicodemo Agiorita," in C. G. Conticello and V. Conticello (eds.), *La théologie byzantine et sa tradition,* vol. 2 (Turnhout, 2002), pp. 919–21. A detailed analysis of the contents of the *Philokalia* is provided by V. Conticello and E. Citterio, "La philokalie et ses versions," in C. G. Conticello and V. Conticello, op. cit., pp. 999–1021.

The most accessible Greek edition of the *Philokalia* is the third, issued in 5 volumes (Athens, 1957–63). There are two English versions. The first, in 2 volumes, is by E. Kadloubovsky and G E. H. Palmer, *Writings from the Philokalia on Prayer of the Heart* (London, 1951); *Early Fathers from the Philokalia* (London, 1954). This is based on the Russian *Dobrotolubiye* edited by St Theophan the Recluse (1815–94), and it contains only selected texts. (The word *Dobrotolubiye* is the Slavonic and Russian equivalent to the Greek word *Philokalia*.) The second English version, based on the original Greek, contains all the texts included in the edition of 1782 (together with certain supplementary material from the second Greek edition): the *Philokalia: The Complete Text . . . translated from the Greek*, by G. E. H. Palmer, P. Sherrard, and K. Ware, 4 vols (London/Boston, 1979–95); vol. 5 is in preparation. References to the *Philokalia* in this chapter are to the third Greek edition, followed (where applicable) by a reference to the English translation (ET) of Palmer, Sherrard, and Ware, or else to the earlier ET of Kadloubovsky and Palmer.

On the theology of the *Philokalia*, see P. Sherrard, "The Revival of Hesychast Spirituality," in L. Dupré and D. E. Saliers (eds.), *Christian Spirituality: Post-Reformation and Modern*, World Spirituality: An Encyclopedic History of the Religious Quest 18 (New York, 1989), pp. 417–31; revised version, "The Renewal of the Tradition of Contemplative Spirituality," in P. Sherrard, *Christianity: Lineaments of a Sacred Tradition* (Edinburgh/Brookline, 1998), pp. 245–67. Cf. A. Louth, "The Theology of the *Philokalia*," in J. Behr, A. Louth, and D. Conomos (eds.), *Abba: The Tradition of Orthodoxy in the West*. Festschrift for Bishop Kallistos (Ware) of Diokleia (Crestwood, NY, 2003), pp. 351–61. See also three articles by K. Ware: "The Spirituality of the *Philokalia*", in *Sobornost incorporating Eastern Churches Review* 13: 1 (1991), pp. 6–24; "Possiamo parlare di spiritualità della Filocalia?," in O. Raquez (ed.), *Amore del bello: Studi sulla Filocalia*, Atti del "Simposio Internazionale sulla Filocalia," Pontificio Collegio Greco, Roma, novembre 1989 (Magnano, 1991), pp. 27–52; "Gerald Palmer, the *Philokalia*, and the Holy Mountain," in G. Speake (ed.), *Friends of Mount Athos: Annual Report 1994* (Oxford, 1995), pp. 23–29.

3. For a brief but sound account of Nikodimos in English, see the book by C. Cavarnos, *St. Nicodemos the Hagiorite*, Modern Orthodox Saints 3 (Belmont, 1974); compare, by the same author, *St. Makarios of Corinth*, Modern Orthodox Saints 2 (Belmont, 1972). There is as yet no full, critical biography of Nikodimos. For the existing bibliography, see D. Stiernon, "Nicodème l'Hagiorite," *Dictionnaire de Spiritualité* 11 (1981), cols. 234–50; I. [=E] Citterio, *L'orientamento ascetico-spirituale di Nicodemo Aghiorita* (Alessandria, 1987), pp. 7–21 (this book is the best study of Nikodimos I know); and E. Citterio, "Nicodemo Agiorita," in C. G. Conticello and V. Conticello, *La théologie byzantine et sa tradition*, vol. 2, pp. 905–78 (esp. pp. 973–98). See also G. E. Marnellos, *Saint Nicodème l'Hagiorite (1749–1809), maître et pédagogue de la nation grecque*, Analecta Vlatadon 64 (Thessaloniki, 2002).

4. *The Gulag Archipelago*, part iv, chapter 1: Fontana edition, vol. 2 (Glasgow, 1976), p. 597.

5. P. Leigh Fermor, *Roumeli: Travels in Northern Greece* (London, 1966), p. 106. On the effects of Neohellenism upon Greek Orthodoxy, see the severe but shrewd assessment by P. Sherrard, *The Greek East and the Latin West. A Study in the Christian Tradition* (London, 1959), pp. 165–95. Compare P. M. Kitromilides, *The Enlightenment as Social Criticism: Iosipos Moisiodax and Greek Culture in the Eighteenth Century* (Princeton, NJ, 1992).

6. On the movement of the Kollyvades, see the well-informed but somewhat hostile account by Ch. S. Tzogas, *I peri ton mnimosynon eris en Agio Orei kata ton 18 aiona* (Thessaloniki, 1969). A briefer but more sympathetic treatment is provided by K. K. Papoulidis, *To kinima ton Kollyvadon* (Athens, 1971). Further bibliography can be found in G. Podskalsky, *Griechische Theologie in der Zeit der Türkenherrschaft (1453–1821)* (München, 1988), pp. 329–85, and in E. Morini, "Il Movimento dei 'Kollyvadhes,' Rilettura dei contesti più

significativi in ordine alla rinascità spirituale Greco-Ortodossa dei secoli xviii–xix," in O. Raquez (ed.), *Amore del bello: Studi sulla Filocalia*, op. cit. (n. 2), pp. 137–77. For Nikodimos's own account of the controversy, see his *Confession of Faith*, ET Fr. George Dokos (Thessaloniki, Uncut Mountain Press, 2007).

7. On frequency of communion in the Christian East, see F. Herman, "Die häufige und tägliche Kommunion in den byzantinischen Klöstern," in *Mémorial Louis Petit*, Archives de l'Orient chrétien 1 (Bucharest, 1948), pp.203–17; R. Taft, *Beyond East and West: Problems in Liturgical Understanding* (Washington, DC, 1984), pp. 61–80; K. Ware, "Prayer and the Sacraments in the *Synagoge*," in M. Mullett and A. Kirby (eds.), *The Theotokos Evergetis and Eleventh-Century Monasticism*, Belfast Byzantine Texts and Translations 6:1 (Belfast, 1994), pp. 325–47, esp. pp. 336–41.

8. The phrase is used originally by St. Ignatios of Antioch, *To the Magnesians* 8.2, where it refers to the person of Christ.

9. *Philokalia* 1, xxii. The introduction by Nikodimos is not included in the ET by Palmer, Sherrard, and Ware.

10. *Cf.* Virgil, *Aeneid*, 2.48.

11. Hieromonk Agapios and Monk Nikodimos, *Pedalion . . . itoi apantes oi ieroi, kai theioi kanones [Rudder . . . or all the holy and divine Canons]* (Leipzig, 1800), p. 36; ET by D. Cummings, *The Rudder* (Chicago, 1957), p.73.

12. *Neon Martyrologion [New Martyrology]* (Venice, 1799). For large portions of this in ET, see L. J. Papadopoulos and G. Lizardos (eds.), *New Martyrs of the Turkish Yoke* (Seattle, 1985). *Cf.* N. M. Vaporis, *Witnesses for Christ. Orthodox Christian Neomartyrs of the Ottoman Period 1437–1860* (Crestwood, 2000).

13. In Ph Meyer, *Die Haupturkunden für die Geschichte der Athosklöster* (Leipzig, 1894), pp. 236–41, esp. pp. 239–40.

14. In J. D. Mansi and L. Petit, *Sacrorum Conciliorum Nova et Amplissima Collectio* 40 (Paris, 1909), pp. 81–82.

15. M.Gedeon, *O Athos: Anamniseis-Engrapha-Simeioseis* (Constantinople, 1885), p. 216.

16. In Cavarnos, *St. Nicodemos the Hagiorite*, p.89.

17. Ibid., p. 93.

18. Evthymios, *Life of Nikodimos*, ed. S. Lavriotis, in the periodical *Grigorios o Palamas*, 4 (1920), pp. 636–41; 5 (1921), pp. 2l0–18; see p. 640. A revised edition of this was edited by N. Bilalis, *O prototypos vios tou agiou Nikodimou tou Agioreitou* (Athens, 1983). Evthymios wrote his biography in 1813, four years after the death of Nikodimos.

19. For an English translation, see Archbishop Chrysostomos and Hieromonk Patapios (eds.), *The Evergetinos: A Complete Text*, 4 vols (Etna, CA: Center for Traditionalist Orthodox Studies, 2008).

20. There exist two English translations of this: (1) Hieromonk Patapios and Archbishop Chrysostomos (trs.), *Manna from Athos: The Issue of Frequent Communion on the Holy Mountain in the Late Eighteenth and Early Nineteenth Centuries* (Oxford, 2006), pp. 53–181. (2) Fr. George Dokos (tr.), *Concerning Frequent Communion of the Immaculate Mysteries of Christ* (Thessaloniki, Uncut Mountain Press, 2006).

For a long time there was considerable doubt about the origin of this work, but the question has now been clarified by the researches of the Athonite monk Theodoritos: see K. Karaisaridis, "Nicodemo l'Aghiorita e Macario di Corinto," in Rigo, *Nicodemo l'Aghiorita e la Filocalia*, op. cit. (n. 2), pp. 62–64; Citterio, "Nicodemo Agiorita," pp. 926–27. The original work, it seems, was written by Neophytos of Kavsokalyvia, and this was published anonymously in Venice in 1777. The 1777 publication was then extensively revised and expanded by Nikodimos, before being reissued, once more anonymously, at Venice in 1783.

For Nikodimos's views on frequent communion, see M.-J. Le Guillou, "L'Athos et la vie eucharistique," in *Le Millénaire du Mont Athos 963–1963*, vol.2 (Venice/Chevetogne, 1964), pp. 111–20; R. A. Klostermann, "Nikodemos Hagiorites über das Abendmahl," *Orientalia Christiana Periodica* 45 (1979), pp. 405–9.

21. Paisy's account of the preparation of the *Philokalia*, together with his description of the translations that he himself made on Athos and in Moldavia, are to be found in the long and important letter that he wrote around 1782 to Archimandrite Theodosy of the St. Sophrony hermitage. For the original text of this letter, see V. Pelin (ed.), "The Correspondence of Abbot Paisie from Neamṭ (III). Letter to Teodosie, Archimandrite at the Sofroniev Hermitage," *Revue des Etudes Sud-Est Européennes* 32: 3–4 (1994), pp. 349–66; certain additional passages are to be found in *Zhitie i Pisaniya Moldavskago Startsa Paisiya Velichkovskago*, edited by the Optina Hermitage (Moscow, 1847), pp 197–217. For a full translation of the letter in Italian, see A. Mainardi (ed.), *Paisij, lo Starec*, Atti del III Convegno ecumenico internazionale di spiritualità russa "Paisij Veličkovskij e il suo movimento spirituale," Bose, 20–23 settembre 1995 (Magnano, 1997), pp. 270–304. Large extracts in English are given in *Blessed Paisius Velichkovsky*, ed. Hieromonk Seraphim (Rose) of the St Herman of Alaska Brotherhood (Platina, 1976), pp. 77–85, 110–13, 117–19, 180–94. Consult also S. Chetverikov, *Starets Paisii Velichkovskii: His Life, Teachings, and Influence on Orthodox Monasticism* (Belmont, 1980), pp. 119–25, 135, 144–51.

22. See K. K. Papoulidis, *Makarios Notaras (1731–1805), Archiepiskopos proin Korinthias* (Athens, 1974), p. 66 and n. 112.

23. Cited by V. Pelin, "L'opera di Nicodemo l'Aghiorita in Romania," in Rigo, *Nicodemo l'Aghiorita e Ia Filocalia*, p. 251.

24. Citterio, *L'orientamento*, pp. 341–72. On Nikodimos's correspondence, see Citterio, "Nicodemo Agiorita," p.939, where doubts are expressed about the actual existence of the manuscript which is supposed to contain the saint's letters.

25. Cavarnos, *St. Nicodemos the Hagiorite*, pp. 96–114. For a full description of Nikodimos's writings, see P. Nikolopoulos, "Vivliographiki epistasia ton ekdoseon Nikodimou tou Agioreitou," in *Praktika symposiou "Nikodimou Agioreitou tou Naxiou pnevmatiki martyria"* (Naxos 8–11 July 1993) (= Epetiris Etaireias Kykladikon Meleton 16 [2000]), pp. 361–667.

26. Nicodemos of the Holy Mountain, *A Handbook of Spiritual Counsel*, ET P. Chamberas, with an introduction by G. Bebis, *The Classics of Western Spirituality* (New York/Mahwah, 1989). Another original work by Nikodimos, also of considerable interest, is *Christoitheia ton Christianon* [*The Good Customs of Christians*], published in 1803: see A.-E. N. Tachiaos, "Nicodemo l'Aghiorita: Un esempio di vita per i laici ortodossi," in Rigo, *Nicodemo l'Aghiorita e Ia Filocalia*, pp. 193–204.

27. See n. 12.

28. See n. 11.

29. *Cf.* Mother Mary and Archimandrite K. Ware, *The Festal Menaion* (London, 1969), p. 18.

30. It appeared in *Ekklesiastiki Alitheia*, year 4, fasc. 7 (Constantinople, 1883), pp. 93–101. On this incident, see A. Rigo, "Nicodemo Aghiorita e la sua edizione delle opere di Gregorio Palamas," in Mainardi, *Paisij, lo Starec*, pp. 165–82. Compare J. Meyendorff, *Introduction à l'étude de Grégoire Palamas*, Patristica Sorbonensia 3 (Paris, 1959), pp. 337–38; Citterio, *L'orientamento*, pp. 350–52; Citterio, "Nicodemo Agiorita," pp. 924–25. On the press of Poulios, see C. M. Woodhouse, *Rhigas Velestinlis: The Proto-Martyr of the Greek Revolution* (Limni, 1995), pp. 36–38, 47, 120, 127, 129, 140.

31. See M. Viller, "Nicodème l'Hagiorite et ses emprunts à la littérature spirituelle occidentale. Le *Combat Spirituel* et *Les Exercises* de S. Ignace dans l'Eglise byzantine," *Revue d'Ascétique et de Mystique* 5 (1924), pp. 174–77, 416; Citterio, *L'orientamento*, pp. 112–36;

B. Bobrinskoy, "Encounter of Traditions in Greece: St. Nicodemus of the Holy Mountain (1749–1809)," in Dupré and Saliers (eds.), *Christian Spirituality: Post-Reformation and Modern*, pp. 447–57; Citterio, "Nicodemo Agiorita," pp. 943–55. It used to be thought that Nikodimos himself translated the works in question from Italian, but now it has been proved that he drew on existing translations made by the Patmian Emmanuel Romanitis. It is doubtful whether Nikodimos in fact knew Italian: see E. N. Phranghiskos, "La questione della conoscenza delle lingue straniere in Nicodemo l'Aghiorita," in Rigo, *Nicodemo l'Aghiorita e la Filocalia*, pp. 205–22.

32. For a reproduction of the title page of the first edition of *Unseen Warfare* (Venice, 1796), see G. G. Ladas and A. D. Chatzidimou, *Elliniki Vivliographia ton eton 1796–1799* (Athens, 1973), p. 16. On the changes made by Nikodimos to Scupoli's text, consult the interesting (but not always accurate) introduction to the English translation, written by H. A. Hodges: *Unseen Warfare: Being the Spiritual Combat and Path to Paradise of Lorenzo Scupoli as edited by Nicodemus of the Holy Mountain and revised by Theophan the Recluse*, ET E. Kadloubovsky and G. E. H. Palmer (London, 1952), pp. 13–67.

33. For a photograph of Fr. Nikon, see G. Speake, *Mount Athos: Renewal in Paradise* (New Haven/London, 2002), p. 228. It was Fr. Nikon who gave his blessing to the two-volume translation of the *Philokalia* made by Kadloubovsky and Palmer, and who selected the texts which they included; he also wrote the anonymous foreword in *Writings from the Philokalia*, pp. 5–7.

34. For an English translation, see Fr. George Dokos (tr.), *Exomologitarion: A Manual of Confession* (Thessaloniki, Uncut Mountain Press, 2006).

35. See n. 20.

36. *Pedalion*, pp. 33–36; *The Rudder*, pp. 68–76. For eighteenth-century Greek views on Latin baptism, see T. [= K.] Ware, *Eustratios Argenti: A Study of the Greek Church under Turkish Rule* (Oxford, 1964), pp. 65–107; G. D. Metallinos, *"Omologo en vaptisma . . . ." Ermineia kai epharmogi tou Z' Kanonos tis B' Oikoumenikis Synodou ypo ton Kollyvadon kai tou Konstantinou Oikonomou* (Athens, 1983; 2nd ed., Athens, 1996); ET by Priestmonk Seraphim, *I Confess One Baptism . . . Interpretation and Application of Canon VII of the Second Ecumenical Council by the Kollyvades and Constantine Oikonomos* (Holy Mountain, Athos, St Paul's Monastery, 1994).

37. "On Prayer" 61; *Philokalia* 1, 182 (under the name of Neilos the Ascetic); ET 1, 62.

38. *Ways of Russian Theology*, Collected Works, vol. 5 (Belmont, 1979), p. 161.

39. See, for example, the explanation given in the introduction to the English *Philokalia*, 1, 13.

40. *Ecclesiastical History* 6.20.2.

41. *The Philokalia of Origen*, ed. J. Armitage Robinson (Cambridge, 1893).

42. *Philokalia* 1, xxii; see n. 9.

43. *Philokalia* 1, xxi.

44. I discuss this possibility more fully in my article, "Possiamo parlare di spiritualità della Filocalia?," pp. 29–35.

45. Evthymios, *Life of Nikodimos*, p. 640 (see n. 18).

46. Daponte, "Istorikos Katalogos," in K. N. Sathas, *Mesaioniki Vivliothiki*, vol. 3 (Venice, 1782), p. 109.

47. "Letter to Archimandrite Theodosy," in Rose, *Blessed Paisius Velichkovsky* (see n. 21), pp. 180–83.

48. Rose, loc. cit.

49. A.-E. Tachiaos, *0 Paisios Velitskophski (1722–1794) kai i askitikophilologiki scholi tou* (Thessaloniki, 1964), p. 111. *Cf.* Tachiaos, "De la *Philokalia* au Dobrotoljubie: la création d'un 'Sbornik'", *Cyrillomethodianum* 5 (1981), pp. 208–13. More recently, P. Géhin has

drawn attention to another Athonite manuscript, Cod. Lavra 54 (1745), of the seventeenth or eighteenth century, whose contents overlap those of the *Philokalia*, although again there is no exact correspondence. Since this manuscript was in Smyrna at the end of the eighteenth century, probably it was not a direct source of the *Philokalia*, but it may well be related to one of the principal sources. In any case, it provides evidence of a "philokalic" tradition prior to the publication of the printed *Philokalia*. See Géhin, "Le Filocalie che hanno preceduto la 'Filocalia'", in Rigo, *Nicodemo l'Aghiorita e la Filocalia*, pp. 83–102, especially pp. 97–8, 100–2.

50. An early example of a "proto-philokalic" collection is the brief anthology of texts to be found in Nikiphoros the Hesychast (late thirteenth century), *On Watchfulness and the Guarding of the Heart* (*Philokalia* 4, 18–28; ET 4, 194–206). Doubtless the hesychast controversy in the mid-fourteenth century greatly encouraged the compilation and dissemination of such "philokalic" anthologies.

51. See Tachiaos, *O Paisios Velitskophski*, pp. 74–5, 109; also his article, "Mount Athos and the Slavic Literatures," *Cyrillomethodianum* 4 (1977), pp. 32–3.

52. Rose, *Blessed Paisius Velichkovsky*, pp.78, 82, 112–13, 117–19.

53. Op. cit., pp. 81, 113.

54. Possibly the revision of Paisy's translations, made on the basis of the printed Greek *Philokalia*, was undertaken not by Paisy himself but by the committee working under the direction of Metropolitan Gabriel of St. Petersburg, which supervised the publication of the *Dobrotolubiye*. On the publication of Paisy's *Dobrotolubiye*, see Nikolaj N. Lisovoj, "Due epoche, due 'Filocalie': Paisij Veličkovskij e Teofano il Recluso," in Mainardi, *Paisij, lo Starec*, pp. 183–215, esp. pp. 185–91.

55. See above, n. 48.

56. Patriarch Kallistos I of Constantinople, *Life of St Gregory of Sinai* 6 (ed. N. Pomialovsky, p. 10, lines 12–16); cited in K. Ware, "The Jesus Prayer in St. Gregory of Sinai," *Eastern Churches Review* 4:1 (1972), p. 5. Eventually Gregory found three monks at the skete of Magoula, not far from Philotheou, who were able to give him guidance. His difficulty in finding an elder experienced in hesychast prayer is puzzling, since he arrived on the Mountain when Nikiphoros the Hesychast was still alive, or at any rate was not long dead. Why did he not turn for help to Nikiphoros or to his disciples? Nikiphoros, however, had settled in later life in what Gregory Palamas terms "the most isolated parts" of Athos (*Triads* 1.2.12; *Philokalia*, ET 4, 341), and this move may explain why the Sinaite failed to make contact with him or his followers.

57. Rose, *Blessed Paisius Velichkovsky*, p. 81.

58. Op. cit., p. 85.

59. *Philokalia* 1, xxi (cf. n. 43).

60. On Elder Basil, who was proclaimed a saint by the Romanian Church in 2003, see D. Raccanello, *La Preghiera di Gesù negli scritti di Basilio di Poiana Mărului* (Alessandria, 1986); D. Raccanello "Vasilij de Pojana Marului," *Dictionnaire de Spiritualité* 16 (1992), cols. 292–8; "A Monk of the Brotherhood of Prophet Elias Skete, Mount Athos," *Elder Basil of Poiana Mărului (1692–1767)* (Liberty, St John of Kronstadt Press, 1996). On the continuing "philokalic" tradition in Romania, see Metropolitan Seraphim Joantă, *Romania: Its Hesychast Tradition and Culture* (Wildwood, St Xenia Skete, 1992).

61. *Elder Basil of Poiana Mărului*, p.27.

62. Op. cit., pp.31–32, 34–35; for ET of the three introductions, see pp. 43–85.

63. "A Century of Spiritual Texts" 40: *Philokalia* 1, 310; ET 2, 21.

64. "Practical and Theological Texts" 16–17: *Philokalia* 3, 239; ET 4, 28.

65. "On Watchfulness and Guarding of the Heart": *Philokalia* 4, 26–27; ET 4, 205.

66. See K. Ware, "Praying with the body: the hesychast method and non-Christian parallels," *Sobornost incorporating Eastern Churches Review* 14.2 (1992), pp. 6–35; note especially the strictures of St. Ignaty Brianchaninov and St. Theophan the Recluse, p. 22.

67. Rose, *Blessed Paisius Velichkovsky*, pp. 191–92; cf Tachiaos, *O Paisios Velitskophsky*, pp. 113–14.

68. *Philokalia* 1, xxiii.

69. *Philokalia* 1, xxiii–iv.

70. "Century" 4: *Philokalia* 4, 199; ET Kadloubovsky and Palmer, *Writings from the Philokalia on Prayer of the Heart*, p. 166. For similar teaching on the recovery of baptismal grace, see Gregory of Sinai, "On the Signs of Grace and Delusion" 1–3: *Philokalia* 4, 66–69; ET 4, 257–59. Nikodimos also speaks of the reactivation of baptismal grace in his introduction: *Philokalia* 1, xx. On the sacramental teaching of the Xanthopouloi, see K. Ware, *A Fourteenth-Century Manual of Hesychast Prayer: The Century of St. Kallistos and St. Ignatios Xanthopoulos* (Toronto, Canadian Institute of Balkan Studies, 1995), pp. 29–32.

71. "Century" 91–92: *Philokalia* 4, 284–89; ET *Writings*, pp. 259–64.

72. *The Mystical Theology of the Eastern Church* (London, 1957), pp. 8–9.

73. *Philokalia* (Venice, 1782), p. 1207. For obvious reasons, this *licenza* does not appear in the later editions of the *Philokalia* published in Athens.

74. The title page of the *Philokalia* refers not only to the threefold Evagrian scheme but also to the somewhat different triadic pattern put forward in the Dionysian writings: purification (*katharismos*), illumination (*photismos*), and perfection (*teleiosis*). Within the *Philokalia* itself the two schemes are sometimes combined, for example, by Nikitas Stithatos (eleventh century). But in general it is the Evagrian terminology that predominates.

75. "On Prayer" 67, 71: *Philokalia* 1, 182; ET 1, 63–64.

76. *Philokalia* 1, 134–35; ET 1, 155–56; ed. G.- M. de Durand, *Sources chrétiennes* 455 (Paris, 2000), pp. 134–40. Fr. de Durand questions the Marcan authorship of the *Letter to Nicolas*, in my view on insufficient grounds.

77. "On Watchfulness and Holiness" 1–6: *Philokalia* 1, 141–42; ET 1, 162–63.

78. *Philokalia* 1, xx.

79. "On Watchfulness and Holiness" 5: *Philokalia* 1, 142; ET 1, 163.

80. "On Prayer" 5: *Philokalia* 4, 82; ET 4, 278; citing St. John Klimakos, *Ladder of Divine Ascent* 27 (*PG* 88.1112A); cf. Evagrios, "On Prayer" 71 (n. 75).

81. "On Prayer" 7: *Philokalia* 4, 85–86; ET 4, 283.

82. "On the Signs of Grace and Delusion" 3: *Philokalia* 4, 68; ET 4, 259.

83. "On Prayer" 7: *Philokalia* 4, 85; ET 4, 283; cf. "On Commandments and Doctrines" 118: *Philokalia* 4, 53; ET 4, 240. A "phantast" is one who depends on the *phantasia* or imagination.

84. On the meaning of the terms *nous* and *kardia*, see K. Ware, "Prayer in Evagrius of Pontus and the Macarian Homilies." in R. Waller and B. Ward (eds.). *An Introduction to Christian Spirituality* (London, 1999), pp. 14–30. For further bibliography on the Jesus Prayer, see K. Ware, "The Beginnings of the Jesus Prayer," in B. Ward and R. Waller (eds.), *Joy of Heaven: Springs of Christian Spirituality* (London, 2003), pp. 1–29.

85. See above, n. 66.

86. The book of E. Wilkins, *The Rose-Garden Game: The Symbolic Background to the European Prayer-Beads* (London, 1969), does not shed much light on this matter.

87. *Philokalia* 1, xix.

88. See Gregory of Nazianzus, *Orations* 43.48. The standard study of deification, old but not outdated, is still J. Gross, *La divinisation du chrétien d'après les Pères grecs* (Paris, 1938); ET by P. A. Onicha, *The Divinization of the Christian according to the Greek Fathers* (Anaheim, 2002). A yet more thorough and detailed treatment is provided by N. Russell, *The Doctrine of Deification in the Greek Patristic Tradition* (Oxford, 2004).

89. For a classic statement of the essence/energies distinction, see Lossky, *The Mystical Theology of the Eastern Church*, pp. 67–90.

90. "On Love" 1.96: *Philokalia* 2, 13; ET 2, 64.

91. "Various texts" 3 [1].7, 9: *Philokalia* 2, 92; ET 2, 165, 166.

92. "Various texts" 6 [4].19: *Philokalia* 2, 150; ET 2, 240.

93. "Topics" 64–150: *Philokalia* 4, 154–87; ET 4, 376–417.

94. *The Pilgrim's Tale*, ed. A. Pentkovsky and tr. T. A. Smith, The Classics of Western Spirituality (New York/Mahwah, 1999), pp. 81–82. The Pilgrim is told to read first of all Nikiphoros the Hesychast; then the "second book" by Gregory of Sinai (i.e., not *On Commandments and Doctrines* and *Further Texts*, but the three treatises that follow); then Symeon the New Theologian, *The Three Methods of Prayer* (spurious) and *On Faith* (genuine); and finally Kallistos and Ignatios Xanthopoulos. I have omitted Nikiphoros and *The Three Methods of Prayer* from my own list because of my reservations about the physical technique that they advocate (see n. 66, p. 283). By the same token I advise the reader, unless under the guidance of a spiritual father, not to follow the directions about the physical technique given by Gregory of Sinai and the Xanthopouloi.

95. Kadloubovsky and Palmer, in their translation *Writings from* the *Philokalia on Prayer of the Heart*, pp. 21–270, open with the same four authors as in the Pilgrim's reading list, given in the same order, but with additional texts taken from Gregory of Sinai and Symeon the New Theologian.

96. See "Un moine de l'Eglise orthodoxe de Roumanie" (Archimandrite André Scrima), "L'avènement philocalique dans l'Orthodoxe roumaine," *Istina* 5 (1958), pp. 295–328, 443–74.

97. "Istorikos Katalogos," in Sathas, *Mesaioniki Vivliothiki*, 3, 109.

98. *Philokalia* 1, xxiii.

99. Nikon Neoskitiotis (not to be confused with Nikon of Karoulia), "La Filocalia al Monte Athosoggi," in Rigo, *Nicodemo l'Aghiorita e la Filocalia*, p. 175.

▪ Chapter 2

1. Clement of Alexandria. *Christ The Pedagogue*. 3.7.

2. Gregory the Theologian. *Epistle*. 33.

3. Epiphanios of Salamis. *Against All Heresies*. 16.1; Cyril of Scythopolis. *Life of St. Saba*. 66; St. Neilos. *Epistle*. 3.25.

4. Epiphanios of Salamis. *Against All Heresies*. 8.8.

5. Cyril of Scythopolis. *Life of St. Saba*. 82.

6. Eusebius of Caesarea. *Church History*. 6.20.

7. St. Athanasius. *Life of Antony*. 4; Epiphanius of Salamis, *Heresies*. 69.4.

8. "Dobrotolubiye" is a Slavonic calque of *Philokalia*. St. Paisy Velichovsky called his edition of 1793 this, echoing the *Philokalia* of Sts. Nikodemos and Makarios, which had been prepared on Athos and had recently appeared in print at Venice. But Paisy's work was not wholly dependent on that of the Athonites.

9. Sometimes "stealing," as several of the "'Tales of the Desert Fathers" refer to the monastic trade in books, and how sometimes laboriously hand-copied (and thus expensive) texts would "go missing" in the satchel of monks.

10. I have treated of his life and times more extensively elsewhere: J.A. McGuckin. "The Life and Mission of St. Paisius Velichovsky: 1722-1794. An Early Modern Master of the Orthodox Spiritual Life." *Spiritus*. 9. 2. 2009. pp. 157–73.

11. Liturgical calendar of the saints: a standard book in monastery churches.

12. cf. Archimandrite Ciprian Zaharia. "Paissij Velichovskij et le role oecumenique de l'Église Orthodoxe roumaine." Irenikon. 58. 1985.

13. 1847, 1890, 1892. The Biography of Platon was edited by A. E. Tachiaos and was included in his study: (in Greek) *The Revival of Byzantine Mysticism among Slavs and Romanians in the 18th century*. Thessalonica. 1966; it was also issued in English by the St. Herman of Alaska Brotherhood from Platina, California, under the mistaken impression that it was the biography of Metrophanes, under the title: *Blessed Paisius Velichovsky*.

14. See J. A. McGuckin. "The Prayer of the Heart in Patristic and Early Byzantine Tradition," pp. 69–108. in P. Allen, W. Mayer, and L Cross (eds.). Prayer and Spirituality in the Early Church. vol. 2. (Centre for Early Christian Studies, Australian Catholic University), Brisbane. 1999.

15. Commonly known as St. Panteleimon Monastery, which was then under Ukrainian direction.

16. Archpriest Sergius Chetverikov (in Romanian), *Paisius: Starets of Neamt Monastery in Moldavia. His Life, Teaching, and His Influence on the Orthodox Church*. Neamt Monastery, Romania.1933. Synopsis and review in Irenikon 11, 1934. 561–72; repr. of Chetverikov in Paris (YMCA Press), 1976; Review: see Irenikon 53, 1980, 113–14.

17. Voivode Grigorie Ghica.

18. The rule of Paisy is discussed in Archbp. Serafim Joanta. *Romania: Its Hesychastic Tradition and Culture*. Wildwood, CA. 1992. pp. 128–57. (see esp. p. 140; and Chetverikov (1933), pp. 110–17.

19. Joanta (1992), p. 147.

20. Discovered in the twentieth century not to be by St. Symeon, but from a slightly later period of the Hesychastic movement. The work describes the physical postures that can be associated with the Jesus Prayer and was very popular on Mount Athos. It can be found in G. Palmer, P. Sherrard, and K.Ware (eds.), *Philokalia*. vol. 4. pp. 64–75. Faber. London. 1995.

21. Joanta (1992), p. 147.

22. *To the Adversaries and Detractors of the Spiritual Prayer that Is the Jesus Prayer*. Text in: I. Smolitsch. *Moines de la sainte Russie*. Paris. 1967, pp. 98–104.

23. cf. Joanta (1992), p. 150.

24. E. Kadloubovsky and G. E. H. Palmer, *Unseen Warfare: The Spiritual Combat and Path to Paradise of Lorenzo Scupoli, ed. Nicodemus of the Holy Mountain and rev. Theophan the Recluse*. Mowbray, Oxford, 1978. See also S. Bolshakoff, *Russian Mystics*. Mowbray. London. 1977.

25. 1762–1867. Important and scholarly Metropolitan of Moscow from 1821.

26. Its leaders were Kireevsky and Aksakov. Its most notable religious thinkers included Khomyakov, Berdyaev, and Soloviev.

27. He composed fifty liturgical hymns.

28. He made contemporary Greek versions of the works of St. Symeon the New Theologian and St. Gregory Palamas, whom he regarded as pillars of the Hesychastic tradition.

29. R. Chamberas (tr.), *Nikodemos of the Holy Mountain: A Handbook of Spiritual Counsel*. Classics of Western Spirituality. Paulist Press. New York. 1989.

30. The title "Kollyvadists" was an ironic slight against them from their opponents. They had advocated a return to stricter, more authentic standards of Orthodox theology, liturgy, and spirituality. Opponents tried to fasten on one aspect only so as to caricature them: their claim that the Kollyva (boiled wheat) memorials for the dead ought to take place only on Saturdays. Among the leading Kollyvadists apart from Nikodemos was Makarios of Corinth, his collaborator in the *Philokalia* project, and Athanasios of Paros.

31. Biography by C. Cavarnos, *St. Macarios of Corinth*, Vol. 2 in Modern Orthodox Saints (Institute for Byzantine and Modern Greek Studies), Belmont, MA, 1993; also S. G Papadopoulos, *Hagios Makarios Korinthou: Ho Genarchēs tou Philokalismou*. Akritas, Athens. 2000.

32. One of the main items in the program of Kollyvadic reform.

33. Newly revised and published in a four-volume set of the 14 original volumes from the Center for Traditionalist Orthodox Studies in California.

34. If they could see it with their material eyes, he argued, it could not be the (immaterial) uncreated light. The apparently abstruse point masked a much wider set of related ideas: was it possible to know God directly in this life. Out of the argument came Palamas's distinction of the Essence and Energies of God. While God was Unknowable and Unapproachable in his Essence, he was discernible and close to his Church through his (Uncreated) Energies. In touching the Energies of God, however, we touched the authentic God, wholly and immediately.

▪ Chapter 3

1. Kallistos Ware, "St. Nikodimos and the *Philokalia*," in Dimitri Conomos and Graham Speake, eds., *Mount Athos the Sacred Bridge. The Spirituality of the Holy Mountain* (Oxford: Peter Lang, 2005), 69–121, here 72. I owe a great deal to this immensely valuable article on the context of the *Philokalia*.

2. Both available in English translations: Hieromonk Patapios and Archbishop Chrysostomos, *Manna from Mount Athos. The Issue of Frequent Communion on the Holy Mountain in the Late Eighteenth and Early Nineteenth Centuries* (Byzantine and Neohellenic Studies 2, Oxford: Peter Lang, 2006), which contains a translation of *Concerning Frequent Communion*; Nicodemos of the Holy Mountain, *A Handbook of Spiritual Counsel*, trans. Peter Chamberas (Mahwah, NJ: Paulist Press, 1989). For most of the facts cited in this paragraph, see Ware, "St. Nikodimos," esp. 85–105.

3. There is no real English equivalent to *Herkunft*: "origin" or "heritage" comes close.

4. *Philokalia* (Venice, 1782), 6.

5. See Placide Deseille, *La Spiritualité orthodoxe et la philokalie* (Paris: Bayard Éditions, 1997), 230.

6. On which see George A. Maloney SJ, *Russian Hesychasm. The Spirituality of Nil Sorsky* (The Hague—Paris: Mouton, 1973).

7. Ware, "St. Nikodimos," 104–5; see also Deseille, *La Spiritualité orthodoxe*, 61–64.

8. Ware, "St. Nikodimos," 101.

9. See, e.g., Ware, "St. Nikodimos," 106–9.

10. See the last two pages of St. Nikodimos" introduction: *Philokalia* (Venice, 1782), 7–8.

11. See Ware, "St. Nikodimos," 108; Deseille, *La Spiritualité orthodoxe*, 64.

12. Deseille, *La Spiritualité orthodoxe*, 235–36.

13. From Kireevsky's "Fragments": translation in *On Spiritual Unity. A Slavophile Reader*, trans. and ed. Boris Jakim and Robert Bird (Hudson, NY: Lindisfarne Books, 1998), 248, 243.

14. O. Clément, "Les Pères de l'Église dans l'Église orthodoxe," in *Connaissance des Pères de l'Église* 52 (December 1993), 25–26, quoted by Boris Bobrinskoy in "Le renouveau actuel de la patristique dans l'orthodoxie," in *Les Pères de l' Église au XXe siècle. Histoire—Littérature – Théologie* (Paris: Cerf, 1997), 437–44, here 440, (though England, as a result of the endeavors of the Fathers of the Oxford Movement, must have run Russia a close second.)

15. *The Way of a Pilgrim* and *The Pilgrim continues his Way*, trans. R. M. French (London: SPCK, 1954), 31.

16. See the introduction to *The Pilgrim's Tale*, trans. Aleksei Pentkovsky (Mahwah, NJ: Pauli St. Press, 1999), and the articles on which it is based in *Simvol* 27 (Paris, 1992).

17. For this, see Deseille, *La Spiritualité orthodoxe*, 245–48, and the article by "Un moine de l'Église de Roumanie" (= André Scrima), "L'avènement philocalique dans l'Orthodoxie

roumaine," in *Istina* (1958), 295–328, 443–74, which is not so much about the philokalic influence in Romania, but a part of it.

18. See *The Way of the Pilgrim*, 38–39. The selection was apparently suggested to Kadloubovsky and Palmer by their spiritual father, Fr. Nikon; it is also very similar to the preliminary reading list given by Metropolitan Kallistos in his article, "St. Nikodimos," 118–19.

19. *The Philokalia. The Complete Text, compiled by St. Nikodimos of the Holy Mountain and St. Makarios of Corinth*, trans. from the Greek and ed. G. E. H. Palmer, Philip Sherrard, and Kallistos Ware, vols. 1–4 (London: Faber & Faber, 1979–95); vol. 5 is still to appear.

20. See my article, "French *Ressourcement* Theology and Orthodoxy: A Living Mutual Relationship," in Gabriel Flynn and Paul Murray (eds.), Ressourcement: *A Movement for Renewal in Twentieth-Century Catholic Theology* (Oxford: University Press, forthcoming).

21. *Petite Philokalie de la Prière du Cœur*, trans. and presented by Jean Gouillard (Documents spirituels 5 (Paris: Cahiers de Sud, 1953); later reissued as livre en poche in Collections Points Saagesse 20, 1979).

22. *Philokalie des Pères neptiques*, presented by Père Boris Bobrinskoy, 11 fascicules (Abbaye de Bellefontaine, 1979–95); *La philokalie*, presented by Olivier Clément, trans. and notes by Jacques Touraille, 2 vols. (Paris, 1995).

23. I owe some of these insights to Fr. Placide Deseille's *La Spiritualité orthodoxe et la philokalie*.

24. See note 13, above.

25. Archimandite Sophrony (Sakharov), *Saint Silouan the Athonite* (Stavropegic Monastery of St. John the Baptist, Essex, 1991), 72, 292; cf. 82–83, 301–2. I am grateful to my colleague, Dr. Krastu Banev, for finding these references.

26. Pavel Florensky, *The Pillar and Ground of the Truth*, trans. Boris Jakim (Princeton, NJ: Princeton University Press, 1997), 8–9.

■ Chapter 4

1. The English reader may consult the article written by Ioan Ică, Jr., "Stăniloae, Dumitru (1903–93)," in Trevor A. Hart (ed.), *The Dictionary of Historical Theology* (Grand Rapids, MI: Pater Noster Press—William B. Eerdmans, 2000), pp. 527–31.

2. For the Protestant contrast brought to this state of affairs, see Earl A. Pope, "Protestantism in Romania," in Sabrina Petra Ramet (ed.), *Protestantism and Politics in Eastern Europe and Russia: The Communist and Post-Communist Eras* (Durham and London: 1992), pp. 157–208.

3. For the Byzantine legacy in the Romanian lands, see the classic work of (Romanian) historian and polymath Nicolae Iorga, *Byzance après Byzance* (Bucharest, 1935).

4. M. Kuehn, *Kant. A Biography* (Cambridge: Cambridge University Press, 2001), p. 371: "Only moral service will make us pleasing to a moral God. Prayer, liturgy, pilgrimages, and confessions are worthless."

5. Andrew Louth, *Discerning the Mystery: An Essay on the Nature of Theology* (Oxford: Clarendon Press, 1983).

6. This process occurs in the whole region of Eastern Orthodoxy, being often dramatized in terms of West versus East tensions. For a specific account related to the Russian theological experience, see "The Ways of Russian Theology" in *The Collected Works of Georges Florovsky*, Vol. IV, *Aspects of Church History* (Belmont, MA: Nordland, 1987). For a more general intellectual history of this inferiority complex toward Westernization, see Martin Malia, *Russia under Western Eyes: From the Bronze Horseman to the Lenin Mausoleum* (Cambridge, MA.: Belknap Press of Harvard University Press, 1999).

7. For the French influence upon this Romanian genealogy of secular culture, see Pompiliu Eliade, *De l'influence française sur l'esprit public en Roumanie. Les origines. Etude sur l'état de la société roumaine, à l'époque des règnes phanariotes* (Paris: Ernest Leroux, 1898).

8. For some profound insights regarding the "Burning Bush Movement," see André Scrima, *Padre spirituale* (Bose: Edizioni Qiqajon, 2001).

9. See André Scrima, "L'avénement philocalique dans l'orthodoxie roumaine," *Istina*, vol. 5 (1958), pp. 295–328 and 343–74.

10. For a more detailed analysis, see the article by Maciej Bielawski, "Dumitru Stăniloae and His *Philokalia*" in Lucian Turcescu (ed.), *Dumitru Stăniloae: Tradition and Modernity in Theology* (Jassy: Center for Romanian Studies, 2002), pp. 25–52; and Maciej Bielawski, the*Philokalical Vision of the World in the Theology of Dumitru Stăniloae* (Bydgoszcz, Poland: Homini, 1997).

11. This was a classical *topos* in the writings of Western foreign travelers, as it is shown by William Wilkinson, *An Account of the Principalities of Wallachia and Moldavia with Various Political Observations Relating to Them* (London, 1820), p. 152 (about superstitions); Felice Caronni, *Mie osservazioni locali, regionali, antiquarie sui Valachi specialmente e Zingari transilvane* (Milan, 1812), p. 15; more accounts on this theme are made available in the rich volume edited by Paul Cernovodeanu et al., *Călători străini despre Țările române în secolul al XIX-lea*, new series, vol. 1 [Foreign Travelers about the Romanian lands in the 19th century] (1801–21) (Bucharest: Editura Academiei, 2004).

12. A classic example is offered by Dumitru Drăghicescu, *Din psihologia poporului român. Introducere* [The Psychology of the Romanian People. An Introduction, 1907] (Bucharest: Albatros Publishers, 1996), p. 288. Here the author (a sociologist) discusses the "wholly pragmatic" and "merely social" character of the Romanian peasants' religious behavior.

13. Fr. Stăniloae's methodology is visible in his 1947 manuscript, published as *Spiritualitatea ortodoxă. Ascetica și mistica* (Bucharest: Ed. Institutului Biblic și de Misiune al Bisericii Ortodoxe Române, [1981], 1992). This book was translated into English under the title: *Orthodox Spirituality. A Practical Guide for the Faithful and a Definitive Manual for the Scholar* (South Canaan, PA: St. Tikhon's Seminary Press, 2002). See also the apt review of Fr. Radu Bordeianu in *Archaeus. Studies in the History of Religions*, vols. 12–13 (2007–8), pp. 414–16, which also lists a number of translation errors.

14. This is a characteristic feature of Orthodox theology, as it is shown by Vladimir Kotelnikov, "The Primacy of Monastic Spirituality," in Giuseppe Alberigo and Oscar Beozzo (eds.), *The Holy Russian Church and Western Christianity* (London: SCM Press, 1996), pp. 21–32.

15. Andrei Pleşu, "Hai să vorbim [Let's talk]," *Ziua*, no. 2867 (November 15, 2003). This text was first delivered by Andrei Pleşu (former Minister of Culture and former Minister of Foreign Affairs) as a presentation on the occasion of Fr. Dumitru Stăniloae's centenary at the Romanian Academy.

16. N 273 (Ward, 40): "every time forgetfulness comes, it engenders negligence; and from negligence, carnal desire proceeds; and desire causes man to fall."

17. *SBo* 118 (Veilleux, 173): "I never corrected any one of you as the one having authority except for the sake of his soul's salvation."

18. Abba Arsenius 40 (Ward, 18): "I have repented of having spoken, but never of having been silent."

19. N 257 (Ward, 37): "do not let your way of life to be seen."

20. St. Pachomius the Great, *ep.* 5.10 (Veilleux, 66), "Having knowledge of the things to come, let us be united with one another in love."

21. Stăniloae, *Filocalia*, vol. 12, p. 119, n. 215. In all subsequent passages I refer to the first edition of each volume of the Romanian *Philokalia*.

22. Stăniloae, *Filocalia*, vol. 12, p. 120, n. 220.

23. Stăniloae, *Filocalia*, vol. 12, p. 118, n. 211.

24. Stăniloae, *Filocalia*, vol. 8, p. 31, n. 30.

25. Stăniloae, *Filocalia*, vol. 8, p. 38, n. 40.

26. Stăniloae, *Filocalia*, vol. 8, p. 42, n. 44.

27. Stăniloae, *Filocalia*, vol. 8, p. 47, n. 49.

28. Here, Fr. Stăniloae's commentaries are close to bishop John Zizioulas's ontological personalism developed in *Being and Communion* (Crestwood, NY: St. Vladimir's Seminary Press, 1984). However, they never lapse into a denigration of nature in opposition to personhood. On this, see more in Nikolaos Loudovikos, "Person Instead of Grace and Dictated Otherness: John Zizioulas' Final Theological Position," *Heythrop Journal*, vol. 48 (2009), pp. 1–16.

29. Stăniloae, *Filocalia*, vol. 8, p. 39, n. 43.

30. Stăniloae, *Filocalia*, vol. 8, p. 48, no. 50.

31. Abba John the Dwarf 35 (Ward, 35): "It was said of the same Abba John that when he returned from the harvest or when he had been with some of the old men, he gave himself to prayer (εἰς τὴν εὐχὴν), meditation (μελέτην), and psalmody (ψαλμῳδίαν), until his thoughts were reestablished (ἀποκατεστάθη) in their previous order."

32. Fr. Stăniloae often reminds us of the danger of confusing the beauty of creation with the very beauty of the Creator or, even worse, to freeze our contemplative gaze at the level of mere aesthetics.

33. Stăniloae, *Filocalia*, vol. 8, p. 62, no. 87.

34. Stăniloae, *Filocalia*, vol. 8, p. 30, n. 29.

35. Stăniloae, *Filocalia*, vol. 8, p. 63, no. 89.

36. Stăniloae, *Filocalia*, vol. 12, p. 121, n. 255.

37. This theme is also developed in the little brochure by Fr. Dumitru Stăniloae, *Victory of the Cross* (Oxford: SLG, 1970).

38. Patristic authors such as St. Athanasius singled out the same vicious propensity. See, for example, Athanasius, *Contra Gentes* 1.9 (Meijering, 45): "[Osiris,] Horus, and now Antinous, lover of the Roman emperor Hadrian whom they worship out of fear of him who gave the decree, although they know that he is a man and not even an honourable man, but full of licentiousness" (ET by R. W. Thomson).

39. Acts 18:9: "And the Lord said to Paul one night in a vision: *Do not be afraid*, but go on speaking and do not be silent" (emphasis mine).

40. Stăniloae, *Filocalia*, vol. 12, p. 117, n. 205.

41. John 18:20: "Jesus answered him, *I spoke openly to the world* (. . .) and in secret have I said nothing" (emphasis mine).

42. For a stark contrast, see the comparison between "ecclesiastical dioceses" and agricultural cooperatives of Communist Romania in the writings of Patriarch Justinian [Marina], *Apostolatul social* [The Social Apostolate], vol. 12 (Bucharest: Institutul Biblic şi de Misiune Ortodoxă, 1976), p. 50 *et passim*.

43. Stăniloae, *Filocalia*, vol. 11, p. 122, n. 226.

44. Stăniloae, *Filocalia vol.* 6, p. 180, n. 299.

■ Chapter 5

1. References to the *Philokalia* are (unless otherwise indicated) to the volume and page of the third Greek edition (Athens: Astir/Papadimitriou, 1957–63), followed by a reference to the English translation (= ET) by G.E.H. Palmer, Philip Sherrard, and Kallistos Ware (London/Boston: Faber & Faber, 1979–95).

2. St. Hesychios the Priest, *On Watchfulness and Holiness, Philokalia*, Vol. 1, p. 147; ET: Vol. 1, p. 168.

3. I am using the word "soul" here to refer broadly to the inner life of the person. The *Philokalia* and the Eastern Christian spiritual tradition as a whole generally prefer "mind"

or "intellect" (most often a translation of the Greek *nous*) when referring to the deepest capacity of the human person for God, and I will also employ this term where appropriate. However, in English "mind" and "intellect" often carry a post–Enlightenment connotation of narrowly rational thought or discourse that is utterly foreign to the way the Eastern Christian spiritual tradition understands these terms. In this sense "soul" can sometimes convey a sense of interiority more effectively and simply.

4. The question of how to describe and interpret the *Philokalia's* distinctive way of reading scripture is complex and requires some comment. Two broad approaches are possible. The first approach, which takes seriously the variety of voices and historical periods represented by the *Philokalia*, would seek to delineate the distinctive interpretive strategies represented by the different teachers of the *Philokalia* and place them in relation to the historical, spiritual, and theological contexts in which they arose. The second approach, more synthetic in character, reads the *Philokalia* as a single work and treats the various interpretive strategies represented by different teachers as part of a whole, if variegated, spiritual vision. Both approaches are legitimate and perhaps necessary. However, in order to do justice to the first approach, one would have to provide an immense amount of historical and theological contextualization, something that is far beyond the scope of this essay. Therefore, I have chosen to adopt the second approach, reading the *Philokalia* as a single work and reading its treatment of scripture as fitting into a common spiritual tradition that has a shared ethos and outlook. Thus, while attending carefully to the way individual writers emphasize particular elements of the interpretive process, I read these different texts as participating in and contributing to a single tradition that has an internal coherence and consistency.

For a good introduction to the role of the Bible in ancient Greek Christianity, see Paul M. Blowers, ed. *The Bible in Greek Christian Antiquity* (Notre Dame, IN: University of Notre Dame Press, 1997). For an analysis of the distinctive approach to biblical interpretation in early Christian monasticism, see: Douglas Burton-Christie, *The Word in the Desert: Scripture and the Quest for Holiness in Early Christian Monasticism* (New York: Oxford University Press, 1993).

5. St. Hesychios the Priest, *On Watchfulness and Holiness*, Philokalia, Vol. 1, p. 52; ET: Vol. 1, p.192. See also Evagrios the Solitary, *Texts on Discrimination in respect of Passions and Thoughts*: "Let us sit still and keep our attention fixed within ourselves, so that we advance in holiness and resist vice more strongly. Awakened in this way to spiritual knowledge, we shall acquire contemplative insight into many things; and ascending still higher, we shall receive a clearer vision of the light of our Saviour" (*Philokalia*, ET: Vol. 1, p. 47).

6. Evagrios the Solitary, *On Prayer: One Hundred and Fifty-Three Texts, Philokalia*, Vol. 1, p. 62. For a thoughtful introduction to Evagrius's approach to psalmody and its importance for his entire system of thought, see Luke Dysinger, OSB, *Psalmody and Prayer In the Writings of Evagrius Ponticus* (New York: Oxford University Press, 2005).

7. Symeon the New Theologian, *One Hundred and Fifty-Three Practical and Theological Texts*, Greek Text: *Chapitres Théologiques Gnostiques et Pratiques*, Introduction, Texte Critique, Traduction et Notes by Jean Darrouzès, (Paris: Cerf, 1980), pp. 176–78; ET: Vol. 4, p. 48.

8. St. John Cassian, *On the Holy Fathers of Sketis and on Discrimination, Philokalia*, Vol 1, pp. 81–82; ET: Vol. 1, p. 95.

9. *A Discourse on Abba Philimon, Philokalia*, Vol. 2, p. 243; ET: Vol. 2, p. 346.

10. St. Mark the Ascetic, *On the Spiritual Law, Philokalia*, Vol. 1, p. 101; ET: Vol. 1, p. 116.

11. St. John of Karpathos, *For the Encouragement of the Monks of India, Philokalia*, Vol. 1, p. 280; ET: Vol. 1, p. 302.

12. St. John Cassian, *On the Eight Vices, Philokalia*, Vol. 1, p. 63; ET: Vol. 1, p. 75.

13. St. Diodochos of Photiki, *On Spiritual Knowledge and Discrimination*, *Philokalia*, Vol. 1, p. 237; ET: Vol. 1, p. 255.

14. St. Maximos the Confessor, *Two Hundred Texts on Theology and the Incarnate Dispensation of the Son of God*, *Philokalia*, Vol. 2, p. 66; ET: p. 134. For an excellent analysis of Maximos's distinctive approach to biblical interpretation, especially as it pertains to the practice of the spiritual life, see Paul M. Blowers, *Exegesis and Spiritual Pedagogy in Maximus the Confessor: An Investigation of the* Quaestiones ad Thalassium, *Christianity and Judaism in Antiquity* 7 (Notre Dame, IN: University of Notre Dame University Press, 1991).

15. St. Maximos the Confessor, *Various Texts on Theology and the Incarnate Dispensation of the Son of God*, *Philokalia*, Vol. 2, p. 124; ET: p. 207.

16. St. Symeon the New Theologian, *One Hundred and Fifty-Three Practical and Theological Texts*, Greek Text: Darrouzès, ed. *Chapitres Théologiques Gnostiques et Pratiques*, p. 114; ET: Vol. 4, p. 36.

17. St. Peter of Damaskos, *A Treasury of Divine Knowledge*, *Philokalia*, Vol. 3, p. 61; ET: Vol. 3, p. 145.

18. St. Peter of Damaskos, *Twenty Four Discourses*, *Philokalia*, Vol. 3, pp. 140–41; ET: p. 246.

19. Nikitas Stithatos, *On the Inner Nature of Things and on the Purification of the Intellect*, *Philokalia*, Vol. 3, p. 321; ET: Vol. 4, p. 133.

20. St. Maximos the Confessor, *Various Texts on Theology, the Divine Economy, and Virtue and Vice*, *Philokalia*, Vol. 2, p. 110; ET: Vol. 2, p. 189.

21. *A Discourse on Abba Philimon*, *Philokalia*, Vol. 2, p. 245; ET: Vol. 2, p. 348.

22. Nikitas Stithatos, *On the Inner Nature of Things and on the Purification of the Intellect*, *Philokalia*, Vol. 3, p. 316; ET: Vol. 4, pp. 127–28.

23. Nikitas Stithatos, *On the Inner Nature of Things*, *Philokalia*, Vol. 3, p. 316; ET: Vol. 4, p. 127.

24. Nikitas Stithatos, *On the Inner Nature of Things*, *Philokalia*, Vol. 3, p. 316; ET: Vol. 4, p. 127.

25. St. Peter of Damaskos, *A Treasury of Divine Knowledge*, *Philokalia*, Vol. 3, p. 99; ET: Vol. 3, p. 194.

26. St. Peter of Damaskos, *Twenty Four Discourses*, *Philokalia*, Vol. 3, p. 156; ET: Vol. 3, p. 264.

27. St. Maximos the Confessor, *Various Texts on Theology, the Divine Economy, and Virtue and Vice*, *Philokalia*, Vol. 2, p. 207.

28. St. Symeon the New Theologian, *One Hundred and Fifty-Three Practical and Theological Texts*, Greek Text: Darrouzès, ed. *Chapitres Théologiques Gnostiques et Pratiques*, pp. 182–84; ET: *Philokalia*, Vol. 4, pp. 49–50.

29. St. Symeon the New Theologian, *One Hundred and Fifty-Three Practical and Theological Texts*, Greek Text: Darrouzès, ed. *Chapitres Théologiques Gnostiques et Pratiques*, pp. 184–86; ET: *Philokalia*, Vol. 4, pp. 49–50. This particular idiom—"Teacher of Spiritual Knowledge—seems to be Symeon's way of referring to the experience of indwelling "divine light" that is so central to his asceticism and theology. In his book, *St. Symeon the New Theologian and Orthodox Tradition* (New York: Oxford University Press, 2000) Hilarion Alfeyev notes that for Symeon the "mystical reading of the scriptures" allows ascent to the 'hidden meaning of Scripture"; then "God himself appears to the man and by the grace of the holy Spirit and through communion with the divine light the man becomes *gnostikos*, that is, acquires perfect meaning of the mystical meaning of the Scripture" (p. 52). Alfeyev gives as a reference Symeon's *Hymn 18*, where Symeon writes: "it [i.e., the divine flame/light] converses with me, enlightens me . . . it reveals the Scriptures to me and increases my knowledge [*gnosin*], it *teaches* [*didaskei*]me mysteries I cannot express" (George Maloney,

Hymns of Divine Love, Dimension Books, 1976). I am grateful to Fr. Luke Dysinger, OSB, for providing this reference.

30. St. Symeon the New Theologian, *One Hundred and Fifty-Three Practical and Theological Texts*, ET: Vol. 4, p. 36.

31. Nikitas Stithatos, *On Spiritual Knowledge, Philokalia*, Vol. 3, p. 340; ET: Vol. 4, p. 157. See also Nikitas Stithatos's observation: "Assimilation to God, conferred on us through intense purification and deep love for God, can be maintained only through an unceasing aspiration towards Him on the part of the contemplative intellect. Such aspiration is born within the soul through the persistent stillness produced by the acquisition of the virtues, by ceaseless and undistracted spiritual prayer, by total self-control, and by intensive reading of the Scriptures" (*On Spiritual Knowledge, Philokalia*, Vol. 3, p. 334; ET: Vol. 4, p. 149).

■ Chapter 6

1. *Counsels on the Spiritual Life: Mark the Monk*, Vol. 1, trans. Tim Vivian and Augustine Casiday, (Crestwood, NY: St. Vladimir's Seminary Press, 2009), 3233. Unless otherwise noted, all English translations of Mark are taken from this volume, which follows the Greek more closely and is based on the most recent critical edition of the Greek text by Georges de Durand, O.P., ed. *Marc le Moine. Traites I. Sources chretiennes* 445 (Paris: Cerf, 1999), 130–201, hereafter abbreviated as SC 445.

2. Very little is known of his life. He was possibly a disciple of St. John Chrysostom, but this is no more than speculation. Henry Chadwick identifies him as a priest and abbot of a monastery near Tarsus in modern-day Turkey. "The Identity and Date of Mark the Monk" *Eastern Churches Review* (Vol. 4.2), 1972, 125–30. (Now Metropolitan) Kallistos Timothy Ware's "The Ascetic Writings of Mark the Hermit" (Oxford, D.Phil. thesis, 1965) remains unpublished. But see his *Introduction* to *Marc Le Moine: Traites spirituels et theologiques*, trans. Sr. Claire-Agnes Zirnheld, *Spiritualite Orientale*, no. 41 (Abbaye De Bellefontaine, 1985), where he agrees with Chadwick's assessment on p. XV.

3. St. Ignatius Briachaninov, a nineteenth-century bishop of Russia, makes an impassioned plea to monks (and all Christians) to practice the teachings of Christ and the apostles before going on to read the writings of church fathers, saints, canons, and rules for worship. They are to make the Gospels, and the New Testament writings generally, their foremost rule. Failure to follow this basic rule was the cause of his own problems given to him by "spiritual directors suffering from blindness and self-delusion." *The Arena: An Offering to Contemporary Monasticism*, trans. Lazarus Moore (Jordanville, NY: Holy Trinity Monastery, 1997). For a wider treatment of the centrality of the gospel in the Orthodox tradition, see our essay "The Evangelical Theology of the Eastern Orthodox Church" in *Three Views on Eastern Orthodoxy and Evangelicalism*, ed. James Stamoolis (Grand Rapids, MI: Zondervan, 2004). Translated into Romanian in *Ortodoxie evanghelism: Trei perspective* (Editura Adoramus, 2009), 27–93.

4. References to *the Philokalia* here and in the footnotes below are from *the Philokalia*, trans. G. E. H. Palmer, Philip Sherrard, Kallistos Ware (London and Boston: Faber & Faber, 1981). *Philokalia*, Vol. 2, p. 335; Vol. 3, p. 74.

5. *The Philokalia*, Vol. 1, pp. 175–76; Vol. 2, pp. 2, 24, 333, 335; Vol. 3, pp. 29, 102; Vol. 4, pp. 17, 200, 261, 269, 320 respectively.

6. *The Philokalia*, Vol. 1, pp. 175–76.

7. *The Philokalia*, Vol. 1, pp. 279–80.

8. *The Philokalia*, Vol. 2, pp. 162–63. On salvation as a free gift of grace with works as a manifestation of our debt to God, see Vol. 2, pp. 336, par. 31; 369, par. 45; Vol. 3, pp. 339–40, par. 123.

9. However, Mark's teaching on the effects of grace in baptism was not accepted by the church. Mark taught that baptism entirely removes from a baptized person the presence of

a sinful nature, and not just past sins, thus restoring human nature to the pristine state of Adam before the Fall. For a comparison of Mark with Sts. Augustine and Gregory of Nyssa, see Kallistos Ware, "The Sacrament of Baptism and the Ascetic Life in the Teaching of Mark the Monk," *Studia Patristica*, Vol. 10 [= *Texte und Untersuchungen* 107] (1970).

10. *Counsels on the Spiritual Life: Mark the Monk*, Vol. 1, pp. 26–34. Tim Vivian informed me in an email (1-12-10) that he was incorrectly credited with writing the Introduction to this volume.

11. A number of Syriac, Greek, Latin, and Slavonic writers ranked Mark alongside Anthony of Egypt, Arsenius, and Isaiah the Solitary. At times, portions of Mark's writings were even integrated into the rules of monasteries because they were seen as providing a wise foundation for the spiritual life (especially *On the Spiritual Law* and *Justified by Works*). The father of Byzantine humanism, Photios the Great (c. 858), regarded Mark's works as worthy of special treatment in codex 200 of his famous *Library*, which was an original and important compilation of literary criticism of early Christian and secular authors.

12. *Counsels on the Spiritual Life: Mark the Monk*, Vol. 1, p. 33.

13. *Counsels on the Spiritual Life: Mark the Monk*, Vol. 1, p. 33.

14. *The Philokalia*, Vol. 1, p. 109.

15. The reliability of the descriptions of Messalian doctrine given through the rebuttals of its opponents are probably correct, even though Columba Stewart rightly cautions us about the methodology we use in defining Messalianism. A flawed approach is one which attempts to construct a unified "Messalian system" that is based on a conflated list of Messalian doctrines that was formulated by its orthodox critics and then to apply that unified system to patristic texts as a way of measuring their "Messalian content." Stewart concludes: "The only safe course is to consider each kind of evidence in turn, recognizing that each provides a particular perspective on the Messalian controversy . . . following each type of evidence only as far as it will lead. The resulting picture of the Messalian controversy will not be like a finely detailed engraving, but like a highly impressionistic painting providing an array of perceptions as it is viewed in different light and from different angles." Columba Stewart, *"Working the Earth of the Heart" The Messalian Controversy in History, Texts, and Language to AD 431*, Columba Stewart OSB (New York: Oxford University Press, 1991), 5–6.

16. The efforts to organize Messalian doctrine into a theological system were first constructed by the condemnations of the Council of Ephesus (431) and the heresiologists Timothy of Constantinople (c. 600) and John of Damaskos (before 750). But the descriptions in these lists may be exaggerated and do not fit every variation of the group called Messalian.

17. For an exploration of Messalianism and its relation to the legacy of Ps.-Macarius of Egypt, see Marcus Plested, *The Macarian Legacy: The Place of Macarius-Symeon in the Eastern Christian Tradition* (New York: Oxford University Press, 2004).

18. John Meyendorff, *The Byzantine Legacy in the Orthodox Church* (Crestwood, NY: St. Vladimir's Seminary Press, 1982), p. 207. Scholars disagree whether the *Liber Graduum* is a Messalian document. Kmosko, the editor of the critical edition of the Syriac, supports its Messalianism while Sebastian Brock disagrees.

19. Kallistos Ware, "The Sacrament of Baptism and the Ascetic Life in the Teaching of Mark the Monk." *Studia Patristica*, Vol. 10 [= *Texte und Untersuchungen* 107] (1970): 442. I am indebted to Ware's article for the narrative of this section, particularly fns. 20–23.

20. The sin of Adam has been removed and nothing but physical death remains as its legacy. Mark's theology contrasts with that of the Messalians, who held to a very strong view of original sin and its ongoing legacy. The Messalians maintained that baptism "profits nothing" or, at best, is severely incomplete. Baptism deals with the symptoms but not the cause of sin. Sin and an indwelling demon remain natural to human nature because of the fall of Adam, and these abide in the soul even after baptism.

21. Mark asserts that as a result of the Fall, humans are born with an inherited inclination towardsevil. We are morally weak and enslaved by disgraceful passions. Baptism, however, delivers us from this inherited slavery to sin and restores us to the same condition Adam enjoyed before the Fall. Post-baptismal humans are liberated from the presence of every evil inclination. In other words, sin and spiritual death are eradicated from human nature. Yet after baptism Christians are still subject to spiritual warfare within and without. Temptations and external demonic assaults continue because free will remains as part of their nature, just as Adam experienced before the Fall. As Mark puts it, "Only baptism is perfect (τέλειον) but it does not make perfect him who does not perform the commandments. . . . Faith consists not only in being baptized into Christ but also in performing His commandments."(Ware, p. 446)

Mark's perspective on the effects of baptism differs from key elements of Messalian, Augustinian, and even Greek patristic thought. As Ware points out, Mark differs from St. Augustine, who views baptism as a sacrament that frees us from the guilt of original sin, but not from sin's evil presence. Mark would have regarded both Messalianism and Augustine's views as a dangerous infringement on the completeness of baptism. A portion of Mark's sacramental theology is also out of step with the mainstream of Greek patristic thought. Gregory of Nyssa represents a more balanced view of the Greek tradition. Unlike Mark, who focuses on the single theme of baptism, Gregory speaks of baptism and the Eucharist. Gregory also differs from Mark by stressing that baptism does not bring about a totally perfected state of restoring the baptized to the status of Adam before the Fall. Evil is not banished from our nature the moment we are baptized, for this is something that can be achieved only gradually through spiritual growth. Gregory also claims that if there is not a morally visible change in the baptized by his keeping of the commandments, we are "only seemingly and not really regenerate."

22. Christ and the Holy Spirit are given to us at the beginning of our Christian life, and no greater experience can be had in our subsequent growth than the full realization of the gift that has already been given in baptism. Mark writes: "However much a man may advance in faith . . . he never discovers nor can he ever discover, anything more than what he has already received secretly through baptism, that is to say, Christ." Ware explains: "Now for the Christian there can obviously be no experience higher than the encounter face to face with the Person of Christ; and this encounter is made possible specifically because Christ is already within our hearts from baptism, although at first we may be unaware of His presence. Our highest experience, then, is simply the full realization of the initial grace of baptism." (Ware, p. 445) In Messalianism, the gift of the Spirit is not given at the beginning of the Christian life through baptism but is reserved for the end as the climax and conclusion of it. It is something we work for. Constant prayer can result in a state of sinless perfection and an absence of the passions (ἀπάθεια).

23. Meyendorff, *The Byzantine Legacy in the Orthodox Church*, p. 210.

24. Andrew Louth, "Messalianism and Pelagianism," *Studia Patristica*, Vol. XVII, Part One, ed. Elizabeth A. Livingstone (Oxford: Pergamon Press, 1982), 127–35.

25. Georges de Durand convincingly demonstrates that the two works are companion pieces based on a close reading of their literary connections, even though he thinks they were originally designed as separate treatises (Photios analyzes them as separate works). *The Spiritual Law* contains an introduction but no ending, while *Justified by Works* has no introduction but a doxological ending that is characteristic of Mark's writings. The "spiritual law," also mentioned at the end of *Justified by Works*, is a theme that unites the treatises as a two-part work. SC 445, 61–3. His hypothesis, however, that the two were originally separate pieces seems unlikely because of the unity of themes and terminology; see Casiday, 89–90. Interestingly, *The Spiritual Law* that Symeon the New Theologian received and read also included the treatise *Justified by Works* (*The Philokalia*, Vol. 4, p. 17).

26. *Marc le Moine*, 41–65.

27. Email correspondence on 3-10-10 with Casiday verified that he and Vivian used the term "justified" simply for practical reasons rather than theological ones. With his permission to reprint the explanation, Casiday explained: "I seriously doubt whether Mark himself would have understood any claim that there was a sharp distinction between the two concepts. Justice and righteousness are approximately equivalent in patristic Greek, according to my experience. Because the word 'justice' carries particular connotations in Western theology, it would not be unreasonable to prefer 'righteous' since there is presumably less risk of eliciting anachronistic associations by using the later rather than the former. On the other hand, from the perspective of a translator, 'justified' is more economical than 'made righteous.' And since the two English concepts both correspond approximately to the Greek, I think in the end you make a choice based on the most relevant criteria."

28. See Plested, *The Macarian Legacy*, pp. 112–15, for the revelation of baptismal grace and the influence of Ps. Makarios of Egypt on Mark.

29. Palmer, Sherrard, Ware translation numbered # 111 in *The Philokalia*, p. 134.

■ Chapter 7

1. I have used the four-volume Greek text published by Astir in Athens; quotations in English are from the four volumes so far published of the translation under the general editorship of G. E. H. Palmer, Philip Sherrard, and Kallistos Ware: *The Philokalia. The Complete Text Compiled by St Nikodimos of the Holy Mountain and St Makarios of Corinth* (London, 1979, 1981,1984, and 1995). References in the text are to the volumes and page numbers of this translation.

2. (London, 1966), p. 138; the work is better known in the United States under its alternative title, *For the Life of the World*.

3. *The Journals of Father Alexander Schmemann, 1973–1983* (Crestwood, NY, 2000).

4. *Journals*, p. 130.

5. For some reflections on this issue in relation to recent discussions, see Rowan Williams, "The Spiritual and the Religious: Is the Territory Changing?" in Tony Blair et al., *Faith and Life in Britain: The Cardinal's Lectures 2008* (London, 2008), pp. 35–48.

6. The most marked instance of this is the paraphrase of the Macarian Homilies made by Symeon Metaphrastes, vol. III of the Greek text, pp. 171–234, vol. III of the English translation, pp. 285–353.

7. I have decided to use "intelligence" to render *nous* rather than the "intellect," preferred by the English translators, on the grounds that "intellect" has for most readers a narrower and more conceptually focused sense than "intelligence."

8. Edited by Paul Gehin and Claire Guillaumont, *Sur les pensees, Sources chretiennes*, 438 (Paris, 1998).

9. An excellent treatment can be found in Reinhard Flogaus, *Theosis bei Palamas und Luther: Ein Beitrag zum Okumenischen Gesprach* (Gottingen, 1997), chapter 2.

10. It is interesting to compare this with the theology of the Anglican layman Charles Williams, who, in his idiosyncratic but powerful and original essay, *He Came Down from Heaven* (London, 1938), writes of the Fall of Adam and Eve: "They knew good; they wished to know good and evil. Since there was not—since there never has been and never will be—anything else than the good to know, they knew good as antagonism" (p. 19).

11. See Teresa's *Spiritual Testimonies* 17 and 37 (in Kieran Kavanaugh, OCD, and Otilio Rodriguez, OCD, trans.: *The Collected Works of St Teresa of Avila*, vol.1 (Washington, 1976), pp. 329 and 341).

12. For a good recent study covering some of this territory, see Paul M. Blowers, "Envy's Narrative Scripts: Cyprian, Basil, and the Monastic Sages on the Anatomy and Cure of the Invidious Emotions," *Modern Theology* 25.1 (2009), pp. 21–43

13. "Love is the daughter of *apatheia*"; Evagrios, *Praktikos*, Prologue 8 and ch. 81.

14. See, among a large literature by these and other writers, Peter Brown, *The Body and Society: Men, Women and Sexual Renunciation in Early Christianity* (New York and London, 1988); Margaret Miles, *Fullness of Life: Historical Foundations for a New Asceticism* (Philadelphia, 1981); *Carnal Knowing: Female Nakedness and Religious Meaning* (Boston 1989); Caroline Walker Bynum, *Holy Feats and Holy Fast. The Religious Significance of Food to Mediaeval Women*, Berkeley (Los Angeles and London, 1987).

15. *Journals*, p. 157.

16. *The Sacred Body: Asceticism in Religion, Literature, Art and Culture* (Baylor University Press, 2009), esp. chapter 1.

17. See *The Pilgrim's Tale*, ed. and introduced by Aleksei Pentkovsky, trans. T. Allan Smith (New York and Mahwah, 1999).

18. I have in mind here especially the work of a theologian like Christos Yannaras: among many works, see particularly his *Ontologia tes scheses* (Ikaros Press, 2004).

19. *The World as Sacrament*, p. 91.

20. It is a pity that the index to volume IV of the English translation has an entry (p. 42) "divine image in man does not involve the body"; there is a difference between saying that the image is not a matter of bodily correspondence or does not primarily relate to any bodily characteristic and denying that the image includes bodily life in some way, as the texts cited under this heading will show.

21. Quoted above, n. 8; see also his contribution to *Orthodox Readings of Augustine*, ed. Aristotle Papanikolaou and George E. Demacopoulos (Crestwood, NY, 2008), "Inspiration—Exploitation—Distortion: The Use of St. Augustine in the Hesychast Controversy," pp. 63–80.

22. David Bentley Hart's essay in *Orthodox Readings of Augustine* ("The Hidden and the Manifest: Metaphysics After Nicaea," pp. 191–226, esp. pp. 221–25) has some illuminating perspectives on parallels between Augustine and Gregory of Nyssa which would bear on the present discussion.

23. See Rowan Williams, "The deflections of desire: negative theology in Trinitarian disclosure," in Oliver Davies and Denys Turner, eds., *Silence and the Word: Negative Theology and Incarnation* (Cambridge, 2002), pp. 115–35.

24. In Adrian Pabst and Christoph Schenider, eds., *Encounter Between Eastern Orthodoxy and Radical Orthodoxy: Transfiguring the World Through the Word* (London, 2009), pp. 271–89.

25. Schneider, op. cit., pp, 285–86.

26. See Loudovikos's essay in Pabst and Schenider, op. cit., pp. 141–55, "Ontology Celebrated: Remarks of an Orthodox on Radical Orthodoxy," esp. p. 146; also his book, *I evcharistiaki ontologia* (Athens, 1992), pp. 229–39

▨ Chapter 8

1. I take this idea from that form of biblical criticism known as "canonical criticism," which was pioneered by Brevard Childs. Canonical criticism sought to move beyond historical-critical work, which concerned itself ultimately with analyszng the text into constituent elements and then interpreting those in isolation from one another in an attempt to discern the pre-history, the "texts behind the text" of Scripture. Childs and his students argued rather that Scripture's "theological" meaning could be accessed only through acceptance of the final form, the groupings and versions in which its various constituent elements have been handed down by tradition. Superficially, the *Philokalia*'s own history resembles that of Scripture: a group of texts written over a millennium, assembled together by self-effacing editors in a "final" list. Yet, the sanction for treating Scripture's "final form" is given by tradition which closes its lists

to new entrants. That has been precisely the opposite case with the *Philokalia*. Moreover, the problems faced by those interpreting the *Philokalia* are almost precisely opposed to those facing biblical critics: if the historical-critical mode with its analytic tendencies has dominated biblical studies, a spiritual-theological mode, keen on synthesis, has dominated philokalic scholarship. In a sense, the problem with the *Philokalia* mirrors that of the canonical critics: we have a final form (of sorts) which has been, if anything, too privileged for interpretation without sufficient attention being paid to its pre-history within Orthodox dogmatic and ascetic theology. Canonical criticism may offer interesting ways forward to readers of the *Philokalia*, but perhaps more in the differences of subject rather than in similarities of form.

2. Kallistos Ware, "The Spirituality of the *Philokalia*," *Sobornost* 13:1 (1991): 6–24 [quotation from 22]. Ware quotes Nikodimos's introduction in *ΦΙΛΟΚΑΛΙΑ ΤΩΝ ΙΕΡΩΝ ΝΗΠΤΙΚΩΝ*, 5 vols. (4th ed.; Athens: Astir-Papadimitriou, 1974–76), 1:xxiii (hereafter "*Philokalia*"). I have had access to vols. 1, 2, and 5; for materials in vols. 3 and 4 I have consulted critical editions where available or, as is sometimes the case, the relevant PG volumes. I have, however, generally quoted from the English translation (hereafter "*Philokalia* ET" or simply "ET") by G. E. H. Palmer, Philip Sherrard, Kallistos Ware, et al., *The Philokalia: The Complete Text*, 4 vols. to date (London: Faber & Faber, 1979–95).

3. Andrew Louth, "Theology of the *Philokalia*," in J. Behr, A. Louth, and D. Conomos, (eds.), *Abba: The Tradition of Orthodoxy in the West. Festschrift for Bishop Kallistos (Ware) of Diokleia* (Crestwood, NY: St. Vladimir's Seminary Press, 2003), 351.

4. Louth, "Theology of the *Philokalia*," 353.

5. Louth, "Theology of the *Philokalia*," 354–55.

6. See, e.g., Ware, "Spirituality of the *Philokalia*," 11.

7. See, e.g., Gregory of Sinai, *On Stillness*, 4, PG 150:1317BC (*Philokalia*, ET 4:265–66), where he quotes Barsanuphius of Gaza as allowing for some flexibility and even variation in the practice of psalmody—a flexibility which Gregory himself approves, though he recommends variation within prescribed practices, i.e., using shortened prescribed prayers (Trisagion and "Our Father") as well as praying "to be delivered from the 'old self'" (Rom 6.6, etc.)," while Barsanuphius, a bit more freely, simply says, "You ought to ask to be delivered and freed from the 'old self,' or say the 'Our Father,' or both." Later in the same work (13–14 [4:272]) Gregory assumes that his readers must undertake all the usual ascetical practices in order to cultivate the spiritual life. His exposition then begins where those virtues, as it were, leave off. For the quotation form Barsanuphius, see F. Neyt (ed. and trans.), *Barsanuphe et Jean de Gaza. Correspondance.* 5 vols., Sources Chrétiennes 426, 427, 450, 451, 468 (Paris: Éditions du Cerf,), I.1, §143.

8. See Ware, "St. Nikodemos and the *Philokalia*," in Dimitri Conomos and Graham Speake (eds.), *Mount Athos: the Sacred Bridge. The Spirituality of the Sacred Mountain* (Oxford: Peter Lang, 2005), 69–122 (esp. 77–81).

9. Gregory of Sinai, *On Stillness*, 11, PG 150:1324C-1325A (*Philokalia*, ET 4:271). His authority, as I mention, is Climacus, who says that ascetics should read ascetical authors (*Scala Paradisi* §27, PG 88:1116C).

10. Louth, "Theology of the *Philokalia*," 355.

11. Carl Laga and Carlos Steel confidently argue for 1105 CE as the *terminus post quem* for the *Capita Varia*'s creation—thus making it rather improbable that Niketas Stethatos (who died twenty years before, c. 1085) would have known them in their present form. See Carl Laga and Carlos Steel, *Maximi Confessoris: Quaestiones ad Thalassium*, vol. 1, CCSG 7 (Leuvain: Brepols, 1980), lxxvi–lxxxii, esp. lxxxi.

12. See Louth, "Theology of the *Philokalia*," 352–53.

13. Placide Deseille, *La Spiritualité Orthodoxe et la* philokalie, L'Aventure Intérieure (Paris: Bayard Éditions, 1997), 59–60. In this regard Aimilianos Tachiaos has ventured to suggest

the mss. from which Paissy and Makarios worked in the Vatopedi library. His suggestion remains, however, merely an interesting speculation. See Ware, "Spirituality of the *Philokalia*," 11, and idem., "*philokalie*," in *Dictionnaire du Spiritualité* 12 (Paris: Beauchesne, 1984), cols. 1338–39. Ware also speculates that Makarios and Nikodemos made their particular selections following "an existing tradition already well established on the Holy Mountain and elsewhere." (Ware, "Nikodemos," 97; he discusses the possibility further at 102–3).

14. For a concise discussion of the history of the *Philokalia*'s creation and Paissy's own work, see Ware, "Nikodemos," 69–122.

15. Nikiphoros the Monk, *On Watchfulness and the Guarding of the Heart*, PG 147:946A-966A (*Philokalia*, ET 4:194–206, esp.); cf. Cyril of Scythopolis, *Vita Sabae*, §28 in E. Schwartz (ed.), *Kyrillos von Skythopolis*, Texte und Untersuchungen 49.2 (Leipzig: Hinrichs, 1939), 113. It is true that in Cyril's telling, Saba is concerned with the watchfulness of his monks, but Cyril, at least, places more emphasis on their learning the liturgical offices and psalms properly!

16. See Ware, "The Spirituality of the *Philokalia*," 7, 10–11: he notes that the lack of editors' names in the original publication allows for (at least some) speculation (given Paissy's silence) as to whether Nikodemos was actually involved in the project.

17. See Ware, "Nikodemos and the *Philokalia*," 77–81.

18. Louth, "Theology of the *Philokalia*," 355.

19. The piece attributed to Isaiah is sourced from across his sermons, cut together and arranged into an entirely new format. Some of the *kephalaia* (this piece was given a form common to many desert writers, such as Evagrius, but not used by Isaiah) are themselves composite. That it was created before the latter thirteenth century and approved by Hesychasts can be deduced from the direct quotation of *On the Guarding of the Intellect* 17 (*Philokalia*, 1:33, ET 1:25) in Nikiphoros the Monk, *On Watchfulness and the Guarding of the Heart*, PG 147:956B-957A (*Philokalia*, ET 4:201).

20. *Philokalia* 1:xxi.

21. See Ware, "Spirituality of the *Philokalia*," 18–19.

22. Ibid., 20–22.

23. I owe the following paragraph to Ware's discussion of the situation in "Nikodemos and the *Philokalia*," 108–9.

24. Ware, "*philokalie*," cols. 1345–46.

25. Of course, my claim here begs the question of whether translators such as Dumitru Staniloae, St. Theophan the Recluse, and Metropolitan Kallistos Ware, have done the right thing in making the *Philokalia* available in the vernacular. It is, I think, an entirely open question, and the crux rests on the extent to which one believes that the content of the *Philokalia* requires safeguarding—or, rather, whether readers require safeguarding from it. I do not propose to answer that question here, only to raise it.

26. Diadochos of Photiki, *One Spiritual Knowledge and Discrimination*, Definitions, in *Philokalia* 1:235 (ET 1:252).

27. Gregory of Sinai, *On Stillness*, 3, in *Philokalia*, ET 4:264. The source in Isaiah is uncertain. The reference to Climacus is to *Scala Paradisi*, §27, PG 88:1112C.

28. Gregory of Sinai, *On Commandments and Doctrines*, 81, PG 150:1261C-1264A (*Philokalia* ET 4:227).

29. See Ware, "*philokalie*," cols. 1345–46 (quotation from col. 1346).

30. Ibid., cols. 1346–47.

31. See the Introduction to *The Philokalia*, ET, vol. 1, pp. 11–12.

▨ Chapter 9

1. *Second Century on Theology*, *Philokalia* 2, 85; ET 2, 158. References to the *Philokalia* are to the volume and page of the third Greek edition (Athens: Astir/Papadimitriou, 1957–63),

followed by a reference to the English translation (ET) by G. E. H. Palmer, Philip Sherrard, and Kallistos Ware (Faber & Faber, London/Boston 1979–95). For basic historical and theological information on the *Philokalia*, see Philip Sherrard, "The Revival of Hesychast Spirituality," in *Christian Spirituality: Post-Reformation and Modern*, Louis Dupré, Don E. Saliers, and John Meyendorff (eds.) (New York: Crossroad Publishing, 1989), 417–31; and Andrew Louth, "The Theology of the *Philokalia*," in *Abba: The Tradition of Orthodoxy in the West: Festschrift for Bishop Kallistos (Ware) of Diokleia* (Crestwood, NY: St. Vladimir's Seminary Press, 2003), 351–61.

2. Regarding the importance of Maximus in the *Philokalia* (as well as key historical and theological matters in his work), see Andrew Louth, "Maximus the Confessor," in *The Study of Spirituality*, Cheslyn Jones, Geoffrey Wainwright, and Edward Yarnold (eds.) (New York: Oxford University Press, 1986), 190–95. Another informative essay on the *Philokalia* and the pervasive influence of Maximus (along with Evagrius Ponticus and Gregory Palamas) in the entire collection is by Kallistos Ware, "The Spirituality of the *Philokalia*," in *Sobornost Incorporating Eastern Churches Review* 13:1 (1991), 6–24. Much of the material in the latter essay is included in Ware's chapter in this book, "St. Nikodimos and the *Philokalia*."

3. Ware argues that theological anthropology will be a primary focus for theological reflection in the twenty-first century. Moreover, he asserts that Christian anthropology (as illustrated in Maximus) is christological and relational in nature, since human beings are created in the image of Christ the Creator Logos and in the image of God the Holy Trinity, "La théologie orthodoxe au vingt-et-unième siècle," *Irénikon* 77, 2–3 (2004): 219–38.

4. For informative surveys of modern scholarship on Maximus, see Paul Blowers, *Exegesis and Spiritual Pedagogy in Maximus the Confessor* (Notre Dame, IN: University of Notre Dame Press, 1991), 1–2; Andrew Louth, "Recent Research on St. Maximus the Confessor: A Survey," *St. Vladimir's Theological Quarterly*, 42:1 (1998): 67–84; Aidan Nichols, *Byzantine Gospel: Maximus the Confessor in Modern Scholarship* (T&T Clark, 1993), 221–52; and Lars Thunberg, *Microcosm and Mediator* (Chicago: Open Court Press, 1995), 12–20.

5. For a detailed analysis of these eight cosmological elements, see Thunberg, *Microcosm and Mediator*, 49–93. Also helpful is Torstein Theodor Tollefsn, *The Christocentric Cosmology of St. Maximus the Confessor* (New York: Oxford, 2008), 40–63, who compares Maximus's doctrine of creation with Platonic, Aristotelian, and Stoic philosophy, as well as the Neoplatonic ideas of Philo of Alexandria and certain Christian theologians who studied Philo.

6. *Fourth Century on Love*, Philokalia 2, 41; ET 2, 100. See Dumitru Staniloae's reflection on *creation ex nihilo*, which includes Maximus's ideas on the world, time, and eternity, *The Experience of God: Orthodox Dogmatic Theology*, vol. 2, *The World: Creation and Deification* (Brookline, MA: Holy Cross, 2000), 7–16.

7. Polycarp Sherwood's discussion on the yawning chasm between God and creatures, and creation out of nothing is particularly helpful, *Saint Maximus the Confessor: The Ascetic Life, The Four Centuries on Charity* (Mahwah, NJ: Newman Press, 1955), 46–51.

8. *Fourth Century on Love*, Philokalia 2, 41; ET 2, 100.

9. Tollefsen argues that the theory of the *logoi* is a kind of Christian exemplarism developed to express the insight that God is the free Creator of everything, *The Christocentric Cosmology of St. Maximus the Confessor*, 65ff. Thunberg explains that the Pseudo-Dionysian dynamism of the emanations of divine grace is combined by Maximus with an emphasis on unity in unviolated diversification, expressed ultimately in the incarnation of the Logos, *Microcosm and Mediator*, 65–66.

10. *Fourth Century on Love*, Philokalia 2, 41; ET 2, 100.

11. For example, Maximus speaks of "the Trinity's creation," *Second Century on Love*, Philokalia 2, 27; ET 2, 82. For an insightful analysis of the trinitarian dimension of Maximus's

theology, see Lars Thunberg, *Man and the Cosmos* (Crestwood, NY: St. Vladimir's Seminary Press, 1985), 31–49.

12. *Second Century on Theology, Philokalia* 2, 70; ET 2, 138. Tollefsen indicates this, as well as the way the circle image coincides with other basic structures of Maximus's metaphysics, including the dual movements of procession and conversion ($\pi\rho\acute{o}o\delta o\sigma$ and $\acute{\epsilon}\pi\iota\sigma\tau\rho o\phi\acute{\eta}$), and of expansion and contraction ($\delta\iota\alpha\sigma\tau o\lambda\acute{\eta}$ and $\sigma\upsilon\sigma\tau o\lambda\acute{\eta}$), *The Christocentric Cosmology of St. Maximus the Confessor*, 69.

13. Using this image from Matthew's Gospel (13:31), Maximus describes the relationship between the Logos and the *logoi*. In those who faithfully cultivate the life of Christian virtue, Christ the Logos, as the grain of mustard seed, grows expansively, so that all the *logoi* come to rest in him, *Philokalia* 2, 70–71; ET, 139–40.

14. See Mark McIntosh's comments on the mystical *logoi* in all created realities as whispers of the Logos, who is the speaking source of all creation. McIntosh provides helpful commentary on various passages in Maximus, including the symbol of the center of the circle and its radii, *Mystical Theology: The Integrity of Spirituality and Theology* (Oxford: Blackwell, 1998), 57–58.

15. Thunberg, *Microcosm and Mediator*, 79. Thunberg also provides an extensive analysis of Maximus's christocentric vision in which the cosmological and historical Logos are not separate elements in Maximus's thinking but are portrayed as one and the same. Thus, according to Maximus, Christ is the center of the universe and the center of the economy of salvation, as illustrated in the threefold embodiment of the Logos: in his coming in the flesh, in the *logoi* of created beings, and in the letters of scripture. Thunberg suggests that through his desire to incarnate himself, the Logos not only unifies the *logoi* of creation, but also the three aspects of creation, revelation, and salvation, 77.

16. For informative commentary on the *logoi* teaching, see Thunberg, *Microcosm and Mediator*, 73–79; John Meyendorff, *Byzantine Theology* (Bronx, NY: Fordham University Press, 1974), 132ff.; and Balthasar, *Cosmic Liturgy*, 116–22.

17. *Fourth Century on Love, Philokalia* 2, 41; ET 2, 100.

18. *Fourth Century on Love, Philokalia* 2, 41; ET 2, 100. See Thunberg's helpful discussion on God's prudence, apophasis, and human astonishment at God's creative wisdom, *Microcosm and Mediator*, 80.

19. On creation as an act of divine condescension and its relation to the concept of motion, see Sherwood, *St. Maximus the Confessor*, 40–45; and Thunberg, *Microcosm and Mediator*, 81–83.

20. *Fourth Century on Love, Philokalia* 2, 41; ET 2, 100.

21. On Maximus's positive evaluation of motion (in opposition to Plotinus, Proclus, and the pantheistic of Origenism), see von Balthasar, *Cosmic Liturgy*, 147–65; and Sherwood, who elucidates Maximus's view that motion is a natural human power tending to its proper end, that is, God, *St. Maximus the Confessor*, 47–51. Also noteworthy is Sherwood's analysis of God's motion, Maximus's appropriation of Pseudo-Dionysius, how God is moved as *eros* and moves as charity, and how creatures are placed outside Godself only that they may be brought back to Godself, 43–45.

22. Thunberg's analysis of this dimension of creaturely existence is especially informative, *Microcosm and Mediator*, 86–89.

23. *Fourth Century on Love, Philokalia* 2, 41, 42, 31; ET 2, 101, 87.

24. Thunberg, *Microcosm and Mediator*, 90–92.

25. Von Balthasar, *Cosmic Liturgy*, 61.

26. For a brief yet potent analysis of the coexistence of body and soul in Maximus, see Thunberg, *Microcosm and Mediator*, 95–97.

27. *Ambigua* 7, PG 91, 1100 D; in Blowers and Wilken, *The Cosmic Mystery of Jesus Christ*, 72.

28. See Adam G. Cooper, *The Body in St. Maximus the Confessor* (New York: Oxford University Press, 2005), for an insightful discussion of the soul–body relationship and its implications for the human vocation, 102–16.

29. For example, see *Th Pol* (*Opuscula theologica et polemica*) 14; PG 91, 152 A; *Th Pol* 23; 261 A; *Ambigua* 7. Thunberg considers this analogy between the union of body and soul in humanity, and the union of the two natures in Christ. In conversation with Sherwood, who finds an inconsistency in Maximus's use of this analogy, Thunberg argues that Maximus is not inconsistent on this point. Thunberg highlights texts like *Amb* 7, where Maximus speaks of *perichoresis* on both the christological and human level, *Microcosm and Mediator*, 101–4.

30. An example of trichotomy in Maximus is found in *Fourth Century on Love, Philokalia* 2, 45; ET 2, 105, while an example of dichotomy is seen in *Philokalia* 2, 4; ET 2, 53–54.

31. On the composition of human being as body and soul, as well as the ways that Maximus constructs his own understanding of human being in dichotomous and trichotmous terms, see Thunberg, *Microcosm and Mediator*, 95–107; Sherwood, *St. Maximus the Confessor*, 47–55; and von Balthasar, *Cosmic Liturgy*, 235–47.

32. For Maximus's teaching on this in the *Philokalia*, see *Philokalia* 2, 188–89; ET 2, 287–88. For excellent discussions on Maximus's teaching on the micocosmic and mediatory roles of the human person, see Thunberg, *Microcosm and Mediator*, 231–330, 331–427; Vladimir Lossky, *Orthodox Theology* (Crestwood, NY: St. Vladimir's Seminary Press, 1978), 74–78; Nonna Verna Harrison, *God's Many-Splendored Image: Theological Anthropology for Christian Formation* (Grand Rapids: Baker Academic, 2010), 131–37.

33. Von Balthasar, *Cosmic Liturgy*, 173–77; Thunberg, *Microcosm and Mediator*, 107–13.

34. For an informative analysis of the threefold approach to the spiritual life in Maximus, see Thunberg, *Microcosm and Mediator*, 330–72, and von Balthasar, *Cosmic Liturgy*, 314–43.

35. Lossky explains that the intellect (*nous*) and spirit (*pneuma*) are synonymous. They represent the highest, most personal part of the human creature, the contemplative faculty by which we are able to seek God, and the principle of our conscience and freedom, *The Mystical Theology of the Eastern Church* (Crestwood, NY: St. Vladimir's Seminary Press, 1976), 201. For a helpful discussion on *nous* in relation to body, soul, and the whole human person, and its Godward orientation, see Thunberg, *Microcosm and Mediator*, 107–13; and Lossky, *The Mystical Theology of the Eastern Church*, 201ff.

36. *First Century on Love, Philokalia* 2, 4; ET 2, 53.

37. *Third Century on Love, Philokalia* 2, 39; ET 2, 85.

38. *Third Century on Love, Philokalia* 2, 32; ET 2, 88.

39. *First Century on Love, Philokalia* 2, 4; ET 2, 53.

40. *First Century on Love, Philokalia* 2, 10; ET 2, 60.

41. *First Century on Love, Philokalia* 2, 11; ET 2, 61, 62.

42. *Fourth Century on Love, Philokalia* 2, 47; ET 2, 108.

43. *Fourth Century on Love, Philokalia* 2, 42; ET 2, 101–2.

44. See Adam G. Cooper, *Life in the Flesh: An Anti-Gnostic Spiritual Philosophy* (New York: Oxford University Press, 2008), 73–74, 153–54.

45. *Second Century on Theology, Philokalia* 2, 74; ET 2, 144.

46. Unless noted otherwise, scripture quotations are from the New Revised Standard Version (NRSV).

47. *First Century of Various Texts, Philokalia* 2, 95; ET 2, 170.

48. *Fifth Century of Various Texts, Philokalia* 2, 180–811; ET 2, 277–78.

49. For succinct and informative discussions on the distinction between the divine image and likeness, see David Cairns, *The Image of God in Man* (London: Collins, 1973); and John McGuckin, *Westminster Handbook to Patristic Theology* (Louisville: Westminster John Knox Press, 2004), 178–80.

50. *Third Century on Love, Philokalia* 2, 30–31; ET 2, 86–87.

51. *First Century on Theology, Philokalia* 2, 53; ET 2, 116.

52. *On the Lord's Prayer*, ET 2, 294.

53. For concise, informative definitions of key terms and concepts in the *Philokalia*, see the glossary near the end of each volume in the English translation.

54. *First Century on Theology, Philokalia* 2, 53; ET 2, 116.

55. *Second Century on Theology, Philokalia* 2, 77; ET 2, 148.

56. *On Spiritual Knowledge*, ET 1, 88.

57. *Makarian Homilies* VIII.8.

58. See the notes on the works of Maximus included in the second volume of the *Philokalia*, ET 49–51. Included in the *Various Texts* are passages from Maximus's *Letters*, from *To Thalassios*, and from the *Ambigua*, where Maximus discusses disputed texts in the works of Gregory of Nazianzus. In the appendix of the ET 2, the translators/editors indicate which texts are from Maximus, from the scholiast, or from Dionysius.

59. *First Century of Various Texts, Philokalia* 2, 102; ET 2, 178.

60. *First Century of Various Texts, Philokalia* 2, 101; ET 2, 177. For a helpful analysis of the "garments of skin," see Panayiotis Nellas, *Deification in Christ: The Nature of the Human Person*, trans. Norman Russell (Crestwood, NY: St. Vladimir's Seminary Press), 43–91.

61. *Fourth Century of Various Texts, Philokalia* 2, 153; ET 2, 243.

62. For an informative analysis of Maximus's sources, see Louth, *Maximus the Confessor*, 19–32.

63. Regarding the creation of human nature with free will and the capacity to obey, see Cooper, *Life in the Flesh*, 77.

64. On the Devil's seduction and humanity's culpability, see Thunberg, *Microcosm and Mediator*, 154–56; regarding self-love, see 231–48.

65. *Fourth Century of Various Texts, Philokalia* 2, 157; ET 2, 248.

66. *First Century of Various Texts, Philokalia* 2, 94; ET 2, 169.

67. *First Century of Various Texts, Philokalia* 2, 96; ET 2, 171.

68. *First Century of Various Texts, Philokalia* 2, 96; ET 2, 171.

69. *Second Century of Various Texts, Philokalia* 2, 114; ET 2, 194. For an informative analysis of the two trees in the garden—including the early Christian interpretations of Origen, Irenaeus, and Gregory of Nyssa, and Maximus's explanation—see Thunberg, *Microcosm and Mediator*, 162–68.

70. *Second Century of Various Texts, Philokalia* 2, 114–15; ET 2, 194–95.

71. *First Century of Various Texts, Philokalia* 2, 100; ET 2, 175.

72. *First Century of Various Texts, Philokalia* 2, 96; ET 2, 171.

73. *Second Century on Theology, Philokalia* 2, 111; ET 2, 139. Maximus, like many of his fellow ascetic theologians, describes the demons who attack human beings, tempting them with impassioned thoughts, contending with them by every possible means in order to separate them from God; *Second Century on Love, Philokalia* 2, 26; ET 2, 80–81. They are those minions who seek to cause disunity in the cosmos, to further what happened at the Fall, to fragment human beings and separate them from communion with God. For an informative and interesting analysis of demons and the Christian ascetic struggle against evil, see Douglas Burton-Christie, *The Word in the Desert: Scripture and the Quest for Holiness in Early Christian Monasticism* (New York: Oxford University Press, 1993), 193–98.

74. Maximus's pneumatology, in my estimation, remains unexplored by contemporary theologians. Thunberg posits that there is nothing remarkable about Maximus's teaching on

the Spirit (*Microcosm and Mediator*, 20), but this claim is difficult to support. Reading his *Mystagogy* alone, attending to his reflection on the Holy Spirit, demonstrates the creative and fertile pneumatological thinking in Maximus. Moreover, in his writings included in the *Philokalia*, Maximus speaks of the Spirit numerous times: the Spirit's ubiquitous presence (ET 2, 180–81); indwelling presence (ET 2, 123, 304); activity as water and fire (ET 2, 152); the law of the Spirit (ET 2, 189); the pledge of the Spirit (ET 2, 110); fruits and gifts (ET 2, 186–87, 217–19); in the Christian life (ET 2, 176, 239); rebirth through the Spirit (ET 2, 256, 284, 287); the Spirit and God's kingdom (ET 2, 290–92).

75. *Fourth Century of Various Texts*, Philokalia 2, 150; ET 2, 239.

76. *Fourth Century of Various Texts*, Philokalia 2, 157; ET 2, 247–48. The implications of this deep connection between humanity and the rest of creation are particularly relevant to contemporary research in eco-theology and eco-spirituality, as I point out in the final section of this essay; cf. Brock Bingaman, "Orthodox Spirituality and Contemporary Ecology: John Cassian, Maximus the Confessor, and Jürgen Moltmann in Conversation," in *Spirit and Nature: The Study of Christian Spirituality in a Time of Ecological Urgency*, ed. Tim Hessel-Robinson and Ray Maria McNamara (Eugene, OR: Pickwick Press, 2011).

77. On the presence of pleasure and pain in human life, see Thunberg, *Microcosm and Mediator*, 159.

78. McGuckin, "Byzantium and the East," in *The Blackwell Companion to Christian Spirituality*, ed. Arthur Holder (Oxford: Blackwell Publishing, 2005), 97.

79. *First Century on Theology*, Philokalia 2, 61–62; ET 2, 127.

80. As Maximus says, the incarnation of the Logos is a *mystery*. Along with the various cataphatic statements being made about the incarnation, we should note the apophatic stance Maximus takes when addressing this great mystery. Accordingly, he asserts that while the Logos is made eternally manifest, he remains eternally invisible, *Philokalia* 2, 92; ET 2, 166; that the Logos always remains a mystery, so that he remains hidden even in the revelation of his enfleshment, *Philokalia* 2, 92; ET 2, 166; and that the great mystery of the incarnation remains a mystery eternally, because even though the Logos came down to the level of human being, he became being in a manner which transcends being, *Philokalia* 2, 93; ET 2, 167.

81. Blowers, *On the Cosmic Mystery of Jesus Christ: Selected Writings from St Maximus the Confessor* (Crestwood, NY: St Vladimir's Seminary Press, 2003), 20. Blowers adds that "Maximus's achievement, from one angle, is a panoramic commentary on the first chapter of Ephesians and on Colossians 1:15–23, the Apostle Paul's reflections on the mystery of Christ as the mystery of the world," 20.

82. *Second Century on Theology*, Philokalia 2, 73; ET 2, 143. Related to the idea of the incarnate Logos as the messenger of God's plan, Maximus explains that he is the mediator between God and humanity (1 Tim. 2:5), because he makes the unknown Father manifest to us through the flesh and gives access, through reconciliation, to the Father through the Holy Spirit (Eph. 2:18). It was on our behalf and for our sake that without changing, the Logos became man, and is now the author and teacher of a great number of new mysteries that remain beyond human understanding, *On the Lord's Prayer*, ET 2, 286.

83. *Fourth Century of Various Texts*, Philokalia 2, 155; ET 2, 246.

84. *First Century of Various Texts*, Philokalia 2, 98; ET 2, 174; cf. where Maximus speaks of the divine incarnation, in which the divine Logos became man for us, as an expression of God's *great generosity* toward us, *First Century of Various Texts*, Philokalia 2, 93; ET 2, 167.

85. *Fifth Century of Various Texts*, Philokalia 2, 169–70; ET 2, 263.

86. *Fifth Century of Various Texts*, Philokalia 2, 181; ET 2, 278.

87. George Berthold, ed. and trans., *Maximus Confessor: Selected Writings*, Classics of Western Spirituality (Mahwah, NJ: Paulist Press, 1985), 7. For further exposition of Maximus by Pelikan, see *The Christian Tradition. A History of the Development of Doctrine, 2:*

The Spirit of Eastern Christendom (600–1700) (Chicago: University of Chicago Press, 1974), 8–36.

88. *On the Lord's Prayer*, ET 2, 286.

89. *On the Lord's Prayer*, ET 2, 289.

90. *On the Lord's Prayer*, ET 2, 287.

91. Blowers says that Maximus's teaching echoes Irenaeus's principle of cosmic *recapitulation*, provides a critical rehabilitation of Origen's masterful insight into the divine interpenetration of all things (1 Cor. 15:28), filtered through a mature trinitarian theology and christology based on insights from the Cappadocian Fathers, *On the Cosmic Mystery of Jesus Christ*, 20–21.

92. *On the Lord's Prayer*, ET 2, 286.

93. Von Balthasar comments on this, saying that the *mysterium magnum*, the great mystery in the divine eternal plan, is rooted in God's determination to bring about the re-creation of all things and their reunion with God, *based on the self-emptying incarnation of Christ, Cosmic Liturgy*, 272.

94. *On the Lord's Prayer*, ET 2, 304.

95. *First Century of Various Texts, Philokalia* 2, 92; ET 2, 165–66.

96. Again, one can hear the echoes of scriptural language within Maximus's reflections, particularly Paul's words in Gal. 4:19: "My little children, for whom I am again in the pain of childbirth until Christ is formed in you."

97. *First Century of Various Texts, Philokalia* 2, 92; ET 2, 166. Maximus explains that this is why the author of Hebrews, "when considering the power of this hidden activity, says, 'Jesus Christ is the same yesterday, and today, and throughout the ages' (Heb. 13:8); for he sees the hidden activity as something which is always new and never becomes outmoded through being embraced by the intellect," 166.

98. *On the Lord's Prayer*, ET 2, 294. Maximus adds that the soul in which Christ is born is made a Virgin Mother, "for such a soul . . . is not conditioned by categories like those of male and female that typify a nature subject to generation and corruption," 294.

99. Thunberg, *Microcosm and Mediator*, 325.

100. In the important essay by Kallistos Ware, he underscores the importance of deification as a unifying theme in the *Philokalia*, "The Spirituality of the *Philokalia*," *Sobornost Incorporating Eastern Churches Review* 13:1 (1991), 6–24.

101. Thunberg, *Microcosm and Mediator*, 430.

102. *Third Century on Love, Philokalia* 2, 30–31; ET 2, 86–87; cf. Russell, *Deification*, 265.

103. Russell, *Deification*, 265.

104. For informative, classic treatments of human participation in the divine nature, see the elucidation of the essence/energies theme in Lossky, *The Mystical Theology of the Eastern Church*, 67–90; Ware's concise section on "Partakers of the Divine Nature," in *The Orthodox Church*, 2313–8; and Panayiotis Nellas, *Deification in Christ: Orthodox Perspectives on the Nature of the Human Person* (Crestwood, NY: St. Vladimir's Seminary Press, 1987.)

105. *Third Century of Various Texts, Philokalia* 2, 134; ET 2, 18–19.

106. *Fourth Century of Various Texts, Philokalia* 2, 150; ET 2, 239–40.

107. *Fifth Century of Various Texts, Philokalia* 2, 185; ET 2, 283.

108. *On the Lord's Prayer*, ET 2, 303–4.

109. *First Century of Various Texts, Philokalia* 2, 101–2; ET 2, 177–78.

110. *Fifth Century of Various Texts, Philokalia* 2, 181; ET 2, 278.

111. See George C. Berthold, "The Cappadocian Roots of Maximus the Confessor," in Heinzer and Schönborn (eds.), *Maximus Confessor: Actes du Symposium sur Maxime le Confesseur, Fribourg, 2–5 septembre 1980*, Paradosis 27 (Fribourg: Éditions universitaires Fribourg Suisse, 1982), 37–49.

112. *On the Incarnation*, 54:107, from *Christology of the Later Fathers*, ed. Edward R. Hardy (Louisville: Westminster John Knox Press, 1977).

113. Regarding this correspondence, see Thunberg, *Microcosm and Mediator*, 329; cf. Russell, *Deification*, 267–68.

114. *First Century of Various Texts*, Philokalia 2, 92; ET 2, 165–66.

115. *First Century of Various Texts*, Philokalia 2, 105; ET 2, 182.

116. *On the Lord's Prayer*, ET 2, 294.

117. Louth, *Maximus the Confessor*, 50–51; cf. Blowers and Wilken, *On the Cosmic Mystery of Jesus Christ*, 16–21; and Ian A. McFarland, "Fleshing Out Christ: Maximus the Confessor's Christology in Anthropological Perspective," *St. Vladimir's Theological Quarterly* 49:4 (2005), 417–36.

118. Meyendorff, *Byzantine Theology*, 38–39.

119. For an insightful analysis of the background of deification, and a comparison between perspectives of the Christian East and West, see Gerhart B. Ladner, *The Idea of Reform: Its Impact on Christian Thought and Action in the Age of the Fathers* (New York: Harper and Row, 1967), 98–107, 153–222.

120. *On the Lord's Prayer*, ET 2, 287.

121. For an insightful discussion of the seven mysteries in relation to deification, see Russell, *Deification*, 267–70.

122. *On the Lord's Prayer*, ET 2, 304.

123. Russell, *Deification*, 270.

124. Von Balthasar explains: "Maximus the Confessor consciously considers whether one should strive to reach God by endeavoring to move backward out of fallen time to Paradise or forward toward the Judgment. Both ways lead to the same goal; the road is blocked, so we have to move forward to get back to our origin and home," *A Theological Anthropology* (New York: Sheed and Ward, 1967), 109.

125. See Jürgen Moltmann's bracing analysis on the new creation, in which he engages Orthodox theologian P. Evdokimov, who says, "The kingdom is not simply a return back toward Paradise, but it's forward-moving creative fulfillment which takes in the whole of creation," *God in Creation* (Minneapolis: Fortress Press, 1985), n. 36, 348.

126. Russell, *Deification*, 292.

127. *First Century on Theology*, Philokalia 2, 60; ET 2, 125.

128. Russell, *Deification*, 292–93.

129. *First Century on Theology*, Philokalia 2, 67; ET 2, 135.

130. *First Century on Theology*, Philokalia 2, 67; ET 2, 135.

131. *Second Century on Theology*, Philokalia 2, 87; ET 2, 160.

132. Meyendorff, *Byzantine Theology*, 164.

133. Regarding the doctrine of *apokatastasis* (universal salvation) in Maximus, see Balthasar, *Cosmic Liturgy*, 354–58; and Brian E. Daley, "*Apokatastasis* Apocalyptic: Eastern Eschatology after Chalcedon," in *The Hope of the Early Church: A Handbook of Patristic Eschatology* (Peabody: Hendrickson Publishers, 2003), 168–204 (esp. 201–2, where he focuses on Maximus).

134. *First Century of Various Texts*, Philokalia 2, 98; ET 2, 173.

135. *First Century of Various Texts*, Philokalia 2, 104–5; ET 2, 182.

136. *Fifth Century of Various Texts*, Philokalia 2, 172–73; ET 2, 267; cf. von Balthasar's informative discussion on the synthesis of the three laws, *Cosmic Liturgy*, 291–303.

137. *Third Century of Various Texts*, Philokalia 2, 133, 135; ET 2, 218, 271.

138. *First Century of Various Texts*, Philokalia 2, 101–2; ET 2, 178.

139. *Second Century of Various Texts*, Philokalia 2, 111; ET 2, 189–90.

140. *Fifth Century of Various Texts*, Philokalia 2, 185; ET 2, 284.

141. Thunberg, *Microcosm and Mediator*, 229.

142. *First Century of Various Texts*, Philokalia 2, 95–96; ET 2, 170–71. As we have seen at other points, note the language used here that is rooted in Maximus's christology: exchange, union, and reciprocity.

143. *First Century of Various Texts*, Philokalia 2, 96; ET 2, 171.

144. *Fifth Century of Various Texts*, Philokalia 2, 184; ET 2, 283.

145. *On the Lord's Prayer*, ET 2, 286.

146. Russell, *Deification*, 267.

147. *On the Lord's Prayer*, ET 2, 304.

148. *On the Lord's Prayer*, ET 2, 297.

149. *On the Lord's Prayer*, ET 2, 297–98.

150. Russell, *Deification*, 269. Some readers of the *Philokalia* might think that the collection is lacking when it comes to ecclesial theology. For an insightful analysis, see the essay in this volume by Krastu Banev, *The Ecclesiology of the Philokalia*.

151. Von Balthasar, *Cosmic Liturgy*, 321–22.

152. Von Balthasar, *Cosmic Liturgy*, 319–20.

■ Chapter 10

1. P. Sherrard and K. Ware, "Introduction," *The Philokalia: The Complete Text. Compiled by St. Nikodimos of the Holy Mountain and St. Makarios of Corinth*. Translated from the Greek by Philip Sherrard and Kallistos Ware, 4 vols. (London: Faber & Faber, 1979–95), 1: 13–15.

2. A concern only partially addressed by other scholars. See K. Ware, "The Spirituality of the '*Philokalia*.'" *Sobornost* 13, no. 1 (1991): 6–24. Id. "St. Nikodimos and the *Philokalia*," in D. Conomos and G. Speake (eds.), *Mount Athos the Sacred Bridge: The Spirituality of the Holy Mountain* (Oxford: Peter Lang, 2005), 69–121. Id., "philokalie," in M. Viller and F. Cavallera (eds.), *Dictionnaire de spiritualité ascétique et mystique, doctrine et histoire*, vol. 12/1 (Paris: Beauchesne, 1984), 1336–52. A. Louth, "The Theology of the *Philokalia*." in J. Behr, A. Louth, and D. Conomos (eds.), *Abba: The Tradition of Orthodoxy in the West. Festschrift for Bishop Kallistos (Ware) of Diokleia* (Crestwood, NY: St. Vladimir's Seminary Press, 2003), 351–61.

3. *The Journals of Father Alexander Schmemann*, 1973–83 (Crestwood, NY: St. Vladimir's Seminary Press, 2000), 18, 295.

4. Ch. Yannaras, КИФА № 12 (38) 2005. Available online at: http://gazetakifa.ru/content/view/335/20/ [10 Dec 2009]. I owe this reference to Mr. Zurab Jashi, research student at Durham University.

5. Ware, "philokalie," 1351.

6. Ch. Yannaras, *Orthodoxy and the West*, trans. Norman Russell (Brookline, MA: Holy Cross Orthodox Press, 2007), 132.

7. *The Philokalia of Origen*, ed. J. Armitage Robinson (Cambridge, 1893).

8. *The Way of a Pilgrim; and, A Pilgrim Continues His Way*. Trans. from the Russian by Olga Savin (Boston: Shambhala, 2001). For more on the intertextuality of *The Way of a Pilgrim*, see A. Golitzen, "Pilgrim and Community," *Spiritus: A Journal of Christian Spirituality* 2, no. 2 (2002): 236–42.

9. Ware, "St. Nikodimos and the *Philokalia*," 72.

10. Ware, "St. Nikodimos and the *Philokalia*," 79–81.

11. St. Nikodimos, "Introduction," *Philokalia*, vol. 1 (Athens: Astir-Papadimitriou, 1957), xxi [in Greek], trans. in Ware, "The Spirituality of the '*Philokalia*,'" 12.

12. Diadochos of Photiki, "On Spiritual Knowledge," 60, in *Philokalia*, 1: 271.

13. The continuity of the tradition is a matter of scholarly debate. For a detailed treatment of the subject see N. Russell, *The Doctrine of Deification in the Greek Patristic Tradition* (Oxford: Oxford University Press, 2004).

14. Cf. Ware, "St. Nikodimos and the *Philokalia*," 108. The relevant letter to Archimandrite Theodosy is extensively quoted in Sergii Chetverikov, *Le starets moldave Païssij Velitchkovskij*, trans. François de Damas (Bégrolles-en-Mauges: Abbaye de Bellefontaine, 1997), 155–62. On the abundance and quality of Paisy's literary activity, see Ibid., 251–66.

15. Translation in Ware, "The Spirituality of the '*Philokalia*,'" 19.

16. See detailed discussion in E. Citterio, "Nicodemo Agiorita." in Carmelo G. Conticello and Vassa Conticello (eds.), *La théologie byzantine et sa tradition* (Turnhout: Brepols, 2002), 936–39, 943.

17. "A Discourse on Abba Philimon," in *Philokalia*, 2:348.

18. "On the Three Stages of Contemplation," in *Philokalia*, 3:138.

19. "Introduction," *Apophthegmata*, Alph., PG 65:73C–76A.

20. "A Discourse on Abba Philimon," in *Philokalia*, 2:351.

21. "A Discourse on Abba Philimon," in *Philokalia*, 2:346.

22. St. Peter of Damaskos, "The Third Stage of Contemplation," in *Philokalia*, 3:116. Citation from the service for Wednesday of Holy Week.

23. St. Peter of Damaskos, "The Third Stage of Contemplation," in *Philokalia*, 3:118–19. Citations from the prayers at the end of Compline and the prayers at the Third Hour.

24. "Trisagion"—the triple '*Holy God, Holy Strong, Holy Immortal, have mercy upon us*'—presumably followed by the prayer "Most Holy Trinity, have mercy upon us . . ." and then by the Lord's Prayer, according to the usual Orthodox practice. The Psalter is divided into twenty sections, each called a "kathisma," and every "kathisma" is divided into subsections called a "stasis" or "antiphon." The Trisagion comes after each antiphon. *Philokalia*, 3:119, nn.1–2.

25. St. Symeon the New Theologian, "Practical and Theological Texts," in *Philokalia*, 4: 25–66. On the difficulties with the appropriation of Symeon's vision of the church, see A. Golitzin, "Hierarchy Versus Anarchy? Dionysius Areopagita, Symeon the New Theologian, Nicetas Stethatos, and Their Common Roots in Ascetical Tradition," *St. Vladimir's Theological Quarterly* 38, no. 2 (1994):131–79.

26. St. Symeon the New Theologian, "Practical and Theological Texts," 144, in *Philokalia*, 4:59.

27. Ibid., 132, in *Philokalia*, 4:54.

28. Ibid., 137, in *Philokalia*, 4:55.

29. Ibid., 142, in *Philokalia*, 4:58. The Apostles' fast in June is not mentioned here.

30. Ibid., 145, in *Philokalia*, 4:59.

31. Ibid., 143, in *Philokalia*, 4:58.

32. Ibid., 61, in *Philokalia*, 4:36.

33. Ibid., 79, in *Philokalia*, 4:41.

34. On the theme of interiorized ecclesiology, see A. Golitzin, *Et introibo ad altare Dei: The Mystagogy of Dionysius Areopagita, with Special Reference to its Predecessors in the Eastern Christian Tradition*, Analekta Vlatadon 59 (Thessalonike: Patriarchikon Hidryma Paterikon Meleton, 1994), 371–85.

35. St. Symeon the New Theologian, "Practical and Theological Texts," 153, *Philokalia*, 4: 62–63.

36. St. Theognostos, "On the Practice of the Virtues," 14, in *Philokalia*, 2:362.

37. Ibid., 21, in *Philokalia*, 2:363.

38. St. Symeon the New Theologian, "Practical and Theological Texts," 55, in *Philokalia*, 4:35.

39. "From the Life of our Venerable Father Maximos of Kafsokalivia." my translation from the second enlarged Russian edition of the *Philokalia* (Moscow, 1900, reprinted in 1992), vol. 5, 473. Cf. also the *Life* of the twentieth-century Russian Athonite, Saint Silouan, who had also received the pure prayer as a young novice "praying before an ikon of the Mother of God." Archimandrite Sophrony, *Saint Silouan the Athonite*, translated from the Russian by R. Edmonds (Crestwood, NY, 1999), 391. For these references, and for kindling my interest in the ecclesial dimensions of the philokalic tradition, I humbly acknowledge my debt to the late father-confessor of the Patriarchal Monastery of St. John the Baptist in Essex, Archimandrite Syméon (1928–2009). I am grateful also to Mr. Francis Garcia, whose comments and editorial skill have greatly improved this text.

■ Chapter 11

1. For a comprehensive up-to-date bibliography and other online resources on Evagrius, see http://www.kalvesmaki.com/EvagPont/.

2. See James J. Stamoolis's excellent review of *The Philokalia: Volume I*, in *Journal of the Evangelical Theological Society*.

3. Twentieth-century Evagrian scholarship, notably Muyldermans, *A travers*, has conclusively demonstrated the authorship of this text by Evagrius. The editors of the seminal English translation of the *Philokalia* have rightfully restored the work to Evagrius.

4. Cf. the English translation of the Philokalia, vol. 1, editors' note p. 21. The English translation editors show the text attributed to St. Anthony to be of a spurious, probably non-Christian Stoic origin, and thus not by St. Anthony at all, while the text of Abba Isaiah to be much later than the fourth century. See the translators' introductions to the work of "St. Anthony" and St. Isaiah the Solitary.

5. See Elm's seminal *"Virgins of God,"* 251–52. Elm points out that the descriptions of Egyptian asceticism in ancient sources have "a consciously crafted normative value." Yet a careful assessment of some of the more esoteric texts stemming from the north-Egyptian milieu, not least those by Evagrius himself, suggests otherwise.

6. Rousseau's classic *Ascetics*, 92–95.

7. C. Guillaumont, Introduction to *Traité Pratique*, SC 170, 34 ff.

8. Cf. Géhin, "Le Filocalie che hanno preceduto la 'Filocalia.'"

9. ***Greek manuscripts of Mt. Athos, Greek manuscripts of Philotheou.

10. The Lavra M 54 contains fourteen of the thirty-six authors within the *Philokalia*, and nineteen texts of its texts. See Géhin, op. cit., p. 100.

11. In the "Mosquensis Bibliothecae Lenineae gr. 126," lf. 102v–103v. On this see M. Richard, "Florilèges spirituals grecs," *DS* 5, cols. 475–512.

12. Evagrius's texts that are found in Nigne's *Patrologia Graeca* generally rely on the editing of Bigot and Cotelier.

13. See Géhin, "Le Filocalie che hanno preceduto Filocalia,"

14. See my *Evagrius Ponticus: the Making of a Gnostic*, pp. 19–22.

15. The work is contained in PG 79.1200D–1233A and PG 40.1240A–1244B. The additional chapters of the work are described by Muyldermans, *A travers la tradition manuscrite d'Évagre le Pontique* (Louvain, 1932), 47–55.

16. See Géhin, Introduction to *Sur les Pensées*, SC 438, pp. 60 and 99.

17. See Géhin's critical edition, in SC 438.

18. Thus, Atheniensis gr. 510 (13th c.) and Dionysiou 271 (Athous 3805) (13th–14th c.). See Géhin, op. cit. p. 59.

19. Cf. Géhin, "Le filocalie che hanno preceduto la 'Filocali,'" p. 88.

20. See catalogues presented in Sophronios Eustratiades and Arcadios of Vatopedi, *Catalogue of the Greek Manuscripts in the Library of Vatopedi on Mt. Athos*, no. 57. Ἑασιλείου

τοῦ Μεγάλου|' paper, end of thirteenth century Tachiaos, *The Slavonic manuscripts of Saint Panteleimon Monastery (Rossikon) on Mt. Athos*, no. 49, paper, end of eighteenth century, Dimitrije Bodnanovic, *Katalog of Cyrillic Manuscripts of the Chilandar Monastery* (Belgrade, 1978), no. 456, *Зборникъ*, papyrus, end of fourteenth century.

21. See D. S. Likhachev (ed.), *Книжные Центры Древней Руси: Иосифо-Волоколамский Монастырь* (Leningrad, 1991).

22. Cf. Metr. Kallistos Ware, "philokalie," DS II, col. 1338.

23. Cf. Géhin, "Le Filocalie che hanno preceduto la Filocalia," pp. 90 ff, notes that Greek ascetical manuscripts predating the tenth century are generally rare. Géhin in fact goes further than this in suggesting that the manuscript collections the philokalic editors used were, in all probability, as late as seventeenth or eighteenth century.

24. Cf. Géhin, op. cit., 91.

25. The three "Palamite" councils, at which Gregory Palamas's views on hesychasm and the Jesus Prayer were vindicated, took place in Constantinople in 1341 and 1351.

26. For the reference see note 21 above.

27. It is not of course possible to establish on the basis of the manuscripts alone when the translations into Slavonic were first produced.

28. Notably chapters 14, on the light of Savior, and 17, reminiscent of Moses's theophanic vision on Sinai.

29. This is not to say that Evagrius considered practical virtues as irrelevant to the more advanced and even perfect. The very *gnôstikoi* are to continue in a measure of asceticism, which remains a precondition to the life of advanced spiritual contemplation. Consequently, the monastic life to Evagrius ever combines negative and positive aspects: renunciation and striving toward a goal. For a valuable summary of the thematic content of this work, see Sinkewicz, *Evagrius of Pontus*, 1–4.

30. This subject is especially developed in other Evagrius works, notably *Skemmata*, not included within the collection.

31. The *Philokalia* is a testimony to a number of spiritual currents merged together in their subsequent Byzantine and Orthodox reception: among them the "Evagrian," "Macarian," and "Dionysian" traditions. See Géhin, *op. cit.* ***

32. Evagrius's other, more esoteric writings, not part of the *Philokalia*, notably the *Great Letter* and the *Gnostic Chapters*, plainly state that, while the Holy Trinity, God the Father, and the Logos are divine, Jesus Christ is not. Neither is Christ numerically identical with God the Logos, but is created and unites with the Logos by a manner of a voluntarist union. See my *Evagrius Ponticus: the Making of a Gnostic*, chapter 5, Christology.

33. Ὅτι αὐτῷ καί πᾶσα ἡ νοερά τῶν' Ἀγγέλων πληθὺς καί χορεία φόβῳ λειτουργοῦσα καί τρόμῳ δοξολογοῦσα, ἀκατάπαυστον ἀναπέμπει τὸν ὕμνον, σὺν τῷ Ἀνάρχῳ αὐτοῦ Πατρί καί τῷ Παναγίῳ καί Συναϊδίῳ Πνεύματι, νῦν καί ἀεί καί εἰς τοὺς αἰῶνας τῶν αἰώνων.' Ἀμην.

34. *Gnostic Chapters* VI.14.

35. *Thoughts* 3.

36. *Thoughts* 3.

37. *Thoughts* 3.

38. Christian ascetic interest in the stirrings of impassioned thoughts within the rational soul may not have started with Evagrius: it was integral to the "Desert Fathers" tradition, of which Evagrius became part as he settled in Egypt in the late 380s. Evagrius, however, elevates this *paideia* of the "guarding of the mind" onto a new rigorous level. Of the numerous Byzantine ascetical authors addressing the matter, it suffices to cite just a few names: Barsanuphius and John, Maximus the Confessor, John of Sinai, John Damascene, Symeon the New Theologian, Gregory of Sinai, Gregory Palamas.

39. Notably by A. Guillaumont, G. Bunge, L. Dysinger, and P. Géhin.

40. Eccl. 3:11.

41. *Thoughts* 16 (17), *Philokalia* vol. 1. This translation is modified from the English translation, *Philokalia: The Complete Text*, vol 1, p. 48.

42. *Thoughts* 20 (19 in the full version).

43. *Thoughts* 20. The translation is from *The Philokalia: the Complete Text*, vol. 1, p. 50.

44. On the Evagrian influence upon later writers, notably St. Maximus the Confessor (*Chapters on Love* III.42, both in the *Philokalia* vol. 2, and in PG 90.1029 A), regarding the distinction between normal and perverse thought activity in the mind, see Törönen, *Union and Distinction*, p. 187. See also Gabriel Bunge, *Earthen Vessels: The Practice of Personal Prayer according to the Patristic Tradition*.

45. As Maximus elaborates on Evagrius, "The monk's whole war is against the demons, that he may separate the passions from the representations," *Chapters on Love*, 3.41, *Philokalia* vol. 2 (PG 90.1029a).

46. Cf. *Thoughts* 23.

47. The editors did not, of course, have the benefit of the evidence brought together by I. Hausherr in his "Le *De oratione* de Nil et Évagre," *Revue d'Ascétique et de Mystique*, 14 (1933), 196–98; "Le *Traité de l'Oraison* d'Évagre le Pontique (Pseudo-Nil)," *Revue d'Ascétique et de Mystique*, 15 (1934), 34–39 ; "Le « De oratione » d'Évagre le Pontique en syriaque et en arabe," *Orientalia Christiana Periodica*, 5 (1939), 7–71.

48. The translation is from *The Philokalia: the Complete Text*.

49. The translation is based on Sinkewicz, *Evagrius of Pontus*, p. 198.

50. *Prayer*, 61.

51. *Prayer* 3.

52. See especially the potent descriptions of the visions of light in his *Skemmata*. Cf. Harmless, "The Sapphire Light of the Mind," pp. 498–500. Likewise my *Evagrius Ponticus: the Making of a Gnostic*, chapter 4, "The Intellect's Vision of Light."

▪ Chapter 12

1. G. E. H. Palmer, P. Sherrard, and K. Ware, trans. and ed., *The Philokalia: The Complete Text*, vol. 1 (London: Faber & Faber, 1979), 15: "Indeed, although the *Philokalia* is concerned with many other matters, it would not be too much to say that it is the recurrent references to the Jesus Prayer which more than anything else confer on it its inner unity."

2. E. des Places, ed., *Diadoque de Photicé: Oeuvres spirituelles*, Sources Chrétiennes 5 (Paris: Éditions du Cerf, 1966, 2nd ed.).

3. J. A. McGuckin. *The Orthodox Church. An Introduction to Its History, Doctrine, and Spiritual Culture* (Oxford: Blackwell Publishing, 2008), 351.

4. See, for example, Hesychios the Priest's treatise, *On Watchfulness and Holiness*, passim; trans. Palmer, Sherrard, and Ware, *The Philokalia*, vol. 1, 162–98; Diadochos of Photike, *On Spiritual Knowledge*; Ibid., 253–96, esp. sections 31–3, 59, 61, 85, 88, 97. Other earlier writers whose texts were not included in the *Philokalia*, such as John Klimakos's *Ladder of Divine Ascent*, also refer to a single phrased invocation of Jesus. See C. Luibheid and N. Russell, trans., *John Climacus. The Ladder of Divine Ascent* (London: SPCK, 1982), 48, 178, and 200.

5. *A Discourse on the Abba Philemon*; trans. Palmer, Sherrard, and Ware, *Philokalia*, vol. 2, 344–57. This tentative dating is proposed by the translators on p. 343.

6. A Monk of the Eastern Church, *The Jesus Prayer* (Crestwood, NY: St. Vladimir's Seminary Press, rev. ed. 1987), 93–106; Bishop Kallistos of Diokleia, *The Power of the Name. The Jesus Prayer in Orthodox Spirituality* (Oxford: SLG Press, 1974; new ed. 1986), 9–11.

7. A Monk of the Eastern Church, *The Jesus Prayer*, 27.

8. I. Hausherr, *The Name of Jesus. The Names of Jesus Used by Early Christians. The Development of the Jesus Prayer*, trans. C. Cummings (Kalamazoo, MI: Cistercian Publications, 1978); A Monk of the Eastern Church, *The Jesus Prayer*, 35–64.

9. St. Diadochos of Photike, *On Spiritual Knowledge* 31; trans. Palmer, Sherrard, and Ware, *Philokalia*, vol. 1, 261.

10. St. Diadochos of Photike, *On Spiritual Knowledge* 33; trans. Palmer, Sherrard, and Ware, *Philokalia*, vol. 1, 263.

11. St. Diadochos of Photike, *On Spiritual Knowledge* 59; trans. Palmer, Sherrard, and Ware, *Philokalia*, vol. 1, 271.

12. St. Diadochos of Photike, *On Spiritual Knowledge* 61; trans. Palmer, Sherrard, and Ware, *Philokalia*, vol. 1, 271.

13. On St. Gregory of Sinai, see K. Ware, "The Jesus Prayer in St. Gregory of Sinai." *Eastern Churches Review* 4:1 (1972), 3–22; David Balfour, ed., *St. Gregory the Sinaïte: Discourse on the Transfiguration* (Athens: Offprint of *Theologia* 52.4–54.1, 1981–83).

14. For example, see St. Gregory of Sinai, *On Stillness* 2; trans. Palmer, Sherrard, and Ware, *Philokalia*, vol. 4, 264.

15. Theoliptos, Metropolitan of Philadelphia, *On Inner Work in Christ*; trans. Palmer, Sherrard, and Ware, *Philokalia*, vol. 4, 181.

16. Unfortunately, owing to limitations of time, it has not been possible to include the fifth volume of *Philokalia* in this study. This volume still awaits publication in an English translation, but it is accessible in the original with a modern Greek translation. See A. G. Galthis, trans., *Φιλοκαλία των Ιερών Νυπτικκών* (Thessalonike: Perivoli tis Panagias Publishers, 3rd ed., 2002).

17. St. Diadochos of Photike, *On Spiritual Knowledge* 31; trans. Palmer, Sherrard, and Ware, *Philokalia*, vol. 1, 261.

18. St. Diadochos of Photike, *On Spiritual Knowledge* 59; trans. Palmer, Sherrard, and Ware, *Philokalia*, vol. 1, 270.

19. St. Hesychios the Priest, *On Watchfulness and Holiness*, passim; trans. Palmer, Sherrard, and Ware, *Philokalia*, vol. 1, 162–98.

20. See, for example, Ibid., chap. 9, 164.

21. See also Peter of Damaskos, *How to Acquire True Faith*; trans. Palmer, Sherrard, and Ware, *Philokalia*, vol. 3, 167.

22. Ilias the Presbyter, *Gnomic Anthology* IV. 65; trans. Palmer, Sherrard, and Ware, *Philokalia*, vol. 3, 56.

23. Nikiphoros the Monk, *On Watchfulness*; trans. Palmer, Sherrard, and Ware, *Philokalia*, vol. 4, 206.

24. St. Gregory of Sinai, *On Prayer*; trans. Palmer, Sherrard, and Ware, *Philokalia*, vol. 4, 277.

25. St. Gregory of Sinai, *On Prayer*; trans. Palmer, Sherrard, and Ware, *Philokalia*, vol. 4, 259.

26. See, for example, St. Diadochos of Photike, *On Spiritual Knowledge* 59; trans. Palmer, Sherrard, and Ware, *Philokalia*, vol. 1, 270–71.

27. St. Hesychios the Priest, *On Watchfulness and Holiness* 5; trans. Palmer, Sherrard, and Ware, *Philokalia*, vol. 1, 163.

28. *A Discourse on the Abba Philemon*; trans. Palmer, Sherrard, and Ware, *Philokalia*, vol. 2, 348.

29. *A Discourse on the Abba Philemon*; trans. Palmer, Sherrard, and Ware, *Philokalia*, vol. 2, 345.

30. *A Discourse on the Abba Philemon*; trans. Palmer, Sherrard, and Ware, *Philokalia*, vol. 2, 356.

31. Theoliptos, Metropolitan of Philadelphia, *On Inner Work in Christ*; trans. Palmer, Sherrard, and Ware, *Philokalia*, vol. 4, 181.

32. Theoliptos, Metropolitan of Philadelphia, *On Inner Work in Christ*; trans. Palmer, Sherrard, and Ware, *Philokalia*, vol. 4, 189.

33. St. Gregory of Sinai, *On Prayer*; trans. Palmer, Sherrard, and Ware, *Philokalia*, vol. 4, 284.

34. Philotheos of Sinai, *The Forty Texts on Watchfulness* 27; trans. Palmer, Sherrard, and Ware, *Philokalia*, vol. 3, 26.

35. For orientation to this topic, see J. Meyendorff, *A Study of Gregory Palamas* (London: Faith Press, 1964); idem., *St. Gregory Palamas and Orthodox Spirituality* (Crestwood, NY: St. Vladimir's Press, 1998); and most recently, D. Krausmüller, "The Rise of Hesychasm," in M. Angold, ed., *The Cambridge History of Christianity: Eastern Christianity* (Cambridge: Cambridge University Press, 2006), 101–26.

36. See the comments made on this subject by Lev Gillet in his *The Jesus Prayer*, 41, 44–860–1. Essentially, Fr. Lev argues that although these Fathers did not mention the prayer explicitly, it was implicit in their thought and practice.

37. R. M. French, trans., *The Way of a Pilgrim* (London: SPCK, 1942; rev. ed. with introduction by Metropolitan Anthony of Sourozh, 1972).

38. Bishop Kallistos of Diokleia, *The Power of the Name*, 5.

39. J. D. Salinger, *Franny and Zooey* (London: Penguin Books, 1955; repr. 2010), 110–11.

▪ Chapter 13

1. Vol. 104, ed./tran. Joseph Paramelle, *Catechesis* (Paris: Editions du cerf, 1964). The English translation by C. J. De Catanzaro, *Symeon the New Theologian: The Discourses* (New York: Paulist Press, 1980) is the one referred to throughout this chapter.

2. De Catanzaro, *Discourses*, n. 1, 243. The patrician's household mentioned may be that of his maternal uncle, according to De Catanzaro, *Discourses*, n. 4, 245.

3. See *Sources Chrétiennes* vol 51, ed./trans. Jacques Darrouzès, *Chapitres théologiques gnostiques et practiques* (Paris: Editions du cerf, 1957). For an English translation, see Paul McGuckin, *Symeon the New Theologian: The Practical and Theological Chapters and Theological Discourses* (Kalamazoo, MI: Cistercian Publications, 1982).

4. This attribution is explored by Hilarion Alfeyev in his article, "St. Symeon the New Theologian, St. Symeon the Pious and the Studite tradition." *Studia Monastica* 36 (1994): 183–222, where he accounts for the manuscript tradition of this text, which he later published as *Syméon le Studite: Discours Ascétique*, trans. Louis Neyrand, *Sources Chrétiennes*, no. 460. (Paris: Editions du cerf, 2001).

5. The contested authorship is debated by Tomáš Špidlík, "Symeon le Nouveau Théologien," in *Dictionnaire de Spiritualité* vol 14 (Paris: Beauchesne, 1990), 1387–401, where he attributes the text to Nikiphorus the Hesychast, a late thirteenth–century mystical writer. The nineteenth-century Russian Orthodox compiler of devotional texts, Igumen Chariton, attributes the text to Nikephoros, commenting that "he may be describing a practice already well established long before his own time." Igumen Chariton, *The Art of Prayer: An Orthodox Anthology* trans. Elizabeth M. Palmer (London, Faber: 1966), 35 and 104. This is discussed (along with the thinness of evidence for authorship by Nicephorus) by Matus at a relatively early stage in twentieth-century debates about the matter. Thomas Matus, "Symeon the New Theologian and the Hesychast 'Method.'" *Diakonia* 10 (1975): 260–70. John Turner emphatically rejects the attribution to Symeon. St. *Symeon the New Theologian and Spiritual Fatherhood* (Leiden: Brill, 1990), 14.

6. *Philokalia* vol. 4, 17, = *Discourse 22*, De Catanzaro, *Discourses*, 244.

7. *Philokalia* vol. 4, 74.

8. Ibid., p. 69.

9. John A. McGuckin, "Symeon the New Theologian's Hymns of Divine Eros: A Neglected Masterpiece of the Christian Mystical Tradition," *Spiritus: A Journal of Christian Spirituality* 5.2 (2005) 182–202.

10. 210 and cf. *On Stillness* in the same volume, 259 and 269.

11. See Matus, op. cit.

12. For example, Olga Louchakova's paper for a conference in psychological method, Olga Louchakova and A. Warner, "Via Kundalini: Pyschosomatic excursions in transpersonal psychology," *The Humanist Pyschologist* 31 (2–3), 2003, 115–58 mentions Symeon in connection with hesychastic prayer.

13. Hilda Graef even calls this "unique," "The Spiritual Director in the Thought of Symeon the New Theologian," *Kyriakon: Festschrift Johannes Quasten*, vol. 2, eds. Patrick Granfield and Josef A. Jungmann (Aschendorff: Münster Westfalen, 1970), 608–14, esp. 608.

14. Symeon's own experience of being a spiritual father is depicted in Nicetas's preface to the *Hymns*, in Louis Neyrand and Joseph Paramelle, (trans.) *Hymnes, Syméon le nouveau théologien* Sources Chrétiennes, 3 vols. 156, 174, 196. (Paris: Editions du cerf, 1969–73) vol. 156, 106–35, 215–23.

15. In addition to *Catechesis 22*, (= *On Faith* in George Palmer, Philip Sherrard, and Kallistos Ware (trans.), *The Philokalia*. 4 vols. London: Faber & Faber, 1979–95, vol. 4),*Hymn 18*, *Catecheses 6* and *17* give accounts of his experiences. We also have less impartial evidence from Stethatos's *Vie* of the visions of light Symeon experienced throughout his life. See Iréné Hausherr and Gabriel Horn, "Un Grand Mystique Byzantin: Vie de Syméon le Nouveau Théologien par Nicétas Stéthatos" (Rome: *Orientalia Christiana* XII ([45] 1928), [herein after *Vie*] *Vie* 1.5, 9–10, *Vie* 2.19, 29, *Vie* 3.23, 33, *Vie* 5, 36, 49, *Vie* 9, 69, 95. There are echoes of the same details in the *Fifth Ethical Discourse*, lines 294–310, Alexander Golitzin, St. *Symeon the New Theologian: On The Mystical Life: The Ethical Discourses*. 3 vols. (Crestwood, NY: St. Vladimir's Seminary Press, 1995–97) vol. 2, 53–54. The autobiographical material is also discussed in Hannah Hunt, *Joy-bearing Grief: Tears of Contrition in the Writings of the Early Syrian and Byzantine Fathers* (Leiden: Brill, 2004), 172.

16. *A New Testament Decalogue, Philokalia* vol. 4, p. 327. Here even the title given to the text suggests the weight to be given to the new commandments of the Christian testament; love of God and neighbor becomes perfected as love of the spiritual family.

17. John A. McGuckin, "Symeon the New Theologian's Hymns of Divine Eros: A Neglected Masterpiece of the Christian Mystical Tradition," *Spiritus: A Journal of Christian Spirituality* 5.2 (2005), 198.

18. Hilarion Alfeyev, St. *Symeon the New Theologian and Orthodox Tradition* (Oxford: Oxford University Press, 2000). Alfeyev gives the most recent analysis of evidence concerning Symeon's dates on pages 28–29. Golitzin, *Mystical v*olume 3 contains a detailed biography of St. Symeon. See also Hannah Hunt, *Joy-Bearing*, 175–79. The majority of modern scholars working on Symeon are orthodox. In the case of the men, most, including McGuckin, Chryssavgis, Steenberg, Golitzin, Alfeyev, and Ware, are ordained as deacon, priest, or bishop.

19. Kurt Holl, *Enthusiasmus und Bussgewalt beim griechischen Mönchtum: Eine Studie zu Symeon dem neuen Theologen* (Leipzig: Hinrichs, 1898). This has been falsely attributed to John of Damascus according to George Maloney's *Introduction* to De Catanzaro, *Discourses*, 12.

20. Golitzin, *Mystical*, vol. 3.

21. H. John M. Turner, *The Epistles of St. Symeon the New Theologian* (Oxford: Oxford University Press, 2009).

22. Alfeyev, *Discours,*

23. Alfeyev, *Tradition*, 10, cf. Golitzin, *Mystical*, 13.

24. Throughout his writings, he refers to Mark the Monk, three of whose texts are included in Volume 1 of the *Philokalia* vol. 4, 109–61 under the name of Mark the Ascetic. This was the book he was given to read by his elder.

25. According to Chryssavgis, this "dialectic or tension between establishment and charisma, between priestly and prophetic function, has never really been resolved, but has in fact characterized the life of the Church at least since the age of Constantine." John Chryssavgis, *Soul Mending: The Art of Spiritual Direction* (Brookline, MA: Holy Cross Orthodox Press, 2000) 50; similar comments may be found in the writings of other Orthodox theologians, such as Golitzin, *Mystical* vol 3, 19, and McGuckin, *Practical*, 18.

26. Chryssavgis, *Soul Mending*, 105.

27. *Discourse 35*, 20–24, de Catanzaro, *Discourses*, 360, Ibid. lines 73–85, 361–62.

28. "Seek out one who is . . . an intercessor, physician, and a good counsellor." *Letter on Confession 7*, Kurt Holl, *Enthusiasmus*, 116–17 = Golitzin, *Mystical* vol. 3, 193.

29. *Seventh Ethical Discourse*, Golitzin, *Mystical* vol. 2, 96.

30. Michael Angold, "The Autobiographical Impulse in Byzantium." *Dumbarton Oaks Papers* 52 (1998): 225–57. The Stoudios where Symeon served his novitiate was noted for producing spiritual autobiographies.

31. Within Symeon's writings it is found in the *Third Discourse*, McGuckin, *Practical*, 139 and Chapter 3.4. McGuckin, *Practical*, 73; it occurs in the title of *Hymn 52*, George Maloney *Hymns of Divine Love by Symeon the New Theologian* (Denville, NJ: Dimension Books, 1975), 263. This issue is explored extensively by Kallistos Ware in his Foreward to Irénee Hausherr, trans. Anthony P. Gythiel, *Spiritual Direction in the Early Christian East* (Kalamazoo, MI 1990), vii, and "The Mystery of God and Man in St. Symeon the New Theologian," *Sobornost* 6/4 (1971): 227–36. It is discussed in the context of *penthos* in Hunt, *Joy-bearing*, 192–95 and 220–21. It is thought the idea consciously invokes the *Celestial Hierarchy* of Dionysius the Areopagite, according to Golitzin, *Mystical* vol. 3, 39–40.

32. Symeon and his biographer refer to his reading of John of the Ladder (Climacos), to be found in Colm Luibheid and Norman Russell, (trans.) *John Klimakos: The Ladder of Divine Ascent* (New York: Paulist Press, 1982), also Mark the Hermit (whose text is represented in *The Philokalia* vol. 1 as Mark the Ascetic); other key exponents of the practice of spiritual fatherhood which are not identified so overtly within Symeon's writings but form part of the tradition are Basil the Great's *Ascetic Discourse* (40) 5. [881A] cited by Alfeyev, *Tradition*, the *Ascetic Discourse* of St. Neilos the Ascetic *The Philokalia* vol 1, 215–24 particularly, Cassian *On the Holy Fathers of Sketis and on Discrimination*, in *The Philokalia* vol 1, 103–7.Turner examines in more detail the heritage of Dorotheus of Gaza, Evagrios, and Ephrem the Syrian. H. John M. Turner, St. *Symeon the New Theologian and Spiritual Fatherhood* (Leiden: Brill, 1990) chapter six.

33. Chapter 16 of St. Anthony's *Life* states that the role of the spiritual father is to share "knowledge and experience" with a pupil. Roy J. Deferrari, *Early Christian Biographies*, Fathers of the Church (Catholic University of America, 1952), 150. In *Catechesis 6(2)*, Symeon recalls the witness of St. Antony as a spiritual father. De Catanzaro, *Discourses*, 120–21. A direct connection to the desert fathers can be found in the writings of Poemen, 65, where we read the advice to "Go, and join a man who fears God, and live near him; he will teach you, too, to fear God." Trans. Benedicta Ward, *The Sayings of the Desert Fathers: The Alphabetical Collection*, (Kalamazoo, MI: Cistercian Publications, 1975), 176.

34. McGuckin, *Practical*, 78, cf Golitzin, *Mystical* vol. 3, 11, and Hunt, *Joy-Bearing*, 187–88.

35. *Catechesis 22*, De Catanzaro, *Discourses*, 251–52 = *Philokalia* vol 4, 22–23.

36. *Letter on Confession*, Golitzin, *Mystical* vol. 3, 202–3. cf *Vie*, 12, 20–26, which is discussed by Alfeyev, *Tradition*, 31.

37. Angold, "Autobiographical," 230.

38. Hannah Hunt, "Byzantine Christianity." In *The Blackwell Companion to Eastern Christianity*, ed. Ken Parry (Oxford, Blackwell Publishing, 2007), 73–93.

39. Rosemary Morris, "Spiritual Fathers and Temporal Patrons: Logic and Contradiction in Byzantine Monasticism in the Tenth Century." *Revue Benedictine* 103 (1993): 283. Morris argues here for an interchange of temporal and spiritual authority, which is peculiarly pertinent in the case of Symeon, who himself enjoyed the benefit of high birth and who juxtaposed secular and monastic life in his early years. John Turner cites Cassian's *Colationes* 14 and 17 as a source of advice on the importance of selecting spiritual children on account of their need for repentance, rather than out of spiritual or temporal ambition. *Fatherhood*, 1990), 92. See also Rosemary Morris, *Monks and Laymen in Byzantium, 843–1118* (Cambridge: Cambridge University Press, 1995), 95–101 on the sociopolitical aspects of spiritual direction.

40. Alexander Kazhdan, "State, Feudal, and Private Economy in Byzantium," *Dumbarton Oaks Papers* 47 (1993), 83–100, 88.

41. McGuckin, *Practical*, 24, cf. Hunt *Joy-Bearing*, 177.

42. Morris, *Monks*, 78, suggests that the educational impetus within monasteries such as the Studios was a significant factor in spiritual direction. As Alfeyev notes, both elder and younger Symeon were involved in educational activities in their monastic life; the *Vita* notes that Symeon the younger was a fine copyist and organizer of the library. *Vie* 1.2, 5 and 3.27, 39. See also *Vie* 24, 9–27, 9. Alfeyev, *Tradition*, 14.

43. Kazhdan, *State*, 87.

44. See Alice-Mary Talbot, "The Byzantine Family and the Monastery," *Dumbarton Oaks Papers* 44 (1990),119–29.

45. Robert Browning, "Enlightenment and Repression in Byzantium in the Eleventh and Twelfth Centuries," *Past & Present* 69 (November 1975), 7.

46. Krausmüller sees such exclusivity as atypical of Byzantine monastic life. Dirk Krausmüller, "The Monastic Communities of Stoudios and St. Mamas in the Second Half of the Tenth Century," in *The Theotokos Evergetis and Eleventh–Century Monasticism*, ed. Margaret Mullet and Anthony Kirby (Belfast: Belfast Byzantine Texts and Translations 6.1, 1994), 67–85.

47. For example, *Catechesis 7* is titled "On attachment to one's kin." De Catanzaro, *Discourses*, 130–42; see also in *On Faith* the comment about not having worn a hairshirt. *Philokalia* vol 4, 19 = De Catanzaro, *Discourses*, 247. *Catechesis 6 (8)* advises the young monk to become "dead to the world." De Catanzaro, *Discourses*, 127.

48. Note also Deuteronomy 32.7 "Ask your father and he will tell you."

49. Kazhdan, *State*, 88.

50. This common practice is nicely placed in its historical context by Rosemary Morris, "The Political Saint of the Eleventh Century," *Studies Supplementary to Sobornost* 5 (1981), 43–50.

51. *Vie* 1, 8, 15–17. It is the subject of the opening section of the Studite's *Ascetic Discourse*, trans. Alfeyev, 73. Alfeyev explores this in more detail in *Tradition*, 136.

52. *Vie* 2,14–16, 23–27. This aspect of the friction between different models of family is discussed by Talbot, "Byzantine," 126.

53. In common with much of the advice on spiritual parenting, this derives from Climacos's *The Ladder*. This detail is from the section on obedience, Luibheid, 104, and is discussed by Chryssavgis, *Soul Mending*, 53. Chapter six of Turner's book deals in detail with "The Spiritual Father's Qualifications," *Fatherhood*. Symeon's *Sixth Ethical Discourse* mentions the compassion of the spiritual physician who shares the burdens of his child. Golitzin, *Ethical* vol. 2, 73–74.

54. *Catechesis 30*, cited Chryssavgis, *Soul Mending*, 55. Symeon even presents his loyalty to his spiritual father as the quality which engendered mercy. *On Faith*, *Philokalia* vol 4, 23 = *Discourse 22*, De Catanzaro, *Discourses*, 251.

55. Golitzin, *Ethical* vol. 3, 58 and see also Ware in his preface to Hausherr, *Spiritual Direction*, xi-xii.. The *Vie* refers directly to Symeon's reading of the *Ladder*: see *Vie* 1.6, p. 13.

56. *Ladder*, Step 15.56.

57. *Ladder* Step 1.15. This common image is found also in the *Second Ethical Discourse*, Goliztin, *Mystical* vol. 1, 115, where repentance is described as the "saving medicine." This theme is developed by Chryssavgis, *Soul Mending*, 64–65, in connection with contemporary examples of spiritual parenting.

58. *Letter on Confession* 5, Golitzin, *Ethical*, vol. 3, 191.

59. The role of mediator is emphasized by Stithatos, *On the Practice of the Virtues*, *Philokalia* vol. 4, 88. Climacos states that it is more important to please your heavenly father than God because he is your intermediary. See Hannah Hunt, *JoyBearing*, 43, for how Climacos integrates and expands desert teaching on this aspect of spiritual fatherhood.

60. See Eulabes, *Ascetic Discourse* 6, 3–4, SC 460, 78 = *Philokalia* vol. 4, 51. Cf. *Chapter 1, 25* in McGuckin, *Practical*, 39.

61. Hunt, *Joy-Bearing*, 190.

62. *Seventh Ethical Discourse*, Golitzin, *Ethical*, vol. 2, 90. The God-like qualities of the spiritual father are also emphasized in *Discourse 14*, De Catanzaro *Discourses*, 186, *Fourth Ethical Discourse*, Golitzin, *Ethical*, vol.2, 17 and *Hymn 4*, Maloney *Hymns* 22. References in the *Theological and Practical Chapters* include 1.28, McGuckin, *Practical*, 40, and 1.55, McGuckin, *Practical*, 47, and *Seventh Ethical Discourse*, Golitzin, *Ethical*, vol. 2, 95. Stithatos also emphasises this in *Vie* 2.10, 19.

63. *Hymn 18*, Maloney, 79–84, is devoted to an extended image of the spiritual father as a new Moses leading the penitent out of sin just as Moses led the Israelites out of Egypt. The correlation of Egypt and sin is a common and regrettably racist *topos* in patristic writing. In the *Fourth Ethical Discourse*, the same image is found, corroborating the need for the guide to be experienced. Golitzin, *Ethical*, vol. 2, 34.

64. Describing the vision of Eulabes in the light, Symeon says he is "equal to the angels," *Catechesis 22*, De Catanzaro, 246 = *On Faith*, *Philokalia* vol. 4, 18.

65. Passim, *Catechesis 22* = *On Faith*.

66. De Catanzaro, *Discourses*, 245. This seems in conscious imitation of Eulabes, *Ascetic Discourse* 3, ed. Alfeyev, *Ascetic*, 75, = *Philokalia* vol. 4. 53–54, and *Ascetic Discourse* 18, ed. Alfeyev, *Ascetic*, 89 = *Philokalia* vol. 4, 55. Similar material is found in the *Ascetic Discourse* 21, ed. Alfeyev, *Ascetic*, 97 = *Philokalia* vol. 4, 57.

67. *Ladder* Step 1, Luibheid, *Ladder*, 77. *Discourse 10* names the Studite as being among the saints and holy, De Catanzaro, *Discourses*, 163, as does *Chapter 1.30*, McGuckin, *Practical*, 41.

68. See *Discourse 1*, De Catanzaro, *Discourses*, 41–42. Krausmüller's comments about the exclusivity of Symeon's model of imitation suggest it provided scope for undue or inappropriate reverence for the elder. See also *Vie* 2.12, 21.

69. *Discourse 36* (=*Eucharistia 2*), De Catanzaro, *Discourses*, 373.

70. De Catanzaro, *Catecheses*, 123. This quotation from Mt. 13.43 consciously places Eulables in an elevated role. The whole of *Discourse Six* is devoted to "The Example and Spirit of Symeon the Pious" and it abounds in such flowery language; the elder is also compared with Anthony of Egypt and Saint Arsenius, 120 and 121.

71. *Seventh Ethical Discourse*, Golitzin, *Ethical*, vol. 2. This is discussed by Chryssagvis, *Soul Making*, 57, and Turner, *Fatherhood*, 88. See also Golitzin, *Mystical*, vol. 2, 95. Symeon may have gotten this idea from John of Damascus, *On Discrimination* Book II, J. R. Sommerfeldt, (ed.),

Abba: Guides to Wholeness and Holiness East and West (Kalamazoo, MI: Cistercian Publications, 1982), 24. It is also found in Nikiphoros the Monk's *On Watchfulness*, to be found in the *Philokalia* vol. 4, 205; note that Nikiphoros was probably the author of the text on methods of prayer attributed here to Symeon, which suggests some common ground.

72. See *Discourse 20*.

73. Alfeyev notes Symeon's use of these ideas in the *Fifth Ethical Discourse*, in *Tradition*, 119. The *Vie* advocates stability *Vie* 2.11, 21.

74. "On the Inner Nature of Things," 53, *Philokalia* vol. 4, 122. John Chryssavgis cites John the Deacon on this, from the *Life of St. Joseph the Hymnographer* 7 (PG 65– 260), in *Soul Mending*, 106, and it is also explored in Hunt, *Joy-Bearing*, 192, and Krivochéine, *Light*, 87.

75. Hyperechius 8, in Ward, *Sayings*, 239. Eulabes's *Ascetic discourse*, 18, invokes the passage from Philippians and exhorts the monk to obey not only his abbot but all the brothers. Alfeyev, *Ascetic*, 89.

76. Chryssavgis, *Soul Mending*, 52.

77. The whole of Step 4 is devoted to obedience. See Luibhied, *Ladder*, 91–120.

78. Mius 1, Ward, *Sayings*, 150.

79. *Vie*, 12, 1–26, and for a discussion of this see Alfeyev, *Tradition*, 34.

80. Alfeyev cites as evidence of this the fact that he encourages his charges to eat and sleep rather than fostering excessive piety. Hilarion Alfeyev, "St. Symeon the New Theologian, St. Symeon the Pious and the Studite tradition," *Studia Monastica* 36 (1994), 191–92.

81. *Saying* 1, Ward, *Sayings*, 85.

82. Symeon, *Chapter* 1, 61, McGuckin, *Practical*, 48.

83. Maloney, *Hymns*, 22.

84. Jean Gouillard *Syméon le Nouveau Théologien* in *Dictionnaire de théologie catholique* vol. 14.2 (Paris, 1941) 2956.

85. *On Commandments and Doctrines* in *Philokalia* vol. 4, 241, and see also *On Stillness* 8, *Philokalia* vol. 4, 268.

86. Kallistos Ware, "Tradition and Personal Experience in Later Byzantine Theology," *Eastern Churches Review* 3.2 (1970), 135; see also Hannah Hunt, "The Reforming Abbot and His Tears: Penthos in Late Byzantium," in *Spirituality in Late Byzantium*, ed. Eugenia Russell (Cambridge: Cambridge Scholars, 2009), 13–20.

87. Golitzin, *Ethical*, vol. 3, 196 and 199. Rosemary Morris claims that the hegoumenoi in coenobitic monasteries were normally the spiritual directors of the monks, so the issue of choice of a spiritual father was not an issue in this context although it was in the more lavriote systems. *Monks*, 56.

88. Alfeyev, *Tradition*, 16–17. Holl details the frequency of such a practice outside the Studious. *Enthusiasmus*, 316–26.

89. *Letter on Confession*, 14, in Golitzin, *Ethical* vol. 3, 201.

90. See the comment by Maloney on this, in his Introduction to De Catanzaro, *Discourses*, 5.

91. Golitzin here, echoing Stithatos, asserts that the vision of God is the" *sine qua non* of authority in the Church." The quotation from Nicetas's *On the Hierarchy* V. 32, is discussed in detail by Golitzin, who believes that Symeon's *Letter on Confession* was influenced by Dionysius's *Eighth Epistle, To Demophilus*. Golitzin also explores here his belief that the "tension between charisma and institution" will not readily be resolved, a prescient observation in the light of the controversy surrounding Father Theologos and his relationship to Elder Ephraim from 1998 onward. Alexander Golitzin, "Hierarchy versus Anarchy? Dionysius Areopagita, Symeon the New Theologian, Nicetas Stethatos and their common roots in Ascetical Tradition." *St. Vladimir's Theological Quarterly* 38.2 (1994), 131 and 138.

92. De Catanzaro, *Discourses*, 126.

93. Ibid., 198.

94. De Catanzaro, *Discourses* 16(2), 199.

95. With regard to the alleged cult, the mere presence of an *akoulouthia* was not remarkable since this did not indicate whether or not the "saint" was canonized, according to Krivochéine, *Light*, 33, 49, and 62. See also Hunt, *Joy-bearing*, 193.

96. Nicholas Oikonomides, "The Holy Icon as an Asset," *Dumbarton Oaks Papers* 45 (1991) 35.

97. The restorative role of "an intercessor and friend of God" is reiterated throughout the *Letter on Confession*, esp. 5, 7, 9 in Golitzin, *Mystical* vol. 3, 191, 193, 195. Symeon's gratitude for the "intercession of this saint" is expressed in *On Faith*, in *Philokalia* vol. 4, 18 = *Discourse 22* De Catanzaro, 246.

98. *Vie* 11, 98, 137; 12, 108, 151; 13.121–22, 173–75; 13,126, 181–83; 14, 130, 187. AnneMarie Weyl Carr's paper touches on the apparently mischievous power of the icon of Symeon himself, referred to in the *Vie* 15.141–43, 207–11 in her paper "Icons and the Object of Pilgrimage in Middle Byzantine Constantinople," *Dumbarton Oaks Papers* 56 (2002) 83–84.

99. See, for example, Alfeyev, *Tradition*, 139 and 141: seeing Eulabes as a Christ-like figure was a type of iconophylia in the face of a "new iconoclasm." This resonates with Symeon's own attempt to portray his spiritual father as Christ-like, as in *Hymn 15*, line 205: "He possessed Christ completely, and was completely Christ," Maloney, *Hymns*, 56.

100. *Catechesis 18* is on "Worthy and unworthy superiors'\" and *Catechesis 20* is on "The ideal spiritual guide."

101. Turner explored this in his article "St. Symeon the New Theologian: His Place in the History of Spiritual Fatherhood," *Studia Patristica* XXIII (1989), 94, and subsequently his monograph and edition of Symeon's letters give a fuller picture.

102. *Letter on Confession*, 2, Golitzin, *Mystical*, vol. 3, 187.

103. Section 7, Golitzin, *Mystical*, vol. 3, 193.

104. *Fourth Ethical Discourse*, Golitzin, *Mystical*, vol. 2, 36.

105. *Sixth Ethical Discourse*, Golitzin, *Mystical*, vol. 2, 76–78.

106. This explicitly biblical inspiration for the practice is made by Priest Alexey Young, in Priest Alexey Young, *"Understandest thou what thou readest?" The Place and Importance of Spiritual Direction*. Online. Available: http://www.roca.org.OA/142/142p.htm. April 19, 2010.

107. 2000, p. 94.

108. Alice-Mary Talbot, *Family*, 126.

109. Jonah Paffhausen, *5 Good Reasons Not to Visit a Monastery*. Again Magazine (issue not stated). Online. Available: http://kiev-orthodox.org/site/english/722/. April 19, 2010, Paffhausen, *5 Good Reasons*.

110. Brief details of this monastery, founded in 1995, are taken from their website, St. Anthony's Greek Orthodox Monastery. Online. Available: http://www.stanthonysmonastery.org/index.php. April 19, 2010.

111. *Soul Mending*, 124.

112. Ibid., 113. The term is symphonia. See Goliztin, *Mystical*, vol. 3, 13, and 17. Gregory of Nyssa first adopts the term, describing how the Emperor's obedience to God's will results in a "symphonia of earth and heaven." Orat Funebris de Flacilla Imperatrice, PG46.889, cited by John McGuckin, "The Legacy of the 13th Apostle: Origins of the East Christian Conceptions of Church and State Relations," in *The Legacy of Constantine* Exeter, UK:Exeter University Press, 2004/5), 16.

113. *Soul Mending*, 121–23.

114. Chryssavgis, *Soul Mending*, 73.

115. Ironically, it was on an internet site that I read: "The Internet is perhaps the worst vehicle for such gossip. This is nothing other than ecclesiastical pornography. It must be avoided at all costs!" See Paffhausen, *5 Good Reasons*.

116. The text of the conversation between John Pantanizopoulos and Theodore Kalmoukos, a journalist of The National Herald, dated October 27, 1998, is available on http://www.rickross.com/reference/ephraim/ephraim8.html, May 14, 2010.

117. Tucson, Arizona. Video footage of this is listed on an old website as being available as http://www.kvoa.com/Global/story.asp?S=4478931&nav=menu216_1 but this appears to have been deleted from the archive by May 14, 2010.

118. "Orthodox Monasticism is not a cult." Athos in America website. Online. Available: http://www.athosinamerica.org/. April 19, 2010. The details which follow are all from this website.

119. For example, http://www.youtube.com/watch?v=iymYaN6SV2s. May, 14, 2010.

120. At a conference of the Orthodox Christian Laity in 2000, ref. www.monachos.net/forum/showthread.php?2198, accessed May 14, 2010. The same site showed a thread entitled "The Ephraim Question." The response to challenges to spiritual authority from Orthodox clergy, such as Father Irénee (formerly Matthew Steenberg, the founder of monachos.net), is to affirm the role of the spiritual father as an authentic means of obtaining illumination, and to reassure laity that when the time is right a spiritual guide will present himself to them.

Chapter 14

1. *On the Inner Nature of Things*, in *The Philokalia*, ed. and trans. G. E. H. Palmer, Philip Sherrard, and Kallistos Ware (London: Faber, 1979–95), 4:131.

2. E.g., for Clement see Salvatore Lilla, *Clement of Alexandria: A Study in Christian Platonism and Gnosticism* (Oxford: Oxford University Press, 1971), 9–59; John Behr, *Asceticism and Anthropology in Irenaeus and Clement* (Oxford: Oxford University Press, 2000); Ulrich Schneider, *Theologie als christliche Philosophie: Zur Bedeutung des biblischen Botschaft im Denken des Clemens von Alexandria* (Berlin and New York: De Gruyter, 1999); Harry Maier, "Clement of Alexandria and the Care of the Self," *Journal of the American Academy of Religion* 62 (1994): 719–45. For Origen see Mark Edwards, *Origen against Plato* (Aldershot, UK and Burlington, VT: Ashgate, 2002); also his "Christ or Plato? Origen on Revelation and Anthropology," in *Christian Origins: Theology, Rhetoric and Community*, ed. Lewis Ayres and Gareth Jones (London and New York: Routledge, 1998), 11–25. Still quite valuable is Werner Jaeger, *Early Christianity and Greek Paideia* (New York: Oxford University Press, 1961), esp. 46–67.

3. For the principal fragments reporting Stoic theories of the passions, see *The Hellenistic Philosophers*, ed. A. A. Long and David Sedley (Cambridge: Cambridge University Press, 1987), 2:65A-Y (pp. 404–18).

4. On the fine points of Stoic teaching here, see Max Pohlenz, *Die Stoa* (Göttingen: Vandenhoeck & Ruprecht, 1948), 1:90–7; Brad Inwood, *Ethics and Human Action in Early Stoicism* (Oxford: Oxford University Press, 1985), 129–32; and Martha Nussbaum, *The Therapy of Desire: Theory and Practice in Hellenistic Ethics* (Princeton, NJ: Princeton University Press, 1994), 359–401.

5. E.g., Cicero, *Tusculanae disputationes* 3.27.64–65 (LCL 141:302); Ibid. 4.31.65 (LCL 141:402); Seneca, *De ira* 2.2.2; 2.4.1 (LCL 214:168, 174).

6. See Andronicus, *De passionibus* 1, in *Hellenistic Philosophers*, 2:65B (p. 405); Ibid. 6, *Stoicorum veterum fragmenta*, 3:432; Stobaeus 2.90–91, in *Hellenistic Philosophers*, 2:65E (pp. 406–7); cf. Clement of Alexandria, *Paedagogus* 1.13.101, ed. Miroslav Marcovich (Leiden: Brill, 2002), 62–63.

7. See Diogenes Laertius 7.116, *Hellenistic Philosophers*, 2:65F (p. 407); also the analysis of additional sources in Richard Sorabji, *Emotion and Peace of Mind: From Stoic Agitation to Christian Temptation* (Oxford: Oxford University Press, 2000), 47–51. These carefully defined states included joy (χαρά), caution (εὐλάβεια), and salutary wishing (βούλησις), each of which subsumed other feelings also. "Wishing," for example, subsumed affections that Christian writers could certainly have deemed virtuous: good will (εὔνοια) or wishing well on others' behalf; kindness (εὐμένεια), a lasting good will; welcome (ἀσπασμός), an uninterrupted good will; and affection (ἀγάπησις).

8. On these "beginner's" emotions see Sorabji, *Emotion and Peace of Mind*, 51–54.

9. Most influential is Plato's portrait (*Phaedrus* 245C-54E) of the tripartite soul as a chariot, with reason as the charioteer harnessing the two horses of the desiring (ἐπιθυμητικόν) and irascible (θυμικόν) functions. Cf. *Rep.* 435B–45B, considering the tripartite soul precisely in the context of the cardinal virtues.

10. Cf. *Symposium* 188D; 205E–12B; *Phaedrus* 249D–52B.

11. Posidonius, frag. 34, in Galen, *De placitis Hippocratis et Platonis* 4.3.2–5, in *Hellenistic Philosophers*, 2:65K (p. 410).

12. *Stromateis* 2.13.59 (GCS 15:145).

13. Ibid., 6.16.135 (GCS 15:500). See also Lilla, *Clement of Alexandria*, 85–86; Behr, *Asceticism and Anthropology in Irenaeus and Clement*, 146–48.

14. For exposition of the relevant texts, see Kamala Parel, "The Disease of the Passions in Clement of Alexandria," in *Studia Patristica* 36, ed. M. F. Wiles and E. J. Yarnold (Leuven: Peeters, 2001), 449–55.

15. On Origen's treatment of the προπάθειαι, see Richard Layton, "*Propatheia*: Origen and Didymus on the Origin of the Passions," *Vigiliae Christianae* 54 (2000): 262–71; on Didymus's treatment, Ibid., 271–81. See also Layton's *Didymus the Blind and His Circle in Late-Antique Alexandria* (Urbana and Chicago: University of Illinois Press, 2004), 114–34.

16. Origen, *Comm. in Matt.* Ser. 92 (GCS 38:205f); also Didymus, *Comm. in Psalmos* (Toura fragments), ed. Michael Gronewald et al., *Psalmenkommentar*, 5 volumes, Papyrologische Texte und Abhandlungen 4–7, 12 (Bonn: Habelt, 1968–70), 293,6–12; Jerome, *Comm. in Matt.* 4.26.38–39 (PL 26:197–98); *Tract. in Psalmos* 108 (CCSL 221:366). See also Layton, *Didymus the Blind and His Circle*, 121–27.

17. *De principiis* 3.2.2 (SC 268:158–62); Ibid. 3.2.4 (SC 268:168–74). See also Sorabji (*Emotion and Peace of Mind*, 346–51) on the comparison here with the Stoic doctrine of προπάθειαι.

18. *Comm. in Ps.*, ed. Michael Gronewald et al., 41,26–42,6; 43,16–20; 263,4–12. See also Layton, "Origen and Didymus on the Origin of the Passions," 274–75; David Brakke, *Demons and the Making of the Monk: Spiritual Combat in Early Christianity* (Cambridge, MA: Harvard University Press, 2006), 54–56.

19. Sorabji (*Emotion and Peace of Mind*, 144–68, 211–27) identifies some examples.

20. *Paed.* 1.12.99–100 (ed. Marcovich, 61,21–62,2). Translation is my own.

21. E.g., the practice of disciplined laughter or even smiling in settings where souls are prone to lose control and lapse into sheer foolery (*Paed.* 2.5.45–48, ed. Marcovich, 96–98); or austere demeanor in the use of public baths where stray lusts run wild (Ibid., 3.5.31–33, ed. Marcovich, 166–68).

22. E.g., *Strom.* 6.13.105 (GCS 15:484–85); Ibid., 7.14.84–88 (GCS 17:60–63); cf. Origen, *Comm. in Matt.* 15.16–17 (GCS 40:395–99). See also Lilla, *Clement of Alexandria*, 106–17; Simo Knuuttila, *Emotions in Ancient and Medieval Philosophy* (Oxford: Oxford University Press, 2004), 113–27; and Róbert Somos, "Origen, Evagrius Ponticus, and the Ideal of Impassibility," in *Origeniana Septima*, ed. Wolfgang Bienert and Uwe Kühneweg (Leuven: Peeters, 1999), 365–73.

23. See the excellent study of Harry Maier, "Clement of Alexandria and the Care of the Self," 719–45, with abundant citations of exemplary texts in Clement.

24. *Strom.* 4.18.117 (GCS 15:300,1–4); cf. Ibid., 2.20.119 (GCS 15:177–78). See also David Hunter, "The Language of Desire: Clement of Alexandria's Transformation of Ascetic Discourse," *Semeia* 57(1992): 99–107.

25. On Aristotle's conception of intellectually educated emotions serviceable for virtue, see Nussbaum, *The Therapy of Desire*, 78–101.

26. *Strom.* 2.8.39 (GCS 15:133–34); Ibid., 2.12.53 (GCS 15:142); *Paed.* 1.9.87 (ed. Marcovich, 53,24–32). On fear in the context of Clement's understanding of spiritual progress, see Piotr Ashwin-Siejowski, *Clement of Alexandria: A Project of Christian Perfection*, (London: T & T clark, 2008), 68–78.

27. See Sorabji, *Emotion and Peace of Mind*, 235, citing Seneca, *Ep.* 101.10; *De beneficiis* 7.2.4–6.

28. *Quaestiones in Genesin* 1.79 (LCL 380:49).

29. *Paed.* 1.6.38 (ed. Marcovich, 25,12–14); cf. *Strom.* 2.12.53 (GCS 15:141–42).

30. *Strom.* 6.9.71 (GCS 15:467,15–20).

31. See Christian Gnilka, *XPHEIE: Die Methode der Kirchenväter im Umgang mit der antiken Kultur* (Basel: Schwabe, 1984), 65–79.

32. *Hom. adversus eos qui irascunter* 5 (PG 31:365C-D); similarly on good use of "hatred," see *Hom. in Psalmos* 44.8 (PG 29:405B).

33. *De virginitate* 18 (GNO 8.1:317–19); *De anima et resurrectione* (PG 46:61B, 65B–68A, 88D-89A); *De mortuis* (GNO 9.1:61).

34. *De hominis opificio* 18 (PG 44:193B-C).

35. On *eros* in Origen and Gregory of Nyssa, see Catherine Osborne, *Eros Unveiled: Plato and the God of Love* (Oxford: Oxford University Pres, 1996), 52–85; Martin Laird, "The Fountain of His Lips: Desire and Divine Union in Gregory of Nyssa's *Homilies on the Song of Songs*," *Spiritus* 7 (2007): 40–57.

36. On human passibility in the theological anthropology of Gregory of Nyssa and Maximus, see Panayiotis Nellas, *Deification in Christ: The Nature of the Human Person*, trans. Norman Russell (Crestwood, NY: St. Vladimir's Seminary Press); Hans Urs von Balthasar, *Presence and Thought: An Essay on the Religious Philosophy of Gregory of Nyssa*, trans. Marc Sebanc (San Francisco: Ignatius Press, 1995), 71–119; J. Warren Smith, *Passion and Paradise: Human and Divine Emotion in the Thought of Gregory of Nyssa* (New York: Crossroad—Herder & Herder, 2004); Morwenna Ludlow, *Gregory of Nyssa: Ancient and (Post)modern* (Oxford: Oxford University Press, 2007), 166–81; Lars Thunberg, *Microcosm and Mediator: The Theological Anthropology of Maximus the Confessor*, 2nd ed. (Chicago: Open Court, 1995), esp. 231–330; Hans Urs von Balthasar, *Cosmic Liturgy: The Universe according to Maximus the Confessor*, trans. Brian Daley (San Francisco: Ignatius Press, 2003), 179–205; Paul Blowers, "Gentiles of the Soul," maximus the confessor on the sub-structure and transformation of Human Passions, "Journal of Early christian studies 4(1994): 57–85.

37. *hom. opif.* 17 (PG 44:189B–192A).

38. Cf. *anima et res.* (PG 46:148C–149A); *Oratio catechetica* 8 (PG 45:33B-D); *mort.* (GNO 9.1:53,9–56,7). For a superb analysis of the "garments of skins," see Nellas, *Deification in Christ*, 43–91.

39. Cf. *virg.* 12 (GNO 8.1:297–300, 301–2); *De vita Moysis* II(GNO 7.1:62–63); *mort.* (GNO 9.1:55); *anima et res.* (PG 46:53C–68A).

40. On this salient theme in Nyssen's anthropology, see von Balthasar, *Presence and Thought*, 111–19.

41. *V. Moysis* II (GNO 7.1:34); cf. *mort.* (GNO 9.1:55,23–56,7; 58,7–8) on free will (προ-αίρεσις) as the "demiurge" of the passions, able to fashion them but also to direct the passible nature toward vice or virtue.

42. Von Balthasar, *Presence and Thought*, 116–18, citing *mort.* (GNO 9:29); *De instituto christiano* (GNO 8.1:40); *Hom. in orationem dominicam* 5 (GNO 7.2:59); and *Hom. de beatitudinibus* 7 (GNO 7.2:151).

43. Rowan Williams, *The Wound of Knowledge: Christian Spirituality from the New Testament to Saint John of the Cross*, 2nd ed. (Cambridge, MA: Cowley Publications, 1990), 66–67, 73.

44. See *mort.* (GNO 9.1:61); also the in-depth analysis of other relevant texts of Gregory in Smith, *Passion and Paradise*, 183–227.

45. *Ambiguorum liber* 7 (PG 91:1072B, 1073B-C).

46. *Qu. Thal.* 61 (CCSG 22:85–7); Ibid. 1 (CCSG 7:47). See also Blowers, "Gentiles of the Soul," 66–71; von Balthasar, *Cosmic Liturgy*, 185–96; and Claire-Agnès Zirnheld, "Le double visage de la passion: malédiction due au péché et/ou dynamisme de la vie: *Quaestiones ad Thalassium* XXI, XXII et XLII," in, *Philohistôr: Miscellanea in honorem Caroli Laga septuagenarii*, ed. A. Schoors and P. van Deun (Leuven: Peeters Press, 1994), 361–80.

47. *Qu. Thal.* 1 (CCSG 7:47–49). Translation here from Paul Blowers and Robert Wilken, *On the Cosmic Mystery of Jesus Christ*, Popular Patristics series (Crestwood, NY: St. Vladimir's Seminary Press, 2003), 98. Cf. also *Amb.* 6 (PG 91:1068A); *Qu. Thal.* 55 (CCSG 7:499); *Ep.* 2 (PG 91:397B); *Centuries on Love* 2.48 (PG 90:1000C-D), *Philokalia* 2:73; *Centuries of Various Texts* 1.60, 65, 66, *Philokalia* 2:177, 178, 179.

48. *Qu. Thal.* 61 (CCSG 22:85); cf. *Amb.* 42 (PG 91:1321B).

49. Cf. *Amb.* 7 (PG 91:1089B); *Opuscula theologica et polemica* 1 (PG 91:9A); cf. Gregory of Nyssa, *v. Moysis* I (GNO 7.1:4).

50. *Expositio orationis dominicae (Commentary on the Lord's Prayer)* (CCSG 23:58), *Philokalia* 2:298.

51. *Qu. Thal.* 22 (CCSG 7:139–41).

52. See Blowers, "Gentiles of the Soul," esp. 79–85.

53. Cf. Gregory of Nyssa, *Contra Eunomium* VI (PG 45:721B-D); *Or. catech.* 13; 15–16; 27 (PG 45:45A-D; 47A–52D; 69C–71D); Maximus, *Qu. Thal.* 21 (CCSG 7:127–33); Ibid., 42 (CCSG 7:285–89); *Amb.* 2–4 (CCSG 48:8–18).

54. Maximus, *Qu. Thal.* 62 (CCSG 22:129); cf. *Amb.* 4 (CCSG 48:13–18).

55. Maximus, *Amb.* 42 (PG 91:1316C–1321B, 1345A, 1348B–1349A).

56. Maximus, *Disputatio cum Pyrrho* (PG 91:297B); cf. *Opusc.* 7 (PG 91:80D); *Commentary on the Lord's Prayer* (CCSG 23:34–35), *Philokalia* 2:288.

57. Maximus, *Qu. Thal.* 42 (CCSG 7:285).

58. For an excellent overview of the Evagrian doctrine of λογισμοί, see Columba Stewart, "Evagrius Ponticus and the 'Eight Generic *Logismoi*,'" in *In the Garden of Evil: The Vices and Culture in the Middle Ages*, ed. Richard Newhauser (Toronto: Pontifical Institute of Medieval Studies, 2005), 3–34.

59. See *Texts on Discrimination* (Περὶ λογισμῶν), *Philokalia* 1:38–52. On the doctrinal background of this text see Antoine Guillamont's Introduction to *Évagre le Pontique: Sur Les Pensées*, SC 438 (Paris: Cerf, 1998), 9–33.

60. These have been helpfully outlined and defined by Palmer, Ware, and Sherrard in the Glossary appended to each of the four volumes of the English *Philokalia*, s.v. "Temptation."

61. Cf. John Cassian, *On the Holy Fathers of Sketis* (=*Conference* 1.16–17, CSEL 13:26–27), *Philokalia* 1:97–98; Mark the Monk, *On the Spiritual Law* 138–41, 151, 175 (=139–42, 152, 176 in SC 445:110–12, 114, 120), *Philokalia* 1:119–20, 122; *Letter to Nicolas the Solitary* (SC 455:130), *Philokalia* 1:153; Hesychius, *On Watchfulness and Holiness* 2, 14, 43–46, 88, 121, 142–43, *Philokalia* 1:162, 164, 169–71, 177, 183, 186–87; Peter Damascene, *A Treasury of Divine Knowledge*, *Philokalia* 3:207–10; also Nicetas Stethatos, *On the Practice of the Virtues* 78, *Philokalia* 4:100, citing Jesus's statement that "temptations" (σκάνδαλα) are inevitable (Matt. 18:7).

62. *On the Virtues and Vices* (PG 95:93A-C), *Philokalia* 2:338 (emphasis added).

63. *No Righteousness by Works* 190 (=178 in SC 445:186), *Philokalia* 1:142.

64. *Texts on Discrimination* 7 (=8 in SC 438:176–78), *Philokalia* 1:42–43; expanded on by Peter Damascene, *Treasury*, *Philokalia* 3:134. Cf. Gregory of Sinai (*On Commandments and Doctrines* 69, *Philokalia* 4:224), who classifies thoughts as "material," "demonic," "natural," and "supernatural."

65. *Texts on Discrimination* 7 (=8 in SC 438:176–78), *Philokalia* 1:42; Ibid., 31 (SC 438:260–62); also Peter Damascene, *Treasury*, *Philokalia* 3:135–36. Cf. also Maximus, *Centuries on Love* 2.32 (PG 90:993D–996A), *Philokalia* 2:71.

66. *Texts on Discrimination* 6 (=7 in SC 438:174–6), *Philokalia* 1:42.

67. *Treasury*, *Philokalia* 3:135, 138–39; cf. Maximus, *Centuries on Love* 4.58 (PG 90:1061A), *Philokalia* 2:197; Hesychius, *On Watchfulness and Holiness* 67, *Philokalia* 1:174; Nicetas Stethatos, *On the Practice of the Virtues* 42, *Philokalia* 4:90.

68. See Evagrius, *Texts on Discrimination* 16 (=17 in SC 438:208–12), *Philokalia* 1:48; also his attack on mental images as undermining "pure prayer" in his *On Prayer* 4, 10, 47, 54, 55, 57, 62, 67, 70, 71, 72, *Philokalia* 1:57–58, 61, 62–63, 63–64; cf. Maximus, *Centuries on Love* 3.49 (PG 90:1032B), *Philokalia* 2:90. On νοήματα and their relation to λογισμοί in Evagrius, see Columba Stewart, "Imageless Prayer and the Theological Vision of Evagrius Ponticus," *Journal of Early Christian Studies* 9 (2001): 186–91. Stewart translates νοήματα "depictions," given their strongly visual power within the mind.

69. See Maximus, *Centuries on Love* 2.15; 2.17; 2.73; 3.1; 3.40–43; 4.66 (PG 90:988C-D; 989A-B; 1008A-B; 1017B; 1064B), *Philokalia* 2:67–68, 77, 61, 66–67, 83. See also Gnilka (*XPHEIE: Die Methode der Kirchenväter*, 96), who notes Maximus's unique appropriation here of the Stoic principle of χρῆσις.

70. Cf. Maximus, *Centuries on Love* 2.17; 2.73; 2.78; 3.3; 3.86 (PG 90:989A-B; 1008A-B; 1009A; 1017C; 1044B), *Philokalia* 2:67–68, 77, 78, 83, 97; *Centuries of Various Texts* 1.31; 3.87, *Philokalia* 2:171, 232; Gregory of Sinai, *On Commandments and Doctrines* 75, *Philokalia* 4:225.

71. *On Commandments and Doctrines* 82, *Philokalia* 4:228; cf. Ps-Macarius, *Hom.* 6.142, *Philokalia* 3:349.

72. E.g., Hesychius, *On Watchfulness and Holiness*, passim, *Philokalia* 1:163–97; Diadochus of Photike, *On Spiritual Knowledge and Discrimination* 59, 61, *Philokalia* 1:270–72; Philotheos of Sinai, *Texts on Watchfulness* 2, *Philokalia* 3:16; Gregory of Sinai, *On Prayer* 4, *Philokalia* 4:277; Theoliptus of Philadelphia, *Texts* 1–2, *Philokalia* 4:188–89. Theoliptus also speaks of prayer invoking the divine name that "assimilates the tripartite soul to the one God in three hypostases" (*On Inner Work in Christ and the Monastic Profession*, *Philokalia* 4:183).

73. See, e.g., Mark the Monk, *Letter to Nicolas the Solitary* (SC 455:136–42), *Philokalia* 1:155–57; Peter Damascene, *Discourse* 9, *Philokalia* 3:234–39.

74. Nicetas Stethatos, *On the Inner Nature of Things* 50, *Philokalia* 4:121; cf. Hesychius, *On Watchfulness and Holiness* 91, *Philokalia* 1:177–78.

75. *To the Most Reverend Nun Xenia* 29, *Philokalia* 4:304; cf. Maximus, *Centuries on Theology* 2.66 (PG 90:1153B), *Philokalia* 2:153.

76. Peter Damascene, *Discourse* 16, *Philokalia* 3:255; cf. Theodoros, *A Century of Spiritual Texts* 23–24, *Philokalia* 2:18–19; Maximus, *Centuries of Various Texts* 2.25, *Philokalia* 2:193.

77. *Texts on Discrimination* 5; 15–16 (=5; 16–17 in SC 438:166–70, 206–8), *Philokalia* 1:40–41, 47–48; cf. John Cassian, *On the Eight Vices* (from *Institutes* 8, CSEL 17:149–65), *Philokalia* 1:82–87. On the dynamics of anger in Evagrius, see Gabriel Bunge, *Dragon's Wine and Angel's Bread: The Teaching of Evagrius Ponticus on Anger and Meekness* (Crestwood,

NY: St. Vladimir's Seminary Press, 2009); and on anger's spiritual utility, see Daniel Dombrowski, "Anger in the *Philokalia*," *Mystics Quarterly* 24 (1998): 101–18.

78. Isaiah the Solitary, *On Guarding the Intellect* 1, 25, *Philokalia* 1:22, 27; Hesychius, *On Watchfulness and Holiness* 30, 34, 126, *Philokalia* 1:167, 168, 184; Diadochus, *On Spiritual Knowledge and Discrimination* 6, 10, 62, 91, *Philokalia* 1:254, 255, 272, 289–90; Peter Damascene, *Discourse* 15, *Philokalia* 3:253; Nicetas Stethatos, *On the Practice of the Virtues* 16–17, *Philokalia* 4:83; Gregory Palamas, *In Defense of Those Who Devoutly Practise a Life of Stillness* 2, *Philokalia* 4:333.

79. *Centuries of Various Texts* 3.54, *Philokalia* 2:223 (emphasis added). Cf. also Gregory Palamas, *Triads* 2.2.19, ed. John Meyendorff, *Défense des saints hésychastes*, 2nd ed. (Leuven: Spicilegium sacrum Lovaniense, 1973), 361–63.

80. Nicetas Stethatos, *On the Inner Nature of Things* 93, *Philokalia* 4:135.

81. *Centuries on Love* 2.48 (PG 90:1000C-D), *Philokalia* 2:73; *Centuries of Various Texts* 2.74; 3.56, *Philokalia* 2:203, 224; *Comm. on the Lord's Prayer* (CCSG 23:58), *Philokalia* 2:298.

82. Mark the Monk, *Letter to Nicolas the Solitary* (SC 455:126), *Philokalia* 1:152; Ps-Macarius, *Hom.* 4.70, *Philokalia* 3:315; Theodore the Great Ascetic, *Theoretikon*, *Philokalia* 2:43; Nicetas Stethatos, *On Spiritual Knowledge* 37, 53, *Philokalia* 4:149, 155.

83. Cf. Diadochus, *On Spiritual Knowledge and Discrimination* 14, 15, 92, *Philokalia* 1:256–57, 290; Maximus, *Centuries on Love* 1.13; 1.16; 1.23–28; 1.53; 1.61, 1.71; 2.8–10; 2.59–60; 3.8; 3.56–57 (PG 90:964B-D; 965A-C; 972A; 973A; 976B-C; 985C–988A; 1004B-C; 1020A; 1033B-C), *Philokalia* 2:54, 55, 58, 59, 60, 66, 75, 84, 92. On this spiritual sociology see Lars Thunberg, *Man and the Cosmos: The Vision of St. Maximus the Confessor* (Crestwood, NY: St. Vladimir's Seminary Press, 1985), 93–112.

84. Cf. Hesychius, *On Watchfulness and Holiness* 201, *Philokalia* 1:198; Maximus, *Centuries of Various Texts* 3.56, *Philokalia* 2:224; Nicetas Stethatos, *On Spiritual Knowledge* 37–38, *Philokalia* 3:149–50; Gregory of Sinai, *On Commandments and Doctrines* 118, *Philokalia* 4:240.

85. *On Spiritual Knowledge and Discrimination* 14, 33–34, *Philokalia* 1:256, 262–63; cf. Nicetas Stethatos, *On Spiritual Knowledge* 38, *Philokalia* 4:149.

86. *Hom.* 16, cited by Peter Damascene, *Treasury*, *Philokalia* 3:175; cf. Ps-Macarius, *Hom.* 5.92–93, *Philokalia* 3:326, noting that ecstasy must not allow the monk to shirk his responsibility to fellow ascetics.

87. Cf. Philotheos of Sinai, *Texts on Watchfulness* 1–2, *Philokalia* 3:16–17; Peter Damascene, *Treasury*, *Philokalia* 3:122–23; Gregory of Sinai, *Further Texts* 1–3, *Philokalia* 4:253. Gregory Palamas ascertains that the rapt ascetic must become "another angel of God on earth" in bearing witness to divine transformative grace (*To the Most Reverend Nun Xenia* 58, *Philokalia* 4:316–17).

88. Gregory of Sinai, *On Commandments and Doctrines* 58–59, *Philokalia* 4:222. He recalls Gregory of Nyssa's (and Philo's) celebrated image of the soul's "sober inebriation" under the influence of divine love (cf. *Hom. in Cant.* 10, GNO 6:308–11).

89. *Conference* 11.11–13 (CSEL 13:325–30), not included in the *Philokalia*.

90. *On Spiritual Knowledge and Discrimination* 16–17, *Philokalia* 1:257–58; cf. Nicetas Stethatos, *On the Practice of the Virtues* 56, *Philokalia* 4:93.

91. *Theoretikon*, *Philokalia* 2:43.

92. Cf. Maximus, *Centuries on Love* 2.81–82 (PG 90:1009B-C), *Philokalia* 2:62; *Comm. on the Lord's Prayer* (CCSG 23:28), *Philokalia* 2:285; *Centuries of Various Texts* 1.69–70, *Philokalia* 2:179–80; *Qu. Thal.* 10 (CCSG 7:83–87); Theodore, *Century of Spiritual Texts* 100, *Philokalia* 2:36–37; Peter Damascene, *Discourse* 3, *Philokalia* 3:216–18. Beyond the *Philokalia*, see also Dorotheus of Gaza, *Didaskaliai* 4.47–49 (SC 92:220–24).

93. *On the Inner Nature of Things* 48, *Philokalia* 4:120.

94. See, e.g., *Strom.* 2.9.45 (GCS 15:136,23–26); Ibid., 2.18.80 (GCS 15:154,24–155,12); also Lilla, *Clement of Alexandria*, 83–84.

95. See Hannah Hunt, *Joy-Bearing Grief: Tears of Contrition and Compunction in the Writings of the East Syrian and Byzantine Fathers* (Leiden: Brill, 2004); also Irénée Hausherr, *Penthos: The Doctrine of Compunction in the Christian East*, trans. Anselm Hufstader (Kalamazoo, MI: Cistercian Publications, 1982); Douglas Burton-Christie, "Evagrius on Sadness," *Cistercian Studies Quarterly* 44 (2009): 395–411.

96. *Scala Paradisi* 7 (PG 88:804B). On Climacus's highly developed and influential "theology of tears," see John Chryssavgis, *John Climacus: From the Egyptian Desert to the Sinaite Mountain* (Aldershot, UK and Burlington, VT: Ashgate, 2004), 131–62; and Hunt, *Joy-Bearing Grief*, 65–93.

97. John Cassian, *On the Eight Vices* (excerpted from *Institutes* 9, CSEL 17:166–71), *Philokalia* 1:87–88; cf. Nicetas Stethatos, *On the Practice of the Virtues* 60, *Philokalia* 4:94–95; Gregory Palamas, *To the Most Reverend Nun Xenia*, 47–56, *Philokalia* 4:312–16. See also Gregory of Nyssa, *De mortuis.* (GNO 9.1:67,5–27).

98. See, e.g., Evagrius, *On Prayer* 78, *Philokalia* 1:64. On *penthos* and tears in Evagrius, see also Jeremy Driscoll, *Steps to Spiritual Perfection: Studies on Spiritual Progress in Evagrius* (New York: Newman Press), 51–65. For Cassian's perspective, see Columba Stewart, *Cassian the Monk* (Oxford: Oxford University Press, 1998), 122–29.

99. On the two kinds of tears (contrite and jubilant), see, e.g., Peter Damascene, *Treasury*, *Philokalia* 3:98–99, 121; *Discourses* 8 and 9, *Philokalia* 3:231, 235; *Discourse* 24, *Philokalia* 3:273; Ps-Macarius, *Hom.* 5, *Philokalia* 3:326–27; Symeon the New Theologian, *Practical and Theological Texts* 67, 69, *Philokalia* 4:38–39; Nicetas Stethatos, *On the Practice of the Virtues* 64–65, 69, *Philokalia* 4:96, 97; Gregory Palamas, *To the Most Reverend Nun Xenia*, *Philokalia* 4:315. On these and other nuances of the penitential emotions, see Hunt, *Joy-Bearing Grief*, 3–9; Kallistos Ware, "The Orthodox Experience of Repentance," in *The Inner Kingdom*, Collected Works 1 (Crestwood, NY: St. Vladimir's Seminary Press, 2000), 55–57; Chryssavgis, *John Climacus*, 144–52.

100. See Peter Damascene, *Treasury*, *Philokalia* 3:109–11.

101. Cf. Theodore, *Century* 57, *Philokalia* 2:25; Theognostus, *On the Practice of the Virtues* 48, *Philokalia* 2:370; Peter Damascene, *Treasury*, *Philokalia* 3:119; Nicetas Stethatos, *On the Inner Nature of Things* 50, *Philokalia* 4:120–21.

102. Ps-Macarius, *Hom.* 5.89, *Philokalia* 3:324.

103. Nicetas Stethatos, *On the Inner Nature of Things* 44–46, *Philokalia* 4:119.

104. Gregory of Sinai, *On the Signs of Grace and Delusion* 4–5, *Philokalia* 4:259–60.

105. Diadochus, *On Spiritual Knowledge and Discrimination* 60, *Philokalia* 1:271; cf. Peter Damascene, *Discourse* 22, *Philokalia* 3:260–63.

106. *Texts for the Monks in India* 85, *Philokalia* 1:318.

107. *No Righteousness by Works* 40 (=39 in SC 445:142), *Philokalia* 1:129.

108. Peter Damascene, *Discourse* 6, *Philokalia* 3:224–27.

109. *On Spiritual Knowledge and Discrimination* 69, *Philokalia* 1:276.

110. *Mystagogia* 8 (PG 91:688C). By "Passion" Maximus means the whole incarnational economy climaxing in Christ's redemptive suffering and death. Cf. also *Amb.* 4 (CCSG 48:15, 58–17, 90).

111. "*Apatheia* and Purity of Heart in Evagrius Ponticus," in *Early Ascetic and Monastic Literature: Essays in Honor of Juana Raasch, O.S.B.*, eds. Harriet Luckman and Linda Kulzer, *Purity of Heart* (Collegeville, MN: Liturgical Press, 1999), 141–59, citing texts from the *Practicus*, *Scholia on Proverbs*, and *Ad Monachos*. This essay is reprinted in Driscoll's *Steps to Spiritual Perfection*, 76–93.

112. *On Prayer* 53–55, *Philokalia* 1:62

113. See, e.g., *On the Holy Fathers of Sketis*, *Philokalia* 1:95, 96, 104. But for his larger conception of purity of heart, see Stewart, *Cassian the Monk*, esp. 42–47, 55–57.

114. *On Watchfulness and Holiness* 67, 109, 113, *Philokalia* 1:174, 181. See similarly Symeon the New Theologian, *Practical and Theological Texts* 73, *Philokalia* 4:39–40. Cf. also Theodore, who equates *apatheia* and purity of heart (*A Century of Spiritual Texts* 25, 66, *Philokalia* 2:19, 27).

115. *Discourse* 14, *Philokalia* 3:252.

116. On *apatheia* as a process and instrumentality, see, e.g., Peter Damascene, *Treasury*, *Philokalia* 3:147–50; *Discourse* 14, *Philokalia* 3:251–53; Nicetas Stethatos, *On the Practice of the Virtues* 41–45, 89–92, *Philokalia* 4:89–90, 103–4. On the indwelling Logos's aid in this process, see Nicetas, *On the Inner Nature of Things* 96–99, *Philokalia* 4:135–37.

117. Cf. Isaiah the Solitary, *On Guarding the Intellect* 14, *Philokalia* 1:25; Diadochus, *On Spiritual Knowledge and Discrimination* 98, *Philokalia* 1:294; Peter Damascene, *Discourse* 14, *Philokalia* 3:251–52.

118. Maximus, *Centuries on Love* 2.34 (PG 90:996B-C), *Philokalia* 2:71; *Centuries on Theology* 2.72 (PG 90:1157A-B), *Philokalia* 2:155; *Centuries of Various Texts* 1.17; 2.58; 2.99, *Philokalia* 2:169, 199, 208.

119. *No Righteousness by Works* 132 (=123 in SC 445:166), *Philokalia* 1:136.

120. E.g., Isaiah the Solitary, *On Guarding the Intellect* 25, *Philokalia* 1:27; Maximus, *Centuries on Love* 1.2; 1.81; 4.91 (PG 90:961B, 977C-D, 1069C-D), *Philokalia* 2:53, 62, 112; Theodore, *A Century of Spiritual Texts* 47, *Philokalia* 2:22–23.

121. E.g., Diadochus, *On Spiritual Knowledge and Discrimination* 89, *Philokalia* 1:288.

122. *Centuries on Love* 2.30 (PG 90:993B), *Philokalia* 2:70.

123. Nicetas Stethatos, *On the Practice of the Virtues* 90, *Philokalia* 4:103.

124. *The Destiny of Man*, trans. Natalie Duddington (New York: Harper & Row, 1960), 187–88.

125. *Centuries on Love* 3.67 (PG 90:1037A-B), *Philokalia* 2:93.

■ Chapter 15

1. *Philokalia* 1: 73–94.

2. *Philokalia* 1: 231 and 234 respectively. See also p. 247, where Neilos refers to possessions as a "source of disease" because they "give rise to all the passions."

3. Paras 46 and 75 respectively (*Philokalia* 1: 308 and 316 respectively). Later he also refers to garrulity as a disease (para 90, see p. 320).

4. Paras 97 and 158 respectively (*Philokalia* 1: 344 and 353 respectively).

5. Para 89 (*Philokalia* 2: 318), cf para 44 (p. 328).

6. *A Discourse on Abba Philimon*, author unknown (*Philokalia* 2: 349).

7. Para 68 (*Philokalia* 2: 375).

8. Para 32 (*Philokalia* 3: 37).

9. Para 72 (*Philokalia* 3: 317).

10. Paras 22, 11, and 55 respectively (*Philokalia* 4: 113, 110, and 122 respectively).

11. Para 41 (*Philokalia* 4: 309).

12. It is also the case, of course, that the passions are associated with pleasure. However, this is understood as inevitably being associated with pain. For example, Maximos argues this in *Various Texts on Theology, the Divine Economy and Virtue and Vice* (e.g., *Philokalia* 2: 175), where he also refers to a "Pleasure-pain syndrome" (2: 246).

13. See, for example, the account by Theodorus, *Philokalia* 2: 15. The notion of the passions as "contrary to nature" is widely encountered in the texts of the *Philokalia*.

14. E.g., *Philokalia* 2: 197.

15. Evagrios, in *Texts on Discrimination in Respect of Passions and Thoughts*, para 15 (*Philokalia* 1: 47).

16. Diadochus of Photiki, in *On Spiritual Knowledge and Discrimination*, para 17 (*Philokalia* 1: 258).

17. John of Karpathos, in *Ascetic Discourse Sent at the Request of the Same Monks in India* (*Philokalia* 1: 325).

18. Philotheos of Sinai, in *Forty Texts on Watchfulness*, para 14 (*Philokalia* 3: 20).

19. Ilias the Presbyter, in Part I of *A Gnomic Anthology*, para 32 (*Philokalia* 3: 37).

20. Nikitas Stithatos, in *On the Practice of the Virtues*, para 75 (*Philokalia* 4: 99).

21. Mark the Ascetic, in his *Letter to Nicolas the Solitary* (*Philokalia* 1: 157); Evagrios, in *Texts on Discrimination in Respect of Passions and Thoughts*, para 13 (*Philokalia* 1: 46); John of Karpathos, in *For the Encouragement of the Monks in India who had Written to Him*, para 37 (*Philokalia* 1: 320); Philotheos of Sinai, in *Forty Texts on Watchfulness*, para 2 (*Philokalia* 3: 16); Gregory Palamas, in *To the Most Reverend Nun Xenia*, para 42 (*Philokalia* 4:310).

22. John Cassian, in *On the Holy Fathers of Sketis and on Discrimination* (*Philokalia* 1: 105), John of Karpathos, in *For the Encouragement of the Monks in India who had Written to Him*, para 37 (*Philokalia* 1: 306), Symeon Metaphrastis, in his *Paraphrase of the Homilies of St. Makarios of Egypt*, para 72 (*Philokalia* 3: 317).

23. Maximos the Confessor, in the third century of *Four Hundred Texts on Love*, para 82 (*Philokalia* 2: 96), Gregory Palamas, in *To the Most Reverend Nun Xenia*, para 42 (*Philokalia* 4: 310).

24. John of Karpathos, in *Ascetic Discourse sent at the Request of the Same Monks in India* (*Philokalia* 1: 325); Maximos the Confessor, in the first century of *Various Texts on Theology, the Divine Economy, and Virtue and Vice*, para 14 (*Philokalia* 2: 168); Peter of Damaskos, in Book I of *A Treasury of Divine Knowledge* (*Philokalia* 3:95).

25. Maximos the Confessor, in the third century of *Various Texts on Theology, the Divine Economy, and Virtue and Vice*, para 36 (*Philokalia* 2: 218).

26. Ilias the Presbyter, in Part I of *A Gnomic Anthology*, para 30 (*Philokalia* 3: 37).

27. Maximos the Confessor, in the first century of *Four Hundred Texts on Love*, para 79 (*Philokalia* 2: 61).

28. Maximos the Confessor, in the second century of *Various Texts on Theology, the Divine Economy, and Virtue and Vice*, para 23 (*Philokalia* 2: 192).

29. Gregory of Sinai, in *On Commandments and Doctrines, Warnings and Promises; On Thoughts, Passions and Virtues, and also on Stillness and Prayer*, para 132 (*Philokalia* 4: 250).

30. Gregory Palamas, in *To the Most Reverend Nun Xenia*, para 36 (*Philokalia* 4: 307).

31. Specifically: The author(s) of the text attributed to Antony the Great, Theodorus the Great Ascetic, Maximos the Confessor, Thalassios the Libyan, Theognostos, Ilias the Presbyter, Nikitas Stithatos, Theoliptos, Gregory of Sinai, and Gregory Palamas.

32. *Philokalia* 2: 139, para 8.

33. In the first century of *Four Hundred Texts on Love*, para 84, and in the first century of *Various Texts on Theology, the Divine Economy, and Virtue and Vice*, para 60 (*Philokalia* 2: 62–63 and 177, respectively).

34. See, for example, the way in which Neilos, in his *Ascetic Discourse*, uses the example of fear of disaster at sea as a way of changing cognitive patterns in relation to fear of God and attitudes toward the spiritual life (*Philokalia* 1: 242–43).

35. Jerome D. Frank, "What Is Psychotherapy?" in *An Introduction to the Psychotherapies*, ed. S. Bloch (Oxford: Oxford University Press, 2006), 62.

36. Ibid., 62–63. Frank suggests a classification according to the primary target of therapy (individual versus family/group), temporal orientation (past versus present), and what they seek to modify (thoughts, emotions, behaviors, etc.).

37. Carl R. Rogers, *On Becoming a Person: A Therapist's View of Psychotherapy* (London: Constable, 1975), 36.

38. Ibid., 31–38.

39. Maximos the Confessor, in the third century of *Four Hundred Texts on Love*, para 87 (*Philokalia* 2: 97).

40. Para 17 (*Philokalia* 2: p. 102).

41. Paras 97–98 (*Philokalia* 2: pp. 134–35).

42. Cf. In the first century of *Various Texts on Theology, the Divine Economy, and Virtue and Vice*, paras 24–25 (*Philokalia* 2: p. 170).

43. See the second century of *Four Hundred Texts on Love*, paras 44 and 91 (*Philokalia* 2: 73 and 81, respectively).

44. See the third century of *Four Hundred Texts on Love*, para 82 (*Philokalia* 2: 96).

45. See the second century of *Four Hundred Texts on Love*, para 46 (*Philokalia* 2: 73) and the first century of *Various Texts on Theology, the Divine Economy, and Virtue and Vice*, para 90 (p. 185).

46. See the third century of *Four Hundred Texts on Love*, para 82 (*Philokalia* 2: 96).

47. See the first century of *Various Texts on Theology, the Divine Economy, and Virtue and Vice*, paras 83 and 86–88 (*Philokalia* 2: 183 and 184).

48. See the first century of *Various Texts on Theology, the Divine Economy, and Virtue and Vice*, para 53 (*Philokalia* 2: 175). In the third century of *Various Texts*, in para 87, Maximos appears to actually identify pain as a passion (p. 232).

49. In the second century of *Four Hundred Texts on Love*, para 46 (*Philokalia* 2: p73)

50. I am referring here to texts which are attributed to Maximos, and in particular paras 7, 8, 10, 33, 35, 37, 39, 42–44. Some texts in this work, as it appears in the *Philokalia*, are known not to be by Maximos (see G. E. H. Palmer, P. Sherrard, and K. Ware, *The Philokalia: The Complete Text Compiled by St. Nikodimos of the Holy Mountain and St. Makarios of Corinth*, vol. 2 (London: Faber & Faber, 1984), 49–50, 391–95).

51. Para 43 (*Philokalia* 2: 246).

52. Cf. Evagrius *On Thoughts* 19 (R. E. Sinkewicz, *Evagrius of Pontus: The Greek Ascetic Corpus* [Oxford: Oxford University Press, 2003], 166).

53. See Nikitas Stithatos in *On Spiritual Knowledge, Love and the Perfection of Living*, para 52 (*Philokalia* 4: 155).

54. Explicit applications of this Christological model are of course also to be found, as for example where Evagrius finds in it a basis for the rejection of thoughts (*Texts on Discrimination in Respect of Passions and Thoughts*, para 1, *Philokalia* 1:38), or where Hesychios the Priest finds in it a model for "humility, fasting, prayer and watchfulness" (*On Watchfulness and Holiness*, para 12, *Philokalia* 1:164), or where John of Damaskos finds an illustration in it for his description of the process of "provocation" (*On the Virtues and the Vices*, *Philokalia* 2:338).

55. See Chris Mace, *Mindfulness and Mental Health* (London: Routledge, 2008). The following account is largely based upon this work.

56. Ibid., 4.

57. See, for example, Peter of Damaskos in *The Seven Forms of Bodily Discipline*, in Book I of his *Treasure of Divine Knowledge* (*Philokalia* 3: 89).

58. See the entry on "stillness" in any of the four published volumes.

59. Mark the Ascetic, in his *Letter to Nikolas the Solitary* (*Philokalia* 1: 159–60); Diadochus of Photiki in *On Spy* 4: 128); Theoliptos in *On Inner Work in Christ and the Monastic Profession* (*Philokalia* 4: 178–89); Nikiphoros the Monk in *On Watchfulness and the Guarding of the Heart* (*Philokalia* 4: 203–4); Gregory of Sinai in *On Commandments and Doctrines, Warnings and Promises; On Thoughts, Passions and Virtues, and also On Stillness and Prayer,*

paras 17, 61 (*Philokalia* 4: 215, 223) as well as in various other works; Gregory Palamus in *Topics of Natural and Theological Science and on the Moral and Ascetic Life*, para 46 (*Philokalia* 4: 367).

60. Andrew Powell and Christopher MacKenna, "Psychotherapy," in *Spirituality and Psychiatry*, ed. Chris Cook, Andrew Powell, and Andrew Sims (London: Royal College of Psychiatrists Press, 2009); J. Moore and C. Purton, *Spirituality and Counselling: Experiential and Theoretical Perspectives* (Ross-on-Wye: PCCS Books, 2006). Also Cook, CCH (2010: *in press*).

61. Charles Taylor, *A Secular Age* (Cambridge: Belknap, 2007).

▨ Chapter 16

1. Maximus the Confessor, *Capita de caritate* 2.97, in *Philokalia*, Vol. 2, ed. G. E. H. Palmer, Philip Sherrard, and Kallistos Ware (London: Faber & Faber, 1981), p. 82.

2. Maximus the Confessor, *Capita theologica et oeconomica* 2.40, 68, in *Philokalia*, Vol. 2, pp. 147, 154.

3. Jason Baehr, "Four Varieties of Character-Based Virtue Epistemology," *Southern Journal of Philosophy* 46 (2008): pp. 469–502; Jason Baehr, "Character in Epistemology," *Philosophical Studies* 128 (2006): pp. 479–514; Robert Roberts and W. Jay Wood, *Intellectual Virtues: An Essay in Regulative Epistemology* (Oxford: Clarendon Press, 2007); and Jonathan Kvanvig, *The Intellectual Virtues and the Life of the Mind* (Savage, MD: Rowman and Littlefield, 1992). For a constructive suggestion about developing a patristic character-based virtue epistemology of deification, see Frederick D. Aquino, "The Healing of Cognition in Deification: Toward a Patristic Virtue Epistemology," in *Immersed in the Life of God: The Healing Resources of the Christian Faith: Essays in Honor of William J. Abraham*, ed. Paul Gavrilyuk, Douglas Koskela, and Jason Vickers (Grand Rapids, MI: Eerdmans, 2008), pp. 123–42.

4. William Alston, *Beyond Justification: Dimensions of Epistemic Evaluation* (Ithaca, NY: Cornell University Press, 2005), pp. 2f., says that some aspects of the cognitive side of human life, from an epistemic point of view, include "the operation and condition of our cognitive faculties—perception, reasoning, belief formation: the products thereof—beliefs, theories, explanations, knowledge; and the evaluation of all that." Moreover, "putting intellectual virtues into the picture will involve adding epistemic *subjects*, cognitive *agents*, *persons* to the list of targets of epistemic evaluation."

5. Jonathan Kvanvig, "Truth Is Not the Primary Epistemic Goal," in *Contemporary Debates in Epistemology*," ed. Matthias Steup and Ernest Sosa (Oxford: Blackwell, 2005), p. 286.

6. Paul Moser, *Philosophy After Objectivity: Making Sense in Perspective* (Oxford: Oxford University Press, 1993), pp. 176f.

7. For a helpful discussion of epistemic value monism and epistemic value pluralism, see Kvanvig, "Truth Is Not the Primary Epistemic Goal," pp. 285–96; Kvanvig, *The Value of Knowledge and the Pursuit of Understanding* (New York: Cambridge University Press, 2003); Alston, *Beyond Justification*; Alston, "Epistemic Desiderata," *Philosophy and Phenomenological Research* 53 (1993): pp. 527–51; Roberts and Wood, *Intellectual Virtues*; Wayne Riggs, "Understanding 'Virtue' and the Virtue of Understanding," in *Intellectual Virtue: Perspectives from Ethics and Epistemology*, ed. Michael DePaul and Linda Zagzebski (Oxford: Clarendon Press, 2003), pp. 203–26; Wayne Riggs, "The Value Turn in Epistemology," in *New Waves in Epistemology*, ed. Vincent F. Hendricks and Duncan Pritchard (New York: Palgrave Macmillan, 2008), pp. 300–23; Moser, *Philosophy After Objectivity*, esp. chapter 4; Richard Foley, "Conceptual Diversity in Epistemology," in *Contemporary Debates in Epistemology*," ed. Matthias Steup and Ernest Sosa (Oxford: Blackwell, 2005), pp.

177–203; and Duncan Pritchard, "Recent Work on Epistemic Value," *American Philosophical Quarterly* 44 (2007): 85–110.

8. Roberts and Wood, *Intellectual Virtues*, pp. 21f. See also Nicholas Wolterstorff, *John Locke and The Ethics of Belief* (Cambridge: Cambridge University Press, 1996).

9. Roberts and Wood, *Intellectual Virtues*, p. 21.

10. Roberts and Wood, *Intellectual Virtues*, p. 323.

11. Roberts and Wood, *Intellectual Virtues*, p. 27.

12. See Andrew Louth, "The Theology of the *Philokalia*," in *Abba: The Tradition of Orthodoxy in the West* (Crestwood, NY: St. Vladimir's Seminary Press, 2003), pp. 351–61. As Norman Russell, *The Doctrine of Deification in the Greek Patristic Tradition* (Oxford: Oxford University Press, 2004), p. 311, points out, "Maximus the Confessor, Symeon the New Theologian, Gregory of Sinai, and Gregory Palamas figure prominently in the *Philokalia*. Their teaching on deification through participation in the divine light became familiar to a wide monastic readership." See also Russell, *Fellow Workers with God: Orthodox Thinking on Theosis* (Crestwood, NY: St. Vladimir's Seminary Press, 2009), pp. 17–29, 80–83.

13. "Introduction," in *Philokalia*, Vol. 1, ed. G. E. H. Palmer, Philip Sherrard, and Kallistos Ware (London: Faber & Faber, 1979), p. 13. See also Kallistos Ware, "The *Philokalia*: A Book for All Christians," *Sourozh* 100 (2005): pp. 5–21.

14. Russell, *The Doctrine of Deification*, p. 262.

15. Paul M. Blowers, "Gentiles of the Soul: Maximus the Confessor on the Substructure and Transformation of the Human Passions," *Journal of Early Christian Studies* 4 (1996): p. 82.

16. Roberts and Wood, *Intellectual Virtues*, p. 40.

17. Maximus the Confessor, *Ambigua* 41.1308A, in Louth, *Maximus the Confessor*, p. 158.

18. Maximus the Confessor, *Capita theologica et oeconomica*, 2.94, 96, in *Philokalia*, Vol. 2, pp. 161–63. Maximus the Confessor, *Ambigua* 10.1129A, in Andrew Louth, *Maximus the Confessor*, p. 110, calls this three-stage process "ethical, natural, and theological philosophy."

19. Maximus the Confessor, *Capita theologica et oeconomica* 1.37, in *Philokalia*, Vol. 2, p. 122.

20. Maximus the Confessor, *Capita de caritate* 3.24, in *Philokalia*, Vol. 2, p. 86.

21. Maximus the Confessor, *Capita de caritate* 2.26, in *Philokalia*, Vol. 2, p. 69.

22. Aidan Nichols, *Byzantine Gospel: Maximus the Confessor in Modern Scholarship* (Edinburgh: T&T Clark, 1993), p. 29. See also Lars Thunberg, *Microcosm and Mediator: The Theological Anthropology of Maximus the Confessor*, 2nd ed. (Chicago: Open Court, 1995), pp. 351–81.

23. Maximus the Confessor, *Quaestiones ad Thalassium* 22.141, in *On the Cosmic Mystery of Jesus Christ*, trans. Paul M. Blowers and Robert Louis Wilken (Crestwood, NY: St. Vladimir's Seminary Press, 2003), pp. 117f.

24. Paul Blowers, "Realized Eschatology in Maximus the Confessor, Ad Thalassium 22," in *Studia Patristica* 32, ed. Elizabeth Livingstone (Leuven: Peeters Press, 1997), p. 262.

25. Blowers, "Realized Eschatology in Maximus the Confessor," p. 262.

26. David Bradshaw, *Aristotle East and West: Metaphysics and the Division of Christendom* (Cambridge: Cambridge University Press, 2004), p. 193. Maximus the Confessor, *Quaestiones ad Thalassium* 60.77, in *On the Cosmic Mystery of Jesus Christ*, pp. 125f., says that the union of Creator and creation enables humans to "acquire, by experience, an active knowledge" of God "in whom they were made worthy to find their stability and to have abiding unchangeably in them the enjoyment of this knowledge." Thunberg, *Microcosm and Mediator*, p. 358, says that the mode of knowledge in *theoria* "has not lost its importance at

the highest stage of perfection, precisely because the highest form of knowledge is of such a different character from all other knowledge that [the self] still needs the support of other insights."

27. Robert Wilken, "Maximus the Confessor on the Affections in Historical Perspective," in *Asceticism*, ed. Vincent L. Wimbush and Richard Valantasis (New York: Oxford University Press, 1995), p. 417.

28. Maximus the Confessor, *Capita theologica et oeconomica*, 1.78, in *Philokalia*, Vol. 2, p. 129.

29. Maximus the Confessor, *Capita theologica et oeconomica* 2.69, in *Philokalia*, Vol. 2, p. 154.

30. Louth, "The Theology of the *Philokalia*," p. 357.

31. Maximus the Confessor, *Quaestiones ad Thalassium* 8.285A.

32. Maximus the Confessor, *Quaestiones ad Thalassium* 63.681A.

33. Maximus the Confessor, *Ambigua* 10.1108A-C, in Louth, *Maximus the Confessor*, p. 97.

34. Maximus the Confessor, *Capita de caritate* 2.56, in *Philokalia*, Vol. 2, p. 75. Polycarp Sherwood, *St. Maximus the Confessor: The Ascetic Life, The Four Centuries on Charity* (New York: The Newman Press, 1955), p. 257 fn. 122, rightly points out that the term "philosopher" here fits the ancient meaning of "a lover of wisdom."

35. On this point, see Maximus the Confessor, *Capita de caritate* 2:8, 59; 3.57, in *Philokalia*, Vol. 2, pp. 66, 75, 92.

36. Maximus the Confessor, *Capita theologica et oeconomica* I. 86, in *Philokalia*, Vol. 2, p. 133.

37. Maximus the Confessor, *Quaestiones ad Thalassium* 58.64–69.

38. Maximus the Confessor, *Capita de caritate* 1.11, in *Philokalia*, Vol. 2, p. 54.

39. Thunberg, *Microcosm and Mediator*, p. 328.

40. Melchisedec Törönen, *Union and Distinction in the Thought of St. Maximus the Confessor* (Oxford: Oxford University Press, 2007), p. 167.

41. Thunberg, *Microcosm and Mediator*, p. 339. The five pairs, for Maximus, are mind and reason, wisdom and prudence, contemplation and action, knowledge and virtue, and enduring knowledge and faith.

42. Sherwood, *St. Maximus the Confessor*, p. 98.

43. Thunberg, *Microcosm and Mediator*, p. 339.

44. Maximus the Confessor, *Mystagogia* 5.60–62, in *Maximus Confessor: Selected Writings*, ed. and trans. George Berthold (Mahwah, NJ: Paulist Press, 1985), p. 191.

45. Maximus the Confessor, *Ambigua* 7.1069B–73B, in *The Cosmic Mystery of Christ*, pp. 46–50.

46. Maximus the Confessor, *Capita de caritate* 3.3–4, in *Philokalia*, Vol. 2, p. 83.

47. Maximus the Confessor, *Quaestiones ad Thalassium* 59.604D–608C. Maximus the Confessor, *Capita theologica et oeconomica* 2.83, in *Philokalia*, Vol. 2, p. 158, says as much: The mind of Christ "does not come to us through the loss of our intellectual power; nor does it come to us as a supplementary part added to our intellect; nor does it pass essentially and hypostatically into our own intellect. Rather, it illumines the power of our intellect with its own quality and conforms the activity of our intellect to its own."

48. In *Ambigua* 10, for example, Maximus draws from Dionysius's teaching about the three motions of the soul and argues that the faculties of the mind, reason, and sense, when properly regulated, "converge into one" (see *Ambigua* 10.1112C–13B, in Louth, *Maximus the Confessor*, p. 100).

49. Roberts and Wood, *Intellectual Virtues*, p. 111. As Blowers, "Gentiles of the Soul," pp. 83f., rightly points out, "virtuous dispositions can never result in virtuous acts without the trained and rallied responses of the soul's full range of faculties and psychosomatic functions."

50. Maximus the Confessor, *Ambigua* 7.1101C, in *On the Cosmic Mystery of Jesus Christ*, pp. 73f.

51. Maximus the Confessor, *Ambigua* 7.1073B, in *On the Cosmic Mystery of Jesus Christ*, p. 50.

52. Maximus the Confessor, *Ambigua* 7.1072A, in *On the Cosmic Mystery of Jesus Christ*, p. 47.

53. Maximus the Confessor, *Ambigua* 7.1069B, in *On the Cosmic Mystery of Jesus Christ*, p. 46.

54. Maximus the Confessor, *Ambigua* 7.1076A, in *On the Cosmic Mystery of Jesus Christ*, p. 51.

55. Maximus the Confessor, *Ambigua* 7.1080C, in *On the Cosmic Mystery of Jesus Christ*, p. 56.

56. Maximus the Confessor, *Ambigua* 7.1076B, in *On the Cosmic Mystery of Jesus Christ*, p. 52.

57. Maximus the Confessor, *Ambigua* 7.1081A, in *On the Cosmic Mystery of Jesus Christ*, p. 57.

58. Thunberg, *Microcosm and Mediator*, p. 370, says that being here "includes *naturally* the power and the faculty" by which humans "move to the second state of well-being."

59. Maximus the Confessor, *Capita de caritate*, 3.24, in *Philokalia*, Vol. 2, p. 86. See also *Ambigua* 42.1325B, in *On the Cosmic Mystery of Jesus Christ*, p. 89.

60. Maximus the Confessor, *Ambigua* 42.1325C, in *On the Cosmic Mystery of Jesus Christ*, p. 89.

61. Maximus the Confessor, *Capita de caritate*, 2.48, in *Philokalia*, Vol. 2, p. 73. On this point, see Wilken, "Maximus the Confessor on the Affections in Historical Perspective," pp. 412–33.

62. Maximus the Confessor, *Ambigua* 10.1112B-C, in Louth, *Maximus the Confessor*, pp. 99f.

63. Maximus the Confessor, *Ambigua* 7.1081D–84A, in *On the Cosmic Mystery of Jesus Christ*, pp. 58f.

64. Maximus the Confessor, *Quaestiones ad Thalassium* 1.49, in *On the Cosmic Mystery of Jesus Christ*, p. 98.

65. Maximus the Confessor, *Ambigua* 7.1080C, in *On the Cosmic Mystery of Jesus Christ*, p. 56.

66. See Maximus the Confessor, *Capita de caritate*, 4.45, in *Philokalia*, Vol. 2, p. 105.

67. For further reflection on the relationship between virtue and perception in Maximus, see Frederick Aquino, "Maximus the Confessor," in *The Perception of God: The Spiritual Senses in the Christian Tradition*, ed. Paul L. Gavrilyuk in collaboration with Sarah Coakley (Cambridge University Press, forthcoming).

68. Maximus the Confessor, *Ambigua* 10.1124D–25A, in Louth, *Maximus the Confessor*, p. 107.

69. Maximus the Confessor, *Epistula* 2.393B, in Louth, *Maximus the Confessor*, p. 85. Sherwood, *St. Maximus the Confessor*, p. 238, says that love is "the defying virtue *par excellence*" for Maximus.

70. Maximus the Confessor, *Epistula* 2.400A, in Louth, *Maximus the Confessor*, p.88.

71. Maximus the Confessor, *Epistula* 2.396B, in Louth, *Maximus the Confessor*, p.86.

72. Maximus the Confessor, *Epistula* 2.404D, in Louth, *Maximus the Confessor*, p. 91.

73. "Introduction," in Louth, *Maximus the Confessor*, p. 38.

74. As Thunberg, *Microcosm and Mediator*, p. 286, points out, Maximus "does not wish to establish an order of superiority as between love and knowledge, since love in a wide sense not only involves a preference for the knowledge of God to anything else, but also carries [the self] in all [its] intellectual activity to full communion with God."

75. Maximus Confessor, *Capita de caritate* 1.1, 4; 3.67, in *Philokalia*, Vol. 2, pp. 53, 93.

76. Maximus the Confessor, *Capita de caritate* 1.9, in *Philokalia*, Vol. 2, p. 54.

77. Maximus the Confessor, *Capita de caritate* 1.31–32, in *Philokalia*, Vol. 2, p. 56.

78. Maximus the Confessor, *Capita de caritate* 2.56, in *Philokalia*, Vol. 2, p. 75.

79. Maximus the Confessor, *Capita de caritate* 4.60, 72, in *Philokalia*, Vol. 2, pp. 107, 109. Maximus also says that without dispassion and humility, "no one will see the Lord" (4.58).

80. Maximus the Confessor, *Capita theologica et oeconomica* 1.55–60, in *Philokalia*, Vol. 2, pp. 125f.

81. For a helpful discussion of the relationship between conceptually loaded (e.g., prior beliefs, expectations, training) and perception, see Jon Greco, "Seeing Good, Seeing God: The Epistemology of Moral and Religious Experience," unpublished paper, pp. 1–15.

82. Maximus the Confessor, *Quaestiones ad Thalassium* 60.77, in *On the Cosmic Mystery of Jesus Christ*, p. 126.

83. Maximus the Confessor, *Quaestiones ad Thalassium* 60.77, in *On the Cosmic Mystery of Jesus Christ*, p. 126.

84. Hans Urs von Balthasar, *Cosmic Liturgy: The Universe According to Maximus the Confessor* (San Francisco: Ignatius Press, 2003), p. 288.

85. On the distinction between experiencing God and providing reasons to justify the belief that God exists, see William Alston, *Perceiving God: The Epistemology of Religious Experience* (Ithaca: Cornell University Press, 1993), and Paul Moser, *The Elusive God: Reorienting Religious Epistemology* (Cambridge: Cambridge University Press, 2008). Paul Moser, "Agapeic Theism: Personifying Evidence and Moral Struggle," *European Journal of Philosophy* (forthcoming Fall 2010), p. 6, says that acquaintance with God "would be *de re*, and not merely *de dicto*, in virtue of being directly agent-to-agent (or person-to person), and not just agent-to-proposition. It would involve the direct acquaintance of one personal agent with another, even if human beliefs accompany the acquaintance."

86. On the role that volitional openness plays in pursuing knowledge of God, see Moser, *The Elusive God*.

■ Chapter 17

1. *Mount Athos: Renewal in Paradise* (New Haven, CT: Yale University Press, 2002), VI.

2. *Letter to Nicholas the Solitary*, *Philokalia* 1:136; ET 1:157–58.

3. *On the Eight Vices*, *Philokalia* 1:64; ET 1:76. This text is actually a Greek summary of Cassian's *Institutes*, bks. V-XII. See the introductory note on Cassian, ET 1:72.

4. *Gnomic Anthology* 3.25, *Philokalia* 2:301; ET 3:50, translation modified.

5. *Second Century on Love* 30, *Philokalia* 2:18; ET 2:70, translation modified.

6. *Third Century of Various Texts* 30–31, *Philokalia* 2:132; ET 2:216–217.

7. "Temper" is my attempt to translate θυμον~, a Greek word that is rendered as "incensive power" in the English translation of the *Philokalia*. This rendering does not have any clear meaning in contemporary English usage, hence it simply stands as a cipher for θυμον~. My translation, "temper," refers to the human capacity for anger and for certain key virtues. Temper can prove to be good or bad. It can lead us into futile or destructive anger, yet by intelligent choice and with God's help it can be redirected, become strong like tempered steel, and provide the necessary energy for perseverance, courage, self-restraint, advocacy for justice, and resistance to evil. See further my "Intro-

duction" to *St. Basil the Great on the Human Condition* (Crestwood, NY: St. Vladimir's, 2005), 22–24.

8. *Texts on Discrimination in Respect to Passions and Thoughts*, 3, *Philokalia* 1:45; ET 1:40, translation slightly modified.

9. *Philokalia* 2:193; ET 2:293, translation slightly modified.

10. *Philokalia* 2:194; ET 2:294.

11. Ibid.

12. Ibid.

13. This homily was well known in the Byzantine world, and Maximus wrote a commentary on difficult passages in Gregory's orations, the *Ambigua*.

14. *On the Nativity of Christ* 1, SC 358:104; Nonna Verna Harrison, trans., *St. Gregory of Nazianzus: Festal Orations* (Crestwood, NY: St. Vladimir's, 2008), 61.

15. *Philokalia* 2:194; ET 2:294.

16. *Philokalia* 2:194; ET 2:195.

17. Ibid.

18. Cited in Kallistos Ware, "The Monk and the Married Christian: Some Comparisons in Early Monastic Sources," *Eastern Churches Review* 6:1 (1974) 72–83, at 80.

19. *Fourth Century of Various Texts* 42–44, *Philokalia* 2:155–156; ET 2:246–47.

20. See my articles, Nonna Verna Harrison "The Feminine Man in Late Antique Ascetic Piety," *Union Seminary Quarterly Review* 48 (1994) 49–71; and "Gender, Generation, and Virginity in Cappadocian Theology," *Journal of Theological Studies*, n.s. 47 (1996), 38–68.

21. *On Virginity* 14, Werner Jaeger, ed. *Gregorii Nysseni Opera* (Leiden: Brill, 1960–), 8.1:308–9, translations mine (henceforth cited as GNO).

22. GNO 7.2:148.

23. *On Virginity* 2, GNO 8.1:253, translation mine.

24. Πρὸ αἰώνων μὲν ἐκ τοῦ πατρὸς γεννηθέντα κατὰ τὴν θεότητα, ἐπ᾿ ἐσχάτων δὲ τῶν ἡμερῶν τὸν αὐτὸν δι᾿ ἡμᾶς καὶ διὰ τὴν ἡμετέραν σωτηρίαν ἐκ Μαρίας τῆς παρθένου τῆς θεοτόκου κατὰ τὴν ανθρωπότητα. Jaroslav Pelikan and Valerie Hotchkiss, eds. *Creeds and Confessions of Faith in the Christian Tradition* (New Haven, CT: Yale, 2003), 1:716. See also my essay, "The Trinity and Feminism," in Gilles Emery and Matthew Levering, eds., *Oxford Handbook of the Trinity* (Oxford: Oxford University Press, forthcoming).

25. Gregory Palamas is a leading fourteenth-century Byzantine theologian. The belief that the Holy Spirit proceeds "from the Father alone" was one Byzantine response to the *filioque* controversy with the Western church. It fits in this passage because it is also the only formula that can be construed in this precise way as virginal. Gregory's understanding of the procession of the Holy Spirit is actually more complex. See John Meyendorff, *A Study of Gregory Palamas*, trans. George Lawrence (Crestwood, NY: St. Vladimir's, 1964), 228–32.

26. *A New Testament Decalogue* 6, *Philokalia* 4:120; ET 4:328.

27. For a fuller discussion, see my article, "The Maleness of Christ," *St. Vladimir's Theological Quarterly* 42 (1998) 111–51.

28. Ps. 109:3 (LXX). For the Christmas services, see Mother Mary and Kallistos Ware, trans. *The Festal Menaion* (London: Faber & Faber, 1969), 221–89.

29. For more on the Father's womb, see my "Trinity and Feminism."

30. *On the Song of Songs* 3, GNO 6:91.

31. *Forty Texts on Watchfulness*, notably 18–40, *Philokalia* 2:280–86; ET 3:23–30.

■ Chapter 18

1. The term literally signifies "not having a vote." In Byzantine times, and by Canon Law to this day, monastics are not permitted to vote.

2. Cf. *Sayings*, Arsenius 9. See B. Ward, *The Sayings of the Desert Fathers: The Alphabetical Collection* (London: Mowbrays, 1975), 9.

3. On the role of demons, see Evagrius, *Chapters on Prayer* 9–10, in *Philokalia*, vol. 1, 58–59.

4. References to the *Letters* of Barsanuphius and John are included throughout the text in parentheses. For a translation of the full text of the spiritual correspondence, see John Chryssavgis, *Barsanuphius and John: Letters*, vols. 1 and 2, *The Fathers of the Church*, 113–14, Washington DC: The Catholic University of America Press, 2006–7. References to the *Philokalia* are taken from the English translation by G. E. H. Palmer, Philip Sherrard, and Kallistos Ware (London/Boston: Faber & Faber, 1979–95).

5. See the introductory note to the writings of Gregory of Sinai in *Philokalia*, vol. 4, 207.

6. *Philokalia*, vol. 1, 14–15.

7. Evagrius of Pontus, *Chapters on Prayer* 124, in *Philokalia*, vol. 1, 69.

8. See *Cyril of Scythopolis, Life of Euthymius*, ed. E. Schwartz (Leipzig, JC Hinrichs Verlag, 1939.

9. Indeed, perhaps in imitation of this lifestyle, the entire community in Thavatha assumed the form of a loose community with many cells, where monks and hermits enjoyed varying degrees of enclosure. In my opinion, it was this intensity of solitude and this primacy of silence that further gave rise to the monastery's outreach within the wider community in the form of its workshops (*Letters* 553–54), guest-houses (*Letters* 570, 595–96), a hospital (*Letters* 327, 548), and a church dedicated to teaching visitors (*Letter* 570).

10. J. Pargoire, *L' Eglise Byzantine de 527 à 847* (Paris, 1905), 274.

11. Other manuscripts are found in Paris, Oxford, Athens, Moscow, Munich, Jerusalem, and Patmos.

12. On the close connection between silence (or stillness) and vigilance (or watchfulness), see Hesychius, *On Watchfulness and Holiness* 1–6, in *Philokalia*, vol. 1, 162–63.

13. On prayer as simply one aspect of silence, see Gregory of Sinai, *Chapters* 5, in *Philokalia*, vol. 4, 278–80.

14. See Symeon the New Theologian, *The Three Methods of Prayer*, in *Philokalia*, vol. 4, 71.

15. Translating the terms *kata monas* (κατα μονας), *kat'idian* (κατ'ιδιαν), *kathisma* (καθισμα), and *kellion* (κελλιον).

16. Translating the terms *sige* (σιγη) and *sigan* (σιγαν), *siope* (σιωπη) and *siopan* (σιωπαν).

17. Translating the terms *hesychia* (ἡσυχια) and *hesychazein* (ἡσυχαζειν).

18. See Gregory of Sinai, *On Prayer*, in *Philokalia*, vol. 4, 285.

19. See Theoleptus of Philadelphia in *Philokalia*, vol. 4, 176–87; and Gregory of Sinai, *On Commandments and Doctrines* 80, in *Philokalia*, vol. 4, 227.

20. On silence and prayer as weapons in the spiritual struggle, see Niketas Stethatos, *On Spiritual Knowledge* 94, in *Philokalia*, vol. 4, 170–71; and Gregory of Sinai, *On Commandments and Doctrines* 113–14, in *Philokalia*, vol. 4, 237–38.

21. On silence and prayer as unceasing, see Kallistos/Ignatios Xanthopouloi, *Century* 90, in *Philokalia*, vol. 5.

22. Cf. Dorotheus, *Teaching 14*, 149–52. Silence is also compared to the construction of a house by Origen of Alexandria, the Desert Fathers, Evagrius of Pontus, and others.

23. The link between silence and faith is emphasized by Gregory of Sinai in his *On Commandments and Doctrines* 103; see vol. 3 of the *Philokalia*, 234.

24. On silence and the senses, see Thalassius, *First Century*, in *Philokalia*, vol. 2, 308; and Second Century, in *Philokalia*, vol. 2, 313.

25. While Barsanuphius and John do not explicitly refer to the invocation of "the name of Jesus" (cf. Niketas Stethatos, *On the Inner Nature of Things* 97, in *Philokalia*, vol. 4, 136; Gregory of Sinai, *On Stillness*, in *Philokalia*, vol. 4, 263–74; and Kallistos/Ignatios Xantho-pouloi, *Century* 22 and 49 in *Philokalia*, vol. 5), they do refer to "invoking" (*Letter* 427) and "saying" (*Letter* 430) "the name of God." See also *Letters* 103, 417, and 424.

26. For an example in the *Philokalia*, see Mark the Monk, *On Those Who Think They Are Made Righteous by Works* 90, in vol. 1, 132.

27. *On the Practice of the Virtues* 75, in *Philokalia*, vol. 4, 98.

28. *The Seven Forms of Bodily Discipline*, in *Philokalia*, vol. 3, 89.

29. *To the Most Reverend Nun Xenia* 1, in *Philokalia*, volume 4, 293.

30. *Ascetic Discourse*, vol. 1, 231. See also 247: "By embracing solitude, let us avoid meeting those who do us no good, for the company of frivolous people is harmful and undermines our state of peace."

31. Alonius, *Sayings* 1. See Ward, op. cit., 30.

32. *Letter* 141 adds that we always have the grace of God; *Letter* 248 notes that we also have the prayer of our spiritual director; and *Letter* 832 observes that we have with us all the communion of saints!

33. *On Commandments and Doctrines* 104, in *Philokalia*, vol. 4, 235.

34. See Igumen Chariton, *The Art of Prayer* (London: Faber, 1966), 51.

35. See also Abba Isaiah of Scetis, *Ascetic Discourse* 13. See J. Chryssavgis and P. Penkett, Abba Isaiah of Scetis: Asectic Discourses (Kalamazoo MI: Cistercian Publications, 2002), 105–9.

36. For the notion of prayer and thanksgiving in the *Philokalia*, see Evagrius, *Praktikos* 42.

37. *A Century of Spiritual Texts*, in *Philokalia*, vol. 1, 31. See also Kallistos/Ignatios Xan-thopouloi, *Century* 24 and 50, in *Philokalia*, vol. 5, as well as Mark the Monk, *On the Spiri-tual Law* 10 and *On Those Who Think They Are Made Righteous by Works* 140, in *Philokalia*, vol. 1, 110 and 136–37. Elias the Presbyter speaks of avoiding talkativeness "like a wild ass that scorns the crowds in a city!" See *A Gnomic Anthology IV*, in *Philokalia*, vol. 3, 57.

38. See Elias the Presbyter, *A Gnomic Anthology I*, in *Philokalia*, vol. 3, 34.

39. See Niketas Stethatos, *On the Practice of the Virtues* 90, in *Philokalia*, vol. 4, 103.

40. See *A Gnomic Anthology* I, in *Philokalia*, vol. 3, 37.

41. On the close link between obedience (*hypakoe*) and silence or stillness (*hesychia*), see Peter of Damascus, in *Philokalia*, vol. 3, 103–8. See also Gregory of Sinai, *On Stillness* 8, in *Philokalia*, vol. 4, 268–69; and Gregory Palamas, *To the Most Reverend Nun Xenia* 34, in *Philokalia*, vol. 4, 306.

42. *Letter to Nicholas the Solitary*, in *Philokalia*, vol. 1, 158. See also *Discourse on Abba Philemon*, in *Philokalia*, vol. 2, 351.

43. See also *Sayings*, Poemen 27. See Ward, op. cit., 143.

44. See Gregory of Sinai, *On Commandments and Doctrines* 99, in *Philokalia*, vol 4, 233. See also Gregory of Sinai, *On Prayer*, in *Philokalia*, vol. 4, 285.

45. *On Stillness*, 15, in *Philokalia*, vol. 4, 274.

46. *On Commandments and Doctrines* 127, in *Philokalia*, vol. 4, 246. Indeed, Gregory states that "stillness gives birth to contemplation, contemplation to spiritual knowledge, and knowledge to the apprehension of the mysteries, which is theology, the fruit of which is love." See *Further Texts 5: On Beneficent Change*, in *Philokalia*, vol. 4, 254.

47. See *Discourse*, in *Philokalia*, vol. 2, 349. It is in this *Discourse on Abba Philemon* that the phrase "Lord Jesus Christ, Son of God, have mercy on me" is encountered for the first time.

48. *On the Inner Nature of Things* 66, in *Philokalia*, vol. 4, 126.

49. *On the Inner Nature of Things* 64, in *Philokalia*, vol. 4, 125. See also Gregory of Sinai, *On Commandments and Doctrines* 115, in *Philokalia*, vol. 4, 238; and *On Stillness*, in *Philokalia*, vol. 4, 266, where Gregory explicitly quotes Barsanuphius.

50. For similar phraseology concerning the gift of prayer and silence, see Evagrius, *Chapters on Prayer* 58 and 69, in *Philokalia*, vol. 1, 62–63.

51. Gregory of Sinai adopts the term "lazy." See *On Stillness* 14, in *Philokalia*, vol. 4, 273.

52. On the connection between prayer and death, see Symeon the New Theologian, *Practical and Theological Texts* 87, in *Philokalia*, vol. 4, 43.

53. See Niketas Stethatos, *On the Inner Nature of Things* 6–8, in *Philokalia*, vol. 4, 108–10.

54. *On Commandments and Doctrines* 103, in *Philokalia*, vol. 4, 234. Gregory cites Barsanuphius when he raises the apophatic notion of "shedding one's thoughts." See his *On Stillness* 9–10, in *Philokalia*, vol. 4, 269–79.

55. *Spiritual Wisdom*, in *Philokalia*, vol. 3, 312.

56. See Niketas Stethatos, *On the Inner Nature of Things* 75–77, in *Philokalia*, vol. 4, 128–29.

57. See his *Second Century*, in *Philokalia*, vol. 2, 314.

58. *On Watchfulness*, in *Philokalia*, vol. 4, 197.

59. See Evagrius, *Historia Ecclesiastica* IV, 33, in PG 87. ii: 2764.

60. See ed. J. E. Bamberger, *Praktikos; Chapters on Prayers* (Kalamazoo MI: Cistercian Publications, 1970).

61. See Niketas Stethatos, *On the Practice of the Virtues* 26, in *Philokalia*, vol. 4, 85–86; and Kallistos/Ignatios Xanthopouloi, *Century* 16, in *Philokalia*, vol. 5.

■ SUBJECT INDEX

CPSIA information can be obtained
at www.ICGtesting.com
Printed in the USA
BVHW082326071218
535061BV00004B/9/P

9 780195 390278